AN ENGLISH LIBRARY

AN ENGLISH LIBRARY
A Bookman's Guide

F. SEYMOUR SMITH

Revised and Enlarged Edition

A GRAFTON BOOK

READERS UNION
ANDRE DEUTSCH
LONDON 1964

This RU edition was produced in 1964 for sale to its members only by Readers Union Ltd at Aldine House, 10–13 Bedford Street, London W.C.2 and at Letchworth Garden City, Herts. Full details of membership may be obtained from our London address. The book is set in 11 point and 9 point Monotype Bembo and has been printed by C. Tinling & Co. Ltd., Liverpool, London and Prescot. It was first published by André Deutsch Ltd.

CONTENTS

CONTENTS

INTRODUCTION

A Backward Glance

An English Library, like wartime willow-herb, grew on a bomb site. Maurice Marston, then Secretary of the National Book Council, invited the compiler to a conference held in the spring of 1941, at which he told his council and members that something should be done to help book buyers who were at that time responsible for an unprecedented demand for the English classics and in particular for the great books of the nineteenth century.

Publishers observed ironically that the dangers of a world war had stimulated interest in the traditional glories of English Literature at the very time when the destruction of a million books by bombing, paper and other shortages, made it difficult, almost impossible, to keep books in print.

But it was agreed that something should and could be done. It was. Conference asked the compiler to produce quickly a guide to the classics for servicemen and the general public, some of whom were perhaps buying books, or borrowing and reading them, for the first time in adult life.

The result was a forty-page quarto booklet about all the volumes then available in the four great series of *Everyman's Library; Collins's Classics; Nelson Classics;* and *Worlds Classics*. It was distributed by the N.B.C. for the British Council. With little or no dissension the war broke down trade conventions and barriers, for this example of co-operative publicity in the book trade was thus officially approved; it quickly justified itself; and *The English Classics* at sixpence a copy became a best-seller. A brief appreciation in Peterborough's column in the *Daily Telegraph* resulted in sackloads of postal orders for Maurice Marston's staff to handle. Many thousands of copies found their way to readers all over the world. Again, ironically, English classics became even more difficult to keep in print.

In 1943 the National Book Council decided to publish something substantial and comprehensive, a handbook not limited to books in the four standard series, but a reference work for librarians; booksellers; book trade students, for whom classes in bookselling were then being organised under the encouraging eyes of John Wilson of Bumpus's; and book-buyers, especially those experiencing for the first time the pleasure of collecting a personal library.

An English Library was the result, the first edition being published in 1943 with a preface by Edmund Blunden, then, as now, always helpful in the cause of books. Wartime difficulties, shortages and perils made it impossible to offer a book worthy of the subject and purpose, but with each edition up to the fourth of 1950 improvements were introduced. That edition has now been out of print for nearly a decade, and encouraging requests for a new one have come, not only from librarians and readers in Great Britain, but also from India and Africa, where new libraries are rapidly developing, and a vast public is eager for English classics and creative literature as well as technical books. Happily, English seems to be a *lingua franca* for this new world of readers. Hence the constant need for a popular reference handbook providing the information and guidance *An English Library* is intended to give.

The Principles of Selection

Using previous editions as a foundation for this fully revised and enlarged edition, the compiler has tried to present within the conventional subject and formal groups of creative literature, bibliographical details of (a) all the books from *The Canterbury Tales*, up to those by writers now dead, of the present century, that by common consent have become classics; (b) a liberal selection of standard books likely to interest general readers; and (c) minor classics of the past that are reprinted, or in the opinion of the compiler deserve to be. It should be emphasised that with the exception of reference books nothing by living writers is included, even though this has meant the omission of books that will probably take their place as twentieth-century classics. The bibliography of living authors is best dealt with separately, and the compiler's own *What Shall I Read Next?* (1953, Cambridge University Press for the National Book League) does offer 'a personal selection of twentieth-century books' as a complementary guide. Some books by authors who have died since 1953 have, however, been transferred from *What Shall I Read Next?* to *An English Library*. This limitation prevents the book from becoming too bulky for a quick-reference guide and restricts entries to those concerning contemporary authors whose place in literature has already been determined by critical and public opinion as likely to be permanent and assured, even though fluctuating taste may from time to time result in wavering popularity.

As before, it has seemed sensible to include nineteenth-century classics in the literature of the United States of America. From

Mark Twain onwards, American literature revealed a characteristic national genius owing little or nothing to the writings of British authors. Only an American author could have written *Tom Sawyer* and *Huckleberry Finn*, and thereafter, American literature, like American language, developed its own idiom, style and unique nature. But the essays of Washington Irving, even the fiction of Nathaniel Hawthorne, and the poetry of Longfellow, are all part of the main traditional stream of English writing. Hence it appears not improper to include American books up to the turn of the century as a convenient compromise.

Children's books find a place in *An English Library* only if they belong to that small but precious class that has given us books we cherish and continue to read throughout life. This has enabled the compiler to include such perennial favourites as *Alice in Wonderland*, *The Wind in the Willows*, *The Happy Prince* and *A Child's Garden of Verses*.

The Arrangement of Entries

The bibliographical information in *An English Library* has been classified in the ten groups (with sub-groups) listed on the contents page. It will be observed that close subject classification has not been attempted. Such an application of a standard scheme was considered quite unnecessary. Hence the broad subject and formal groups adopted will serve the general public and booksellers equally well, and should not prove inconvenient to librarians.

Critical monographs on authors, together with literary histories, will be found in the group headed *Essays, Belles Lettres and Literary Criticism*. Here too have been included omnibus volumes and collected works of a miscellaneous nature, with cross-references in other sections when this has been considered necessary. A few translations from Greek and Latin classics, and from such foreign classics as the *Essays of Montaigne*, are arranged under the names of the translators, because these books find a place in *An English Library*, and are discussed in standard histories of English literature, owing to the classic stature of the English translator's work. Thus North's *Plutarch*, being recognised beyond question as a classic of Tudor prose in its own right, is included in *Biography* under North, but with an index reference from Plutarch.

Political philosophy has been grouped under the main heading of *Philosophy and Religion*; and the *History* section embraces social and political histories, as well as rhetoric and speeches.

A*

Arnold Bennett would have approved of the separation of *Poetry and Poetic Drama* from *Prose Drama*, and it is hoped that users of *An English Library* will also find this to their liking. Books by scientists have been brought within the scope of this bibliography only when they have the sort of literary distinction that gives them a right to discussion in a history of English literature. Their classification has presented difficulties because they were too few to justify a separate group. Some, therefore, will be found under *Essays and Belles Lettres*; others, less inappropriately, under *Philosophy and Religion*. Thus Draper's book on the conflict between religion and science attracted such epoch-making books as Darwin's *Origin of Species* and *The Universe Around Us* to *Philosophy*, but Faraday's pioneer little work of popular science and T. H. Huxley's books are with *Essays and Belles Lettres*.

Within each section or sub-group all entries are arranged under the surnames of authors, or for anthologies, under editors. This arrangement is adhered to even in the section dealing with *Biographies*. George Cavendish's life of Cardinal Wolsey is there, not because it is an important biography, but because Wolsey's contemporary Cavendish wrote it. Many modern biographies have superseded older books, but these continue to be worth reading.

Each section is preceded by a short introductory essay which should be useful to those requiring a summary, together with some information on books about the specific subjects or forms of literature. To assist those who may be perplexed by too many choices and the exhilarating wealth of genius in English books, the compiler's personal first choice is indicated by the use of asterisks. These are placed against books one would recommend as of prime importance to those starting a library—public, personal or school; they are books that for many readers have become lifetime companions. Individual tastes differ widely, but it is thought there may be general acceptance of the practical advantages in adopting this indication of *primus inter pares* in each group.

Style of Entry

With few exceptions all entries are annotated, the notes emphasising historical and literary importance, and conveying as much as possible the compiler's own appreciation of those books that have meant much to him during his reading life. Dates of first editions in book form and important revisions, if any, have been given within parentheses ( ); followed by the date of a recent, or often the latest, edition or reprint up to 1962, together with the 1962 price. Books with no current price are thought to be out of print in 1962, or as far as can be traced, not available in any British edition. Public librarians, who have been so helpful to publishers and bookmen since 1945 in this respect, may perhaps remember these when they are compiling from time to time their lists of books they would like to see reprinted, with the support of Members of the Library Association behind their recommendations. The public book supply is now an important factor in every publisher's office, and the knowledge that librarians would support the republication of certain out-of-print books by buying copies is sometimes a deciding factor in the maintenance of a back list.

Editions in the standard hard-cover series have been included as a matter of course. Many others are noted, including some paperbacks, especially when these are the only ones available. But this paperback coverage is not complete, because it fluctuates so much. The current position can be checked by reference to *Paperbacks In Print*, published twice-yearly by Whitaker, price 3s 6d, and available for consultation at all booksellers and libraries. Here and there an American reprint or paperback is noted because it happens to be the only edition available. Briefly, the compiler's aim throughout has been to include all good editions and most minor ones, in order to provide information within a fairly extensive range of prices. At the time of going to press certain price increases were announced by series publishers. These were approximately about ten per cent. on the prices given in the imprint details: e.g., the 11s 6d *Everyman* volumes have been increased to 12s 6d; *Worlds Classics* now cost from 6s 6d to 12s 6d, the majority being 8s 6d instead of 7s 6d as stated.

The collation of each book is for the most part limited to the above details, but the number of pages is stated when 500 or over, illustrations being added only when they are a notable feature.

There remains the indexes to explain. The author index includes editors of anthologies, collections and reference works, but not of specific authors, and, like the main entries, is concerned with the best-known names of authors using pen-names, with cross-references added. Thus S. L. Clemens, Eric Blair and C. L. Dodgson are entered respectively under Twain, Mark, Orwell, George, and Carroll, Lewis. Other surnames follow the conventional usage of indexers, double-barrelled names under the first part; prefixes according to codified rules: de la Mare under 'de'; De Morgan under 'De'; both preceding Defoe. This word-by-word order is followed throughout.

It should be noted that the title index does not include formal titles such as 'Essays', 'Collected Poems', 'Plays', by . . . and so on. Such books are self-indexing, and the reader should refer direct to the appropriate group or section under the author. From a count of the indexes it appears that 1170 authors are within the scope of *An English Library* and that the total number of books included is approximately 2630, which will be considered, one hopes, a fair and comprehensive coverage.

Acknowledgements

The compiler gratefully acknowledges the advice and useful suggestions he has received from time to time from former colleagues in libraries, and from many unknown correspondents all over the world who have taken the trouble to write about former editions. Apart from kindly expressed appreciation, these letters nearly all contained useful suggestions regarding omissions. Even the solitary letter of downright abuse for venturing to offer guidance in the formation of a library and in reading was encouraging, since it was evidence that *An English Library* was not being used only by the converted.

Every volume listed in the last section, *A Bookman's Reference Library*, has been useful for checking, evaluating, factual details and bibliographical information. These reference books will be found in every public reference library, and are indispensable.

A few years after the end of the last war, the compiler received a letter from a town clerk who wrote to say that his corporation's public library was pleasant, well-built and nearly worthy of the historically-interesting town for which he worked; but to his dismay, on checking the stock with *An English Library*, he found that he had in his personal library a greater selection of the books than was available to the public using the library. 'What,' he asked in despair, 'can I do?' The compiler, having confirmed from a reference book that the corporation had the usual pension scheme for retired officials, made an appropriate suggestion, reminding the town clerk that the celebrated Rev. William Spooner had once employed with effect on some undergraduate guests who had stayed long after tea-time, his well-known nervous habit of transposition in speech; by asking 'Oh! Must you stay? Can't you go?'

But those days are over; almost every town now has a public

book supply worthy of the great literature in English produced from Chaucer to G. M. Trevelyan, Virginia Woolf, James Joyce and Dylan Thomas, in all its rich variety of genius, form and talent. It is the compiler's hope that this revised and enlarged edition of *An English Library* will continue to do its work as a sort of superior bookman's shopping-list at its most modest level, and at its highest, as a working bibliographical tool supplementing critical histories of English literature.

F. SEYMOUR SMITH

AUTOBIOGRAPHIES AND MEMOIRS
(*including Diaries, Journals and Letters*)

JOHN BYNG, fifth Viscount Torrington, hit the nail on the head: 'All diaries are greedily sought for, let them be ever so ill and foolish written; as coming warm from the heart.' His own journal, known to us as the *Torrington Diaries*, happens to be a good example of a form of literature characteristically mingling historical record of social life, topography, and those spontaneous thoughts or observations which, 'coming warm from the heart', retain the interest of posterity, as Byng hoped his own work would do.

Diaries, journals and letters, conveniently classed with autobiographies, are strictly in a class of their own. They attract the amateur writer as much as the professional, and depend less on literary skill than any other literary form. A single thread links them with autobiography proper: egotism.

Cowper's 'divine chit-chat' enchanted Coleridge and Lamb. He elevated gossipy letters to the eminence of a world classic; the suffering of 'Barbellion' gave us a self-portrait of a man of talent of our own time; the shrewd sanity and common sense of Arnold Bennett raised the trivia of daily life to the level of literature: and as readers, we are delighted that the vanity of such diverse human beings impelled them to keep these informal records, whether they were written deliberately for general publication, or for private solace.

The diary kept by Samuel Pepys is probably the most widely-read book of its kind in European literature, although we still lack a complete, definitive transcription. Valuable as this document is as an historical record, most of us read it for its indiscretions and amusing self-portraiture. Pepys created himself in his shorthand jottings with such fidelity that he lives in the minds of his readers with the vitality of a masterpiece of fictional characterisation. But his contemporary, John Evelyn, left a diary read more for its historical value than for its interest as a human document. Thus some diaries would be as much at home in the *History* section as here, but it may be agreed that form is paramount and so we include historical works, such as *The Creevey Papers*; travel diaries, such as the *Torrington Diaries*; and writings of spiritual profundity such as George Fox's *Journal*, as well as simpler works like Francis Kilvert's charming diary, so recently published, yet so quickly established as a classic. All of these books abound in entertainment, and like so many in this section were not the work of professional writers.

Even when we consider the full-scale autobiography, written for publication, we observe the same diversity, and the same attractive egotism producing classics and minor classics from amateurs as well as established men of letters. The Chartist, William Lovett, depicts his 'Life and Struggles', and the record becomes part of social history; G. K.

Chesterton gave us one of his best books because we needed his 'Auto-biography' to complete the portrait he left us in his hundreds of essays, poems, and political works. Everything he wrote put in a touch or two; the 'Autobiography' gave us the background; it is an extended essay by G.K.C. written by himself as a character already partly portrayed in his other books.

Trollope's book has survived as a classic, not because it offers a profound insight into the novelist's character, nor for any unusual experiences recorded, but because of its absolute honesty as a narrative recording the development of a public servant into a novelist of enduring qualities.

If we except that strange religious document known as *The Book of Margery Kempe*, set down for posterity in the far-off years of the Lancastrian kings, then the earliest autobiography that has come to light so far is that of Thomas Whythorne, discovered by accident even more recently than Margery Kempe's manuscript. Between these two early examples of autobiographical writing and Flora Thompson's delightful evocation of country life in the last decades of the nineteenth century, we have a diversity of interest as fascinating as human nature itself; enabling us to skip in one page from amusing trivia to profound personal statements revealing piercing insight into the human soul.

Autobiography has attracted few monographs, but the research of Margaret Bottrall has produced two books of outstanding interest: *Every Man A Phoenix*, John Murray, 1958, 18s, and the complementary volume of *Personal Records*, Hart-Davis, 1961, 25s.

Every Man A Phoenix is a series of studies in seventeenth-century autobiographical writings, aptly termed 'strange hybrids', thus emphasising the many strands that go to the making of personal documents and statements 'coming warm from the heart' as confessions of faith or self-interpretation. Specifically, the writer selects Browne's *Religio Medici*, Lord Herbert of Cherbury's *Autobiography*, and Richard Baxter's *Reliquiae* to illustrate her theme.

Personal Records, being the perfect introduction to this section of *An English Library*, because it offers well-chosen extracts from many of the books included here, is entered and described below. These two books are indispensable to students but are also recommended with confidence to general readers. Seldom has the theme been so well discussed and exemplified. An older book, now out of print, was well entitled *Inside Out*: an introduction to autobiography, by E. Stuart Bates, Blackwell, 1936; and the latest analysis was *Design and Truth in Autobiography*, by Roy Pascal, Routledge, 1960, 25s.

Asquith, Margot (Countess of Oxford and Asquith) (1864-1945)
AUTOBIOGRAPHY 2 vols. (Butterworth, 1920-2) ed. with an introduction by Mark Bonham Carter *Eyre and Spottiswoode* 1962 30s Illus.

Skilful abridgement of one of the most amusing, gay and diverting autobiographies of the century. When first published it was something of a *succès de scandale*. It may now take its place firmly as a minor classic of its kind as a witty picture of Victorian and Edwardian society by a most individual and spontaneous personality.

Austen, Jane (1775-1817) LETTERS ed. by R. W. Chapman *O.U.P.* (1932) 1952 45s *Illus.*
LETTERS, 1796-1817 Selected by R. W. Chapman *O.U.P.* (*Worlds Classics*) 1956 7s 6d
The complete edition was acclaimed as a masterpiece of editing when it was first published in the 1932, two-volumed, edition. The last edition, in one volume of 728 pages, has minor corrections, small improvements, additional illustrations, and one newly-discovered letter. Nearly all of Jane Austen's letters were written to her sister Cassandra.

Barbellion (Bruce Frederick Cummings) (1889-1919) THE JOURNAL OF A DISAPPOINTED MAN *Chatto* (1919); *Penguin* 1948
'Barbellion' was a scientist with an artist's sensitivity; a literary man with scientific training. Struck down by an incurable malady, he created this 'Journal' to analyse and dissect his emotions and agonising experiences, conscious always of 'time's hurrying chariot'. H. G. Wells introduced this book; and A. J. Cummings, a distinguished journalist, and brother of 'Barbellion', contributed a preface to the posthumous *Last Diary* Chatto, 1920.

Baring, Maurice (1874-1945) THE PUPPET SHOW OF MEMORY *Heinemann* (1922)
Like 'Barbellion', Baring had to endure the pain of a grievous, incurable illness, but this autobiography records his happier years. His wit, grace, and intellectual distinction gave his novels and occasional writings a high place in twentieth-century literature. See Laura Lovat's *Maurice Baring: a postscript*, Hollis and Carter, 1948, for the poignant record of his fortitude in the last years of his life.

Baxter, Richard (1615-91) AUTOBIOGRAPHY ed. and abridged by J. M. Lloyd Thomas *Dent* (*Everyman*) (1925) 1931 6s 6d
Standard abridgement of the folio of 1696, *Reliquiae Baxterianae*. It helps to keep alive the memory of the army chaplain for the Puritans, who later suffered from the wrath and severity of Judge Jeffreys, and was imprisoned. His most widely-read work was *The Saints' Everlasting Rest*, 1650.

Beckford, William (1759-1844) LIFE AT FONTHILL, *1807-1822* ed. and trans. by Boyd Alexander *Hart-Davis* 1957 35s
'Letters to Francis, to be seen by no one.' They provide amusing light reading, now that the editor's research and scholarship have made them available in English. Apart from the 'interludes' in London and Paris, these letters of an eccentric add to our knowledge of the building of Fonthill.

Bell, Gertrude Lowthian (1868-1926) LETTERS ed. by Lady Bell
Benn (1927; 1937); *Penguin* 2 vols. 1939; SELECTED LETTERS
Penguin 1953
In addition to the interest arising from their vivid, personal style, these
famous letters must always be a prime source of information about the
Arab world. Of even greater importance as historical documents are the
two volumes edited by Elizabeth Burgoyne, *Gertrude Bell: From Her
Personal Papers, 1893-1914*, Benn, 1958, 42s; and the same title dealing
with the years *1914-1926*, Benn, 1961, 45s. The latter volume records her
work in the Arab intelligence bureau, the creation of the new state of
Iraq, and the founding of the Baghdad Museum. 'I don't think I ever
met anyone more entirely civilised,' wrote T. E. Lawrence.

Belloc, Hilaire (1870-1953) LETTERS FROM HILAIRE BELLOC sel. and
ed. by Robert Speaight *Hollis and Carter* 1958 30s
The choice is from letters written to Belloc's many friends and contemporaries, including Maurice Baring and other authors, during the
period from 1914 to the early forties. Many letters are not given in full,
the selection concentrating on the passages likely to have permanent and
general interest.

Bennett, Arnold (1867-1931) JOURNALS ed. by Newman Flower
3 vols. *Cassell* 1932-3; sel. by Frank Swinnerton *Penguin* 1954
Vol. I is concerned with the formative years, 1896 to 1910; vol. 2 with
the period of success and mature achievement, 1911 to 1921; and the
final vol. from 1921 to 1928, the brief period of established authority.
As a gifted journalist, Bennett had a flair for sensing 'the news' and an
eye for the unusual in everyday life; as a great novelist, aware of his
genius, he displayed an engaging egotism. Hence the attraction his
journals have for the average reader.

*Bewick, Thomas (1753-1828) A MEMOIR (1862) ed. by Selwyn
Image *Bodley Head* (1924); ed. by Montague Weekley *Cresset
Press* 1961 18s Illus.
'Written by himself, 1822-8, simply for his daughters' and his sons'
sake.' This is indeed 'a golden book', simple and homely as the artist-
craftsman was himself, and is a minor classic of heart-warming charm.
The edition in the *Cresset Library* is slightly abridged, and embellished
with many delightful wood-engravings by Bewick.

Blake William (1757-1827) LETTERS ed. by Geoffrey Keynes
Hart-Davis 1956 50s Illus.
The definitive edition. Refer also to Gilchrist's *Life of Blake* which
includes a selection of letters, and to the *Essays and Belles Lettres* section
for details of omnibus editions.

Blunt, Wilfrid Scawen (1840-1922) MY DIARIES 2 vols. (1919-20);
new edn. in 1 vol. *Secker* 1932
'A personal narrative of events, 1888-1914', of historical interest in the
present era of radical changes in Egypt, Africa, the Middle East and Asia.

Poet, rebel, wealthy diplomat and sportsman, Blunt opposed the traditional policy of nineteenth-century British imperialism, 'pleading the cause of the backward nations of the world, and especially those of Africa and Asia, from their slavery to Europe'.

Boswell, James (1740–95) THE BOSWELL PAPERS ed. by F. A. Pottle and Frank Brady *Heinemann* 1950 *in progress* Illus.

Vol. 1: London Journal, 1762–3 1950 25s; *Ace Books* 3s 6d

Vol. 2: In Holland, 1763–4 1952 8s 6d

Vol. 3: On the Grand Tour, vol. 1, 1764: Germany and Switzerland 1953 12s 6d

Vol. 4: On the Grand Tour, vol. 2, 1765–6: Italy, Corsica and France 1955 12s 6d

Vol. 5: In Search of a Wife, 1766–9 1957 30s

Vol. 6: Boswell for the Defence, 1769–74 1960 30s

Limited editions of the above contain additional material and illustrations. In the first volume the publisher's note sets out the full story of the most extraordinary 'find' in English literary history, with details of the plan to publish the complete series of the *Boswell Papers* found at Malahide Castle, and purchased from Colonel Isham by Yale University.

JOURNAL OF A TOUR TO CORSICA (1768) ed. by S. C. Roberts *C.U.P.* 1923 12s 6d

*JOURNAL OF A TOUR TO THE HEBRIDES WITH SAMUEL JOHNSON, 1773 (1785) ed. by F. A. Pottle and C. H. Bennett *Heinemann* 1936

This definitive edition gave for the first time the text of the original manuscript found at Malahide Castle. Of the many other editions there are *Collins* (*Classics*), 1955, 6s; *Dent* (*Everyman*), 1958, 8s 6d (text from third edition, with intro. by L. F. Powell); *Nelson* (*Classics*), 1954, 5s; *Macdonald* (*Illustrated Classics*), 1956, 15s; and *O.U.P. Standard Authors*, ed. by R. W. Chapman, 1924, 12s 6d. This edition includes Johnson's *Journey to the Western Islands of Scotland* (1775).

*Bottrall, Margaret (Editor) PERSONAL RECORDS *Hart-Davis* 1961 25s

'A gallery of self-portraits chosen by Margaret Bottrall.' This systematically arranged anthology of extracts from autobiographies, journals and letters presents in a single volume the whole range of writing in this form from the most distinguished and famous to the little-known and obscure. Starting in the seventeenth century and proceeding to the twentieth the contributions take us from Sir Thomas Browne to W. B. Yeats, H. G. Wells, 'Barbellion', G. K. Chesterton and the late Edwin Muir, grouped in seven sections that include 'Women In Love'; and the 'Afflicted and Distressed'.

Browne, Sir Thomas (1605–82) RELIGIO MEDICI (1642; 1643) *C.U.P.* (1953) 1955 10s 6d

For annotated entry and other editions see under *Essays and Belles Lettres* section.

*Browning, Elizabeth Barrett (1806-61) and Robert Browning (1812-89) THE BROWNING LOVE LETTERS, 1845-6 *Murray* (1899) 1923 21s 1176 pp.

Letters exchanged during the period of courtship that ended with the romantic elopement and marriage in 1846, when the two poets fled to Florence. They are probably the most widely-read letters in the language.

Bunyan, John (1628-88) GRACE ABOUNDING TO THE CHIEF OF SINNERS (1666) *Dent (Everyman)* (1907) 1954 8s 6d

For annotated entry and other editions see under *Philosophy and Religion* section.

*Burney, Fanny (Madame D'Arblay) (1752-1840) DIARY AND LETTERS, 1778-1840 ed. by her niece Charlotte Barrett (1842-6); ed. by Austin Dobson 6 vols. *Macmillan* 1904-5; THE DIARY ed. by Lewis Gibbs *Dent (Everyman)* (1940) 1961 12s 6d

A lively picture of eighteenth-century intellectual society from January 1778 (when Fanny Burney's *Evelina* was published) to February 1823. Her circle included celebrated literary and social personalities, such as Dr. Johnson, Mrs. Thrale, and people at the court of George III; and many French political *émigrés*. The standard biography of Madame D'Arblay draws upon hundreds of unpublished letters and other material: *The History of Fanny Burney*, by Joyce Hemlow, O.U.P., 1957, 35s.

Burns, Robert (1759-96) SELECTED LETTERS ed. by J. de Lancey Ferguson *O.U.P. (Worlds Classics)* 1953 7s 6d

A choice of about 200 letters from the standard edition in 2 vols. O.U.P., 1931, 63s.

Butler, Samuel (1835-1902) LETTERS BETWEEN SAMUEL BUTLER AND MISS E. M. A. SAVAGE, 1871-1885 ed. by Geoffrey Keynes and Brian Hill *Cape* 1935 7s 6d

Includes three sonnets by Samuel Butler on Miss Savage, his closest woman friend whom he portrayed in *The Way of All Flesh* as Alethea Pontifex.

THE FAMILY LETTERS OF SAMUEL BUTLER, 1841-1886 ed. by Arnold Silver *Cape* 1962 30s Illus.

An important redaction for students of Butler's *The Way of All Flesh*, for which see under *Fiction* section. Most of these letters have never been published before, and only now, therefore, is it possible to estimate the autobiographical element in the novel at its full value. In addition to the correspondence between father and son there is a selection of letters to and from Butler s mother and sisters.

Buxton, Sir Thomas Fowell (1786-1845) MEMOIRS ed. by Charles Buxton (1848); and with intro. by Earl Buxton for *Dent (Everyman)* 1925

Includes some of the letters and the speeches of this philanthropist whose work for reform of the criminal law proved to be of permanent importance. His sustained advocacy for the emancipation of slaves gave him world-wide renown.

Byron, Lord (George Gordon Noel Byron) *6th Baron* (1788-1824)
*LETTERS ed. by R. G. Howarth *Dent (Everyman)* (1933) 1962
12s 6d

A selection, introduced by André Maurois, from the standard edition in six volumes, Murray, 1897-1904. Annotations and index add greatly to the pleasure of the general reader.

*BYRON: A SELF PORTRAIT 2 vols. ed. by Peter Quennell *Murray* 1950 45s 826 pp.

Here the journals are reprinted in full, together with the editor's selection of Byron's most characteristic letters, covering between them the period 1798-1824. The preface and commentaries to this 'self-portrait' make this set of volumes of epistolary wit and lively gossip the best introduction to Byron's life and character we have had.

Carlyle, Jane Welsh (1801-66) LETTERS TO HER FAMILY, 1836-1863 ed. by Leonard Huxley *Murray* 1924 25s

'These letters, I perceive, equal and surpass whatever of best I know to exist, in that kind.' So wrote Carlyle himself, after the death of his wife. Froude's edition, published in 1883, and prepared by Carlyle, introduced readers to these witty, acute letters, with many salty comments on everyday social affairs and people.

*LETTERS selected by Trudy Bliss *Gollancz* (1949) 1954 21s; *Grey Arrow* 1959 3s 6d

'A new selection' of letters, collated with the originals, and with passages omitted by Froude, restored to the text as written.

Carlyle, Thomas (1795-1881) LETTERS TO HIS WIFE ed. by Trudy Bliss *Gollancz* 1953 25s

Over 700 letters are here, copied from the vast collection in the National Library of Scotland. Most of them have not been published before. The sequence is linked by an editorial commentary, with a glossary of names.

*REMINISCENCES (1881) ed. by C. E. Norton (1887) *Dent (Everyman)* 1932

Abounds with interest, with some extraordinarily vivid pen-portraits of literary contemporaries, such as De Quincey, and of Carlyle's family and friends.

Chesterfield, Philip Dormer Stanhope (4th Earl of) (1694-1773) LETTERS TO HIS SON AND OTHERS (1774) ed. by R. K. Root *Dent (Everyman)* (1929) 1957 8s 6d

A standard selection of the most characteristic letters, taken from the complete edition, ed. by Bonamy Dobrée, 6 vols. Eyre and Spottiswoode, 1932, published in a limited edition only. The worldly-wise epistles to the young Philip were intended to educate Chesterfield's son in the correct conduct of a gentleman's life in matters of etiquette, morals and behaviour. They and the other letters have been admired for their occasional wit, axiomatic, if cynical, wisdom, and the common sense of many of the precepts.

*Chesterton, Gilbert Keith (1874-1936) AUTOBIOGRAPHY *Hutchinson* (1936); *Grey Arrow* 1959 3s 6d; *Penguin* 1958 3s 6d
Of all his many books, this is perhaps the best of G.K.C., displaying his characteristic wit, paradoxical sense of fun, Christian virtues, tolerance, shrewdness, gaiety and the many other qualities that made him beloved by a wide circle of readers.

Cibber, Colley (1671-1757) AN APOLOGY FOR THE LIFE OF COLLEY CIBBER, COMEDIAN (1740) *Dent (Everyman)* 1914
Includes Hazlitt's 'Appreciation' of this actor and playwright, immortalised by Pope in the *Dunciad* of 1743. Dull his plays may have been, and his verse written as poet laureate doubltess merited Pope's lash; yet in this autobiography he provided a prime source of information on the stage of his time, with memorable pages on many famous players.

Clare, John (1793-1864) LETTERS ed. by J. W. and Anne Tibble *Routledge* 1951
'A representative collection; 249 in all, perhaps half Clare's known letters . . . In Clare's letters there is . . . something of the same "living" quality as in his poetry . . . this daring to be true to the life in him, driving the creative artist always deeper, even though not intellectually stated, is seen to be in Clare's letters with more deliberation than in the poems.'— *From the editors' preface. Sketches In the Life of John Clare*, written by himself and addressed to his friend John Taylor (the recipient of many of the letters), in March 1821, was first published with an introduction and notes by Edmund Blunden, in 1931.

Clarendon, Edward Hyde, *Earl of* (1608-74) THE LIFE OF EDWARD, EARL OF CLARENDON (1759) *O.U.P. (Worlds Classics)* 1955 9s 6d
Written in the third person for his children, and published posthumously. The only modern reprint contains also a selection from Clarendon's *History*, for which see under the *History* section.

Cobbett, William (1763-1835) AUTOBIOGRAPHY ed. by William Reitzel *Faber* (1933) 1947 8s 6d
'The progress of a ploughboy to a seat in Parliament.'

Coleridge, Samuel Taylor (1772-1834) COLLECTED LETTERS 4 vols. ed. by Earl Leslie Griggs *O.U.P.* 1956-9 Vols. 1-2, 105s; vols. 3-4, 105s
'These letters are particularly rich in biographical information. Coleridge continues to be his own best biographer.' Many of the letters are here published for the first time, and the editor has taken the text from the original manuscripts.

Collingwood, Robin George (1889-1943) AN AUTOBIOGRAPHY
O.U.P. 1939 15s Penguin 1945
The personal statement of a philosophical historian and archaeologist,
discussing for the general reader as well as the scholar, his intellectual
development and his political ideals, the latter being expressed in books
with a more restricted interest, in the question/answer form developed
by him with cogency in *The New Leviathan*.

Conrad, Joseph (1857-1924) A MIRROR OF THE SEA (1906) *Methuen
1950 6s*

A PERSONAL RECORD (1912) *Dent 1946 10s 6d*
Both essays in autobiography are bound together in the uniform edition
published by Dent.

*Cowper, William (1731-1800) SELECTED LETTERS ed. by W.
Hadley *Dent (Everyman)* 1926 6s 6d*; ed. by E. V. Lucas *O.U.P.*
(*Worlds Classics*) 1907
The chronological arrangement of the letters from 1758 to 1799 provides
a background to the poems, which, as E. V. Lucas averred, merit
Coleridge's praise 'divine chit-chat' as much as *The Task* and the other
quiet poems that Coleridge had in mind.

Creevey, Thomas (1768-1838) THE CREEVEY PAPERS ed. by John
Gore *Murray 1948 25s*; *Batsford 1963 18s* and 12s 6d (paperback)
The standard selection from the correspondence and diaries was edited
by Sir Herbert Maxwell, and published by Murray in 1903. These two
volumes, writes John Gore, have been 'a source of endless entertainment
to the reading public, of considerable value to the social historian and of
much interest to the student of politics'. The 1948 selection from the
main work and from a supplementary volume edited by John Gore in
1934, may be regarded as 'the cream of Creevey', with a biographical
commentary on this gossipy politician and man of fashion.

Darwin, Charles (1809-82) AUTOBIOGRAPHY (1887) ed. by Nora
Barlow *Collins 1958 16s*
A new edition, presenting for the first time the full, unabridged text,
with some notes and appendices, giving much information about
Darwin's early life, and his quarrel with Samuel Butler. Lady Barlow is
Darwin's granddaughter. A reprint of the 'autobiographical chapter'
originally included in the *Life and Letters*, 3 vols. ed. by Sir Francis
Darwin in 1887, was published in the *Thinkers Library*, Watts, 1949, 2s 6d.

*Davies, William Henry (1871-1940) AUTOBIOGRAPHY OF A SUPER-
TRAMP (1908) *Cape 1955 15s*; *Digit Books 3s 6d*
Five characteristic poems, exhibiting the same directness of observation
and simplicity of style that have made the prose work a twentieth-
century classic, are included in the standard edition.

*De Quincey, Thomas (1785-1859) CONFESSIONS OF AN ENGLISH
OPIUM EATER (1821; 1856) ed. by J. E. Jordan *Dent (Everyman)*

(1907) 1960 8s 6d; ed. by Malcolm Elwin *Macdonald (Illustrated Classics)* 1956 15s; *O.U.P. (Worlds Classics)* (1902) 1960 6s
Some readers prefer the 1821 text, contributed to the *London Magazine*, and published in book form in 1822, rather than the revised and enlarged edition of 1856. The edition in Macdonald's *Illustrated Classics* gives both texts, with some famous essays, portraits, and reproductions from contemporary engravings.

REMINISCENCES OF THE ENGLISH LAKE POETS (1834) ed. by J. E. Jordan *Dent (Everyman)* 1961 15s
Journalism, but of a frank, personal type that makes this a most important, as well as a most interesting, and even amusing book. Flashes of autobiography mingle with vivid accounts of the Wordsworths (not always flattering); of life at Dove Cottage (which De Quincey took over from the Wordsworths); of Coleridge, 'the sublime somnambulist', and of Southey. Professor Jordan's new edition is the best ever published of a difficult text, and is offered as a definitive one.

Defoe, Daniel (1661-1731) LETTERS ed. by George Harris Healey O.U.P. 1955 42s 528 pp
These letters reveal Defoe the journalist and pamphleteer, the political schemer, rather than the man of letters.

Evelyn, John (1620-1706) DIARY 6 vols. ed. by E. S. De Beer O.U.P. 1955 £15 15s the set; and *Oxford Standard Authors* 1959 30s; ed. by William Bray (1818-19) 2 vols *Dent (Everyman)* 1907 6s 6d each
The standard edition in *Oxford English Texts* provides for the first time the full text edited from manuscripts in possession of the diarist's descendant, Mr. John Evelyn. The cheaper edition, a volume of 1037 pages, has some omissions, but few of any great importance.

Fanshawe, Lady Anne (1625-80) MEMOIRS (1830) *Bodley Head* 1905
Charming account of Caroline life and of Spain and Portugal, written to narrate the events of the daily life of Lady Anne and her husband Sir Richard Fanshawe (1608-66) for their son. After the Restoration, Sir Richard, who had served under Prince Rupert, was appointed ambassador to Madrid and Lisbon.

Field, Michael (Katherine Harris Bradley—1846-1914; and Edith Emma Cooper—1862-1913) WORKS AND DAYS ed. by T. and D. C. Sturge-Moore *Murray* 1933 10s 6d Illus.
A selection from the journal, with some letters, kept jointly by the aunt and her niece, who collaborated in all their literary work, including their poetry and dramas, so closely and for so long, that under the joint pen-name of Michael Field they created an individual *persona* . To their circle of literary and artistic acquaintances they attracted most of the distinguished writers of the day.

FitzGerald, Edward (1809-83) LETTERS ed. by J. M. Cohen
Centaur Press 1960 21s
This selection fills the gap left by the out-of-print standard editions that
used to delight previous generations of readers (Macmillan, 1894, 1895,
and 1901), by the wit, lively style and individuality of the eccentric
translator of Omar Khayyám's *Rubáiyát*. But see also under *Essays and
Belles Lettres* section for a generous selection included in the *Reynard
Library* omnibus published in 1962.

Fleming, Margaret ('Marjorie') (1803-11) THE COMPLETE MARJORIE
FLEMING: her journals, letters and verses transcribed and edited
by Frank Sidgwick *Sidgwick and Jackson* 1935
Sir Walter Scott's 'Pet Marjorie'; the subject of a charming essay by Dr
John Brown (see *Essays and Belles Lettres* section); in this edition all that
this gifted wonder-child wrote is gathered together.

Fox, Caroline (1819-71) MEMORIES OF OLD FRIENDS 2 vols. ed. by
Horace N. Pym 1882
In this somewhat scarce Smith, Elder edition there are also fourteen
letters from John Stuart Mill. He was one of many friends among the
intellectually eminent who valued, and were inspired by, the conversation and character of this remarkable Quaker. In his *Caroline Fox*, by
Wilson Harris, Constable, 1944, the author allows the subject of his
biography to tell her own story by quoting abundantly from her journals.

Fox, George (1624-91) JOURNAL prepared by Thomas Ellwood in
1694 2 vols. ed. by Norman Penney *C.U.P.* 1911 75s; rev. edn.
by John L. Nickalls *C.U.P.* 1952 22s 6d; *Dent (Everyman)* (1924)
1962 10s 6d
The standard revised edition in one volume is slightly modernised for
the general reader. Since George Fox, the celebrated Quaker, was un-
lettered, his work was dictated, but the style of his *Journal* is Biblical in
its nobility, and has taken its place as one of the most beloved spiritual
revelations in modern European literature. Norman Penney also edited
Fox's *Short Journals and Itinerary Journals*, C.U.P., 1925, 25s, and prepared the *Everyman* edition noted above.

Franklin, Benjamin (1706-90) AUTOBIOGRAPHY ed. by John
Bigelow (1868) *Dent (Everyman)* (1908) 1960 8s 6d; *O.U.P.
(Worlds Classics)* 1924 7s 6d
John Bigelow's first authentic edition of this famous personal narrative
of the making and maturity of the apprentice who became a renowned
political philosopher and diplomat, was published in Great Britain in
1905 by Dent. W. T. Franklin's edition of 1817 was abridged. The
Everyman edition contains also what amounts to a biography of the
statesman's later life, by W. Macdonald.

*Gibbon, Edward (1737-94) AUTOBIOGRAPHY (1796) *Dent (Every-
man)* 1911; *O.U.P. (Worlds Classics)* (1907) 1960 8s 6d

Follows the text of Lord Sheffield's edition published after the historian's death. Introduction by J. B. Bury, who was the editor of the definitive edition of the *Decline and Fall of the Roman Empire*. This is one of the most famous autobiographies in the language.

LETTERS 3 vols. ed. by J. E. Norton *Cassell* 1956 168s
The first collected edition, containing all the letters extant from 1750 to 1794.

Gill, Eric (1882–1940) AUTOBIOGRAPHY *Cape* 1940 12s 6d
As artist and thinker Gill made notable contributions to his age, and as a typographer he influenced a whole generation.

★Gosse, Sir Edmund (1849–1928) FATHER AND SON *Heinemann* (1907) 1958 12s 6d
'Surely among the half dozen English prose masterpieces of the twentieth century: as much a classic among autobiographies as *Lord Jim* among novels or *Zuleika Dobson* among fantasies.'—*Lord David Cecil, Sunday Times, 12 May, 1957.*

Grant, Elizabeth (1797–1885) MEMOIRS OF A HIGHLAND LADY, 1797–1827 ed. by Lady Strachey (1898); new edition by Angus Davidson *Murray* 1950 12s 6d
A narrative of individual charm, with value as social history. The current edition omits parts of little interest nowadays.

★Gray, Thomas (1716–1771) LETTERS ed. by John Beresford *O.U.P.* (*Worlds Classics*) 1925 7s 6d; *Dent* (*Everyman*) 1955 10s 6d
In the *Everyman* volume, Lewis Gibbs includes some of Gray's essays, and all the poems, together with a selection of the entertaining letters, which, by common consent, are amongst the best in the language. The standard edition of Gray's *Correspondence* is in three volumes of 1480 pages, edited by Paget Toynbee, O.U.P., 1935, 100s.

Grenfell, Sir Wilfred Thomason (1865–1940) A LABRADOR DOCTOR *Hodder* 1948 15s; paperback edn. 4s 6d
Contains *Forty Years for Labrador* (1932) and *A Labrador Doctor* (1920) recording his devoted work in the dual roles of physician and Christian missionary.

Greville, Charles Cavendish Fulke (1794–1865) MEMOIRS 8 vols. ed. by Lytton Strachey and Roger Fulford *Macmillan* 1938; ed. by Roger Fulford *Batsford* 1963 18s and 12s 6d (paperback)
An entertaining source book of social and political gossip of the period —George IV to the early years of Queen Victoria's reign. The limited edition is the only complete text.

Guest, Lady Charlotte (1812–95) DIARIES ed. by the Earl of Bessborough *Murray* 1950
These extracts from her journals, 1833–52, were followed by a companion volume for the years 1853–91, when she was Lady Charlotte Schreiber,

Murray, 1952, 21s. Lady Guest was a celebrated linguist; she translated the ancient Welsh *Mabinogion*; wrote a technical treatise on iron processing; reared a family of ten children; kept these interesting journals; and lived to the age of 83: thus her diaries present a full portrait of Victorian life.

Hare, Augustus John Cuthbert (1834-1903) THE STORY OF MY LIFE 6 vols. (1896-1900); 2 vols. ed. and abridged by Malcolm Barnes *Allen and Unwin* 1952-3 30s each

In the abridgement volume 1 deals with 'The Years With Mother'; volume 2 with the period 'In My Solitary Life'. Augustus Hare's *Walks in Rome* and *Wanderings in Spain*, are minor classics, still read with enjoyment by travellers. This immense autobiography offers an insight into the mind and way of life of a Victorian middle-class worthy; the abridgement excludes all the padding, and everything 'that has lost its value with the years'.

*Haydon, Benjamin Robert (1786-1846) AUTOBIOGRAPHY AND JOURNALS (1853) *Macdonald (Illustrated Classics)* 1950 15s

For many readers this is the most delightful literary journal ever published. Tom Taylor edited the first edition. The best ordinary edition, in two volumes, with introduction by Aldous Huxley, 1926, Peter Davies, is out of print. The 1950 edition is a pleasure to handle. For scholars, the definitive edition edited by Willard Bissell Pope, now in progress, will publish everything extant. Two volumes were published in 1960: 1: 1808-15; 2: 1816-24; 1080 pages, O.U.P., 160s. Scarcely a great artist, Haydon was certainly a considerable writer, and through his pages passes almost every great contemporary of this golden age.

Hazlitt, William (1778-1830) LIBER AMORIS (1823) *Peter Nevill* 1948 15s

The story of his heart, frank, bitter and anguished. The only recent edition also contains some *Dramatic Criticisms*, and an introduction by Charles Morgan.

Herbert, Edward (Lord Herbert of Cherbury) (1583-1648) AUTOBIOGRAPHY (1764) ed. by Sir Sidney Lee *Routledge* 1886

A minor work, but, presenting as it does, the self-portrait and experiences up to 1624, of a brilliant character whose poems have a sure place in literature, and whose career as a soldier and a diplomatist was passed during an era of crisis, one which is of considerable historical interest.

Hervey, Lord (1696-1743) MEMOIRS (1848; 1931) ed. by Romney Sedgwick *Batsford* 1963 18s Illus.

A revised edition of the 1952 text which was a selection of the 3 volumes of the 1931 edition. Lord Hervey's memoirs of the first ten years of the reign of George II (1727-1737), ending with the death of the Queen, are not only an invaluable source book on court life but are rated as an 'historical masterpiece', ranking Hervey, states the editor, 'with Saint Simon among the great memoir writers'.

*Hickey, William (1749-1830) MEMOIRS 4 vols. (1913-25); ed. by Peter Quennell *Hutchinson* 1960 42s
Racy, frank, amusing and revealing, these memories of a lawyer, socialite and womaniser, whose life and work took him from London to the East, and particularly to India, where he became a leading attorney, have been rightly evaluated as 'one of the most fascinating autobiographies of its kind ever published in the English language'. In the reprint, the original four volumes are brought within the compass of a single volume by the elimination of repetitious passages and 'by closing the story at the end of the most interesting early period of Hickey's life'.

*Hillary, Richard (*d.* 1943) THE LAST ENEMY *Macmillan* 1942 15s (*St. Martins Library*) 1962 4s
A poignant, moving narrative, cast in the form of a novel, largely factual. The author was a young flying officer in the R.A.F., who fought gallantly, and suffered much. In recovery he again experiences the perils of war in the air, and meets the last enemy.

Hoby, Margaret (Lady) (1571-1633) DIARY, 1599-1605 ed. by Dorothy M. Meads *Routledge* 1930
Edited from the manuscript in the British Museum. It is the earliest extant diary written by an Englishwoman, and its interest lies in the revelation of the domestic life of a gentlewoman of the time of Queen Elizabeth I.

Holcroft, Thomas (1745-1809) MEMOIRS (1816) 2 vols. ed. by Elbridge Colby *Constable* 1925; *O.U.P.* (*Worlds Classics*) 1925
'The life of Thomas Holcroft written by himself, continued to the time of his death from his diary, notes and other papers, by William Hazlitt.' This picturesque narrative of the progress of a stable boy who became an actor, a novelist, and author of more than thirty plays, has outlived its author's other work, though his *Road To Ruin* is still remembered.

*Hopkins, Gerard Manley (1844-89) LETTERS TO ROBERT BRIDGES 2 vols. ed. by Claude Colleer Abbott *O.U.P.* (1935) 1955 50s; FURTHER LETTERS ed. by C. C. Abbott *O.U.P.* (1938) 1956 50s
These three volumes are the most creative, revealing and analytical collection of a poet's letters since those of Keats. Wherever they are opened one is brought into communication with a powerful intellect and a poetic thinker of high critical integrity. They include the correspondence of Hopkins with a fellow poet, R. W. Dixon, and the last volume contains letters discovered in 1952, and Hopkins's correspondence with Coventry Patmore.

A HOPKINS READER ed. by John Pick *O.U.P.* 1953
Interesting selection, with an introduction by the poet's biographer, of some characteristic letters, some of the poetry, and a choice from Hopkins's fugitive, cogent notes, providing an introduction for those lacking the leisure or without the opportunity to consult the standard volumes.

*Hudson, William Henry (1841-1922) FAR AWAY AND LONG AGO (1918) *Dent* 1953 11s 6d; *Everyman* 1953 8s 6d
'A history of my early life' in South America. Probably the most popular of all the naturalist's non-fiction books, introduced in the standard edition by R. B. Cunninghame Graham; and in *Everyman* by John Galsworthy.

Hunt, James Henry Leigh (1784-1859) AUTOBIOGRAPHY (1850; 1860) ed. by J. E. Morpurgo *Cresset Press* 1949 12s 6d
Leigh Hunt's friendships formed a stimulating background to his own creative and journalistic writing, but his autobiography is pleasant and interesting reading for its own sake.

Hutchinson, Sara (1775-1835) LETTERS, 1800-1835 ed. by Kathleen Coburn *Routledge* 1954
The first publication of letters of prime interest because of their references to Sara's circle, which included her brother-in-law Wordsworth, Charles Lamb, Southey, and Coleridge. Lively and vivid, they convey the personality of the writer across the lapse of years. The interested reader may be referred also to George Whalley's *Coleridge and Sara Hutchinson; and the Asra Poems*, Routledge, 1955, 21s.

James, Henry (1843-1916) AUTOBIOGRAPHY ed. by Frederick W. Dupee *W. H. Allen* 1956
Collects three autobiographical works, first published separately by Macmillan: *A Small Boy and Others* (1913); *Notes of a Son and a Brother* (1914); and, *The Middle Years* (1917).

SELECTED LETTERS ed. by Leon Edel *Hart-Davis* 1956 16s
A choice by James's biographer, of 120 letters, some of which have not been published before. Those that have, are taken from Percy Lubbock's first collection, 2 vols. Macmillan, 1920.

*Jefferies, Richard (1848-87) THE STORY OF MY HEART (1883) *Eyre and Spottiswoode* 1949 5s
A poignant personal document, somewhat over-sensitively expressed.

Johnson, Samuel (1709-84) THE LETTERS OF SAMUEL JOHNSON 3 vols. ed. by R. W. Chapman *O.U.P.* 1952 160s *SELECTED LETTERS *O.U.P.* (*Worlds Classics*) 1925 7s 6d
The collected edition includes 'Mrs. Thrale's genuine letters to him', and runs to 1516 pages. A great edition of Dr. Johnson's complete works was inaugurated in 1958 by the publication for the first time in one volume, of the *Diaries, Prayers, and Annals*, that is, of all the autobiographical writings, edited by E. L. McAdam and two others, Yale, and O.U.P., 80s.

Joyce, James (1882-1941) LETTERS ed. by Stuart Gilbert *Faber* 1957 42s
Few of these 400 letters and notes had appeared in print before this collection was published. Written to a large circle of friends as well as to

relatives, they enable the reader to watch the development of *Ulysses* through the eight years of its writing, and to understand Joyce as a man apart from his writings.

*Keats, John (1795-1821) LETTERS ed. by Maurice Buxton Forman *O.U.P.* (1931) 1952 45s 640 pp
The definitive edition of all the extant letters. By common consent they are unequalled in English literature for the insight they give us into poetic development. Memorable phrases, flashes of piercing insight and critical analysis, abound in these pages.

SELECTED LETTERS ed. by Frederick Page *O.U.P.* (*Worlds Classics*) 1954 8s 6d; ed. by Hugh I'Anson Fausset *Nelson* (*Classics*) 1929 6s
See also *Biography* section for Houghton's *Life and Letters of John Keats* (1848).

Kempe, Margery (*fl.* 1370) THE BOOK OF MARGERY KEMPE ed. by W. Butler-Bowdon *O.U.P.* (*Worlds Classics*) 1954 7s 6d
The original was found by chance in 1934. 'The discovery . . . is of the very greatest importance for the history of English literature. The book is a biography or autobiography, written when kings of the House of Lancaster were on the throne.' So wrote R. W. Chambers introducing the first publication of the modernised version, Cape, 1936. Obsolete words have been retained when their meanings are clear, and replaced by modern equivalents when obscure or when they have changed their meanings. For a literal copy of the manuscript, see the edition in the Early English Texts Society series, O.U.P., 1940, 30s.

Kilvert, Francis (1840-79) DIARY, 1870-1879 3 vols. ed. by William Plomer *Cape* (1938-40); 1961 105s (the set) 1308 pp; SELECTIONS *Cape* (1944) 1960 18s
A new minor classic was added to English literature by the discovery of twenty-two notebooks, the complete diary kept by a young Victorian curate. The editor has made a selection for the larger edition, abridged in the smaller volume, to give the best of a charmingly revealing personal document. This simple, unaffected, hard-working parish priest gives us some poignant sketches of the peasants for whom he toiled, and his descriptions of country life and love in Clyro (Radnorshire) and Langley Burrell (Wiltshire) endear his book to readers now that it has been so admirably presented by publisher and editor.

Kipling, Rudyard (1865-1936) SOMETHING OF MYSELF *Macmillan* (1937) 1951 10s 6d
An unfinished fragment, intended to 'deal with his life from the point of view of his work'. So writes his biographer, Charles Carrington, adding, 'There are few dates, and those not always accurate . . . as a record of self-criticism it is worth much.'

*Lamb, Charles (1775-1834) LETTERS 3 vols. ed. by E. V. Lucas *Methuen and Dent* 1935; 2 vols. chosen and arranged by Guy Pocock *Dent* (*Everyman*) 1945 6s 6d each

The selection of 738 letters from Lucas's complete edition contains the annotations that are so necessary for the enjoyment of these incomparable and diverting epistles addressed to most of Lamb's immortal contemporaries during the great period of the romantic revival, from 1796 to 1834.

*Lawrence, David Herbert (1885-1930) COLLECTED LETTERS 2 vols. ed. by Harry T. Moore *Heinemann* 1962 84s (the set) 1307 pp
LETTERS ed. by Aldous Huxley *Heinemann* 1932 30s 925 pp
Few writers have left more intense, revealing letters than these; they are thus the best introduction to Lawrence's ideas and character, in spite of the many good books he has already attracted. The two-volumed collections supersedes the earlier, and is offered as the definitive edition, with an introduction, and a 'Who's Who'.

Lawrence, Thomas Edward (1888-1935) SELECTED LETTERS ed. by David Garnett *Cape* (1938) 1952 18s
Biographies and controversies continue to arouse public interest in the enigmatic personality of 'Lawrence of Arabia'. Hence the importance of this selection of letters, some of which are included in the *Essential T. E. Lawrence*, Cape, 1951, 18s. Lawrence's brother, A. W., has edited a volume of *Letters To T. E. Lawrence*, Cape, 1962, 35s, 'as a corrective' to some popular misconceptions and simplifications. These letters are of great interest, for Lawrence's circle was wide, and included eminent statesmen, authors, and artists.

Le Gallienne, Richard (1866-1947) FROM A PARIS GARRET *Unicorn Press* 1936 21s
Grant Richards introduced this pleasant autobiographical narrative of life in the nineties by a charming writer, bohemian and romantic novelist, whose *Quest of the Golden Girl* (1896) may still be read with the nostalgic pleasure evoked by the period of the *Yellow Book*.

Lovett, William (1800-87) THE LIFE AND STRUGGLES OF WILLIAM LOVETT by himself 2 vols. *Bell* (1876); ed. by R. H. Tawney 1920
The personal narrative of a famous Chartist whose struggles 'in pursuit of bread, knowledge and freedom' are of considerable importance in the social and economic history of the nineteenth century.

Ludlow, Edmund (c. 1617-92) MEMOIRS, 1625-1672 (1698-9) 2 vols. ed. by Sir Charles Firth *O.U.P.* 1894
Ludlow was Lieutenant-General of the Horse in the army of the Commonwealth; his memoirs are therefore 'at once an autobiography and a history of Ludlow's own times'.

Machen, Arthur (1863-1947) AUTOBIOGRAPHY *Unicorn Press* 1951 15s
When Machen died, the last representative of the old-fashioned, traditional, bohemian man of letters left the literary scene. Yet he found

writing for a living arduous and until the last few decades, financially unrewarding. His autobiographical volumes and his tales of the supernatural will probably always find interested readers.

Mansfield, Katherine (Kathleen Mansfield Beauchamp) (1888-1923) JOURNAL ed. by J. Middleton Murry *Constable* (1927) 1954 30s.
The last edition was definitive. This journal of a literary woman, kept from 1904 to 1922, has a singular poignancy, because the reader is always aware of the cruel fate that was to limit the life of a genius just at the moment of maturity and fame.

LETTERS ed. by J. Middleton Murry *Constable* (1928) 1951 45s 701 pp
This revised and enlarged edition supersedes the earlier collection done in two volumes.

Mendoza, Daniel (1764-1836) MEMOIRS ed. by Paul Magriel *Batsford* 1951
These lively memoirs are a classic of boxing literature. The modern edition reprinted the champion's *Observations On the Art of Pugilism* (1789) a book of instruction that emphasised, what Mendoza's fights had demonstrated, perhaps for the first time, the advantage of systematic defence over mere brute force.

*Mill, John Stuart (1806-73) AUTOBIOGRAPHY (1873) ed. by J. J. Coss *O.U.P.* 1924 20s; ed. by H. J. Laski *O.U.P.* (*Worlds Classics*) 1924 7s 6d
For the series edition, H. J. Laski wrote a preface, and included an appendix of hitherto unpublished speeches by Mill.

Montagu, (Lady) Mary Wortley (1689-1762) LETTERS, 1709-1762 (1763-7) ed. by R. Brimley Johnson *Dent* (*Everyman*) 1906
Acute observation, eighteenth-century wit, and the fact that the writer lived in Turkey for a period of two or three years, when her husband was ambassador in Constantinople, give these letters a special place in literature and social history.

Moore, George (1852-1933) CONFESSIONS OF A YOUNG MAN (1888) *Heinemann* 1952 15s; *Digit Books* 1961 3s 6d
HAIL AND FAREWELL 3 vols. *Heinemann* (1911-13) 1947 15s each
A fusion of fiction and autobiographical narrative, the first being reminiscent in style and tone of that earlier period work, Alfred de Musset's *Confession d'un Enfant du Siècle*; the second introducing in its three parts many of Moore's Irish and other contemporaries: *Ave* (1911); *Salve* (1912); and *Vale* (1914).

Morris, William (1834-96) LETTERS TO HIS FAMILY AND FRIENDS ed. by Philip Henderson *Longmans* 1950 25s Illus.
The first collection to be published.

*Muir, Edwin (1887-1959) AN AUTOBIOGRAPHY *Hogarth Press* (1940) 1954 21s

A poet's portrait of himself tracing his intellectual development, against the background of his life in Germany and Austria, and other countries of Europe, and his literary work as a critic and a gifted translator of Kafka.

Nelson, Horatio (*Lord*) (1758-1805) LETTERS ed. by Geoffrey Rawson *Dent* (*Everyman*) 1961 12s 6d

A selection from Sir Harris Nicolas's edition of 1844-6, and from the Morrison collection of correspondence between Lord Nelson and Lady Hamilton privately printed in 1894, with editorial notes, some supplementary letters and a few official dispatches.

Newman, John Henry (1801-90) LETTERS ed. by Derek Stanford and Muriel Spark *Peter Owen* 1957 25s

Presented as a selection with an autobiographical pattern: one editor is an Anglican and was responsible for the choice from Cardinal Newman's Church of England period; the other is a Catholic, and chose the letters written after his conversion.

North, Roger (1653-1734) AUTOBIOGRAPHY ed. by A. Jessop 1887 LIVES OF THE NORTHS 3 vols. ed. by A. Jessop *Bell* 1890

The writer was the youngest of six brothers in one of the greatest families of their times. It included the illustrious Sir Thomas North, translator of Plutarch's *Lives*. Roger North's eulogies of his family (the 1890 edition includes the *Autobiography*) are not without interest. See also Lytton Strachey's essay on Roger's elder brother, Dr. John North.

O'Crohan, Tomas (1856-1937) THE ISLANDMAN translated from the Irish by Robin Flower (1934) *O.U.P.* 1951 15s Illus. *Penguin* 1943

The simplicity of this narrative and the remote experience of the writer created a classic unique in literature. O'Crohan was shrewd, hardworking, and God-fearing, and he was born, lived all his life, and died, on the Great Blasket Island.

*Orwell, George (Eric Arthur Blair) (1903-50) DOWN AND OUT IN PARIS AND LONDON *Secker and Warburg* (1933) 1949 15s

A grim and realistic chapter in the autobiography of Eric Blair, author of *1984* and *Animal Farm*, whose literary work was written under the pen-name which he made world-famous.

*Osborne, Dorothy (Lady Temple) (1627-95) LETTERS ed. by Sir Edward Parry (1888); ed. by G. C. Moore Smith *O.U.P.* 1928 30s; Parry's edition *Dent* (*Everyman*) 1914

These letters written to Sir William Temple between 1652 and 1654 have a charm and interest that have endeared them to readers from the time when Judge Parry first edited them. His introduction and notes were reprinted in the *Everyman* edition.

O'Sullivan, Maurice (1904-50) TWENTY YEARS A-GROWING trans. from the Irish (1933) Revised edition O.U.P. (*Worlds Classics*) 1953 7s 6d
When Chatto published the first edition this autobiography was recognised as a classic, and in the *Worlds Classics* edition, was introduced as such by E. M. Forster.

Pattison, Mark (1813-84) MEMOIRS *Macmillan* 1885
Frank self-analysis of a great scholar, thought at one time to have been the model taken by George Eliot for her classic portrait of the type of devoted pedant, in Mr. Casaubon of *Middlemarch*.

*Pepys, Samuel (1633-1703) DIARY 10 vols. ed. by H. B. Wheatley *Bell* (1893-9); 3 vols. (India paper) 84s
The standard edition, with Braybrooke's notes, whose original edition was published in 1825, after the first deciphering of the manuscript by the Rev. J. Smith. This fascinating, world-famous personal record of public matters and private experiences from 1660 to 1669 (a period that included the Great Plague and the Great Fire of London) has probably been read more widely than any other diary in European literature. Its uninhibited, racy freedom of expression, amusing trivia, as well as its documentary value as a subjective narrative of public affairs in an era of extraordinary interest, give it a unique place in literature. A complete, definitive text is still awaited.

3 vols. ed. by John Warrington *Dent* (*Everyman*) 1953 10s 6d each 1532 pp
This selected text is based on one first transcribed by Mynors Bright in 1875-9. A popular selection, entitled *Everybody's Pepys*, being an abridgement by O. F. Morshead, with illustrations by E. H. Shepard, Bell, 1926, 18s, offers the most entertaining and generally interesting entries.

LETTERS OF SAMUEL PEPYS AND HIS FAMILY CIRCLE ed. by Helen Truesdell Heath O.U.P. 1955 35s
Collects the letters that passed between Pepys and his close relatives. Of the 188 documents, 162 are here printed in full for the first time, though many have been quoted.

Pilkington, Laetitia (1712-50) MEMOIRS (1748-54) ed. by Iris Barry *Routledge* 1928
Of minor interest as literature, but a lively narrative of an unsettled life typical of the period. As this adventuress formed a close friendship with Dean Swift, her memoirs have a special value for the information they afford the student on his later years.

Pope, Alexander (1688-1744) LETTERS selected by John Butt O.U.P. (*Worlds Classics*) 1960 8s 6d
Based on the great edition in five volumes of Pope's *Correspondence*, a work of consummate scholarship, prepared for the press by George Sherburn, O.U.P., 1956, 210s.

Raleigh, Sir Walter Alexander (1861-1922) LETTERS, 1879-1922
2 vols. ed. by Lady Raleigh *Methuen* 1926; SELECTED LETTERS,
1880-1922 *Methuen* 1928
Sir Walter's wine merchant once confessed to having been guilty of
concocting unnecessary letters sent to his customer with the sole object
of eliciting a characteristic and thereafter treasured reply. Sir Walter
Raleigh was a gifted teacher, and his letters are certainly amongst the
best published in the first half of the twentieth century.

Reid, Forrest (1876-1947) APOSTATE *Constable* (1926); *Faber* 1947
10s 6d
A self study in spiritual and mental development by an Irish novelist.

Ruskin, John (1819-1900) PRAETERITA: an autobiography 3 vols.
Allen and Unwin (1899) 1949 7s 6d each; *Hart-Davis* 1949 7s 6d
'Scenes and thoughts perhaps worthy of memory in my past life.' First
published 1885-9. The Hart-Davis edition is introduced by Sir Kenneth
Clark.

Scott, Sir Walter (1771-1832) JOURNAL (1890) 3 vols. ed. by
J. G. Tait *Oliver and Boyd* 1939; 1941; 1946 5s; 7s 6d; and 10s;
one-volume edition 1950 25s
A self-portrait of great charm: 'by general consent a great book'. This
is the definitive edition, the revised text having been established by
photostat.

Shaw, George Bernard (1856-1950) SIXTEEN SELF SKETCHES
Constable 1949 15s
Collects into one volume fragments of autobiography scattered here and
there in Bernard Shaw's writings.

Shelley, Percy Bysshe (1792-1822) LETTERS 2 vols. ed. by Roger
Ingpen *Bell* 1915; ed. by F. L. Jones *O.U.P.* 1963 50s 600 pp
For details of a selection of the poet's letters see the *Nonesuch* Shelley,
entered in the *Essays and Belles Lettres* section.

Smith, Logan Pearsall (1865-1946) UNFORGOTTEN YEARS *Constable*
1938 10s
Characteristic sketches of family and friends, with some account of the
writer's experiences and growth, written in that cultivated, quietly ironic
prose style readers of his *Trivia* would expect.

*Smith, Sydney (1771-1845) LETTERS 2 vols. ed. by Nowell
Charles Smith *O.U.P.* 1953 105s; SELECTED LETTERS *O.U.P.*
(*Worlds Classics*) 1956 7s 6d
The complete edition runs nearly to 900 pages; but the editor made an
enjoyable selection, with interesting notes, for the *Worlds Classics*.
Sydney Smith was unquestionably one of the most delightful letter-
writers in literature; much of the spontaneous wit and gaiety, and the
character of the man who was so loved by his family and circle, found
expression in his letters.

Somerville, Alexander (1811-85) THE AUTOBIOGRAPHY OF A WORK-ING MAN (1848) ed. by John Carswell *Turnstile Press* 1951 10s 6d
A social document of considerable interest. The savage treatment meted out to Somerville, who, as a soldier, was punished by flogging (a hundred strokes of the cat) for the trivial offence of writing a letter of complaint to the Press, aroused the conscience of many liberal-minded people.

Soutar, William (1898-1943) DIARIES OF A DYING MAN *Chambers* 1954
A record of fourteen bedridden years, by one who was considered by good judges to be the best modern Scottish poet.

Southey, Robert (1774-1843) LETTERS ed. by Maurice H. Fitz-gerald *O.U.P.* (*Worlds Classics*) 1912
'Southey's letters show his true character' quotes the editor from Walter Savage Landor, adding 'they offer us a complete self-revelation of one of the most remarkable men of his day'.

Stephen, Sir Leslie (1832-1904) SOME EARLY IMPRESSIONS *Hogarth Press* 1924
A fragment written in 1903, but never published in book form until this edition. It offers a sketch of the life of an intellectual at Cambridge, where the writer resided for fourteen years.

Stevenson, Robert Louis (1850-94) LETTERS TO HIS FAMILY AND FRIENDS, 1868-1894 4 vols. ed. by Sir Sidney Colvin *Methuen* 1911
VAILIMA LETTERS *Methuen* (1895) 1926; *Nelson* (*Classics*) 1928
Addressed to Colvin, November 1890-October 1894, from Stevenson's house 'Vailima', in Samoa, where he died.

Sturt, George (George Bourne) (1863-1927) JOURNALS ed. by Geoffrey Grigson *Cresset Press* 1941
In these pages are recorded some of the changes that took place in the English countryside and in village life between 1890 and 1902. See also Sturt's book entered in the *History* section.

A SMALL BOY IN THE 60's *C.U.P.* 1927
A minor masterpiece, introduced by Arnold Bennett. For other books by this craftsman-teacher, who, writing under the pen-name of 'George Bourne', expressed the very essence of a vanished but traditional English country life, see the *Essays and Belles Lettres* section.

Sullivan, John William Navin (1886-1937) BUT FOR THE GRACE OF GOD *Cape* 1932
A poignant fragment by a man who was dogged by ill-health. His occasional writings (especially his journalism on music) were much prized, for he was gifted both as a scientist and a writer.

*Swift, Jonathan (1667-1745) JOURNAL TO STELLA (1766-8) 2 vols.
ed. by Sir Harold Williams *O.U.P.* 1948 60s Illus.; ed. by
J. K. Moorhead *Dent (Everyman)* 1955 10s 6d
An intimate, fascinating journal in the form of letters, written, without
thought of subsequent publication, to 'Stella' (i.e. Esther Johnson), and
dispatched regularly from London to Dublin while Swift was separated
from his friend during the period 1710 to 1713. By this means he gave
Stella a record of his life. His spontaneous thoughts and comments on
acquaintances, and on topics of the day, often expressed in his 'little
language' or 'prittle prattle', to be fully enjoyed, need both commentary
and notes. These are supplied by the great authority on Swift, in the
standard edition, which also includes a long introduction, clues to obscure
allusions to people and events, seven documentary appendices, a facsimile
of one letter, six portrait plates, together with a full and analytical index.
The *Everyman* is the best ordinary edition, with entries 'newly de-
ciphered'. See also the *Essays and Belles Lettres* section for selections in
omnibus editions.

Swinburne, Algernon Charles (1837-1909) THE SWINBURNE
LETTERS. 6 vols. ed. by Cecil Y. Lang *Yale; O.U.P.* 1959-62
252s (the set) 2162 pp
A superb example of modern editorial scholarship, in which the poet's
letters from 1854 to 1909 are made available for the leisured to dip into,
finding much to delight and a good deal of perceptive criticism, and the
learned historian to study.

Terry, Dame Ellen (1848-1928) ELLEN TERRY AND BERNARD SHAW:
a correspondence ed. by Christopher St. John *Constable* (1931);
Reinhardt 1949 25s Illus.
'A correspondence unique in the annals of the theatre . . . the letters were
evidently written without a thought of their possible publication . . .
Mr. Shaw consented to contribute the preface.'—*Publisher's note* (1931).

THE STORY OF MY LIFE (1908); ed. by Edith Craig and Chris-
topher St. John *Gollancz* 1933
The new edition, with preface, notes and biographical chapters by
Edith Craig and her co-editor, was published as *Ellen Terry's Memoirs.*
Part Two, from pages 279 to 354, provide a biography of this great and
much-loved actress from 1906 (when her own book ended), to 1928.

Thackeray, William Makepeace (1811-63) LETTERS AND PRIVATE
PAPERS 4 vols. ed. by Gordon N. Ray *O.U.P.* 1946-7 126s
2857 pp
Includes some diaries and sketches. As Thackeray disliked the idea of a
biography, he did little to help posterity to compile one, and this
masterly edition is therefore the principal source of knowledge of the
novelist's life story.

Thirkell, Angela (1890-1961) THREE HOUSES *O.U.P.* 1931 15s
'Memories of childhood days', by the popular novelist who recreated
Barsetshire country-town life in a series of widely-read novels. This

autobiographical volume is worthy of a place with *Lark Rise to Candle-ford*, by Flora Thompson, which see below.

*Thompson, Flora (1877-1947) LARK RISE TO CANDLEFORD *O.U.P.* (*Worlds Classics*) 1954 8s 6d
A trilogy originally published in separate volumes: *Lark Rise* (1939); *Over to Candleford* (1941); and *Candleford Green* (1943). It is a beautifully written piece of work, endearing and unaffected, offering a picture of country life in England in the 1870's and 80's.

Thoreau, Henry David (1817-62) A WRITER'S JOURNAL ed. by Laurence Stapledon *Heinemann* 1961 25s; *Constable* (*Dover Paperback*) 1961 12s 6d
A selection from the extensive journal kept by the American essayist and nature-lover, from 1834 to his death. In these pages he made the first notes for all his written work. Refer also to *The Heart of Thoreau's Journals*, edited by O. Shepard, Constable (Dover Paperback), 1961, 12s.

Torrington, John Byng *5th Viscount* (1740-1813) THE TORRINGTON DIARIES 4 vols. ed. by C. Bruyn Andrews *Eyre and Spottiswoode* (1934-8) ed. and abridged into one volume by Fanny Andrews 1954 528 pp Illus.
A selection from the record kept by John Byng, later fifth Viscount Torrington, of tours in England and Wales between 1781 and 1794. Entertaining and self-revealing, these selections from his travel diaries, with informal items on inns, bad food, prices, and similar grumbles, are prime sources for the social historian working in this period of revolutionary change in town and country. Indeed, Sir Arthur Bryant, in his preface to the abridgement, says: Torrington's diary gives us 'a picture of England which is among the great treasures of our social history'.

Trelawney, Edward John (1792-1881) THE ADVENTURES OF A YOUNGER SON (1831); ed. by E. C. Mayne *O.U.P.* (*Worlds Classics*) 1925
Accepted as in the main autobiographical, although some of the material may have been romantically based on youthful experiences rather than accurately recollected. Trelawney was a friend of Shelley and Byron, and was with Shelley when he visited Italy for the last time.

Trollope, Anthony (1815-82) AUTOBIOGRAPHY (1883) ed. by Frederick Page *O.U.P.* 1950 18s Illus.; ed. by Michael Sadleir *O.U.P.* (*Worlds Classics*) 1947 7s 6d; *Collins* (*Fontana*) 1962 6s
The standard edition, with a preface by Frederick Page, is uniform with the novels published in the *Oxford Illustrated Trollope*. Frederick Page writes: 'It has been my pleasant task to bring for the first time a printed text of the *Autobiography* into accordance with Trollope's manuscript, now in the British Museum. The first edition of 1883 needed to be altered in 544 places.'

LETTERS ed. by Bradford Allen Booth *O.U.P.* 1951 35s 550 pp

Tully, Miss (*fl.* 1780–96) LETTERS WRITTEN . . . AT THE COURT OF TRIPOLI (1816) ed. by Seton Dearden *Arthur Barker* 1957 42*s*
Miss Tully wrote these remarkably interesting letters to her family in England, 'simply to relate facts as they occur, without the least embellishment'. She had accompanied her brother Richard to take up residence at the British Consulate, Court of Tripoli, for the ten years, 1783–93. The letters relate in a vivid, spontaneous style, events at court of political intrigue, murder, the plague and many other horrors, and have provided posterity with a picture of semi-oriental squalor in this Moorish city under the rule of Bashaw.

Victoria, Queen (1819–1901) EARLY LETTERS ed. by John Raymond *Batsford* 1963 18*s* Illus.
A selection for a new series. These letters deal with the period 1821 to 1861, and were originally published by John Murray in 1907.

Walpole, Horace (1717–97) CORRESPONDENCE *In progress* ed. by W. S. Lewis and others. *O.U.P.* 1937– 80*s* to 120*s* each volume (*The Yale Edition*)
The greatest editorial achievement of twentieth-century publishing. Here already are more than 11000 pages of letters, arranged according to the correspondents, and the Press estimates that when the vast work is completed in 1973 it will extend to about fifty volumes. Volumes 30 and 31 were published in 1961. This is a monument to a cultivated and amusing man, who was himself perhaps the greatest letter-writer in English literature, and who attracted from his wide and brilliant circle letters of superlative social, literary and historical interest. For full details and prices, see the *Oxford Catalogue*, 1963, pages 305–6.

LETTERS 16 vols. ed. by Mrs. Paget Toynbee; with supplement of 3 vols. ed. by Paget Toynbee *O.U.P.* 1903–5; 1918–25
Lytton Strachey referred in one of his essays to 'the Palladian beauty' of of this great edition, in which Walpole's own letters are arranged in chronological order.

*SELECTED LETTERS ed. by William Hadley *Dent* (*Everyman*) (1926) 1959 12*s* 6*d*
This choice of 434 letters is arranged in classified groups, including one on historical events of the period, with an introduction and notes.

Washington, Booker Taliaferro (1856–1915) UP FROM SLAVERY (1901) *O.U.P.* (*Worlds Classics*) 1946 7*s* 6*d*
'The story of my life.' This gifted negro was born a slave. As an adult he gave his time and powerful personality to the education of negroes in the U.S.A., and became the first Principal of the Um Tuskagee Institute, Alabama, a college for coloured men and women.

Webb, Beatrice (1858–1943) MY APPRENTICESHIP *Longmans* 1926 18*s*; OUR PARTNERSHIP ed. by Barbara Drake and Margaret I. Cole *Longmans* 1948 25*s*

In her chosen field of work—social surveying, political economy, and practical political and economic science—Beatrice Webb was the greatest woman of her time. In these two books she makes a substantial contribution to the social history of the period that she and her husband, Sidney Webb helped to mould. The second volume takes the narrative up to 1912. To complete the record, there were published posthumously *Diaries, 1912-1924*, and *Diaries, 1924-1932*, both edited by Margaret I. Cole, Longmans, 1952 and 1956, 24s and 25s respectively.

Wells, Herbert George (1866-1946) EXPERIMENT IN AUTOBIOGRAPHY 2 vols. *Gollancz and Cresset Press* 1934
Here the famous writer recreated, informally, his years of development and maturity, painting in the background of the social structure of the world he grew up in, and which he himself did so much to shape, as he educated himself and generations of readers, stimulating with ideas the minds of people of many nations.

Wesley, John (1703-91) JOURNAL (1849) 4 vols. *Dent (Everyman)* 1906; SELECTION ed. by Hugh Martin *S.C.M. Press* 1955 9s 6d SELECTED LETTERS ed. by Frederick C. Gill *Epworth Press* 1956 15s
For complete editions of the above works see the catalogue of the Epworth Press, in which are listed all of John Wesley's works and occasional writings on Methodism, which he and his brother Charles founded as part of their evangelical work.

White, William Hale (Mark Rutherford) (1831-1913) PAGES FROM A JOURNAL (1900) *O.U.P.* 1910
Followed by *More Pages* (1910) and *Last Pages* (1915). For the semi-autobiographical writings of this man of powerful intellect and spiritual independence, which he cast in the form of fiction, see under that section.

Whythorne, Thomas (1528-?) AUTOBIOGRAPHY ed. by James M. Osborn *O.U.P.* 1962 30s
A volume of quite exceptional interest on two counts: it is the earliest extant autobiography in the language; and it was written in 'new orthografye', that is, in spelling according to sound. The manuscript did not come to light until 1955, and the first publication of 1961, edited by James M. Osborn, was in the original 'orthografye'. The new edition in modern spelling will reach a wider public, who will enjoy what a reviewer in *The Times Literary Supplement* praised as 'a fascinating picture of wealthy middle-class Elizabethan society'.
Whythorne's *Songes* (1571) is the earliest separate book of English madrigals we have, and is included in the *Cambridge Bibliography of English Literature*.

*Wilde, Oscar (1854-1900) DE PROFUNDIS (1905) ed. by Vyvyan Holland *Methuen* 1949 12s 6d

'The first complete and accurate version of *Epistola: in Carcere et Vinculis*.' But see below, and also in *Essays and Belles Lettres* section, for other editions, including those contained in omnibus editions of Wilde's collected works. The 1905 text is reprinted in a Unicorn Press volume, 1947, 5s.

LETTERS ed. by Rupert Hart-Davis *Hart-Davis* 1962 84s 984 pp
A masterly example of redaction and editing. With few exceptions, the 1098 letters are here published complete for the first time, making a volume of exceptional interest. The complete text is given of *De Profundis*, because of its conception in epistolary form, this being taken from an exact transcript of the British Museum holograph.

Wilson, Harriette (1789-1846) MEMOIRS OF HERSELF AND OTHERS (1825) *Peter Davies* 1929; ed. and abridged by Lesley Blanch *Murray* 1957 Illus.
A *succès de scandale*; entertaining; sometimes outrageously frank, life-story and memoirs of 'a daughter of the game' from the age of fifteen to maturity. The 'others' of her title included many famous men of the early nineteenth century. Lesley Blanch's diverting abridgement is entitled *The Game of Hearts*. Other selections are sometimes available in popular paperbacks.

*Wood, Anthony à (1632-95) THE LIFE AND TIMES OF ANTHONY WOOD ed. by Llewelyn Powys (1932) and *O.U.P.* (*Worlds Classics*) 1961 8s 6d
This delightful abridgement of Andrew Clark's edition (Oxford, 5 vols. 1891-1900) was first published by Wishart and Company, and well deserves a permanent place in the series. In part an informal autobiography, in part 'notes, jottings, scraps', it provides posterity with a store of anecdotes and racily recounted episodes of the time of Charles I, the Commonwealth and Charles II, with chapters on the reigns of James II and William and Mary. 'A unique contribution, the value of which can never be overestimated', wrote the editor.

*Woodforde, James (1740-1803) THE DIARY OF A COUNTRY PARSON, 1758-1802. Selected and edited by John Beresford *O.U.P.* (*Worlds Classics*) 1949 9s 6d 640 pp
Thanks to the work of John Beresford, whose brilliant redaction of the complete set of diaries in five volumes, O.U.P., 1924-31, entertained a wide circle of readers as they appeared, we now have in 'Parson Woodforde' a diarist to compare with Pepys.

Woolf, Virginia (1882-1941) A WRITER'S DIARY ed. by Leonard Woolf *Hogarth Press* 1953 21s
In 1915 the novelist and critic started to keep a regular diary and continued it until her death. The extracts chosen for publication contain all that she wrote referring to her own literary work, her creative and critical methods and standards. Hence the title given to the book by the editor.

B*

Woolman, John (1720-72) JOURNAL AND OTHER WRITINGS *Dent* (*Everyman*) 1910

'Get the writings of John Woolman by heart; and love the early Quakers' wrote Charles Lamb. Woolman was an American of humble birth, who preached and wrote against slavery. His journal was first published posthumously in 1774.

Wordsworth, Dorothy (1771-1855) JOURNALS (1897) 2 vols. ed. by Ernest de Selincourt *Macmillan* 1941 63s 878 pp Illus.

The standard and only complete edition, containing, with illustrations and map, about twice the material in the earlier edition by William Knight, last reprinted in 1934 by Macmillan.

*JOURNALS ed. by Helen Darbishire *O.U.P.* (*Worlds Classics*) 1958 7s 6d

A selection from the Alfoxden Journal of 1798, and the Grasmere Journal, 1800-3, with a long introduction by the greatest living authority on the Wordsworths, and co-editor of the definitive edition of Wordsworth's Poems, with Ernest de Selincourt. An interesting feature of this selection is the appendix of shorter poems by Wordsworth referred to in his sister's Journals.

Wordsworth, William (1770-1850) LETTERS selected by Philip Wayne *O.U.P.* (*Worlds Classics*) 1954 7s 6d

A masterly choice from an enormous mass of material, not only from the great edition (see next entry), but also from a collation of other editions, and from two volumes published in America. The selection presents Wordsworth the poet, the man, the friend and the thinker.

Wordsworth, William (1770-1850) and Dorothy (1771-1855) LETTERS, 1787-1850 6 vols. arranged and edited by Ernest de Selincourt *O.U.P.* 1935-9 160s Illus.

A monumental work of redaction, extending to over 3000 pages.

Wynne, Elizabeth (1779-1857) THE WYNNE DIARIES, 1789-1820 3 vols. *O.U.P.* 1935-40; SELECTED PASSAGES ed. by Anne Fremantle *O.U.P.* (*Worlds Classics*) 1952 9s 6d 568 pp

These diaries were kept from childhood, and offer a lively, spontaneous picture of life in the Napoleonic period and after, with interesting details of naval affairs. On their first publication, Sir Arthur Bryant wrote: 'scarcely a page that does not hold out some delight in the genre of Pepys or Boswell'.

*Yeats, William Butler (1865-1939) AUTOBIOGRAPHIES *Macmillan* 1955 36s Illus. 592 pp

Collects in one volume autobiographical writings formerly published separately, and some essays, notably *Reveries Over Childhood and Youth* (1916); *The Trembling of the Veil* (1922); and *Dramatis Personae* (1936).

BIOGRAPHIES
(Individual and Collective)

AUTOBIOGRAPHIES, diaries and letters are the material from which the biographer draws the facts in his search for the truth about his subject. It is his task then to assemble, collate, emphasise and above all, to interpret. To produce a 'Proper Study' he must be objective, balanced, fair, and free from bias. Sometimes the lives of scoundrels must be written, and the full record of the deeds of monsters has to be set down. It would seem, therefore, that on occasion a biographer must play the parts of counsel for the prosecution as well as for the defence; adding eventually to these roles by acting as both jury and judge.

A distinguished living biographer, whose best works will almost certainly achieve the status of classics, once affirmed in a lecture to booksellers that he doubted if he could write a good biography of a man whose character he disliked. One gathered he drew the line at Karl Marx. This probably reflects the opinion of most practitioners of the art, although it may be remembered that in recent years we have had a standard life of Hitler, who was universally detested; in the past we have had good books on Genghis Khan and many another historical candidate for a chamber of horrors. J. T. Smith's masterpiece is the work of a writer who had cause to dislike his subject, and indeed has attracted readers by the candour of its approach to the failings of Nollekens.

In collective form, biographical writing has come down to us from ancient Greece and Rome. The term itself was not used until Dryden coined it in the introduction he wrote for an English translation of Plutarch's *Lives* first published in 1683, defining the term as 'the history of particular men's lives'. Plutarch's *Lives of the Noble Grecians and Romanes*, written in parallel series for contrast and comparison, is not only the earliest, but also the greatest example of collective biography, and in the English dress fashioned for it by Sir Thomas North, out of the French version done by Jacques Amyot, is a classic with a special niche in our literature, because it was the source from which Shakespeare drew the plots, the inspiration, and sometimes the language, for his Roman historical plays, notably *Julius Caesar*, *Antony and Cleopatra* and *Coriolanus*, and for *Timon of Athens*. North's *Plutarch* came at a time of flowering in English prose. Its continued absence from *The Worlds Classics* leaves a lamentable lacuna in that admirable series.

The only comparable work from the ancient world is *The Lives of the Twelve Caesars* by the Roman Suetonius, Englished notably by 'the translator-generall of his age'; while for the first example of a biographical monograph, devoted to one person only, we have to turn again to Greek literature in which Xenophon's *Memorabilia of Socrates* has survived to add to the portrait of the philosopher already immortalised in the Platonic dialogues.

In English, the books by Thomas Fuller and his contemporary John Aubrey are examples of the first collective biographies, soon to be followed by Izaak Walton's beautiful, simple work. Aubrey's *Brief Lives* is a treasure, posthumously published, and not revealed in its full brilliance until O. L. Dick's masterly redaction appeared in 1949. From the period of long neglect and obscurity of his complete work, Aubrey now emerges as a considerable artist.

In Johnson's *Lives of the Poets* we have an example of the triumph of author over subject. The work is read for Johnson's sake. Hence one of the reasons for the eminence of Boswell's *Johnson*, which towers over all other biographies in world literature. Boswell did something that had not been attempted before, and did it with exceptional skill; but in Dr. Johnson he had a subject of extraordinary individuality, capable of inspiring affection to a degree unparalleled in literary history. Boswell's *Johnson* has given more delight and entertainment to a world audience than anything written by Johnson himself; truly a superb achievement, resulting from a unique sort of collaboration between biographer and subject. One must applaud the sure touch that made the founder of *Everyman's Library* choose this work to inaugurate the series, EML numbers 1 and 2, in May 1906, then to be purchased for one shilling the pair; now for twenty-five shillings, with a cheaper paperback for fifteen shillings.

Boswell's contribution to the biographer's art is necessarily one of the principal topics discussed in many monographs, of which Leon Edel's *Literary Biography*, Hart-Davis, 1957, 10s 6d, is notable for its analysis of the nature of biography, the question of relation between biographer and subject, the aim of the biographer, and the related, diverse types of biography, from the old-fashioned 'Life and Letters' (so often a second burial for Victorian worthies), to the imaginative, creative interpretation of which Virginia Woolf's *Flush*, and Geoffrey Scott's *The Portrait of Zélide* are brilliant examples from twentieth-century literature.

'The material is gathered,' writes Leon Edel. 'Our great table, piled high with documents, confronts the biographer.' His lectures given in 1955-6, and now printed as *Literary Biography*, show with the authority of the author of the standard life of so complicated a writer as Henry James what happens as the work takes shape and emerges as a full-scale biography.

Sir Harold Nicolson's *The Development of English Biography*, Hogarth Press, 1927, 8s 6d, also in the lecture form, cannot be bettered as a concise introduction to the theme. This author of many modern classics, discusses the origins and progress of the art of biography to his own time; severely critical as he is of 'the Boswell formula', Sir Harold's lectures can scarcely be neglected by any reader wishing to establish standards of value. Perhaps the most important lesson of this short but important book is the warning that 'It is a mistake to confuse charm with value'.

Two other books will be enjoyed by the inquiring reader, interested in the assessment of standard and modern work: André Maurois examines *Aspects de la biographie* (Paris, 1928), translated by S. C. Roberts, C.U.P., 1929; and the general theme is discussed in some detail in *The Nature of Biography*, by John A. Garraty, Cape, 1958.

Then as a background to the inquiry we have in J. L. Clifford's anthology, for which see below, a remarkable survey in the form of statements by biographers of the past and the present on their art.

The extracts are comprehensive and enlightening, and as one would expect, about half the contents are devoted to twentieth-century writers, but amongst the earlier statements are 'long passages' from an eighteenth-century manuscript by Roger North, here published for the first time; and lengthy extracts from 'An Essay On the Study and Composition of Biography', by James Field Stanfield, 1813, this being 'the first comprehensive study of the art'. From this interesting compilation the reader may therefore learn much about the fine distinction between biography and history; the place of anecdote (in, for example, the work of Lytton Strachey); and related topics. The editor is himself a biographer of distinction, much praised for his book on *Young Samuel Johnson*, Heinemann, 1955, 30s, and *Mercury Books*, 1962, 10s 6d, in which he deals with Johnson's life up to the age of forty.

Many twentieth-century biographies must necessarily supersede older monographs. New facilities for research, new discoveries made by scholars delving into archives recently made available to students, and new standards of scholarship set by such distinguished writers as Dr. C. V. Wedgwood, Sir Harold Nicolson, and Carola Oman, have enriched current literature, by producing masterpieces praised for their scholarship, and acclaimed by the general public to a degree that has made many of them best sellers.

That is one reason for arranging the following section under authors rather than subjects. These biographies are not always the best, but if new books have superseded some of them, they have not submerged the older classics. Indeed contemporary biographers do not hesitate to express their indebtedness to and their appreciation of the enduring qualities of their predecessors' work. Carola Oman, whose life of Nelson is certainly one of the greatest modern biographies, unlikely ever to be superseded, pays generous tribute to the classic nature of Southey's ever-popular and delightful biography. 'He brought greatness to his great task,' she writes in her preface to the last edition of Southey's *Life of Horatio, Lord Nelson* in *Everyman's Library*.

When Lytton Strachey's *Eminent Victorians* shocked and delighted critics and readers in 1918 by its display of irreverent irony, witty detachment, satiric attention to flaws, and to the men behind the masks worn in public, it was soon apparent that this new development was more than a passing *succès de scandale*. It was a highly individual performance on the part of the biographer, illuminating both author and subject, and likely to influence fellow-craftsmen for many generations to come.

Aldington, Richard (1892-1962) PORTRAIT OF A GENIUS, BUT . . .
Heinemann 1950 15s
Interesting and important biography of D. H. Lawrence by one of his
most distinguished contemporaries and acquaintances.

*Aubrey, John (1626-97) BRIEF LIVES (1813) ed. by O. L. Dick
Secker and Warburg (1949) 1959 50s; *Penguin Books* 1962 12s 6d
A masterly redaction, superseding the former text edited in 1898 by
Clark. The editor has for the first time collated all of Aubrey's notes,
drafts, supplementary versions and manuscript sources, skilfully producing a complete, final text of these biographical brevities varying
from a few paragraphs to much longer biographies, material for which
John Aubrey collected throughout his adult life from friends and contemporaries. Diverting and entertaining as they are, the *Brief Lives* are
often of prime importance as sources of information about Shakespeare,
Sir Walter Raleigh, Hobbes, Sir Thomas More, John Milton, and many
other illustrious men. This edition is prefaced by a considerable biography of Aubrey himself.

Austen-Leigh, James Edward (1798-1874) A MEMOIR OF JANE
AUSTEN ed. by R. W. Chapman *O.U.P.* (1926) 1951 12s 6d
A portrait written by Jane Austen's nephew.

Belloc, Hilaire (1870-1953) MARIE ANTOINETTE *Methuen* (1910)
1951 30s
Complementary to this full-length biographical study of Louis XVI's
queen (1755-93), Belloc wrote a short monograph on the French Revolution, for details of which see under the *History* section.

Boas, Frederick Samuel (1862-1957) CHRISTOPHER MARLOWE
O.U.P. 1940 25s
A notable biographical and critical monograph for students.

*Boswell, James (1740-95) THE LIFE OF SAMUEL JOHNSON, LL.D
(1791) 6 vols. ed. by Birkbeck Hill *O.U.P.* (1887); revised
edition by L. F. Powell 1934-50 240s Illus.
The last two volumes of this definitive edition, which is annotated
throughout, with full details of textual variants, allusions, and the
critical apparatus of modern scholarship, contain *A Tour to the Hebrides*
(1785), and a *Diary of a Journey Into Wales*. There is a table of anonymous persons, and an index to the complete set.

Other editions:
O.U.P. (*Oxford Standard Authors*) 1953 25s 1516 pp
The text is the third (1799), with footnotes by Boswell and Malone;
Greek and Latin quotations are translated by R. W. Chapman.
2 vols. ed. by S. C. Roberts *Dent* (*Everyman*) (1906) (1949) 1960 12s 6d
each.
Text: Malone's sixth; with a 36-page index compiled by Alan Dent

3 vols. ed. by Clement K. Shorter *Navarre Society* 1924 Illus. Text: the first edition of 1791, reprinted verbatim, with the appendix of principal corrections and additions of 1793; illustrated with twenty photogravure etchings, fifty half-tone plates, and facsimile autograph letters

EVERYBODY'S BOSWELL ed. by A. C. Ward *Bell* (1930) 1956 18s 6d 610 pp Illus. by E. H. Shepard
The most popular abridgement; includes *A Tour to the Hebrides.*

Buchan, John (1st Baron Tweedsmuir) (1875-1940) MONTROSE *Hodder* 1928 4s 6d; *Nelson* 1913 18s and 12s 6d; O.U.P. (*Worlds Classics*) 1957 9s 6d
A life of the Marquis of Montrose, 1612-50, the Covenanter who was at the same time a passionate Royalist, presented 'in its appropriate setting' . 'Probably the most enduring of his serious works.'—*Keith Feiling,* in his introduction to the *Worlds Classics* edition.

SIR WALTER SCOTT *Cassell* (1932) 1961 21s
'It is not only the best one-volume book on Scott, but the best one-volume biography in the language.'—*G. M. Trevelyan.*

Carlyle, Thomas (1795-1881) LETTERS AND SPEECHES OF CROMWELL (1845) ed. by Mrs. S. C. Lomas *Methuen* (1904); 3 vols. *Dent* (*Everyman*) (1908)
A creative redaction in which Carlyle presents a history of Cromwell's life and times by his arrangement of the letters and speeches into a continuous narrative, 'with elucidations and an introductory essay'. He added to his first edition some seventy-five items, and later, Mrs. Lomas, re-editing the work for her standard edition, made still further additions. The definitive edition of Cromwell's *Letters*, 4 volumes, edited by Wilbur Cortez Abbott and Catherine W. Crane, appeared from 1937 to 1947, Harvard University Press, but is now out of print.

THE HISTORY OF FREDERICK THE GREAT (1858-65) ed. and abridged by A. M. D. Hughes O.U.P. 1916
The abridgement reduced this little-read work from six volumes to one of 400 pages.

LIFE OF JOHN STERLING (1851) O.U.P. (*Worlds Classics*) 1907
A masterpiece of the biographer's art, preserving for all time the name, character and work of Carlyle's friend, 1806-44. 'The quietest, and in the common sense, most human, of all his books.'—*George Saintsbury.*

Cavendish, George (*c.* 1500-62) THE LIFE AND DEATH OF CARDINAL WOLSEY (1641) O.U.P. (*Early English Text Society*) 1959 35s
The E.E.T.S. edition was prepared from the autograph manuscript in the British Museum, retaining the spelling and punctuation of the early or middle sixteenth century. The work was written from 1554-8, but circulated in manuscript only, until 1641. Singer's edition of 1815 has been reprinted but is now out of print. Cavendish was a loyal servant of Wolsey even in the period of the Cardinal's disgrace. His picturesque style is best left untouched by editorial improvements. It seems almost

certain that Shakespeare read the work in manuscript when he was writing *Henry VIII*. Also available in *Two Early Tudor Lives*, Yale University Press, 1962, 48s. The other life is Roper's *Life of Sir Thomas More*, for which see under Roper.

Chambers, Sir Edmund Kerchever (1866-1954) SAMUEL TAYLOR COLERIDGE *O.U.P.* 1938 30s
'A biographical study.'

WILLIAM SHAKESPEARE 2 vols. *O.U.P.* 1930 70s (the set) 1058 pp Illus.
'A study of facts and problems.' This is the great, standard work to which all other modern writers on Shakespeare are indebted. See under Charles Williams for the abridgement, entitled *A Short Life of Shakespeare*.

Chambers, Raymond Wilson (1874-1942) THOMAS MORE *Cape* 1935 30s; *Penguin Books (Peregrine)* 1963 8s 6d
A standard work, gaining for its author the James Tait Black Memorial Prize for 1935.

Charnwood, Godfrey Rathbone Benson, *1st Baron* (1865-1945) ABRAHAM LINCOLN *Constable* (1916); 1947
First published in the *Makers of the Nineteenth Century* series, when it was judged to be the best single-volume biography of Lincoln by an English writer. The later reprint was out of series.

Colvin, Sir Sidney (1845-1927) KEATS *Macmillan* (1887) 1957 7s 6d
Originally a monograph in the series of biographical and critical volumes known as *The English Men of Letters*, but now reprinted out of series as a standard work of permanent value as a summary by an authority on Keats, whose major study, *John Keats: his life and poetry, contemporaries and after-fame*, Macmillan, 1917, revised edition 1925, has long been out of print.

*Cooper, Sir Alfred Duff (1st Viscount Norwich) (1890-1954) TALLEYRAND *Cape* 1932 (*Bedford Historical Series*) 1950 30s
The standard biography of the French statesman, 1754-1838, whose complicated political manoeuvres during the Napoleonic domination of Europe offered an ideal subject to the English statesman, who was a distinguished francophile all his political life.

Crabbe, George (1785-1857) LIFE OF CRABBE (1834) *Cresset Press* 1947 10s 6d
Introduction by Edmund Blunden. This delightful biography of the poet, written by his son, was originally prefixed to the collected edition in eight volumes, of Crabbe's works.

De Selincourt, Ernest (1870-1943) DOROTHY WORDSWORTH *O.U.P.* 1933 35s
Standard biographical study by the greatest authority on the Wordsworths in modern scholarship.

Dowden, Edward (1843-1913) LIFE OF ROBERT BROWNING (1904)
Dent (Everyman) 1915
A well-proportioned and sympathetic portrait, by a biographer who
knew Browning personally.

LIFE OF PERCY BYSSHE SHELLEY *Routledge* (1886) 1951 25s
Considered to be the best of all nineteenth-century biographies of the
poet. The 1951 edition is abridged, with an introduction by Sir Herbert
Read, who writes: 'Later and fuller biographies have been published,
but they have not substantially altered the portrait drawn by Dowden.
Its great virtue lies in its impartiality'.

Forster, John (1812-76) THE LIFE OF DICKENS 3 vols. (1872-4);
2 vols. *Dent (Everyman)* 1926 6s 6d each
The series edition of a Victorian classic has an appreciation by G. K.
Chesterton.

THE LIFE AND TIMES OF GOLDSMITH (1848; 1854) *Hutchinson* 1903
During the nineteenth century this was said to be Forster's most popular
book, yet it has not found a place in any standard series. It certainly has
enduring qualities as a picture of an age, as well as a sympathetic portrait
of a man of great charm, of whom his biographer says, 'No man ever
put so much of himself into his books as Goldsmith'.

Froude, James Anthony (1818-94) A HISTORY OF THE FIRST FORTY
YEARS OF CARLYLE'S LIFE *Longmans* (1882)
CARLYLE: THE HISTORY OF HIS LIFE IN LONDON, 1834-1881 2 vols.
Longmans (1884)
The second part of this standard work aroused controversy, because of
its subjective judgements and critical tone. For this reason it is considered
by eminent critics to be the first 'modern' biography. It was based on
correspondence, and the writer had an intimate personal knowledge of
Carlyle's life and character. Now superseded by the definitive life by
D. A. Wilson, 6 volumes, Kegan Paul, 1923-34.

THE LIFE OF BENJAMIN DISRAELI, EARL OF BEACONSFIELD (1890)
Dent (Everyman) 1914
A biographical sketch that aroused criticism from Disraeli's admirers.

Fuller, Thomas (1608-61) THE WORTHIES OF ENGLAND (1662;
1840) ed. by John Freeman *Allen and Unwin* 1952 42s
A long, leisurely work of over 700 pages, once a familiar household
volume and bedside companion. Part biographical, part topographical,
it is still of interest as a source book and a miscellany to dip into now and
again.

*Gaskell, Elizabeth Cleghorn (1810-65) THE LIFE OF CHARLOTTE
BRONTË (1857) *Dent (Everyman)* (1908) 1960 10s 6d; *O.U.P.*
(Worlds Classics) 1919 7s 6d
A biography by the novelist's friend that can never be superseded.
Published only two years after Charlotte Brontë's death, it is a poignant,

sympathetic and moving portrait of the Brontë sisters as well as a detailed life of the eldest and most mature of the three geniuses of Haworth Parsonage.

*Gilchrist, Alexander (1828-61) THE LIFE OF WILLIAM BLAKE (1863) ed. by Ruthven Todd *Dent (Everyman)* 1942 Illus.
Notable new edition of the first biography of Blake, based on the second edition of 1880, with notes and emendations and illustrations reproducing Blake's woodcuts made for Thornton's *Virgil*. Mrs. Gilchrist completed the original text after her husband's death.

Gleig, George Robert (1796-1888) THE LIFE OF ARTHUR, DUKE OF WELLINGTON (1862) *Dent (Everyman)* 1909 6s 6d
The author served under Wellington in the Peninsular War, and was able to work partly from prime sources for the final edition of this first substantial biography of the Iron Duke.

Godwin, William (1756-1836) MEMOIR OF MARY WOLLSTONECRAFT (1798) *Constable* 1928
The story of the brief but rewarding life of Mary Wollstonecraft Godwin (1759-97) whose celebrated and influential *Vindication of the Rights of Women* (1792) is a landmark in sociology.

Graham, R. B. Cunninghame (1852-1936) JOSE ANTONIO PAEZ *Heinemann* 1929
The life and times of the Venezuelan cowboy (1790-1873) who led his country's revolt against Spain in 1823, became first President of Venezuela, but was later overthrown.

Guedalla, Philip (1889-1944) THE DUKE *Hodder* (1931) 1946 21s
A popular biography of the Duke of Wellington, told in glittering, epigrammatic style.
PALMERSTON *Benn* (1926); *Hodder* 1937 21s
Guedalla's method of writing history and biography attracted the general reader but was often attacked by scholars. Nevertheless, he always tried to evoke the past in sympathy with the times and the people he was writing about, not as a twentieth-century critic.

Hammond, John Lawrence (1872-1949) and Barbara Hammond LORD SHAFTESBURY *Longmans* 1923; *Penguin Books* 1939
A biographical study of the great philanthropist, Anthony Ashley Cooper, seventh Earl of Shaftesbury (1801-85), whose work for the betterment of the conditions of the poor, the underprivileged and the labouring classes, has given him a secure place amongst the makers of the nineteenth century. The Hammonds' classic trilogy, to which this volume is complementary, will be found listed in the *History* section.

Harpsfield, Nicholas (1519?-1575) LIFE OF SIR THOMAS MORE (1877) For reprint see under *Roper, William* below

Hawkins, Sir John (1719-89) THE LIFE OF SAMUEL JOHNSON (1787)
ed. by Bertram H. Davis *Cape* 1962 42s
This interesting first biography of Dr. Johnson (it preceded Boswell's
by four years), contains many of Johnson's most famous extempore
remarks and sayings, as well as anecdotes about contemporaries such as
Garrick and Goldsmith. But Hawkins, being 'a very unclubbable man',
had to contend with Boswell's jealousy, and his book has been unjustly
pushed into the background. Here, at last, is a modern edition, skilfully
abridged by the omission of minor material, with an introduction by
the editor.

Holland, Philemon (1552-1637) THE LIVES OF THE FIRST TWELVE
CAESARS translated from Suetonius by Philemon Holland (1606)
See under *Essays and Belles Lettres* for other translations by Holland.

Holmes, Edward (1797-1859) A LIFE OF MOZART (1845) *Dent*
(*Everyman*) 1912
The first English biography of the composer, reprinted in the series,
with an introduction by Ernest Newman, who praised it in superlative
terms.

Hone, Joseph (1873-1950) W. B. YEATS, 1865-1939 *Macmillan*
(1943) 1962 30s 504 pp
The standard biography of the Irish poet by a friend who had the
assistance of Mrs. Yeats, and access to private papers in order to make his
work authoritative and accurate. Although special monographs may
add much to our appreciation of the poet's achievement, it is therefore
unlikely that this volume will ever be superseded.

Houghton (Richard Monckton Milnes), *1st Baron* (1809-85) THE
LIFE AND LETTERS OF JOHN KEATS (1848) *Dent* (*Everyman*) 1954
8s 6d; *O.U.P.* (*Worlds Classics*) 1931 7s 6d
The first biography of the poet, based on materials made available to
Lord Houghton by Charles Brown, Keats's friend. The series reprint has
an introduction by Robert Lynd, with notes on the letters by Lewis
Gibbs.

Howe, Percival Presland (1886-1944) THE LIFE OF WILLIAM HAZLITT
(1922) *Hamish Hamilton* 1947 15s; *Penguin* 1949
P. P. Howe edited the definitive, centenary edition of Hazlitt's complete
works (see under *Essays and Belles Lettres* section); and completed his work
on the great essayist and critic by writing this standard biography, not
likely to be superseded.

Hutchinson, Francis Ernest (1871-1947) HENRY VAUGHAN, 1622-
1695 *O.U.P.* 1947 21s
'A life and an interpretation.' It is accepted as the standard biography of
the poet.

Hutchinson, Lucy (1620-80?) MEMOIRS OF THE LIFE OF COLONEL HUTCHINSON (1806) 2 vols. ed. by Sir Charles H. Firth (1885); *Dent (Everyman)* 1908

Colonel John Hutchinson, Governor of Nottingham, was a distinguished Puritan who was one of the judges at the trial of Charles I. His widow wrote this pleasant record and narrative of their life together for their children. The *Everyman* edition contains F. P. G. Guizot's essay, and a fragment of autobiography.

James, Henry (1843-1916) WILLIAM WETMORE STORY AND HIS FRIENDS (1903) *Thames and Hudson* 1957 35s

Written when James was at the height of his powers, this biography of an American expatriate (his life nearly spanned the century—1819-95) has considerable interest for readers of *Roderick Hudson*. The character of Story was similar to that of James's creation. William Wetmore Story had a wide circle of friends in Rome, including the Brownings, Landor, and Lowell. His magnificent salon in his Palazzo Barberini was the focus for the famous in Rome.

Johnson, Samuel (1709-84) THE LIVES OF THE ENGLISH POETS (1779-81) 2 vols. *Dent (Everyman)* (1925) 1954 8s 6d each; 2 vols. *O.U.P. (Worlds Classics)* (1906) 1959 7s 6d each; 2 vols. *W. H. Allen (Dolphin Series)* 1962 10s each

Originally contributed to a series of selections from the works of the English poets, including many who were minor poets even in their own time, these biographies in brief are read for the pleasure to be derived from Dr. Johnson's style, and the individual critical approach he made to each of his subjects, whether they were great poets or mere versifiers.

Jones, Henry Festing (1851-1928) LIFE OF SAMUEL BUTLER 2 vols. *Macmillan* 1919

The biographer was Butler's closest friend and constant companion. This is therefore a subjective work, but essential reading for the student and often attractively amusing.

Keynes, John Maynard, *1st Baron* (1883-1946) ESSAYS IN BIOGRAPHY (1933, *Macmillan*); *Hart-Davis* 1951 12s 6d; *Heinemann (Mercury Books)* 1961 7s 6d

The last edition, edited by Geoffrey Keynes, included three new essays; all fifteen, chiefly 'Sketches of Politicians' and 'Lives of Economists', were written with few exceptions from personal knowledge, and are refreshingly spontaneous and shrewd.

TWO MEMOIRS *Hart-Davis* 1949 7s 6d

'Dr. Melchior: a defeated enemy; and, My Early Beliefs', with an introduction by David Garnett. Originally read to friends, and not intended for publication during the author's lifetime. Dr. Melchior was the leader of the financial delegation from defeated Germany to the peace conference after World War I; the second piece is a frank examination of the author's beliefs when he was a student at Cambridge soon after the turn of the century.

Leslie, Charles Robert (1794-1859) MEMOIRS OF THE LIFE OF JOHN
CONSTABLE (1843) ed. by Jonathan Mayne Phaidon Press 1951
12s 6d Illus.
An intimate biography 'composed chiefly of his letters', and of reports
of his conversations. Leslie was himself a genre painter of some distinction. This edition contains 14 plates in colour, and 58 other illustrations.

Lewes, George Henry (1817-78) THE LIFE AND WORKS OF GOETHE
(1855) Dent (Everyman) (1908) 1959 12s 6d
With an introduction by Havelock Ellis, who accords it a very high place.
By common consent, it is still the best short biography in English, and
'with sketches of his (Goethe's) age and contemporaries' is indispensable
to the student.

Lockhart, John Gibson (1794-1854) HISTORY OF NAPOLEON
BUONAPARTE (1829) Dent (Everyman) 1906 6s 6d 512 pp

LIFE OF ROBERT BURNS (1828) Dent (Everyman) (1907) 1959 12s 6d
Contains diaries of the Border and Highland Tours, and a selection of
Burns's letters and journals.

LIFE OF SIR WALTER SCOTT (1838) Dent (Everyman) (1906) ed. by
W. M. Parker 1957 12s 6d 675 pp
Contains Scott's fragment of autobiography (forty-seven pages), with
Lockhart's own approved abridgement of the original work which he
published from 1836 to 1838 in seven volumes. The biography is a
complete portrait of a great man of letters, can never be superseded, and
is second only to Boswell's *Johnson* as a biographical masterpiece.

Lucas, Edward Verrall (1868-1938) LIFE OF CHARLES LAMB
2 vols. Methuen 1905
The standard biography by the greatest authority on Charles Lamb, the
editor of his letters, himself an essayist who was once called 'the
sophisticated Elia'.

Macaulay, Dame Rose (1881-1958) MILTON Duckworth (1934)
1958 6s
A short biographical monograph in the *Great Lives* series.

Mackail, John William (1859-1945) THE LIFE OF WILLIAM MORRIS
2 vols. Longmans (1899); O.U.P. (Worlds Classics) 1950 9s 6d
The standard biography; introduced in the series edition by Sir Sydney
Cockerell, who knew both author and subject.

Maude, Aylmer (1858-1938) THE LIFE OF TOLSTOY O.U.P. (1909-
10) revised and enlarged 1930; (Worlds Classics) (1918) 1957
10s 6d 1060 pp
The standard biography by Tolstoy's friend and translator. Tolstoy himself contributed to it, and Countess Tolstoy revised it. 'Much of the
story is told in extracts from Tolstoy's own writings.'

Mayne, Ethel Colburn (1870-1942) BYRON 2 vols. *Methuen* (1912);
revised edition, 1 vol. 1924

It is not likely that the last word will ever be written on Byron, for, as
he prophetically wrote, 'there is that within me that shall tire Torture
and Time, and breathe when I expire'. This notable full-scale biography
should be supplemented, the author suggested, by Sir Harold Nicolson's
Byron: the Last Journey, Constable, 1924, 10s; it is surpassed only by
L. A. Marchand's new, immense work of 1071 pages, *Byron: a biography*,
3 vols., Murray, 1958, 147s, illustrated.

Moore, Thomas (1779-1852) LIFE, LETTERS AND JOURNALS OF
BYRON *Murray* (1830) 1932 21s

'The foundation-stone for all,' wrote Ethel Colburn Mayne. She pointed
out the surprising fact that Moore's pioneer work was the only full-
length *Life and Letters* of Byron to which she could refer.

Murry, John Middleton (1889-1957) KEATS: A BIOGRAPHY (*Cape*
1955 25s

SON OF WOMAN *Cape* (1931) 1954 25s

Two biographical studies of enduring worth, the latter being a biography of D. H. Lawrence, who was Murry's intimate friend. Of the
many books written on D. H. Lawrence, this is certainly one of the most
essential for the understanding of that complex writer. The later edition
contains a new introduction.

Newcastle, Margaret Cavendish (Duchess of) (1624?-74) THE LIFE
OF THE DUKE OF NEWCASTLE (and other writings) (1667) *Dent*
(*Everyman*) 1915

The edition included the Autobiography of the Duchess of Newcastle,
and some letters. This was one of Charles Lamb's 'jewels' of literature.

Newman, Ernest (1868-1959) THE LIFE OF RICHARD WAGNER
4 vols. *Cassell* (1933-7) 1961 200s 2674 pp Illus.

The most detailed, comprehensive music biography of the century,
unequalled in its scholarship and understanding of one of the most
controversial composers of the nineteenth century.

*North, Sir Thomas (1535-1601) LIVES OF THE NOBLE GREEKS AND
ROMANS translated from the French of Amyot's *Plutarch* (1579)
8 vols. *Blackwell* 1928; 5 vols. *Nonesuch Press* 1930; ed. and sel.
by Paul Turner *Centaur Press* 1962 126s (limited edn.)

North's version of Plutarch's *Parallel Lives* is a magnificent example of
Tudor prose, and the work is also of exceptional interest as the source of
Shakespeare's Roman plays.

Pattison, Mark (1813-84) LIFE OF CASAUBON (1875)

A minor classic of the biographer's art. In the life of the famous classical
scholar (1559-1614) who became Royal Librarian in Paris and produced many standard texts, Mark Pattison found a subject which exactly
suited his own character.

Pinto, Vivian de Sola (Editor) ENGLISH BIOGRAPHY IN THE SEVEN-
TEENTH CENTURY *Harrap* (*Life, Literature and Thought Library*)
1951 7s 6d
An anthology of characteristic selections, with an introduction and
notes, forming a useful survey for students.

Pollard, Albert Frederick (1869-1948) THOMAS CRANMER AND THE
ENGLISH REFORMATION *Putnam* (1904) 1926; WOLSEY *Longmans*
(1929) 1954 30s
Monographs by an authority on Tudor history; they supplement his
historical works, for which see in the *History* section.

Roberts, Morley (1857-1942) THE PRIVATE LIFE OF HENRY MAIT-
LAND (1912) *Unicorn Press* 1958 21s
A definitive edition edited by Morchard Bishop, with introduction and
notes. Originally published and read as fiction, attracting praise as a
roman à clef, it is now recognised as a poignant biographical study of
Morley Roberts's friend, the novelist George Gissing.

Roper, William (1496-1578) THE LIFE OF SIR THOMAS MORE (1626)
Dent (*Everyman*) (1906) 1962 15s
A modern spelling edition of the E.E.T.S. edition of 1935, together with
Nicholas Harpsfield's *Life of Sir Thomas More* published by the Society
in 1932. This first example of the biographer's art (but see Sir Harold
Nicolson's book noted in the introduction to this section), is also re-
printed in an edition of *Utopia*, together with a selection of More's
Letters, ed. by Mildred Campbell, Van Nostrand, 1947, 14s. See also
Cavendish's *Life of Wolsey* for the other early biography in English.

Sackville-West, Victoria (1892-1962) ST. JOAN OF ARC *Cobden-
Sanderson* (1936); *Michael Joseph* 1948 12s 6d; *Penguin Books*
1955 3s 6d

Scott, Geoffrey (1885-1929) THE PORTRAIT OF ZELIDE *Constable*
(1925) 1934 7s 6d
A charming sketch of the life and character of Isabella Van Tuyll, or
Isabella de Zuylen, afterwards Madame de Charrière, the learned, witty
girl whom James Boswell wooed with misgivings when on his 'grand
tour'. After this episode 'Zélide' endured, or enjoyed, a passionate
friendship with Benjamin Constant.

Scott, Sir Walter (1771-1832) LIVES OF THE NOVELISTS (1821)
Dent (*Everyman*) 1910; O.U.P. (*Worlds Classics*) 1907
Biographical essays commissioned to preface a collected edition
fiction by major and some minor, now forgotten, writers. The former
included Fielding, Richardson, Goldsmith, Smollett, Sterne, Walpole,
Mrs. Radcliffe, and Defoe.

Smith, John Thomas (1766-1833) NOLLEKENS AND HIS TIMES
2 vols. (1828); ed. by Wilfred Whitten *Bodley Head* (1920);
Turnstile Press 1949

A candid, amusing study of the sculptor who made a fortune from his art, which produced for posterity many busts of famous literary and other contemporaries, including Fox, Pitt, Sterne, Garrick, and Dr. Johnson.

*Southey, Robert (1774-1843) THE LIFE OF HORATIO, LORD NELSON (1813) *Dent* (*Everyman*) (1906) 1962 10s 6d; *Macdonald* (*Illustrated Classics*) 1953 15s
'Beyond all doubt, the most perfect and the most delightful of all Southey's works. No writer, perhaps, ever lived whose talents so precisely qualified him to write the history of the great naval warrior. The character of the hero lay on the surface. The exploits were brilliant and picturesque. It would not be easy to find, in all literary history, an instance of a more exact hit between wind and water.'—*Macaulay*.

THE LIFE OF WESLEY (1821) 2 vols. *O.U.P.* 1925; Warne 1926
Intermingled with the biography is a history of 'the rise and progress of Methodism'.

Stanhope, Philip Henry (5th Earl of) (1805-75) NOTES OF CONVERSATIONS WITH THE DUKE OF WELLINGTON, 1831-1851 (1886) *O.U.P.* (*Worlds Classics*) 1938 7s 6d
Interesting source of anecdotes about the Great Duke. The author, Lord Mahon, statesman and scholar, became 5th Earl Stanhope in 1855; he wrote a number of historical works, and helped to found the National Portrait Gallery.

Strachey, Giles Lytton (1880-1932) BIOGRAPHICAL ESSAYS *Chatto* 1948 12s 6d
Collected from *Portraits in Miniature* (1931) and other volumes of essays.

*EMINENT VICTORIANS *Chatto* (1918) 1949 10s 6d; *Collins* (*Classics*) 1959 6s
Studies of General Gordon, Cardinal Manning, Florence Nightingale, and Dr. Arnold of Rugby. These four 'Eminent Victorians' are here subjected to an ironic scrutiny, presented in a highly individual style that influenced many other biographers.

*QUEEN VICTORIA *Chatto* (1921) 1949 10s 6d; *Collins* (*Classics*) 1958 6s
Another characteristic study in irony. It delights; it shocks; it charms; for eventually, as readers come to the last chapters, 'Old Age', and 'The End', they perceive the author's ironic detachment giving place to affection, and even reverence.

Swinburne, Algernon Charles (1837-1909) WILLIAM BLAKE *Heinemann* (1868) 1925
A brief life, and a glowing appreciation, written with sympathy, and rare understanding of Blake's strange mind and genius. It followed quickly on Gilchrist's pioneer, full-scale biography, and the two books did a great deal to arouse public interest in Blake's work.

A STUDY OF BEN JONSON *Chatto* (1889)

Symons, Arthur (1865-1945) AUBREY BEARDSLEY: A MEMOIR (1898) *Unicorn Press* 1948 10s
A sympathetic, personal portrait of the artist of the *Yellow Book* period, by a gifted contemporary.

Terry, Charles Sanford (1864-1936) J. S. BACH: A BIOGRAPHY O.U.P. (1928) 1933 35s
Acknowledged to be a standard contribution to the literature on Bach and his music.

Tovey, Sir Donald Francis (1875-1940) BEETHOVEN O.U.P. 1944 12s
A monograph by a distinguished critic and music historian, whose writings are valued as much by listeners as they are by professional musicians.

Trelawney, Edward John (1792-1881) RECOLLECTIONS OF THE LAST DAYS OF SHELLEY AND BYRON (1858; 1878) O.U.P. 1906; ed. by J. E. Morpurgo, *Doubleday: Mayflower Press* 1961 12s; *W. H. Allen (Anchor Books)* 1962 7s 6d
Sometimes published as *Recollections of Shelley, Byron, and the Author*, this memoir was also reprinted in a volume containing Thomas Jefferson Hogg's *Life of Shelley* (1851) and *Memoirs of Shelley*, by Thomas Love Peacock (1858), 2 volumes, with an introduction by Humbert Wolfe, Dent, 1933.

Trevelyan, George Macaulay (1876-1962) GREY OF FALLODON *Longmans* 1937 15s
The life of Sir Edward Grey, afterwards Viscount Grey of Fallodon, 1862-1933.

LORD GREY OF THE REFORM BILL *Longmans* (1920) 1929 30s
The life of Charles, second Earl Grey, 1764-1845.

Trevelyan, Sir George Otto (1838-1928) THE LIFE AND LETTERS OF LORD MACAULAY (*Longmans*, 1876) 2 vols. O.U.P. (1932) 1961 21s (the set) 972 pp
With preface by G. M. Trevelyan. 'It was at once hailed as a great biography, and is still, I think, so regarded . . .' 'The strong interest of this book derives in part from the double thread of literature and politics.' A reprint of the Longmans edition is still listed, price 105s.

Trotter, Lionel James (1827-1912) THE BAYARD OF INDIA (1903) *Dent (Everyman)* 1909 6s 6d
A life of General Sir James Outram (1803-63).

WARREN HASTINGS (1878) *Dent (Everyman)* 1910

Verney, Frances Parthenope (1819-90) and Margaret Maria Verney (1844-1930) MEMOIRS OF THE VERNEY FAMILY 4 vols. *Longmans* (1892-9) 2 vols. 1925

Compiled from the family archives at Claydon House, Buckingham-shire, the seat of one of the oldest families in England. A Ralph Verney was Lord Mayor of London in 1465. These *Memoirs* are, however, limited to the story of the Verneys in the seventeenth century, but Lady Margaret later published two volumes of *Verney Letters of the 18th Century*, Longmans (1930); reprinted Benn, 1932.

Wallas, Graham (1858-1932) THE LIFE OF FRANCIS PLACE, 1771-1854 *Allen and Unwin* (1898) 1919 16s
Standard life of a great social reformer, whose ideas on the control of population were some generations in advance of his own time.

*Walton, Izaak (1593-1683) LIVES OF DONNE, WOTTON, HOOKER, HERBERT AND SANDERSON (1640-78) *Nelson* (*Classics*) 1954 6s; *O.U.P.* (*Worlds Classics*) 1927 7s 6d
These graceful pages from 'Walton's heavenly memory' are early examples of the biographer's art that time has outdated in many respects, yet they continue to charm readers by the sweet beauty of Walton's prose. They were only occasional writings (the Donne, for example, prefaced an edition of the poet's Sermons), but, as Walton himself said, they were written 'with all truth and equal plainness'.

*Williams, Charles (1886-1945) A SHORT LIFE OF SHAKESPEARE *O.U.P.* 1933 12s 6d Illus.
An abridgement of the standard work by Sir Edmund K. Chambers: *William Shakespeare: a Study of Facts and Problems*, 2 volumes, O.U.P., 1930, 70s, a great illustrated monograph of 1058 pages. Sources are noted in *The Short Life*, which is probably the best work for the general reader, and the best introduction of its kind for the student.

*Woolf, Virginia (1882-1941) FLUSH *Hogarth Press* 1933 8s 6d
The theme of this essay in imaginative reconstruction is the elopement of Elizabeth Barrett with Robert Browning, and especially the flight from the house of her father with her maid, and the pet dog, Flush.

ESSAYS, BELLES LETTRES AND LITERARY CRITICISM
(including critical monographs, collected works of individual authors, and omnibus volumes)

HERE is a miscellany, a convenient gathering together of volumes of essays in the strictly limited sense; of fugitive prose; works of literary criticism; selections in the form of anthologies; pamphlets and tracts; and omnibus collections of voluminous writers whose varied output has contributed writing of distinction in many forms of literature.

Collections such as *The Nonesuch Library* and *The Reynard Library*, together with certain volumes in *Everyman*, enable readers to have in one volume, sometimes the complete text, more often a well-chosen selection, of many great writers. Blake; Oscar Wilde; Milton; De Quincey; Swift; and the others listed below, are examples of authors whose work lends itself to this treatment.

Montaigne, the innovator, used the essay as a convenient form for communicating his personal philosophy. European civilisation owes much to his choice. Had he written many learned, forbidding folios, systematically propounding his thoughts and reflections, his work might have reached only a very limited audience. As it was, the briefer, informal, casual method he developed from 1580 to 1588 for his *Essais* endeared him to a wide circle of cultivated readers, and must have contributed much to the encouragement of the good life of the tolerant, kind, contemplative and shrewdly inquiring sort of gentleman Western culture was slowly producing after the Dark Ages.

In English literature Sir Francis Bacon was the first to use the form, and the appearance in 1597 of his celebrated ten essays, followed later by two enlarged editions, showed what could be done with the essay form in a style that was useful in the development of English prose. Bacon, too, displayed a remarkable diversity in his choice of theme. If his temperament avoided the occasional excursions of the French master into indiscreet literary by-ways (see for example, Montaigne's amusing *Sur des Vers de Virgile*), his didactic nature enabled him to offer wise counsel on the conduct of life in an axiomatic style that still makes his best essays remembered as quotations now passed into common usage. Sentences from the essays on Death, Revenge, Atheism, and *Of Studies*, to specify a few, are as familiar and oft quoted as proverbs, bringing his wisdom and 'counsels, civill and morall' truly 'home, to mens businesse, and bosomes', as he observed with pleasure, while in the essay *Of Gardens* he was able to relax and to give posterity one of the most delightful essays in the language.

Essays, by their personal, wayward, random nature and growth, developing from Bacon's work, and the 'Character Books' of the seventeenth century to our own time, allow their writers to wander where they will, from a trifle such as *On Nothing* (Belloc), to profound wisdom, touched with the jester's wit (G. K. Chesterton); from essays in literary appreciation that whet the appetite and lead the reader to widen his own horizon (Virginia Woolf), to vigorous political and social controversy, pamphleteers' tracts, satire, and amusing fantasy (Bernard Shaw, Dean Swift, Carlyle).

Even then the variety and diversity of the English essay has only been hinted at, for we have said nothing of Charles Lamb (beloved by all); nor of kindly, smiling Robert Lynd (immortally 'Y.Y.' of the *New Statesman*); nor of 'the inimitable Max' (what a pity somebody with talent doesn't try); nor of the journalism of that greatest of all journalists William Hazlitt; nor of the lapidary prose of Landor.

There remains *Belles Lettres*, a happy term, enabling the compiler to bring together in this section such unclassifiable joys as Sterne's *Sentimental Journey* (if that isn't *Belles Lettres* the thing doesn't exist); Samuel Butler's *Notebooks* by means of which we are able to overhear this highly individual author talking to himself before the days of tape-recorders); and the quiet *Trivia* of Logan Pearsall Smith, which, although it may be merely the tinkle of the spoon in the teacup, is not less important in the reader's life than the impassioned rhetoric of a Carlyle, or the winding, allusive discourses of a Robert Burton anatomising melancholy for all time.

Abercrombie, Lascelles (1881-1938) THE ART OF WORDSWORTH
O.U.P. 1952
Five lectures delivered in 1935, with an additional essay on *Peter Bell*.

THE IDEA OF GREAT POETRY *Secker* 1925

PRINCIPLES OF LITERARY CRITICISM *Gollancz* (1932); *High Hill Books* 1961 12s 6d
A notable and stimulating discussion, of interest to general readers as well as to academic students, critics, and teachers. The art of literature is discussed, with special reference to Aristotle's *Poetics* and to later theories.

Addison, Joseph (1672-1719) and Sir Richard Steele (1672-1729)
THE SPECTATOR (1711-12) 4 vols. ed. by C. Gregory Smith *Dent*
(*Everyman*) (1907) 1958 11s 6d each
The best modern edition, being a reprint of Professor Gregory Smith's edition of 1897-8, with notes to each volume, a biographical and a general index. These essays by the principal contributors to *The Spectator* are a landmark in the development of this form of literature.

SELECTED ESSAYS ed. by J. R. Green *Macmillan* (*Golden Treasury series*) 1880 7s 6d

*SIR ROGER DE COVERLEY and other essays *Nelson* (*Classics*) 1956 6s

THE COVERLEY PAPERS from *The Spectator* ed. (with those of Steele and Budgell) by O. M. Myers O.U.P. 1908 6s 6d

Agate, James (1877-1947) AN ANTHOLOGY ed. by Herbert van
Thal *Hart-Davis* 1961 21s
A choice of characteristic journalism, dramatic criticism, and extracts
from the *Ego* series of diaries, that enlivened the national newspapers
week by week. Agate was one of the wittiest critics of his age. This
selection has an introduction by his friend and colleague Alan Dent.

Aldis, Harry Gidney (1853-1919) THE PRINTED BOOK (1916)
Revised by John Carter and Brooke Crutchley *C.U.P.* 1947
The history of the development of printed books from the first examples.
A standard book for students of librarianship, printing and bibliography;
an interesting survey for readers and book collectors.

Amarasinghe, Upali (*d.* 1960) DRYDEN AND POPE IN THE EARLY
NINETEENTH CENTURY, 1800-1830 *C.U.P.* 1962 27s 6d
The only published work of a promising young Sinhalese scholar. It is a
salutary study of changing literary taste, correcting the superficial idea
that after Wordsworth's preface on poetic diction (1800) there was a
quick response leading to a swing towards romanticism. He points out
that it was not until about 1820 that *Blackwood's Magazine* and the other
critical magazines indicated that Wordsworth had succeeded in creating
readers for the new type of poetry.

Arnold, Matthew (1822-88) CULTURE AND ANARCHY (1869) ed.
by J. Dover Wilson *C.U.P.* 1932 15s; 1960 8s 6d (paperback)
A standard edition in a series *Landmarks in the History of Education*. These
essays attacked in forthright style the materialism and philistinism of the
age; Arnold pleaded for the pursuit of culture as a means of avoiding the
deterioration of society which he foresaw would result from unchecked
tendencies in English society and thought.

ESSAYS IN CRITICISM 2 series *Macmillan* (1865; 1888) 2nd series
1938 6s
Influential essays on literature and authors, that were widely read and
influential up to our time. Selections are noted below.

ESSAYS IN LITERATURE *Dent* (*Everyman*) (1907) 1954
Includes the essay *On Translating Homer*, with F. W. Newman's reply.
Introduction by G. K. Chesterton.

*SELECTED WORKS ed. by John Bryson *Hart-Davis* (*Reynard
Library*) 1954 26s
Of the 800 pages of this omnibus 500 are of prose, and the remainder
poetry, with introduction and notes.

POETRY AND PROSE ed. by Sir Edmund Chambers *O.U.P.* 1939
8s 6d
Includes critical essays on Arnold's achievement by Lionel Johnson and
by H. W. Garrod.

NOTEBOOKS ed. by H. F. Lowry and two others *O.U.P.* 1952
Arnold kept records of everything that took his fancy in his daily reading

in English, French, German and Italian and in the classics of Greek and Latin literature. In his daughter's selection from his notebooks, published in 1902, she stated: 'My father used often to say half-jokingly, that if anyone would ever take the trouble to collect all the extracts from various writers which he had copied in his notebooks, there would be found a volume of priceless worth.'

ON THE CLASSICAL TRADITION ed. by R. H. Super *Angus and Robertson* 1960 27s 6d
Volume 1 of an American edition from Ann Arbor, University of Michigan Press, of the *Complete Prose Works* of Matthew Arnold. It includes prefaces, and the essay *On Translating Homer*.

Ascham, Roger (1515-68) ENGLISH WORKS ed. by Aldis Wright *C.U.P.* 1904
Contains *Toxophilus*, a dialogue on archery (1545); *The Scholemaster*, a treatise on the education of boys (1570); and, *A Report of Affaires of State*. Apart from their antiquarian interest, these prose pieces are important landmarks in the making of English, because Ascham was one of the few learned men of his age who deliberately chose his native tongue instead of Latin for his didactic writings.

*Bacon, Sir Francis (Lord Verulam) (1561-1626) ESSAYS: CIVIL AND MORAL (1597; 1625) ed. by Oliphant Smeaton *Dent* (*Everyman*) (1906) 1955 6s 6d; *Macmillan* 1889 6s; *Nelson* (*Classics*) 1954 6s; *O.U.P.* (*Worlds Classics*) (1902) 1959 6s
The *Worlds Classics* edition 'reproduces the spelling and typographical features of the 1625 edition, and carries an appendix containing the text of the version of 1597 . . . The fragment *Of Fame* is reprinted from Dr. Rawley's *Resusitatio* (1657).' *Everyman* provides an index of quotations and foreign phrases used in the fifty-eight essays, with a glossary, and the fragment. The text of the third edition of 1625 is given, with spelling modernised, in an edition of Bacon's *The New Atlantis*, edited by Gordon S. Haight, Van Nostrand, 1942, 14s.

Bagehot, Walter (1826-77) LITERARY STUDIES (1879) 2 vols. ed. by George Sampson *Dent* (*Everyman*) 1911 6s 6d each
The creative criticism of a general reader; stimulating essays in appreciation by a writer with interest in many walks of life. Of special note are the essays on Gibbon, on the Waverley novels, Dickens, Macaulay, Crabb Robinson, and the poetry of Clough.

Bailey, John Cann (1864-1931) DR. JOHNSON AND HIS CIRCLE *O.U.P.* (*Home University Library*) (1913) 1944 8s 6d
MILTON *O.U.P.* (*Home University Library*) 1915 8s 6d
Two examples of the critical appreciations of an urbane critic whose essays on literary themes, contributed over a long period to *The Times Literary Supplement*, were amongst the best literary journalism of their time. The first monograph has been revised with additional material by L. F. Powell.

Baring, Maurice (1874-1945) LANDMARKS IN RUSSIAN LITERATURE *Methuen* (1910) (*University Paperbacks*) 1960 7s 6d
An outline by a gifted diplomatist, journalist and creative writer, who worked for a time in Russia.

Barkley, Henry C. (1871-1940) STUDIES IN THE ART OF RAT-CATCHING: A MANUAL FOR SCHOOLS (*Murray* 1891) *Methuen* (*Venture Library*) 1960 5s
The modern reprint is entitled *Rat-Catching For the Use of Schools*. The author, who also wrote *My Boyhood: a story book*, put down in simple prose, reminiscent of W. H. Davies's style in *Autobiography of a Super-tramp*, the results of a lifetime of experience in rat and rabbit catching in the countryside of late nineteenth-century England. The book is a minor classic in its small class.

*Barrie, Sir James (1860-1937) PLAYS AND STORIES *Dent* (*Everyman*) 1962 12s 6d
An addition to the series, providing an omnibus selection of Barrie's most characteristic work. Details under *Prose Drama* section.

Beckford, Peter (1740-1811) THOUGHTS ON HUNTING (1781) ed. by J. Otho Paget *Methuen* (1899) 1951 10s 6d Illus.
A frequently reprinted classic on fox and hare hunting, written in the form of a series of 'familiar letters to a friend'.

Beerbohm, Sir Max (1872-1956) *AND EVEN NOW *Heinemann* (1920) 1950 15s
This volume contains the two essays that for many admirers of Beerbohm's delicate art are the two best examples of ironic wit in the language: *No. 2 The Pines* (1914), and *A Clergyman* (1918).

AROUND THEATRES 2 vols. *Heinemann* (1924); *Hart-Davis* 1953 30s
A collected edition of 583 pages of all Beerbohm's dramatic criticism and essays. Witty, creative criticism to be read with enjoyment, even if the plays discussed are no longer in the repertory.

A CHRISTMAS GARLAND *Heinemann* (1912) 1950 15s
Classic parodies in prose of Henry James, H. G. Wells, Arnold Bennett and other contemporaries. The last edition contains an additional piece 'On the Art of a Certain M...r...ce B...r...ng'.

MAINLY ON THE AIR *Heinemann* 1946 15s
Collection of radio talks and essays broadcast.

*SEVEN MEN—AND TWO OTHERS *Heinemann* (1919) 1950 10s 6d; *Penguin Books* 1956 2s 6d
The last standard edition of these amusing studies in character contained 'the two others', making eight in all. The missing man is presumably Sir Max, about whom nothing is offered explicitly.

A VARIETY OF THINGS *Heinemann* 1953 15s
A late gathering, including some broadcast scripts.

WORKS AND MORE *Bodley Head* (1930) 1952 8s 6d
With characteristically gay wit in early flower, the essayist published his
firstlings (seven essays) in 1896, followed by *More* (twenty essays) in 1899.
Here they are together in one volume.

*YET AGAIN *Heinemann* 1920 15s
Originally published by Chapman and Hall in 1909. In the second group
of essays are the notable set of nine 'Words For Pictures'.

*THE INCOMPARABLE MAX: a selection, edited by S. C. Roberts
Heinemann 1962 36s
Thirty-two choice pieces, arranged chronologically in order of publica-
tion or broadcast date, including a selection of dramatic criticsm from
Around Theatres, together with an introduction by Sir Sydney Roberts.

Behn, Aphra (1640–89) SELECTED WRITINGS *John Calder* (*Evergreen*)
1950 10s 6d
Mrs. Aphra Behn was the first woman in English literature to write
professionally for a living. Her novel *Oroonoko* (1688); her one beautiful
poem; and some of her coarse comedies, have a place in literature for the
student.

Belloc, Hilaire (1870–1953) *AN ANTHOLOGY OF HIS PROSE AND
VERSE Selected by W. N. Roughead *Hart-Davis* 1951; *Heinemann* (*Mercury Books*) 1962 12s 6d
'Poetry, essays, history, fiction, satire, travel, biography, sociology, sea-
faring, religion, literary criticism, comic verse—all have their place in
the catalogue of this vigorous and versatile genius, almost all are represented in this anthology . . .' In the *Mercury* paperback reprint the
volume is called *Selected Writing*.

SELECTED ESSAYS *Methuen* 1948 12s 6d
With an introduction by J. B. Morton.

SELECTED ESSAYS ed. by J. B. Morton *Penguin Books* 1958 2s 6d

*STORIES, ESSAYS AND POEMS *Dent* (*Everyman*) (1938) 1957 11s 6d
The last edition has an introduction by J. B. Morton ('Beachcomber'),
who has made a new selection of poems, together with an extended
'selection from the celebrated Epigrams'.

Bennett, Arnold (1867–1931) LITERARY TASTE (1912) *Cape* 1937;
Penguin Books 1938 2s 6d
An introduction to the pleasures of reading with a purpose, still stimulating, and useful to beginners for its advice on the development of a
critical sense, with specific recommendations regarding the formation of
a personal library of English and some European classics.

*Blake, William (1757-1827) COMPLETE WRITINGS ed. by Geoffrey
Keynes *Nonesuch Press* 1957 63s 968 pp
Bicentenary omnibus volume of everything Blake is known to have
written, including variant readings and some of his letters. The previous

collection, entitled *Complete Poetry and Prose*, was last published in 1939, Nonesuch Press, 30s.

Boas, Frederick Samuel (1862-1957) AN INTRODUCTION TO TUDOR DRAMA O.U.P. 1933 15s
AN INTRODUCTION TO STUART DRAMA O.U.P. 1946 25s
AN INTRODUCTION TO EIGHTEENTH CENTURY DRAMA, 1700-1780 O.U.P. 1953 30s
A standard trilogy for students, by one of the greatest literary historians of his time.

Bolingbroke, Henry St. John, *1st Viscount* (1678-1751) LETTERS ON THE SPIRIT OF PATRIOTISM; and ON THE IDEA OF A PATRIOT KING (1749) O.U.P. 1917 5s
Enduring prose of a rhetorician who attracted superlative praise from his contemporaries, notably Chesterfield and Pope. 'He held Pope, as it were, by a spell, and the spell was never broken.' *Memoir of Pope, by Robert Carruthers.*

Boswell, James See under Johnson below, for an edition of A TOUR TO THE HEBRIDES: Johnson and Boswell

Bradley, Andrew Cecil (1851-1935) OXFORD LECTURES ON POETRY *Macmillan* (1909) 1950 21s; and 1962 (*Papermac series*) 12s 6d
SHAKESPEAREAN TRAGEDY *Macmillan* (*St. Martins Library*) 1904 18s; 1957 6s
Lectures on *Hamlet, Othello, King Lear,* and *Macbeth,* that have maintained a high place in critical literature in the estimation of teachers and general readers. The notes on specific points are useful for reference when reading, or before seeing productions of, these four major tragedies.

Bradley, Henry (1845-1923) THE MAKING OF ENGLISH *Macmillan* 1904 7s
Standard work by one of the greatest lexicographers of his time. He was joint-editor, later senior editor, of the *Oxford English Dictionary.*

Brailsford, Henry Noel (1873-1958) SHELLEY, GODWIN AND THEIR CIRCLE O.U.P. (*Home University Library*) (1913) 1951 8s 6d
VOLTAIRE O.U.P. (*Home University Library*) 1935
Two brilliant examples of compression of great subjects to the limits of a pocket book series. Brailsford's cogent style was well-suited to the persuasive exposition of controversial political topics.

Brooke, Rupert (1887-1915) PROSE ed. by Christopher Hassall *Sidgwick and Jackson* 1956 15s
Essays on travel, the arts and democracy, poetry and drama, concluding with a poignant valedictory essay written for the *New Statesman,* dated 29 August, 1914.

C

Brown, John (1810-82) HORAE SUBSECIVAE (1858) *O.U.P. (Worlds Classics)* 1907

Of these half-forgotten essays for 'leisure hours' two are to be found in selections made from the three original series of 1858, 1861, and 1882, and in many prose anthologies: *Rab and his Friends* (an anecdotal sketch of a favourite dog); and *Marjorie Fleming* (an affectionate portrait of the talented child who was Sir Walter Scott's little friend).

Browne, Sir Thomas (1605-82) RELIGIO MEDICI (1642; 1643) ed. by Jean-Jacques Denonain *C.U.P.* (1953) 1955 10s 6d

The editor of this definitive text, who is Professor of English Literature, University of Algiers, discovered in 1946 that W. A. Greenhill's standard edition (Macmillan, 1881, 5s) had been based on early printed editions, not on manuscripts. His own collation of all extant manuscripts and editions disclosed passages never before printed, and many important variants. His new edition therefore offers the text 'as nearly what Browne actually wrote as may be wished'.

*RELIGIO MEDICI AND OTHER WRITINGS ed. by C. H. Herford *Dent (Everyman)* (1906) 1956 6s 6d

This edition includes, in addition to the principal work, all of Browne's stately, allusive prose that the general reader requires; namely: *Hydriotaphia; or, Urn Burial*; *The Garden of Cyrus*; *Christian Morals*; and, *Letter To a Friend*.

RELIGIO MEDICI AND CHRISTIAN MORALS ed. by Geoffrey Keynes *Nelson (Classics)* 1940 6s

The second work consists of short notes and brief observations, and should be read as a complementary essay to *Religio Medici*. The editor has taken his standard text for this edition, from his uniform set of Browne's *Collected Works*, 6 volumes, Faber, 1928-31.

URNE BURIALL, and THE GARDEN OF CYRUS (1658) ed. by John Carter *C.U.P.* 1958 12s 6d

A tercentenary edition in similar format to Denonain's edition of *Religio Medici*. The editor's revised text, based on his 1932 edition published by Cassell, was prepared in the light of 'recently found copies of the first edition corrected by Browne himself'.

*Browning, Robert (1812-89) POETRY AND PROSE ed. by Simon Nowell-Smith *Hart-Davis (Reynard Library)* 1951 25s

A selection of 776 pages, containing a liberal choice of Browning's letters, the essay on Shelley, and about 600 pages of poetry, including extracts from *The Ring and the Book*.

Bulfinch, Thomas (1796-1867) THE AGE OF FABLE (1855) *Dent (Everyman)* 1910 6s 6d

Standard introduction, suitable for young readers, to classical and Nordic mythology, by an American writer. A revised and enlarged edition, now out of print, was published under the title of *The Golden Age of Myth and Legend*, Harrap, 1913.

*Burton, Robert (1577-1640) THE ANATOMY OF MELANCHOLY
(1621; 1651-2) 3 vols. ed. by Holbrook Jackson *Dent* (*Everyman*)
(1932) 1961 11s 6d each
A digressive, allusive discourse, analysing and commenting on the causes
and symptoms of melancholy, its cure and consequences. To illustrate
and embroider his theme Burton quotes from a whole library of ancient
authors. In this modern edition the spelling has been modernised and the
Latin quotations translated, the text being that of the sixth, published in
1651. Through the centuries many poets and other writers have drawn
rich inspiration from this extraordinary work.

Butler, Samuel (1612-80) CHARACTERS, AND PASSAGES FROM NOTE-
BOOKS ed. by A. R. Waller *C.U.P.* 1908 30s
Although the satirist is remembered for his mock-epic *Hudibras* (see
under *Poetry* section), he is worth reading also for his proverbial wisdom,
to be found in his occasional essays and the formal 'characters' after the
fashion set by Overbury.

Butler, Samuel (1835-1902) THE AUTHORESS OF THE 'ODYSSEY'
(1897) *Cape* 1922 7s 6d
An original theory (as indicated by the title), put forward with persuasive vigour and clarity.

THE ESSENTIAL SAMUEL BUTLER ed. by G. D. H. Cole *Cape* 1950
6s
Presents in 544 pages a fair proportion of Butler's miscellaneous prose,
including biological essays and extracts from longer works such as *The
Fair Haven*, some poetry, and a substantial selection from the two great
works of fiction, *The Way of All Flesh*, and *Erewhon*.

EX VOTO (1888) *Cape* 1928 7s 6d
'An account of the Sacro Monte or New Jerusalem at Varallo-Sesia;
with a note of Tabachetti's remaining work at Crea.'

*NOTE-BOOKS ed. by Geoffrey Keynes and Brian Hill *Cape*
1951 18s
The definitive edition, presenting the cream of Butler's characteristic
comments on life, people, and ideas, set down with brevity, dry wit,
and acute, though sometimes perverse, shrewdness. First selected by
Butler's friend and biographer, Festing Jones, who published a volume
in 1912, and a further selection in 1934.

SELECTIONS FROM THE NOTE-BOOKS ed. by A. T. Bartholomew
Cape 1930 4s 6d

SHAKESPEARE'S SONNETS RECONSIDERED (1899) *Cape* 1927 7s 6d
Highly controversial and individual view of the many problems
presented by the sonnets, including that concerned with the 'correct'
order; and those relating to the identity of 'Mr. W.H.', and the meaning
of certain obscure allusions. Even if they do not convince the reader, the
arguments will engage his interest and illuminate the text. The modern
edition has a photographic reproduction of the Grenville copy of the
1609 edition of Shakespeare's *Sonnets*, now in the British Museum.

Byron, George Gordon Noel, *6th Baron* (1788-1824) BYRONIC
THOUGHTS ed. by Peter Quennell *Murray* 1960 10s 6d
A gleaning of Byron's maxims, reflections and portraits from his prose
and poetry, correspondence and notebooks, displaying his genius in a
new light.

*SELECTIONS FROM POETRY, LETTERS AND JOURNALS ed. by Peter
Quennell *Nonesuch Press* 1949 21s
An 'omnibus' selection of 880 pages.

Carlyle, Thomas (1795-1881) *A CARLYLE ANTHOLOGY ed. by
G. M. Trevelyan *Longmans* 1953 18s
Classified extracts selected to display Carlyle's characteristic view of
history, philosophy, human nature and the shape of things to come.
'It is my hope,' writes the editor, 'that this anthology will help some to
whom Carlyle is little more than a great name to realise the nature of his
fiery art, its power, its perceptiveness, its humour and at times its strange
beauty.'

ESSAYS 2 vols. *Dent* (*Everyman*) 1912 6s 6d each
Vol. 1: Scottish and other miscellanies; Burns, Scott; and occasional
pieces. *Vol. 2:* English and other critical miscellanies: Boswell's *Johnson*;
Biography; History; Corn Law Rhymes; Chartism; Cagliostro; The
Nigger Question; The Opera; Petition on the Copyright Bill.

SARTOR RESARTUS (1838) and ON HEROES AND HERO WORSHIP
(1841) *Dent* (*Everyman*) (1908) 1954 7s 6d
Of all Carlyle's writings, the two brought together in this volume are
the most widely read now, the first being an ironic, satiric essay in social
philosophy; the second, originally a series of six lectures delivered in
1840, offered to students of history a powerful argument in favour of
authoritarian government and emphasised what to Carlyle seemed to be
the inevitableness of dominance by Great Men, if mankind were to
progress. He drew examples from mythical heroes, from great men of
literature, religion and military history, including Dante, Mahomet,
Luther, Cromwell, Rousseau, and Napoleon. Published separately
O.U.P. (*Worlds Classics*) 1961, 6s.

*SELECTED WORKS ed. by Julian Symons *Hart-Davis* (*Reynard
Library*) 1956 27s 6d
An omnibus of 784 pages, providing a comprehensive choice from a
wide range of work, from the earliest to *Frederick the Great* (1865) and
with some *Reminiscences* and *Letters*.

SELECTIONS ed. by A. M. D. Hughes *O.U.P.* 1957 9s 6d
Some essays; extracts from all the major works; from *Chartism*; *Latter-
Day Pamphlets*; some historical essays; and the *Reminiscences*, together
with essays in appreciation of Carlyle by Edward Caird, Mazzini,
Matthew Arnold, Harriet Martineau, George Meredith, Professor
Saintsbury, and Frederic Harrison.

*Carroll, Lewis (Charles Lutwidge Dodgson) (1832-98) COMPLETE
WORKS *Nonesuch Press* 1939 32s 6d illustrations by John Tenniel

An omnibus introduced by Alexander Woollcott. In addition to the two stories about Alice, this volume of 1293 pages contains less popular long stories, poems, puzzles, 'phantasmagoria', college rhymes and notes, acrostics, inscriptions, and miscellany: 'bubbling laughter . . . Carroll's legacy to the world'.

Chambers, Raymond Wilson (1874-1942) MAN'S UNCONQUERABLE MIND *Cape* 1939 30s
'Studies of English authors from Bede to A. E. Housman and W. P. Ker.'

Chapman, Robert William (1881-1960) JANE AUSTEN: FACTS AND PROBLEMS *O.U.P.* 1948 15s
The Clark Lectures, 1948; not biographical; not entirely criticism: but a mingling of both elements by the greatest modern authority on the novelist.

JOHNSONIAN AND OTHER ESSAYS AND REVIEWS *O.U.P.* 1953 15s
Collected essays of the Johnsonian scholar whose editorial work and urbane learning placed all who enjoy Dr. Johnson's writings and Jane Austen's novels in his debt.

Chesterton, Gilbert Keith (1874-1936) *AN ANTHOLOGY ed. by D. B. Wyndham Lewis *O.U.P.* (*Worlds Classics*) 1957 7s 6d
A dazzling display of G. K. Chesterton's wit, exuberance, militant, but genial faith, and optimism. The volume includes some letters, one short story, some essays, and extracts from his longer books, a broadcast talk, some of his best poetry, and the last act of his play, *Magic*.

CHARLES DICKENS *Methuen* (1906) 1956 9s 6d
A study in appreciation revealing Chesterton's complete enjoyment of, and sympathy with, Dickens's novels and gifts.

*CHAUCER *Faber* (1932) 1960 21s; 1962 9s 6d (paperback)
An appreciation and study of the period, life and achievement, of the first great English poet.

ESSAYS AND POEMS ed. by Wilfrid Sheed *Penguin Books* 1958 2s 6d

GEORGE BERNARD SHAW *Bodley Head* (1909) 1935 7s 6d
A witty, stimulating, and critical appreciation by a friendly, but very shrewd critic. The last edition has an additional chapter on some of Shaw's later plays.

HERETICS *Bodley Head* (1905) 1950 7s 6d
A series of studies. The essay on Bernard Shaw is notable, and may be read as complementary to the monograph above.

THE MAN WHO WAS ORTHODOX ed. by A. L. Maycock *Dobson* 1963 30s
A selection of writings not hitherto published in book form.

ORTHODOXY *Bodley Head* 1908 9s 6d
Perhaps the best of all G.K.C's personal statements. From these essays on spiritual problems and related topics, there emerges a clear impression of his faith and optimistic temperament.

*ROBERT BROWNING *Macmillan* (1903) 1952 7s 6d
A brief biographical sketch, followed by a critical discussion of the
characteristic poems of Browning. This monograph (formerly in the
English Men of Letters series) is of great value to those who find Browning's
poetry difficult to enjoy and sometimes to understand.

SELECTED ESSAYS *Methuen* 1951 12s 6d

*STORIES, ESSAYS AND POEMS *Dent* (*Everyman*) (1935) 1953 7s 6d
A comprehensive omnibus, with an introduction by Maisie Ward, the
author of the standard biography of Chesterton.

THE VICTORIAN AGE IN LITERATURE *O.U.P.* (*Home University
Library*) (1913) 1961 8s 6d
Within the limits of the series, this summary is an illuminating, although
individual and controversial, sketch, summarising the main currents of
nineteenth-century thought as expressed by the major authors.

Clare, John (1793-1864) PROSE ed. by J. W. and Anne Tibble
Routledge 1951
The most interesting piece in this gathering of essays and fragments, and
letters on natural history, is Clare's autobiographical sketch, *Sketches in
the Life of John Clare*, written by himself, first edited by Edmund Blunden,
with notes and additions, Cobden-Sanderson, 1931.

Coleridge, Samuel Taylor (1772-1834) ANIMA POETAE *Heinemann*
1895
Extracts from notebooks, posthumously published, and perhaps revised
by E. Hartley Coleridge. Brief, fragmentary and unsystematic, but yet
offering informal comments to the reader, of a very illuminating nature,
on creative literature and ideas.

*BIOGRAPHIA LITERARIA (1817) 2 vols. ed. by J. Shawcross
O.U.P. 1907 30s (the set); *Dent* (*Everyman*) (1906) 1956 7s 6d
'Biographical sketches of my literary life and opinions.' The standard
edition in two volumes of 704 pages includes 'Aesthetical Essays'. *Biographia Literaria* is the most important index to Coleridge's philosophy,
critical theories, and intellectual development. From it, the student is
able to estimate the influence on Coleridge of German writers and
philosophers, and to observe the growth of the ideas that flowered in
the *Lyrical Ballads*, published by Wordsworth and Coleridge in 1798.

*COMPLETE POETRY AND SELECTED PROSE ed. by Stephen Potter
Nonesuch Press (1933) 1950 21s
In an omnibus volume of 880 pages the editor gives not only the poetry,
but also a selection of Coleridge's *Letters*, the most important of the
fugitive writings and critical essays.

INQUIRING SPIRIT ed. by Kathleen Coburn *Routledge* 1951
A presentation of Coleridge's thought in passages chosen from both
published and unpublished prose.

THE NOTEBOOKS ed. by Kathleen Coburn *In progress Routledge* 1957- Vol. 1 (in 2 parts): 1794-1804 75s (the set); Vol. 2 (in 2 parts): 1804-8 90s (the set)
A double volume inaugurating the first publication of the complete edition of Coleridge's Notebooks, 'hitherto inaccessible to scholars, and, except for *Anima Poetae*' (see above) 'the limited selection made by E. H. Coleridge in 1895, unpublished'. The full text, with editorial notes and indexes, will be completed in five or six double volumes.

POETRY AND PROSE ed. by Kathleen Raine *Penguin Books* 1957 3s 6d

PROSE AND POETRY ed. by H. W. Garrod *O.U.P.* 1925 8s 6d
A selection, with essays on Coleridge by Hazlitt, De Quincey, Jeffrey, and Carlyle.

*SHAKESPEAREAN CRITICISM 2 vols. ed. by T. M. Raysor (1930) revised edition *Dent (Everyman)* 1961 11s 6d each
The notable addition to *Everyman* is a recension of Professor Raysor's first collection of all of Coleridge's lectures, his notes, fragments, essays, and critical miscellany relating to Shakespeare, and may be regarded as the definitive edition of a work of such eminence that the editor claims Coleridge to be 'the greatest of English critics'.

Cotton, Charles (1630-87) THE ESSAYS OF MONTAIGNE translated by Charles Cotton (1685) 3 vols. revised by W. C. Hazlitt *Bell* 1892
There is no modern edition of this translation, which, although it lacks the picturesque style of Florio's, is preferred by some readers as a pleasant rendering of Montaigne's familiar, discursive essays.

Cowley, Abraham (1618-67) ESSAYS (1668) ed. by A. R. Waller *C.U.P.* 1906 30s
In contrast to his poetry, Cowley's prose is in an easy-flowing style, well-suited to the essay form, of which the volume contains many pleasant examples such as *Of My Self* and *The Garden*.

Davies, William Henry (1871-1940) THE ESSENTIAL DAVIES selected by Brian Waters *Cape* 1951 6s
Contains extracts from the *Autobiography* (q.v.); *A Poet's Pilgrimage*; *Later Days*; some poems, and a memoir by the editor.

de la Mare, Walter (1873-1956) A SELECTION FROM HIS WRITINGS ed. by Kenneth Hopkins *Faber* 1956 18s
Presents aspects of the whole genius of the writer in chosen essays, short stories, and poetry.

*STORIES, ESSAYS AND POEMS *Dent (Everyman)* 1937

*De Quincey, Thomas (1785-1859) THE ENGLISH MAIL COACH and other writings *Dent (Everyman)* (1912) 1961 9s 6d
A selection of De Quincey's best prose pieces, including the long and most famous essay, *On Murder, Considered as one of the Fine Arts*. In his introduction Professor J. E. Jordan says: 'This edition is a sort of minia-

ture *Selections Grave and Gay*, for it shows De Quincey in both his lightest and most solemn moods . . . the seven selections range from 1823 to 1849'.

*Defoe, Daniel (1661?-1731) A JOURNAL OF THE PLAGUE YEAR (1722) *Dent (Everyman)* (1908) 1953 6s 6d
Presented as if 'written by a citizen who continued all the while in London', and accepted for some time as an authentic account of an eye-witness of the events of 1665. Yet Defoe was but four years old at the time of the Great Plague of London. Thus it is enjoyed as one of the most remarkable examples of vivid journalism in the history of literature.

Dekker, Thomas (1570?-1632) THE GULL'S HORNBOOK (1609) *Dent (Temple Classics)* 1905
A racy piece of Elizabethan prose, describing manners and customs of rakes and gallants by means of ironic instructions to typical characters on the way to behave and the places in London to frequent. Two related examples of Dekker's prose are included in the reprint: *The Belman of London*; and, *Lanthorne and Candlelight* (1608).

Dobson, Henry Austin (1840-1921) EIGHTEENTH CENTURY VIGNETTES 3 vols. (1892-96) O.U.P. (*Worlds Classics*) series 1 and 2 1924 9s 6d
Studies of men and books written in a light, pleasant style, characteristic of the author when dealing with his favourite century.

*Donne, John (1573?-1631) COMPLETE POETRY AND SELECTED PROSE ed. by John Hayward *Nonesuch Press* 1929 21s
The prose includes *Paradoxes and Problemes*; *Letters*; *Meditations from 'Devotions Upon Emergent Occasions'*; passages from *Sermons*; *Death's Duel*, with textual and explanatory notes. 814 pages.
POETRY AND PROSE ed. by Desmond Hawkins *Nelson (Classics)* (1938) 1955 7s
Poems: pp 1-401; Sermons and Letters: 402-79.

Dowden, Edward (1843-1913) SHAKESPEARE *Routledge* (1875;1912) 1949 21s
'A critical study of his mind and art.' Although there are so many critical works on Shakespeare this is still a standard book, and is notable for its influence on later critics.

Drummond, William (1585-1649) CONVERSATIONS WITH JONSON IN 1618 (1711; 1842) *Dent (Everyman)* 1954
Included in Thornton's *Table Talk*, for which see next section. Ben Jonson's visit to Hawthornden resulted not only in the receipt of high civic honours at Edinburgh, but also in a number of intimate conversations with his host. Drummond kept a private memorandum of the poet's opinions and observations, to which he added his own views of Jonson's character. Posthumously published, these notes have not been regarded as completely reliable, but if accepted with some reservations, they have considerable interest.

Dryden, John (1631-1700) *OF DRAMATIC POESY AND OTHER
CRITICAL ESSAYS 2 vols. ed. by George Watson *Dent (Everyman)*
1962 15s each
A comprehensive collection, with notes and glossary. For the first time
the editor gives us Dryden's complete criticism: prefaces; essays, prologues; epilogues; even critical letters and occasional notes. School and
students' editions of the principal work, *An Essay of Dramatic Poesy*
(1668) are usually available in other editions.

POETRY AND PROSE ed. by D. Nichol Smith O.U.P. 1925 8s 6d
Includes the essays on Dryden by Congreve, Dr. Johnson, and Sir
Walter Scott.

*SELECTED WORKS ed. by Douglas Grant *Hart-Davis (Reynard
Library)* 1955 25s
An omnibus of 896 pages: essays, some of the plays; and a generous
selection of Dryden's best poetry and verse satires. The same editor has
also published a selection of Dryden's *Poems and Prose*, Penguin Books,
1955, 3s 6d.

Ellis, Havelock (1859-1939) SELECTED ESSAYS *Dent (Everyman)*
1936 6s 6d
Havelock Ellis chose this selection himself. The sixteen pieces offer some
of his best work from *Affirmations* (1898) and *The Philosophy of Conflict*
(1919) to *The Dance of Life* (1923) and *Little Essays of Love and Virtue* (two
series, 1922 and 1931).

*Elton, Oliver (1861-1945) A SURVEY OF ENGLISH LITERATURE
6 vols. *Edward Arnold* 1912-28 180s (the set) 1370 pp
A masterly survey, free from pedantry, balanced and shrewd in judgement. Hence of importance as a reference text for students but at the
same time interesting and readable enough for leisured general study.
The set is in three pairs of two volumes each, sold in these three periods
thus: 1730-80 (1928) 84s; 1780-1830 (1912) 84s; and 1830-80 (1920) 84s.

Elyot, Sir Thomas (1490-1546) THE BOKE NAMED THE GOVERNOUR
(1531) *Dent (Everyman)* (1907) ed. by S. E. Lehmberg 1962 15s
One of the first English treatises on education, being advice on the
training of a young man to fit him for positions of authority as master
or ruler. Sir Thomas was an ambassador, and his book was widely read
by those concerned in the sixteenth and seventeenth centuries. The new
edition in *Everyman* is the first to have modern spelling and punctuation.

Emerson, Ralph Waldo (1803-82) THE CONDUCT OF LIFE (1860)
W. H. Allen (Dolphin Books) 1962 7s 6d; *Dent (Everyman)* (1908)
1963 10s 6d

ENGLISH TRAITS; REPRESENTATIVE MEN; AND OTHER ESSAYS *Dent
(Everyman)* 1906
The series of essays on *English Traits* (1856) was the sequel to the American
philosopher's visit to England, during which he delivered some lectures,
published in 1850 as *Representative Men*.

ESSAYS 2 series (1841-4) *Dent (Everyman)* (1906) 1955 8s 6d;
ESSAYS, POEMS AND ADDRESSES ed. by Gordon S. Haight *Van
Nostrand* 1941 14s

The essays from lectures on didactic themes, emphasise the harmony as
well as the contrast between the American and his famed English friend,
Thomas Carlyle.

*ESSAYS; REPRESENTATIVE MEN; AND POEMS ed. by G. F. Maine
Collins (Classics) 1954 7s

Faraday, Michael (1791-1867) THE CHEMICAL HISTORY OF A CANDLE
(1861) *N.Y. Viking Press (Mayflower)* 1960 18s
ON THE VARIOUS FORCES OF NATURE (1860) *N.Y., Crowell* (1957)
1961 $2·75

The only editions now available of Faraday's scientific writings suitable
for popular reading. He was the first scientist to write scientific monographs for the educated layman. The second work, above, gives the text
of his Christmas Lectures at the Royal Institution, London, 1859-60:
'a course of six lectures on the various forces of nature and their relations
to each other'. *Everyman's Library* includes his historic lectures on *Experimental Researches in Electricity* (1839-55), Dent, 1912, 6s 6d.

FitzGerald, Edward (1809-83) SELECTED WORKS ed. by Joanna
Richardson *Hart-Davis (Reynard Library)* 1962 35s 776 pp
Based on the standard *Letters and Literary Remains*, edited by W. Aldis
Wright, 1902-3. Following FitzGerald's memoir of his father-in-law,
Bernard Barton, the Quaker poet, this much-needed collection reprints
almost everything likely to interest the general reader, including
Euphranor (1851) the *Rubáiyát* (first and fourth editions) (1859 and 1879);
Agamemnon, and above all, a generous selection of the delightful letters,
pages 457 to 760.

Florio, John (1553?-1625) THE ESSAYS OF MONTAIGNE translated by
John Florio (1603) 3 vols. *O.U.P. (Worlds Classics)* 1906; *Dent
(Everyman)* 1910
Of all the great Tudor translations Florio's *Montaigne* has perhaps been
the most widely read by the general public. The familiar style of the
original was here rendered into euphuistic prose with the freedom
characteristic of the age. Refer also to Cotton's version above.

Ford, Ford Madox (F. M. Hueffer) (1873-1939) THE MARCH OF
LITERATURE *Allen and Unwin* 1939 21s
An individual, sometimes idiosyncratic survey of world literature 'from
Confucius to modern times', seldom attempted by one who is a creative
writer himself. Ford's stimulating criticism and evaluations (extending
to 807 pages) provoke the reader into the formation of independent
judgements, and lead him to the books discussed with such gusto and
vitality.

Fortescue, Sir John William (1859-1934) THE STORY OF A RED DEER *Macmillan* (1897) 1950 7s 6d
A minor classic for younger readers, but also enjoyed by adults. It is the story of an Exmoor stag from birth to the last run.

FROUDE, James Anthony (1818-94) SHORT STUDIES ON GREAT SUBJECTS *Longmans* (1867-83) 2 vols. *Dent* (*Everyman*) 1907; ed. and selected by David Ogg *Collins* (*Fontana*) 1963 7s 6d
This series of essays, chiefly historical, was contributed to magazines, and was admired for generations because of the brilliant, lucid style maintained by the author year by year. In spite of the 'slips of detail' referred to by Hilaire Belloc in his introduction, *The Short Studies* deserve their permanent place in readers' affections. Of the literary essays, that reviewing Matthew Arnold's *The Strayed Reveller and Other Poems* (1854) is of particular interest.

Fry, Roger (1866-1934) TRANSFORMATIONS *Chatto* 1926
'Critical and speculative essays in art,' with illustrations to exemplify the critic's argument.

*VISION AND DESIGN *Chatto* (1920) 1957 10s 6d
An influential volume of essays on painting and art theory, by a persuasive teacher who was himself an artist of charm and accomplishment. He could fill the largest lecture halls in London when he spoke at length on the appreciation of painting and sculpture.

Gill, Eric (1882-1940) ESSAYS *Cape* 1947 8s 6d
A posthumously published collection, with an introduction by Mary Gill, of essays from the volume *Last Essays* (1942), together with fourteen other essays taken from *In a Strange Land* (1944). Eric Gill combined the creative gifts of a sculptor and typographer, with the vigorous temperament of a born controversialist holding individual views on art and modern life, religion and art, and on more general topics of the day.

Gissing, George (1857-1903) CHARLES DICKENS *Blackie* (1898)
'A critical study', of which Professor Cunliffe wrote: 'by far the best analysis of the genius of Dickens'.

*THE PRIVATE PAPERS OF HENRY RYECROFT *Constable* (1903); *Phoenix House* (1953) 1961 10s 6d
Readers in maturity return to this volume for its quiet, ironic discussion of problems of a democratic civilisation, and for its wisdom as a personal statement or idealised autobiography. Selected by *The Sunday Times* literary staff as one of the *101 Great Books Of Our Time*.

*Goldsmith, Oliver (1728-74) SELECTED WORKS ed. by Richard Garnett *Hart-Davis* (*Reynard Library*) 1950 25s
Essays, extracts from longer prose works, the two plays, and all of the novel, *The Vicar of Wakefield*, an abridgement of the *Life of Nash*, poems, some letters, and most readable chapters from *Polite Learning*, make up an omnibus volume of 898 pages.

Gordon, George (1881-1942) THE DISCIPLINE OF LETTERS *O.U.P.* 1946 15s

SHAKESPEARIAN COMEDY AND OTHER STUDIES *O.U.P.* 1944 12s 6d
A posthumous volume of critical essays, edited by the great Shakespearian scholar Sir Edmund Chambers.

*Granville-Barker, Harley (1877-1946) PREFACES TO SHAKESPEARE
2 vols. (1946-7); *Batsford* 1958 42s each; 1963 paperback editions 4 vols. 12s 6d each Illus.
Originally published by Sidgwick and Jackson in a series of five volumes; later published in America in the two-volume definitive edition, with some revision. Of great practical value to producers and actors, these essays are also illuminating to readers and students of the plays. *Contents:* Vol. 1: *Hamlet* (a book of over 200 pages); *King Lear*; *The Merchant of Venice*; *Antony and Cleopatra*; and *Cymbeline*. Vol. 2: *Othello*; *Coriolanus*; *Romeo and Juliet*; *Julius Caesar*; and *Love's Labour's Lost*. This distinguished producer and playwright also published in collaboration with G. B. Harrison, *A Companion To Shakespeare Studies*, C.U.P., 1934, 30s. His essay *On Dramatic Method* (1931) has been reprinted in *Dramabooks* series, MacGibbon and Kee, 1956, 9s 6d.

Gray, Thomas (1716-71) POEMS, WITH A SELECTION OF LETTERS
AND ESSAYS *Dent (Everyman)* (1912) 1955 10s 6d
A choice of letters from the period 1735 onwards, with some literary essays including *Metrum: Observations On English Metric* . . . and one on the poems of Lydgate.

Grey, Edward (1st Viscount Grey of Fallodon) (1862-1933) THE
CHARM OF BIRDS *Hodder* (1927) 1937 4s 6d
FALLODON PAPERS *Constable* (1926) 5s Illus.
FLY FISHING *Dent* (1899) 1947 15s Illus.
Three books indicating the recreations of the famous Liberal statesman. They continue to be enjoyed as modern classics on angling and bird life. *Fallodon Papers* is embellished with woodcuts by Robert Gibbings; *Fly Fishing* with wood engravings by Eric Fitch Daglish.

Grierson, Sir Herbert John Clifford (1866-1960) THE BACK-
GROUND OF ENGLISH LITERATURE *Chatto* 1934 21s
CROSS-CURRENTS IN ENGLISH LITERATURE *Chatto* 1929 21s
MILTON AND WORDSWORTH: POETS AND PROPHETS *Chatto* (1937) 1950 16s
Five of seven chapters are on Milton. The theme is the reactions of these poets to the politics of their times.

RHETORIC AND ENGLISH COMPOSITION *Oliver and Boyd* (1944) 1952 7s 6d
A severe, didactic title: but Professor Grierson's treatment of the subject lifts the book from the classroom to the private library of the reader interested in style.

Grierson, Sir Herbert John Clifford and James Cruickshank Smith (1867-1946) A CRITICAL HISTORY OF ENGLISH POETRY *Chatto* (1944) 1947 30s 548 pp; *Penguin Books (Peregrine)* 1963 12s 6d

Hardy, Thomas (1840-1928) NOTEBOOKS ed. by Evelyn Hardy *Hogarth Press* 1955 12s 6d
Two unpaged notebooks, with extracts from a third, 1867 to 1927; and some letters to Hardy from Julia Augusta Martin, 'the lady of Kingston Maurward who did so much to foster his talent in boyhood'.

Hazlitt, William (1778-1830) COMPLETE WORKS 21 vols. ed. by P. P. Howe *Dent* 1930-4

The centenary edition with much previously uncollected material, edited by the author of the standard biography of Hazlitt (for which see under *Biography* section). This great edition of the foremost essayist and literary journalist of his brilliant age was based on A. R. Waller's and Arnold Glover's edition in 12 volumes, published 1902-6.

*CHARACTERS OF SHAKESPEARE'S PLAYS (1817-18) O.U.P. (*Worlds Classics*) (1917) 1960 7s 6d; and with *The Round Table* in *Dent (Everyman)* (1906) 1957 12s 6d
Hazlitt's most important work, and one of the best volumes of Shakespearian criticism and appreciation in the language. The *Worlds Classics* reprint has an introduction by Sir Arthur Quiller-Couch; and the *Everyman* edition one by C. M. Maclean, the author of a standard biography of Hazlitt. *The Round Table* is a collection of forty 'essays on literature, men and manners' from *The Examiner*. These, said Hazlitt, were 'the thoughts of a metaphysician expressed by a painter'.

CONVERSATIONS OF JAMES NORTHCOTE, ESQ., R.A. (1830) ed. by Frank Swinnerton *Hutchinson* 1952 6s
Northcote lived from 1746 to 1831.

ESSAYS AND CHARACTERS ed. by Stanley Williams *Nelson (Classics)* 1937 6s
A selection of twenty-four of the most well-known and favourite essays.

*LECTURES ON THE ENGLISH COMIC WRITERS (1819) *W. H. Allen (Dolphin Books)* 1962 7s 6d; *O.U.P. (Worlds Classics)* 1907 6s; and with *Miscellaneous Essays* in *Dent (Everyman)* 1910 6s 6d

*LECTURES ON THE ENGLISH POETS (1818) *O.U.P. (Worlds Classics)* 1924 6s; and with *The Spirit of the Age* in *Dent (Everyman)* (1910) 1955 8s 6d

ON THE THEATRE ed. by William Archer and Robert Lowe *MacGibbon and Kee (Dramabooks)* 1958 10s
Collects in one volume all the essays Hazlitt wrote on plays, players and the theatre.

*SELECTED ESSAYS ed. by C. M. Maclean *Macdonald* (*Illustrated Classics*) 1948 15s; ed. by Geoffrey Keynes *Nonesuch Press* 1930 21s 808 pp

*THE SPIRIT OF THE AGE (1825) *Dent* (*Everyman*) with *Lectures q.v.* above; *O.U.P.* (*Worlds Classics*) (1904) 1961 6s; *W. H. Allen* (*Dolphin Books*) 1962 7s 6d
'Contemporary Portraits', of Wordsworth, Coleridge, Byron, Scott, Canning, Wilberforce, Brougham, Godwin, Cobbett, Malthus, Bentham, and others. These essays contain some of Hazlitt's most trenchant personal criticism.

TABLE TALK (1821-4) *Dent* (*Everyman*) (1908) 1960 12s 6d
'Original Essays', written in maturity, producing, writes C. M. Maclean, in her appreciation, contributed to the new edition in *Everyman*, 'one of those rare books, of which the reader might say:' 'Here I am heart to heart, hand to hand, with a real human being" '.

*WINTERSLOW (1839) *O.U.P.* (*Worlds Classics*) 1902
'Essays and characters written there.'

Hills, John Waller (1867-1938) A SUMMER ON THE TEST (1924-30) *Bles* 1946
A modern classic in the literature of angling, comparable, say those competent to judge, with Izaak Walton's masterpiece.

Hoby, Sir Thomas (1530-66) THE COURTIER translated by Sir Thomas Hoby (1561) *Dent* (*Everyman*) (1928) 1956 8s 6d
The introduction by W. H. D. Rouse and critical notes by Professor Henderson emphasise the literary importance of this notable example of Tudor prose. It is probable that it was known to Shakespeare, for the Shakespearian ideal of 'scholar-prince' can be observed clearly in Baldassare Castiglione's *Il Cortegiano* (1528), and the influence of this courtly dialogue has been traced in many other sixteenth-century poets.

Holland, Philemon (1552-1637) THE LIVES OF THE FIRST TWELVE CAESARS translated from Suetonius by Philemon Holland (1606)

THE MORALS OF PLUTARCH translated by Philemon Holland (1603) *Dent* (*Everyman*) 1912
Two examples of the work of 'the translator-generall of his age', as he was termed by Thomas Fuller. Holland also published an English version of William Camden's topographical folio *Britannia* (1610). Plutarch's *Moralia* consists of twenty essays on Flattery, Curiosity, Garrulity, Naughty Bashfulness, and related topics.

THE NATURAL HISTORY OF PLINY translated by Philemon Holland (1601) selected by Paul Turner *Centaur Press* 1962 84s
Selected passages from this vast 'History of the World' as Holland called it. It is a most entertaining repository of fact and fancy, enlivened by digressions, and has been a source book for generations of writers from Shakespeare onwards.

Holmes, Oliver Wendell (1809-94) THE AUTOCRAT OF THE BREAK-
FAST TABLE (1858) *Dent (Everyman)* (1906) 1960 10s 6d; *W. H.
Allen (Dolphin Books)* 1962 7s 6d
The first of a once-popular trilogy of essays in conversation by an
American physician, distinguished for his genial wit and wisdom. The
new edition has an introductory appreciation by Van Wyck Brooks.
Companion volumes were *The Poet at the Breakfast Table* (1872); and
The Professor at the Breakfast Table (1859).

Hopkins, Gerard Manley (1844-89) A HOPKINS READER ed. by
John Pick *O.U.P.* 1953
A selection with an introduction, of poems, characteristic letters, and
literary notes, presenting the poet's most generally interesting work in a
single volume of 346 pages.

JOURNALS AND PAPERS ed. by Humphry House, completed by
Graham Storey *O.U.P.* 1959 63s 614 pp Illus.
The first edition of Humphry House's redaction was published in 1937,
and is now superseded by this much enlarged edition resulting from
many years of research that continued up to House's death in 1955. It
gives a collection of Hopkins's drawings and sketches, an appendix on
his music, with the poet's settings to songs, some hitherto unpublished
poems, and the Journal for 1866 to 1868, discovered in 1947.

Housman, Alfred Edward (1859-1936) THE NAME AND NATURE OF
POETRY *C.U.P.* 1933 3s 6d
The text of the Leslie Stephen Lecture. This attracted attention from
readers because of the personal nature of the statement from a poet whose
work is enjoyed by a wide public drawn from every walk in life.

SELECTED PROSE ed. by John Carter *C.U.P.* 1961 10s 6d (paperback)
Learned prefaces; reviews of classical texts and editions; letters to the
Press; ceremonial addresses; and the above essay-lecture reprinted.

Hudson, William Henry (1841-1922) ADVENTURES AMONG BIRDS
(1913) *Dent* 1951 10s 6d
A HIND IN RICHMOND PARK *Dent* 1922 10s 6d
NATURE IN DOWNLAND (1900) *Dent* 1951 10s 6d
*A SHEPHERD'S LIFE (1910) *Dent (Everyman)* (1936) 1961 12s 6d
Of all the naturalist's books, the last is the most lovable, recalling as it
does, a countryside and a way of life now vanished from the downs of
Wiltshire and from the cottages of peasant-farmers, for ever. 'In its own
discursive, easy, itinerant way, I suppose this is the best prose pastoral
we have in English,' wrote Ernest Rhys, who introduces the reprint,
which now also contains that poignant narrative *An Old Thorn*, based
on records of the judicial murder of a peasant convicted of sheep stealing
in 1821, and recalling a rare survival of tree worship in Wiltshire.
Details are given in Dent's current catalogue of Hudson's complete
collected work, published in fourteen uniform volumes.

*Hunt, James Henry Leigh (1784-1859) SELECTED ESSAYS ed. by
J. B. Priestley *Dent (Everyman)* 1929 6s 6d
A choice from the work of a prolific and gifted journalist whose prose
style retains its charm, and whose friendships with the most famous
writers of his time give him a secure place in literary history. Lawrence H.
Houtchens and Carolyn Washburn Houtchens have collected Leigh
Hunt's *Literary Criticism* from various journals, O.U.P., 1956, 45s. The
volume has more than antiquarian and academic interest because of the
soundness of Hunt's judgements on the work of his contemporaries.
The same editors have also published his *Dramatic Criticism, 1808-1831*,
O.U.P., 1950, 36s.

Huxley, Thomas Henry (1825-95) LECTURES AND LAY SERMONS
(1870) *Dent (Everyman)* 1910

MAN'S PLACE IN NATURE AND OTHER ESSAYS (1863) *Dent (Everyman)* 1906
Notable volumes in the popularisation of scientific writing, by eminent
scientists, addressing the educated layman. See also Michael Faraday,
above.

Irving, Washington (1783-1859) SKETCH BOOK (1819-20) *W. H.
Allen (Dolphin Books)* 1962 7s 6d; *Dent (Everyman)* (1906) 1963
12s 6d
Full title: *The Sketch Book of Geoffrey Crayon, Gent*, being a volume of
miscellany, some short stories and essays, once immensely popular in
America and England. The two stories that have continued to be read
are *The Legend of Sleepy Hollow*, and *Rip van Winkle*, both frequently
reprinted separately for young readers, or in collectors' editions, as, for
example, *Rip van Winkle*, illustrated with eighty coloured plates by
Arthur Rackham, Heinemann, 1960, 30s.

*Jackson, Holbrook (1874-1948) THE READING OF BOOKS *Faber*
1946 8s 6d
A great bookman here discussed the reading of books as an art, to be
pursued with enjoyment by readers as cultivated artists, touching also
on many allied themes, such as the communication between author and
reader, the cult of ambiguity, books as intoxicants, the whole being
presented with many aptly chosen quotations. Of his other books, two
deserve special mention: *The Eighteen Nineties* (1913; 1927) and *The
Anatomy of Bibliomania* (1930).

James, Henry (1843-1916) THE ART OF THE NOVEL *Scribners* (1948)
1960 10s 6d (paperback edition)
Prefaces to the collected edition of James's fiction brought together in
one volume. Apart from their interest as revelations of Henry James's
methods and exercise of his craft as a writer, they illuminate the whole
subject of creative writing.

THE HOUSE OF FICTION ed. by Leon Edel *Hart-Davis* 1957 25s;
Heinemann (Mercury Books) 1962 12s 6d

James's biographer and bibliographer here collects the novelist's thoughts and essays on the art of fiction, scattered in letters and in fugitive writings. Thus this volume is complementary to the one above. In addition it includes four reviews by James of novels by Dickens, George Eliot, Thomas Hardy and Zola, with some other essays selected from the book *Partial Portraits*, published in 1888.

LITERARY REVIEWS AND ESSAYS ON AMERICAN, ENGLISH AND FRENCH LITERATURE ed. by Albert Mordell *Calder (Evergreen Books)* 1959 17s 6d

*NOTEBOOKS ed. by F. O. Matthiessen and Kenneth B. Murdock *O.U.P.* (1947) 1962 15s (paperback)
Some first drafts of short stories, together with notes made on novels and stories as first conceived. Indispensable to students and literary critics.

THE PAINTER'S EYE ed. by John L. Sweeney *Hart-Davis* 1956 20s
Thirty 'notes and essays on the pictorial arts' written between 1868 and 1897.

THE SCENIC ART ed. by Allan Wade *Hart-Davis* 1949 21s
'Notes on the drama, 1872-1901', with reviews of plays, collected from American periodicals, with editorial notes on the actors and plays mentioned.

SELECTED LITERARY CRITICISM ed. by Morris Shapira *Heinemann* 1962 25s

Jefferies, Richard (1848-87) THE AMATEUR POACHER *Murray* (1880) *O.U.P. (Worlds Classics)* with *The Gamekeeper at Home* 1948 7s 6d

FIELD AND HEDGEROW (1889) ed. by S. J. Looker *Lutterworth Press* 1948 3s 6d Illus.
Last essays, originally collected for posthumous publication by Mrs. Jefferies, and here reprinted, with illustrations by Agnes Miller Parker, for a centenary edition.

*THE GAMEKEEPER AT HOME (1878) *Eyre and Spottiswoode* 1948 5s; *O.U.P. (Worlds Classics)* with *The Amateur Poacher* 1948 7s 6d

HODGE AND HIS MASTERS (1880) ed. by Henry Williamson *Faber* 1947; *Eyre and Spottiswoode* 1948 5s
'A classic of English farming.'—*Henry Williamson*.

*THE LIFE OF THE FIELDS (1884) ed. by S. J. Looker *Lutterworth Press* 1947 3s 6d Illus. by Agnes Miller Parker and C. F. Tunnicliffe

*THE OPEN AIR (1885) *Eyre and Spottiswoode* 1948 5s

ROUND ABOUT A GREAT ESTATE (1880) *Eyre and Spottiswoode* with *Red Deer* (1884) 1948 5s

The sub-title of *The Gamekeeper at Home: Sketches of Natural History and Rural Life*, is an apt description of all the above books by a writer whom the late Professor Saintsbury evaluated as 'the greatest minute describer of English country life since White of Selborne'.

Jeffrey, Francis (1773-1850) LITERARY CRITICISM (1844-53) *O.U.P.* 1910

For a period, the Lord Advocate was editor of the *Edinburgh Review*. These contributions were nearly all on poets and poetry, and have permanent interest for posterity because they enable readers to judge how the works of Byron, Thomas Campbell, Crabbe, Felicia Hemans, Keats, Southey and Wordsworth struck a contemporary, when they were first published.

Johnson, Samuel (1709-84) *A JOURNEY TO THE WESTERN ISLANDS OF SCOTLAND (1775) *O.U.P.* (*Standard Authors*) with Boswell's *Journal of a Tour to the Hebrides* (1785) (1924) and 1961 with the cover title of *A Tour to the Hebrides: Johnson and Boswell* 16s

A volume edited by Dr. R. W. Chapman, bringing the two works together, with an introduction, a threefold index, a map, and seven illustrations.

*ON SHAKESPEARE ed. by W. K. Wimsatt *MacGibbon and Kee* (*Dramabooks*) 1960 18s; ed. by Sir Walter Raleigh *O.U.P.* 1908 10s 6d

The *Dramabooks* edition reprints two essays from *The Rambler* (1751); the Dedication to *Shakespeare Illustrated* (1753); and the two principal items: *Proposals For Printing By Subscription* (1756), and the famous *Preface* to Johnson's edition of 1765, with his notes on twenty-eight plays. Writing on the *Preface*, D. Nichol Smith, the editor of Worlds Classics *Shakespeare Criticism*, said 'By common consent nowadays it is one of the greatest essays on Shakespeare that has ever been written.'

*PROSE AND POETRY ed. by Mona Wilson *Hart-Davis* (*Reynard Library*) 1950 25s

The most comprehensive omnibus collection, totalling nearly 1000 pages.

THE RAMBLER (1750-2) ed. by S. C. Roberts *Dent* (*Everyman*) 1953 7s 6d

These are the essays contributed by Johnson to his Journal, which was published every Tuesday and Friday at the time when his main work was the compilation of his *Dictionary*. The subjects are sometimes didactic, sometimes on general literary themes, such as criticism, plagiarism, and biography, and sometimes on current topics such as living in a garret, and on 'the art of living at the cost of others'.

*SELECTIONS ed. by R. W. Chapman *O.U.P.* 1955 15s; (*Worlds Classics*) 1962 8s 6d

An anthology of choice pieces, wherein the full range of Dr. Johnson's genius in prose and poetry is displayed. Only the poem *The Vanity of*

Human Wishes is given complete, but there are characteristic specimens of other poems; selections from *Lives of the Poets*; *Table Talk*; some prayers, essays; and a choice from his tale of *Rasselas*.

Jonson, Ben (1572-1637) TIMBER; OR DISCOVERIES (1640-1) *Dent* (*Temple Classics*) 1898 7*s*
Being sundry observations on men and manners. This interesting collection seems to have been Ben Jonson's notebook into which he jotted brief observations and reflections from and upon Latin and Greek authors.

*Joyce, James (1882-1941) THE ESSENTIAL JAMES JOYCE ed. with notes, by Harry Levin *Cape* 1948 21*s*
A selection of 534 pages, giving some short stories from the volume *Dubliners*; the short novel, *A Portrait of the Artist as a Young Man*; the play *Exiles*; poems from *Chamber Music*; together with extracts from *Ulysses* and from *Finnegans Wake*, and a few scattered pieces.

Junius (perhaps Sir Philip Francis) (1740-1818) LETTERS TO THE PUBLIC ADVERTISER, 1769-1772 ed. by C. G. Everrett *Faber* 1927
Francis never acknowledged the authorship of these satirical essays on contemporary politics. The best modern edition, noted above, is a reprint of H. S. Woodfall's standard text of 1772, but excludes doubtful material of the 1812 edition edited by Woodfall and Mason Goad. The editor advances a strong case for assigning authorship to the Earl of Shelburne, afterwards Marquis of Lansdowne.

Ker, William Paton (1855-1923) THE ART OF POETRY *O.U.P.* 1923
Seven lectures, delivered between 1920 and 1922.

COLLECTED ESSAYS 2 vols. ed. by Charles Whibley *Macmillan* 1925

THE DARK AGES (*Blackwood*, 1904) *Nelson* 1955 15*s*
The standard history of European literature from the fifth century to the renaissance. The reprint of this classic work was a centenary tribute to a great literary historian and critic.

MEDIAEVAL ENGLISH LITERATURE *O.U.P.* (*Home University Library*) 1912 8*s* 6*d*

ON MODERN LITERATURE ed. by Terence Spencer and James Sutherland *O.U.P.* 1955 35*s*
Unpublished lectures on the literature of seventeenth, eighteenth and nineteenth centuries, delivered at University College, London, and taken down by shorthand writers.

Kingsmill, Hugh (1889-1949) PROGRESS OF A BIOGRAPHER *Methuen* 1949
'The best literary criticism in the language, at least if there is anything to compare with these essays for imaginative insight, unfailing common sense, careful appraisement, spiritual illumination, and sustained humour, I should like to hear of it.'—*Hesketh Pearson*, in *About Kingsmill*, Methuen, 1951, 10*s* 6*d*.

Lamb, Charles (1775-1834) *THE ESSAYS OF ELIA; AND LAST ESSAYS
OF ELIA (1823; 1833) *Dent (Everyman)* (1906) 1954 7s 6d; *Mac-
donald (Illustrated Classics)* 1952 15s *(Nelson (Classics)* 1954 6s;
O.U.P. (Worlds Classics) (1901) 1961 6s

Essays contributed to the *London Magazine* between 1820 and 1822 under
the pen name of 'Elia'. By his characteristic humour and style, Charles
Lamb created almost a new form of the essay in English. The illustrated
edition contains reproductions from prints and engravings, and from
some of Hogarth's pictures.

ESSAYS, LETTERS AND POEMS *Collins (Classics)* 1953 6s

EVERYBODY'S LAMB ed. by A. C. Ward *Bell* (1933) 1953 580 pp
Illus. by E. H. Shepard

A popular, standard selection of essays, letters and miscellany, with
drawings.

*Lamb, Charles (1775-1834) and Mary Lamb (1764-1847) TALES
FROM SHAKESPEARE (1807) *Collins (Classics)* 1953 5s; *Dent
(Children's Illustrated Classics)* 1957 15s; and *(Everyman)* (1906)
1960 7s 6d *Nelson (Classics)* 1960 6s 6d

Originally written for *Godwin's Juvenile Library*, and thus assured of a
permanent place in the history of books written for young readers. But
apart from this, the *Tales* have always charmed readers of all ages, and
cannot be equalled as prose introductions to the plays and their plots
and characters. The illustrations to both Dent editions are by Arthur
Rackham.

*Lamborn, Edmund Arnold Greening (1887-1950) THE RUDIMENTS
OF CRITICISM *O.U.P.* (1916) 1926 8s 6d

An introduction to the enjoyment of poetry and to appreciation of the
poet's craft.

Landor, Walter Savage (1775-1864) *IMAGINARY CONVERSATIONS
(1824; 1848) *Dent (Everyman)* with *Poems* 1933 6s 6d; *O.U.P.
(Worlds Classics)* 1915

Both of the above editions are selections. The classic mould and lapidary
prose of everything that Landor wrote limits his readers to the small
circle for whom he knew he was writing: 'Let us love those that love us,
and be contented to teach those that will hear us.'

POETRY AND PROSE ed. by Sir Edmund K. Chambers *O.U.P.*
1946 8s 6d

A small selection of the complete works, which, in the definitive edition
by T. E. Welby and Stephen Wheeler, totalled sixteen volumes, 1927-
1936, Chapman and Hall. Of this set, volumes 1-12 were the prose works;
and the remainder poetry. The latter were afterwards published separately by O.U.P., for which see under the *Poetry* section.

Lawrence, David Herbert (1885-1930) PHOENIX: POSTHUMOUS PAPERS *Heinemann* 1961 42*s*; (*Mercury Books*) 1962 12*s* 6*d*
A collection of 880 pages of essays and miscellaneous writings, contributions to magazines, and other pieces.

*SELECTED LITERARY CRITICISM ed. by Anthony Beal *Heinemann* 1956 21*s*; (*Mercury Books*) 1962 12*s* 6*d*
In 435 pages the editor gives us the best of Lawrence's literary journalism, his prefaces and occasional writings on books and authors, divided into six groups: Autobiographical; Puritanism and the Arts (this includes the well-known essay on Pornography and Obscenity); On Verse; Contemporaries and the Importance of the Novel; Continentals; and, Americans.

SEX, LITERATURE AND CENSORSHIP ed. by Harry T. Moore *Heinemann* 1955 21*s*
A collection of essays and pamphlets, uniform with the above.

*STORIES, ESSAYS AND POEMS *Dent* (*Everyman*) 1953 10*s* 6*d*
A remarkably comprehensive selection of 84 items, including stories, essays, 30 poems, and 40 letters from 1911 to 1930.
Refer also to *A D. H. Lawrence Miscellany*, edited by Harry T. Moore, Heinemann, 1962, 35*s*, in which there is 'a representation of the best recent work on Lawrence'.

*Lawrence, Thomas Edward (1888-1935) THE ESSENTIAL T. E. LAWRENCE ed. by David Garnett *Cape* 1951 18*s*; *Penguin Books* 1956 3*s* 6*d*
Extracts from *Seven Pillars of Wisdom*; *The Mint*; some letters and diaries, 'together with a composite biography by his friends'.

Leacock, Stephen Butler (1869-1944) THE BODLEY HEAD LEACOCK ed. by J. B. Priestley *Bodley Head* 1957 20*s*
'The main emphasis' in this selection from *Literary Lapses*, *Nonsense Novels* (1910 and 1911), and from other books of lighthearted foolery and parody, 'is on Leacock the essentially Canadian humorist, dry and droll, half-clown, half-satirist, whose irony reflects no anger, whose wit is sharp but leaves no sting'.

Lear, Edward (1812-88) *COMPLETE BOOK OF NONSENSE ed. by Holbrook Jackson *Faber* 1947 15*s*
Assembles the contents of all the nonsense books written and illustrated by Lear, and published during his lifetime from 1846 onwards, or posthumously by his executors.

NONSENSE OMNIBUS ed. by Sir E. Strachey *Warne* 1943 10*s* 6*d*
A complete edition of the four principal books with all the original pictures by Lear: *Nonsense Songs and Stories* (1871); *The Jumblies*; and *Pelican Chorus*, all of which are also available in separate editions. Lear's *Book of Nonsense* (1846; 1863) forms a substantial part of an *Everyman* collection of that title, 1928, 6*s* 6*d*, which includes other nonsense rhymes and stories by Lewis Carroll, W. B. Rands, D'Arcy W. Thompson, Heinrich Hoffman, and others, with illustrations.

Lewes, George Henry (1817-78) ON ACTORS AND THE ART OF
ACTING (1875) *John Calder (Evergreen)* 1957 14s 6d
This gifted journalist's early attempts on the stage, although of no value
to him at the time, later made him an excellent dramatic critic. Next to
his standard life of Goethe, this volume of criticism is his only work to
survive.

Lewis, Percy Wyndham (1884-1957) THE LION AND THE FOX
Richards (1927); *Methuen* 1951 21s
A subtle analysis of the influence of Machiavelli and his *Il Principe* (1532)
on Elizabethan drama, and in particular on the role of the Shakespeare
hero.

Lucas, Edward Verrall (1868-1938) CRICKET ALL HIS LIFE *Hart-
Davis* 1950 4s
'Cricket writings in prose and verse assembled and arranged' by the
publisher.

SELECTED ESSAYS ed. by H. N. Wethered *Methuen* 1954 10s 6d
Lucas, the writer of many charming, urbane essays, and editor of the
definitive edition of Charles Lamb's Letters, was once termed 'the
sophisticated Elia'.

Lyly, John (1554?-1606) COMPLETE WORKS 3 vols. ed. by R. W.
Bond *O.U.P.* 1902 1752 pp.
In addition to the plays, contains the two examples of fictional narrative,
written in that high-flown style of 'taffeta phrases, silken terms precise,
Three-piled hyperboles, spruce affecttation, Figures pedantical . . .' that
has become a literary term, derived from the name of the young Athenian
hero, Euphues. In *Euphues: the Anatomy of Wit* (1578), and *Euphues and
his England* (1580), we have an Elizabethan gentleman's view of the life
and character of the ideal courtier. Refer also to the next section of
Anthologies and Collections for an edition of *Euphues* in James Winny's
The Descent of Euphues.

Lynd, Robert (1879-1949) ESSAYS ON LIFE AND LITERATURE *Dent
(Everyman)* (1951) 1955 6s 6d
A selection made by Lynd's friend, Sir Desmond MacCarthy, of 38
essays from 30 books published between 1908 and 1945. Most of these
essays were contributed to periodicals, and in particular to the *New
Statesman*, week by week, under the pseudonym of 'Y.Y.'

Macaulay, Dame Rose (1881-1958) SOME RELIGIOUS ELEMENTS IN
ENGLISH LITERATURE *Hogarth Press* 1931 6s
A monograph in the *Hogarth Lectures on Literature* series.

Macaulay, Thomas Babington *Baron* (1800-59) CRITICAL AND
HISTORICAL ESSAYS (1843) 2 vols. *Dent (Everyman)* (1907) 1961
12s 6d each
Biographical and thematic essays written during the period 1825 to 1844
in Lord Macaulay's brilliant, lucid style. These essays have no equal as

introductions to the understanding and appreciation of great writers, and as imaginatively presented summaries of important historical subjects.

*PROSE AND POETRY ed. by G. M. Young *Hart-Davis* (*Reynard Library*) 1953 26s
Of these 856 pages, 200 are from *Macaulay's History of England*, and the remainder from the *Essays*, together with characteristic speeches and the *Lays of Ancient Rome*.

MacCarthy, Sir Desmond (1878-1952) PORTRAITS (*Putnam*, 1931) *MacGibbon and Kee* 1949 12s 6d

*THEATRE *MacGibbon and Kee* 1954 12s 6d
Next to Bernard Shaw, Desmond MacCarthy ('Affable Hawk') was the best dramatic critic of his time. His witty, genial essays on contemporaries offer diverting reading and shrewd, tolerant judgements.

Mackail, John William (1859-1945) LATIN LITERATURE *Murray* 1895 8s 6d
Accepted as one of the best short histories of Latin literature in English.

Mair, George Herbert (1887-1926) ENGLISH LITERATURE: MODERN, 1450-1959 O.U.P. (*Home University Library*) (1911) 1960 8s 6d
A concise summary, with an epilogue by A. C. Ward, bringing the original text up to date.

Malory, Sir Thomas (*fl.* 1470) WORKS ed. by Eugène Vinaver O.U.P. (*Oxford Standard Authors*) 1954 25s 938 pp
Text taken from the unique Winchester College manuscript of the fifteenth century. This great edition was first published in 1947 in three volumes, 210s (1858 pp), and its inclusion in OSA series places it within the reach of all students and libraries. A few essential notes from the larger edition are retained, as is the old spelling of the original.

*LE MORTE D'ARTHUR 2 vols. *Dent* (*Everyman*) (1906) 1953 8s 6d each
Follows Caxton's text of 1485, with modernised spelling and punctuation, and a glossary.

Meredith, George (1828-1909) AN ESSAY ON COMEDY *Constable* (1897); *W. H. Allen* (*Anchor Books*) 1962 7s 6d
A classic discussion and analysis of 'the comic spirit'. Useful not only to the student of, for example, the plays of Congreve and dramatists of the early eighteenth century, but also to the general reader of Meredith's own work. The American paperback reprint is bound with Bergson on *Laughter*.

Milton, John (1608-74) *COMPLETE POETRY AND SELECTED PROSE ed. by E. H. Visiak *Nonesuch Press* 1938 21s 896 pp
SELECTED PROSE ed. by M. W. Wallace O.U.P. (*Worlds Classics*) (1925) 1961 6s

88 AN ENGLISH LIBRARY

In addition to the great prose utterance 'for the liberty of unlicensed printing', known as *Areopagitica* (1644) and ever since its first deliverance before the Lords and Commons of England accepted as one of the noblest discourses in the history of Western civilisation, this selection includes *The Doctrine and Discipline of Divorce*, *Of Reformation Touching Church Discipline*, and *The Reason of Church Government*.

PROSE WRITINGS ed. by Kathleen Burton *Dent (Everyman)* (1927) 1958 12s 6d
A fuller selection, with an index. Milton's *Complete Prose Works*, edited by Don M. Wolfe and Ernest Sirluck, is in progress, for great libraries and scholars: Vol. 1, 1624-42, O.U.P., 1953, 100s (1092 pp). Vol. 2, 1643-8, O.U.P., 1959, 100s (854 pp).

Mitford, Mary Russell (1787-1855) BELFORD REGIS 3 vols. (1835-49) ed. by L. Stanley Jast *Werner Laurie* 1939
'Or, Sketches of a Country Town'; that is, of the borough of Reading in Berkshire. Miss Mitford preferred this book to all her others.

*OUR VILLAGE (1824-32) ed. by Sir John Squire *Dent (Everyman)* (1936) 1963 12s 6d; ed. by W. J. Roberts *Harrap* 1947 10s 6d Illus. by Joan Hassall
Stories and essays originally contributed to a magazine from 1819 onwards, as 'Sketches of Rural Character and Scenery', in which the author drew upon recollections of life and her circle of acquaintances in the neighbourhood of Reading. The charming, simple humour of these pieces has endeared them to generations of readers.

Montague, Charles Edward (1867-1928) DISENCHANTMENT *Chatto* 1922
One of the few classics of World War I. The book relates personal experiences against a background of hope and promises during 1914 and 1915; followed by that sad period of disillusionment as the war dragged on to its slaughtering close.

A WRITER'S NOTES ON HIS TRADE *Chatto* 1930; *Penguin* 1949 2s 6d
A discussion of the kind of skill and personal discipline required of a journalist of integrity, and of a writer determined to use words with care, knowledge and effect, and to reverence his daily work as a craft.

Morgann, Maurice (1726-1802) THE CHARACTER OF FALSTAFF (1777)
An early essay in Shakespearean criticism, included in D. Nichol Smith's anthology entered in the next section.

*Morris, William (1834-96) STORIES IN PROSE AND OTHER WORKS ed. by G. D. H. Cole *Nonesuch Press* 1934 20s
An omnibus collection of 695 pages, published as a centenary edition of Morris's best and most characteristic work, including his *Stories In Verse*; some *Shorter Poems*; *Lectures and Essays*.

Muir, Edwin (1887-1959) ESSAYS ON LITERATURE AND SOCIETY *Hogarth Press* 1949 10s 6d

THE ESTATE OF POETRY *Hogarth Press* 1962 16s

THE STRUCTURE OF THE NOVEL *Hogarth Press* 1928 8s 6d
Substantial critical work by a metaphysical poet of a high order. The posthumous volume prints the text of the Charles Eliot Norton Lectures for 1955-6. The poet was much concerned with the relationship between the public and the poet in a century which appeared to encourage the latter to take refuge in isolation from the mechanical society characteristic of the world of today.

Murray, Gilbert (1866-1957) AESCHYLUS: THE CREATOR OF TRAGEDY *O.U.P.* (1940) 1962 6s (paperback)

*EURIPIDES AND HIS AGE *O.U.P.* (*Home University Library*) (1911) 1946 8s 6d
An introduction for general readers. Gilbert Murray's translations of twenty-six classical Greek plays into English rhyming verse brought the work of Aristophanes, Euripides, Aeschylus, Sophocles and Menander to many thousands of unacademic readers.

*HELLENISM AND THE MODERN WORLD *Allen and Unwin* (1953) 1960 3s 6d (paperback)
Brief discussion on the meaning and message of Greek culture and civilisation.

THE RISE OF THE GREEK EPIC *O.U.P.* (1907) 1960 8s 6d (paperback)
A course of lectures delivered at Harvard

Murry, John Middleton (1889-1957) *KEATS AND SHAKESPEARE *O.U.P.* 1925 21s
A study of the development of the poet's mind and art, and of the influence of Shakespeare.

*THE PROBLEM OF STYLE *O.U.P.* 1922 10s 6d; and 1960 (paperback) 5s
Critical essays on prose style of great value to readers, and to young writers when they are developing their individual tastes and are learning to exercise discrimination as readers.

*SELECTED CRITICISM, 1916-1957 ed. by Richard Rees O.U.P. 1960 30s
A choice of Murry's critical essays likely to have permanent value.

*SHAKESPEARE *Cape* 1936 30s

Nashe, Thomas (1567-1601) WORKS 5 vols. ed. by R. B. McKerrow (1904-10); and F. P. Wilson *Blackwell* 1958 252s (the set) 2137 pp
The definitive edition, collated from the original texts, with F. P. Wilson's supplementary editorial notes. Writing of McKerrow's work, the editor of the new edition states: 'Set a new standard in editorial

method . . . The edition has long been recognised as one of the greatest
of any English writer and an essential work of reference for students of
Elizabethan life, language and literature.'

Newman, Ernest (1868-1959) TESTAMENT OF MUSIC ed. by Herbert
Van Thal *Putnam* 1962 30s
Selected writings of the leading music critic of his time, whose biography of Wagner is the standard work. The selection includes autobiographical essays.

Newman, John Henry (1801-90) THE IDEA OF A UNIVERSITY (1873)
ed. by C. F. Harrold *Longmans* 1947 25s
The complete edition of 'The Idea of a University Defined and
Illustrated': being the revised texts of nine discourses addressed to the
Catholics of Dublin; together with 'Occasional Lectures and Essays
addressed to Members of the Catholic University'.

ON THE SCOPE AND NATURE OF UNIVERSITY EDUCATION (1852)
ed. by Wilfrid Ward *Dent* (*Everyman*) 1915 6s 6d
This edition of the eight original lectures includes the text of *Christianity
and Scientific Investigations*.

*SELECTED WORKS ed. by Geoffrey Tillotson *Hart-Davis*
(*Reynard Library*) 1957 30s
A volume of 842 pages: it includes four characteristic sermons; lengthy
extracts from the *Apologia* (revised second edition), *On the Scope and
Nature of University Education* (first text), and from *The Dream of
Gerontius*); together with the full text of the scarce novel, *Loss and Gain*,
published anonymously in 1848, and last reprinted in 1904.

Orwell, George (1903-50) *COLLECTED ESSAYS *Secker and Warburg*
1961 30s; *Heinemann* (*Mercury Books*) 1961 12s 6d
SELECTED ESSAYS *Penguin Books* 1957 2s 6d
Many of these literary and social judgements, tipped with satire, have
become famous. They represent the journalism of a powerful writer
whose individual and characteristic view of contemporary problems
made whatever he wrote worth preserving.

Osler, Sir William (1849-1919) A WAY OF LIFE *Dover; Constable*
1959 12s (paperback)
Introduction by Dr. G. L. Keynes is followed by a selection of sixteen
essays displaying the diverse gifts of a great physician. The essays include
writings on Sir Thomas Browne, Richard Burton, on bookworms, the
student life, the collecting of a library, teaching, thinking, and the
growth of truth.

Paget, Violet (Vernon Lee) (1856-1935) THE BEAUTIFUL *C.U.P.*
1913 7s 6d
A brief study of the aesthetic by a gifted writer whose devotion to art,
Italy, and 'the handling of words', resulted in a number of essays, belles-
lettres, and miscellaneous works on 'the gardening of life'.

Pater, Walter (1839-94) APPRECIATIONS *Macmillan* 1889
Includes a famous essay on style. The other essays in this once widely-read volume are on Charles Lamb, Rossetti, William Blake, and Sir Thomas Browne.

MISCELLANEOUS STUDIES *Macmillan* 1895 3s 6d
Further examples of Pater's polished and disciplined prose style, cast in classic mould.

*THE RENAISSANCE *Macmillan* (1873) 1924; *Collins (Fontana)* 1961 6s; *Muller (Mentor Books)* 1959 4s
'Studies in art and poetry.' One of the influential books of the nineteenth century. Generations of intellectuals accepted its teachings and message: summed up, perhaps, by one sentence from an essay in the volume: 'For art comes to you, proposing frankly to give nothing but the highest quality to your moments, as they pass, and simply for those moments' sake'.

Peacock, Thomas Love (1785-1866) THE FOUR AGES OF POETRY (1820) ed. by H. F. B. Brett-Smith *Blackwell (Percy Reprints of English Classics)* 1921 7s 6d
An essay that provoked a reply and counter-attack in Shelley's *A Defence of Poetry* (1821), reprinted in the above volume, with an essay on Shelley by Robert Browning. H. F. B. Brett-Smith and C. E. Jones were editors of the definitive *Helliford Edition* of Peacock's *Works*, including letters, and a biography, bibliographical details and textual notes, 10 volumes, Constable, 1924-34.

Penn, William (1644-1718) AN ESSAY TOWARDS THE PRESENT AND FUTURE PEACE OF EUROPE (1693), and, SOME FRUITS OF SOLITUDE (1693) *Dent (Everyman)* 1915
The two most famous works of the Quaker-preacher, who voyaged to America with fellow Quakers, and there founded Pennsylvania. The second major work in this edition consists of moral axioms, precepts and wise thoughts, 'relating to the conduct of human life'. It was a work beloved by R. L. Stevenson, to whom it was ever 'a sweet, dignified and wholesome book', and 'in all times and places a peaceful and sweet companion'.

Phillipps, Lisle March (1863-1917) THE WORKS OF MAN *Duckworth* (1911) 1950 15s
A critical survey of development of styles, and of appreciation of architecture and art. The second edition of 1932 and the reprint contian an introduction by Sir Herbert Read.

Poe, Edgar Allan (1809-49) TALES, POEMS, AND ESSAYS *Collins (Classics)* 1953 7s
Poe's most widely-read essay was on *The Poetic Principle*, included in an *Everyman* edition of his *Poems and Essays*, and also in the *Oxford Standard Authors* volume of *Poems and Miscellanies*, for details of which see under

Poetry section. The other critical essays include some lengthy, and often biased, studies of Poe's contemporaries, such as Elizabeth Barrett Browning, Charles Lever, Bayard Taylor and Macaulay.

Prior, Matthew (1664-1721) DIALOGUES OF THE DEAD ed. by A. R. Waller *C.U.P.* 1907 32s 6d
Prior's best known prose work, being early examples in English literature of the imaginary conversation form, first used by Lucian.

LITERARY WORKS 2 vols. ed. by H. Bunker Wright and Monroe K. Spears *O.U.P.* 1959 126s (the set) 1156 pp
Prose and verse; Latin and English: collected after collation of extant manuscripts.

Puttenham, George (*d.* 1590) THE ART OF ENGLISH POESIE (1589) ed. by G. D. Willcock and J. A. Walker *C.U.P.* 1936
The first substantial treatise in English on the nature of poetry, poetic ornament and rhyme, with a survey of poetry up to the author's time.

Quiller-Couch, Sir Arthur Thomas (1863-1944) *CAMBRIDGE LECTURES *Dent* (*Everyman*) 1943 6s 6d
A selection of addresses on literature delivered at Cambridge University. Some of these are also published in two books: *On the Art of Reading*, C.U.P. 1920, 2s; and *On the Art of Writing*, C.U.P., 1916, 2s.
CHARLES DICKENS AND OTHER VICTORIANS *C.U.P.* 1925 10s 6d
SHAKESPEARE'S WORKMANSHIP *C.U.P.* 1918 10s 6d
*STUDIES IN LITERATURE 3 series *C.U.P.* 1918; 1922; 1929 10s 6d each
Delightful discourses in appreciation, most of which were, he writes, 'given to my pupils in the New Arts Schools at Cambridge'. They range over the English classics, from balladry to 'The Poetry of Thomas Hardy', with occasional references to the Greek masterpieces and to general literary themes such as romanticism, 'Patriotism in English Literature', and 'The New Reading Public'.

Raleigh, Sir Walter (1861-1922) ON WRITING AND WRITERS *Edward Arnold* 1926 6s
'Extracts from his notebooks selected by George Gordon.'

*SHAKESPEARE *Macmillan* (1907) 1951 7s 6d

Reynolds, Sir Joshua (1723-92) DISCOURSES ON ART (1794) *O.U.P.* 1960 80s Illus.
A handsome library quarto edition of a document that the editor, from the Huntington Library, California, regards as one of the most important in the history of European art. It is embellished with a series of reproductions of pictures, with many learned notes for academic students and teachers. The lectures were delivered between 1769 and 1791 to members of the then newly-established Royal Academy of Art.

PORTRAITS *Heinemann* 1952
A collection of miscellaneous prose: character sketches of contem-
poraries, including Goldsmith, Dr. Johnson and Garrick, an essay on
Shakespeare, together with the well-known dialogues illustrating Dr.
Johnson's manner of speaking. This volume was edited from the redac-
tion of the Boswell papers at Malahide Castle.

Richard de Bury (Richard Aungervyle of Bury) (1281-1345)
PHILOBIBLON: THE LOVE OF BOOKS (1473) ed. and trans. by E. C.
Thomas (1903) Oxford, Shakespeare Head Press Blackwell 1961
73s 6d quarto
A beautiful edition in honour of Sir Basil Blackwell's seventieth birthday; original Latin text parallel with Thomas's standard translation, his
introduction and some of his notes, extended and added to by Michael
Maclagan. Richard de Bury's much-loved book treats of the writing of
new books, of 'showing due propriety in the custody of books', 'of the
manner of lending all our books to students', and of allied themes dear to
the bibliophile.

Robinson, Henry Crabb (1775-1867) ON BOOKS AND THEIR
WRITERS 3 vols. ed. by Edith Morley *Dent* (1938) 1950 25s (the
set) 1136 pp
Anecdotes, gossip, informal criticism and entertaining chit-chat,
admirably edited from notebooks and memoranda. From these pages,
we learn, for example, how the genius of William Blake struck his
contemporaries; receive first-hand accounts of the man himself; read
about the lectures of Coleridge from the pen of one who actually heard
them; and enjoy recollections of Wordsworth and Charles Lamb by a
man who talked with them and listened to their conversation.

Rogers, Samuel (1763-1855) RECOLLECTIONS OF THE TABLE TALK
OF SAMUEL ROGERS by Alexander Dyce (1856) ed. by Morchard
Bishop *Unicorn Press* 1952 12s 6d
Noted by Dyce (1798-1869) over a period of years, and probably written
down at intervals soon after the conversations occurred. It was a happy
partnership, since Rogers was a born talker and his Boswell had the
knack of recording. The result is a little book that abounds in vivid
recollections of Byron, Wordsworth, Fox, Sheridan, Coleridge, Wellington and other famous contemporaries with whom Rogers was acquainted
during his long literary and social life.

Ruskin, John (1819-1900) THE CROWN OF WILD OLIVE (1866)
Allen and Unwin 3s 6d; ed. by J. H. Fowler *Macmillan* 1962 4s
Lectures on work, traffic, war, and the future of England.

THE ETHICS OF THE DUST (1866) *Allen and Unwin* 2s 6d
'Ten lectures to little housewives on the elements of crystallisation.'

A JOY FOR EVER (1857) *Allen and Unwin* 2s 6d
Lectures on 'the political economy of art', which was the first title,
changed in the 1880 edition, to *A Joy For Ever: and its price in the market.*

MODERN PAINTERS 6 vols. (1843) Allen and Unwin 2s 6d each
Illustrated and indexed.

*SESAME AND LILIES (1865) *Allen and Unwin* 3s 6d; and *Dent*
(Everyman) with *The Two Paths*, and, *The King of the Golden*
River (1907) 1953 8s 6d
Sesame and Lilies is perhaps the most widely-read of Ruskin's books. In
three lectures, and a long preface, he stated in oft-quoted, eloquent
sentences, his thoughts on the value of reading: what books to choose;
how to read one's choice; to which he added powerful pleas for the
widest diffusion of good literature, the personal ownership of books
as opposed to borrowing, the principles of the education of girls, and
their duties, as 'the Lilies in Queens' Gardens' of his title.

THE SEVEN LAMPS OF ARCHITECTURE (1849) *Allen and Unwin*
3s 6d; and *Dent (Everyman)* (1907) 1956 10s 6d Illus.
In praise of the Gothic style in cathedral and other architecture, with an
analysis of general principles.

THE STONES OF VENICE 3 vols. (1851-53) *Allen and Unwin* 25s
(the set); edited and abridged by J. G. Links *Collins* 1960 21s
Continues arguments in favour of the Gothic, and attacks the style of
Italian Renaissance as exemplified in Venice. The abridgement of the
half-million words of this classic work skilfully offers to the modern
traveller and holiday-maker in Venice and Verona the essence and the
most important chapters.

TIME AND TIDE (1867) *Allen and Unwin* 2s 6d
Letters to working men on the laws of work, embodying Ruskin's
ideas for the making of a better England by means of a programme of
social reform leading to what the twentieth century regards as the
welfare state.

*UNTO THIS LAST (1860) *Dent (Everyman)* 1907
'Four essays on the first principles of political economy.' A notable, and
fundamental utterance of permanent value. Reprinted in the *Everyman*
edition with *A Joy For Ever*, which see above.
The above list is but an essential selection from Ruskin's astonishing
output, which, in the great library edition published by Allen and
Unwin, 1903-12, extends to thirty-nine volumes (£50 the set). The
index volume to the 2,700 items in this edition is encyclopaedic, and of
the 2,100 illustrations, about 270 are by Ruskin himself.

*THE LAMP OF BEAUTY ed. by Joan Evans *Phaidon Press* 1959
32s 6d Illus.
The editor's apt title to a much-needed volume of selections, with many
plates in full colour and other illustrations, from Ruskin's works, noted
above. This handsome quarto displays Ruskin's genius in interpretation,
appreciation and his gift for instruction in art, especially painting and
architecture.

Sadleir, Michael (1888-1957) TROLLOPE: A COMMENTARY *Constable*
(1927) 1945 8s 6d Illus.

The best monograph on the man and his major fiction. This distinguished bibliographer and authority on nineteenth-century novelists edited with the late Frederick Page the *Oxford Illustrated Trollope* series.

Saintsbury, George (1845-1933) A HISTORY OF ENGLISH CRITICISM *Blackwood* 1911 18s
'The English chapters' from the standard work, *A History of Criticism and Literary Taste in Europe*, 3 vols., Blackwood, 1900-4, 25s each.

*THE PEACE OF THE AUGUSTANS (1916, Bell) O.U.P. (*Worlds Classics*) 1946 7s 6d
'A survey of eighteenth-century literature as a place of rest and refreshment.' Here, Professor Saintsbury was assuredly at his best as an interpretative critic and appreciative historian.

*A SHORT HISTORY OF ENGLISH LITERATURE *Macmillan* (1896) 1913 *Macmillan* 30s; (*Papermacs*) 1963 20s
'Short' is here used comparatively, for this masterly survey extends to 818 pages. It continues to hold its own as one of the best histories of English literature from Anglo-Saxon poetry to the end of the nineteenth century. In spite of highly individual judgements and prejudices, Professor Saintsbury's salty humour and parenthetic style, enabled him to offer students a most readable text, packed with information and criticism, shrewdly expressed.

Scott, Geoffrey (1885-1929) THE ARCHITECTURE OF HUMANISM *Constable* (1914) 1924 12s 6d
A study in the history of taste.

Selden, John (1584-1654) TABLE TALK (1689)
The Selden Society was named after this erudite lawyer and parliamentarian. His *Table Talk* is reprinted in Thornton's collection of *Table Talk from Ben Jonson to Leigh Hunt* for which see next section.

Seton-Thompson, Ernest (1860-1946) THE BEST OF SETON-THOMPSON ed. by W. Kay Robinson *Hodder* 1949 12s 6d
A selection of the best animal stories and nature studies by the Founder of the Boy Scouts of America. He spent his boyhood in Canada, and was the author of some books of permanent value for open-air youth, especially *Lives of the Hunted* (1901) and *Wild Animals I Have Known* (1898).

Shaw, George Bernard (1856-1950) DOCTORS' DELUSIONS *Constable* 1932 15s
A volume of prefaces, tracts, and prose pieces arising from the plays, and current controversies, gathered together for the standard edition. The contents also include *Crude Criminology*; and *Sham Education*.

HOW TO BECOME A MUSICAL CRITIC *Hart-Davis* 1961 25s
'Hitherto uncollected writings' from 1876 to 1950, edited and entitled by Dan Lawrence. In addition to some lively controversial exchanges with other critics, notably with Ernest Newman on the first London

performance of the *Elektra* of Richard Strauss, these fugitive writings sparkle with shrewd judgements on music, musical form, and composers.

LONDON MUSIC IN 1888-9 *Constable* 1937 15s
'As heard by Corno di Bassetto (later known as Bernard Shaw) with further autobiographical particulars and a portrait.'

MAJOR CRITICAL ESSAYS *Constable* 1932 15s
Collects *The Quintessence of Ibsenism* (1891); *The Perfect Wagnerite* (1898); and *The Sanity of Art* (1895).

MUSIC IN LONDON 3 vols. *Constable* 1932 15s each
A collection totalling 960 pages of lively criticism written during the years 1890-4.

OUR THEATRES IN THE NINETIES 3 vols. *Constable* 1932 15s each
Reprinted criticisms totalling 1000 pages. First collected in 1907 as *Dramatic Opinions and Essays*.

PEN PORTRAITS AND REVIEWS *Constable* 1932 15s

*PLAYS AND PLAYERS *O.U.P.* (*Worlds Classics*) 1952 7s 6d
'Essays on the theatre' selected with an introduction by A. C. Ward. The volume contains some of the best dramatic criticism in the English language.

SELECTED PROSE *Constable* 1953
A liberal choice in a volume of 1004 pages, made by Diarmuid Russell, from the non-dramatic prose, and arranged in groups: biography; fiction; music criticism; dramatic criticism; socialism; and miscellany. The choice was made from the ten volumes of prose works in the uniform edition of Shaw's Complete Works, and the five novels.

Shelley, Percy Bysshe (1792-1822) LITERARY AND PHILOSOPHICAL CRITICISM ed. by J. Shawcross *O.U.P.* (*Oxford Miscellany*) 1909 10s 6d

*SELECTED POETRY, PROSE AND LETTERS ed. by A. S. B. Glover *Nonesuch Press* 1951 25s 1142 pp
The prose includes *The Necessity of Atheism* (1811); *A Philosophical View of Reform*; the translation of Plato's *Banquet*; and *A Defence of Poetry*. See also Ernest Rhys's *The Prelude to Poetry* in the next section, and under White, R. J. in the *Philosophy and Religion* section.

Sidney, Sir Philip (1554-86) AN APOLOGIE FOR POETRIE (1595) ed. by E. S. Shuckburgh *C.U.P.* 1891 6s; ed. by D. M. Macardle *Macmillan* 1919 3s 6d
Sometimes entitled *The Defence of Poetrie*. This vigorous statement of the function of the poet, and the importance of his art, is of more than antiquarian interest. See also Ernest Rhys' *The Prelude To Poetry* in the next section.

PROSE WORKS 4 vols. ed. by Albert Feuillerat *C.U.P.* (1912-26) 1962 1588 pp
Vol. 1: *The Countesse of Pembrokes Arcadia* (1590; 1593; 1598) 37s 6d; vol. 2: *The Last Part of the Countesse of Pembrokes Arcadia*; and *The Lady of May* 30s; vol. 3: *The Defence of Poesie*; *Political Discourses*; *Correspondence*; Philip of Mornay's *Of the Trewnesse of the Christian Religion*, translated 25s; vol. 4: *The Countess of Pembroke's Arcadia*, being the original version, 30s.

*Smith, James Cruickshank (1867-1946) A STUDY OF WORDSWORTH (1944) *Oliver and Boyd* 1955 5s
Notable study of Wordsworth's theories of poetry and of his political ideas, religious emotions and related themes, as they affected his poetry.

Smith, Logan Pearsall (1865-1946) *ALL TRIVIA *Constable* 1933 7s 6d
Collects in a single volume two books published separately: *Trivia* in 1917, and *More Trivia* in 1921. In these concise essays the writer offered his comments on human foibles, the passing moment (the chance remark overheard) and the behaviour of human beings as observed by an ironic wit with a lapidary style and the detachment of an intellectual.

THE ENGLISH LANGUAGE *O.U.P.* (*Home University Library*) (1912) 1952 8s 6d
On the genius and growth of the English language, and its use in the hands of great writers. The second edition has 'an epilogue' by R. W. Chapman.

ON READING SHAKESPEARE *Constable* 1933 7s 6d

*WORDS AND IDIOMS *Constable* 1925 12s 6d
Allusive, erudite essays on meanings (surface and hidden) of certain selected words, some in general use, others half-forgotten except by scholars, together with material on the origins of phrases. This is an illuminating complement to *The English Language*, noted above.

Smith, Sydney (1771-1845) *SELECTED WRITINGS ed. by W. H. Auden *Faber* 1957 30s
This representative choice includes some letters, together with a long introduction in appreciation of Sydney Smith 'as an exemplar of the liberal mind'.

Southey, Robert (1774-1843) THE DOCTOR (1834-47) ed. and abridged from J. W. Warter's edition of 1848 by M. H. Fitzgerald *Bell* 1930
A pleasantly varied miscellany, containing the children's story of *The Three Bears*. This may or may not have been invented by Southey, but from the time of its appearance in *The Doctor* it became a classic of the nursery.

LETTERS FROM ENGLAND (1807) ed. by Jack Simmons *Cresset Press* 1952 12s 6d

D

Using a convention established in the eighteenth century, Southey adopted the pose of translator of letters supposedly written by a foreigner on a visit to England. The volume presents a witty picture of English life, manners and customs at the beginning of the nineteenth century.

Steele, Sir Richard (1672-1729) *THE TATLER ed. by Lewis Gibbs Dent (Everyman) 1953 8s 6d
A selection of essays from the periodical from 1709 to 1711. Refer also to Addison for details of essays from *The Spectator* written by Addison and Steele.

Stephen, Sir Leslie (1832-1904) ENGLISH LITERATURE AND SOCIETY IN THE 18TH CENTURY (1904) Methuen (University Paperbacks) 1963 7s 6d
The *Ford Lectures*, offering a happy combination of literary history, the analysis of society and ideas, and the interplay of social forces and the written word, in the age of Swift, Dr. Johnson and Rousseau.

HOURS IN A LIBRARY 3 vols. Murray 1874-9 8s 6d each
Essays on books and authors.

MEN, BOOKS AND MOUNTAINS ed. by S. O. A. Ullman. Hogarth

Press 1956

*Stephens, James (1882-1950) A SELECTION ed. by Lloyd Frankenberg Macmillan 1962 30s
In a volume of 490 pages the editor provides Stephens's first novel *The Charwoman's Daughter* (Mary, Mary) in full, short stories and episodes from all his other books, including fairy tales, a little-known essay *On Prose and Verse* (hitherto privately printed), and a selection of poetry.

Sterne, Laurence (1713-68) *SELECTED WORKS ed. by Douglas Grant Hart-Davis (Reynard Library) 1951 25s
In 750 pages the editor has been able to give two works unabridged: *Tristram Shandy* in the first edition text; and *A Sentimental Journey*; with a selection of sermons; some letters; and the autobiographical essay, *Memoirs of Mr. Laurence Sterne*, written in 1767 for his daughter Lydia.

A SENTIMENTAL JOURNEY THROUGH FRANCE AND ITALY By Mr. Yorick (1768) ed. by Wilbur L. Cross Chapman and Hall 1947 15s; ed. by George Saintsbury Dent (Everyman) (1927) 1960 8s 6d; ed. by John Cowper Powys Macdonald (Illustrated Classics) 1948 15s; Nelson (Classics) 1941 5s; O.U.P. (Worlds Classics) 1928 6s
This witty, graceful trifle has diverted readers for nearly 200 years. Professor Cross's edition includes selections from journals, sermons, and correspondence; The *Everyman* new edition has an introduction by Daniel George, and includes the *Journal to Eliza* (1767) and *Letters to Eliza*; Nelson's edition is illustrated by Gwen Raverat; and *Worlds Classics* is graced by an appreciation by Virginia Woolf.

Stevenson, R. A. M (1847-1900) THE ART OF VELASQUEZ *Bell* (1895) 1962 21s Illus.
R. A. M. Stevenson was a cousin of R.L.S. This monograph was considered by D. S. MacColl to be 'the most substantial contribution to the theory and defence of modern painting since Ruskin'. The new edition has a sketch of the author's life by Denys Sutton and an outline of twentieth-century research on Velasquez by Theodore Crombie.

Stevenson, Robert Louis (1850-94) *SELECTED ESSAYS ed. by Malcolm Elwin *Macdonald (Illustrated Classics)* 1950 15s
Forty-four essays selected from *Familiar Studies, Virginibus Puerisque* and other volumes.

VIRGINIBUS PUERISQUE (1881) and FAMILIAR STUDIES OF MEN AND BOOKS (1882) ed. by Ernest Rhys *Dent (Everyman)* (1925) 1963 10s 6d; *Nelson (Classics)* 5s
Virginibus Puerisque, the most enduring of all Stevenson's collections of essays, contains *On Falling In Love*; *Crabbed Age and Youth*; *An Apology for Idlers*; *Walking Tours*; and *A Plea for Gas Lamps*. *Familiar Studies*, formerly contributed to monthly periodicals, include essays on *Victor Hugo's Romances*; *Some Aspects of Robert Burns*; *Walt Whitman*; *Thoreau*; *Francois Villon*, and *Samuel Pepys*.

Strachey, Giles Lytton (1880-1932) *LANDMARKS IN FRENCH LITERATURE *O.U.P. (Home University Library)* 1912 8s 6d, and *Chatto (Uniform Edition)* 1949 10s 6d
Stimulating introduction to some great authors and their books up to 1896.

*LITERARY ESSAYS *Chatto* 1949 10s 6d
In the uniform collected edition this volume is made up of essays from *Characters and Commentaries* (1933); and from *Books and Characters: French and English* (1922). See also under *Biography* section.

Sturt, George (George Bourne) (1863-1927) THE WHEELWRIGHT'S SHOP *C.U.P.* 1923 16s
Studies in this ancient craft, made with the knowledge of, and the affection for English village life, that were characteristic of George Bourne, who lived as a schoolmaster among the folk he wrote about in this book, *The Bettesworth Book: Talks With a Surrey Peasant* (Duckworth, 1901); and *Change In the Village* (Duckworth, 1912 and 1955).

Swift, Jonathan (1667-1745) *GULLIVER'S TRAVELS AND SELECTED WRITINGS IN PROSE AND VERSE ed. by John Hayward *Nonesuch Press* 1934 21s 868 pp
The prose includes selections from *A Tale of a Tub* (1704), a masterpiece of irony cast in the form of an allegory with 'digressions', in which three brothers represent respectively the Church of England, the Church of Rome, and the Dissenters; selections from *The Conduct of the Allies* (1711); *The Drapier's Letters* (1724); the savage satire *A Modest Proposal* (1729); and *Polite Conversation* (1738).

*POLITE CONVERSATION (1738) ed. by Eric Partridge *André Deutsch (Language Library)* 1962 18*s*
A new edition, with an introduction and annotations by an authority on language and slang, of what the editor evaluates as 'the most faithful and comprehensive record of the conversation of eighteenth-century England that anyone has ever made . . . even the tempo of colloquial conversation comes alive'. Short title of: *A Complete Collection of Genteel and Ingenious Conversation, According To the Most Polite Mode . . .* in three dialogues.

SELECTED PROSE WORKS ed. by John Hayward *Cresset Press* 1950 12*s* 6*d*
A volume of nearly 500 pages, with a complete, unabridged text of *Gulliver's Travels*, some *Irish Tracts*—including *A Modest Proposal*; some *Religious Writings*, and *Miscellanies*.

A TALE OF A TUB AND OTHER SATIRES *Dent (Everyman)* (1909) 1953 8*s* 6*d*
The 'other satires' are *The Battle of the Books* (1704); *The Bickerstaff Papers* (1709-11); and *Polite Conversation* (1738).

A TALE OF A TUB ed. by A. C. Guthkelch and D. Nichol Smith *O.U.P.* (1920) rev. edn. 1957 50*s*
The standard edition for students, with other pieces such as Curll's *Complete Key*, Wotton's *Observations*, etc., and notes historical and explanatory.

The standard edition of Swift's *Prose Writings*, published by Shakespeare Head Press, Blackwell, 1939- (in progress) is under the authoritative editorship of Herbert Davis. Volume 14 is an index to the complete set, in which the works are arranged chronologically. This beautiful set is now complete, at 30*s* each volume, with the exception of volume 14 in preparation (1963). See also under *History* section for further details.

Note too the Swift editions in *Oxford Standard Authors* series, 12*s* 6*d* each, one being *Gulliver's Travels: The Tale of a Tub*; and *The Battle of the Books*, 608 pp; and the other **Satires and Personal Writings*, edited by W. A. Eddy, 532 pp.

Swinburne, Algernon Charles (1837-1909) *POEMS AND PROSE ed. by Richard Church *Dent (Everyman)* 1940
Critical and literary essays, with a selection of lyrics and from longer poems, originally issued in the collected works, *The Golden Pine edition*, Heinemann, 1917.

Symonds, John Addington (1840-93) STUDIES OF THE GREEK POETS *A. and C. Black* (1873; 1893) 1920 25*s*

*Synge, John Millington (1871-1909) PLAYS, POEMS AND PROSE *Dent (Everyman)* 1954 8*s* 6*d*
All the plays, *Poems and Translations* (1909) and a selection from *The Aran Islands* (1907).

Temple, Sir William (1628-99) EARLY ESSAYS AND ROMANCES ed. from manuscripts by G. C. Moore Smith *O.U.P.* 1930
ESSAYS ON ANCIENT AND MODERN LEARNING AND ON POETRY ed. by J. Spingarn *O.U.P.* 1908
Sir William's writings collected. Remembered chiefly for the charming letters written to him by Dorothy Osborne (Lady Temple), his best essays are often to be found in anthologies, especially those on gardens, on poetry and on health and long life. His prose style was agreeable, fluent, and free from prolixity, attracting praise from Dr. Johnson.

Thackeray, William Makepeace (1811-63) THE BOOK OF SNOBS (1848) *W. H. Allen (Dolphin Books)* 1962 7s 6d
Satircial essays collected from contributions to *Punch* (1846-7) on *The Snobs of England.*

THE FOUR GEORGES (1860) AND THE ENGLISH HUMOURISTS (1853) *Dent (Everyman)* 1912 6s 6d
The text of lectures on the Hanoverian kings from George I to George IV, with some minor lectures of little interest now on Swift, Congreve, Addison, Steele, Prior, Gay, Pope, Hogarth, Smollett, Fielding, Sterne and Goldsmith.

Thomas, Dylan (1914-53) QUITE EARLY ONE MORNING *Dent* 1954 12s 6d
Talks and essays broadcast on the B.B.C. radio.

Thoreau, Henry David (1817-62) *WALDEN; OR, LIFE IN THE WOODS (1854) ed. by Basil Willey *Dent (Everyman)* (1908) 1955 8s 6d
Description of Thoreau's life of solitude in a hut, where he retired for two years and two months, supporting himself with very little money, spent only when absolutely necessary. This little book has interested and sometimes inspired readers of every generation, for the individualistic author rebelled against many aspects of American life, going so far on occasion as to refuse to pay taxes.

A WEEK ON THE CONCORD AND MERRIMAC RIVERS (1849) *Dent* 1932 Illus.
The author takes his readers through the week from Saturday to Sunday, somewhat sententiously, but allusively, with quotations from his favourite poets, and with flashes of the same genius in the descriptions of nature that make *Walden* his masterpiece.

Tilley, Arthur Augustus (1851-1942) THE DECLINE OF THE AGE OF LOUIS XIV *C.U.P.* 1929 50s
French literature from 1687 to 1715. The author edited two 'Companions to French Studies', collective works for students entitled: *Medieval France*, C.U.P., 1922; and, *Modern France*, C.U.P., 1922.

Torr, Cecil (1857-1929) SMALL TALK AT WREYLAND 3 series *C.U.P.*
1918; 1921; 1923 15s each
Commonplace books, appreciated by a small circle of readers for the
author's individual outlook and his pointed style. A selection in one
volume was published in 1933.

Trench, Richard Chevenix (1807-86) *ON THE STUDY OF WORDS
(1851) *Dent (Everyman)* 1927 6s 6d
Eminent men in literary and legal life have paid tribute to this delightful
introduction, originally in the form of lectures, to the meanings and
etymology of certain words in the English language. Here bound with a
kindred work on *English Past and Present* (1855), with an introduction by
George Sampson.

Trevelyan, George Macaulay (1876-1962) CLIO, A MUSE; AND
OTHER ESSAYS *Longmans* (1913) 1930 10s 6d
Occasional pieces by the great historian. The later edition contained an
essay on *The Present Position of History*, which is the original *Clio*, rewritten in maturity. Throughout his writing Dr. Trevelyan adhered to
his belief that history should be so written that it would be enjoyed by
general readers as well as by academic students.

A LAYMAN'S LOVE OF LETTERS *Longmans* 1954 11s 6d
The text of the Clark Lectures, delivered at Cambridge, October-
November, 1953.

Tytler, Alexander Fraser (1747-1813) ESSAY ON THE PRINCIPLES OF
TRANSLATION (1791) *Dent (Everyman)* 1907 6s 6d
An early discussion still of interest to students. It held the field in this
subject until Matthew Arnold's well-known essay.

Walton, Izaak (1593-1683) and Charles Cotton (1630-87)
*THE COMPLEAT ANGLER (1653; 1676; 1678) *A. and C. Black*
1945 6s Illus.; *Dent (Everyman)* (1906) 1953 7s 6d; *Nelson
(Classics)* 1954 5s; *O.U.P. (Worlds Classics)* (1935) 1961 7s 6d
'The contemplative man's recreation, being a discourse of rivers, fish-
ponds, fish and fishing'; in part two of this much-loved classic, that is,
Cotton's part, which appeared for the first time in the 1678 printing of
Walton's fifth edition, the angler is given 'instructions how to angle for
a trout or grayling in a clear stream'. The new edition in *Worlds Classics*
is notable for its inclusion of a modernised text of *The Arte of Angling*,
'by an unknown hand' (1577), a unique copy of which was discovered
by an American. This pioneer work appears to have been the inspiration
and perhaps even the source-book of Walton's masterpiece.

Weekley, Ernest (1865-1954) THE ENGLISH LANGUAGE (Benn, 1928);
André Deutsch (The Language Library) 1952 9s 6d
*THE ROMANCE OF WORDS *Murray* (1912) 1961 12s 6d
Ivor Brown introduces this most popular of all of Weekley's books,
sometimes also available in a cheap paperback edition (Guild Books).

WORDS ANCIENT AND MODERN *Murray* 1947 12s 6d
These three books by a distinguished lexicographer introduce general readers to the history of the development of English from Anglo-Saxon and Middle English periods to current forms, and so uncover the original meanings of selected words that time has buried by changing usage.

Welch, Denton (1917–48) EXTRACTS FROM HIS PUBLISHED WORKS ed. by Jocelyn Brooke *Chapman and Hall* 1963 25s
The publication of *Maiden Voyage* (Routledge, 1943) revealed something of the suffering and poignancy of a young, rebellious writer with more than a touch of genius. It was followed by the posthumous autobiographical novel, *A Voice Through a Cloud* (1950); the *Journals* (1952); and a volume of short stories, *Brave and Cruel* (1949).

Weston, Jessie Laidlay (1850–1928) FROM RITUAL TO ROMANCE *C.U.P.* (1920); *W. H. Allen (Anchor Books)* 1960 8s
An influential history and discussion of the development of the legend of the Holy Grail in the Middle Ages, and its literary treatment in the Arthurian cycle of romance.

Whibley, Charles (1859–1930) LITERARY STUDIES *Macmillan* 1919 STUDIES IN FRANKNESS *Macmillan* 1926
Literary criticism that has the persuasive power to send readers to the books discussed. Largely classical in his interests and learning, Whibley could also respond to writers of his own age and the nineteenth and eighteenth centuries. Though the merits of Disraeli and Sterne were appreciated, Petronius, Heliodorus, Lucian, Herondas, Apuleius and the noble prose of the Tudor translators drew from him his finest essays.

Whistler, James McNeill (1834–1903) THE GENTLE ART OF MAKING ENEMIES (1890) *Heinemann* 1903 21s
Waspish stings and sharp-tongued sarcasm directed against fake art and *bourgeois* lack of standards of value. Somewhat dated now, but not without interest and amusement for twentieth-century readers.

*White, Gilbert (1720–93) THE NATURAL HISTORY OF SELBORNE (1789) ed. by James Fisher *Cresset Press* (1947) 1960 15s Illus. with wood engravings by Claire Oldham; *Dent (Everyman)* (1906) 1950 6s 6d; *O.U.P. (Worlds Classics)* (1902) 1958 7s 6d Illus.
'The parish of Selborne lies in the extreme eastern corner of the county of Hampshire . . .' So start these letters to Thomas Pennant, dated from 1767-87, and offered by the naturalist as a 'parochial history', which, said Selborne, 'ought to consist of natural productions and occurrences as well as antiquities'. Selborne combined minute and loving observation of nature with a charming style. The best edition of his much-loved book, embellished with wood engravings, is based on a former *Penguin* edition. *Worlds Classics* edition has illustrations by Edmund H. New, follows the first edition text, but also contains the poems from the second edition of 1813.

*Whitehead, Alfred North (1861-1947) THE AIMS OF EDUCATION
AND OTHER ESSAYS *Benn* (1932) 1959 15s; 1962 9s 6d (paperback)
'The whole book is a Protest against dead knowledge, that is to say,
against inert ideas.'—Professor Whitehead's preface to the original
edition, published by Williams and Norgate. 'These essays express the
views of a great man, whose immense knowledge, with accomplish-
ments in all fields of human inquiry, were combined with a singular
gift of direct intuition, an extraordinary freshness of view.'—*Preface by
Lord Lindsay of Berker*, to the paperback reprint.

*Whitman, Walt (1819-92) *COMPLETE POETRY AND SELECTED
PROSE ed. by Dr. Emory Holloway *Nonesuch Press* 1938 25s
In a volume of 1120 pages there are some characteristic letters, extracts
from *Specimen Days*, and from *Democratic Vistas*, and the complete text
of *Leaves of Grass*. For Dr. Holloway's separate edition of the last, and
for details of other standard editions, see under *Poetry* section.

Wilde, Oscar (1854-1900) ESSAYS ed. by Hesketh Pearson *Methuen*
1951 10s 6d
Nine of the longer essays, including *The Soul of Man Under Socialism*,
and, *The Decay In the Art of Lying*, selected from the volume *Intentions*,
see below, and from other volumes.

ESSAYS AND POEMS *Collins* (*Classics*) 1954 6s

INTENTIONS *Methuen* 1891 5s; *Unicorn Press* 1945 8s 6d
Four long essays.

PLAYS, PROSE WRITINGS AND POEMS ed. by Hesketh Pearson
Dent (*Everyman*) (1931) 1955 7s 6d
Includes *The Critic as Artist* (from *Intentions*), the novel *The Picture of
Dorian Gray*, *The Soul of Man under Socialism*, *The Ballad of Reading
Gaol*, and two plays.

*WORKS: STORIES, PLAYS, POEMS, ESSAYS ed. by G. F. Maine
Collins (1931) 1948 16s
The complete works in an omnibus of 1119 pages.

Williams, Charles (1886-1945) THE IMAGE OF THE CITY ed. by
Anne Ridler *O.U.P.* 1958 25s
A selection of characteristic essays grouped under headings: Literary;
The Incarnation; The City; Pardon and Justice; Exchange and the
Affirmative Way; On the Arthurian Myth; Collects; and a critical
introduction with a bibliography.

Wilson, John (1785-1854) NOCTES AMBROSIANAE (1822-35)
Essays by the principal journalist of *Blackwood's Magazine*, known under
his pen-name of 'Christopher North'. Others of the Blackwood group,
notably Maginn and Hogg, contributed critical essays and discussions, but
it is thought that those collected under the fanciful title of *Noctes Ambrosianae* (gatherings of the group in Ambrose's Tavern in Edinburgh) were
probably all by Wilson himself. These miscellanies are seldom read now,

but they contain trenchant criticisms of contemporaries, such as, for example, Wordsworth 'Wordsworth often writes like an idiot', Scott, and of Scottish politics and themes.

Woolf, Virginia (1882-1941) THE CAPTAIN'S DEATH BED *Hogarth Press* 1950 8s 6d
A final collection of essays, including a much-discussed, long essay on trends in modern fiction, *Mr. Bennett and Mrs. Brown*, first published in 1924.

*THE COMMON READER 2 series *Hogarth Press* 1925; 1932 9s 6d each
Essays in criticism and appreciation, addressed to Dr. Johnson's 'common reader', who reads for pleasure, 'rather than to impart knowledge or correct the opinions of others'. Although these delightful essays are chiefly on English authors, there are some on general themes, such as 'Modern Fiction', and 'The Russian Point of View'.

THE DEATH OF THE MOTH *Hogarth Press* 1947 8s 6d; *Penguin Books* 1961 3s 6d
A volume of essays.

GRANITE AND RAINBOW *Hogarth Press* 1958 18s
Twenty-seven essays on the art of fiction and the art of biography, contributed to journals anonymously. They have only recently been identified as the work of Virginia Woolf.

THE MOMENT AND OTHER ESSAYS *Hogarth Press* 1947 8s 6d

A ROOM OF ONE'S OWN *Hogarth Press* 1929 8s 6d
A discussion, tinged with irony, on the position of the intellectual woman in England, at home, at the university (of the twenties), fending often for herself, compared with the traditional masculine conception of individual freedom.

THREE GUINEAS *Hogarth Press* 1938 10s 6d
'A tract against war and dictatorship.'

*Wordsworth, William (1770-1850) POETRY AND PROSE ed. by W. W. Marchant *Hart-Davis (Reynard Library)* 1955 27s 6d 885 pp
A liberal selection of the poetry, with some letters, essays, and some miscellaneous prose.

LITERARY CRITICISM ed. by Nowell C. Smith *O.U.P.* 1906
Contains the 1800 preface to the *Lyrical Ballads*, the later addition, some letters of a critical nature, and miscellaneous prose.

Wyld, Henry Cecil Kennedy (1870-1945) THE GROWTH OF ENGLISH *Murray* 1907 6s
'An elementary account of the present form of our language, and its development.' The author was a distinguished lecturer and lexicographer.

D*

A HISTORY OF MODERN COLLOQUIAL ENGLISH *Blackwell* (1920) 1936 27s 6d
'An epoch-making work highly valued by scholars all over the world.' —*The Annual Register*, 1945.

A SHORT HISTORY OF ENGLISH *Murray* (1914) 1927 12s 6d
'With a bibliography of recent books on the subject, and lists of texts and editions.'

Yeats, William Butler (1865-1939) *ESSAYS AND INTRODUCTIONS *Macmillan* 1961 36s
A collection in one volume of 530 pages of the essays formerly published in three separate volumes: *Ideas of Good and Evil* (1896-1903); *The Cutting of an Agate* (1903-15); and, some later essays and introductions contributed to various books, with three hitherto unpublished items, being Yeats's introduction to these essays, a general introduction to his collected works, and his introduction to the volume containing all the plays. Notable literary essays include those on Shelley, Blake, Spenser, and Synge.

EXPLORATIONS ed. by Mrs. W. B. Yeats *Macmillan* 1962 35s
Collects into one volume various prefaces to books Yeats admired, and many other prose pieces, hitherto unpublished in book form, the whole forming a contribution of great interest to the history of the Irish Dramatic Movement from 1901 to 1919.

A VISION (1925) *Macmillan* (1938) 1962 30s
Original edition was a private, limited publication. In this volume the poet discussed and explained the experiences and esoteric teachings that inspired some of his poetry and prose writings.

PROSE ANTHOLOGIES AND COLLECTIONS
(including miscellanies of prose and poetry)

Agate, James THE ENGLISH DRAMATIC CRITICS, 1660-1933 *MacGibbon and Kee (Dramabooks)* 1958 12s 6d
A selection from Restoration times to the best work of Agate's contemporaries.

*Allott, Kenneth THE PELICAN BOOK OF ENGLISH PROSE 5 vols. *Penguin Books* 1956 3s 6d each
Vol. 1: Elizabethan Jacobean (1550-1620); vol. 2: Seventeenth Century (1620-1700); vol. 3: Eighteenth Century (1700-80); vol. 4: The Romantic Period (1780-1830); vol. 5: Victorian Prose (1830-80). Arranged chronologically with an introduction to each volume on the characteristic styles of each period, and with biographical notes.

Baring, Maurice HAVE YOU ANYTHING TO DECLARE? *Heinemann* 1936 25s
Chosen pieces from the author's wide reading in both classical and modern literature, with scholarly comments. The title derives from the

form in which the anthology is cast: across the Styx, the editor is asked
to declare the literary baggage he had travelled with during his lifetime.

Brett-Smith, H. F. B. PEACOCK'S FOUR AGES OF POETRY; with
Shelley's *Defence of Poetry*, and Browning's *Essay on Shelley*
Blackwell (*Percy Reprints of English Classics*) 1921 7s 6d
Collects three short works related to each other, as indicated by the
titles. Shelley's *Defence* was provoked by Peacock's summary classification of the rise, golden age and modern 'decline' to the 'brazen age'
(i.e. his own) of poetry.

Bullough, Geoffrey NARRATIVE AND DRAMATIC SOURCES OF
SHAKESPEARE 6 vols. *in progress Routledge* 1957- 45s each
Vol. 1: Early Comedies, Poems and *Romeo and Juliet* (1957); vol. 2: The
Comedies, 1597-1603 (1958); vol. 3: Earlier English History Plays:
Henry VI; *Richard III*; *Richard II* (1960); vol. 4: Later English History
Plays: *King John*; *Henry IV*; *Henry V*; *Henry VIII* (1962). Each volume
in this set totals over 500 pages. There is no modern collection of the
major sources and analogues of Shakespeare's plays . . . 'The work will
bring together in six volumes the major sources probably used by
Shakespeare for plots and characters, together with similar works which
he may have consulted. The texts will usually be based closely on Elizabethan editions; foreign works will be printed in English translation.
Whole works will be given wherever possible, and long significant
extracts from such works as . . . Ovid's *Metamorphoses*.'

*Davies, Hugh Sykes (Editor) THE POETS AND THEIR CRITICS
2 vols. *Hutchinson* 1960; 1962 13s 6d; 21s
Vol. 1: Chaucer to Collins; vol. 2: From Blake to Browning. The first
volume was originally issued as a *Pelican* in 1943. Each section, devoted
for example, in the larger supplementary volume 2 to the seven great
Romantic poets, is prefaced by editorial comment; then follow extracts
from notable critics, emphasising modern criticism from T. S. Eliot,
W. H. Auden, Dr. Leavis and others.

Edwards, S. L. AN ANTHOLOGY OF ENGLISH PROSE FROM BEDE TO
STEVENSON *Dent (Everyman)* (1914) 1953 8s 6d
This selection reveals the development of English prose styles.

*Enright, D. J. and Ernst de Chickera ENGLISH CRITICAL TEXTS:
16TH TO 20TH CENTURY *O.U.P.* 1962 18s
A notable collection for students, with notes and extracts from classical
writers on the theory of criticism, from Aristotle (*The Poetics*) to Lon-
ginus (*On the Sublime*). The volume gives authoritative texts of: Sidney's
An Apology for Poetry; Dryden's *An Essay of Dramatic Poesy*; Pope's *An
Essay on Criticism*; Johnson's *Preface to Shakespeare*; Wordsworth's
Preface to The Lyrical Ballads; Coleridge's *Biographia Literaria* (chapters
XIV, XVII and part of XVIII); Shelley's *A Defence of Poetry*; extracts
from some of Keats's *Letters*; Matthew Arnold on *The Study of Poetry*;
D. H. Lawrence's essay on *Why the Novel Matters*; T. S. Eliot (two
essays); and F. R. Leavis on *Keats*.

*Ford, Boris THE PELICAN GUIDE TO ENGLISH LITERATURE 6 vols.
Penguin Books 1954-8 3s 6d to 5s each; *Cassell* (Library, cloth-
bound, crown octavo editions) 1961-1962 15s, 18s and 21s
In part, the separate volumes of this standard set are anthologies of
representative prose and poetry of each period, together with bibliographies, historical and critical discussion by authorities. Some of the
texts quoted (especially in volume 1) are not otherwise easily come by.
Vol. 1: The Age of Chaucer (5s); vol. 2: The Age of Shakespeare (5s);
vol. 3: From Donne to Marvell (3s 6d); vol. 4: From Dryden to Johnson (5s); Vol. 5: From Blake to Byron (5s); vol. 6: From Dickens to
Hardy (5s).

*George, Daniel A PECK OF TROUBLES *Cape* 1936 10s 6d
'An anatomy of woe': arranged alphabetically under subjects, and
chosen to display writers known and unknown, or half-forgotten, with
masterly skill, and an extraordinary knowledge of the by-ways of
English literature, in grumbling, complaining, 'wearisome condition of
humanity' moods. A rare anthology for those in search of diversion.

Hibbard, G. R. THREE ELIZABETHAN PAMPHLETS *Harrap* (*Life,
Literature and Thought* series) 1951 7s 6d
Greene's *The Third and Last Part of Cony-Catching* (1592); Nashe's *Pierce
Penilesse* (1592) and, Dekker's *The Wonderful Year 1603* with an intro-
ductory essay and a bibliography.

*James, Eirian AN ANTHOLOGY OF ENGLISH PROSE, 1400–1900
C.U.P. 1951 12s 6d
The extracts range from Malory to Samuel Butler, and are planned
primarily to introduce foreign readers to characteristic specimens of
English prose. The second section of the book provides a commentary
on each extract. The pieces selected are also available as 'a talking book',
the British Council having had them recorded at Cambridge, read by a
group of senior members of the University. Thirty 78 r.p.m. records, or
five LP. Book also published in soft covers, for class use, 6s.

*Jones, Edmund David ENGLISH CRITICAL ESSAYS 2 vols. *O.U.P.*
(*Worlds Classics*) (1922; 1916) 1961
Vol. 1: XVI-XVIII Centuries (8s 6d); vol. 2: 19th Century (7s 6d).

*Jones, Phyllis M. ENGLISH CRITICAL ESSAYS *O.U.P.* (*Worlds
Classics*) 1938 7s 6d
A standard series, offering a choice of the best and most representative
critical essays from Sir Philip Sidney, through Dryden's and Dr. Johnson's period, and the great critics of the nineteenth century, to living
writers, such as T. S. Eliot, E. M. Forster, and Sir Herbert Read.

Lucas, Edward Verrall THE OPEN ROAD *Methuen* (1899) 1949 8s 6d
A perennial favourite, devoted to prose and verse inspired by the
countryside, walking, and enjoyment out of doors. The last edition was
the forty-fifth.

Makower, S. V. and B. H. Blackwell ENGLISH ESSAYS, 1600-1900 O.U.P. (*Worlds Classics*) 1912 7s 6d

Milford, Sir Humphrey MODERN ENGLISH ESSAYS 2 series O.U.P. (*Worlds Classics*) 1925; 1932
1: Mark Rutherford to J. Middleton Murry (8s 6d); 2: Mark Rutherford to Virginia Woolf (7s 6d).

*Newbolt, Sir Henry AN ENGLISH ANTHOLOGY OF PROSE AND POETRY *Dent* 1921 15s
A collection of 1024 pages, 'showing the main stream of English literature through the six centuries, fourteenth to nineteenth, with students' notes and indices separately, 2s 6d. Also usually available for presentation, bound in full morocco, 84s.

Nugent, Elizabeth M. THE THOUGHT AND CULTURE OF THE ENGLISH RENAISSANCE *C.U.P.* 1956 37s 6d
Tudor prose from 1481 to 1555, selected in a volume of 703 pages, and introduced in seven essays by Cambridge scholars, prefacing the seven groups: Humanists; Grammarians; Politicians; Physicians; The Divines; The Chroniclers and The Romancers; and the Historians.

Peacock, William ENGLISH ESSAYS O.U.P. (*Worlds Classics*) 1903 7s 6d
'From Bacon to Stevenson.'
ENGLISH PROSE 5 vols. O.U.P. (*Worlds Classics*) 1921-2 8s 6d each
Vol. 1: Wycliffe to Clarendon; vol. 2: Milton to Gray; vol. 3: Walpole to Lamb; vol. 4: Landor to O. W. Holmes; vol. 5: Mrs. Gaskell to Henry James.

*Quiller-Couch, Sir Arthur Thomas THE OXFORD BOOK OF ENGLISH PROSE O.U.P. 1925 25s
From Wycliffe to Rupert Brooke, in a volume of 1112 pages.

Read, Sir Herbert and Bonamy Dobrée THE LONDON BOOK OF ENGLISH PROSE *Eyre and Spottiswoode* 1932 18s
Introduction; extracts from Malory to Peter Quennell, arranged in formal groups.

Redman, Ben Ray READING AT RANDOM O.U.P. (*Worlds Classics*) 1933 7s 6d
Prose and verse selected from volumes in the *Worlds Classics*.

*Reeves, James GREAT ENGLISH ESSAYS *Cassell* 1961 30s
Authoritative, standard selection in one volume of 442 pages, ranging in time from Sir Francis Bacon to living writers, including humorists such as Paul Jennings.

Rhys, Ernest A CENTURY OF ENGLISH ESSAYS *Dent (Everyman)*
(1939) 1955 8s 6d
One hundred authors, from Caxton to the twentieth century.

THE PRELUDE TO POETRY *Dent (Everyman)* (1927)
Collects the writings from twenty-one poets 'in defence and praise of
their own art': Chaucer, Spenser, Sidney (*An Apologie for Poetry*),
Campion, Daniel, Jonson, Milton, Dryden, Pope, Gray, Burns, Scott,
Wordsworth, Coleridge, Shelley (*Defence of Poetry*), Byron, Keats,
Landor, Browning, Arnold, and Robert Bridges.

*Ridler, Anne SHAKESPEARE CRITICISM, 1919-1935 *O.U.P.* (*Worlds
Classics*) 1936 7s 6d; SHAKESPEARE CRITICISM, 1935-1960 1963
9s 6d
Companion to D. Nichol Smith's anthology, which see below. Essays
and criticsms are here collected from scholars and other critics of various
schools and of sometimes widely varying methods of approach to
Shakespearian problems.

Smith, D. Nichol CHARACTERS FROM THE HISTORIES AND MEMOIRS
OF THE SEVENTEENTH CENTURY *O.U.P.* 1918 18s

EIGHTEENTH CENTURY ESSAYS ON SHAKESPEARE (1903) *O.U.P.*
1963 50s
From Nicholas Rowe (1709) and Dr. Johnson (1765), to Maurice
Morgann (1777).

*SHAKESPEARE CRITICISM, 1623-1840 *O.U.P.* (*Worlds Classics*)
1916 7s 6d
'Aims to assemble the greatest pieces of Shakespeare criticism from 1623
to 1840 as well as to represent the general movement in critical opinion
and method: among those whose criticism is contained in this anthology
are Ben Jonson, Milton, Dryden, Addison, Steele, Pope, Gray, Johnson,
Lamb, Coleridge, Hazlitt, De Quincey, Landor, and Carlyle.' For companion volume see Ridler, above.

*Smith, G. Gregory ELIZABETHAN CRITICAL ESSAYS 2 vols. *O.U.P.*
1904 45s (the set)
A standard collection of 1048 pages. For the companion work on the
seventeenth century, see Spingarn below.

Smith, Logan Pearsall *A TREASURY OF ENGLISH APHORISMS
Constable 1928 7s 6d
A diverting choice. The compiler's individual taste and wide reading
enabled him to display the riches of English writers in this concise form
not only from well-known sources, but from less obvious sources.

A TREASURY OF ENGLISH PROSE *Constable* 1920 8s 6d
In this anthology the compiler's appreciation of wit and irony is
emphasised by his choice.

*Spingarn, J. E. CRITICAL ESSAYS OF THE SEVENTEENTH CENTURY
3 vols. *O.U.P.* (1908-9) 1958 84s (the set)
Collects in 1104 pages, all the material ('save the writings of Dryden')
necessary for a thorough study of the development of English criticism
in the seventeenth century, with annotations and comments. It is a
complementary companion to Gregory Smith's *Elizabethan Critical
Essays*, see above. Verse is included; some of the material is not easily
obtained elsewhere. Vol. 1: 1605-50; vol. 2: 1650-85; vol. 3: 1685-1700.

Stone, J. A. PERIODICAL ESSAYS OF THE EIGHTEENTH CENTURY
O.U.P. 1954 6s
About thirty essays by Addison, Steele, Goldsmith and Johnson, with
notes to explain for what public they were originally intended, and the
authors' purpose in writing these pieces.

*Sutherland, James THE OXFORD BOOK OF ENGLISH TALK *O.U.P.*
1953 21s
A unique and entertaining anthology, being a collection of recorded
talk gathered from an extraordinarily wide range of sources: memoirs;
letters; trials; newspaper reports; and similar out of the way material,
including even the drama and novels. The extracts display the conversational powers and characteristics of people in every walk of life, from
the humblest to the most famous, from about A.D. 1500 to the present
day.

Thornton, James Cholmondeley TABLE TALK *Dent* (*Everyman*)
(1934)
'From Ben Jonson to Leigh Hunt': that is, from Ben Jonson's well-
known *Conversations with Drummond of Hawthornden*, and Selden's *Table
Talk* (both given complete), to extensive selections from the recorded
talk of Pope, Swift, Byron, Coleridge, and Leigh Hunt.

Thorpe, James MILTON CRITICISM *Routledge* 1951 23s
Covers four centuries, from the seventeenth to the twentieth, of writing
on Milton. Useful as a display of changing taste, as well as a key to the
full understanding and appreciation of Milton and his works.

Ward, Alfred Charles A MISCELLANY OF TRACTS AND PAMPHLETS
O.U.P. (*Worlds Classics*) 1927
From John Knox to H. G. Wells: political, social and topical writings,
loosely classified as tracts, or other didactic pieces, written with a
purpose.

SPECIMENS OF ENGLISH DRAMATIC CRITICISM *O.U.P.* (*Worlds
Classics*) 1945 7s 6d
From the seventeenth to the twentieth centuries.

Williams, W. E. A BOOK OF ENGLISH ESSAYS *Penguin Books* (*Pelican*)
1943 3s 6d
From Bacon to the present day.

Williams, W. T. and G. H. Vallins GRAY, COLLINS, AND THEIR CIRCLE *Methuen* 1937 4s
'A selection of prose and poetry, representing a not inconsiderable part of mid-eighteenth century literature.'

Williamson, Claude C. H. READINGS ON THE CHARACTER OF HAMLET, 1661-1947 *Allen and Unwin* 1951 45s
In a substantial volume of 783 pages the editor provides extracts that vary in length from about 100 words to 3,000, of critical and appreciative writings, including some of the greatest Shakespearian criticism in English literature.

Wilson, John Dover LIFE IN SHAKESPEARE'S ENGLAND *C.U.P.* (1911) 1913 10s; and *Penguin Books* 1944 3s 6d Illus.
'An anthology collected from contemporary sources to present the daily life of a great period. Useful for students of history as well as of literature, as a book that illustrates the social background of Elizabethan and Jacobean drama.

Winny, James THE DESCENT OF EUPHUES *C.U.P.* 1957 16s
Under this collective title the editor provides, with introductory essay and a glossary, the text of three Elizabethan romances: *Euphues: the Anatomy of Wit*, by John Lyly (1578); *Pandosto: the Triumph of Time*, by Robert Greene (1588); and, *Piers Plainness: Seven Years' Prenticeship*, by Henry Chettle (1595). This last, a charming pastoral in picturesque prose, is transcribed from a unique quarto in the Bodleian Library. It is the only reprint.

FICTION
(*Novels and Short Stories*)

'THE novel is dying.' 'The novel is dead.' Assertions made by writers in conference may be thrown off for effect and platform provocation. The two quoted also reflect the opinions of a handful of critics, as well as creative writers, who, unlike critics, do not always read their contemporaries' books.

Such statements are very much of our times: they would be unthinkable in the nineteenth century, the greatest of centuries so far as English fiction is concerned. If 'the novel' was given any special attention then, and it was occasionally in the nineties, the resultant book would usually be historical, a survey of development, or an inquiry into function, as in F. Marion Crawford's *The Novel: What It is*, published in 1893.

The nineteenth-century novel was normally a substantial affair. Its origins in Defoe, Fielding, Richardson and Smollett encouraged the large canvas, but Jane Austen set an example by showing what the perfect artist could achieve by choosing a more exacting, limited genre, and Emily Brontë later offered a tragic masterpiece beyond the range of her more prolific predecessors and contemporaries.

Problems confronting the modern novelist are largely the result of the creation of an industry now connected with mass entertainment. Behind the writing of most novels lurk what literary agents term 'subsidiary rights'. Novelists must live: films from their tales; television plays from their short stories; and so on, must be borne in mind when these are being created. There is no reason to think Dickens and Wilkie Collins would have not welcomed such aids to even greater publicity and incomes than they enjoyed in their own period. Both authors would have been godsends to the B.B.C. and British film makers. But the rewards for success are now so considerable that inevitably the industry has attracted writers who are not creative artists. Their books tend to swamp those by writers of talent trying to express a view of life in their own way, regardless of the commercial aspects of literature.

On the other hand, a century that has novelists of genius who have been able to command a world audience cannot be accused of killing the novel. One would not be far out by evaluating the best work of Graham Greene, Somerset Maugham, Angus Wilson, and many others, as on the level of the fiction produced by Victorian novelists whose books have found permanent places in *Everyman*, *Worlds Classics* and other series.

But the temptation to encourage the production of the branded commodity type of fiction is certainly not repulsed by all publishers. It has been advocated as the only sensible, business policy by a well-known industrialist addressing a meeting of publishers and authors. Concentrate on a few books; advertise efficiently; exploit the potential markets: this, in brief was the advice. The result: bigger profits; happier booksellers;

more authors paying supertax. There is not the slightest evidence that anybody present took this advice seriously except those who already conducted publishing firms on the principles advocated. They were in the minority. The remainder continue to publish books they respect, and encourage authors whose work will never make big money for anybody. Some live happily in both worlds, like the recording companies, and this is probably the best method for everybody concerned.

The novel in European literature is the most informal branch of imaginative writing we have produced. That other form of fiction, the play, must submit to the requirements of the theatre or remain for ever in the library. But a Marcel Proust may decide to ignore everything written before and to impose on his readers an endless series of introspective analyses, create enough characters to populate a large village, pack his multi-volumed masterpiece with philosophic essays, internal monologues and cinematic flash-backs: and the result is still called 'a novel'. Joyce dispenses with punctuation, coherent diction, and even the vocabulary of the normal writer; George Moore talks to himself with Irish garrulity; Samuel Richardson writes hundreds of letters; the translators of Rabelais transfer into English a gigantic, fantastic joke with the aid of the unlimited vocabulary of a lexicographer on the grand scale; Fielding intermingles with his sturdy, forthright and picaresque comedies, essays and digressions on human frailties and passions; Henry James circumambulates the essential truth about his themes and characters with fascinating leisure; Peacock flings narrative out of the door and conducts his readers to the dinner-table and library to overhear aristocratic conversation with an edge to it; while Jane Austen keeps to the point with matchless perfection. And their books are all novels. If the novel is dead, something different has taken its place with the same name. To generalise about 'the novel' is indeed a very singular critical proceeding.

Lack of imagination, mistrust or ignorance of the emotional springs of human behaviour have led some readers to declare that they never read novels. Let the tale to be told be put into the form of a drama or a television script, and the librarian is then allowed to add the book to his 'non-fiction' stock, attracting praise for its issue to his public. But if the same tale is later rewritten as a novel, it will be depreciated as 'Fiction', lending fuel to library critics who so often deplore the preponderance of 'fiction issues' in the annual reports from their librarians.

Yet these seekers after truth, and nothing but the truth, will sometimes naïvely go in search of it to newspapers, revelations of strange occult experiences in Tibet, dream books, the autobiographies of 'self-made' business men, and narratives of adventures with flying saucers.

If such critics of the whole idea of fiction in novels and short stories be tempted to pass over the wealth of genius and talent recorded in this largest of all groups in *An English Library*, one would ask them to read some of the brilliant and illuminating 'non-fiction' books that have been written on 'the novel' before finally dismissing this gallery of authors from Defoe to Virginia Woolf and Rose Macaulay from their minds.

The theme attracts historical and critical monographs by the score every year, embracing studies of form, function and interpretation. In 1961 there were forty-two books of which twelve were devoted solely to critical analysis of two authors: James Joyce and D. H. Lawrence.

Of the older books, now matured into standard works not likely ever to be superseded, *Aspects of the Novel*, by E. M. Foster, Edward Arnold (1927) 1949, 7s 6d, is supreme. These *Clark Lectures* on Plot, People, Fantasy, and allied themes, discuss and answer many fundamental questions about the writing, and the reading, of fiction. Percy Lubbock's *The Craft of Fiction*, Jonathan Cape (1921) 1954, 16s, continues to instruct and illuminate both novelist and reader; Robert Liddell's *A Treatise On the Novel*, Cape, 1947, 15s, and its complementary study of *Some Principles of Fiction*, Cape, 1953, 15s, were well received, and are further evidence of their distinguished publisher's devotion to the art which has added so much to the brilliance of a back list of fiction itself worthy of a monograph in praise of perception and literary taste of the highest order.

Miriam Allott's *Novelists On the Novel*, Routledge, 1959, 30s, is an anthology of surpassing interest, ranging as it does from Richardson and Fielding to the European novelists of the twentieth century. It might well be studied with that other compilation, selected with rare knowledge and judgement, for *Writers on Writing*, by Walter Allen, Phoenix House (1948) 1958, 16s. This is a book worthy of *Everyman*, where it could take its place next to *The Prelude to Poetry*. Walter Allen has also written a concise, fluent study, now in *Penguin Books*, on *The English Novel: a Short Critical History* (1954), 1958, 4s, and his stimulating, provocative *Reading A Novel*, Phoenix House (1949; 1956), in its latest edition, 1962, 6s, includes an examination of Iris Murdoch's *The Bell* (Chatto, 1958) to help critical readers in their approach to understanding and appreciation of a distinguished newcomer of the post-war decades.

Monographs abound. Kathleen Tillotson's *Novels of the 1840's*, O.U.P. 1954, 21s and 1961 Paperback, 8s 6d, is accepted as a study of permanent value to students; F. R. Leavis on *The Great Tradition* should not be neglected by any reader who enjoys George Eliot, Henry James, and Joseph Conrad. It has been widely discussed since 1948, when it was first published by Chatto, 18s, and will now reach a greater public in the *Peregrine Paperback* reprint of 1962, 9s 6d. The same series has a new work for Janeites, in Andrew H. Wright's *Jane Austen Novels: a Study In Structure*, 1962, 7s 6d; while the series from America, in progress from Thames and Hudson, known as the *Reader's Guides*, has already made available to students notable monographs on Herman Melville, Joseph Conrad, James Joyce, W. B. Yeats, and a valuable survey in Karl and Magalaner's *Great Twentieth-Century English Novels*. A reference dictionary of *Literary Terms* is included in the final section of suggestions for *A Bookman's Library*.

Richard Church's compact, but quite outstanding, little study of *The*

Growth of the English Novel, Methuen, 1951, 8s 6d, is now also in *University Paperbacks*, 6s: it well repays reading by both students and general readers. Of the detailed histories, Arnold Kettle's *An Introduction to the English Novel*, 2 vols. Hutchinson (University Library), 1951-3, 12s 6d each, may be recommended with confidence; and the recent stimulating survey for the common reader of masterpieces in English fiction from Defoe to Thomas Hardy and D. H. Lawrence, entitled *Masters of the English Novel*, by Percy Marshall, Dennis Dobson, 1962, 12s 6d, should be especially useful for its bibliographical information.

Novels and Short Stories

Adlington, William (*fl.* 1560) THE GOLDEN ASSE OF APULEIUS (Metamorphoses) translated by William Adlington (1566) *Heinemann (Loeb Classics)* 1915 18s; *New York, Macmillan* 1962 5s (Paperback)

A parallel Latin and English edition in a standard series, revised by Stephan Gaselee, of one of the most popular of the great Tudor translations: 'simple, direct and fresh, and yet possesses that picturesque happiness of phrase which is the crown of a growing language . . . It is, indeed, as well rounded and as pleasant a piece of prose as you will meet in our tongue.'—*George Saintsbury*: Preface to a 1922 reprint, now out of print.

Ainsworth, William Harrison (1805-82) THE LANCASHIRE WITCHES (1848 *Nelson (Classics)* 1937 6s

A vivid tale of Lancaster at the beginning of the seventeenth century.

OLD ST. PAUL'S (1841) *Collins (Classics)* 1953 6s; *Dent (Everyman)* 1911 6s 6d; *Nelson (Classics)* 1920 6s

ROOKWOOD (1834) *Dent (Everyman)* 1931 6s 6d

THE TOWER OF LONDON (1840) *Collins (Classics)* 1953 6s; *Dent (Everyman)* 1910 6s 6d; *Nelson (Classics)* 1928 6s

WINDSOR CASTLE (1843) *Collins (Classics)* 1953 5s; *Dent (Everyman* 1915 6s 6d; *Nelson (Classics)* 1923 6s

These five historical romances are the best of the prolific output of a once immensely popular novelist. *Old Saint Paul's* is a colourful and exciting tale of the City of London at the time of the Great Plague and the Great Fire. *Rookwood* is based on the more or less legendary exploits of Dick Turpin, a popular hero, although a highwayman, of the eighteenth century; and *The Tower of London* has for central theme the story of the unhappy Lady Jane Grey, who was beheaded at the Tower in 1554. For his *Windsor Castle*, Ainsworth took the reign of Henry VIII in the years of his marriage to Anne Boleyn, and later, to Jane Seymour, mother of Edward VI.

Alcott, Louisa May (1832-88) LITTLE WOMEN (1867); GOOD WIVES (1869) *Collins (Classics)* 1954 6s; *Dent (Children's Illustrated Classics)* 1953 10s 6d each

The sequel, sometimes entitled *Little Women Married*, is often bound with *Little Women*, as in *Collins Classics* edition. These are but two of many reprints of a perennial favourite with adolescent readers, which is re-read with pleasure in mature years because of its charming simplicity in portraying family life, based largely, it is said, on the writer's life at Concord and Boston.

Aldington, Richard (1892-1962) DEATH OF A HERO *Chatto* (1929); *Penguin Books* 1939
One of the most enduring novels to come from the bitterness and frustration engendered in the minds of many poets and novelists who survived the war of 1914-18.

Anstey, F. (Thomas Anstey Guthrie) (1856-1934) VICE VERSA *Murray* (1882) 1949 7s 6d
Popular humorous fantasy in which a father changes place with his son at school, and by the working of the same charm, the son assumes his father's role at home. But each retains his mental age, thus provoking many amusing episodes, not without psychological significance for the attentive reader.
The author's other great success was *The Brass Bottle* (1900) a pantomimic fantasy about a genie released from an old bottle by a purchaser in an auction sale. This is sometimes available as a paperback, notably in Penguin Books, 1946, 2s 6d.

*Austen, Jane (1775-1817) EMMA (1816) MANSFIELD PARK (1814) NORTHANGER ABBEY (1818) PERSUASION (1818) PRIDE AND PRE-JUDICE (1813) SENSE AND SENSIBILITY (1811) MINOR WORKS
The standard, definitive edition of the above is that edited by R. W. Chapman, 6 vols. O.U.P. (1923); 1933 5 vols. 15s each; *Minor Works* 1954, 21s. Illustrated with reproductions of contemporary engravings and plates; fully collated texts with all editions published in Jane Austen's lifetime, and with hitherto unpublished manuscripts. Punctuation and spelling of original editions retained; with editorial notes and appendices. The volume of *Minor Works*, 486 pages, contains juvenilia: *Volume the First*; *Volume the Second* (that is, *Love and Freindship*); *Volume the Third* (that is, *Lady Susan*, 1805 and *The Watsons*, 1803, and a charming, mature fragment, *Sanditon*, 1817); together with Verses and Prayers, and some Early Miscellanea.

Standard editions in series of the six novels include: *Chatto* (*Zodiac Press*) 12s 6d each; *Collins* (*Classics*) 5s and 6s each; *Dent* (*Everyman*) 7s 6d and 8s 6d each; *Nelson* (*Classics*) 5s and 6s each; *Macdonald* (*Illustrated Classics*) 15s each; and O.U.P. (*Worlds Classics*) 6s each. There is also a pleasant presentation set with coloured illustrations and line-drawings by C. E. Brock, Dent, 6 vols. 10s 6d each (boxed as a set, 63s). The texts of the first editions, with minor corrections, are given in Macdonald's set, completed in 1961.

Bage, Robert (1728-1801) HERMSPRONG (1796) ed. by Vaughan Wilkins *Turnstile Press* 1951

A novel with a purpose, that is indicated by its sub-title: *Man as he is not*. It is concerned with the social injustices of the eighteenth century, and above all, was radical in tone. The American-born hero, 'taught only to distinguish men by virtue', surveys the English social scene with irony and Peacockian aloofness.

Ballantyne, Robert Michael (1825-94) MARTIN RATTLER (1858) *Collins (Classics)* 1961 5s; *Dent (Everyman)* 1907 6s 6d; *Nelson (Classics)* 1923 6s
A boy's adventures 'through the romantic forests of Brazil': written for youth, but a perennial favourite long afterwards.

Banks, Isabella (1821-97) THE MANCHESTER MAN (1876) *Harrap* 1932
Presents with fidelity the era of industrial strife from about 1799 to 1831. The central episode is the Peterloo Massacre. Sometimes reprinted in Lancashire, e.g. Sherratt of Altrincham, 1954, 10s 6d.

Barrie, Sir James (1860-1937) PLAYS AND STORIES *Dent (Everyman)* 1962 12s 6d
Barrie's fiction appears to be the least likely to survive of all his work, but this latest addition to the series includes a story from *Auld Licht Idylls* (1888), and a short story much admired when it was first published: *Farewell, Miss Julie Logan* (1928).

Beaconsfield, *1st Earl of* (Benjamin Disraeli) (1804-81) *CONINGSBY (1844) *Dent (Everyman)* (1911) 1959 12s 6d
In the modern edition B. N. Langdon-Davies provides a useful, essential introduction and notes to assist readers in a full appreciation of this auto-biographical novel, the first of its kind in English literature. It is still the best political novel in the language. Sub-titled 'The New Generation', it is a *roman à clef*, addressed by the young Disraeli to members of the Tory Party of his time who believed in a Tory democracy as the best form of government for the country and the Empire.

LOTHAIR (1870) *Nelson (Classics)* 1957 7s
Introduced by A. Norman Jeffares, who says it is 'the richest expression of its author's own personality and ideas'.

*SYBIL (1845) *Nelson (Classics)* 1957 7s; *O.U.P. (Worlds Classics)* 1926 7s 6d; *W. H. Allen (Dolphin Books)* 1962 10s
The most enduring of all Disraeli's novels, and complementary to *Coningsby*. Sub-titled 'The Two Nations' to indicate the theme: the social inequalities in England in the forties; the 'two nations', rich and poor, landlord and farmer against labourer, engaged in a struggle, fraught with evil if not comprehended by political leaders.

TANCRED (1847) *Bodley Head* 1927
Completion of the trilogy of which *Coningsby* and *Sybil* are the first two. Sub-titled 'The New Crusade', being a prophetic indication of the great opportunity awaiting British youth ready to respond to enterprising, inspired leadership.

Becke, George Louis (1855-1913) BY REEF AND PALM (1894)
Angus and Robertson 1955 10s 6d
Fourteen stories by an Australian writer, 'vigorous, sometimes violent',
of life in the Pacific Islands about a century ago.

Beckford, William (1759-1844) VATHEK (1786)
See under Saintsbury and Henderson, joint editors of *Shorter Novels*,
entered in the next section.

Beerbohm, Sir Max (1872-1956) *THE HAPPY HYPOCRITE *Bodley
Head* (1897) 1959 6s
' A fantastical allegory.'

*ZULEIKA DOBSON *Heinemann* (1911) 1947 12s 6d; *Penguin
Books* (1952) 1961 3s 6d
An Edwardian masterpiece of wit and irony, in which Zuleika, a Helen,
not of Troy but of Oxford, drives undergraduates to madness and
suicide.

Bellamy, Edward (1850-98) LOOKING BACKWARD (1888) *Redman*
1948 7s 6d; *W. H. Allen (Dolphin Books)* 1963 7s 6d
An early, once very popular, example of science fiction, in which the
Radical author offers a view of life in Boston, U.S.A., in the year
A.D. 2000. He did foresee some of the mechanical developments of the
twentieth century, but his book is notable for the vision he had of the
true nature of an authoritarian government in the coming century, with
state ownership playing an important part in the economy.

Bennett, Arnold (1867-1931) *CLAYHANGER *Methuen* (1910) 1952
10s 6d; *Penguin Books* (1954) 1961 7s 6d

HILDA LESSWAYS *Methuen* (1911) 1951 7s

THESE TWAIN *Methuen* (1916) 1955 10s 6d
A trilogy of 1508 pages, tracing in leisurely detail, the course of Edwin
Clayhanger's life in the Five Towns, from youth to married strife with
Hilda.

*THE CARD *Methuen* (1911) 1956 10s 6d
An adventure in the Five Towns. The hero is an engaging, impudent,
lucky fellow. Nothing stops his rise to the top, where he makes or finds
plenty of room. This is a perennial favourite and is Bennett's best comedy.

*THE OLD WIVE'S TALE *Hodder* (1908) 1945 12s 6d; *Dent (Everyman)* (1935) 1954 10s 6d; *Nelson (Classics)* 1961 8s 6d
Bennett's masterpiece. It is a realistic portrait of two women, Constance
and Sophia Baines: their lives from youth to middle age and beyond, are
depicted with a craftsman's delight in vivid detail and authenticity. Set
partly in the Five Towns and partly in Paris.

THE PRETTY LADY *Unicorn Press* (1918) 1950 12s 6d
Frank Swinnerton introduces the new edition and writes: 'It is one of
the three most seriously undervalued novels Bennett ever wrote.'

THE REGENT *Methuen* (1913) 1955 6s

The 'Card', hero of the novel of that title (see above), pursues his way upward for this 'Five Towns story of adventure in London'. *The Regent* is the name of his Piccadilly theatre.

*RICEYMAN STEPS *Cassell* (1923) 1951 12s 6d; *Collins (Classics)* 1956 7s

An endearing novel, and in the opinion of some, likely to be Bennett's most enduring masterpiece. It is the study of a miser, set in Clerkenwell, close to the City of London. Since the publication of this novel, Riceyman Steps has become a place-name to Londoners who know the neighbourhood. In the *Collins Classics* reprint, there is included a long-short story of *Elsie and the Child* (1925) another beautifully conceived piece of work. This poignant masterpiece is a study of a simple soul, the Elsie who worked as a 'domestic' for Mr. Earlforward, the miserly book-seller of *Riceyman Steps*.

WHOM GOD HATH JOINED *Methuen* (1906) 1952 8s 6d

Introduced by Sir Desmond MacCarthy. It is an admirably characterised study of a divorce, and must be classed high in the serious fiction of the Edwardian era.

The above nine books, selected from Bennett's prolific output, seem likely to endure for many generations to come. Amongst his lesser, but still popular tales, kept in print owing to demand, are *Anna of the Five Towns*, Methuen (1902) 1955, 10s 6d; *A Great Man*, Methuen (1904) 1950, 10s 6d; and *Buried Alive*, the amusing novel from which Bennett made a popular comedy called *The Great Adventure*, Methuen (1908) 1951, 10s 6d.

Benson, Stella (1892-1933) TOBIT TRANSPLANTED *Macmillan* 1931
'A re-reading of the Apocrypha, while I was living in Kanto, Manchuria, some years ago, seemed to me to show a curiously exact parallel between the position of the exiled Jews of Tobit's day and that of the exiled White Russians in ours.'—*From the preface*.

*Bentley, Edmund Clerihew (1875-1956) TRENT'S LAST CASE *Nelson* (1913) (*Classics*) 1955 6s; *Dent* 1950 7s 6d
A classic of detective fiction, described by enthusiasts as 'epochal'.

*Beresford, John Davys (1873-1947) THE HAMPDENSHIRE WONDER (1911) Intro. by Walter de la Mare *Eyre and Spottiswoode* 1948 6s
A story of an infant prodigy, told with imaginative insight, humour and pathos. Of all Beresford's fiction, this seems to be his masterpiece.

*Bierce, Ambrose (1842-1914?) IN THE MIDST OF LIFE (1891) *Chatto (New Phoenix Library)* 1950 6s
Classic American short stories. Some of the themes, like the author's life, are macabre; some are episodes of the American Civil War; many have a sustained power in spite of brevity: a notable example being *The Horseman In The Sky*.

Blackmore, Richard Doddridge (1825-1900) *LORNA DOONE (1869) *Collins (Classics)* 1953 7s; *Dent (Everyman)* (1908) 1956

10s 6d; *Macdonald (Illustrated Classics)* 1949 15s; *Nelson (Classics)* 7s; *O.U.P. (Worlds Classics)* 1957 7s 6d

'A romance of Exmoor' in the last quarter of the seventeenth century, and of the legendary outlawed Doones, in the valley of the River Lyn. The attractive setting, and the fresh, simple, old-fashioned style of the narrative have made it one of the most popular nineteenth-century novels in the language. The Collins series reprint contains eighteen photographs of famous scenes in Devonshire visited by tourists for their romantic beauty and as part of 'the Doone country'.

SPRINGHAVEN (1887) *Dent (Everyman)* 1909
'A tale of the Napoleonic wars.' It has never achieved the popularity of *Lorna Doone*, but Blackmore considered it to be his best novel.

Blackwood, Algernon (1869-1951) THE EMPTY HOUSE (1906) *Unicorn Press* 1948 12s 6d

Ghost stories by a modern master of the supernatural in fiction.

JOHN SILENCE (1908) *Unicorn Press* (1947) 1962 18s
John Silence is a 'Physician Extraordinary', who, by developing and using those strange powers that the author thought might be more common than is generally supposed, was able to unravel mysteries beyond the normal comprehension. These five long stories include the well-known variation on the Vampire theme, *The Camp of the Dog*.

*Boldrewood, Rolf (T. A. Browne) (1826-1915) ROBBERY UNDER ARMS (1888) *Collins (Classics)* 1954 6s; *Macmillan (St. Martins Library)* 1958 6s; *O.U.P. (Worlds Classics)* 1950 8s 6d

A classic adventure story of Australian literature. Captain Starlight, bushranger, his life and exploits in the bush and in the goldfields of Australia, are now as legendary as Dick Turpin, but the novel is accepted also as a fairly authentic account of early days in the country.

*Borrow, George (1803-81) LAVENGRO (1851) *Dent (Everyman)* (1906) 1961 10s 6d; *Nelson (Classics)* 1954 7s; *O.U.P. (Worlds Classics)* (1906) 1958 7s 6d

The story of Lavengro, 'The Scholar, the Gypsy, and the Priest', based partly on Borrow's own picaresque life and wanderings amongst gypsies.

THE ROMANY RYE (1857) *Cresset Press* 1949 12s 6d; *Dent (Everyman)* (1906) 1961 10s 6d; *Nelson (Classics)* 1922 7s; *O.U.P. (Worlds Classics)* (1906) 1958 7s 6d

A sequel to *Lavengro*. The term 'Romany Rye' was Borrow's gypsy name, and means 'The Gypsy Gentleman'. Unrivalled for their romantic atmosphere and evocation of the wanderer's life on the road and in the open air, these two novels are unique in nineteenth-century fiction. Dr. Walter Starkie, the distinguished authority on gypsy lore, contributes a long introduction to the *Everyman* editions, in which he writes of both books as if they were one work.

Bowen, Marjorie (1888-1952) THE VIPER OF MILAN *Bodley Head* (1906) 1960 12*s* 6*d*
A romance of Lombardy in the fourteenth century, and of the Duke Visconti. First of many successful historical novels, it has maintained a place as a minor classic of its kind. 'Marjorie Bowen' wrote under other pseudonyms, and as 'George Preedy', and 'Joseph Shearing' made new reputations as a born storyteller. The reprint is introduced by Graham Greene.

Bramah, Ernest (Ernest Bramah Smith) (1868-1942) KAI LUNG BENEATH THE MULBERRY TREE *Unicorn Press* 1940 12*s* 6*d*

KAI LUNG UNROLLS HIS MAT *Unicorn Press* (1928) 12*s* 6*d*; *Penguin Books* 1937 2*s* 6*d*

*KAI LUNG'S GOLDEN HOURS *Unicorn Press* (1922) 12*s* 6*d*; *Penguin Books* 1937 2*s* 6*d*

*THE WALLET OF KAI LUNG *Unicorn Press* (1900) 12*s* 6*d*; *Penguin Books* 1936 2*s* 6*d*
The last in the series as listed was the first to be published by Grant Richards, who was delighted with the charming style of these short stories, with their neat plots, gentle characterisation, and inimitable humour derived from traditional Chinese traits. The Richards Press, now Unicorn Press, continued at intervals to add further to the collection which now seems to be firmly established and likely to continue to give pleasure to new generations.

*Brontë, Anne (1820-49) AGNES GREY (1847) *Nelson* (*Classics*) (1933) 1956 5*s*; *O.U.P.* (*Worlds Classics*) (1907) 1960 7*s* 6*d*; and with *The Tenant of Wildfell Hall*; for which editions see below
The story of a governess, whose sad lot it was to care for 'a family of odious children'. Agnes Grey falls in love, however, with Mr. Weston, a kindly curate. This simple tale was written in part from the author's own experiences.

THE TENANT OF WILDFELL HALL (1848) *Chatto* (*Zodiac Press*) 1954 12*s* 6*d*; *Nelson* (*Classics*) (1933) 1956 6*s*; *O.U.P.* (*Worlds Classics*) (1906) 1960 8*s* 6*d*; and, with *Agnes Grey* in *Collins* (*Classics*) 1954 6*s*; and *Dent* (*Everyman*) (1914) 1954 12*s* 6*d*
A strongly characterised novel, with a plot of some power. The mysterious widow of Wildfell Hall is suspected of double-dealing, but she clears her reputation by giving her lover, who tells the tale, a sight of her diary. The character of Arthur Huntingdon, her first husband, seems to have been based on that of Branwell Brontë, whose weakness and excessive drinking habits caused the Brontë sisters grave concern.

*Brontë, Charlotte (1816-55) JANE EYRE (1847) *Chatto* (*Zodiac Press*) 1946 12*s* 6*d*; *Collins* (*Classics*) 1953 6*s*; *Dent* (*Everyman*) (1908) 1953 7*s* 6*d*; *Macdonald* (*Illustrated Classics*) 1955 15*s*; *Nelson* (*Classics*) 1954 6*s*; *O.U.P.* (*Worlds Classics*) (1901) 1960 6*s*

From its first (anonymous) publication, this powerful story of a governess, her unhappy childhood and somewhat sombre life, until she gains a post in the macabre household of the sardonic Mr. Rochester, was popular with every class of reader, in spite of critical controversy aroused by the heroine's strongly frank character. It was the first volume to be issued in the *Worlds Classics* series.

THE PROFESSOR (1857) *Collins (Classics)*—with *Some Angrian Tales*, and *Poems* 1954 6s; *Dent (Everyman)* (1910) 1954 7s 6d; *Nelson (Classics)* 1929 5s; *O.U.P. (Worlds Classics)* 1959 6s
This first novel, written in 1846, but posthumously published, is partly autobiographical. It was written when Charlotte's Brussels student life with Emily, were fresh in mind. Her chief character, William Crimsworth, is memorable. Some of the material was recast to help in the making of *Villette*.

SHIRLEY (1849) *Collins (Classics)* 1953 6s; *Dent (Everyman)* (1908) 1955 10s 6d; *Nelson (Classics)* 1923 6s; *O.U.P. (Worlds Classics)* 1902 7s 6d
The character of Shirley Keeldar, proud, single-minded Shirley, was drawn from that of Charlotte's sister, Emily. But the background of the tale is industrial, centring on the Yorkshire mill workers, the Luddite riots in opposition to new machinery, and the mill owner's determination to use the latest equipment to help his diminishing trade.

VILLETTE (1853) *Chatto (Zodiac Press)* 1948 12s 6d; *Collins (Classics)* 1954 6s; *Dent (Everyman)* (1909) 1957 10s 6d; *Nelson (Classics)* 1954 6s; *O.U.P. (Worlds Classics)* (1908) 1959 6s
The heroine is again a governess, who tells her story in the first person. She takes up a position at Villette, in Belgium, under a formidable Madame Beck, one of the most firmly drawn characters in the book, next to that of the complex little professor, Paul Emanuel.

*Brontë, Emily (1818-48) WUTHERING HEIGHTS (1847) *Collins (Classics)* 1953 5s; *Dent (Everyman)* (1907) 1955 7s 6d; *Macdonald (Illustrated Classics)* 1955 15s; *Nelson (Classics)* 1954 5s; *O.U.P. (Worlds Classics)* (1901) 1957 6s
The *Worlds Classics* and *Everyman* editions reprint the text as the author originally left it, not the one as revised later by her sister Charlotte. *Worlds Classics* also contains a preface and memoir of Emily and Anne Brontë, written by Charlotte; together with a general introduction by H. W. Garrod, and the textual variants in an appendix. This wild, passionate and haunting novel, a classical tragedy set in the bleak moors of Yorkshire, is the most widely read of all nineteenth-century tales written by a woman. About sixty of Emily Brontë's poems are included in *Everyman* at the end of the volume.

Brooke, Henry (*c.* 1703-83) THE FOOL OF QUALITY (1766) *Routledge* 1906
Sub-title: 'Or, The History of Henry, Earl of Moreland'. It is one of the earliest English didactic novels, much admired by some nineteenth-

century writers, notably by Charles Kingsley. It is the first English book in which the influence of Rousseau's teachings and ideas on education can be clearly seen.

Buchan, John *(1st Baron Tweedsmuir)* (1875–1940) *THE FOUR ADVENTURES OF RICHARD HANNAY *Hodder* 1924 21s
An omnibus volume of 1216 pages, containing the four immensely popular thrillers of secret service and intelligence work, all of which are usually available separately in many other editions, including Penguin Book paperbacks: *The Thirty-Nine Steps* (1915); *Greenmantle* (1916); *Mr. Standfast* (1919); and *The Three Hostages* (1924). *Nelson Classics* include the first three, 5s, 6s, 7s respectively.

FOUR TALES OMNIBUS *Blackwood* 1936 12s 6d 640 pp
The Thirty-Nine Steps (1915); *The Power House* (1916); *The Moon Endureth* (1912); and, *The Watcher By the Threshold* (1902).

PRESTER JOHN (1910) *Nelson* (*Classics*) 1954 5s; *Penguin Books* 1956 2s 6d
A smuggling romance of South Africa and of the legendary Prester John. Refer also to Nelson's current stock list for the titles of the uniform edition of John Buchan's novels and tales, 25 volumes, 10s 6d each. Popular novels in the first series are also frequently reprinted in library editions: for example, *Mr. Standfast*, 31st reprint, Hodder, 1962, 15s; and the Scottish adventure of *The Island of Sheep*, Nelson (1936), was added to *Nelson Classics* in 1962, 6s.

Burney, Frances (Madame D'Arblay) (1752–1840) CECILIA (1782) 3 vols. *Dent* 1893
'Memoirs of an Heiress.' An amusing novel with a lively plot about the heroine's quest for a husband who will adopt her name, to enable her to enjoy an inheritance left to her on this condition. But the chance of sharing the money attracts several undesirable adventurers before she succeeds.

*EVELINA (1778) *Dent* (*Everyman*) (1909) 1958 8s 6d; ed. by Sir Frank Mackinnon *O.U.P.* 1930
'The History of a Young Lady's Entrance Into the World.' A novel of manners, presented in a series of letters. The heroine of this diverting comedy is Sir John Belmont's daughter; her youth is spent with a guardian, who introduces the story, but the greater part is related by Evelina, whose lively letters narrate her trials and the progress of her love affair with Lord Orville.

***Burton, Sir Richard Francis** (1821–90) THE ARABIAN NIGHTS ENTERTAINMENTS Translated into English by Sir Richard Burton (1885–8) Selections ed. by P. H. Newby 2 vols. *Arthur Barker* 1950; 1957 18s each
The standard English translation, more free and racy in style than the somewhat old-fashioned version by E. W. Lane, Chatto (1838) frequently reprinted. See also under Mathers for a twentieth-century version from the French.

*Butler, Samuel (1835-1902) EREWHON (1872) *Cape* (1922) 1960
16s; *Nelson (Classics)* 1954; *Penguin Books* 1956 2s 6d

EREWHON REVISITED (1901) *Cape* 1921 10s 6d; *Dent (Everyman)*—
with *Erewhon* (1932) 1959 10s 6d
The original satire, revised in 1901, and its sequel, are masterpieces of
irony in which Butler criticised many aspects of Victorian morality and
current ideas. Erewhon is 'Nowhere', and this fantasy about a remote
country, revisited by the narrator's son in the sequel, was Butler's only
popular success in his own lifetime.

THE WAY OF ALL FLESH (1903) *Cape* (1921) 1961 18s Illus. by
Donia Nachshen; *Collins (Classics)* 1934 6s; *Dent (Everyman)*
(1933) 1954 8s 6d; *O.U.P. (Worlds Classics)* 1933 7s 6d
The *Worlds Classics* edition of this posthumously published masterpiece
has an introduction by Bernard Shaw, who emphasised his indebtedness
to Butler's thought and writings. The novel sharply attacks the Victorian
attitude to conventional family life, especially the father-son relationship.
Some of the material is autobiographical. It is told in the first person, and
is supposed to have been written in 1867.

*Carroll, Lewis (Charles Lutwidge Dodgson) (1832-98) ALICE'S
ADVENTURES IN WONDERLAND *Macmillan* (1865) 1953 15s and 6s
Illus. by Sir John Tenniel

THROUGH THE LOOKING-GLASS, and What Alice Found There
Macmillan (1871) 1953 16s and 6s Illustrated by Sir John Tenniel
Standard editions of these two world-famous fantasies, enjoyed as much
in maturity as in childhood, with the original illustrations in both the
quarto and the crown octavo editions. The quartos have coloured plates.
Many other editions are always available, including the *Everyman* edition,
1930, 6s 6d, which gives both stories in one volume, together with *The
Hunting of the Snark*, with Carroll's illustrations from which Tenniel
did his familiar drawings for the first editions. In 1958 the two stories
were added to Macmillan's paperback series, *St. Martins Library*, one
volume, illustrated, 3s 6d.

*Cary, Joyce (1888-1957) A HOUSE OF CHILDREN *Michael Joseph*
(1941) 1951 15s
Awarded the James Tait Black Memorial Prize.

HERSELF SURPRISED; TO BE A PILGRIM; THE HORSE'S MOUTH *Michael
Joseph* (1941; 1942; 1944) 1951 16s; 15s; 15s
A notable contribution to the twentieth-century novel in the form of a
trilogy. It is high comedy, garnished with satire and drollery. The period
covers about sixty years and the novelist 'Designed to show three
characters, not only in themselves but as seen by each other'. There are
eleven novels in the uniform *Carfax* edition, for details of which see the
publisher's current catalogue.

*Chesterton, Gilbert Keith (1874-1936) THE CLUB OF QUEER
TRADES (1905) *Darwen Finlayson* 1960 10s 6d

Highly diverting fantasy: a set of short stories on a linking theme, commencing with one of Chesterton's most original stories: *The Tremendous Adventures of Major Brown*.

THE FATHER BROWN STORIES *Cassell* (1929) 1955 25s
A perennial favourite, being an omnibus collection of forty-nine short stories (in a volume of 718 pages), originally published in five volumes, available separately from time to time in *Penguin* and other paperback editions: *The Innocence of Father Brown* (1911); *The Wisdom of Father Brown* (1914); *The Incredulity of Father Brown* (1926); *The Secret of Father Brown* (1927); and, *The Scandal of Father Brown* (1935). Father Brown playing the part of amateur detective is now one of the immortals of the English gallery of characters. His kindly, shrewd, semi-mystical approach to crime and its problems, unmasking the international thief Flambeau, reveals something of Chesterton's own Catholic faith in God and man.

FATHER BROWN: SELECTED STORIES O.U.P. (*Worlds Classics*) 1955 7s 6d
Eighteen characteristic stories, with an appreciation by Monsignor Ronald Knox.

THE FLYING INN *Methuen* (1911) 1954 7s 6d; *Penguin* 1958 2s 6d
Hilarious fantasy in which an imaginary English law, abolishing inns, is evaded ingeniously by the keeper of a 'flying inn', on the run, so to speak, to preserve his licence to sell beer and other intoxicating liquor.

A G.K.C. OMNIBUS *Methuen* 1953 21s
In one volume of 726 pages we have more characteristic fantasies: *The Napoleon of Notting Hill* (1904); *The Man who was Thursday* (1908); and, *The Flying Inn*.

THE MAN WHO KNEW TOO MUCH (1922) *Darwen Finlayson* 1961 12s 6d
A volume of short stories. See also under *Essays and Belles Lettres* section for the *Everyman* volume of *Stories, Essays and Poems*.

MANALIVE (1912) *Darwen Finlayson* 1962 12s 6d
An extravaganza with characteristic reflections on things as they were and things as they ought to be.

Childers, Erskine (1870–1922) THE RIDDLE OF THE SANDS (1903)
Hart-Davis (*Mariners' Library*) 1955 10s 6d; *Penguin Books* 1952 2s 6d
Before the 1914 war this tale of German plans for the invasion of England, the discovery of a secret naval base by two Englishmen, and their subsequent adventures, had a sensational success, and it still attracts readers as one of the best books of its kind in twentieth-century fiction.

Clarke, Marcus (1846–81) FOR THE TERM OF HIS NATURAL LIFE (1874)
Collins (*Classics*) 1953 6s; O.U.P. (*Worlds Classics*) 1952 8s 6d
Classic Australian novel about early convict settlements. The author's style is realistic, and his characters are drawn with great power.

Cobbold, Richard (1797-1877) THE HISTORY OF MARGARET CATCH-
POLE (1845) *O.U.P. (Worlds Classics)* 1907
Based on the true story of a Suffolk girl who was imprisoned for a petty
offence at the end of the eighteenth century. Later, she was transported,
married a settler, and died in Sydney.

*Collins, William Wilkie (1824-89) THE MOONSTONE (1868)
Collins (Classics) 1953 6s; *Dent (Everyman)* (1944) 1957 10s 6d;
Nelson (Classics) 1954 6s; *O.U.P. (Worlds Classics)* (1928) 1957
7s 6d; *Penguin Books* 1956 3s 6d
'The classic forerunner of modern detective fiction.' Dorothy L. Sayers
thus described this ingeniously constructed story about the disappearance
in an English country house of a precious stone called the Moonstone.
Sergeant Cuff is the first of his kind in English fiction. The *Worlds Classics*
edition has an introduction by T. S. Eliot; *Everyman* one by Dorothy
Sayers.

THE WOMAN IN WHITE (1864) *Collins (Classics)* 1954 7s; *Dent
(Everyman)* (1910) 1955 10s 6d; *Nelson (Classics)* 1954 7s
The story, and the mystery surrounding the woman in white, are unfolded in masterly style, through the personal narratives of the principal
characters, which include the immortal Count Fosco. The novel has been
a popular thriller for a century.

Conrad, Joseph (1857-1924) ALMAYER'S FOLLY (1895) *Collins
(Classics)* 1955 7s; *Dent* 1948 11s 6d; *Nelson (Classics)* 1957 6s
'A story of an Eastern river'; bound in Collins's edition with the sequel,
An Outcast of the Islands; in Dent's Collected Edition, with *Tales of
Unrest*; and in Nelson's edition with *Last Essays*. These are varied in
subject; some geographical, others, such as the essay on Stephen Crane,
on authors and books.

THE ARROW OF GOLD (1919) *Dent* 1947 11s 6d; *Nelson (Classics)*
1959 6s
A romance of love and political plotting concerned with the Carlist
conspiracy for the Spanish throne in the 1870's.

*CHANCE (1913) *Dent* 1949 11s 6d; *Methuen* 1956 8s 6d
This ingenious love story presents the characters and events in a subtly
oblique style of narration. It was one of Conrad's great popular successes.

*FOUR TALES *O.U.P. (Worlds Classics)* 1950 7s 6d
Sir David Bone introduces a choice of four of Conrad's characteristic
tales: *The Nigger of the Narcissus*; *Youth*; *The Secret Sharer* (1910); and,
Freya of the Seven Seas (1912).

*LORD JIM *Blackwood* 1900 6s; *Collins (Classics)* 1957 6s; *Dent*
1946 10s 6d; *Dent (Everyman)* (1946) 1957 11s 6d; *Nelson
(Classics)* 1955 6s; *Penguin* 1961 3s 6d
Conrad's masterpiece. It is the tale of a young naval officer who is
cashiered, and who then strives to regain his lost self-respect. The scene
is set in the East Indies.

*THE NIGGER OF THE NARCISSUS (1897) *Dent* 1951 11s 6d; *Dent (Everyman)* (1945) 1956 8s 6d; *Nelson (Classics)* 1958 6s; *O.U.P. (Worlds Classics)* 1962 7s 6d
A very popular and enduring 'tale of the forecastle', bound in all editions with other works, notably in Nelson's edition, with *A Mirror of the Sea* (1913), a book of 'memories and impressions', and 'a very intimate revelation'; and in *Worlds Classics* with other tales and an introduction by Sir David Bone.

*NOSTROMO (1904) *Dent* 1947 11s 6d; *Dent (Everyman)* 1957 10s 6d
'A tale of the seaboard', and Conrad's most sustained and difficult romance. It concerns an imaginary South American republic (Costaguana), and the political intrigue associated by tradition with such countries. The theme, linked with one about buried treasure, is developed with such power and significance that the novel reaches great heights of imaginative fiction. Lord David Cecil wrote of it: 'It is a wonderful achievement: grander, if not more perfect, than anything in twentieth century fiction.' In his introduction to the *Everyman* edition, Richard Curle, a close friend of Conrad, states that the novelist regarded this book as his greatest achievement.

*AN OUTCAST OF THE ISLANDS (1896) *Collins (Classics)* 1955 7s; *Dent* 1949 11s 6d; *Nelson (Classics)* 1956 6s
Sequel to *Almayer's Folly*, which see above, and with which it is bound in Collins's edition. The tale, one of a mixed marriage that brings suffering and anguish, is set in Borneo: 'Certainly,' said Conrad, 'the most tropical of my Eastern tales.'

THE RESCUE (1920) *Dent* 1949 11s 6d
A tale of the South Seas.

ROMANCE (1903) *Dent* 1949 11s 6d
Written in collaboration with Ford Madox Ford.

THE ROVER (1923) *Benn* 1956 8s 6d; *Dent* 1948 11s 6d; *Nelson (Classics)* 1955 6s
Study of a brooding French sea captain in the time of Nelson's blockading of French ports.

*THE SECRET AGENT (1907) *Dent* 1948 11s 6d; *Dent (Everyman)* 1961 10s 6d; *Methuen* 1948 10s 6d; *Nelson (Classics)* 1955 6s
'A Simple Tale'; a melodrama; told with powerful insight into character and with skilful suspense. It concerns a sinister attempt to blow up a famous London building.

*A SET OF SIX (1908) *Dent* 1951 11s 6d; *Methuen* 1948 6s
Cleverly contrasted in moods, each one specifically designated. *Gasper Ruiz*; *The Informer*; *The Brute*; *The Duel*; *The Anarchist*; and, *Il Conde*.

*THE SHADOW LINE (1917) *Dent* 1951 11s 6d; *Dent (Everyman)* (1945) 1956 8s 6d

'A confession': a strange story of a haunted ship in Far Eastern seas, where she has mysterious difficulty in passing latitude 8° 20'. The little masterpiece was likened when it first enthralled readers, to a prose *Ancient Mariner.*

SUSPENSE (1925) *Dent* 1951 11s 6d; *Nelson* (*Classics*) 1958 6s
A posthumous, unfinished novel about Napoleonic times. In the Nelson edition it is printed with *Tales of Hearsay.*

TALES OF HEARSAY *Dent* (1924) 1955—With *Last Essays* 11s 6d
Four short stories, all that Conrad left of a volume of stories to be entitled *Tales of Hearsay,* and hence printed with other work of last years. One of the tales is about the author's native country of Poland.

*TALES OF UNREST (1898) *Dent* 1948—With *Almayer's Folly* 11s 6d; *Nelson* (*Classics*) 1957—With *Typhoon* 7s
Five great short stories, one, *The Idiots,* an outstanding piece of work in realism; and another, *An Outpost of Progress,* a masterpiece of its kind.

*'TWIXT LAND AND SEA (1912) *Collins* (*Classics*) 1955—With *The Nigger of the Narcissus,* and *Typhoon* 7s; *Dent* 1948 11s 6d
Three long-short stories of the Far East.

*TYPHOON AND OTHER STORIES (1903) *Dent* 1951 11s 6d; *Dent* (*Everyman*) (1945) 1956 8s 6d
Four long-short stories. *Typhoon,* as noted above, is often bound with other stories, as it is one of Conrad's greatest tales, containing the finest description of a storm at sea in English fiction. The other tales are *Falk*; *Amy Foster*; and, *To-Morrow.*

UNDER WESTERN EYES (1911) *Dent* 1947 11s 6d; *Methuen* 1949 6s; *Nelson* (*Classics*) 1956 6s
Subtle analysis of Russian political conspirators.

*VICTORY (1915) *Dent* 1948 11s 6d; (*Everyman*) 1962 10s 6d; *Methuen* 1957 10s 6d; *O.U.P.* (*Worlds Classics*) 1957 8s 6d
'An island tale,' with an interesting preface by the author on chance glimpses of people who inspired his romance of love and evil.

*WITHIN THE TIDES (1915) *Dent* 1951—With *The Shadow Line* 1951 10s 6d
The Planter of Malaya and three shorter tales.

*YOUTH: A NARRATIVE (1902) *Dent* 1946 11s 6d; *Nelson* (*Classics*) 1955 6s; *O.U.P.* (*Worlds Classics*)—With *The Nigger of the Narcissus* 1962 7s 6d
A masterpiece, and one of the most read of all Conrad's stories, published with two other tales, both of high quality: *The Heart of Darkness*; and, *The End of the Tether. Youth* is a sustained narrative of a man's unceasing struggle with the sea. In the above list of this great twentieth-century writer the volumes published by Dent, 11s 6d each, are all in the uniform, standard collected edition. There is also a centenary selection in the *Mariners Library, Sea Stories,* Hart-Davis, 1957, 10s 6d. This brings four masterpieces together: *The Nigger of the Narcissus*; *Youth*; *Typhoon*;

and, *The Secret Sharer*. The last is considered by some readers to be the best short story he wrote. It is included, with *Freya of the Seven Isles*, and *Youth*, in the *Worlds Classics* edition of *The Nigger of the Narcissus*, for which see above.

Cooper, James Fenimore (1789-1851) *THE DEERSLAYER (1841) *W. H. Allen (Dolphin Books)* 10s
The first in the series of 'Leatherstocking' novels about Red Indians and the early settlers' struggles to subdue them.

*THE LAST OF THE MOHICANS (1826) *Collins (Classics)* 1954 5s; *Dent (Everyman)* (1906) 1957 10s 6d; *Nelson (Classics)* 1955 6s
'A narrative of 1757,' and the most popular of all the 'Leatherstocking' novels. It is the sequel to *The Deerslayer*.

*THE PATHFINDER (1840) *Nelson (Classics)* 1955 7s
'Or, The Inland Sea'; Sequel to the above, and next in popularity to it.

THE PRAIRIE (1827) *W. H. Allen (Dolphin Books)* 1962 10s; *Dent (Everyman)* 1907 6s 6d
The fifth and last of the series. No edition of the fourth novel, *The Pioneers* (1823), is in print at present (1962).

Coppard, Alfred Edgar (1878-1957) THE BLACK DOG *Cape* 1924 9s 6d

*SELECTED TALES *Cape* 1946 9s 6d
Coppard remained faithful to the form of the short story all his life, and produced some masterpieces, such as *The Higgler*, to be found in the selection.

Craik, Mrs. (Diana Maria Mulock) (1826-87) JOHN HALIFAX, GENTLEMAN (1857) *Collins (Classics)* 1954 6s; *Dent (Everyman)* (1906) 1961 12s 6d; *Nelson (Classics)* 1955 6s
The favourite story of the popular nineteenth-century type, in which orphan boy, underprivileged, but hard-working, capable, and honest, rises to success and a happy marriage with Ursula, the heroine. A simple tale, but the idealism and didactic tone are not allowed to overburden the characters.

Crane, Stephen (1871-1900) *THE RED BADGE OF COURAGE (1895) *O.U.P. (Worlds Classics)* 1960 8s 6d
In addition to the title story, the new edition includes six other stories, one of which, *Maggie: a Girl of the Streets* (1893) was an early example of American realism in fiction. The title story was Crane's greatest work, and is probably the best psychological analysis of a soldier's mental conflict under fire in a prolonged battle, in English fictional writing. The volume has an introduction by V. S. Pritchett.

STEPHEN CRANE OMNIBUS ed. by R. Wooster Stallman *Heinemann* 1954 21s
Contains extracts from longer works, some poems, and *The Red Badge of Courage*.

Crockett, Samuel Rutherford (1860–1914) THE RAIDERS (1894)
Collins (Classics) 1954 7s
A tale of the Scottish border fighting and smuggling, at the beginning of
the eighteenth century. In this edition it is bound with *The Lilac Sun-
bonnet*, a sentimental story of Galloway folk.

THE STICKIT MINISTER AND SOME COMMON MEN (1893) *Benn* 1929
A typical example of the sentimental 'Kailyard' school of Scottish fiction:
hence it has some literary importance for students.

Dawson, A. J. (1872–1951) FINN THE WOLFHOUND (*Richards*, 1908)
Brockhampton Press 1962 15s
A dog story, challenging comparison with animal stories by Jack London
and Rudyard Kipling. 'This must surely be one of the best, and most
sensitively-written animal stories in the English language,' wrote Henry
Treece, when the new, abridged edition was published.

de la Mare, Walter (1873–1956) *BEST STORIES *Faber* (1942) 1957
15s
Sixteen short stories selected from four volumes: *The Riddle* (1923);
The Connoisseur (1926); *On the Edge* (1930); and, *The Wind Blows Over*
(1936).
'The best . . .' wrote de la Mare, 'merely implies a personal preference.'
MEMOIRS OF A MIDGET *Faber* (1921) 1945 12s 6d
The world seen through the eyes and mind of a diminutive woman. Her
story is told with such delicate sensitivity that fantasy becomes reality;
the normal is minified for the reader so acutely that detail is presented
with the significance of a Japanese print.
SOME STORIES *Faber (Paperbacks)* 1962 6s
A selection of eight stories.

De Morgan, William (1839–1917) ALICE-FOR-SHORT *Heinemann*
1907
A long Victorian novel written out of period.

JOSEPH VANCE *Heinemann* (1906) O.U.P. (*Worlds Classics*) 1954
9s 6d
'An ill-written autobiography,' of Dickensian amplitude and realism.
In the reprint, A. C. Ward introduces to a new generation De Morgan's
first novel, and his masterpiece, published when he was sixty-seven.
Joseph's career from poverty to middle-class security is related episodic-
ally, supported by a great gallery of portraits of family, friends, relations
and acquaintances.

Defoe, Daniel (1661?–1731) CAPTAIN SINGLETON (1720) *Dent
(Everyman)* (1906) 1962 12s 6d; *Methuen (Venture Library)* 1960
5s
Picaresque novel displaying Defoe's astonishing gift for the presentation
of imaginary episodes as actual happenings. The narrative concerns the
progression of a kidnapped child to a career of piracy. Full title *The Life,
Adventures and Piracies of the Famous Captain Singleton*.

*A JOURNAL OF THE PLAGUE YEAR (1722) *Dent (Everyman)* (1908) 1953 6s 6d; *Nelson (Classics)* 1936

The Nelson reprint is slightly abridged. This extraordinary reconstruction of events from September 1664 to the end of 1665, written as if Defoe had experienced them himself, although this was impossible as he was only four years of age at the time, was accepted for long as a true, eyewitness account of the Great Plague of London. It may still be read as such, so vividly and accurately are the details set before the reader in Defoe's matter-of-fact, homely style.

MEMOIRS OF A CAVALIER (1724) *Dent (Everyman)* 1908

Historical romance of the time of Charles I and Gustavus Adolphus. Sub-titled 'A Military Journal'.

*MOLL FLANDERS (1721-2) *Chatto (Zodiac Press)* 1962 15s; *Dent (Everyman)* 1955 6s 6d; *O.U.P. (Worlds Classics)* 1961 7s 6d

The Fortunes and Misfortunes of the Famous Moll Flanders. The *Worlds Classics* reprints the first edition text established for a limited edition published by Constable in 1923. The introduction by Bonamy Dobrée is supplemented by a note on the text pointing out that the so-called 'corrected third edition' of 1722 was probably not the result of Defoe's own correction, although it is the text usually reprinted. Professor Dobrée discusses the astonishing realism of this picaresque novel, declaring 'it can be claimed that it is the fountain-head of the vast flood of what we have come to call "novels". There had been nothing like it before.'

*ROBINSON CRUSOE (1719) *Collins (Classics)* 6s 6d; *Dent (Everyman)* (1906) 1956 7s 6d; *Nelson (Classics)* 1954 6s; *O.U.P. (Worlds Classics)* (1902) 1960 6s

Both *Collins* and the *Everyman* editions include the sequel, Part Two, of this most popular of all classic novels of adventure. The 'Further Adventures' take Robinson Crusoe to China and Russia. The *Everyman* edition gives the complete, unabridged text from the original edition, with a glossary of unfamiliar and obsolete words and phrases.

ROXANA, THE FORTUNATE MISTRESS (1724) *Constable* (1929) *Elek (Bestseller Library)* 1960 3s 6d (paperback)

Here once again, Defoe presented a picaresque romance in the first person. It is the story of a kept woman who achieves success and acquires considerable money. More to blame than Moll Flanders, she is eventually overtaken by misfortune. Sometimes entitled *The Fortunate Mistress; or, Roxana.*

Deloney, Thomas (1543-1600?) THE NOVELS OF THOMAS DELONEY ed. by Merritt E. Lawlis *Indiana Univ Pr.*, *O.U.P.* 1961 100s 492 pp

A handsome edition for scholars and libraries of the original texts, fully annotated, with an editorial introduction of thirty-two pages.

WORKS ed. by F. O. Mann *O.U.P. (Oxford English Texts)* 1912 30s

A standard collection of 644 pages. The 'novels' written by this silk-weaver from Norwich, who became a prolific writer of ballads, are of interest because they were craftsmen's novels, all written from 1596 onwards. The two most famous are *Jack of Newberie* (1597), on the weaver's art; and *Thomas of Reading* (1612), on the clothier's craft. Both of these are in *Shorter Novels* edited by Saintsbury and Henderson, for which see next section. A third in the series, called *The Gentle Craft* (1598), on the shoemaker's craft, may have furnished material for Dekker's popular play, *The Shoemakers Holiday*; or, *The Gentle Craft*.

*Dickens, Charles (1812–70)

BARNABY RUDGE (1841)
CHRISTMAS BOOKS (1843–8)
DAVID COPPERFIELD (1849–50)
EDWIN DROOD (1870)
HARD TIMES (1854)
MARTIN CHUZZLEWIT (1843–4)
NICHOLAS NICKLEBY (1838–9)
THE OLD CURIOSITY SHOP (1841)
OUR MUTUAL FRIEND (1864–5)
REPRINTED PIECES (1835–6)
A TALE OF TWO CITIES (1859)

BLEAK HOUSE (1852–3)
CHRISTMAS STORIES (1850–67)
DOMBEY AND SON (1846–8)
GREAT EXPECTATIONS (1861)
LITTLE DORRIT (1857)
MASTER HUMPHREY'S CLOCK (1840–1)
OLIVER TWIST (1838)
THE PICKWICK PAPERS (1836–7)
SKETCHES BY BOZ (1835–6)
THE UNCOMMERCIAL TRAVELLER (1860–6)

Standard editions of the complete fictional works of Dickens are now available in two new sets: *The New Oxford Illustrated Dickens*, in twenty-one volumes, 17s 6d each (with a few at 15s); the complete set cloth bound £15 15s; separate volumes bound in leather from 30s each. This set is notable for its introductions by Dickensian scholars, and for the illustrations taken from contemporary sources, re-made specially for this edition.

The other post-war set is a reprint of Macmillan's standard *Illustrated Dickens* in sixteen volumes, 15s each. Macdonald's *Illustrated Classics* contains in ten volumes the most popular stories, 15s each. The majority of Dickens's novels and stories are also included in the four series of classics: *Collins*—sixteen volumes (5s to 8s each according to length, and a *Blue Canterbury* set, in slipcase, 6½ guineas, or a set bound in full leather, with slipcase, £10); *Everyman*—twenty volumes (6s 6d to 12s 6d each) each with an introduction by G. K. Chesterton; *Nelson*—fifteen volumes (5s to 8s 6d), and *Worlds Classics*—four novels only, 6s each. The *Collins* edition of *Edwin Drood* has an introduction by Cecil Day Lewis, with a possible solution by the American critic Edmund Wilson. The minor non-fiction works will be found in *Everyman*, including *A Child's History of England* (1854). In the Oxford set this is bound with *Master Humphrey's Clock*. The story for children, *The Magic Fish-bone*, will be found in Dent's *Children's Illustrated Classics*, bound with Thackeray's *The Rose and the Ring*.

*Douglas, George (i.e. George Douglas Brown) (1869–1902) THE HOUSE WITH THE GREEN SHUTTERS (1901) *Nelson* (*Classics*) (1929) 1958 7s

A powerful study of small-town characters in Scotland. This minor classic is a contrast to the 'Kailyard' school of fiction, for an example of which, see Crockett above.

Douglas, Norman (1868-1952) SOUTH WIND *Martin Secker* (1917) *Secker and Warburg* 1946 18s
The new edition corrects a number of misprints, and is divided into the fifty chapters as originally planned by the author. It is a novel of a vanished world of wit, allusive conversation, leisure and indiscreet diversion on the island of 'Nepenthe' near Sicily (possibly Capri), told in a style to appeal to devotees of Peacock. For Professor Saintsbury, who had read thousands of novels, *South Wind* was one of the two novels of 'this so-called age' which he felt he could recommend to a friend.

*Doyle, Sir Arthur Conan (1859-1930) THE COMPLETE NAPOLEONIC STORIES *Murray* 1956 20s 672 pp
Collects in one volume *The Exploits of Brigadier Gerard* (1896); *Uncle Bernac* (1902); *The Adventures of Gerard* (1903); and, *The Great Shadow* (1912).

THE COMPLETE PROFESSOR CHALLENGER STORIES *Murray* 1952 18s 577 pp
An omnibus collection of three examples of imaginative 'science fiction': *The Lost World* (1912); *The Poison Belt* (1913); and, *The Land of Mist* (1926), together with two shorter tales, *The Disintegration Machine*, and, *When the World Screamed*. See also the last entry, below.

THE CONAN DOYLE STORIES *Murray* 1929 20s 1202 pp
Collection of six volumes of stories of adventure, terror, mystery, medical life, boxing, and the supernatural.

HISTORICAL ROMANCES 2 volumes *Murray* 1931-2 20s each 1644 pp; 820 pp
Volume 1: *The White Company* (1890); *Sir Nigel* (1906); *Micah Clark* (1888); and, *The Refugees* (1893). Volume 2: *Rodney Stone* (1896); *Uncle Bernac* (1902); *The Adventures of Gerard* (1903); and, *The Exploits of Brigadier Gerard* (1896).

SHERLOCK HOLMES: LONG STORIES *Murray* 1929 20s 640 pp
Collects four novels: *A Study In Scarlet* (1887); *The Sign of Four* (1890); *The Hound of the Baskervilles* (1902); and, *The Valley of Fear* (1915).

SHERLOCK HOLMES: SHORT STORIES *Murray* 1938 20s 1336 pp
Comprising *The Adventures of Sherlock Holmes* (1892); *The Memoirs of Sherlock Holmes* (1894); *The Return of Sherlock Holmes* (1905); *His Last Bow* (1917); and, *The Case-Book of Sherlock Holmes* (1927).

SHERLOCK HOLMES ed. by S. C. Roberts *O.U.P.* (*Worlds Classics*) 1951 7s 6d 460 pp
A selection of perennial favourites, with an introduction. Chosen from the preceding omnibus of short stories.

THE LOST WORLD and THE POISON BELT *Eyre and Spottiswoode* 1958 7s 6d

These two Professor Challenger stories are here bound together, with an introduction by John Dickson Carr, who discusses the astonishing realism of the 'science fiction' of this great storyteller. *The Lost World* and several of the Sherlock Holmes books are also available from time to time in John Murray's Paperback series, 2s 6d to 3s 6d each.

Du Maurier, George (1834–96) PETER IBBETSON (1891) *Cape* 1931
A novel of sentiment and the supernatural. Thought by some readers to be superior in merit to *Trilby*.

TRILBY (1894) *Collins (Classics)* (1927) 1953 5s; *Dent (Everyman)* (1931) 1956 6s 6d Illustrated by the author; *W. H. Allen (Anchor Books)* 1962 7s 6d; *Unicorn Press* 1954 12s 6d
A very popular novel about a Paris artist's model who is enabled to acquire a beautiful singing voice under the mesmeric influence of Svengali. Her tragedy is told poignantly, for without his will and control she is unable to sing; and in the end, even unable to live.

Eden, Emily (1797–1869) THE SEMI-DETACHED HOUSE (1859) ed. by Anthony Eden *Nicholson and Watson* 1928

THE SEMI-ATTACHED COUPLE (1860) ed. by John Gore *Nicholson and Watson* 1927
The author was sister of a Governor-General of India (1835–41). She accompanied him to India when he took up his duties there. These two charming novels are comedies of manners enjoyed by those who like Jane Austen's stories. An illustrated edition of the second was published in 1955 by the Folio Society, 18s 6d. This can only be obtained through the society.

Edgeworth, Maria (1767–1849) CASTLE RACKRENT (1800) *Dent (Everyman)* (1910) 1960 10s 6d; *Nelson (Classics)* 1953 6s
Lively story of spendthrift, hard-living Irish landlords, related by a servant of a typical Irish family. In *Everyman* it is bound with *The Absentee* (1812), one of a series of 'Tales of Fashionable Life' concerned with the career of an extravagant Irish landlord, who neglects his estate by living a fashionable life in London to please a foolish, self-willed wife. In *Nelson Classics* edition *Castle Rackrent* also includes two shorter stories, *Emilie de Coulanges*, and, *The Birthday Present*.

Eliot, George (Mary Ann Evans) (1819–80) *ADAM BEDE (1859) *Chatto (Zodiac Press)* 1952 15s; *Collins (Classics)* 1953 6s; *Dent (Everyman)* (1906) 1960 10s 6d; *Nelson (Classics)* 1954 6s
The story of a village carpenter, and of his love for Hetty Sorrell, who is led astray by a man of social standing, but of little integrity.

DANIEL DERONDA (1876) *Collins (Classics)* 1923; intro. by F. R. Leavis *Hamish Hamilton (Harper Torchbooks)* 1961 16s
George Eliot's last, and least popular novel. It has been praised for the firmness of characterisation in the contrasting portraits of Daniel Deronda, a dignified, idealistic Jew; Klesmer, a Jewish musician; and of Mrs. Grandcourt, the tragic heroine whose unhappy marriage mars her life.

FELIX HOLT, THE RADICAL *Blackwood* (1866) 7s 6d and 5s
A didactic novel concerned with industrial and social problems following the Reform Bill of 1832.

*MIDDLEMARCH (1871) *Chatto (Zodiac Press)* 1950 15s; 2 vols. *Dent (Everyman)* (1930) 1962 8s 6d each; *O.U.P. (Worlds Classics)* 1947 10s 6d
'A study of provincial life.' It is one of the greatest novels in European literature, and George Eliot's masterpiece. Middlemarch is a small town in the Midlands, peopled by the writer with families and conflicting characters that are famous in fiction. It is an example of the novel of intellectual discussion rare in nineteenth-century English fiction.

*THE MILL ON THE FLOSS (1860) *Chatto (Zodiac Press)* 1951 15s; *Collins (Classics)* 1930 6s; *Dent (Everyman)* (1908) 1956 8s 6d; *Nelson (Classics)* 1930 6s; *O.U.P. (Worlds Classics)* 1929 7s 6d
The tragic story of Maggie Tulliver and of her brother Tom. It is George Eliot's most popular novel, preferred by many to *Middlemarch*.

ROMOLA (1863) *Dent (Everyman)* (1907) 1956 10s 6d; *O.U.P. (Worlds Classics)* 1957 8s 6d
An historical novel with Savonarola in the background, playing a subsidiary part with Machiavelli. The main story deals with Romola and Tito Melema, and with Florentine events at the end of the fifteenth century.

SCENES OF CLERICAL LIFE *Blackwood* (1858) 1923 4s; *Nelson (Classics)* 1923 6s
Three long stories: *The Sad Fortunes of the Rev. Amos Barton*; *Mr. Gilfil's Love Story*; and, *Janet's Repentance*.

*SILAS MARNER (1861) *Chatto (Zodiac Press)* 1954 12s 6d; *Collins (Classics)*—with Poems 1954 5s; *Dent (Everyman)* (1906) 1958 7s 6d; *Nelson (Classics)* 1955 5s; *O.U.P. (Worlds Classics)* (1906) 1957 7s 6d
The story of 'The Weaver of Raveloe', and of provincial life, depicted with humour and realism. This dramatic masterpiece is bound in both Collins' edition and in *Worlds Classics* with *The Lifted Veil* (1859) and *Brother Jacob* (1860).

Falkner, John Meade (1858-1932) *MOONFLEET *Edward Arnold* (1898) 1955 10s 6d Illustrated, and 7s 6d; *Penguin Books* 1962 3s 6d
A minor classic of adventure, concerned with smuggling in Dorset, 1757. Enjoyed by readers of all ages, from youth upwards, it has been reprinted throughout the century.

THE NEBULY COAT (1903) and THE LOST STRADIVARIUS (1895) *O.U.P. (Worlds Classics)* 1954 9s 6d
Introduction and appreciation by G. M. Young. The first novel is in the style of Wilkie Collins's romances, and concerns a family coat-of-arms,

a shaky claim to estate, and allied themes. The second is a tale of the supernatural concerned with the spell exercised by an old violin.

Ferrier, Susan Edmonstoune (1782-1854) THE INHERITANCE (1824) 2 vols. *Dent* 1894
Romance of an heiress and of her love for a worthless fortune hunter. Miss Pratt has a place as a minor character in the English gallery of gossiping, garrulous women.

MARRIAGE (1818) *Nelson* (*Classics*) 1953 7s
Much admired by Sir Walter Scott. This is a story that displays Miss Ferrier's gift for social satire, and for the creation of eventful plots.

*****Fielding, Henry** (1707-54) AMELIA (1751) 2 vols. *Dent* (*Everyman*) (1930) 1959 10s 6d each
Fielding's last novel begins where many novels end: with the marriage of hero and heroine. The character of Amelia is drawn with tenderness and charm. She remains loyal to her wayward husband, whose misfortunes and debts provided Fielding with themes that enabled him to expose faults and injustices in the law and the prison conditions of his time. *Amelia* is not so popular as Fielding's other novels, but it is a major and lovable work.

JONATHAN WILD (1743) *Dent* (*Everyman*) (1932) 1958 8s 6d; *O.U.P.* (*Worlds Classics*) 1932 7s 6d
The mock biography of a rogue and a robber, 'Jonathan Wild, The Great' from youth to death on the gallows. In this satirical, picaresque novel, Fielding protests against the glorification of wicked men, and the popular misuse of the epithet 'great'. In the *Everyman* edition the novel is bound with *The Journal of a Voyage to Lisbon*, for which see under *Travel* section.

JOSEPH ANDREWS (1742) *Dent* (*Everyman*) (1910) 1961 7s 6d; *O.U.P.* (*Worlds Classics*) (1929) 1952 6s
A masterpiece of comedy, in which Fielding reverses satirically the situation in Richardson's *Pamela*, for here it is Jonathan's virtue that is in danger. Lady Booby's amorous pursuit of her manservant frightens him into flight. Parson Adams dominates the story, emerging as one of the greatest characters in English fiction.

TOM JONES (1749) *Collins* (*Classics*) 1956 8s; 2 vols. *Dent* (*Everyman*) (1909) 1960 7s 6d each; *Macdonald* (*Illustrated Classics*) 1953 15s
One of the greatest and most popular novels in the language. The heroine, Sophia Western, is Fielding's charming and beautiful creation, to be paired with the eponymous hero in the long run, but not until they both have many racy adventures and escapades. Squire Western shares with Parson Adams of the earlier novel (see above) a place at the head of the most famous characters in fiction.

Firbank, Arthur Annesley Ronald (1886-1926) THE COMPLETE RONALD FIRBANK *Duckworth* 1961 42s

E*

In one omnibus volume of 768 pages, here are eight novels, some short stories, and the play *The Princess Zoubaroff*, together with a biographical and critical introduction by Anthony Powell. Firbank's bright, brittle wit, sly, saucy and indiscreetly oblique, seems to have sprung from too slender a talent to fill a large book, but for those who appreciate innuendo and grace of an uncommon kind, there is much pleasure to be sipped by dipping into his work from time to time. The novels and stories were previously published in a uniform edition, 1929-30. They include: *The Artificial Princess* (1920); *Valmouth* (1919); *Concerning the Eccentricities of Cardinal Pirelli* (1926); *Prancing Nigger* (1925); *The Flower Beneath the Foot* (1923); *Caprice* (1919); *Inclinations* (1916); and, *Vainglory* (1915).

Fitzpatrick, Sir James Percy (1862-1931) JOCK OF THE BUSHVELD
Longmans (1907) 1948 30s Illus.
The story of a dog, probably more fact than fiction, at least in those pages concerned with Jock's master, whose adventures in South Africa at the turn of the century have long been enjoyed by readers of all ages. The book is usually available in cheaper school editions.

Ford, Ford Madox (F. M. Hueffer) (1873-1939) THE GOOD SOLDIER
Bodley Head 1915
'A tale of passion'; '. . . the saddest story I have ever heard': thus the opening page sets the tone of this distinguished novel.

LADIES WHOSE BRIGHT EYES *Constable* (1911) 1931
Ingenious romance in which the reader is transferred backwards and forwards from the twentieth to the thirteenth century.

*SOME DO NOT (1924) NO MORE PARADES (1925)

A MAN COULD STAND UP (1926) LAST POST (1928)
4 volumes *Duckworth* 1924-8; *Penguin Books* 1948 2s 6d each
A tetralogy of fiction about the period 1913 to 1919: the break-up of the Edwardian world, and the vacuum that followed the holocaust. Ford's insight, his technical virtuosity, his masterly characterisation, and many unforgettable chapters on the infantryman's war in France, with an epilogue depicting anguished disillusion following the armistice of November, 1918, place this set of novels at the peak of twentieth-century fiction. Tietjens is one of the major characters of the modern novel.

*THE BODLEY HEAD FORD 4 vols. ed. by Graham Greene *Bodley Head* 1962-3 25s each
Vol. 1: *The Good Soldier; Selected Memories; Poems;* Vol. 2: *The Fifth Queen:* trilogy; Vols. 3-4 *Parades End.*
Offers a new generation of readers a choice of some of Ford's best writing. The trilogy consists of three historical novels: *The Fifth Queen* (1906); *Privy Seal* (1907); *The Fifth Queen Crowned* (1908), these being the story from 1540 onwards to death, of Henry VIII's queen, Katherine Howard. *Parades End* reprints the first three parts of the Tietjeni tetralogy.

Galsworthy, John (1867-1933) CARAVAN *Heinemann* 1925 15s
'Omnibus of short stories': that is, assembled tales in 870 pages, published between 1900 and 1925.

THE COUNTRY HOUSE *Heinemann* 1907; *Dent (Everyman)* (1935) 1953 8s 6d
A story of landed gentry of Edwardian England and the last decade of the Victorian era; restrained social satire.

*THE FORSYTE SAGA *Heinemann* 1922 21s; illustrated by Anthony Gross 1950 21s
A trilogy of 821 pages, generally accepted as Galsworthy's best work. The three novels, here reprinted with connecting interludes, are: *The Man of Property* (1906); *In Chancery* (1920); *To Let* (1921).

A MODERN COMEDY *Heinemann* 1929 21s
A sequel omnibus of 736 pages, with two interludes: *The White Monkey* (1924); *The Silver Spoon* (1926); *Swan Song* (1928).

END OF THE CHAPTER *Heinemann* 1935 21s
Completion of the series, comprising the final three novels (859 pages) in: *Maid in Waiting* (1931); *Flowering Wilderness*; *Over the River* (1933).

Galt, John (1779-1839) THE ANNALS OF THE PARISH (1821) *Nelson (Classics)* 1928 6s

THE AYRSHIRE LEGATEES (1821)—with *The Annals of the Parish* *Dent (Everyman)* 1910
'Among his sixty volumes . . . an astonishing output . . . there was one masterpiece, a work fit to make any writer immortal, because it is a simple joy for ever. Neither time nor taste, nor even the union of the English and Scottish Churches will cause to wither the force or charm of *Annals of the Parish*'—'Oliver Edwards', writing in *The Times*, 18 July, 1957. The book thus praised so unreservedly, is the recollection of an old minister of an Ayrshire parish, who looks back on fifty years of work for his flock, presenting in this form some of the most picturesque and characteristic men and women of Scotland in the reign of George III.
Other once popular novels by Galt, notable *The Entail* (1823), *The Provost* (1822), and *The Last of the Lairds* (1826), will be found in a uniform edition in ten volumes, illustrated, and published by Grant of Edinburgh in 1935, 70s the set. This may sometimes be picked up in antiquarian and second-hand booksellers.

Garnett, Richard (1835-1906) THE TWILIGHT OF THE GODS, AND OTHER TALES *Bodley Head* (1888); *Watts (Thinkers Library)* 1949 2s 6d
A volume of studies in irony, inspired by classical legends.

Garnett, Mrs. Robert Singleton (1869-1946) THE INFAMOUS JOHN FRIEND *Duckworth* (1909); *Cape (Travellers Library)* (1927) 1959 18s
Engrossing and skilful study of two sides of a man's nature. Before the era of Quislings, so-called John Friend exemplified the type, by be-

coming a spy for France during the Napoleonic wars. He is ready to betray his country if Napoleon invades England. But in domestic, everyday life, he is a good man.

Garstin, Crosbie (1887-1930) THE OWL'S HOUSE *Bodley Head* (1923) 1956 10s 6d

HIGH NOON *Bodley Head* (1925) 1958 12s 6d

WEST WIND *Bodley Head* (1926) 1958 12s 6d

A Cornish trilogy of adventure concerning smuggling, gypsies, romance and voyaging. The reprint of the first novel has an appreciation by J. H. Williams. Formerly published by Werner Laurie, these three popular novels were also published in one omnibus volume entitled *The Penhales*, Heinemann, 1933, 1002 pages.

Gaskell, Elizabeth Cleghorn (1810-65) COUSIN PHILLIS AND OTHER TALES *Dent (Everyman)* 1912

The other tales include *My Lady Ludlow*; *Half-a-Life-Time Ago*; *Right at Last*; and, *The Sexton's Hero*. These were contributions to magazines during the period 1847 to 1864.

*CRANFORD (1853) *Collins (Classics)* 1953 5s; *Dent (Everyman)* (1906) 1955 7s 6d; *Harrap* 1940 10s 6d Illus.; *Nelson (Classics)* 1954 5s; *O.U.P. (Worlds Classics)* 1916 7s 6d

Charming, amusing sketches of life in Knutsford, originally contributed to *Household Words*, 1851-3. *Worlds Classics* includes *The Cage at Cranford* (1863) and, *The Moorland Cottage* (1850). *Everyman* has an appreciation by Frank Swinnerton.

MARY BARTON (1848) *Dent (Everyman)* (1911) 1961 10s 6d

'A Tale of Manchester Life.' Mrs. Gaskell's first novel. It has a strong plot, characteristic of the novel at that time, and presented the lives and hardships of Manchester's industrial workers 'in the cruel thirties and the hungry forties' so forcibly that it aroused hostile criticism, but also attracted the attention and friendship of Charles Dickens.

*NORTH AND SOUTH (1855) *Dent (Everyman)* (1914) 1962 10s 6d

Here the way of life in London and of Hampshire in southern England is contrasted with that of the industrial North, whither the delightful heroine, Margaret Hale, is sent by a change in circumstances. She falls in love with an employer of hostile labour. This is a major novel.

RUTH (1853) *O.U.P. (Worlds Classics)* 1906

Tragic story of an unmarried mother.

SYLVIA'S LOVERS (1863) *Dent (Everyman)* 1911

A story of the Whitby coast and the North Sea.

*WIVES AND DAUGHTERS (1866) *O.U.P. (Worlds Classics)* 1910

A posthumously published, unfinished novel, now neglected, but so mature, sustained, and rich in characterisation and humour, that distinguished critics have declared it to be Mrs. Gaskell's masterpiece. In addition there is a reprint of a story *Lois the Witch*, taken from *Right At Last* (see above), Methuen, *Venture series*, 1960, 5s.

Gibbs, Sir Philip Hamilton (1877-1962) THE STREET OF ADVENTURE
Hutchinson (1900) 1954
Of all the considerable output by this popular author, critics single this
early novel about journalistic struggles in London's Fleet Street as likely
to continue to be read for its permanent value as an authentic picture of a
hazardous but exciting period.

Gilchrist, Robert Murray (1868-1917) A PEAKLAND FAGGOT *Faber*
1926
Collected short stories. '. . . no record or estimate of the *conte* in English
letters can be complete without study of his contributions thereto, and
one may reasonably hope that this book will challenge attention for
many unknown masterpieces.'—*From the preface by Eden Phillpotts.*

Gissing, George Robert (1857-1903) DEMOS (1886) *Grayson* 1928
'A study of English socialism.' Didactic novel, written with realism and
great sincerity. Of permanent value as a picture of late Victorian, post-
Dickensian working-class life.

*NEW GRUB STREET (1891) O.U.P. (Worlds Classics) (1940) 1958
9s 6d; W. H. Allen (Dolphin Books) 1962 10s
Introduction by G. W. Stonier. It is a novel of the literary life of late
Victorian England, as seen, somewhat pessimistically, by the author,
during his grim years of poverty and struggle.

THE TOWN TRAVELLER (1898) *Methuen* 1956 7s 6d
Good-humoured portraits of the London cockney: the familiar types
include commercial travellers and the inmates of boarding houses, south
of the River Thames, towards the end of the last century.

WILL WARBURTON *Constable* (1905) 1915
'A romance of real life.' It is Gissing's lightest and happiest novel.

Godwin, William (1756-1836) CALEB WILLIAMS; or, *Things As
They Are* (1794) *Routledge* 1904
'The question now afloat in the world respecting *Things As They Are* is
the most interesting that can be presented to the human mind. While
one party pleads for reformation and change, the other extols in the
warmest terms the existing constitution of society.'—Author's original
preface (withdrawn): An avowedly didactic novel, reviewing in striking
fashion, 'the modes of domestic and unrecorded despotism, by which
man becomes the destroyer of man'.

*Goldsmith, Oliver (1728-74) THE VICAR OF WAKEFIELD (1766)
Collins (Classics) 1953 5s; *Dent (Everyman)* (1908) 1956 7s 6d;
Nelson (Classics) 1954 5s; *O.U.P. (Worlds Classics)* (1901) 6s
A much-loved, simple story of Rev. Dr. Primrose, who tells his own
story, relating his undeserved misfortunes, and the progress of his family:
Olivia, Sophia, Deborah, his wife, and Moses, his easily taken-in son.
Other works are included in Collins's edition, notably the play *She
Stoops To Conquer*, and some poems.

Graham, R. B. Cunninghame (1852-1936) RODEO Selected by
A. F. Tschiffely *Heinemann* 1936

Tales and sketches from a number of books by a writer whose life itself
might well have been the creation of an author of genius, and whose
character inspired even the mediocre to dreams of the gallantry of a
former age. A selection by Edward Garnett, of *Thirty Tales and Sketches*,
was published by Duckworth, 1929.

Grahame, Kenneth (1859-1932) THE WIND IN THE WILLOWS (1908)
Methuen 1950 25s Illus. by Arthur Rackham; 21s Illus. in
colour by E. H. Shepard; 15s and 8s 6d Illus. (line-drawings) by
E. H. Shepard

*THE KENNETH GRAHAME BOOK *Methuen* 1953 16s

An omnibus volume of *The Wind In the Willows*, and some short
stories published in separate volumes as *The Golden Age* (1895); and
Dream Days (1898). The last contains the delightful story of *The Reluctant
Dragon*. All of these charming stories and fantasies were written for
children, but they belong to the small, immortal class of nursery
favourites that please and entertain throughout a reading life.

Graves, Richard (1715-1804) THE SPIRITUAL QUIXOTE (1772)
2 vols. *Peter Davies* 1926

The sub-title indicates the informal, episodic style, of this 'Comic
Romance': *Or, The Summer's Ramble of Mr. Geoffry Wildgoose*. The
theme is an account of the hero's efforts to spread the teachings of
Methodism, and the humour and satire arise from his wayside misadventures, largely at the expense of Whitefield and his Methodist
converts.

Grossmith, George (1847-1912) and Weedon (1854-1900) THE
DIARY OF A NOBODY (1894) *Collins* (*Classics*) 1955 6s; *Dent*
(*Everyman*) (1940) 1962 10s 6d

Both reprints have the original illustrations by Weedon Grossmith.
Everyman has an appreciation by Sir John Squire. This diary of Mr.
Pooter, originally contributed to *Punch*, has never been without admirers,
and its satire on Victorian suburban types and middle-class snobbery
must therefore be evergreen for many readers.

Haggard, Sir Henry Rider (1856-1925) *ALLAN QUATERMAIN
(1887) *Collins* (*Classics*) 1955 5s 6d; *Macdonald* 1949 10s 6d;
Nelson (*Classics*) 1957 5s 6d

A sequel to *King Solomon's Mines* (q.v.) below.

AYESHA (1905) *Collins* (*Classics*) 1957 5s 6d; *Macdonald* 1956
10s 6d; *Ward Lock* 1950 6s

'The Return of She.' A sequel to *She* (q.v.) below.

*KING SOLOMON'S MINES (1885) *Cassell* 1952 12s 6d; *Collins*
(*Classics*) 1955 5s 6d; *Macdonald* 1956 10s 6d; *Nelson* (*Classics*)
1956 5s

See *Allan Quatermain*, above, for sequel.

*NADA THE LILY (1892) *Collins (Classics)* 1957 5s 6d; *Macdonald* 1949 10s 6d
A novel of African adventure with a Zulu hero. It is linked with *Allan Quatermain* (q.v.) above.

THE PEOPLE OF THE MIST (1894) *Macdonald* 1951 10s 6d
SHE (1887) *Macdonald* 1948 10s 6d; *Nelson (Classics)* 1957 5s 6d; *Hodder (paperback)* 1961 3s 6d
See *Ayesha*, above, for sequel. This selection of five is from a large number of novels of exciting adventure, chiefly in Africa. Nine other volumes are available in the illustrated uniform edition published by Macdonald.

Hardy, Thomas (1840-1928) A CHANGED MAN and other tales *Macmillan* (1913) 1951 15s
'Minor novels', including *The Waiting Supper*, and *The Romantic Adventures of a Milkmaid*.

DESPERATE REMEDIES *Macmillan* (1871) 1951 15s; 1907 7s 6d

*FAR FROM THE MADDING CROWD *Macmillan* (1874) 1949 15s; 1906 7s 6d; 1962 (*St. Martins Library*) 4s 6d
One of Hardy's major novels, and the first in which he used the term 'Wessex' for the Dorset and surrounding region which he has immortalised. It is the story of Gabriel Oak and of his love for Bathsheba.

A GROUP OF NOBLE DAMES *Macmillan* (1891) 1952 15s; 1907 7s 6d
Ten stories narrating central episodes in the lives of women of the past in Wessex, as if from the lips or notebooks of an old chronicler or local historian.

THE HAND OF ETHELBERTA *Macmillan* (1876) 1951 15s; 1907 7s 6d
'A comedy in chapters': a minor work.

*JUDE THE OBSCURE *Macmillan* (1895) 1949 15s; 1906 7s 6d; 1962 (*St. Martins Library*) 4s
A tragedy of classic stature. Jude, the stonemason, marries unwisely and unhappily; his instinctive love of learning and idealisation of Christminster (Oxford University); his disastrous passion for Sue Bridehead; and ill-luck, all play their part in the final agony.

A LAODICEAN *Macmillan* (1881) 1951 15s
'Or, The Castle of the De Stancys: a story of today.' A minor novel.

LIFE'S LITTLE IRONIES *Macmillan* (1894) 1952 15s; 1907 7s 6d
Characteristic short stories, concluding with *A Few Crusted Characters*.

*THE MAYOR OF CASTERBRIDGE *Macmillan* (1886) 1950 15s; 1906 7s 6d; 1962 (*St. Martins Library*) 4s
One of the greatest of the Wessex novels. At the height of the Mayor's career (Casterbridge being the county town of Dorset, Dorchester), a sinful, selfish deed done in his drunken youth confronts him and ruins him.

A PAIR OF BLUE EYES *Macmillan* (1873) 1952 15s; 1906 7s 6d
An ironic romance, set in Cornwall. A minor work.

*THE RETURN OF THE NATIVE *Macmillan* (1878) 1949 15s; 1906
7s 6d; 1962 (*St. Martins Library*) 4s
The greatest of all of the Wessex novels. Here Egdon Heath (an
imaginative region fusing a number of actual landscapes in Dorset) is a
sombre background to the passionate story of Clym, of his mother, and
of the brilliant Eustacia.

*TESS OF THE D'URBERVILLES *Macmillan* (1891) 1949 15s; 1906
7s 6d; 1962 (*St. Martins Library*) 4s and a special edition,
illustrated with sixteen plates of the Hardy country, 1953, 18s;
Collins (*Classics*) 1958 7s
The classic story of the simple 'pure woman' of the country: her
betrayal, brief happiness, and final, heartbreaking tragedy, when 'the
President of the Immortals' (in Hardy's Aeschylean phrase) 'had ended
his sport with Tess'.

*THE TRUMPET MAJOR *Macmillan* (1880) 1950 15s; 1907 7s 6d
A lovable, amusing comedy, set in the days of the Napoleonic scare in
the south-west, 'founded more largely on testimony—oral and written—
than any other in this series'. It is Hardy's happiest novel, set in the town
of Budmouth (Weymouth) and the surrounding villages.

TWO ON A TOWER *Macmillan* (1882) 1952 15s; 1906 7s 6d
A minor romance of an astronomer who inspires love in a lady of
quality.

*UNDER THE GREENWOOD TREE *Macmillan* (1872) 1949 15s;
1907 7s 6d; 1962 (*St. Martins Library*) 3s; *Collins* (*Classics*)
1958 6s
A pastoral of the rural year through the four seasons. The 'Mellstock'
village choir, village lovers, and the Shakespearean sub-characters,
harmonise to form a perfect bucolic comedy.

THE WELL-BELOVED *Macmillan* (1897) 1952 15s; 1907 7s 6d
'A sketch of a temperament' in search of an ideal. A minor work.

WESSEX TALES *Macmillan* (1888) 1952 15s; 1907 7s 6d
Six short stories: *The Three Strangers*; *The Withered Arm*; *The Melancholy Hussar*; *Interlopers at the Knap*; *Fellow-Townsmen*; and, *The Dis-
tracted Preacher*.

*THE WOODLANDERS *Macmillan* (1887) 1949 15s; 1906 7s 6d;
1962 (*St. Martins Library*) 4s
A great novel, much loved by readers of the Wessex novels. Hardy himself thought it was his best work. It is the romance of two passionate
natures, set in the sombre, green woodlands of Dorset, in which noble
loyalty and unregarded love mingle poignantly to a tragic end, one of the
most moving in the whole of English literature.
Of the editions noted above, the 15s reprints are in the standard library
edition, the editions priced 7s 6d each in a uniform, pocket set were
increased to 8s 6d each in Jan., 1963; *St. Martins Library* is a paperback
series.

FICTION

*Harris, Joel Chandler (1848–1908) THE ESSENTIAL UNCLE REMUS
ed. by George van Santvoord and Archibald C. Coolidge *Cape*
1949 15s
A selection, with illustrations by A. B. Frost, for adult readers, of those
favourites of the nursery, the folk stories of Brer Rabbit, told in negro
idiom and dialect from Georgia, U.S.A., in a series of *Nights With Uncle
Remus* (1883) and succeeding volumes.

Harte, Francis Bret (1836–1902) TALES OF THE WEST *Nelson* (*Classics*)
1957 6s
A selection of the best work of a popular American writer of short
stories and parodies of his contemporaries. His tales of gold-rush days
and mining camps have an authentic background, and in this selection
have been chosen from *M'liss* (1857); *The Luck of Roaring Camp* (1870);
and *The Outcasts of Poker Flat*. The parodies come from a volume called
Condensed Novels (1867), together with some poems.

Harvey, William Fryer (1885–1937) THE BEAST WITH FIVE FINGERS
AND OTHER TALES *Dent* (1928); *Aldine* (*Paperbacks*) 1962 5s
From the volume of *Midnight Tales* (*Dent, 1946*), this selection reprints
the classic short story of the macabre, and nineteen other stories, by a
twentieth-century master in the Le Fanu tradition.

Hawthorne, Nathaniel (1804–64) THE HOUSE OF SEVEN GABLES
(1851) *Dent* (*Everyman*) (1907) 1954 7s 6d
A romance of a New England family and Hawthorne's best work after
his masterpiece.

*THE SCARLET LETTER (1850) *Dent* (*Everyman*) (1906) 1957 7s 6d;
Nelson (*Classics*) 1955 5s
This tragic story of Boston in the puritan age of severity in mid-
eighteenth century is Hawthorne's greatest and most enduring novel.
It is the story of Hester Prynne and her husband Roger Chilling-
worth, who finds his young wife in the pillory when he returns home
from Amsterdam. She has her baby Pearl in her arms, and the scarlet
letter 'A' proclaims her sin to all.

TWICE-TOLD TALES (1837–42) *Dent* (*Everyman*) (1911) 1955 10s 6d
Stories and sketches of New England people, originally contributions in
series, to a periodical: hence the title when collected into a volume. For
standard editions of Hawthorne's evergreen favourites for children:
Tanglewood Tales (1853), and *The Wonder Book* (1852), retold tales of the
Greek myths and legends, refer to Dent's *Children's Illustrated Classics*
series, 10s 6d each volume.

COMPLETE SHORT STORIES *W. H. Allen* 1962 30s 615 pp

Henry, O. (William Sydney Porter) (1862–1910) *THE BEST OF
O. HENRY *Hodder* 1929 21s 1140 pp
The selection of 100 stories was done by 'Sapper', H. C. McNeile.

*MORE O. HENRY *Hodder* 1933 21s 1428 pp
100 more of the master's stories, with an introduction by James Hilton.
These two volumes are the standard collections.

FIFTY-EIGHT SHORT STORIES *Collins* (*Classics*) 1956 6s
Contains all the stories in three volumes: *Heart of the West* (1907); *The Gentle Grafter*; and, *The Voice of the City* (1908).

SIXTY-NINE SHORT STORIES *Collins* (*Classics*) 1954 6s
Contains all the stories from *Cabbages and Kings* (1905); *The Four Million* (1906); and, *The Trimmed Lamp* (1907). Most of these slick, slangy stories of American life and character have a twist at the end, characteristic of O. Henry's magazine technique and humour.

Hewlett, Maurice Henry (1861-1923) THE FOREST LOVERS *Macmillan* (1898) 1951 7s 6d
High romance in the fourteenth century; the forest scenes are set in the New Forest, Hampshire.

THE QUEEN'S QUAIR *Macmillan* 1904
'Or, The Six Years' Tragedy'—of Mary, Queen of Scots.

Hichens, Robert (1864-1950) THE GREEN CARNATION (1894) *Unicorn Press* 1949 8s 6d
A brilliant, epigrammatic novel, satirising Oscar Wilde and the other aesthetes of the nineties in a style worthy of the principal victim.

Hogg, James (1770-1835) THE PRIVATE MEMOIRS AND CONFESSIONS OF A JUSTIFIED SINNER (1824) *Cresset Press* 1947 10s 6d
The series reprint has an introductory essay by André Gide, writing as an admirer of this strange story by Sir Walter Scott's friend, known as 'The Ettrick Shepherd'. Once entitled *The Confessions of a Fanatic*, this is a powerful story of a murderer, driven to commit his crimes by an evil spirit that haunts him.

Holme, Constance (1881-1955) THE LONELY PLOUGH (1914) *O.U.P.* (*Worlds Classics*) (1931) 1962 8s 6d
THE SPLENDID FAIRING (1919) *O.U.P.* (*Worlds Classics*) 1937 7s 6d
A choice of two simply-told, peasant and farming novels, from many others reprinted in series. *The Splendid Fairing*, awarded the *Femina Vie-Heureuse* prize, has a tragic theme, set in a landscape as dark and over-hanging as the moorland background of *Wuthering Heights*. Constance Holmes was a regional novelist, her stories being set in the English Lake District of Westmorland. *The Lonely Plough*, often reprinted, is the story of a landed estate in that Northern region of England.

*Hope, Anthony (Sir Anthony Hope Hawkins) (1863-1933) THE PRISONER OF ZENDA (1894) *Dent* 1949 7s 6d; (*Children's Illustrated Classics*) 1962 12s 6d
RUPERT OF HENTZAU (1898) *Dent* 1949 7s 6d; 1963 15s Illus.

Perennial favourites of high romance and adventure in an imaginary European country, Ruritania. The first, 'the history of three months in the life of an English gentleman' concerns a royal impersonation, the Princess Flavia, Black Michael, and Colonel Sapt, all household names since 1894.

Horniman, Roy (1872-1930) ISRAEL RANK (1907) *Eyre and Spottiswoode* 1948 6s
A neglected masterpiece of Edwardian social comedy, introduced in the reprint, in an appreciation by Hugh Kingsmill.

Hornung, Ernest William (1866-1921) RAFFLES, THE AMATEUR CRACKSMAN (1899) *Collins (Classics)* 1955; *Eyre and Spottiswoode* 1956 7s 6d

A THIEF IN THE NIGHT (1905) *Eyre and Spottiswoode* 1950 7s 6d
Short stories recording the popular, improbable adventures of a 'gentleman' crook, engaged in thefts and burglaries, whilst living in a fashionable flat in the Albany. His passion for cricket endeared him to a wide variety of tolerant readers.

Howard, Edward (?-1841) RATTLIN THE REEFER ed. by Captain Marryat (1836) by Guy N. Pocock *Dent (Everyman)* 1930 6s 6d
Captain Marryat's sub-editor wrote this one story in a style similar to that of his famous chief. Based on his own experiences of life at sea, it was for a time attributed to Marryat.

Howells, William Dean (1837-1920) THE RISE OF SILAS LAPHAM (1884) *O.U.P. (Worlds Classics)* 1948 7s 6d; *W. H. Allen (Dolphin Books)* 1962 7s 6d
An American classic. The novel concerns a family that prospers and rises in the social scale from humble farm to wealthy household in Boston. The girls of the family attempt to enter the highest social circles. It is regarded as the best novel of the many written by Howells, who was at one time American consul at Venice, and who received an honorary doctorate from Oxford University.

Hudson, William Henry (1841-1922) EL OMBÚ *Duckworth* (1922)
'Tales of the pampas.' Time early nineteenth century.

*GREEN MANSIONS *Collins (Classics)* 1957 6s; *Duckworth* 1904 7s 6d; *Dent* 1951 10s 6d
'A romance of the tropical forest' of Venezuela, in which the strange, mystical character of Rima, half human, half bird of the forest, living in communion with birds and beasts, attracts a white man as if by a spell.

*THE PURPLE LAND (1885) *Duckworth* 1904 7s 6d; *Dent* 1951 10s 6d
'The Purple Land That England Lost'; or, 'The Narrative of one of Richard Lamb's adventures in the Banda Oriental, in South America, as told by himself.' Both the stories in Dent's uniform edition of Hudson's works are introduced by Edward Garnett.

Hughes, Thomas (1822-96) *TOM BROWN'S SCHOOLDAYS (1857)
   Collins (Classics) 1953 5s; *Dent (Everyman)* (1906) 1955 6s 6d;
   Macmillan (St. Martins Library) 1962 4s; *Nelson (Classics)* 1955 5s
Life at Rugby during the formative period of Dr. Thomas Arnold's
headship. Also included in Dent's *Children's Illustrated Classics*, 1949,
10s 6d.

TOM BROWN AT OXFORD (1861) *Nelson (Classics)* 1956 7s
The sequel, comparatively little read by young people.

Inchbald, Elizabeth (1753-1821) A SIMPLE STORY (1791) *O.U.P.*
   1908
Early example of the didactic novel with a melodramatic plot. The
author was an actress and wrote minor pieces for the stage.

Jacobs, William Wymark (1863-1943) CAPTAINS ALL *Methuen*
   (1905) 1951 6s
DIALSTONE LANE *Methuen* (1904) 1951 6s
*THE LADY OF THE BARGE *Methuen* (1902) 1951 6s
In this volume is included a famous story of the macabre, *The Monkey's
Paw*.

*MANY CARGOES (1896) *Methuen* 1951 6s
SEA URCHINS (1898) *Methuen* 1951 7s
SEA WHISPERS *Methuen* (1926) 1951 7s
*THE SKIPPER'S WOOING (1897) *Methuen* 1951 7s
The above is a selection of the most popular of eighteen volumes of
humorous, semi-farcical stories about unscrupulous longshoremen and
their boon companions in Wapping and home ports. The narrator is
often 'The Night Watchman', who seldom judges the genial rascals,
and assumes a similar tolerance in his listeners. The stories are still
diverting and continue to be in sufficient demand to be reprinted.

James, Henry (1843-1916) *THE AMBASSADORS (1903) *Dent (Everyman)* 1957 10s 6d
Introduced by Frank Swinnerton in whose opinion it is 'one of the
richest and most sustained performances in modern fiction'. The ambassadors (one of whom is the famous character Lewis Lambert Strether)
are sent from America to 'rescue' Chadwick Newsome from the cultural
and emotional allurements of Europe, and especially of Paris—a theme
that evoked James's finest and most mature art.

THE COMPLETE TALES 12 vols. ed. by Leon Edel *Hart-Davis*
1962—*in progress* 35s each
The standard New York edition of 1907-9 included fifty-nine short
stories and *nouvelles*; but the great undertaking under the editorship of
James's biographer and bibliographer will include everything he wrote
in this form, 112 items in total. Vol. 1 starts with *A Tragedy of Error*,
dating from 1864, and contains eleven tales up to 1868; vol. 2 continues
with *Osborne's Revenge* (1868), containing eight tales up to *Guest's Con-*

fession (1872); vol. 3 contains eight stories from 1873-5; vol. 4: eleven from 1876-82, including *Daisy Miller* and *An International Episode*.

★THE GOLDEN BOWL *Methuen* (1905) 1956 18s

'The Prince had always liked his London, when it had come to him.' So starts one of James's most subtle novels, said by some, to be his greatest. It sets the tone for a long, psychological study of complex characters moving in highly civilised circles.

★IN THE CAGE (1898) *Hart Davis* 1958 21s

Collects eight stories belonging to the richest period of James's life, including *Brooksmith* (1891); *The Jolly Corner*; that masterpiece *The Altar of the Dead* (1895); and *The Figure In the Carpet* (1896).

THE OTHER HOUSE (1896) *Hart-Davis* 1948 10s 6d

'For all its resemblances to Ibsen, *The Other House* stands on its own feet as a distinct Jamesian work.' So writes Leon Edel, discussing the play (originally called *The Promise*) that James wrote from his notes for the novel. It is the nearest approach he made to writing a psychological thriller, with a melodramatic plot and strong characterisation.

★THE PORTRAIT OF A LADY (1881) *O.U.P.* (*Worlds Classics*) (1947) 1957 8s 6d; *Penguin Books* 1963 7s 6d

Graham Greene introduces this new edition of an early masterpiece. Isabel Archer's 'portrait' is a full-length, detailed study of an American girl in England and Europe. She remains loyal to the man she had married, although it proves a most unfortunate choice, until at the end, the barren soulless life she is compelled to lead forces her to irrevocable changes.

THE PRINCESS CASAMASSIMA (1886) 2 vols. *Macmillan* 1948 *Hamish Hamilton* (*Harper Torchbooks*) 1961 14s

This sequel to *Roderick Hudson* is introduced by Lionel Trilling.

THE REVERBERATOR (1888) *Hart-Davis* 1949 10s 6d

A social comedy. The theme is one that recurs in James's work: the clash between vulgarity and highly civilised behaviour.

★RODERICK HUDSON (1875) *Hart-Davis* 1961 25s

James's first great novel. The story is told from the viewpoint of Rowland Mallet, the rich patron of the eponymous artist, who falls tragically in love in Rome with an aloof beauty, later in life, the Princess Casamassima. Her married life is described in the sequel of that name.

THE SACRED FOUNT (1901) *Hart-Davis* 1959 16s

On the popular theme that age may be rejuvenated by 'the sacred fount' of youth.

★SELECTED STORIES ed. by Gerard Hopkins *O.U.P.* (*Worlds Classics*) 1957 9s 6d

Sixteen shorter stories, well chosen to display 'the growing complexity of the author's style'.

★SELECTED TALES *Richards Press* (1947) 1962 18s

Six masterpieces, all long-short stories, selected from Macmillan's New York edition of 1907-9, and including *Daisy Miller* (1878) one of James's

most delightful stories, and perhaps the best introduction to his work;
The Death of the Lion (1894); *The Lesson of the Master* (1892); *The Figure
In the Carpet* (1896); *The Beast In the Jungle* (1903); and *The Turn of the
Screw* (1898).

THE SPOILS OF POYNTON (1897) *Penguin Books* 1963 3s 6d

THE TRAGIC MUSE (1901) *Hart-Davis* 1948; *Hamish Hamilton
(Harper Torchbooks)* 1961 17s 6d
A novel of theatrical art, and in particular of a woman's place in the
world of the theatre. Set in Paris and London.

*THE TURN OF THE SCREW (1898) *Collins (Classics)* 1956 7s;
Dent (Everyman) (1935) 1957 8s 6d; *Penguin Books* 1947 2s 6d
A masterpiece of the macabre, and James's most widely-read story. It
has been dramatised; was used for the libretto of Benjamin Britten's
opera; and has been made into a notable film. The narrator tells the story
of the haunting of two children, little Miles and his sister, by Peter Quint,
a former valet, and Miss Jessel, a governess, both dead before the story
opens. A new governess strives to free her charges from this dreadful
link with the vicious dead. In both of the series reprints, this long story
is coupled with *The Aspern Papers* (1888), set in Venice. This too, has
been successfully adapted for radio drama. Collins *Classics* edition also
includes seven other stories.

WASHINGTON SQUARE (1880) *Penguin Books* 1963 3s 6d

WATCH AND WARD (1878) *Hart-Davis* 1960 16s
Of great interest to students of James's work, for this was his first novel,
written in 1870 for serialisation, and later revised for publication in
book form in 1878. It thus preceded *Roderick Hudson*. Introduced by
Leon Edel.

*THE WINGS OF A DOVE (1902) *Eyre and Spottiswoode* (1948) 1957
7s 6d
Introduced by Sir Herbert Read. It is a subtle study of Milly Theale (the
doomed dove of the title), and of her two, scheming, callous 'friends'.
The above selection includes all of James's fiction readily available in
modern editions.

James, Montague Rhodes (1862-1936) *COLLECTED GHOST STORIES
Edward Arnold (1931) 1961 12s 6d 647 pp
The author was a Provost of Eton College. The collection brings
together the stories in three popular volumes: *Ghost Stories of an
Antiquary* (1905); *More Ghost Stories* (1911); and, *A Warning to the
Curious* (1925). The first two are available separately, Penguin Books,
1937 and 1959, 2s 6d each.

Jefferies, Richard (1848-87) AFTER LONDON (1885) *Dent (Everyman)*
1939 6s 6d
This novel is an imaginative work, of what would now be called
'science fiction', about Wild England, set in a period of the future,
when the countryside has gone back to a primitive state. Forests have

grown in the thoroughfares of what was once the capital city. In the *Everyman* reprint the story is bound with a slighter work, a tender picture of English country family life, *Amaryllis At the Fair* (1886).

*BEVIS, THE STORY OF A BOY (1882) *Cape* 1932 13s 6d Illustrated by E. H. Shepard; *Dent (Everyman)* 1930 6s 6d
Mark and Bevis explore the countryside of Wiltshire, transforming it in their boyish imaginations to what they need for full enjoyment of their spirit of adventure and capacity for wonder. This is a masterpiece that is read in youth, but is enjoyed to the full in maturity.

WOOD MAGIC (1881) *Longmans* 1934
The boy Bevis, younger than he was in the above book, drinks in the magic of the Wiltshire woods and meadows. Even squirrels and mice, in this 'fable', are able to speak to him to unfold their secrets.

*Jerome, Jerome Klapka (1859-1927) THREE MEN IN A BOAT (1889) *Collins (Classics)* 1957 6s Illus.; *Dent (Everyman)* 1957 10s 6d
A perennially popular comedy by a Victorian journalist. Its period style enhances the evergreen humour of this record of misadventures of three friends (to say nothing of the dog), holidaymaking on the River Thames. In the *Everyman* edition it is bound with a sequel *Three Men on the Bummel* (1900), in which semi-farcical exploits on a cycling tour through Germany are recounted in similar style. (*Bummler:* an idler, loafer; hence *Bummel:* a stroll or promenade.)

Jewett, Sara Orne (1849-1909) THE COUNTRY OF THE POINTED FIRS (1896) *Cape* 1927 4s 6d; *W. H. Allen (Anchor Books)* 1962 7s 6d
Willa Cather, the distinguished American novelist, introduced these 'Tales of New England' in Cape's pocket edition.

*Johnson, Samuel (1709-84) RASSELAS (2 vols. 1759) ed. by R. W. Chapman *O.U.P.* 1927; school edition, ed. by G. Birkbeck Hill 1927 7s 6d
See also the Everyman *Shorter Novels*, vol. 3, in next section, under Saintsbury and Henderson. Dr. Johnson's only fictional work, written in a week. It is a moral, didactic tale, of wit and irony, in which the son of the Emperor travels forth with Imlac, an old philosopher, and a sister, in search of a community where man is truly happy. Full original title: *The Prince of Abissinia: a tale.*

Joyce, James (1882-1941) *DUBLINERS (1914) *Cape* 1924 16s Illus. by Robin Jacques
Fifteen short stories, one of which is a masterpiece entitled *The Dead.*

FINNEGANS WAKE *Faber* 1939 42s
The strangest, most original and poetic novel in English. Its 628 pages are difficult to read, being 'anti-novel' in style, and artificial in vocabulary. Yet they convey a vision of Irish life and character, with 'the rivering waters of, hitherandthithering waters of' the *Liffey* ever in the background, ending evocatively, musically, with 'We pass through grass behush the bush to. Whish! A gull. Gulls. Far calls. Coming, far!

End here. Us then. Finn, again! Take. Bussoftlhee, mememormee! Till
thousandsthee. Lps. The keys to. Given! A way a lone a last a loved a
long the . . .' Readers who find this dying fall difficult are referred to
A Skeleton Key to 'Finnegans Wake', by Joseph Campbell and H. M.
Robinson, Faber (1947) 1954, 30s.

★A PORTRAIT OF THE ARTIST AS A YOUNG MAN (1917) *Cape* (1924)
1956 16s Illus. by Robin Jacques
An autobiographical novel revealing in a series of episodic chapters the
character of Stephen Daedalus, from boyhood to student days in Dublin.
See also *Stephen Hero*, below.

STEPHEN HERO *Cape* (1944) ed. by Theodore Spencer 1956 16s
The definitive edition, with additional material, and a foreword by
John J. Slocum and Herbert Cahoon. The novel is part of the first draft
of the work published as *A Portrait of the Artist as a Young Man*, for which
see above.

★ULYSSES (Paris, 1922) *Bodley Head* (1936) 1960 25s
A landmark in twentieth-century world literature. The best book providing the general reader with a critical appreciation of and an explanatory commentary on this extraordinary novel, which is not, however, so
difficult and esoteric in style as *Finnegans Wake*, is Stuart Gilbert's *James
Joyce's 'Ulysses': A Study*, Faber (1930) 1952, 30s. The 1936 edition of the
novel, in handsome quarto, limited to 1,000 copies, includes appendices
of documents in the cases heard in New York in 1928 and 1933, with
Judge M. Woolsey's famous decision: '*Ulysses* may, therefore, be
admitted into the United States' of which Morris L. Ernst, Counsel for
the Defence, rightly remarked: 'It would be difficult to overestimate the
importance of Judge Woolsey's decision.'

Kingsley, Charles (1819–75) ALTON LOCKE, TAILOR AND POET
(1850) *Dent (Everyman)* 1910
The tragedy of an idealist and a Chartist, whose struggles for the sweated,
underpriviliged working classes, land him in prison. Before death, he
finds in Christian Socialism the answer to some of his problems. The
story is told in autobiographical form.

★HEREWARD THE WAKE (1866) *Collins (Classics)* 1955 6s; *Dent
(Everyman)* (1908) 1961 12s 6d; *Nelson (Classics)* 1955 6s
Imaginative reconstruction of the fighting life of 'The Last of the English'
in the eleventh century; his outlawry; and his refusal to accept Norman
rule after the Conquest.

THE HEROES (1856) *Macmillan* (1928) 1954 12s 6d; *Nelson
(Classics)* 1925 5s; *Dent* 1963 15s. Illus.
'Greek fairy tales for my children.' The Macmillan edition is a quarto,
illustrated by H. M. Brock.

HYPATIA (1853) *Dent (Everyman)* 1927; *O.U.P. (Oxford Standard
Authors)* 1915
'Or, New Foes With an Old Face'. A dramatic tale of fifth-century
Egypt, under Christian influence. Hypatia, a beautiful woman phil-

osopher, believes in, and dies for, Neoplatonism, and is torn to pieces by an Alexandrian Christian mob.

*THE WATER BABIES (1863) *Allen and Unwin* 1948 6s; *Collins (Classics)* 1955 5s; *Dent (Everyman)* 1908 6s 6d; *O.U.P. (Illustrated Classics)* 1948 10s 6d

Evergreen 'fairy tale for a land baby'. All editions are illustrated, and the four noted above are but a few of many.

*WESTWARD HO! (1855) *Collins (Classics)* 1953 7s; *Dent (Everyman)* (1906) 1955 12s 6d; *Macdonald (Illustrated Classics)* 1948 15s; *Nelson (Classics)* 1955 7s

Romantic historical tale of the days of Drake. Young adventurers sail from Westward Ho! in North Devonshire, to the Spanish Main, and return in time to share in the national joy at the defeat of the Armada. Woven into this colourful tale is the story of Sir Amyas Leigh.

Kingsley, Henry (1830–76) RAVENSHOE (1881) ed. by Griselda Taylor *O.U.P.* 1956 6s 6d

The new edition is abridged for younger readers, who may be interested in this once popular romance of a man, who, deceived on all sides, and betrayed by a friend, joins the army, and fights at Balaclava. All comes right in the end.

THE RECOLLECTIONS OF GEOFFREY HAMLYN (1859) *O.U.P. (Worlds Classics)* 1925 8s 6d

Spirited adventures of a family who emigrate from Devon to New South Wales. The life of these early settlers is presented with the authenticity that the author's personal knowledge of the country gave him.

Kipling, Rudyard (1865–1936) A CHOICE OF KIPLING'S PROSE selected by W. Somerset Maugham *Macmillan* 1952 15s

A representative selection of short stories, with an introductory essay in appreciation.

ACTIONS AND REACTIONS (1909)
THE DAY'S WORK (1898)
A DIVERSITY OF CREATURES (1917)
*JUST SO STORIES FOR LITTLE CHILDREN (1902)
LAND AND SEA TALES FOR SCOUTS AND GUIDES (1923)
THE LIGHT THAT FAILED (1891)
MANY INVENTIONS (1893)
*PUCK OF POOK'S HILL (1906)
*THE SECOND JUNGLE BOOK (1895)
*STALKY AND CO. (1899)
TRAFFICS AND DISCOVERIES (1904)

*CAPTAINS COURAGEOUS (1897)
DEBITS AND CREDITS (1926)
*THE JUNGLE BOOK (1894)
*KIM (1901)
LIFE'S HANDICAP (1891)
LIMITS AND RENEWALS (1932)
*PLAIN TALES FROM THE HILLS (1888)
*REWARDS AND FAIRIES (1910)
*SOLDIERS THREE (1888)
THY SERVANT A DOG; AND OTHER DOG STORIES (1930)
*WEE WILLIE WINKIE (1888)

This uniform set of all of Rudyard Kipling's short stories and novels in twenty-three volumes, with *The Naulahka*, written in collaboration with Wolcott Balestier (1892), is published by Macmillan: Library edition,

12s 6d each; pocket edition (of the most popular volumes) 9s 6d each. For other editions, including the *Young People's Edition*, nine volumes, 12s 6d each; quarto collections, illustrated, of *All the Mowgli Stories* (1933); and *Animal Stories* (1932) 17s 6d each, refer to the publisher's current catalogue. *St. Martins Library* paperback editions included up to December 1962: *Kim* 5s; *Puck of Pook's Hill* 4s; *The Jungle Book* 3s; *Just So Stories* 3s 6d; *The Second Jungle Book* 3s 6d; and *Stalky and Co.*, 3s 6d.

Knox, Ronald Arbuthnott (1888-1957) THE FOOTSTEPS AT THE LOCK *Methuen* (1928) 1950 6s
Regarded by connoisseurs of modern detective fiction as 'a classic'.

*Lamb, Charles (1775-1834) and Mary Lamb (1764-1847) TALES FROM SHAKESPEARE (1807) *Collins* (*Classics*) 1953 5s; *Dent* (*Everyman*) (1906) 1960 7s 6d; (*Children's Illustrated Classics*) 1957 12s 6d
Both Dent series editions illustrated by Arthur Rackham. See also *Essays and Belles Lettres* section.

Lawrence, David Herbert (1885-1930) AARON'S ROD (1922) *Heinemann* 1956 12s 6d

KANGAROO (1923) *Heinemann* 1956 12s 6d; *Penguin Books* 1956 3s 6d

LADY CHATTERLEY'S LOVER (Florence, 1928) *Heinemann* 1960 15s and 16s; *Penguin Books* 1960 3s 6d
These are the unexpurgated editions of the famous erotic novel that will always have a place in literary, legal, and social history, although as a novel, it is one of Lawrence's lesser works of fiction. Heinemann's also publish the expurgated edition, 12s 6d.

THE LOST GIRL (1920) *Heinemann* 1956 12s 6d
Awarded the James Tait Black Memorial Prize.

*THE PLUMED SERPENT (1926) *Heinemann* 1956 12s 6d

THE RAINBOW (1915; 1926) *Heinemann* 1956 12s 6d; *Penguin Books* 1956 5s
Suppressed when first published.

*SONS AND LOVERS (1913) *Heinemann* 1956 15s; *Collins* (*Classics*) 1955 7s; *Penguin Books* 1956 5s
One of Lawrence's greatest novels. Largely autobiographical, it is the story of Paul Morel and his mother. They dominate the story, and it is their deep bond that is so powerfully and poignantly expressed.

*THE TRESPASSER (1912) *Heinemann* 1956 12s 6d; *Penguin Books* 1956 2s 6d

THE WHITE PEACOCK (1911) *Heinemann* 1956 12s 6d

*WOMEN IN LOVE (1920) *Heinemann* 1956 12s 6d; *Penguin Books* 5s

Considered by many readers as Lawrence's best novel, or as next to *Sons and Lovers*. The novelist himself rated it as with his best work.

All of the above are in the uniform *Phoenix Edition*. Most of them were originally published by Martin Secker. Some of the novels are also available in a pocket edition, published by Heinemann, 8s 6d each (*Sons and Lovers*, 12s 6d).

*THE COMPLETE SHORT STORIES 3 vols. *Heinemann* (1934) 1955 12s 6d each

In 880 pages, this collection, originally in one volume, includes many masterpieces, such as, for example, *The Rocking-Horse Winner*. The volume *England My England* (1924) is also available separately, Heinemann, 8s 6d; and Penguin Books, 2s 6d.

*THE SHORT NOVELS 2 vols. *Heinemann* 1956 12s 6d each

Brings together in the uniform edition *novellen* originally published separately or included in other volumes: Vol. 1: *Love Among the Haystacks*; *The Ladybird*; *The Fox*; and, *The Captain's Doll* (1923); vol. 2: *St. Mawr* (1925); *The Virgin and the Gypsy* (1930); and, *The Man Who Died* (1931). The three stories in the volume entitled *The Ladybird*, are also available in Penguin Books, 3s 6d.

Le Fanu, Joseph Sheridan (1814-73) IN A GLASS DARKLY (1872) (1947)

A collection of five stories of the supernatural and the macabre, of vampires and familiars.

*UNCLE SILAS (1864) *Cresset Press* 1948 12s 6d

Elizabeth Bowen introduces the series reprint of the best novel by this Irish writer. It is a major example of the suspense and terror school of writers, and narrates the sinister machinations of Uncle Silas in his endeavours to marry his ward to a cousin, in order to obtain control of her fortune.

Lever, Charles James (1806-72) HARRY LORREQUER (1839) *Dent* (*Everyman*) 1907

The best of a number of popular military sketches and romances, richly packed with old-fashioned comedy and farce, and some amusing minor characters. Probably a fair picture of rough garrison life in Cork. Full title *The Confessions of Harry Lorrequer*.

Leverson, Ada (1862-1933) THE LITTLE OTTLEYS *MacGibbon and Kee* 1962 30s 542 pp

This modern reprint collects into one volume a trilogy of three novels of social comedy and witty dialogue concerning Bruce and Edith Ottley, who are introduced to the reader in their small, white Knightsbridge flat, in the third year of marriage. The three novels are: *Love's Shadow* (1908); *Tenterhooks* (1912); and *Love At Second Sight* (1916). The author, Oscar Wilde's 'dear Sphinx', gracious and courageous friend, stood firmly by the playwright and wit in his misery and disgrace, and these three Edwardian comedies fully support the opinion of Colin MacInnes, who says in his preface that Ada Leverson was 'in her own right and by her own achievement a very great artist indeed'. All six of her novels were reprinted in 1950-1 by Chapman and Hall.

Lewis, Matthew Gregory (1775-1818) THE MONK (1796) *Mark Paterson* 1956 38s; *Calder (Evergreen Books)* 1952 17s 6d
Notable example of the Gothic novel. The depraved Ambrosio seeks to possess a penitent; his lust leads to murder, and to a horrible death. Lurid, but powerfully written, sometimes unpleasantly overwritten to the point of pornography, the novel has an antiquarian interest for literary students, though 'Monk' Lewis's best work was not fiction. See also the *Travel* section.

Lewis, Wyndham (1884-1957) *THE HUMAN AGE 2 vols. *Methuen* 1955-6 25s; 30s 968 pp Illustrated by Michael Ayrton
This lengthy, sometimes savage, satire and fantasy on the human race was given the definitive edition and collective title long after the first book (*Childermass*) was published in 1928. Books two and three contain the completion *Monstre Gai*, and *Malign Fiesta*, published together in the second volume in 1955.

TARR (*Egoist Press*, 1918); *Methuen* 1951
Tarr, by 'Percy Wyndham Lewis', introduced a new satiric novelist to a small, intellectual public. His journalism in *Blast* and powerful paintings were soon to give him a European reputation.

Lodge, Thomas (1558-1625) ROSALYNDE (1590) ed. by W. W. Greg O.U.P. (1907) 1931
'Euphues Golden Legacie.' From this charming pastoral Shakespeare took the main plot for his *As You Like It*.

London, Jack (1876-1916) *THE CALL OF THE WILD (1903) *Methuen* 1950 7s 6d
The tale of a dog who escapes from human bondage, and, lured back to the woods, becomes the leader of a pack of wolves.

WHITE FANG (1906) *Collins (Classics)* 1953 6s; *Methuen* 1950 9s 6d; *Nelson (Classics)* 1956 5s
Here it is a wolf which forsakes its native woods and pack, preferring the company and care of humans. In the Collins' edition it is bound with *The Call of the Wild*, and a notable short story, *The Scarlet Plague*. Jack London's *Best Short Stories* were collected in an American edition, obtainable in Great Britain in 1955 from Bailey Bros., and Swinfen, 17s 6d.

*THE BODLEY HEAD JACK LONDON ed. by Arthur Calder-Marshall *Bodley Head* 1962 25s 450 pp
A selection displaying London's narrative genius.

THE FITZROY EDITION *in progress* Arco 1962- 12s 6d each
This new uniform edition, reprinting some of Jack London's once popular adventure stories is in progress, starting with *The Cruise of the 'Dazzler'* (1906) reprinted in 1962, 12s 6d, followed by *A Daughter of the Snows* (1904) and *The Son of the Wolf* (1900) and others.

Lover, Samuel (1797-1868) HANDY ANDY (1842) *Dent* (*Everyman*) (1907) 1954 10s 6d

'A tale of Irish life,' still enjoyed for the high-spirited farce, lively characterisation and boisterous humour. Its eponymous hero is the classic example of the clumsy, well-meaning, unlucky clown, always striving to do his best for master, but usually making a mess of everything he puts his hand to. Nevertheless, he ends up as a peer with the title of Lord Scatterbrain.

Lucas, Edward Verrall (1868-1938) OVER BEMERTON'S *Methuen* (1908) 1950 6s

'An easy-going chronicle', informally commenting on life in London. Urbane in style, part fiction, part essay, it might be used by historians of the social life of Edwardian London as an authentic picture of the middle-class world before the summer of 1914 ushered in the new era.

Lytton, Edward Bulwer, *1st Baron* (1803-73) HAROLD, THE LAST OF THE SAXONS (1848) *Dent* (*Everyman*) 1906

An historical novel on the reign and defeat of 'the last of the Saxon kings'.

*THE LAST DAYS OF POMPEII (1834) *Collins* (*Classics*) (1907) 1953 6s; *Dent* (*Everyman*) (1906) 1957 8s 6d; *Nelson* (*Classics*) (1906) 1953 7s

Unsurpassed fictional reconstruction of A.D. 79 in the Roman world, and of the catastrophe that overwhelmed the city of Pompeii. The above are the best of a large series of historical romances, once enormously popular, and collected in the *Knebworth* edition, sets of which may still be obtained from second-hand booksellers.

Macaulay, Dame Rose (1881-1958) *ORPHAN ISLAND *Collins* (1924) 1961 18s

This may prove to be the writer's most enduring satire. It is a witty, diverting fantasy, in which the discovery in the 1920's of a matriarchal society on a lonely Pacific island enables a sharp contrast to be delineated between the ideas of two periods of social history, for the inhabitants have developed from a shipload of orphans, wrecked in the 1850's, and left undisturbed.

*THEY WERE DEFEATED *Collins* (1932) 1960 21s

A great historical novel, in which this gifted author reconstructs life at her beloved Cambridge during the Civil War. Introduced by the distinguished historian C. V. Wedgwood.

THE TOWERS OF TREZIBOND *Collins* 1956 13s 6d; (*Fontana Books*) 1962 3s 6d

Macdonald, George (1824-1905) PHANTASTES (1858) and LILITH (1895) *Gollancz* 1962 25s

An introduction by Dr. C. S. Lewis to the only modern reprint of these two remarkable 'visionary novels' draws attention to their qualities. Imaginative masterpieces in the style of the novels of Charles Williams, with a weird touch of horror such as Edgar Allen Poe conveyed, they have long had their admirers, especially *Phantastes: a Faerie Romance* for adults.

*Macdonnell, Archibald Gordon (1895-1941) *ENGLAND, THEIR ENGLAND *Macmillan* (1933) 1949 7s 6d; (*St. Martins Library*) 1957 3s 6d

A Scotsman's tolerant view of the English, in a novel of high comedy and satire, including a classic account of a cricket match, the best in modern fiction.

Machen, Arthur (1863-1947) TALES OF HORROR AND THE SUPER-NATURAL *Unicorn Press* 1949 15s

Machen was the greatest modern master of this type of fiction, and this collection is likely to endure.

Mackenzie, Henry (1745-1831) THE MAN OF FEELING (1771) *Routledge* 1906

An example of the cult of excessive sentimentality characteristic of the author's age, when the heroes of minor fiction were seldom far from tears or suicide. In the last reprint the tale is bound with *The Man of the World* (1773), a picaresque narrative.

Mallock, William Hurrell (1849-1923) THE NEW REPUBLIC (1877) *Michael Joseph* 1937

'Culture, Faith and Philosophy in an English Country House.' The last reprint of this ironic, polished and witty novel had an appreciation by Sir John Squire. It has found admirers in every generation, especially among readers who enjoy Peacock's novels, to which it is akin. Many eminent Victorians appear in disguise, notably Pater and Ruskin, Matthew Arnold and Jowett.

*Malory, Sir Thomas (*d.* 1470) LE MORTE D'ARTHUR trans. by Sir Thomas Malory (1485) 2 vols. *Dent* (*Everyman*) (1906) 1962 8s 6d each

This romance cycle came to us from the Middle Ages, in French, and sometime about the year 1470, Malory's prose translation presented it in a redaction for English readers. From the time of Caxton's first printing of the romance (1485), reprinted in *Everyman*, with spelling and punctuation modernised, it has inspired poets and artists, and enthralled readers of all types. Introduced by Sir John Rhys, with a glossary.

THE TALE OF THE DEATH OF KING ARTHUR ed. by Eugene Vinaver *O.U.P.* 1955 15s

The *Morte D'Arthur*, Caxton's title for the whole Arthurian romance, belongs strictly only to the last of Malory's eight prose romances. It is a beautifully composed, tragic story, and may be regarded as the turning point between medieval and modern fiction. In the above edition it is reprinted in revised form from the editor's major publication of the complete *Works*, entered below. Commentary, notes and glossary included.

WORKS 3 vols. ed. by Eugene Vinaver O.U.P. (*Oxford English Texts*) 1947 160s (the set) 1858 pp; (*Oxford Standard Authors*) 1954 25s 938 pp
This great edition of Malory's *Romances* was made possible by the discovery in 1934 of a fifteenth-century manuscript in the Fellows' Library of Winchester College, providing a fuller and more authentic text than that given in Caxton's edition. The editor gives a long, critical introduction; volume 3 has a commentary and an essay on each of the eight romances; and there is a glossary by Professor G. L. Brook. The illustrations include collotype reproductions of the Winchester MS and of a hitherto unknown MS of the French Arthurian cycle. In the OSA one-volume edition the plain text is given, with a glossary, thus offering a student's edition at low cost.

Manning, Anne (1807-79) THE HOUSEHOLD OF SIR THOMAS MORE (1851) *Dent* (*Everyman*) 1906
The edition included the *Life of Sir Thomas More* by his son-in-law, William Roper, which see under *Biography* section, but the volume is now replaced in the series by another edition which no longer reprints Anne Manning's little story, put into the form of a diary kept by More's daughter, Margaret.

Mansfield, Katherine (1888-1923) *COLLECTED SHORT STORIES *Constable* 1946 16s 6d 794 pp

THE GARDEN PARTY AND OTHER STORIES (1922) *Penguin Books* 1951 2s 6d

*SELECTED STORIES O.U.P. (*Worlds Classics*) 1953 7s 6d

THIRTY-FOUR SHORT STORIES ed. by Elizabeth Bowen *Collins* (*Classics*) 1957 6s 6d
During her brief writing life, Kathleen Beauchamp, publishing under the pen-name of Katherine Mansfield, produced five volumes of short stories, each containing masterpieces, and all giving evidence of a writer of genius with an individual style. *Prelude*, *Sun and Moon*, and *The Fly*, to name only t hree, must be placed with the best short stories in the language.

Marryat, Frederick (1792-1848) THE CHILDREN OF THE NEW FOREST (1847) *A. and C. Black* 1952 10s 6d; *Collins* (*Classics*) 1955 5s; *Dent* (*Children's Illustrated Classics*) 1955 12s 6d; *Nelson* (*Classics*) 1955 5s
Delightful story of a family of Royalists who have to live near Lymington, Hampshire. The historical element is slight.

MASTERMAN READY (1841) *Dent* (*Everyman*) 1907 6s 6d; *Nelson* (*Classics*) 1955 5s
'Or, The Wreck of the *Pacific*.' A much-loved tale for boys and girls of the life of a family on an island.

*MR. MIDSHIPMAN EASY (1836) *Collins (Classics)* 1955 6s; *Dent* *(Everyman)* (1906) 1954 10s 6d; *Nelson (Classics)* 1955 6s
The most popular of all Captain Marryat's manly naval stories based largely on the author's own experiences. Here Marryat did for the naval novel, the kind of thing his younger contemporary Charles Lever was doing for the novel of military life. The new *Everyman* edition is introduced by Oliver Warner, the authority on this author and his books.

*PETER SIMPLE (1834) *Dent (Everyman)* 1907
Oliver Warner considers this to be Marryat's best work. It is a lively picture of life in the British Navy, as experienced by Peter Simple, who is not so simple as his name might imply, since he rises from midshipman to high rank.

THE SETTLERS IN CANADA (1844) *Dent (Everyman)* (1909) 1956 8s 6d
Introduced by Oliver Warner. It is a vivid tale of adventure of settlers in the Province of Canada.

Martineau, Harriet (1802-76) FEATS ON THE FIORD (1841) *Collins* 1955 2s; *Dent (Everyman)* 1910 6s 6d
Stories for young people originally published with *Settlers At Home*; *The Crofton Boys*; and *The Peasant and the Prince*, under a series title *The Playfellow*. In the *Everyman* edition the volume includes *Merdhin* (1852).

Mathers, Edward Powys (1892-1939) THE BOOK OF THE THOUSAND NIGHTS AND ONE NIGHT 4 vols. translated by E. Powys Mathers *Routledge* 1925 126s
Powys Mathers, known as 'Torquemada' to crossword puzzlers, made this masterly translation of *The Arabian Nights Entertainments* from a classic French version done by J. C. Mardrus. This is said to be the best translation of the original in any European language. The tales are given in a frank style, perhaps more suited to a modern reader than Burton's extant version.

Maturin, Charles Robert (1782-1824) MELMOTH, THE WANDERER (1820) 2 vols. *Macmillan* 1892
Considered to be the best of all the Gothick novels of terror and mystery. Melmoth is an eighteenth-century Faust, who has sold his soul to the Devil a century ago. When the story opens he seems doomed to live, as he bargained, for many centuries to come, leading, like the Wandering Jew, or Wagner's *Flying Dutchman*, a homeless, journeying life. The set of tales that comprise the novel range from the horrific to the pathetic.

Melville, Herman (1819-91) *FOUR SHORT NOVELS *Transworld* (Bantam Books)* 1959 4s
Benito Cereno; *Billy Budd, Foretopman*; *Bentleby*; and *The Encantadas*; or, *Enchanted Isles*.

*MOBY DICK; OR, THE WHALE (1851) *Collins (Classics)* 1953 6s; *Dent (Everyman)* (1907) 1961 8s 6d; *Macdonald (Illustrated Classics)* 1952 15s; *O.U.P. (Worlds Classics)* 1920 7s 6d

The greatest American novel of the nineteenth century, and indubitably a world classic. The prose style has Biblical grandeur and intensity; the characterisation has the power of great dramatic poetry. Captain Ahab's obsession with, and pursuit of, the White Whale is often interpreted symbolically. The *Worlds Classics* edition has an appreciation by Viola Meynell, indicating that this novel is one of the greatest experiences of a reading life.

The *Everyman* edition has an especially useful introduction by Professor Sherman Paul, with illuminating notes on the text, and extracts from literature on the theme of whales.

PIAZZA TALES (1856)—with *Billy Budd W. H. Allen (Dolphin Books)* 1962 7s 6d

REDBURN: HIS FIRST VOYAGE (1849) *W. H. Allen (Anchor Paperbacks)* 1962 7s 6d

Based on the author's experiences, and in particular, on his first voyage from America to Liverpool.

SHORTER NOVELS *Mayflower (Universal Series)* 1961 10s

*TYPEE (1846) *Dent (Everyman)* 1960 12s 6d; *O.U.P. (Worlds Classics)* 1924 7s 6d

'A Peep at Polynesian Life': being a narrative based on Melville's own voyage to the South Seas in 1841-2, and to the Marquesas Islands. The sequel is *Omoo* (1847), a continuing narrative of adventures in the South Seas, *Dent (Everyman)* 1908. In this series *Typee* is bound with *Billy Budd*, for which see also above under *Four Short Novels*. This great *novella* is a symbolic interpretation of a young sailor's tragic fate during a mutiny. It is based on true events that occurred in 1797 in a section of the Royal Navy, and was not published until 1924. Benjamin Britten wrote his opera from a libretto based on the story. The editor, Milton R. Stern, reprints the definitive text from the University of Harvard editions of 1948 and 1956.

Meredith, George (1828-1909) THE AMAZING MARRIAGE *Constable* (1895)

Epigrammatic comedy of a marriage that failed.

*BEAUCHAMP'S CAREER *Constable* (1875) *O.U.P. (Worlds Classics)* 1950 8s 6d

A political novel, and one of Meredith's major works, introduced by G. M. Young. The romantic element is nearly as powerful as the radicalism, and the complicated plot is managed with skill.

DIANA OF THE CROSSWAYS *Constable* (1885)

Meredith's most brilliant heroine dominates the novel, which is said to be a *roman à clef*, Lady Caroline Norton appearing as Diana.

*THE EGOIST *Constable* (1879) *O.U.P. (Worlds Classics)* 1947 9s 6d

'A comedy in narrative', introduced by Lord Dunsany. For most readers of our time, *The Egoist* is Meredith's masterpiece. It is a witty, but merciless

F

exposure of masculine egoism, as observed in the person of Sir Willoughby Patterne in his courtship of Clara Middleton and two others.

EVAN HARRINGTON *Constable* (1861)
An autobiographical comedy, largely conversational, with a strong plot.

HARRY RICHMOND *Constable* (1871)
A romance of a lighter type, episodic and rapidly developed.

*THE ORDEAL OF RICHARD FEVEREL *Constable* (1859) *Dent* (*Everyman*) (1935) 1955 10s 6d
Of all Meredith's novels, this is the most easily read, with sustained passages of lyrical rapture. The story is a 'history of a father and son', and is the vehicle of many memorable epigrams.

RHODA FLEMING *Constable* (1865)
A country tragi-comedy: dramatic, with strongly-drawn characters of farmers, yeomen and country folk.

*THE SHAVING OF SHAGPAT *Constable* (1855)
'An Arabian entertainment', consisting of over a score of tales told with Oriental exuberance and delightful extravagance of style, in a sort of burlesque of *The Arabian Nights Entertainments*.

THE TALE OF CHLOE *Constable* (1895)
Four examples of Meredith's genius as a short story teller. Apart from the title story, there are three others: *The House on the Beach*; *Farina*; and, *The Case of General Ople and Lady Camber*. The above are the most important in the set of Meredith's complete fiction known as the *Mickleham* edition, published by Constable in 1924, reprinted in 1946, 6s each. This uniform set is now out of print, but those not noted in the selection above are: *Celt and Saxon* (1910-unfinished); *Lord Ormont and His Aminta* (1894); *One of Our Conquerors* (1891); *Sandra Belloni* (1864—originally entitled *Emilia in England*); its sequel *Vittoria* (1866), a masterly study of Italian politics during the rising of 1848; and, *The Tragic Comedians* (1880).

Merrick, Leonard (1864-1939) LEONARD MERRICK OMNIBUS *Cassell* 1950
A collection (619 pages) made by the author's daughter from five of her father's best books, with four stories of Paris: *The Man Who Understood Women* (1908); *While Paris Laughed* (1918); *A Chair on the Boulevard* (1919); *To Tell You the Truth* (1922); and, *The Little Dog Laughed*. Merrick never achieved great popularity, but his contemporaries admired his art, and those who read him were delighted with his grace, wit and Gallic charm.

Merriman, H. Seton (Hugh Stowell Scott) (1862-1903) BARLASCH OF THE GUARD *Nelson* (1903) (*Classics*) 1957 5s; *Collins* (*Classics*) 1956 5s
A tale of the Napoleonic wars of 1812, and in particular of the defence of Dantzig.

WITH EDGED TOOLS *Murray* (1894) 1957 11s 6d

An adventure of the African jungle. The hero and a companion are lured by a half-caste in search of a rare plant, said to yield a new drug with fantastic commercial possibilities.

Montague, Charles Edward (1867-1928) FIERY PARTICLES *Chatto* 1923

Notable volume of short stories by a distinguished journalist who was for many years associated with the *Manchester Guardian*.

Moore, George (1852-1933) *THE BROOK KERITH *Heinemann* (1916) 1927; *Penguin* 1952 2s 6d

'A Syrian story' of a shepherd who is a member of the Essenes. He is crucified, but does not die on the cross.

CELIBATE LIVES *Heinemann* 1927

Short stories, originally published in a first version as *Celibates* (1895), the title indicating the unifying theme.

*ESTHER WATERS *Heinemann* (1894) 1920 15s; *Dent (Everyman)* (1936) 1962 12s 6d; *Digit Books* 1961 3s 6d; *Penguin* 1936 2s 6d

'An English story', and Moore's best novel. Esther is a domestic servant. Most of the characters are men of the turf, stablemen and jockeys.

HELOISE AND ABELARD *Heinemann* 1921 15s

A reconstruction of the romance of the two lovers of the twelfth century, immortalised in the famous *Letters*.

*A MUMMER'S WIFE *Heinemann* (1884) 1918

A major novel of realism, tracing the gradual decay of an errant wife who runs off with a touring actor, and thereafter finds solace in gin, to compensate for the neglect of her husband.

*A STORYTELLER'S HOLIDAY 2 vols. *Heinemann* (1918) 1928 15s each

Stories told for 'Alec', inspired by Moore Hall, and the Irish legends, fancies and folk tales of the countryside. These pages contain some of Moore's most exquisite writing in a mood of nostalgia and reminiscence. The *Ebury* edition of George Moore's work, published by Heinemann in a uniform set, 1936-8, is now out of print. In addition to the above, it contained a beautiful Englishing of the *Daphnis and Chloe* of Longus, first published in 1924, and *Aphrodite in Aulis* (1931), as well as the belles-lettres.

*Morier, James (1780?-1849) THE ADVENTURES OF HAJJI BABA OF ISPAHAN (1824) ed. by Richard Jennings *Cresset Press* 1949 12s 6d; *O.U.P. (Worlds Classics)* 1923 8s 6d

A picturesque, episodic and amusing Persian pastiche, in which Hajji Baba attains to a post of some importance by way of a picaresque career of robber, barber and executioner. The author had an unusually intimate knowledge of Persia, and his comic masterpiece became so popular that he turned the scales with a sequel, *Hajji Baba in England* (1828), reprinted last in 1943.

Morris, William (1834-96) THE DREAM OF JOHN BALL *Longmans*
(1888) *Central Books: Collet* 1958 2s 6d
Idealisation of the Kentish Rising of 1381.

NEWS FROM NOWHERE *Longmans* (1890)
'Or, An Epoch of Rest: some chapters from a Utopian romance'. This
was published two years after Bellamy's popular *Looking Backward*, which
see above, and it is possible that Morris, the artist-craftsman, wished to
offer in contrast, a more ideal future state, by creating a race of art-loving,
anti-commercial men and women.

THE STORY OF THE GLITTERING PLAIN *Longmans* (1891)
Another story of a Utopian state. For reprints and selections from
Morris's work, refer to the omnibus editions noted in the *Essays and Belles
Lettres* section.

Morrison, Arthur (1863-1945) A CHILD OF THE JAGO *Methuen*
(1896)
A powerful, Zolaesque study of the degrading life of a boy thief, brought
up in vile, Victorian slums.

THE HOLE IN THE WALL *Methuen* (1902) *Eyre and Spottiswoode*
1947 7s 6d
Low life on the Ratcliff Highway, London Docks, 1865, with principal
characters selected from a typical group of thieves, receivers, and
murderers.

TALES OF MEAN STREETS *Methuen* (1894)
Remarkable stories of the East End of London, and particularly of
Bethnal Green and Stepney, accurate in detail and psychology. Now
that the conditions, most of the streets, and all of the poverty have gone
forever, these books by Morrison survive as social documents.

Munro, Hector Hugh ('Saki') (1870-1916) THE BEST OF 'SAKI' ed.
by Graham Greene *Bodley Head* 1952 6s

*COMPLETE SHORT STORIES *Bodley Head* (1930) 1948 15s 720 pp

THE NOVELS AND PLAYS OF 'SAKI' *Bodley Head* 1933 12s 6d

SEVENTY-SIX SHORT STORIES *Collins* (*Classics*) 1956 7s
All of the stories in *The Chronicles of Clovis* (1912); *Reginald* (1904); and,
The Toys of Peace (1919).
The Bodley Head omnibus is introduced by an appreciation by Christopher Morley. 'Saki's' short stories were characterised by an individual
wit, a diverting twist at the end, and sometimes by an unpleasant, almost
cruel, grotesque touch.

Munro, Neil (1864-1930) DOOM CASTLE *Blackwood* 1901 6s
Historical romance of the aftermath of the '45 Rebellion in Scotland.

JOHN SPLENDID *Blackwood* 1898 7s 6d
'The tale of a poor gentleman and the little wars of Lorn: Montrose and
the Royalists.

THE NEW ROAD *Blackwood* 1914 6s
Historical tale of Field-Marshal George Wade (1673-1748), who did much to open up the Highlands to military transport by making the great roads during the decades following the Rebellion of '15.

PARA HANDY TALES *Blackwood* 1955 10s 6d
An omnibus collecting Neil Munro's humorous writings. Other volumes in the uniform *Inveraray* edition are available, a total of eleven in the complete set, 6s each.

*Myers, Leo Hamilton (1881-1944) THE NEAR AND THE FAR *Cape* (1940) 1956 25s 950 pp
The first part of this tetralogy, *The Near and the Far*, was published separately in 1927 under this title, now used for the complete work. *Prince Jali* followed in 1931; *Rajah Amar* (1934) was followed by the final instalment *The Pool of Vishnu* (1940). The 1956 definitive edition in one volume is introduced by L. P. Hartley, who states: 'there is nothing like it in the field of English fiction'. The author said of his vast novel that 'it is not an historical novel, although the action is placed in the time of Akbar the Great Mogul (who was a contemporary of Queen Elizabeth)'. Refer also to *L. H. Myers: a critical study*, by G. H. Bantock, Cape, 1956, 15s.

Nashe, Thomas (1567-1601) THE UNFORTUNATE TRAVELLER (1594) ed. by H. F. B. Brett-Smith *Blackwell* (*Percy Reprints*) 1927 9s 6d
An episodic, picaresque narrative of power, written in a picturesque style. Sub-titled: *Or, The Life of Jacke Wilton*, it is similar to some of Defoe's books, though it preceded them by 120 years. See also Saintsbury and Henderson's collection of *Shorter Novels*, in next section.

Nesbit, Edith (1858-1924) FIVE CHILDREN AND IT (1902) *Benn* 1957 11s 6d
THE PHOENIX AND THE CARPET (1904) *Benn* 1956 13s 6d
THE RAILWAY CHILDREN (1906) *Benn* 1961 12s 6d
THE STORY OF THE AMULET (1906) *Benn* 1957 11s 6d
THE STORY OF THE TREASURE SEEKERS (1899) *Benn* 1958 11s 6d
THE WOULDBEGOODS (1901) *Benn* 1958 12s 6d
Being further adventures of the Treasure Seekers.
*THE NEW TREASURE SEEKERS (1904) 1949 11s 6d
A few of sixteen endearing and very amusing comedies of childhood, centred for the most part on the Bastable children, read today with as much enjoyment by adults as by children. They are all illustrated, some with the original drawings; others, for example *The Railway Children*, by distinguished contemporaries such as Lynton Lamb.

Noonan, Robert ('Robert Tressall') (?-1911) THE RAGGED TROUSERED PHILANTHROPISTS *Richards* (1914); *Unicorn Press* 1949 12s 6d; *Lawrence and Wishart* 1955 30s
A remarkable Edwardian 'working-class' novel written by a self-educated house-painter (hence the pen-name). Published posthumously, it imme-

diately attracted attention as a classic of its kind, and it is said that about
150,000 copies have been sold, quite apart from the full version published
in 1955.

Oliphant, Laurence (1829–88) PICCADILLY *Blackwood* (1870)
Constable 1928
A brilliant, satirical novel on Victorian society. The dialogue gives
pleasure even today, for its wit and irony. The author was a much-
travelled barrister, diplomat, and journalist; somewhat eccentric, and an
idealist. His *Episodes of a Life of Adventure* (1887) is now scarce, but his
cousin's *Memoir*, 2 vols. 1891, can sometimes be obtained second-hand.
See next author.

Oliphant, Margaret (1828–97) THE BELEAGUERED CITY (1880)
Macmillan 1910
Imaginative story on a supernatural theme: the siege of a city by hosts of
the dead. It was the best work of a gifted woman, cousin of Laurence
Oliphant (see above). Her industry, courage and individuality were
remarkable.

SALEM CHAPEL (1863) *Dent* 1907
One of a series of four novels, *Chronicles of Carlingford*, dealing with the
problems and dissenters of a small provincial community in the 1850's.
Formerly included in *Everyman*, and still useful to students of social and
political history.

Olivier, Edith (1879–1948) THE LOVE CHILD (1927) *Unicorn Press*
1951 7s 6d Illustrated by Rex Whistler
A delicate fantasy, of which Lord David Cecil wrote in the preface to the
the reprint, that it is 'a masterpiece of its kind'.

*Orczy, Baroness Emmuska (1865–1947) THE SCARLET PIMPERNEL
Hodder (1930) 1961 25s 1279 pp
The omnibus edition in one volume of four popular novels in which the
central character is Sir Percy Blakeney, the 'Scarlet Pimpernel' who
rescues aristocrats from the French revolutionaries during the Reign of
Terror, outwitting the French with cool nonchalance and the sort of
cleverness that has enthralled generations of readers of all ages. The four
separate novels are: *The Scarlet Pimpernel* (1905); *I Will Repay* (1906);
Eldorado (1913); and, *Sir Percy Hits Back* (1927).

*Orwell, George (1903–50) ANIMAL FARM *Secker and Warburg*
1945 8s 6d; *Penguin Books* 1951 2s 6d
The most celebrated satirical fable in twentieth-century fiction. Current
ideologies and the antics of political theorists are here reduced to the
level of nonsense.

NINETEEN EIGHTY-FOUR *Secker and Warburg* 1949 18s; *Penguin
Books* 1954 3s 6d
A horrifying glimpse into the possible future. It has taken its place with
Huxley's *Brave New World* and *Ape and Essence* as a powerful object lesson
to all political thinkers with a liking for totalitarian government, and a
warning to those whose acquiescence makes dictatorship workable.

Paget, Violet ('Vernon Lee') (1856-1935) SUPERNATURAL TALES
Peter Owen 1955
'Vernon Lee' was steeped in the art and atmosphere of Italy, where she
spent most of her life. These tales of the macabre were written from
about 1886 to 1927, and were published in her various volumes of
miscellaneous essays and writings.

Pain, Barry Eric Odell (1864-1928) HUMOROUS STORIES *Werner
Laurie* 1930 744 pp
A memorial omnibus volume to a writer of whom Alfred Noyes said
in his preface: 'In France he would long ago have been recognised as a
great artist who combines the gifts of the author of *Tartarin de Tarascon*
with some of those of de Maupassant'.

Painter, William (1540?-94) THE PALACE OF PLEASURE (1566-7)
3 vols. ed. by J. Jacobs (1890); 4 vols. ed. by Hamish Miles
Cresset Press 1930 (limited edition for collectors; eight guineas)
'Pleasaunt Histories and Excellent Novelles selected out of divers good
and commendable authors.' This rich collection of stories from Italian,
Spanish and classical sources, including Herodotus and Boccaccio, was
used by many English authors of the sixteenth and seventeenth centuries
as a source for plots for plays and themes for poems.

Paltock, Robert (1697-1767) THE LIFE AND ADVENTURES OF PETER
WILKINS, A CORNISHMAN (1751) *Dent* (*Everyman*) 1914
Inspired perhaps by *Robinson Crusoe* or *Gulliver's Travels* Paltock sends
his Cornishman off on a voyage that lands him in country where there
are 'flying Indians', one of whom he marries.

Parker, Sir Gilbert (1862-1932) THE BATTLE OF THE STRONG (1898)
Harrap 1926
'A romance of two kingdoms': Brittany and the island of Jersey, during
the wars that followed the French Revolution.

THE SEATS OF THE MIGHTY (1896) *Nelson* 1929
An historical romance of Wolfe at Quebec, and the defeat of the French
army in Canada. It is probably the best of the many historical novels
written by this Canadian-born writer, who lived in England, and had a
seat in the House of Commons.

Pater, Walter (1839-94) MARIUS THE EPICUREAN *Macmillan* (1885)
Dent (*Everyman*) (1934) 1960 8s 6d
Introduction by Osbert Burdett. This philosophical novel relates, with
many discursive pages, the reflective life of Marius, who, as secretary to
the Emperor Marcus Aurelius observed the Stoic philosophy of the
Emperor, against a background of the new Christianity of the second
century. The prose style has been admired by many distinguished
authors and critics.

Peacock, Thomas Love (1785-1866) CROTCHET CASTLE (1831) and
MAID MARIAN (1822) *Macmillan* 1955 7s 6d
GRYLL GRANGE (1861) *Macmillan* 1927 4s 6d
MELINCOURT; OR, SIR ORAN HAUT- ON (1817) *Macmillan* 1927 4s 6d
THE MISFORTUNES OF ELPHIN (1829) and RHODODAPHNE (1818)
Macmillan 1927 4s 6d
All the above editions are introduced by George Saintsbury, and are
illustrated. Other editions:

*NIGHTMARE ABBEY (1818) and HEADLONG HALL (1816) *Dent*
(*Everyman*) (1907) 1961 8s 6d
Nightmare Abbey is a satire notable for its witty portraits of Shelley,
Byron and Coleridge, who in thinly disguised characterisation all figure in
the story.

*THREE NOVELS *Nelson* (*Classics*) 1940 7s
These are: *Headlong Hall*; *Nightmare Abbey*; and *Crotchet Castle*. These
are the three novels that are read today with keen enjoyment by a small
but devoted group of Peacockians, who prize them as incomparable
satires in dialogue (for Peacock was a master of the conversational novel),
that are unique in English literature. Peacock's complete works were
edited in ten volumes for a definitive edition by H. F. B. Brett-Smith
and C. E. Jones, Constable, 1924-34, published as a set for 189s. The seven
novels, ed. by David Garnett, are now available in 2 vols. Hart-Davis
(Paperbacks) 1963 14s each.

Pettie, George (1548-89) A PETITE PALLACE OF PETTIE HIS PLEASURE
(1576) 2 vols. ed. by Sir Israel Gollancz *Chatto* 1908; ed. by
H. Hartman *O.U.P.* 1938
As the sub-title has it, here is an old book 'contayning many pretie
Hystories by him set foorth in comely colours and most delightfully
discoursed'. The twelve narratives are retold from classical sources in the
euphuistic style of the period. See also William Painter, above, for
another example of this kind of Tudor compilation.

Pickthall, Marmaduke William (1875-1936) SAĪD THE FISHERMAN
Methuen 1903
A sympathetic interpretation of the mind of the Arab. It is said to have
been recommended to those who, as officials, went to work and live in
the countries of the Near East, as a brilliant introduction to the Oriental
character, unsurpassed in English.

*Poe, Edgar Allan (1809-49) TALES OF MYSTERY AND IMAGINATION
(1840-5) *Collins* (*Classics*) 1953 7s; *Dent* (*Everyman*) (1908) 1955
8s 6d; *Nelson* (*Classics*) 1923 6s; *O.U.P.* (*Worlds Classics*) 1927
7s 6d
In the Collins' reprint, the tales are included with some essays and Poe's
Poems. All editions include the famous stories; e.g. *The Purloined Letter*;
the horrific *The Murders in the Rue Morgue*, and the macabre *The Fall of*

the House of Usher; *The Gold Bug*; and *The Pit and the Pendulum*. For the long story known as *The Narrative of Arthur Gordon Pym*, see the *Oxford Standard Authors* edition of Poe's *Poems and Miscellanies*, O.U.P., 1909, 12s 6d

Porter, Jane (1776-1850) THE SCOTTISH CHIEFS (1810) *Hodder* 1921
Of antiquarian interest only, as an early example of the historical novel, that, four years later, was to achieve its greatest popularity as a form of fiction, by the publication of Sir Walter Scott's *Waverley*. Jane Porter's story, in spite of its stilted, artificial style, is, however, still readable. It is a tale of Wallace, 'Governor of Scotland'.

Powys, Llewelyn (1884-1939) LOVE AND DEATH *Bodley Head* 1950 5s
'An imaginary autobiography', with an introduction by Alyse Gregory. Written in 1933 when Powys was very ill, the novel is an ecstatic, passionate love idyll, set in the Somerset countryside. A critic of the first edition said he thought it had 'a claim to immortality'.

*Powys, Theodore Francis (1875-1953) MR. WESTON'S GOOD WINE *Chatto* (1927) 1950
An allegory, unique in twentieth-century fiction, in the novelist's use of an early form of fiction.

Quiller-Couch, Sir Arthur (1863-1944) *THE ASTONISHING HISTORY OF TROY TOWN (1888) *Dent* 1928 7s 6d; *Penguin* 1950 2s 6d
Amusing stories of the Cornish people and of life in Polperro, a small seaside village, in the literary tradition of Miss Mitford's *Our Village*, and Mrs. Gaskell's *Cranford*.

FORT AMITY (1904) *Dent* 1928 7s 6d
Historical tale of a young English ensign who takes part in the battle for Ticonderoga in 1758, under General Howe. After the defeat, he takes refuge among the Canadian Indians.

*HETTY WESLEY (1903) *Dent* 1928 7s 6d; (*Everyman*) 1931 6s 6d
A sad story, based on the life of the evangelist's sister. Both John and Charles Wesley figure in the story, in which there is little fiction. There is a preface by the author, to this, his most serious novel.

*THE MAYOR OF TROY (1905) *Dent* 1928 7s 6d
Diverting comedy of the affairs and deeds of Troy's Voluntary Artillery Company, during the Napoleonic scare.

MYSTERY STORIES *Dent* 1937 10s 6d
Collects short stories from other volumes.

POISON ISLAND (1907) *Dent* 1928 7s 6d
Remarkable story of a treasure island.

SHORTER STORIES *Dent* 1944 6s
The author's own choice of his best work, excluding those included in *Mystery Stories*, which see above.

F*

THE SPLENDID SPUR (1889) *Dent* 1928 7s 6d

Historical romance of Charles I, in the traditional style, indicated by the sub-title: *Being memoirs of the adventures of Mr. John Marvel, a servant of his late Majesty King Charles I in the year 1642-3.* 'Written by himself and edited in Modern English by "Q".'

The above are the principal novels in the uniform *Duchy* edition, in twenty-eight volumes. *A 'Q' Anthology*: a representative collection of Q's best work, edited by F. Brittain, Dent, 1953, 6s, 425 pages, and the two volumes of short stories noted above, complete Dent's edition of all his fiction.

Radcliffe, Ann (1764-1823) THE MYSTERIES OF UDOLPHO (1794) 2 vols. *Dent (Everyman)* (1931) 1959 10s 6d each

Notable examples of the English Gothick romance, introduced in the reprint by R. Austin Freeman. In *Northanger Abbey*, Jane Austen gently satirised some characteristics of this once popular novel. Mrs. Radcliffe's *The Italian; or, The Confessions of the Penitent*, a romance of Sicily (1797), has been reprinted only once in recent years, and that was in 1956, when the Folio Society published it in a handsome edition, illustrated by Philip Ross, 22s 6d, for members of the society only.

*Raspe, Rudolf Erich (1737-94) SINGULAR TRAVELS, CAMPAIGNS AND ADVENTURES OF BARON MUNCHAUSEN (1785) ed. by John Carswell *Cresset Press* 1948 10s 6d; *Max Parrish (Classics in Colour)* 1950 10s 6d, with eight plates in colour

A famous collection of extravagant episodes, originally attributed to Karl Friedrich Hieronymus, Baron von Munchausen (1720-97). The editor of the best modern edition, in the *Cresset Press* series, provides a bibliography of early editions and an introduction. John Carswell has written a biography of Rudolf Raspe, called *The Prospector*, Cresset Press, 1950, 21s.

Raymond, Walter (1852-1931) TWO MEN O' MENDIP (1899) *Dent* 1933

A tale of the lead mines of the Mendip country in the author's native Somerset, set in the early nineteenth century. Nearly all of Raymond's work was regional, and he did much to preserve items of Somerset folklore. For a delightful appreciation of this neglected author, see Richard Church's *A Window On the Hill*, published by Robert Hale, 1951, 15s.

Reade, Charles (1814-84) *THE CLOISTER AND THE HEARTH (1861) *Collins (Classics)* 1953 7s; *Dent (Everyman)* (1906) 1955 12s 6d; *Nelson (Classics)* 1906 8s 6d

'A tale of the Middle Ages.' It recreates the atmosphere of Renaissance Europe with splendid exuberance. The hero is based on what is known about the father of Erasmus, Gerrit Elias, who falls in love with a doctor's daughter, by whom he has a child, later to become the great humanist of his century.

IT IS NEVER TOO LATE TO MEND 1856 *Chatto* 1932
Exposed the horrors of prison conditions in the English Midlands of the times. The scene is then shifted to Australia, where the life of settlers and prospectors in the gold fields is colourfully reproduced, with considerable sentiment.

PEG WOFFINGTON (1852) *Nelson (Classics)* 1955 6s
A popular romance of the stage, based on Reade's play, *Masks and Faces*.

Reid, Forrest (1876-1947) UNCLE STEPHEN *Faber* 1931

THE RETREAT; OR, THE MACHINATIONS OF HENRY *Faber* 1936
12s 6d

YOUNG TOM; OR, VERY MIXED COMPANY *Faber* 1944 12s 6d
A trilogy intended to be read in the above order. Thus the development of young Tom may be observed in reverse, and these studies in the sunshine of youth may be fully appreciated.

DENIS BRACKNEL (1911) *Faber* 1947 9s 6d
Original title *The Bracknels: a Family Chronicle*. This was completely rewritten. It is a realistic story of a family of contrasting characters, some harsh, one idealistic, and all in conflict each with the other.

*Richardson, Dorothy Miller (1873-1957) PILGRIMAGE 4 vols.
Dent 1938 9s 6d each (35s the set, boxed) 2,000 pp
A landmark in the twentieth-century novel. From 1915 onwards in a series of novels about Miriam, Dorothy Richardson developed the technique known later as the interior monologue and the stream of consciousness. The series, from *Pointed Roofs* (1915) to *Dimple Hill* (1938) was originally published by Duckworth.

Richardson, Ethel Florence Lindsay ('Henry Handel Richardson')
(1870-1946) *THE FORTUNES OF RICHARD MAHONY *Heinemann*
1930 18s
A trilogy of 990 pages, by the principal Australian novelist of her time. Separately: *Australia Felix* (1917); *The Way Home* (1925); and *Ultima Thule* (1929). The power of the series springs from the central character.

MAURICE GUEST *Heinemann* (1908) 1950
'It is a chapter in the spirit of youth, a history of the romance of youth with its waywardness, its sadness, and its beauty.'—*John Masefield* (1908).

*Richardson, Samuel (1689-1761) CLARISSA HARLOWE (1747-8)
4 vols. *Dent (Everyman)* (1932) 1962 12s 6d each

PAMELA (1740-1) 2 vols. *Dent (Everyman)* (1914) 1962 10s 6d
each

SIR CHARLES GRANDISON (1753-4) *Routledge* 1895
Three epistolary novels, the first of their kind in English literature, where character is pre-eminent and plot subordinate. They were widely read and admired all over Europe. The modern standard edition of these novels was published in eighteen volumes by the Shakespeare Head Press,

1930-2. Of the three, it is said that *Clarissa* is the masterpiece. The American scholar A. C. Baugh says of it: 'If the novel is read slowly and reflectively . . . its effect is even today overwhelming.'—*A Literary History of England*, Routledge, 1950.

Rigg, James (1855-1926) THE DECAMERON OF BOCCACCIO translated by James Rigg (1903) 2 vols., with an introduction by Edward Hutton *Dent* (*Everyman*) 1930 7s 6d each
The standard translation, sometimes reprinted in illustrated editions.

Rolfe, Frederick ('Baron Corvo') (1860-1913) THE DESIRE AND PURSUIT OF THE WHOLE *Cassell* (1934) 1953 15s
'A romance of modern Venice,' written in 1909. In his introduction, A. J. A. Symons, says: it is 'an incongruous compound of an exquisite romantic dream-tale with undramatic and sordid details from Rolfe's life'.

DON TORQUINIO (1905) *Chatto* 1957 12s 6d
'A kataleptic, phantasmatic romance.'

HADRIAN VII (1904) *Chatto* 1929 15s
See A. J. A. Symon's brilliantly absorbing *Quest For Corvo*, Cassell (1934) 1955, 18s, for details of the life of this extraordinary man, which must be known before the full flavour of this, his best novel, can be enjoyed. His hero, here, is himself, scoring off those who had slighted him, revealing disappointments endured with bitterness, but, in the novel, triumphing in papal glory—for at least a brief interval.

*Sackville-West, Victoria (1892-1962) ALL PASSION SPENT *Chatto* (1931) 1950 (*New Phoenix Library*) 6s
THE EDWARDIANS *Hogarth Press* (1930) *Hutchinson* (*Arrow Books*) 1960 3s 6d
A comedy of manners and morals. A period piece and perhaps the author's best novel, displaying her gift of satire directed against her own social class.

*Sayers, Dorothy (1893-1957) MURDER MUST ADVERTISE *Gollancz* (1933) *Four Square Books* 1959 2s 6d

THE NINE TAILORS *Gollancz* (1934) *Four Square Books* 1959 2s 6d
Two of many detective stories by a modern master, selected because they are judged by connoisseurs of this type of fiction to be twentieth-century contributions of the first order.

Schreiner, Olive (1855-1920) THE STORY OF AN AFRICAN FARM (1883) *Benn* 1951 4s 6d; *Collins* (*Classics*) 1954 6s
A powerful novel. The characters have been likened to Emily Brontë's Catherine and Heathcliff, although the background is an ostrich farm in the veld. The philosophy and didactic purpose of the writer were much admired in Victorian times, and her Edwardian study of *Woman and Labour* (1911) gave her an enduring place in the pioneer struggle for the rights of women.

Scott, Michael (1789–1835) TOM CRINGLE'S LOG (1829) *Dent* (*Everyman*) 1915
A midshipman's adventures from 1812 onwards, full of lively scenes, picturesque characters, dare-devil escapades, and thrilling sea-fights with American frigates and privateers.

Scott, Sir Walter (1771–1832) THE ABBOT (1820)
Sequel to *The Monastery*.

ANNE OF GEIERSTEIN (1829)
'Or, The Maiden of the Mist.' Continues the historical events narrated in *Quentin Durward*

*THE ANTIQUARY (1816)
Scott's own favourite of his Waverley novels. The affectionate portrait of the Antiquary, drawn from the life, and the eventful plot, have endeared it to all readers.

THE BETROTHED (1825)
A romance of the time of Henry II, and the second of the pair of novels known as *Tales of the Crusaders*.

THE BLACK DWARF (1816)
The first of the series *Tales of My Landlord*. It is a melodrama of Scottish life in the first decade of the eighteenth century.

*THE BRIDE OF LAMMERMOOR (1819)
Third of *Tales of My Landlord*. It is the tragedy of Lucy Ashton, and the young Master of Ravenswood, used as the theme for the libretto of Donizetti's opera, *Lucia di Lammermoor*.

CASTLE DANGEROUS (1832)
The fourth (and final) *Tales of My Landlord*: a romance of Robert the Bruce and 'the Black Douglas', 1306–7.

*COUNT ROBERT OF PARIS (1831)
The second of the fourth (and final) series of *Tales of My Landlord*. It is a romance of Constantinople and the Crusaders, 1080–1120.

*THE FAIR MAID OF PERTH (1828)
'Or, St. Valentine's Day.' Romance of the time of Robert III of Scotland.

*THE FORTUNES OF NIGEL (1822)
A brilliant portrait of the times of James I of England.

*GUY MANNERING (1815)
'Or, The Astrologer.' Scotland and the Border country from 1750; notable for the famous characters of Meg Merrilies, the gypsy; and Dominie Sampson, the tutor. John Buchan ranked *Guy Mannering* as certainly among the first three of the Waverley novels.

*THE HEART OF MIDLOTHIAN (1818)
One of Scott's most popular novels, being the second series of *Tales of My Landlord*. Period George II and Queen Caroline; scene: Edinburgh and the Lowlands at the time of the Porteous Riots, and London.

THE HIGHLAND WIDOW (1827)
Chronicles of the Canongate: first series.

*IVANHOE (1819)
The most popular of all the Waverley novels, being a romance of
England in the days of Richard Coeur de Lion and the Crusaders.

*KENILWORTH (1821)
The story of Amy Robsart, ill-fated wife of the Earl of Leicester, favourite
at the court of Queen Elizabeth I. This major novel incorporates in its
colourful pages the legend of Wayland the Smith.

A LEGEND OF MONTROSE (1819)
The second romance of the third series of *Tales of My Landlord*. It is a
tale of 1644, depicting the bitter struggles between the Covenanters and
the Highlanders who were loyal to Charles I, under command of Earl
Montrose, a complex character of his period.

THE MONASTERY (1820)
The first part of the narrative continued in *The Abbot*.

OLD MORTALITY (1816)
From the first series of *Tales of My Landlord*, on the Covenanters and
their struggles with John Grahame of Claverhouse up to William III.

PEVERIL OF THE PEAK (1822)
On the time of Titus Oates and the Popish Plot.

THE PIRATE (1822)
A tale of Shetland and Orkney in the middle of the seventeenth century.

*QUENTIN DURWARD (1823)
The first of two romances of the time of Charles the Bold of Burgundy
and Louis XI of France. Continued in *Anne of Geierstein*. This novel
attained great popularity on the continent of Europe.

*REDGAUNTLET (1824)
In this major romance, the famous story *Wandering Willie's Tale* appears.
Redgauntlet is the name of a Jacobite who came to England after the '45
Rebellion to work again for a return of the Young Pretender.

*ROB ROY (1817)
Period: the decade preceding the 1715 rising. It is one of the most widely-
read of all the Waverley novels. Famous characters abound: the charming
Diana Vernon; Francis Osbaldistone; Bailie Nicol Jarvie of Glasgow;
Andrew Fairservice; and the Scottish Robin Hood, Rob Roy Macgregor.

ST. RONAN'S WELL (1824)
Scott's only novel of manners, set in his own times, with a conventional
plot, centred on the social life of a fashionable Scottish spa.

THE SURGEON'S DAUGHER (1827)
Dramatic tale of an adventurer. Janet Gray, the Scottish surgeon's
daughter, is the victim of a plan to lure her to Tippoo Sahib, enemy of the
British in India.

THE TALISMAN (1825)
The second of the Tales of the Crusaders.

*WAVERLEY (1814)
Romance of a young man whose loyalties are divided between his duties
as an officer in the king's army, and his desire to help Charles Edward,
the Young Pretender. The battle of Prestonpans is a climax to this first
of the Waverley novels, that swept through Europe and made literary
history.

*WOODSTOCK (1826) 'Or, The Cavalier: a Tale of the Year
1651.'
The above briefly sets out details of the series that comprise the
Waverley novels. In addition there are some short stories, usually bound
in the volume containing *The Highland Widow*; see *The Short Stories of
Sir Walter Scott*, O.U.P. (*Worlds Classics*) 1924, 7s 6d. The fullest set
available at January, 1962, was the twenty-three volumes in the A. and C.
Black standard edition, 8s 6d each (a few 7s 6d). Dent's *Everyman* Scott is
in progress of reprinting, twelve volumes being available, 8s 6d to 12s 6d
each.
The most popular are available in *Collins* (*Classics*), and there are fifteen
in *Nelson* (*Classics*).

*Sewell, Anna (1820-1878) BLACK BEAUTY (1877) *Collins* (*Classics*)
    1923 5s; *Dent* (*Children's Illustrated Classics*) 1950 10s 6d; (*Every-
    man*) 1921 6s 6d; *Nelson* (*Classics*) 1954 5s
'The autobiography of a horse.' This perennial favourite of the nursery,
often reread with pleasure in later life, is available in many other
editions.

*Shaw, George Bernard (1856-1950) THE BLACK GIRL AND SOME
    LESSER TALES *Constable* 1934 15s Illus.
'With a preface.' The major tale was first published, with decorations by
John Farleigh, who designed the handsome volume, in 1932, entitled
The Adventures of the Black Girl In Her Search For God. It is an amusing
satire in the style of Voltaire's *Candide*. Shaw's other fiction, written in
his 'nonage', comprises four novels reprinted for inclusion in the uniform
edition of the Complete Works.

Shelley, Mary Wollstonecraft (1797-1851) FRANKENSTEIN (1818)
    Dent (*Everyman*) (1912) 1959 8s 6d; *W. H. Allen* (*Dolphin Books*)
    1960 7s 6d
Shelley's wife recounts in her preface to this ever-popular tale of terror,
in which a student named Frankenstein creates a monster, how Byron
and Shelley and she spent a wet summer holiday in Switzerland writing
ghost and horror tales of the supernatural. Mrs. Shelley offered this wild
story of 'The Modern Prometheus' as her contribution.

Shelton, Thomas (*fl.* 1616) CERVANTES: HISTORY OF DON QUIXOTE
    DE LA MANCHA translated by Thomas Shelton (1612) *Constable*
    1922

A notable Tudor translation, now superseded by that of P. A. Motteux (1712) available in two volumes in *Everyman's Library*, 10s 6d each, with notes added by J. G. Lockhart and L. B. Walton.

Sheppard, Elizabeth Sara (1830–62) CHARLES AUCHESTER (1853) *Dent (Everyman)* 1911
A *roman à clef*, with Mendelssohn as the musician presented in a glowing portrait rather larger than life.

Shiel, Matthew Phipps (1865–1947) THE PURPLE CLOUD (1901) *Gollancz* (1929) 1963 18s
A masterpiece of 'science fiction' by a contemporary of that other English pioneer of the genre, H. G. Wells. After the scientist-explorer has unleashed the purple cloud he finds that all human life, save his own and that of one other, has been obliterated from a ruined Europe.

Shorthouse, Joseph Henry (1834–1903) JOHN INGLESANT *Macmillan* (1880; 1881) 1905; *S.C.M. Press* 1961 13s 6d
Historical novel of grave and enduring charm. The eponymous hero serves Charles I with loyalty and at great risk. He visits the community of Mr. Nicholas Ferrar at Little Gidding, and describes the life of the devoted few, who pass their time in prayer and contemplation, with bookbinding as their only relaxation. Later the scene shifts to Italy, where Inglesant becomes involved in political and religious intrigues. The reprint is slightly abridged.

Smollett, Tobias (1721–71) *THE EXPEDITION OF HUMPHRY CLINKER (1771) *Collins (Classics)* 1954 6s; *Dent (Everyman)* (1943) 1961 10s 6d; *Nelson (Classics)* 1936 6s; *O.U.P. (Worlds Classics)* 1925 6s
If only one of Smollett's novels is read, it is usually this one, because it is his best. Thackeray admired it as one of the funniest novels in the language. It is in epistolary form, like Richardson's novels, and relates how Lieutenant Obadiah Lismahago and a party of travellers ramble through many towns from Bath to London and Scotland. Notes on places and persons are provided in *Collins's* and *Everyman's* library.

THE ADVENTURES OF PEREGRINE PICKLE (1751) 2 vols. *Dent (Everyman)* (1930) 1956 8s 6d each
'In which are included the Memoirs of a Lady of Quality.' Introduction by Walter Allen.

THE ADVENTURES OF RODERICK RANDOM (1748) *Dent (Everyman)* (1927) 1958 8s 6d; *O.U.P. (Worlds Classics)* 1930 7s 6d
Picaresque adventures, modelled on the *Gil Blas* of Le Sage, translated from the French by Smollett, in 1750. For other, and minor novels by this writer see the uniform, standard edition of his *Complete Works*, 11 volumes Shakespeare Head Press, Blackwell, 1925–6. Smollett also translated Voltaire's *Candide* included in J. C. Thornton's revised edition in *Everyman*, 1937, 8s 6d.

Somerville, E. Œ. and 'Martin Ross' (1858-1949; 1865-1915) THE
IRISH R.M. COMPLETE *Faber* (1928) 1956 15s
Edith Œnone Somerville and her cousin Violet Martin, were notable
Irish sportswomen, ardent foxhunters, yet with considerable intellectual
gifts. These stories of Irish life and sport abound in vivid talk, reproduced with fidelity, and in lively humour and characterisation. The first
volume, *Some Experiences of an Irish R.M.* (1899), and *Further Experiences* (1908) are available in one volume of *Everyman*, Dent (1944) 1953,
8s 6d.

THE REAL CHARLOTTE (1894) *O.U.P.* (*Worlds Classics*) 1948 8s 6d
Regarded as the best of the novels written by these collaborating
authors.

*Stephens, James (1882-1950) THE CROCK OF GOLD *Macmillan*
(1912) 1961 10s 6d
Fantasy, myth and legend, semi-philosophic parables—all these went to
the making of this 'novel-cum-fairy-story' as the publisher so aptly
describes it.

*Sterne, Laurence (1713-68) TRISTRAM SHANDY 9 vols. (1760-7)
Collins (*Classics*) 1955 7s; *Dent* (*Everyman*) (1912) 1956 8s 6d;
Macdonald (*Illustrated Classics*) 1948 15s; *O.U.P.* (*Worlds
Classics*) (1903) 1958 7s 6d
The Life and Opinions of Tristram Shandy, Gent., to give this extraordinary
book its full title, is like no other in the language. Discursive, eccentric,
episodic, wayward, sometimes coarse, sentimental and tender: it is all
these, and richly humorous.

Stevenson, Robert Louis (1850-94) *THE BLACK ARROW (1888)
Collins (*Classics*) 1953 6s; *Dent* (*Children's Illustrated Classics*)
1957 10s 6d; *Nelson* (*Classics*) 1955 5s

Historical romance of the Wars of the Roses, and Richard III. In the
Collins Classics edition it is bound with *Prince Otto* (1885), a social comedy
set in an imaginary kingdom, notable as a departure from Stevenson's
usual style.

*CATRIONA (1893) *Nelson* (*Classics*) 1956 5s; *O.U.P.* (*Illustrated
Classics*) 1947 8s 6d
Frequently bound with *Kidnapped*, to which it is a sequel.

*DR. JEKYLL AND MR. HYDE (1886) *Collins* (*Classics*) 1953 6s;
Dent (*Everyman*) (1925) 1962 7s 6d; *Macdonald* (*Illustrated*) 1950
15s; *Nelson* (*Classics*) 1949 5s
A popular masterpiece of the macabre. Bound with other works: *The
Merry Men*; and *The Island Nights' Entertainments*: Collins; *The Merry
Men and other stories*: Everyman; *The Pavilion On the Links, The Merry
Men, The Treasure of Franchard, The Beach of Falesá*, and ten other stories,
with an introduction by Sir Compton-Mackenzie: Macdonald; *Weir of
Hermiston*: Nelson.

ISLAND NIGHTS' ENTERTAINMENTS (1893) *Nelson* (*Classics*) 1925 5s
Long-short stories of the South Seas. See also above.

*KIDNAPPED (1886) *Collins* (*Classics*) 1953 6s; *Dent* (*Everyman*)
1962 12s 6d; *Nelson* (*Classics*) 1926 5s; *O.U.P.* (*Worlds Classics*)
1926 6s
Catriona, the sequel to this story of high adventure and romance after the
'45 Rebellion, is bound with *Kidnapped* in all the above editions except
Nelson. Also available separately in Oxford *Illustrated Classics*, O.U.P.,
1946, 8s 6d.

*THE MASTER OF BALLANTRAE (1889) *Collins* (*Classics*) 1953 6s;
Dent (*Everyman*) 1956 7s 6d
The steward of a declining family tells this story of the period of the
'45 Rebellion: two brothers take opposite sides. Bound with *Weir of
Hermiston* in both the above editions. Separately in *Nelson* (*Classics*)
1926 5s; and O.U.P. (*World's Classics*) 1957 6s.

THE MERRY MEN AND OTHER TALES AND FABLES (1887)
See above for editions that include these short stories.

*THE NEW ARABIAN NIGHTS (1882) *Collins* (*Classics*) 1925 6s;
Nelson (*Classics*) 1925 5s
Amusing fantasies, the most famous being *The Suicide Club*, the adven-
ture of *The Cream Tarts*, and a romance *The Pavilion On the Links*. The
Collins edition also includes *The Dynamiter* (1885), a volume of stories in
similar style, some being the work of Mrs. Stevenson.

ST. IVES (1897) *Dent* (*Everyman*) (1934) 1955 8s 6d
The adventures of a French prisoner of war who is sent to Edinburgh
Castle. Sir Arthur Quiller-Couch completed this novel, left unfinished.

*TREASURE ISLAND (1883) *Collins* (*Classics*) 1953 5s; *Dent* (*Everyman*) 1962 12s 6d; *Nelson* (*Classics*) 1954 5s; *O.U.P.* (*Illustrated
Classics*) 1944 8s 6d
The most popular of all Stevenson's novels, with readers in every land,
and of all ages, is reprinted in many other editions. In *Everyman* it is
bound with *The New Arabian Nights*, for which see above.

*WEIR OF HERMISTON (1896) *Collins* (*Classics*) 1953 6s; *Dent*
(*Everyman*) 1956 7s 6d
Bound in both the above editions with *The Master of Ballantrae*, which
see above. Although unfinished, this grimly powerful fragment of what
was obviously planned as a major novel is mature, and seems to have
been Stevenson's finest character study. Archie Weir is the son of a
'hanging judge', and takes refuge away from a home that revolts him.
Kirstie, his kinswoman and housekeeper, and Christina, with whom
Archie falls tragically in love, are characters drawn with romantic and
passionate understanding.

THE WRECKER (1892) *O.U.P.* (*Worlds Classics*) 1950 8s 6d
A modern adventure and mystery novel, written in collaboration with
Stevenson's son-in-law, Lloyd Osborne (1868-1947).

*THE WRONG BOX (1889) *O.U.P.* (*Worlds Classics*) 1954 7s 6d
A comedy, bordering upon extravaganza, concerned with the endeavours of fortune-hunters to get rid of a corpse, and of two men struggling to acquire the legacy of two tontine holders.

Stoker, Bram (1847-1912) DRACULA (1897) *Rider* 1950 7s 6d; *Hutchinson* (*Arrow Books*) 1957 2s 6d
This horrific story has established itself as a minor classic of its blood-curdling type, and indeed has become almost folk-lore.

THE LAIR OF THE WHITE WORM (1911) *Hutchinson* (*Arrow Books*) 1960 2s 6d

*Stowe, Harriet Beecher (1811-96) UNCLE TOM'S CABIN (1852) *Dent* (*Everyman*) (1909) 1961 10s 6d; *Nelson* (*Classics*) 1930 7s
This world-famous story of 'life among the lowly' has been translated into more than twenty languages. The Fugitive Slave Law of the Southern States of America was itself, practically outlawed, so powerful was the influence of this moving novel, exposing the cruelties and injustices of the slave system.

Sturgis, Howard Overing (1855-1920) BELCHAMBER (1904) *O.U.P.* (*Worlds Classics*) 1935
Gerard Hopkins introduced this reprint of a minor novel in the style of Henry James. It concerns an estate, Belchamber, and two brothers, of contrasting temperaments and characters.

Surtees, Robert Smith (1803-64) ASK MAMMA (1858) *Methuen* 1949 8s 6d
HANDLEY CROSS (1843) *Methuen* 1850 9s 6d
HAWBUCK GRANGE (1847) *Methuen* 1950 9s 6d
HILLINGDON HALL (1845) *Methuen* 1950 8s 6d

*JORROCKS'S JAUNTS AND JOLLITIES (1838) *Methuen* 1950 15s Illus.; *Dent* (*Everyman*) 1928 6s 6d
The most popular of the Surtees sporting novels.

MR. FACEY ROMFORD'S HOUNDS (1865) *Methuen* 1950 9s 6d

*MR. SPONGE'S SPORTING TOUR (1853) *Methuen* 1949 21s Illus.; *O.U.P.* (*Worlds Classics*) 1958 9s 6d Illus.
'. . . a masterpiece in its own way. It is the story of a crook . . . solid Surtees; he comes through every line . . .'—*Joyce Cary* in his appreciative introduction to the *Worlds Classics* edition. Both editions reproduce the original illustrations by John Leech.

PLAIN OR RINGLETS? (1860) *Methuen* 1950 9s 6d Illus.
A limited edition for collectors of these popular sporting novels was published in ten volumes, by Eyre and Spottiswoode, 1930, £17 10s the set. Methuen's standard set reproduces hundreds of woodcuts made by John Leech and others for the first editions, and some of the colour

plates. A characteristic selection will be found in *Hunting With Jorrocks*, edited by Lionel Gough from *Handley Cross*, with illustrations by Edward Ardizonne, O.U.P. (*Illustrated Classics*) 1956, 12s 6d.

*Swift, Jonathan (1667-1745) GULLIVER'S TRAVELS (1726) *Collins* (*Classics*) 1953 5s; *Dent* (*Everyman*) (1906) Preface by Harold Williams 1961 7s 6d; *Nelson* (*Classics*) 1920 5s; ed. by A. B. Gough O.U.P. (*Standard Authors*) 1919 12s 6d; (*Worlds Classics*) 1902 6s

The *Everyman* edition gives the complete text from Swift's own revised edition, published in Dublin, 1735 (including six plans and maps). *Oxford Standard Authors* edition includes *A Tale of a Tub*, and other pieces.

Taylor, Philip Meadows (1808-76) CONFESSIONS OF A THUG (1839) O.U.P. (*Worlds Classics*) 1916

Written as a romance of adventure in India, but it was based on long experience of the country and of the violent deeds of the ruffians and assassins banded together by some secret semi-religious oaths until they were suppressed.

Thackeray, William Makepeace (1811-63) THE ADVENTURES OF PHILIP (1861) 2 vols. *Murray* 1887 2s 6d each

Thackeray's last novel, continued from *A Shabby Genteel Story* (1840) which in the pocket reprint is included with the sequel.

BARRY LYNDON (1844) *Murray* 30s
A satirical novel first called *The Luck of Barry Lyndon*.

THE BOOK OF SNOBS (1848) *Murray* 30s; *W. H. Allen* (*Dolphin Books*) 1962 7s 6d

Contributions to *Punch* reprinted, with omissions. 'The Snobs of England, By One of Themselves', is not strictly fiction, but satirical journalism.

*HENRY ESMOND (1852) *Collins* (*Classics*) 1954 6s; *Dent* (*Everyman*) (1906) 1955 10s 6d; *Nelson* (*Classics*) 1955 6s; O.U.P. (*Worlds Classics*) 1903 7s 6d

A masterpiece of historical fiction. Period: the beginning of the eighteenth century. The characters include the brilliantly-drawn heroine, Beatrix Esmond, and many great men of Queen Anne's reign, such as Swift and Steele.

*THE NEWCOMES (1853-5) 2 vols. *Dent* (*Everyman*) (1910) 1962 12s 6d each

A story told by Pendennis, and one of Thackeray's five major novels. The character of Colonel Newcome is drawn with loving detail.

*PENDENNIS (1848-50) 2 vols. *Dent* (*Everyman*) (1910) 1959 10s 6d each

Arthur Pendennis and Captain Shandon provide the material for one of Thackeray's liveliest and most amusing novels of social satire, largely autobiographical.

THE ROSE AND THE RING (1855) *Macmillan* (1908) 1958 6s Illus.; *Nelson* (*Classics*) (1940) 1957 5s
Charming 'fireside pantomime', being 'the History of Prince Giglio and Prince Bulbo, by Michael Angelo Titmarsh'. Nelson's edition includes a companion piece for children, *The Alphabet*, with the author's grotesque illustrations.

*VANITY FAIR (1847-8) *Chatto* (*Zodiac Press*) 1948 15s; *Collins* (*Classics*) 1954 7s; *Dent* (*Everyman*) (1908) 1957 10s 6d; *Macdonald* (*Illustrated Classics*) 1950 15s; *Nelson* (*Classics*) 1955 8s 6d
One of the most popular classics in the language. It is a social satire, a comedy of manners, and a domestic comedy, with the most famous fictional characters of Becky Sharp and Josh Sedley adding their names to the great gallery of portraits started by John Fielding in *Tom Jones* exactly a century before. In this 'Novel Without a Hero' some of the characters are drawn from the life.

THE VIRGINIANS (1857-9) 2 vols. *Dent* (*Everyman*) (1911) (1961) 10s 6d each
A sequel to *Henry Esmond*, relating the careers of the descendants of Esmond in Virginia and later, in London. Some chapters deal with the American War of Independence, and introduce Wolfe and Washington.

*Thomas, Dylan (1914-53) PORTRAIT OF THE ARTIST AS A YOUNG DOG *Dent* 1940 12s 6d
'A fictional autobiography.'

A PROSPECT OF THE SEA ed. by Daniel Jones *Dent* 1955 12s 6d
'Stories and other prose writings.'

*Tomlinson, H. M. (Henry Major Tomlinson) (1873-1958) GALLIONS REACH *Heinemann* (1927) *Hart-Davis* (*Mariners Library*) 1950 10s 6d
A sea adventure by a great prose writer who was himself a sailor and traveller. It was awarded the *Femina Vie-Heureuse* prize, and is now included in the standard series usually reserved for non-fiction, and personal narratives.

Trollope, Anthony (1815-82) *THE BARSETSHIRE NOVELS 6 vols.
Vol. 1: *The Warden* (1855); vol. 2: *Barchester Towers* (1857); vol. 3: *Dr. Thorne* (1858); vol. 4: *Framley Parsonage* (1861); vol. 5: *The Small House At Allington* (1864); vol. 6: *The Last Chronicle of Barset* (1867).
Chatto (*Zodiac Press*) 1946-8 72s (the set, boxed); *Dent* (*Everyman*) 7s 6d to 10s 6d each (set, of 7 vols. 54s 6d); *O.U.P.* (*Worlds Classics*) 46s 6d (set); *Nelson* (*Classics*) 43s (set); (*Oxford Illustrated Trollope*) *The Warden* (15s); *Barchester Towers* 2 vols. (25s); *Collins* (*Classics*) *The Warden* (5s); *Barchester Towers* (6s).

*THE PALLISER SERIES *O.U.P.* (*Oxford Illustrated Trollope*)
1: *Can You Forgive Her?* (1864-5) 2 vols. 1948 30s (the set); 2: *Phineas Finn, the Irish Member* (1866) 2 vols. 1949 30s (the set); 3: *The Eustace Diamonds* (1872) 2 vols. 1950 30s (the set); 4: *Phineas Redux* (1874) 2 vols.

1951 30s (the set); 5: *The Prime Minister* (1876) 2 vols. 1952 36s (the set); 6: *The Duke's Children* (1880) 1954 25s.

The *Palliser* series of political novels narrates the career of Plantagenet Palliser, later Duke of Omnium and of his wife, Glencora. The Oxford set is introduced in the first novel by Michael Sadleir; the others each have an introduction by either an English or an American critic; the illustrations are by Lynton Lamb and others. The set is also reprinted in *Worlds Classics*, 6 vols. 10s 6d each. This series also contains many other favourite Trollope novels: *The American Senator* (1877) 8s 6d; *Ayala's Angel* (1881) 9s 6d; *The Belton Estate* (1866) 7s 6d; *The Claverings* (1867) 8s 6d; *Dr. Wortle's School* (1881) 6s; *He Knew He Was Right* (1865-9) 10s 6d; *Is He Popenjoy?* (1877-8) 9s 6d; *John Caldigate* (1878-9) 9s 6d; *The Kellys and the O'Kellys* (1848) 8s 6d; *Lady Anna* (1874) 7s; *Miss Mackenzie* (1865) 8s 6d; *Nina Balatka* (1867) and *Linda Tressel* (1868) 7s 6d; *An Old Man's Love* (1884) 6s; *Orley Farm* (1862) 9s 6d; *Rachel Ray* (1863) 7s 6d; *Ralph the Heir* (1870-1) 9s 6d; *The Three Clerks* (1858) 8s 6d; *The Vicar of Bulhampton* (1869-70) 7s 6d; *The Way We Live Now* (1874-5) 10s 6d.

*Twain, Mark (Samuel Langhorne Clemens) (1835-1910) THE ADVENTURES OF HUCKLEBERRY FINN (1884) *Chatto* (*Zodiac Press*) 1962 15s; *Collins* (*Classics*) 1953 6s; *Cresset Press* 1950 10s 6d; *Dent* (*Children's Illustrated Classics*) 1955 10s 6d; (*Everyman*) (1944) 1954 10s 6d; *Harrap* 1924 8s 6d; *Nelson* (*Classics*) 1953 5s

Probably the first novels by an American with a quality purely national and home-bred; and in an idiomatic style owing nothing to the classics of English literature, were *Tom Sawyer* and the above story. To some extent autobiographical, this novel of youth has delighted readers of all ages and of every generation. In *Collins Classics* and the *Everyman* edition, it is bound with the companion story of *Tom Sawyer*, for which see below. T. S. Eliot contributes an appreciation in the preface to the *Cresset Press* reprint.

THE ADVENTURES OF TOM SAWYER (1876) *Chatto* (*Zodiac Press*) 1962 12s 6d; *Harrap* 1924 8s 6d; *Nelson* (*Classics*) 1953 5s

See also above for two editions bound with *Huckleberry Finn*. In *Tom Sawyer* the hero and his friend Huck are in company on the Mississippi: the first the leader in all escapades, the other more thoughtful. Sequels were *Tom Sawyer Abroad* (1894) and *Tom Sawyer, Detective* (1897), but these are now seldom read.

PUDD'NHEAD WILSON (1894) *Chatto* (*Zodiac Press*) 1955 12s 6d

Introduced in the reprint by F. R. Leavis. It is the story of a lawyer in a small town in Missouri, and of his ultimately successful struggle to assert his character in a community where he is disregarded and undervalued.

A YANKEE AT THE COURT OF KING ARTHUR (1889) *Chatto* (*Zodiac Press*) 1957 12s 6d

Fantastic farce, guying with a broad, effective humour the absurdities of some minor, but popular costume pieces and historical romances.

*Urquhart, Sir Thomas (1611-60) THE HEROIC DEEDS OF GAR-
GANTUA AND PANTAGRUEL By Rabelais, translated by Sir
Thomas Urquhart and Peter Le Motteux (1653-94) 2 vols.
Dent (Everyman) (1929) 1954 8s 6d each
Introduction by D. B. Wyndham Lewis. This extraordinary satire of
sixteenth-century French literature found inspired translators using
English seventeenth-century prose with an exuberance well-suited to the
original, which, in Chamber's *Biographical Dictionary* is aptly summed up
as 'the most astonishing treasury of wit, wisdom, common sense, and
satire that the world has ever seen'.

Wallace, Edgar (1875-1932) *THE FOUR JUST MEN *Hodder* (1905)
Pan Books 1959 2s 6d
A thrilling novel of crime and punishment well-established from the
author's prolific output as one of his best inventions. It has a world-wide
sale in many languages.

Wallace, Lewis (1827-1905) BEN HUR (1880) *Blackie* 1956 6s;
Collins (Classics) 1930 6s; *W. H. Allen (Dolphin Books)* 1962 10s
'A tale of the Christ.' This immensely popular American novel on the
days of the Messiah in Judaea is a world bestseller, and has been adapted
for both stage and screen with notable success.

Walpole, Horace (1717-97) THE CASTLE OF OTRANTO (1765)
Included in volume 3 of *Shorter Novels*, for which see in next section
under Saintsbury and Henderson. This Gothick Romance has a secure
place in literary history. It is a tale of thirteenth-century Italy, with the
sensational, supernatural common to all novels of this type emphasised.
Saintsbury says of it: 'The story is a clumsy one, and its wonders are
perpetually hovering on the verge of the burlesque. But its influence,
though not immediate, was exceedingly great.'—*A Short History of
English Literature*.

Walpole, Sir Hugh Seymour (1884-1941) THE CATHEDRAL *Macmillan* (1922) 1950 7s 6d
A study in spiritual conflict, and the nearest thing to Trollope's Barchester novels in fiction. The author grew up in a New Zealand cathedral
city, but the scene of his novel is probably Polchester, in Cornwall.
Sequels entered below.

THE DARK FOREST *Macmillan* (1916); *Hart-Davis* 1949 3s 6d
The sequel is *The Secret City*, entered below.

HARMER JOHN *Macmillan* 1926
The third of the series started in *The Cathedral*.

JEREMY *Macmillan* (1919) 1949 7s 6d; *(St. Martins Library)* 1957
3s 6d

JEREMY AND HAMLET *Macmillan* (1923) 1951 7s 6d

JEREMY AT CRALE *Macmillan* (1927) 1952 7s 6d
Trilogy devoted to the childhood and gradual growing-up of Jeremy,
'his friends, his ambitions, and his one great enemy'.

*MR. PERRIN AND MR. TRAILL *Macmillan* (1911) 1949 3s 6d;
Dent (Everyman) (1935) 1955 8s 6d
The *Everyman* edition of this masterpiece, has a special introduction by
the author. The 'tragi-comedy' depicts the hatred and the meannesses
lurking beneath the normal jealousies of two teachers in a small private
school in the West country.

THE OLD LADIES *Macmillan* (1924) *Hart-Davis* 1949 3s 6d
The second in the Trollopian series, started in *The Cathedral*.

*PORTRAIT OF A MAN WITH RED HAIR *Macmillan* (1925) *Hart-
Davis* 1949 3s 6d
Walpole's best work in the sinister, macabre vein.

*ROGUE HERRIES *Macmillan* (1930) 1948 12s 6d (*St. Martins
Library*) 1957 5s
The first of a popular regional series of romances, known as *The Herries
Chronicle*. The sequels are: *Judith Paris*, Macmillan, 1931, 12s 6d (*St.
Martins Library*) 1958, 6s; *The Fortress*, Macmillan, 1932, 12s 6d; and,
Vanessa, Macmillan, 1933, 12s 6d. The *Chronicle* begins with the 1745
Rebellion, centred on the border town of Carlisle; but it is Borrowdale,
in the English Lake District, that provides most of the regional scenes.

THE SECRET CITY *Macmillan* 1919
'A novel in three parts', and a sequel to *The Dark Forest*. The city was
Petrograd in the time of the revolution.

Ward, Mrs. Humphrey (1851-1920) ROBERT ELSMERE 2 vols.
Murray (1888) *Nelson (Classics)* 1952 7s
A didactic novel by the granddaughter of Dr. Arnold of Rugby. It is a
once popular and controversial study in conflict between loyalty to an
institution and a creed, and agnosticism.

Watts-Dunton, Theodore (1832-1914) AYLWIN (1898) *O.U.P.
(Worlds Classics)* 1929 7s 6d
A poetically conceived novel, with some autobiographical elements
mingled in the pattern of the story. Characters in the author's circle
(including William Morris) are identifiable. The description of Snowdon
and other parts of Wales were once much admired, though time has
thrust the book into the background of fiction.

*Webb, Mary (1881-1927) PRECIOUS BANE *Cape* 1924 13s 6d
The uniform edition of six novels, known as *The Sarn* edition, is published by Jonathan Cape, who also publishes a volume of characteristic
prose with some poems, in *The Essential Mary Webb*, with an introduction
by Martin Armstrong, 1949, illustrated, 12s 6d. *Precious Bane*, the story
of Prudence Sarn, was awarded the *Femina Vie-Heureuse* prize. Next to
it in popularity is *Gone To Earth*, 1917, also available in a *Foursquare*
paperback edition, 2s 6d. These sombre, regional novels contain many
notable descriptions of the author's native Shropshire.

*Wells, Herbert George (1866-1946) ANN VERONICA (1909) *Dent* (*Everyman*) (1944) 1962 12s 6d
'A modern love story', and a landmark in Edwardian fiction, dealing with problems of the individual woman involved in the contemporary struggle for emancipation from Victorian ideas and ideals about 'the proper place' of an intelligent woman in social and professional spheres.

BEALBY *Methuen* (1915) (*Venture Library*) 1958 5s
'A holiday'; light-hearted comedy for pastime reading.

THE FIRST MEN IN THE MOON (1901) *Collins* (*Classics*) 1930 6s
A famous example of 'science fiction' that nowadays has a topical interest.

THE FOOD OF THE GODS (1904) *Collins* (*Classics*) 1926 6s
An imaginative fantasy developed with extraordinary power.

THE HISTORY OF MR. POLLY (1910) *Collins* (*Classics*) 1926 6s
One of Wells's early masterpieces, and still, probably his most popular social comedy.

IN THE DAYS OF THE COMET (1906) *Collins* (*Classics*) 1927 6s
An example of science fiction on a Utopian theme; replanning for Utopia is made possible by changes on earth caused by the passage of a comet.

THE INVISIBLE MAN (1897) *Collins* (*Classics*) 1926 6s
Wells's most amusing and convincing fantasy, developed with great skill and verisimilitude.

THE ISLAND OF DR. MOREAU (1896) *Heinemann* 1960 12s 6d
An engrossing and somewhat macabre story, in which the horrific Dr. Moreau experiments on gorillas to produce a kind of semi-human monster.

KIPPS (1905) *Collins* (*Classics*) 1926 6s
'The story of a simple soul.' This major novel has some autobiographical elements.

LOVE AND MR. LEWISHAM (1900) *Collins* (*Classics*) 1926 6s
A minor, but enjoyable romance, with scenes of realistic comedy.

MEANWHILE *Benn* (1927) 1962 16s
'The picture of a lady.' Written as a topical novel with the central event based on the General Strike of 1926.

THE SEA LADY *Methuen* (1902) 1948 7s
'A tissue of moonshine': a fantastic comedy concerned with the arrival on the beach at Sandgate of a mermaid.

SHORT STORIES *Benn* (1927) 1947 15s
Am omnibus collection of 1030 pages of 63 masterly short stories, chiefly 'science fiction' or imaginative fantasies.

THE SLEEPER AWAKES (1899) *Collins* (*Classics*) 1926 6s
A scientific romance, forecasting the London of the year 2000.

TALES OF LIFE AND ADVENTURE *Collins* (*Classics*) 1927 6s

TALES OF THE UNEXPECTED *Collins* (*Classics*) 1927 6s

TALES OF WONDER *Collins (Classics)* 1927 6s
In these three volumes are reprinted the short stories, arranged in groups, indicated by the collective titles.

THE TIME MACHINE (1895) *Dent (Everyman)* (1935) 1954 10s 6d; *Heinemann* 1945 7s 6d
The earliest 'science fiction', and one of the most brilliant stories ever written in this genre. In *Everyman* it is bound with

THE WHEELS OF CHANCE (1896)
A charming comedy about a cycling holiday, nowadays read for its period flavour.

Weyman, Stanley (1855-1928) CHIPPINGE *Murray* 1906; OVINGTON'S BANK *Murray* 1922; THE GREAT HOUSE *Murray* 1919
A trilogy on life in the first decade of the nineteenth century. Sir Keith Feiling, in a volume of biographical essays called *In Christchurch Hall*, Macmillan, 1960, 25s, evaluates this as Weyman's best work. He also rates highly *Count Hannibal*, Nelson, 1901, a tale of the massacre of St. Bartholomew; *The Long Night*, 1903; and *The Castle Inn*, 1898.

*UNDER THE RED ROSE (1894) *Collins (Classics)* (1926) 1958 6s; *Penguin Books* 1962
Historical romance of the time of Cardinal Richelieu, and perhaps Weyman's most popular novel of intrigue, adventure and swashbuckling drama.

Wharton, Edith (1862-1937) ETHAN FROME (1924) *Penguin Books* 1938 2s 6d
A novel in the style of Henry James. This gifted American writer here forsook her usual social comedy, and created this tragic story of people in a remote village in Massachusetts.

*THE HOUSE OF MIRTH (1905) *O.U.P.* (*Worlds Classics*) 1936 7s 6d; *Corgi* 1962 4s 6d
A brilliantly satirical novel on the smart set of New York.

*White, William Hale ('Mark Rutherford') (1831-1913) THE AUTOBIOGRAPHY OF MARK RUTHERFORD (1881) *O.U.P.* 1936 MARK RUTHERFORD'S DELIVERANCE (1885) *O.U.P.* 1936
Two autobiographical novels of spiritual significance for those who sometimes doubt if Christianity provides answers to problems of life involving suffering and poverty.

THE REVOLUTION IN TANNER'S LANE (1887) *O.U.P.* 1936
A study of radicalism in the days of the Bread Riots, and of the sufferings of social workers among the very poor from 1814 to about 1825. Although 'Mark Rutherford' is now neglected, André Gide, Arnold Bennett, and D. H. Lawrence all thought highly of his work, and considered him a major figure in nineteenth-century fiction. See Irvin Stock's excellent critical study *William Hale White*, Allen and Unwin, 1956, 25s, with an introduction by Lionel Trilling.

Whyte-Melville, George (1821-1878) THE GLADIATORS (1863)
Dent (Everyman) 1911
'A tale of Rome and Judaea in the first century A.D.'

KATERFELTO (1875) *Ward Lock* 1921
A sporting novel of Exmoor in the mid-eighteenth century, characteristic of this writer's popular stories of hunting, here mingled with slight historical background.

*Wilde, Oscar (1854-1900) THE HAPPY PRINCE AND OTHER STORIES
(1888) *Duckworth* 1928 10s 6d Illus.
An edition of the complete fairy stories. It thus includes those in the volume published as *A House of Pomegranates*, below.

A HOUSE OF POMEGRANATES (1892) *Unicorn Press* 1949 8s 6d
LORD ARTHUR SAVILE'S CRIME AND OTHER STORIES (1891) *Methuen*
1949 5s; *Unicorn Press* 1949 8s 6d
The title story is an amusing skit on crime stories; among the other stories is *The Canterville Ghost*, and, *The Portrait of Mr. W. H.*, which see also below.

THE PICTURE OF DORIAN GRAY (1891) *Collins (Classics)* 1953 6s;
Dent (Everyman) 1931 7s 6d; *Penguin* 1956 2s 6d; *Unicorn Press*
1947 8s 6d
In both Collins's edition and *Everyman*, this epigrammatic novel is bound with short stories and other works.

THE PORTRAIT OF MR. W. H. ed. by Vyvvan Holland *Methuen*
1958 15s
The first publication of the full version, nearly twice as long as the 1889 edition. The editor states that his father was fascinated by the theme, and as it grew in his imagination, he rewrote it. It develops a theory on the identity of the mysterious 'Mr. W. H.' of Shakespeare's Sonnets, published in 1609.

Williams, Charles (1886-1945) ALL HALLOW'S EVE *Faber* (1945)
1947 15s
DESCENT INTO HELL *Faber* (1937) 1949 12s 6d
THE PLACE OF THE LION (1931) *Faber* 1932 12s 6d
WAR IN HEAVEN (1930) *Faber* 1947 15s; *(paperbacks)* 1962 6s
These may be read as thrilling stories on supernatural themes. But Charles Williams, the poet, offered in his fiction some discussion of spiritual problems, and it is this serious element that attracts many readers today.

Wister, Owen (1860-1938) THE VIRGINIAN *Macmillan* (1902) 1949
(St. Martins Library) 1961 6s
A classic of the American Wild West, being a romance of Wyoming and of 'the Horsemen of the Plains', with their great cattle herds in 1870 onwards.

Wood, Mrs. Henry (1814-87) EAST LYNNE (1861) *Collins (Classics)*
(1924) 1954 7s; *Nelson (Classics)* 1906 7s
Once a very popular domestic novel, with a strong, melodramatic plot,
this is still read with enjoyment.

MRS. HALLIBURTON'S TROUBLES (1862) *Nelson (Classics)* 1924 7s
The characterisation may be outmoded, but craftsmanship in telling a
good story is there. Mrs. Henry Wood's output was prolific; many
readers judge this book to be her best and most enduring.

Woolf, Virginia (1882-1941) BETWEEN THE ACTS *Hogarth Press*
1941 9s 6d A HAUNTED HOUSE AND OTHER STORIES *Hogarth Press*
1944 8s 6d
JACOB'S ROOM *Hogarth Press* 1922 8s 6d
*MRS. DALLOWAY *Hogarth Press* 1925 8s 6d
NIGHT AND DAY *Hogarth Press* 1919 10s 6d
*ORLANDO *Hogarth Press* 1928 10s 6d
*TO THE LIGHTHOUSE *Hogarth Press* 1927 10s 6d; *Dent (Everyman)*
(1938) 1961 7s 6d
THE VOYAGE OUT *Hogarth Press* 1915 10s 6d
*THE WAVES *Hogarth Press* 1931 8s 6d
THE YEARS *Hogarth Press* 1937 10s 6d
Volumes of the uniform collected edition of one of the most intellectual
writers of the century. Her novels and stories are all delicate and sensitive
studies in character, developed by the exercise of a technique in narration
that has given Virginia Woolf a distinguished place in European literature as an innovator. *To the Lighthouse, Mrs. Dalloway, The Waves,* and
the delightfully ingenious *Orlando,* may be selected as examples of her
art at its greatest.

Yonge, Charlotte Mary (1823-1901) THE HEIR OF REDCLYFFE
Macmillan (1853)
A didactic novel, sentimental, but once very popular: it is a fair example
of the work of a prolific novelist, somewhat similar to Mrs. Henry
Wood.

THE LITTLE DUKE (1854) *O.U.P.* 1959 5s; *Dent* 1962 10s 6d
A story of Richard the Fearless and Normandy from A.D. 942 to 996.
It is still enjoyed by young readers, and may be reread with pleasure by
adults.

Young, Emily Hilda (1880-1949) THE CURATE'S WIFE *Cape* (1934)
1950 7s 6d
MISS MOLE *Cape* (1930) 1950 7s 6d
Awarded the James Tait Black Memorial Prize, 1930.
Two in the uniform edition of domestic novels and romances by 'E. H.
Young' whose work is much appreciated by those who enjoy well-
written, quiet fiction of everyday life.

Young, Francis Brett (1884-1954) MY BROTHER JONATHAN *Heinemann* (1928) 1947 12s 6d

PORTRAIT OF CLARE *Heinemann* (1927) 1950 12s 6d 873 pp
Two selected from the uniform *Severn* edition of a very popular regional novelist, whose *Portrait of Clare*, and *Dr. Bradley Remembers*, Heinemann, 1938, both very long novels, were amongst the bestsellers of their time. The former was awarded the James Tait Black Memorial Prize.

Zangwill, Israel (1864-1926) THE CHILDREN OF THE GHETTO (1892)
'Pictures of a Peculiar People'; that is, of the immigrant Jews of London in the late Victorian era.

THE KING OF SCHNORRERS (1894) *Pordes* 1954 12s 6d; *Rodale Press* 1954 21s
Jewish 'grotesques and fantasies' of an old-fashioned type, by a well-known Zionist and Anglo-Jewish writer.

SHORT STORIES
(*A selection of some standard collections and anthologies*) (arranged under names of editors)

Cournos, John AMERICAN SHORT STORIES OF THE NINETEENTH CENTURY *Dent* (*Everyman*) (1930) 1961 8s 6d

Davin, D. M. NEW ZEALAND SHORT STORIES *O.U.P.* (*Worlds Classics*) 1953 7s 6d

Hampden, John GHOST STORIES *Dent* (*Everyman*) 1939 10s 6d
GREAT ENGLISH SHORT STORIES *Penguin Books* 1929 2s 6d

*Hudson, Derek MODERN ENGLISH SHORT STORIES: second series *O.U.P.* (*Worlds Classics*) 1956 7s 6d

Jones, Gwyn WELSH SHORT STORIES: *O.U.P.* (*Worlds Classics*) 1956 7s 6d

*Jones, Phyllis M. MODERN ENGLISH SHORT STORIES: first series *O.U.P.* (*Worlds Classics*) 1939 7s 6d

*Milford, Sir Humphrey SELECTED ENGLISH SHORT STORIES: 3 series *O.U.P.* (*Worlds Classics*) 1914; 1921; 1927 7s 6d

Murdoch, Walter and H. Drake-Brockman AUSTRALIAN SHORT STORIES *O.U.P.* (*Worlds Classics*) 1951 7s 6d

*O'Connor, Frank MODERN IRISH SHORT STORIES *O.U.P.* (*Worlds Classics*) 1957 7s 6d
An anthology designed to display the individual genius of Irish writers in this form. The editor, indeed says that it is 'a distinct art form', and to

prove his assertion provides some example of the work of George Moore, Somerville and Ross, Daniel Corkery, James Joyce, James Stephens, and some other twentieth-century writers.

*Saintsbury, George and Philip Henderson SHORTER NOVELS 3 vols. *Dent (Everyman)* 1920-30

Vol. 1: *Eliabethan*; introduction by Saintsbury; notes by Henderson. Thomas Deloney: *Jacke of Newberie* (1597); and *Thomas of Reading* (1612); Thomas Nashe: *The Unfortunate Traveller* (1594); Robert Greene: *The Carde of Fancie* (1584).

Vol. 2: *Seventeenth Century:* Emanuel Ford: *Ornatus and Artesia* (1595); Aphra Behn: *Oroonoko* (1688); Henry Neville: *The Isle of Pines* (1668); William Congreve: *Incognita* (1692).

Vol. 3: *Eighteenth Century:* William Beckford: *Vathek* (1786); Horace Walpole: *The Castle of Otranto* (1765); Dr. Johnson: *Rasselas* (1759). Reprinted 1962, 7s 6d.

A most useful collection for the student, and the general reader, for the tales included are not easy to come by elsewhere, especially Greene's *Carde of Fancie* (*Chart of Love*), and Henry Neville's *The Isle of Pines*. Vols. 2 and 3 are edited by Philip Henderson.

Stern, Philip van Doren THE MIDNIGHT READER *Bodley Head* 1948 5s 512 pp

Horror stories by six authors: Henry James, Rudyard Kipling, Hugh Walpole, Oliver Onions, Sheridan le Fanu, and Edgar Allan Poe.

Thoms, William John EARLY ENGLISH PROSE ROMANCES *Routledge* 1924

Includes *Reynard the Fox; Robert the Devil; The History of Hamlet; Friar Bacon; Guy, Earl of Warwick; Thomas of Reading; Robin Hood; Dr. Faustus,* and six minor tales. This collection reprinted Henry Morley's original preface.

*Wilson, Richard ENGLISH SHORT STORIES *Dent (Everyman)* (1921) 1957 8s 6d

By its chronological arrangement this collection of thirty-six stories reveals the development of this form of fiction from the Middle Ages (folk tales), to John Galsworthy.

Wise, Herbert A. and Phyllis Fraser GREAT TALES OF TERROR AND THE SUPERNATURAL *Hammond, Hammond* (1947) 1957 21s 832 pp

Fifty-two classic and modern short stories by American and British authors, from Poe to Edith Wharton and O. Henry, and from Sheridan le Fanu and Wilkie Collins to Walter de la Mare.

HISTORY

(including social and political history, rhetoric and speeches)

To young students history is one of the simplest subjects in the curriculum. A matter of dates, a collection of names, a story of achievement, a narrative of deeds: the whole garnished with anecdotes that may or may not be true, but are certainly too interesting and amusing to part with. Many never get beyond this stage.

So there is something to be said for G. K. Chesterton's idea that history should be learnt backwards: begin with yesterday's newspaper and work back to King Alfred and his cakes. It must be admitted that this might mean we would start with a lie and end with a fairy tale.

'What is history?' asked Napoleon. ' 'Tis but a fable agreed upon,' was his reputed answer. In our time we have seen how difficult it has been to arrive at the truth even about events that have taken place within the last twenty-five years. Affirmations are followed by contradictions; rumours by denials; denials are refuted; lies 'nailed', as the current cant has it, only to be repeated, and later declared to be the truth, the whole truth and nothing but the truth.

What chance then, does the modern historian have in his search for the truth about men and women, and events of the past, however scholarly, patient and gifted he may be? Only the great historians can answer this question, but it is clear that history has to be constantly rewritten and interpreted afresh. Hence, although the mere chronology, the record, is the framework of the whole structure, historical inquiry in works of permanent value must consist to a great extent of the results of the historian's philosophy and interpretation. In that monument of learning and philosophy, *A Study of History*, Professor A. J. Toynbee offers the modern world the greatest contribution yet made in English to historiography, or the philosophy of history. Already the ten volumes of the main work have provoked sufficient world-wide controversy to justify the author in publishing a long book devoted entirely to replies and 'Reconsiderations'.

Toynbee's view of history, its meaning and nature, so brilliantly abridged by D. C. Somervell, is now available in what must be the most distinguished paperback of the post-war era. The purpose of this vast work of 6294 pages, plus the atlas and gazetteer, is to enable us to consider the complete pattern of human endeavour; to provide a map of the way already traversed through the centuries; and to help the historian to forecast the probable future of man's destiny by assessing the significance of what has gone before.

The philosopher-historian confessed to apprehension as he watched 'the Recording Angel's moving finger indefatigably going on writing'; in *Reconsiderations*, O.U.P., 1961, 45s, among many other criticisms, he answers the inevitable one of pessimism. Scholars will debate Toynbee's conclusions until the discussion is overtaken by historical development and the hidden road has emerged from the darkness. For historians, *A Study of History* must be the background to their own special inquiries; for readers, it is an achievement which helps towards the establishment of a standard of values. Whether the conclusions prove to be valid or not, the importance of this great work lies in the speculation and discussion, the argument and its influence.

Polybius, the earliest Greek historian to evolve a scientific method of personal research into prime sources, urged historians, in their quest for truth, to forget all considerations such as love of friends and hatred of enemies: it might sometimes be proper to praise the latter and blame the former.

In history, then, as in biography, the work of contemporary historians may supersede the classics of the past; but some remain, like Gibbon's great work, immune from the effects of time, monumental and for ever supreme.

Other books retain their status as classics of historical writing, but should be supplemented by later histories. Thus Carlyle's *French Revolution* cannot now be accepted as a fully adequate and completely satisfactory treatment of its subject. J. M. Thompson's masterpiece, *The French Revolution*, Blackwell, 1943, 37s 6d, is generally accepted as the best work in English, and with its companion volumes, even perhaps the best in any language. Yet the exhilarating effect of Carlyle's book more than compensates for the subjective distortion one is conscious of as one enters into the excitement of his highly-coloured, powerfully vivid narrative, with its extraordinary and poetic metaphors that live in the mind long after the book is finished. Perhaps the final impression Carlyle's history leaves with his readers, is, after all, as near to the reality of that world-shaking upheaval as any historian can hope to achieve.

Fortunately English historical writing abounds in examples of brilliant work enjoyed by the general reader but which at the same time attracts the praise of academic scholars because of the accuracy, scholarship and research displayed by the historian.

There is an established tradition dating from the publication of Macaulay's *History of England* in mid-nineteenth century that has been an example to the world of letters in the popularisation of history on the grand scale. Macaulay's work is said to have been as popular as a novel. Fragment though it is, eminent modern historians regard it as a brilliant, immortal example of the historian's art. Supplemented by Macaulay's *Historical Essays*, such an introduction to history has never been bettered.

From Macaulay to Dr. Trevelyan and to living writers the tradition has been notably followed. In his *English Social History*, Dr. Trevelyan rivalled the success of his great predecessor, for his book made publishing history, and during the paper shortage created by wartime conditions, it was impossible to satisfy the enormous and sustained demand for copies.

Again, H. A. L. Fisher's *A History of Europe*, is valued alike by university students as well as the common reader: both are helped by the publication of this standard survey and interpretation in a paperback edition. Fisher found no pattern in the course of history, and is therefore an historian to study in conjunction with Toynbee's work.

Apart from these comprehensive histories, we have scores of monographs that time has not removed from the student's bookshelf. Consider, for example, Warde Fowler's *The City State of the Greeks and the Romans*, first published in 1893. It has been reprinted for every new generation of students as essential reading. It is but a chapter in the history of the ancient world, but of permanent importance. Included in the section are some examples of standard work by twentieth-century historians, intended primarily for university and other students, but read for enjoyment as well as information by general readers. A. J. Grant, H. W. Temperley, Z. N. Brooke, Sir Charles Oman, H. W. C. Davis and W. F. Reddaway, are a few such authors selected at random from the list.

The reader will find details below of the other types of specific historical writing, essential to this present century of specialisation. Social history has been mentioned in connection with Dr. Trevelyan's book; one should not forget that earlier history in this genre: Green's *Short History of the English People* was itself an historic publication. It is still in print in a standard series. Then there are the specialised accounts of aspects of history such as Edward Jenks on English Law, A. V. Dicey on the Constitution and the interesting by-ways of Law and Public Opinion.

Famous personal narratives must necessarily belong partly to autobiography and partly to history. T. E. Lawrence's masterpiece is a notable modern example and Clarendon's *History of the Great Rebellion* has few parallels in our literature.

Collections of speeches are included when they are read for literary enjoyment, as well as sources of history; but anthologies in the standard series find a place as reference books for students as a matter of course, and one or two collections of documents valuable as prime sources come into the same category.

A specialised branch of social history, known as economic history, is now receiving far greater attention than it did in the nineteenth century. It has already attracted standard books for students, and some notable, well-illustrated popularisations.

Meanwhile, history is being made, historians are writing history, and many of them take time off to continue the discussion about their art and science with scholarly vigour. Readers who are interested in theory as well as practice may be recommended to consult Pieter Geyl's *Debates With Historians*, Batsford, 1955, 25s; Collins (Fontana), 1962, 7s 6d. This is an illuminating professional survey of modern historical writing from the German Leopold von Ranke (1795-1886) to Professor Arnold Toynbee.

Let us pay a tribute to the monkish tradition that started British writers on this long, unending quest for historical truth in the earliest chronicles.

G

They may still be read for pleasure. *The Anglo-Saxon Chronicle* is the chief source of information about events before the Norman Conquest; but it is a delight to read for the slyly amusing asides, the brief comments the old chroniclers so wisely allowed to creep in to clothe the skeleton of their record of events. The brevity is part of the charm, for it often gives a somewhat pointed remark an air of finality. The curtain falls on an episode as in a theatre; nothing more is uttered until the curtain rises and the next act begins.

⋆Acton, John E. E. Dalberg *1st Baron* (1834-1902) ESSAYS ON FREE-DOM AND POWER ed. by Gertrude Himmelfarb *Thames and Hudson* 1956 12s 6d

A selection containing the famous Inaugural Lecture, eight other chapters on freedom, political causes of the American and French Revolutions, and one chapter of selections from the Acton-Creighton correspondence.

LECTURES ON MODERN HISTORY *Macmillan* (1906) 1950 16s; *Collins* (*Fontana*) 1960 6s

Seminal lectures delivered from 1899-1901, and the Inaugural Lecture on the study of history delivered 11 June, 1895. Lord Acton planned the *Cambridge Modern History*, a standard work of collective scholarship, now under revision.

⋆THE ANGLO-SAXON CHRONICLE trans., with intro. by G. M. Garmonsway *Dent* (*Everyman*) 1953 7s 6d

'The most important single source for the pre-Conquest history of England.' These documents were edited by Charles Plummer and J. Earle, for the Oxford University Press, 1892-1900, and the new *Everyman* translation, for which this edition was used as a basis, is the best for the general reader. Scholars and students may also wish to consult the notable quarto edition, done in a revised translation by Dorothy Whitelock, David C. Douglas, and Susie I. Tucker, Eyre and Spottiswoode, 1962, 50s. The period covered by the old chroniclers was A.D. 450 to 1154.

⋆Bagehot, Walter (1826-77) THE ENGLISH CONSTITUTION (1867) *O.U.P.* (*Worlds Classics*) 1928 7s 6d; *W. H. Allen* (*Dolphin Books*) 1962 7s 6d; *Collins* (*Fontana*) 1963 7s 6d

A standard introduction for lay readers, with an appreciation by the Earl of Balfour, written for the *Worlds Classics* edition.

Barker, Sir Ernest (1874-1960) BRITAIN AND THE BRITISH PEOPLE *O.U.P.* (1942) 1955 12s 6d Illus.

POLITICAL THOUGHT IN ENGLAND, 1848-1914 *O.U.P.* (*Home University Library*) (1915) 1928 8s 6d

This is the final monograph in a series, each written by an authority on different periods of English political history. See also under Laski, below.

Barrow, Sir John (1764-1848) THE EVENTFUL HISTORY OF THE
MUTINY OF H.M.S. BOUNTY (1831) *O.U.P.* (*Worlds Classics*) 1914
7s 6d

The first full account of the most famous mutiny in naval history. Under
the leadership of Fletcher Christian, the crew mutinied in 1789 after
leaving Tahiti, and cast Captain Bligh (see also below), with eighteen
members of the crew who refused to join the mutineers, adrift in an
open boat. The mutineers settled on Pitcairn Island in the Pacific, where
their descendants live to this day. Sir John Barrow was assistant secretary
to the Admiralty, and founded the Geographical Society. For his own
travel narratives refer to entries in the *Travel* section.

*Bede (The Venerable) (673-735) THE ECCLESIASTICAL HISTORY OF
THE ENGLISH NATION translated by Thomas Stapleton (1565);
by J. Stevens (1723) *Dent* (*Everyman*) (1910) 1954 8s 6d

Bede, living a scholar's life in a monastery at Jarrow, wrote his famous
work in Latin. It is much more than its title indicates, and is the chief
source of information on the early history of Britain, the coming of
Augustine and of Christianity, the invasions and other early events, to
about A.D. 730. Minor pieces are included in the *Everyman* edition, that
reprints the translation by Stevens, revised by J. A. Giles in 1847 for
Bohn's Library, with notes by L. C. Jane (1903). There is a modern version
under the title of *A History of the English Church and People*, translated by
L. Sherley Price, Penguin Books, 1955, 3s 6d.

Bell, Walter George (1870-1942) THE GREAT FIRE OF LONDON IN
1666 *Bodley Head* (1920) 1951 25s Illus.

THE GREAT PLAGUE OF LONDON IN 1665 *Bodley Head* (1924) 1951
25s Illus.

Two popular monographs based on a study of contemporary records by a
London antiquarian.

UNKNOWN LONDON *Bodley Head* (1919) 1951 25s Illus.

Old buildings, nooks and corners, alleys and out-of-the-way curiosities
described for visitors to London.

Belloc, Hilaire (1870-1953) THE FRENCH REVOLUTION *O.U.P.*
(*Home University Library*) 1911 8s 6d

A masterly summary in 215 pages, of the causes, personalities and
development of the events of the decade from May 1789.

HOW THE REFORMATION HAPPENED *Cape* (1928) 1950 18s

A Catholic's view; regarded by many readers as Belloc's best historical
monograph.

*Berners, Lord (John Bourchier) (1467-1533) THE CHRONICLES OF
FROISSART trans. by Lord Berners (1523) ed. by G. C. Macaulay
Macmillan (*Globe Library*) 1895

Froissart's *History of His Own Times* (1338-1410) is usually called in English
translation *The Chronicles of England, France and Spain*. The popular
edition in the *Globe Library* is abridged to keep it within the scope of a
single volume, and the spelling modernised.

Bligh, William (*c.* 1753-1817) BLIGH AND THE BOUNTY *Methuen* 1936

'Narrative of the voyage to Otaheite, with an account of the Mutiny, and of his boat journey to Timor.' Refer also to Barrow above, for the classic account of the mutiny.

A BOOK OF THE BOUNTY ed. by George Mackaness *Dent* (*Everyman*) 1938

An edition of Bligh's *Voyage* and his *Narrative of the Mutiny*; together with a Report of the Court Martial, Correspondence, and a bibliography.

Bradford, William (1589-1657) THE HISTORY OF PLYMOUTH COLONY, 1606-1646 (1856) ed. by G. E. Willison *Van Nostrand* 1948 14*s*

An historic document of very great interest, being the story of the Pilgrim Fathers, told by their leader, Governor William Bradford. The original has been modernised by Harold Paget for this reprint in the *Classics Club College Editions*. Fully annotated, with list of *Mayflower* passengers. Two maps, with facsimiles of the original Bradford journal, add to the usefulness of this edition.

Breasted, James Henry (1865-1935) THE HISTORY OF EGYPT FROM THE EARLIEST TIMES TO THE PERSIAN CONQUEST *Hodder* (1905) revised edition 1946 84*s* 634 pp Illus.

Standard work by an American historian. The volume is notable for its production, with 200 illustrations, some coloured, and many maps.

Bright, John (1811-89) SELECTED SPEECHES ON PUBLIC QUESTIONS *Dent* (*Everyman*) 1907

Delivered between 1858 and 1878 on foreign policy, the land question, peace, free trade, the Crimean War (which he opposed) and Ireland. Bright was an eloquent speaker, and as M.P. for Durham became famous for his strong opposition to the Corn Laws.

Brooke, Zachary Nugent (1883-1946) A HISTORY OF EUROPE, 911-1198 *Methuen* (1938) 1951 35*s*

A standard volume for students, by an authority on the Middle Ages.

Brown, Peter Hume (1849-1918) A SHORT HISTORY OF SCOTLAND *Oliver and Boyd* (1908) revised edition by Henry W. Meikle 1955 21*s* Illus.

The best of the older short histories, abridged from the author's classic work, *A History of Scotland*, 3 vols. C.U.P., 1899-1909, 50*s* each. Vol. 1: To the accession of Mary Stewart; vol. 2: The Revolution of 1689; vol. 3: 1689-1910.

Bryce, James (1st Viscount) (1838-1922) THE HOLY ROMAN EMPIRE *Macmillan* (1864) 1950 24*s*

Scholar and ambassador, Lord Bryce here wrote a book that time has not superseded. It is generally accepted as a well-balanced survey in a single volume, of the central European states whose rulers from the eighth century A.D. successively claimed the authority of Rome as spiritual and temporal supports.

Buckle, Henry Thomas (1821-62) THE HISTORY OF CIVILISATION IN ENGLAND (1857; 1861) 3 vols. O.U.P. (Worlds Classics) 1903-4
This first history of its kind immediately brought Buckle European fame as an initiator in historiography, and it exerted considerable influence on other historians because of his conception of a quasi-scientific examination of historical changes in thought and the development of epochs in the history of a nation.

Burke, Edmund (1729-97) REFLECTIONS ON THE REVOLUTION IN FRANCE, 1790, and other writings ed. by A. J. Grieve Dent (Everyman) (1910) 1953 7s 6d; ed. by E. J. Payne O.U.P. (1875) (Worlds Classics) 1907 6s
The other essays include Thoughts on French Affairs, 1791. The main work is an impassioned, eloquently expressed denunciation of the French Revolution, romantic in tone, and remarkable more for its style than content.

*SELECTIONS ed. by A. M. D. Hughes O.U.P. (Clarendon English Series) 1921 8s 6d
Includes essays on Burke by Hazlitt, Matthew Arnold, and others.

SELECTIONS FROM POLITICAL WRITINGS AND SPEECHES ed. by Sir Henry Newbolt Nelson (Classics) 1925 7s

SPEECHES AND LETTERS ON AMERICAN AFFAIRS Dent (Everyman) (1908) 1955 7s 6d
Under the title of The Philosophy of Burke, Louis I. Bredvold and Ralph G. Ross have edited a volume of selections of his speeches and writings for University of Michigan Press (in Great Britain, Cambridge University Press), 1960, 35s (cloth), 21s (student's paperback).

Burnet, Gilbert (1643-1715) HISTORY OF HIS OWN TIME 2 vols. (1724; 1734) 2 vols. ed. by O. Airy O.U.P. 1897-1900; supplement ed. by H. C. Foxcroft O.U.P. 1902; ed. and abridged by Thomas Stackhouse (1677-1752) Dent (Everyman) 1906
A personal account of the events of the period 1659 to 1713, published posthumously. 'It seems,' said Horace Walpole, 'as if Burnet had just come from the King's closet or from the apartments of the men whom he describes, and was telling his readers, in plain honest terms, what he had seen and heard.'

Burns, Cecil Delisle (1879-1942) THE FIRST EUROPE Allen and Unwin 1947 30s 700 pp Illus. Maps
'A study of the establishment of medieval Christendom, A.D. 400-800.'

Bury, John Bagnell (1861-1927) A HISTORY OF THE LATER ROMAN
EMPIRE, A.D. 395-565 2 vols. *Macmillan* (1889) rev. edn. 1923;
Constable (Dover Books) 1958 16s each

The paperback edition is an unabridged reprint, with notes, of this
standard work. Bury takes the narrative of events from the death of
Theodosius I (A.D. 395) to the death of Justinian (A.D. 565). Bibliography;
Greek-English index.

A HISTORY OF THE EASTERN ROMAN EMPIRE, A.D. 802-867 *Macmillan* 1912

A HISTORY OF GREECE TO THE DEATH OF ALEXANDER THE GREAT,
323 B.C. 2 vols. *Macmillan* (1900) rev. edn. 1913; ed. in 1 vol.
by Russell Meiggs 1951 21s 968 pp Illus.; abridged edition,
Macmillan (1903; 1927) 1962 15s as *A History of Greece For
Beginners*

THE INVASION OF EUROPE BY THE BARBARIANS *Macmillan* 1928

Bury was Professor of Greek and of Modern History at Dublin, and
later at Cambridge. His edition of Gibbon's *Decline and Fall* is the standard
set, for which see under Gibbon.

Callcott, Maria (Lady) (1785-1842) LITTLE ARTHUR'S HISTORY OF
ENGLAND *Murray* (1835) 1962 8s 6d Illus.

A classic of the Victorian nursery. About 800,000 copies of this amusing,
simple introduction to the history of England had been printed up to the
Century edition of 1936, and the latest edition has now been revised and
brought up to date.

*Carlyle, Thomas (1795-1881) THE FRENCH REVOLUTION (1837)
2 vols. *Dent (Everyman)* (1906) 1955 10s 6d each

Introduction by Hilaire Belloc. Twentieth-century scholarship has
superseded Carlyle's once widely-read masterpiece, but it can be read
today for its poetic, almost intuitive interpretation of events, characters
and motives, for its gallery of portraits presented in the glowing vitality
of Carlyle's style at its best.

PAST AND PRESENT (1843) *Dent (Everyman)* (1912) 1960 8s 6d;
O.U.P. (Worlds Classics) 1912 6s

Introduced in *Everyman* by G. K. Chesterton, who was in sympathy with
Carlyle's praise of the best in the Middle Ages, although in this work it
is tinged with Carlyle's romantic idealisation. He uses as an object lesson
for the politicians and policy-makers of 'the present', an old *Chronicle
of Jocelin of Brakelond*, which tells the story of Samson, Abbot of St.
Edmondsbury, as set down by his chaplain, 1173-1202. By contrast
Carlyle exposed aspects of democracy that he mistrusted, such as vote-
catching parliamentary speeches and panaceas of popular politicians.

Charlesworth, Martin Percival (1895-1951) THE ROMAN EMPIRE
O.U.P. (Home University Library) 1951 8s 6d

Companion summary to Fowler's classic *Rome*, written for the same
series, and entered below. The period covered is 21 B.C. to A.D. 476.

Chesterton, Cecil Edward (1879-1918) A HISTORY OF THE UNITED
STATES (1919) ed. by D. W. Brogan *Dent (Everyman)* 1940 6s 6d
The series edition, with annotations, bibliography and a chronological
table of events, makes this little survey a model of its kind. The author
was the brother of G. K. Chesterton, and was killed in the First World
War.

Clapham, Sir John (1873-1946) *A CONCISE ECONOMIC HISTORY OF
BRITAIN TO 1750 *C.U.P.* 1949 30s
Continued from 1750 in a companion book, by W. H. B. Court, C.U.P.,
1954, 32s 6d. The two books are founded on the great parent work by
Sir John Clapham.

THE ECONOMIC HISTORY OF MODERN BRITAIN 3 vols. *C.U.P.*
1926-38 57s 6d each
Vol. 1: The Early Railway Age, 1820-50; vol. 2: Free Trade and Steel,
1850-86; vol. 3: Machines and National rivalries, 1887-1914; with an
Epilogue, 1914-29.

*Clarendon, Edward Hyde (Earl of) (1608-74) THE HISTORY OF
THE GREAT REBELLION (1702-4) 7 vols. *O.U.P.* (1849); 6 vols.
1888 126s (the set) 3094 pp; selected by G. Huehns (*Worlds
Classics*) 1955 9s 6d 542 pp
A personal narrative of great events, without parallel in English historical
writing until Sir Winston Churchill's *The Second World War*. Like Sir
Winston, Clarendon related in glowing style, events in which he himself
had played a leading part. Full title *History of the Rebellion and Civil Wars
in England*, together with *An Historical View of the Affairs of Ireland*. The
Worlds Classics double volume includes the charming *Life (by himself)*,
written for his children.

Clark, Cecily (Editor) THE PETERBOROUGH CHRONICLE, 1070-1154
O.U.P. 1957 30s
A source book for historians of the early Norman period. The editor
gives a commentary, and introduction, and an appendix on the inter-
polations.

*Cole, G. D. H. (1889-1958) A SHORT HISTORY OF THE BRITISH
WORKING CLASS MOVEMENT, 1789-1947 *Allen and Unwin* (3 vols.
1925-7) rev. edn. 1 volume 1948 25s 500 pp
A major work by a prolific writer on co-operation, trade unionism, the
Labour Party, and other topics in sociology.

*Collingwood, Robin George (1889-1943) ROMAN BRITAIN
Oxford University Press 1932 15s
Collingwood was part author, with J. N. L. Myres, of volume 1 of the
Oxford History of England: Roman Britain and the English Settlements,
O.U.P., 1937, 30s.

Connell, Brian (Editor) REGINA V. PALMERSTON *Evans* 1962 42*s*
'The correspondence between Queen Victoria and her foreign and prime minister, 1837-1865.' Most of these letters have never before been published. They form a prime source book for historians and may be read with pleasure by the general reader.

*Coulton, George Gordon (1858-1947) CHAUCER AND HIS ENGLAND *Methuen* (1908) 1937 25*s*; (*University Paperback*) 1963 15*s* Illus.
An unrivalled monograph for literary students and for students of the history of the Middle Ages, especially of the reign of Edward III.

THE MEDIAEVAL PANORAMA *Cambridge University Press* 1938 Illus.; 2 vols. *Collins* (*Fontana Books*) 1961 9*s* 6*d* each
'The English scene from Conquest to Reformation.'

THE MEDIAEVAL SCENE *Cambridge University Press* (1930) 1960 10*s* 6*d* Illus. (paperback)
Can scarcely be bettered as 'an informal introduction to the Middle Ages' for both students and the general readers for whom these broadcast talks were first delivered by this eminent authority on the period.

SOCIAL LIFE IN BRITAIN FROM CONQUEST TO REFORMATION *Cambridge University Press* (1918) 1938 45*s* 566 pp
Extracts from books and documents of the period, presented to supplement formal histories. For Coulton's masterpiece see under *Philosophy and Religion* section.

*Creasy, Sir Edward Shepherd (1812-78) THE FIFTEEN DECISIVE BATTLES OF THE WORLD (1851) *Dent* (*Everyman*) (1908) 1960 12*s* 6*d*
From Marathon, through the centuries, to Waterloo: that is, from 400 B.C. to A.D. 1815: Syracuse; Arbela; Metaurus; the victory of Arminius, A.D. 9; Chalons; Tours; Hasting; Orleans; The Defeat of the Armada; Blenheim; Pultowa; Saratoga; Valmy.

Cruttwell, Charles (1887-1941) A HISTORY OF PEACEFUL CHANGE IN THE MODERN WORLD *O.U.P.* 1937
A HISTORY OF THE GREAT WAR, 1914-1918 *O.U.P.* (1934) 1936 25*s*
A standard summary in 670 pages, with 34 maps.

Davis, Henry William Carless (1874-1928) THE AGE OF GREY AND PEEL *O.U.P.* 1929
ENGLAND UNDER THE NORMANS AND THE ANGEVINS, 1066-1272 *Methuen* (1905) 1949 30*s*
*MEDIAEVAL EUROPE *O.U.P.* (*Home University Library*) (1911) 1960 8*s* 6*d*
Revised edition, with an epilogue by R. H. C. Davis.

*Dicey, Albert Venn (1835-1922) INTRODUCTION TO THE STUDY OF THE LAW OF THE CONSTITUTION *Macmillan* (1885) 1959 35s; (*Papermacs*) 1961 21s 536 pp
A standard textbook for students, revised for the 10th edition, by E. C. S. Wade.

LAW AND PUBLIC OPINION IN ENGLAND *Macmillan* (1905; 1914) 1962 30s; (*Papermac*) 1962 18s 506 pp
Full title: *Lectures on Relation Between Law and Public Opinion in England During 19th Century*. This is a standard work that can be read without a student's specialised knowledge of the subject. The reprint has a preface by Professor E. C. S. Wade, in which he emphasises that this is not a textbook, like the first book entered above. He considers it to be 'indispensable reading' for the political history of the nineteenth century.

*Dickinson, Goldsworthy Lowes (1862-1932) THE INTERNATIONAL ANARCHY, 1904-1914 *Allen and Unwin* 1926
Summarises and discusses foreign policies of the powers, resulting in World War I.

REVOLUTION AND REACTION IN MODERN FRANCE, 1789-1871 *Allen and Unwin* (1892) 1927 9s 6d

Draper, John William (1811-82) A HISTORY OF THE INTELLECTUAL DEVELOPMENT OF EUROPE 2 vols. *Bell* (1863) 1904
A monograph by a British-born American scientist, whose view of history was characteristic of a rationalist's interpretation.

Evelyn, George Palmer (1823-89) A DIARY OF THE CRIMEA ed. by Cyril Falls *Duckworth* 1954 12s 6d
Colonel Evelyn of the Rifle Brigade served with the Turkish Army. This contemporary document displays his lively interest in all that he witnessed, and his considerable literary ability.

Finlay, George (1799-1875) A HISTORY OF GREECE UNDER THE ROMANS, 146 B.C. to A.D. 716 (1844-1861) *Dent* (*Everyman*) 1906
THE HISTORY OF THE BYZANTINE EMPIRE, 716-1057 (1854) *Dent* (*Everyman*) 1906
The author was a Scottish historical scholar who lived most of his life in Greece, taking part in the War of Independence, 1823-4, during which he met Byron. He was one of the first English Philhellenes, and died at Athens. The first part of his standard history has been withdrawn from the *Everyman* series.

*Firth, Sir Charles Harding (1857-1936) CROMWELL'S ARMY *Methuen* (1902) 1962 25s; (*University Paperbacks*) 1962 14s
The Ford Lectures delivered at the University of Oxford, 1900-1. The fourth edition has a new introduction by P. H. Hardacre. This monograph on the formation of Cromwell's 'New Model' of 1645, and of contrasting military systems of the Stuarts preceding Cromwell's era, provides in effect 'a history of the English soldier during the Civil Wars, the Commonwealth, and the Protectorate'.

THE LAST YEARS OF THE PROTECTORATE, 1656-8 2 vols. *Longmans* 1909
Completes Gardiner's *History*, which see below.

OLIVER CROMWELL AND THE RULE OF THE PURITANS IN ENGLAND (1900; 1947); *O.U.P.* (*Worlds Classics*) 1953 8s 6d
Originally one of the *Heroes of the Nation* series, published by Putnam. The reprint has an appreciation by G. M. Young.

*Fisher, Herbert Albert Laurens (1865-1940) A HISTORY OF EUROPE *Eyre and Spottiswoode* (3 vols. 1935) 2 vols. (1938) 1952 25s each; one volume edition *Edward Arnold* 35s 1300 pp; *Collins* (*Fontana series*) 2 vols. 1960 9s 6d each (paperback)
One of the great historical surveys of the twentieth century. It has become a standard work for students and a popular one with general readers. This distinguished humanist and liberal historian wrote: 'I begin this book with neolithic man and conclude with Stalin and Mustapha Kemal, Mussolini and Hitler ... Men wiser and more learned than I have discerned in history a plot, a rhythm, a predetermined pattern. These harmonies are concealed from me.' Vol. 1: From the earliest times to 1713; vol. 2: From the beginning of the eighteenth century to 1935.

*Fowler, William Warde (1847-1921) THE CITY STATE OF THE GREEKS AND ROMANS *Macmillan* (1893) 1952 15s
A classic 'survey introductory to the study of ancient history' used by every generation of students.

ROME *O.U.P.* (*Home University Library*) (1911) Revised edition by M. P. Charlesworth 1947 8s 6d

SOCIAL LIFE AT ROME IN THE AGE OF CICERO *Macmillan* (1908) 1963 25s

Fox, Charles James (1749-1806) SPEECHES DURING THE FRENCH REVOLUTIONARY WAR PERIOD *Dent* (*Everyman*) 1924
Fox's attitude as a statesman, to the main events of the period, would now be described as that of a 'non-interventionist'. He consistently opposed the French war.

Freeman, Edward Augustus (1823-92) A HISTORY OF THE NORMAN CONQUEST 6 vols. *O.U.P.* 1867-79
'One of the greatest monuments of English historical learning.'— Chambers's *Biographical Dictionary*.

OLD ENGLISH HISTORY FOR CHILDREN *Macmillan* (1869) *Dent* (*Everyman*) 1911
Learning lightly conveyed for readers of all ages. Withdrawn from *Everyman* series.

Froude, James Anthony (1818-94) A HISTORY OF ENGLAND (1856-70) 10 vols. *Dent* (*Everyman*) 1909-12

A glowing narrative of events from the fall of Cardinal Wolsey to the defeat of the Spanish Armada. Read in its sections, it may be enjoyed by the general reader as four separate works: Vols. 1-3: Henry VIII; Vol. 4: Edward VI; vol. 5: Mary Tudor; vols. 6-10: Queen Elizabeth I.

Gardiner, Samuel Rawson (1829-1902) HISTORY OF THE COMMON-WEALTH AND THE PROTECTORATE, 1649-1656 4 vols. *Longmans* (1894-1901)
This standard history was completed by Sir Charles Firth's book, for which see above.

THE FIRST TWO STUARTS AND THE PURITAN REVOLUTION, 1603-1660 *Longmans* (1876) 1888
A student's textbook, noted for objective impartiality, and documentation.

Geoffrey of Monmouth (*c.* 1100-1154) HISTORIES OF THE KINGS OF BRITAIN *Dent* (*Everyman*) (1912) 1962 12s 6d
The Welsh chronicler's *Historia Regnum Britanniæ*, in the standard translation by Sebastian Evans (1904), revised for the new edition by C. W. Dunn. This twelfth-century chronicle is an important part of the Arthurian literature. It was published in 1508.

*Gibbon, Edward (1737-94) THE HISTORY OF THE DECLINE AND FALL OF THE ROMAN EMPIRE (1776-88) 6 vols. *Dent* (*Everyman*) (1910) 1954 8s 6d each; 7 vols. ed. by J. B. Bury *Methuen* 1909-10; 7 vols. O.U.P. (*Worlds Classics*) 50s (the set in slipcase); *Abridgement* in one volume, by D. M. Low *Chatto* 1960 36s 924 pp
For students, J. B. Bury's edition is regarded as the standard set; the abridgement by D. M. Low, author of the standard biography of Gibbon, was praised by critics as a masterly undertaking for readers lacking the leisure or inclination to read the whole of this 'greatest historical book of the century, if not of all time'—*Professor Saintsbury*.

*Grant, Arthur James (1862-1948) A HISTORY OF EUROPE, 1494-1610 *Methuen* (1931) 1954 30s

Grant, Arthur James and Harold William Temperley (1879-1939) EUROPE IN 19TH AND 20TH CENTURIES, 1789-1950 *Longmans* (1926) 1950 30s
Two standard texts for students. The sixth edition of the latter was revised by Lillian M. Penson. See also under Temperley, below.

*Green, John Richard (1837-83) A SHORT HISTORY OF THE ENGLISH PEOPLE *Macmillan* (1874); 2 vols. *Dent* (*Everyman*) (1915) ed. by L. C. Jane 1960 12s 6d each
The first book of its kind, and the most popular social history until Trevelyan's *English Social History* appeared in 1942. The new *Everyman*

edition continues the story in summary up to 1960. The best edition of Green's work was that edited by Mrs. J. R. Green and Kate Norgate, 4 vols. illustrated quartos, Macmillan, 1893-4, with about 1400 illustrations from contemporary sources, and some coloured maps. This handsome library set may sometimes be obtained second-hand from antiquarian booksellers.

Grote, George (1794-1871) HISTORY OF GREECE 10 vols. *Murray* (1846-56) 12 vols. *Dent (Everyman)* 1907
Grote was an amateur historian, being a banker, and a member of Parliament. Yet he found time to produce his vast history, taking the narrative up to the death of Alexander the Great. He viewed men and achievements with philosophic vision, and in politics, showed himself to be a pronounced believer in democracy. Some of his judgements have been criticised, but viewed as a whole, his history is considered by scholars to have maintained its place as a major work of permanent value.

Haddon, Alfred Cort (1855-1940) A HISTORY OF ANTHROPOLOGY *Watts* (1910) 1934
THE WANDERINGS OF PEOPLES *C.U.P.* 1911 7s 6d
Brief monograph on European tribes and communities, their nomadic wanderings and settlements, written as a prelude to the study of history.

Hall, Edward (*c.* 1499-1547) CHRONICLE OF HENRY VIII, 1509-1547 2 vols. ed. by Charles Whibley *Nelson* 1904
Picturesque contemporary narrative of events, from a section of Hall's *The Union of the Two Noble and Illustre Famelies of Lancastre and Yorke*, 1548 and 1550.

Hallam, Henry (1777-1859) THE CONSTITUTIONAL HISTORY OF ENGLAND 3 vols. (1827) *Dent (Everyman)* 1912
The period is 'from the accession of Henry VII to the death of George II'. Time has not superseded this authoritative study, based on Hallam's original research. Introduced in the reprint by Professor J. H. Morgan.

A VIEW OF THE STATE OF EUROPE DURING THE MIDDLE AGES 3 vols. *Murray* (1818) 1901
Hallam's learning brought him international fame. He followed the above two works with a four-volumed *Introduction to the Literature of Europe in the 15th, 16th, and 17th Centuries* (1837-9), still valuable as a work of reference.

Hamilton, Alexander (1757-1804) THE FEDERALIST (1787) ed. by M. Beloff *Blackwell* 1948; ed. by William B. Brock *Dent (Everyman)* (1911) 1961 12s 6d
Essays on 'The New Constitution', some of which were written by James Madison and John Jay, published to influence the State of New York to ratify the constitution drawn up by the Convention. Their effect on statesmen and federal policies generally have made these essays a classic of international importance.

*Hammond, John Lawrence (1872-1949) and Barbara Hammond
THE AGE OF THE CHARTISTS, 1832-1854 *Longmans* 1930
'A study in discontent.' Complementary to the trilogy noted below.
THE RISE OF MODERN INDUSTRY *Methuen* (1925) 1951 18s
THE VILLAGE LABOURER, 1760-1832 *Longmans* (1911) 2 vols. 1948
1s 6d each (paperbacks)
THE TOWN LABOURER, 1760-1832 *Longmans* (1917) 2 vols. 1950
1s 6d each (paperbacks)
'The new civilisation.'
THE SKILLED LABOURER, 1760-1832 *Longmans* 1919
This standard trilogy is the principal study of working-class life, labour,
wages and conditions in the industrial and economic history of Britain
before the Reform Bill.

*Haskins, Charles Homer (1870-1937) STUDIES IN MEDIAEVAL
CULTURE *Constable* (1929) 1958 45s
Portrays the civilisation of the Middle Ages through Latin literature,
particularly 'unofficial' Latin. These essays received superlative praise by
authorities: e.g., 'immune from the corrosive touch of time . . . a work
beyond the reach of criticism . . .'—*The English Historical Review*.

Henderson, George Francis Robert (1854-1903) STONEWALL
JACKSON AND THE AMERICAN CIVIL WAR *Longmans* (1898) (1936)
1961 50s
A long, detailed biography of 737 pages, regarded by both American
and British General Staffs as a military classic. Colonel Henderson was
able to gather material for his book from eye-witnesses of many of the
great Southern leader's most brilliant engagements.

Hennell, Thomas (1903-45) CHANGE ON THE FARM *C.U.P.* 1934
THE COUNTRYMAN AT WORK *Architectural Press* 1947
The last book by this countryman-craftsman, published posthumously,
was illustrated by the author himself. It is prefaced by a memoir by
H. J. Massingham. Hennell's love of ancient country crafts, and deep
knowledge of the countryman's traditional skills, from the making of a
farmer's cart to the thatching of a cottage, enabled him to produce these
two books, worthy to be classed with those by Richard Jefferies, and
George Sturt's *The Wheelwright's Shop*.

Hodgkin, Thomas (1831-1913) ITALY AND HER INVADERS, A.D. 376-
814 8 vols. *O.U.P.* 1879-99 5000 pp Illus.
Excepting volumes 3 and 4 (out of print), this work is sold in pairs of
volumes 1-2; 5-6; 7-8; at 42s each pair.

Hogarth, David George (1862-1927) THE ANCIENT EAST *O.U.P.*
(*Home University Library*) (1914) 1945
The last edition was slightly revised and amended by Sir John L. Myres.

Holdsworth, Sir William (1871-1944) SOME MAKERS OF ENGLISH
LAW *C.U.P.* 1938
The distinguished legal historian's masterpiece was the great *History of
English Law*, 13 volumes, published by Methuen, and revised for the 7th
edition in 1956 by A. L. Goodhart and H. G. Hanbury.

*Holinshed, Raphael (*d.* 1580?) CHRONICLES (1577-87) ed. and
sel. by Allardyce and Josephine Nicoll *Dent* (*Everyman*) (1927)
1955 7s 6d
A collective work named after the Elizabethan translator who was
responsible for its planning and publishing. From its pages many
dramatists drew characters and plots for their plays; and Shakespeare's
debt to these *Chronicles* when writing his incomparable series of English
historical plays, is emphasised by the *Everyman* title of the selection:
Holinshed's Chronicle As Used in Shakespeare's Plays.

Hovell, Mark (1888-1916) THE CHARTIST MOVEMENT ed. and completed by T. F. Tout *Manchester University Press* (1918) 1951 21s
Hovell, a gifted young student, was killed in World War I; his only
book was greatly admired by Professor Tout, who completed it for
publication as a standard monograph, which place it has maintained.

Howard, John (1726?-90) THE STATE OF THE PRISONS (1777; 1784)
Dent (*Everyman*) 1929 6s 6d
Pioneer reformer's inquiry into conditions in English prisons, based
on first-hand knowledge. It had great influence. The abridged text in
Everyman includes Howard's *Account of Lazarettos*, and some extracts
from other minor writings.

Hume, Martin Andrew Sharp (1847-1910) SPAIN: ITS GREATNESS
AND DECAY, 1479-1788 *C.U.P.* (1898) 1913 22s 6d
The third, posthumous edition of this standard work for students, was
revised by E. Armstrong.

James II (1603-1701) THE MEMOIRS OF JAMES II trans. and ed. by
A. Lytton Sells, with an intro. by Sir Arthur Bryant *Chatto*
1962 42s
James II served under Turenne from 1652 to 1655. These memoirs were
presented in 1696 by James himself, to Cardinal de Bouillon, nephew of
Turenne. The manuscript—a 'priceless document', as Sir Winston
Churchill has termed it, was lost, and given up as lost forever. But in
1954 it was discovered and identified by David Randall and Percy Muir,
rare book experts, who found it in a château in the south of France.

*Jenks, Edward (1861-1939) THE BOOK OF ENGLISH LAW *Murray*
(1928) 1953 24s
The fifth edition was revised by J. L. Davies. It is considered to be the
best introduction for general readers as well as first-year students. The
revised text takes the commentary up to the end of 1952.

Johnson, Charles (*fl.* 1730) A GENERAL HISTORY OF THE ROBBERIES
AND MURDERS OF THE MOST NOTORIOUS PYRATES (1724) ed. by
A. L. Hayward *Routledge* 1926 30s 603 pp Illus.
Generally accepted as the most straightforward, if picturesque, account
of the misdeeds and careers of both famous and lesser-known pirates of
seventeenth and early eighteenth centuries. The modern edition, often
reprinted, is a quarto illustrated with reproductions of old engravings and
prints.

Jowett, Benjamin (1817-1893) THE HISTORY OF 'THE PELOPON-
NESIAN WAR' OF THUCYDIDES translated by Benjamin Jowett
2 vols. *O.U.P.* (1881) 1900
Said to be the first 'critical' historian, Thucydides, in his account of the
disastrous war that broke out in 431 B.C., wrote a military and political
history of twenty-seven years of his own life time. Macaulay's superlative praise of the narrative, and the high place it has maintained through
the centuries, are evidence of its enduring greatness. In Jowett's Ruskinian
prose it seemed to have found its final English form; but Richard
Crawley's (1874) is preferred by many, and indeed is used, with Richard
Feetham's revision, in both *Everyman's Library* and *Worlds Classics*.

King, Bolton (1860-1937) A HISTORY OF ITALIAN UNITY 2 vols.
Nisbet (1899) 1934 30s
A political history of the period during which modern Italy was created:
1814-71. For the author's complementary monograph on Mazzini, one
of the makers of modern Italy, see under the *Biographies* section.

Laski, Harold Joseph (1893-1950) A GRAMMAR OF POLITICS
Allen and Unwin (1925) 1938 30s 700 pp

LIBERTY IN THE MODERN STATE *Allen and Unwin* (1930) 1948 9s 6d

POLITICAL THOUGHT IN ENGLAND: LOCKE TO BENTHAM *O.U.P.*
(*Home University Library*) 1920 8s 6d
One of a series of five monographs. See also under Barker above.

REFLECTIONS ON THE REVOLUTION OF OUR TIME *Allen and Unwin*
(1943) 1952 21s

THE RISE OF EUROPEAN LIBERALISM *Allen and Unwin* 1936 16s;
1962 6s (paperback)
'An essay in interpretation.'

*Lawrence, Thomas Edward (1888-1935) SEVEN PILLARS OF
WISDOM (1926) *Cape* 1935 25s Illus.
This famous personal narrative of events in Arabia during the 1914-18
War in the Near East, apart from its historical importance, will rank as
one of the greatest prose publications of the twentieth century.

Lea, Henry Charles (1825-1909) THE INQUISITION OF THE MIDDLE
AGES 3 vols. (1887-8) ed. with an historical introduction by
Walter Ullmann *Eyre and Spottiswoode* 1963 25s

A modern edition, unabridged, of those chapters in volume 1 'dealing with the organisation and operation of the Inquisition throughout Europe'. This controversial American classic, praised by Lord Acton, 'still forms to-day', writes Dr. Ullmann, 'the basis of research into the subject.'

Lecky, William Edward (1838-1903) A HISTORY OF ENGLAND IN THE EIGHTEENTH CENTURY 8 vols. *Longmans* (1878-90); 12 vols. (1899) 7 vols. 1913
Much admired for its scientific approach to historical events, its firmly drawn and balanced estimates of the principal figures, its depiction of social details, and for the detachment shown by the author (who was Irish) in the last volumes dealing with Ireland.

Lincoln, Abraham (1809-65) SPEECHES AND LETTERS, 1832-1865 ed. by Paul M. Angle *Dent (Everyman)* (1907) 1957 10s 6d
A new selection, designed by the editor, Director of Publications, Chicago Historical Society, to cover the whole of Lincoln's public career, up to the last speech the President made a few days before his assassination.

Lingard, John (1771-1851) A HISTORY OF ENGLAND TO 1688 (1819-30) 6th edn. 10 vols. *Bell* (1854-5) 1915
Little-read now, but referred to by students as the best of the older histories written from the point of view of a Roman Catholic. It was admired for its judicial, balanced judgements of controversial issues, and for Lingard's research, which included the study of Vatican documents not normally made available to scholars.

Lloyd, Sir John Edward (1861-1947) THE HISTORY OF WALES *Longmans* (1911) 1939 63s 810 pp
The best work on the history of the early period up to the Edwardian conquest.

London, Jack (1876-1916) THE PEOPLE OF THE ABYSS (1903) *Arco* 1962 12s 6d
A grim picture of the appalling lives of the outcast and the very poor people of London, as observed by this American writer during a visit in the year 1902. The reprint is one of the new uniform edition of Jack London's best work, known as the *Fitzroy Edition.* For the others, see note under this author in the *Fiction* section.

*Macaulay, Thomas Babington (Baron) (1800-59) CRITICAL AND HISTORICAL ESSAYS (1843) 2 vols. *Dent (Everyman)* (1907) 1961 12s 6d each
THE HISTORY OF ENGLAND FROM THE ACCESSION OF JAMES II (1848-61) 4 vols. *Dent (Everyman)* (1906) 1953 10s 6d each
The best edition of this brilliant, fluent and enjoyable work was edited by Sir Charles Firth, 6 vols., Macmillan, 1913-15, with 900 illustrations, quarto. This may still be seen in second-hand booksellers' stocks. Macaulay's *History of England* was unfinished. It does not go beyond

1700 and the end of the reign of William III. It was criticised for its Whig bias, but never before, and seldom since, has an historical work of this popular nature displayed such superb gifts of narrative and such a masterly comprehension of the English historical scene. Sir Charles Firth pays tribute, as a professional historian, to its enduring qualities. The *Historical Essays* have opened the door of the historical library to generations of students, and introduced general readers to the persons and events of history in the same fluent, readable style.

SELECTED SPEECHES (1854) ed. by G. M. Young O.U.P. (*Worlds Classics*) 1935 7s 6d
Includes Macaulay's *Minute on Indian Education*, 1835.

Macdonnell, Archibald Gordon (1895-1941) NAPOLEON AND HIS MARSHALS *Macmillan* 1934 10s 6d
A notable study in strategy and personalities, interesting as a footnote to general histories and to biographical studies of the Napoleonic period.

Mackinder, Sir Halford John (1861-1947) BRITAIN AND THE BRITISH SEAS O.U.P. (1902; 1907) 1950
Seminal work linking geography with history; environment and climate with the development of national character and destiny.

*Maine, Sir Henry James Sumner (1822-88) ANCIENT LAW (1861) *Dent* (*Everyman*) (1917) 1954 8s 6d; ed. by Sir C. K. Allen O.U.P. (*Worlds Classics*) 1931 6s
A classic study of primitive law, 'its connection with the early history of society, and its relation to modern ideas'.

*Maitland, Frederick William (1850-1906) DOOMSDAY BOOK AND BEYOND: THREE ESSAYS (1897) *Collins* (*Fontana*) 1960 9s 6d
Maitland was 'England's greatest historian since Gibbon and Macaulay'. —*Thomas Seccombe*.

SELECTED HISTORICAL ESSAYS ed. by Helen M. Cam C.U.P. 1957 27s 6d

SELECTIONS FROM THE WRITINGS OF ENGLAND'S GREAT HISTORIAN ed. by Robert Livingston Schuyler (University of California) C.U.P. 1960 14s (paperback)
The above two volumes offer a representative choice of shorter work by Maitland, whose legal training enabled him to prepare authoritative essays on legal aspects of history, including the growth of townships and boroughs, the history of law, the renaissance, the reformation and allied topics.

Marriott, Sir John Arthur Ransome (1859-1945) ENGLAND SINCE WATERLOO, 1815-1900 *Methuen* (1913) 1943 30s
A student's text in the standard series, *Oman's History of England*.

ENGLISH HISTORY IN ENGLISH FICTION *Blackie* 1940
See note for duplicate entry of this book in the last section: *A Bookman's Library*.

ENGLISH POLITICAL INSTITUTIONS *O.U.P.* (1910) 1938 15*s*
An introductory study, with a chapter on the constitution.

THE EVOLUTION OF MODERN EUROPE, 1453-1939 *Methuen* (1932)
1948 25*s*

*A HISTORY OF EUROPE FROM 1815 to 1939 *Methuen* 1943

*MODERN ENGLAND, 1885-1945 *Methuen* (1934) 1948 30*s*
'A history of my own times.'

Masterman, Charles Frederick Gurney (1873-1927) THE CONDITION
OF ENGLAND *Methuen* (1909) 1960 9*s* 6*d*
A notable study, of permanent value to students of social history, con-
cerned with life and labour in England in the Edwardian period. This
penetrating study and discussion of affairs before the break-up of the
world in 1914, has further interest for students of literature in that
Masterman tried to guess from such novels as *Tono Bungay*, by H. G.
Wells, what kind of England was coming in the decades ahead.

Mayhew, Henry (1812-87) LONDON'S UNDERWORLD ed. by Peter
Quennell *Kimber* 1950 Illus.
Selections from the fourth volume of Mayhew's *London Labour and the
London Poor, 1851-1861*. It is a grim, unique account of social life and
customs among the poor and the outcasts of London in the Dickensian
age, often quoted for its shrewd documentary journalism. The above
selection was remaindered and may be picked up cheaply at book sales
and in second-hand bookshops.

Merivale, Charles (1803-93) A HISTORY OF THE ROMANS UNDER THE
EMPIRE (1850-64) *Dent* (*Everyman*) 1910
The reprint omits the eleven concluding chapters of this work, intended
by Merivale to be a prelude to Gibbon's *Decline and Fall*, by taking the
story of Rome up to the fall of Trajan.

Mitchell, James Leslie (1901-35) THE CONQUEST OF THE MAYA
Jarrolds 1934
Standard work, with an introduction by Sir G. Elliott Smith. The author
wrote fiction under the pseudonym of Lewis Grassic Gibbon; see also
under *Fiction* section.

Moodie, Susanna (1803-85) LIFE IN THE CLEARINGS (VERSUS THE
BUSH) (1853) ed. by Robert L. McDougall *Macmillan* 1959 35*s*
Describes in a vivid, alert style, the social scene and religious sects, popular
education and dominant personalities, in the days of the pioneers of the
St. Lawrence and Lake Ontario regions. Mrs. Moodie, a minor novelist,
and sister of Agnes Strickland, the once-popular biographical historian,
was well-equipped to observe for posterity this interesting phase in the
social history of Canada.

More, Sir Thomas (1478-1535) THE HISTORY OF RICHARD III
(1543) ed. by J. R. Lumby *C.U.P.* 1883

This interesting work was used by the old chroniclers. Apart from its historical importance, it has literary significance in that it is one of the first pieces of prose historical writing in English, and hence did something to develop style.

Motley, John Lothrop (1814-77) THE RISE OF THE DUTCH REPUBLIC (1856) 3 vols. *Dent (Everyman)* 1906 6s 6d each
This standard work by an American historian deals with the thirty years' period of the Netherlands from 1555. Time has not superseded it.

*Namier, Sir Lewis Bernstein (1888-1960) ENGLAND IN THE AGE OF THE AMERICAN REVOLUTION *Macmillan* (1930) 1962 50s; *(Papermac)* 25s
The revision for the second (posthumous) edition of this modern classic was carried out by Lady Namier and John Brooke.

THE STRUCTURE OF POLITICS AT THE ACCESSION OF GEORGE III *Macmillan* (1928) 1957 50s; *(Papermacs)* 1951 25s 514 pp
A major historical study of the first importance, to which the first book above is a companion. The author's method of approach profoundly influenced other historians and students.

Napier, Sir William (1785-1860) THE HISTORY OF THE PENINSULAR WAR 6 vols. (1828-40) Warne 1890
Napier was a General who saw active service in the war about which he afterwards wrote this work, for long the only comprehensive monograph. Now superseded by Sir Charles Oman's *History*, mentioned below.

Newton, Arthur Percival (1873-1942) THE EUROPEAN NATIONS IN THE WEST INDIES, 1493-1688 *A. and C. Black (Pioneer Histories)* 1933

A HUNDRED YEARS OF THE BRITISH EMPIRE *Duckworth* 1940 21s
A series history of the Empire and the Commonwealth into which it merged, from Queen Victoria to 1939, intended as a survey for the general reader.

Oliver, Frederick Scott (1864-1934) ALEXANDER HAMILTON *Macmillan* (1906) 1931
'An essay on American Union,' seen largely as the work of the American statesman (1757-1804) who wrote most of *The Federalist* (which see above), and who was the architect of the American constitution.

THE ENDLESS ADVENTURE 3 vols. *Macmillan* 1931-5
'Personalities and practical politics in eighteenth-century England.'

*Oman, Sir Charles William Chadwick (1860-1946) ENGLAND BEFORE THE NORMAN CONQUEST *Methuen* (1910) 1949
'The Celtic, Roman, and Anglo-Saxon periods down to the year A.D. 1066.'

THE GREAT REVOLT OF 1381 *O.U.P.* 1906
An historical monograph on the Peasants' Revolt and Wat Tyler.

A HISTORY OF THE ART OF WAR IN THE MIDDLE AGES, A.D. 378-1515 *Methuen* (1898; 1924) revised and enlarged by John H. Beeler *O.U.P.* 1953 24s

A HISTORY OF THE ART OF WAR IN THE 16TH CENTURY *Methuen* 1937 50s

SEVEN ROMAN STATESMEN OF THE LATER REPUBLIC *Edward Arnold* (1902) 1921 16s
'The Gracchi, Sulla, Crassus, Cato, Pompey, Caesar.'
Sir Charles Oman was one of the greatest specialist historians of his time, and the above books are likely to be standard for many generations of students to come. They may also be read with pleasure by the general reader. But Oman's masterpiece was his *The History of the Peninsular War*, 7 vols. O.U.P. 1903-31, of interest principally only to students of military history.

*Pares, Sir Bernard (1867-1949) A HISTORY OF RUSSIA *Cape* (1926; 1947) 1955 42s 684 pp; *Methuen* (*University Paperbacks*) 1962 15s
The last, posthumous revision, contains an introduction by Richard Pares. It is probably the best work in one volume, and is certainly one of the most authoritative books on the subject. The author was Professor of Russian Language, Literature, and History at the University of London.

*Parkman, Francis (1823-93) FRANCE AND ENGLAND IN NORTH AMERICA 7 vols. (1851-92) *Macmillan* 1917
Parkman's life work was to write a complete history of the struggle for Canada and North America. Certain volumes of this great work are usually available in good editions in Great Britain. These are detailed below in chronological order:

THE DISCOVERY OF THE GREAT WEST: LA SALLE (1869; 1879) *Eyre and Spottiswoode* 1962 25s Illus.
La Salle (1643-87) explored the whole length of the Mississippi, and founded Louisiana in honour of Louis XIV. The new edition reprints the revised text of the 11th, 1879, edition, but reverts to the title of the first.

MONTCALM AND WOLFE (1884) 2 vols. *Dent* (*Everyman*) 1908
On the campaigns between Wolfe and the French general Montcalm, ending in Wolfe's victory at Quebec in 1759.

THE CONSPIRACY OF PONTIAC (1851) 2 vols. *Dent* (*Everyman*) 1908
On the Indian war after the conquest of Canada. Pontiac, the leader of the Indians, attacked the settlers in 1763, but was afterwards finally defeated by the British in 1766. *Everyman* editions temporarily out of print, but all four volumes still in series.

Petrie, Sir William Flinders (1853-1942) A HISTORY OF EGYPT 6 vols. *Methuen* 1923
From the earliest times to the 16th dynasty. The author was the greatest Egyptologist of his time.

Pitt, William (1759-1806) ORATIONS ON THE FRENCH WAR *Dent* (*Everyman*) 1906
Pitt the Younger made many notable speeches on the war he deplored, up to the temporary cessation agreed at the Peace of Amiens, March, 1802.

THE WAR SPEECHES ed. by Sir Reginald Coupland O.U.P. 1940 10s
A selection, with a foreword by Sir Winston Churchill.

Pollard, Albert Frederick (1869-1948) THE EVOLUTION OF PARLIAMENT *Longmans* (1920) 1938
A notable study in the growth of parliamentary government, but, stated the author, evidence of the research still required is revealed by his own work.

FACTORS IN AMERICAN HISTORY *C.U.P.* 1924

FACTORS IN MODERN HISTORY *Constable* (1907; 1932) 1949

*HENRY VIII *Longmans* (1902; 1913) 1951 30s

Power, Eileen (1889-1940) MEDIAEVAL ENGLISH NUNNERIES, 1275-1535 *C.U.P.* 1922
This was the masterpiece of a distinguished historian, and is the most detailed specialised monograph on the subject.

*MEDIAEVAL PEOPLE *Methuen* (1924) 1950 Illus. *Penguin Books* 1937 2s 6d
Written for a popular audience, but displaying the same scholarly attention to detail as the specialised work on nunneries. It is a picture of life in the Middle Ages, emphasising the daily round of typical people by the specific example of a characteristic household.

*Prescott, William Hickling (1796-1859) THE HISTORY OF THE CONQUEST OF MEXICO (1843) *Allen and Unwin* (1949) 1960 18s; 2 vols. *Dent* (*Everyman*) (1909) 1957 12s 6d each 843 pp

THE HISTORY OF THE CONQUEST OF PERU (1847) *Allen and Unwin* 1959 25s; *Dent* (*Everyman*) (1908) 1962 15s; *W. H. Allen* (*Dolphin Books*) 1962 10s
The pair of standard histories are also published boxed, by Allen and Unwin, 42s the set. These carefully documented historical narratives of two sixteenth-century conquests by the Spanish invaders under Hernando Cortes and the Pizarro brothers, have not been superseded by later researches, although they were written under the almost insuperable difficulties of blindness.

THE HISTORY OF THE REIGN OF FERDINAND AND ISABELLA THE CATHOLIC (1837) *Allen and Unwin* ed. and abridged by C. Harvey Gardiner 1962 35s
The historian's first work, recognised immediately as an historical narrative of the greatest period of Spanish civilisation (1452-1516) not likely ever to be superseded.

*Previté-Orton, Charles William (1877-1947) A HISTORY OF
EUROPE, 1198-1378 *Methuen* (1937) 1951 32s 6d

THE SHORTER CAMBRIDGE MEDIAEVAL HISTORY 2 vols. *C.U.P.*
1952 80s (the set) 1202 pp Illus. Maps
An abridgement of the collective work in eight volumes. Previté-Orton
was one of the original editors. With its 300 illustrations it has been
described as 'almost an encyclopaedia of the European Middle Ages'.

THE STUDY OF MEDIAEVAL HISTORY *C.U.P.* 1937 3s 6d
An Inaugural Lecture addressed to students.

Ralegh, Sir Walter (1552?-1618) SELECTIONS FROM HIS HISTORIE
OF THE WORLD (1614) ed. by G. E. Hadow *O.U.P.* 1917
Notable example of Elizabethan prose, with some letters and other pieces,
selected by the editor to present Ralegh's genius as a writer. There is a
long introduction and notes.

Ramsay, Edward Bannerman (1793-1872) REMINISCENCES OF
SCOTTISH LIFE AND CHARACTER (1857) *Nelson* 1947
Dean Ramsay's Scottish classic has delighted generations of his fellow
Scots, who relish the racy stories gathered by this divine from the
peasantry, during the first half of the nineteenth century.

Rawlinson, George (1812-1902) THE HISTORY OF HERODOTUS translated by George Rawlinson (1858) 2 vols. *Dent* (*Everyman*) 1910
E. H. Blakeney, who edited the series reprint, wrote of Rawlinson's
version that it was itself 'well-nigh an English classic'.

Reade, William Winwood (1838-75) THE MARTYRDOM OF MAN
(1872) *Watts* (1923) 1931
A seminal work that influenced rationalists and other writers, including
H. G. Wells. Reade was the nephew of Charles Reade, the novelist. His
explorations in West Africa, neglected by his contemporaries as they
were, yet gave him some of the material for this somewhat gloomy
survey of man's development along a course mapped out for him by
wars, religions, and aspirations towards liberty and freedom. Nothing
like this had appeared for the general reading public before, and his book
is still read with admiration for its imaginative grasp of great themes.

*Reddaway, William Fiddian (1872-1949) FREDERICK THE GREAT
AND THE RISE OF PRUSSIA *Putnam* (1935) 1948
A HISTORY OF EUROPE, 1610-1715 *Methuen* 1948 30s
A HISTORY OF EUROPE, 1715-1814 *Methuen* (1936) 1951 30s
The author stated in his preface to the last of these standard histories,
that he 'seeks a middle course between mere annals and a series of separate
essays'. The volumes contain bibliographies to aid students in further
reading.

Rose, John Holland (1855-1942) THE REVOLUTIONARY AND
NAPOLEONIC ERA, 1789-1815 *C.U.P.* (1894) 1935

A monograph providing a background to the author's biographies of Napoleon and William Pitt.

*Sackville-West, Victoria (1892-1962) KNOLE AND THE SACKVILLES *Heinemann* (1922); *Benn* 1958 7s 6d Illus.
The fifth, paperback edition of this brilliant history of the great house at Knole, in Kent, the home of the writer's ancestors from Thomas Sackville, First Earl of Dorset, 1536-1608, testifies to its enduring qualities.

Steed, Henry Wickham (1871-1956) THE HAPSBURG MONARCHY *Constable* 1913
A monograph on the dynasty, its rise to power, decline and fall. Wickham Steed was a distinguished foreign correspondent and at one time, was Editor of *The Times*.

*Stobart, John Clarke (1878-1933) THE GLORY THAT WAS GREECE (1921) 3rd rev. edn. by F. N. Pryce *Sidgwick and Jackson* (1933) 1946 35s Illus.

THE GRANDEUR THAT WAS ROME *Sidgwick and Jackson* (1912) 4th rev. edn. by W. S. Maguiness and H. H. Scullard 1961 45s Illus.
Notable popularisations, revised in the light of modern scholarship, with additional illustrations.

*Strachey, Giles Lytton (1880-1932) ELIZABETH AND ESSEX *Chatto* 1928 10s 6d
Presented as 'a tragic history', interpreting the inner thoughts and motives of the two protagonists, and of the statesman, Robert Cecil, Earl of Salisbury, written in a persuasive, pellucid style. The narrative ends with the death of Elizabeth.

Stubbs, William (1825-1901) THE CONSTITUTIONAL HISTORY OF ENGLAND 3 vols. *O.U.P.* (1874-8) 1880

SELECT CHARTERS ed. by William Stubbs *O.U.P.* (1870) 9th edn. rev. by H. W. C. Davis 1913 15s 548 pp
A students' classic, and its complementary book of sources, illustrating English constitutional history from Edward I.

*Sturt, George (1863-1927) CHANGE IN THE VILLAGE *Duckworth* (1912) ed. by Geoffrey Grigson 1955 10s 6d
'A study of the English village.' The changes in the Surrey village in the nineteenth century are a part of social history and all of the books of this sensitive observer, writing under the pen-name of 'George Bourne' have this linking theme. See also his books listed in the *Autobiography* section.

Swift, Jonathan (1667-1745) PROSE WRITINGS ed. by Herbert Davis *Shakespeare Head Press; Blackwell* 1939-59 30s each
Vol. 6: Political Tracts, 1711-13. 1952.
Vol. 7: History of the Four Last Years of the Queen. 1951.

Vol. 8: Tracts Relating to England, 1713-19. 1953.
Vol. 9: Irish Tracts and Sermons. 1948.
Vol. 10: Drapier's Letters. 1941.
Vol. 12: Irish Tracts, 1728-33. 1955.

These are the volumes in the standard set relating to historical events, political topics, and related affairs. The others (*Gulliver's Travels*, for example) will be found in their appropriate sections: *Fiction*; *Essays and Belles Lettres*. The complete set is to be in fourteen volumes; the last will be an index volume to the whole.

Sykes, Sir Percy Molesworth (1867-1945) A HISTORY OF PERSIA
2 vols. *Macmillan* (1915) 1951 70s 1180 pp
The author of this standard work was a noted explorer and traveller in Persia and the Near East.

Symonds, John Addington (1840-93) RENAISSANCE IN ITALY 7 vols.
Murray 1875-86 15s each
Vol. 1: The Age of the Despots; vol. 2: The Revival of Learning; vol. 3: The Fine Arts; vols. 4 and 5: Italian Literature; vols. 6 and 7: The Catholic Reaction; Index to complete work. Vols. 5, 6, and 7 were out of print in 1961.

*Tawney, Richard Henry (1880-1962) THE ACQUISITIVE SOCIETY
Bell 1921 7s 6d; *Collins (Fontana)* 1961 5s
EQUALITY *Allen and Unwin* (1931) 1952 18s
RELIGION AND THE RISE OF CAPITALISM *Murray* (1923) 1948
10s 6d; *Penguin* 1938 4s 6d
The text of the Holland Memorial Lectures, 1922; 'An historical study', with a preface by Bishop Gore. The above three books are the most widely studied and influential writings of one of the greatest Socialist teachers of the century. His work and thought on economic history and socialism gave him an international reputation.

Temperley, Harold William Vazeille (1879-1939) THE FOREIGN POLICY OF CANNING, 1822-1827 *Bell* 1925
Expanded from the author's contribution to the second volume of the *Cambridge History of British Foreign Policy*. The period covered is from Canning's acceptance of the post of minister for foreign affairs after Castlereagh's suicide. Canning's policy helped considerably towards the creation of independent South American states.

Temple, Sir William (1628-99) OBSERVATIONS UPON THE UNITED PROVINCES OF THE NETHERLANDS (1673) ed. by G. N. Clark
C.U.P. 1932
Although of interest chiefly to students it is a noteworthy example of seventeenth-century prose in presenting a sustained theme, as compared with Temple's charming essays. This long, historical essay and commentary is worth attention for its reflective wisdom and statesmanlike apothegms: 'Many things seem true in reason, and prove false in experience: Many, that are weakly consulted, are executed with success.'

Terry, Charles Sanford (1864-1936) A HISTORY OF SCOTLAND
C.U.P. 1920

THE RISING OF 1745 *C.U.P.* (1900) 1922

A SHORT HISTORY OF SCOTLAND *C.U.P.* 1921

*Trevelyan, George Macaulay (1876-1962) BRITISH HISTORY IN
THE NINETEENTH CENTURY AND AFTER, 1782-1919 *Longmans*
(1922; 1937) 1960 32s Maps

ENGLAND IN THE AGE OF WYCLIFFE *Longmans* (1899; 1904; 1909)
1948 18s Maps

ENGLAND UNDER QUEEN ANNE 3 vols. *Longmans* (1930; 1932;
1934) 1948 21s each
Dr. Trevelyan regarded this trilogy as his best work, and it is not likely
to be superseded. Praised as a masterpiece for its scholarship; widely
enjoyed by the general public; it is one of those twentieth-century classics
that have made English historical writing world-famous both with
academic students and with the ordinary reader. The three volumes are
divided thus: *Blenheim* (1930); *Ramillies and the Union with Scotland* (1932);
The Peace and the Protestant Succession (1934).

ENGLAND UNDER THE STUARTS *Methuen* (1904) 1949 30s
This monograph for students is volume V of *Methuen's History of England*,
edited by Sir Charles Oman.

THE ENGLISH REVOLUTION, 1688-1689 *O.U.P.* (*Home University
Library*) 1938 8s 6d

ENGLISH SOCIAL HISTORY *Longmans* (1944; 1946) 1958 30s 628 pp
'A survey of six centuries: Chaucer to Queen Victoria,' and the most
widely-read historical narrative of the century. There is another edition
in four volumes, known as *Illustrated English Social History*, Longmans,
1949-52, with coloured plates and many other illustrations, 27s 6d each
volume, or boxed edition bound in leather, £9 19s 6d the set.

GARIBALDI 3 vols. *Longmans* (1907; 1909; 1911) 1948-9 21s each
A masterly mingling of historical narrative and biographical writing,
being a trilogy on the life and achievements of the maker of modern
Italy. Available in three separate volumes: *Garibaldi's Defence of the
Roman Republic, 1848-1849*; *Garibaldi and The Thousand, May 1860*; and
Garibaldi and the Making of Italy (June-November, 1860).

THE HISTORY OF ENGLAND *Longmans* (1926; 1945) 1956 35s
758 pp 37 maps
The last edition has four additional chapters, bringing the narrative to
Peace of 1919. Also available in another edition, *Illustrated History of
England*, Longmans, 1956, 42s, with 4 coloured plates and 150 black and
white illustrations.

Trevelyan, Sir George Otto (1838-1928) THE EARLY HISTORY OF
CHARLES JAMES FOX *Longmans* 1880

THE AMERICAN REVOLUTION 4 vols. *Longmans* (1899-1907) 1905-12

GEORGE III AND CHARLES FOX 2 vols. *Longmans* (1912-14); 1920-2
A trilogy on the political history of the second half of the eighteenth
century.

Turberville, Arthur Stanley (1888-1945) ENGLISH MEN AND
MANNERS IN THE EIGHTEENTH CENTURY *O.U.P.* (1926) *Galaxy
Books* 1957 15s
THE SPANISH INQUISITION *O.U.P.* (*Home University Library*) 1932
*JOHNSON'S ENGLAND 2 vols. edited by A. S. Turberville *O.U.P.*
1933 70s (the set) 846 pp Illus.
A standard work of social history, contributed to by specialists on
various aspects, with 180 illustrations.

Vinogradoff, Sir Paul (1854-1925) COMMONSENSE IN LAW *O.U.P.*
(*Home University Library*) (1913) rev. edn. by H. G. Hanbury
(1946) 1959 8s 6d
THE GROWTH OF THE MANOR *Allen and Unwin* (1904; 1911)
1951 18s
The author was recognised as the greatest authority on this specialised
topic in the social and agricultural history of England.

Wakefield, Edward Gibbon (1796-1862) A LETTER FROM SYDNEY
AND OTHER WRITINGS (1829) *Dent* (*Everyman*) 1929 6s 6d
A volume of historic essays on colonisation, the most important being
the *Letter*, which Wakefield wrote in gaol. On release he became an
influential, practical exponent of his own ideas for successful colonisation
by sale of holdings to colonists at state-controlled prices, and other
measures which he advocated in these writings.

Webster, Sir Charles Kingsley (1886-1961) THE CONGRESS OF
VIENNA (Bell, 1919) *Thames and Hudson* 1963 21s
A masterly study of the organisation, methods and techniques of the
epoch-making Congress held in 1815 to settle some of the problems
resulting from the final defeat of Napoleon. It was originally written for
the Foreign Office to provide historical background for officials and
statesmen confronted with the settlement of international problems in
the aftermath of World War I.

*Wells, Herbert George (1866-1946) THE OUTLINE OF HISTORY
Cassell (1920) rev. from time to time by Raymond Postgate
1961 36s 1280 pp Illus. Maps
The most widely-read survey of its kind, and the begetter of many
similar outlines of great subjects for the general reader. Wells starts with
'primordial life'; in the latest revision the record is taken up to 1960, with
maps and pictures by J. F. Horrabin.
A SHORT HISTORY OF THE WORLD (1922) *Collins* (*Classics*) 1953
6s; *Penguin Books* (1936) 1937 3s 6d
This is not an abridgement of the *Outline*, but a summary from prehistory
to 1936, written as a separate work.

Woolley, Sir Charles Leonard (1880-1960) DIGGING UP THE PAST
  Benn (1930) 1954 10s 6d Illus.; *Penguin Books* 1937 3s 6d

  HISTORY UNEARTHED *Benn* (1958) 1960 12s 6d Illus. quarto
  Two major works by an eminent archaeologist, whose excavations at
  Ur over a period of twelve years unearthed valuable information about
  the early civilisation of Mesopotamia.

*Young, George Malcolm (1882-1959) CHARLES I AND CROMWELL
  Hart-Davis 1950 7s 6d
  VICTORIAN ENGLAND: THE PORTRAIT OF AN AGE *O.U.P.* (1936)
  1960 6s (*paperback*)
  An extension of a famous last chapter in G. M. Young's *Early Victorian
  England, 1830-1865*, a work of collective scholarship that he edited in
  two volumes, O.U.P., 1934, 63s, 1006 pages, with 138 plates. The separate
  work takes the portrait up to 1901.

  VICTORIAN ESSAYS ed. by W. D. Handcock *O.U.P.* 1962 7s 6d
  (paperback)
  '. . . contains the Victorian pieces from the three volumes of essays that
  Young published in his lifetime.'—*Intro.* by W. D. Handcock, who adds
  that 'The *Portrait* has established itself as the most penetrating and comprehensive account that we have of the Victorian age'.

*Zimmern, Alfred (1879-1957) THE GREEK COMMONWEALTH
  O.U.P. (1911) 1931 25s; 1961 10s 6d (paperback)
  A masterly study of politics and economics in fifth-century Athens.

HISTORY
(*Anthologies and Collections*)

Barker, Sir Ernest (Editor) THE CHARACTER OF ENGLAND *O.U.P.*
  1947 608 pp Illus.
  Collective work on specific aspects of English social history, consisting
  of contributions by distinguished specialists: for example, Sir Francis
  Meynell writes on *The Making of Books*; C. T. Onions on *The English
  Language*.

Bell, K. N. and W. P. Morrell (Editors) SELECT DOCUMENTS ON
  BRITISH COLONIAL POLICY, 1830-1860 *O.U.P.* 35s 622 pp

Birley, Robert (Editor) SPEECHES AND DOCUMENTS IN AMERICAN
  HISTORY, 1776-1939 4 vols. *O.U.P.* (*Worlds Classics*) 1942-4
  7s 6d each
  Vol. 1: 1776-1815; vol. 2: 1818-65; vol. 3: 1865-1913; vol. 4: 1914-39.

Clark, Manning (Editor) SOURCES OF AUSTRALIAN HISTORY *O.U.P.*
  (*Worlds Classics*) 1957 9s 6d

The history of Australia from its foundation to the Treaty of Versailles, presented by the Professor of History, Canberra University College, in a series of documents on political and social history, including material from newspaper files, poems and ballads.

Emden, Cecil Stuart (Editor) SELECTED SPEECHES ON THE CONSTITU-TION 2 vols. *O.U.P.* (*Worlds Classics*) 1939 7s 6d each

*Hassall, W. O. (Editor) THEY SAW IT HAPPEN: 55 B.C.–A.D. 1485 *Blackwell* 1957 15s
An anthology of eye-witness accounts of events in British history from Julius Caesar to the Battle of Bosworth. The sources drawn upon include the chroniclers, official documents, and the early historians. The series is continued in three supplementary anthologies: 1485-1688, edited by C. R. N. Routh (15s) 1956; 1689-1897, edited by T. Charles-Edwards and Asa Briggs (21s) 1958; and 1898-1945, edited by B. Richardson (30s), published 1960.

Keith, Sir Arthur Berriedale (1879-1944) (Editor) SPEECHES AND DOCUMENTS ON BRITISH COLONIAL POLICY, 1763-1917 *O.U.P.* (*Worlds Classics*) 1918 9s 6d
An anthology edited by one of the most distinguished constitutional historians of his time, whose classic work on *Responsible Government In the Dominions*, 2 vols. O.U.P., 1928, 1432 pp, has guided official opinion in this present century of political evolution and development within the nations of the Commonwealth.

*Newman, Bertram (Editor) ENGLISH HISTORIANS: SELECTED PASSAGES *O.U.P.* 18s; school edition 13s 6d
Introduction by C. V. Wedgwood. This anthology 'illustrates the pro-gress of English historical writing since the sixteenth century, from More and Holinshed to Sir Winston Churchill and G. M. Trevelyan. These typical extracts from the work of more than sixty historians, are, as far as possible, self-contained.'

*Paston Family, The (1378-) PASTON LETTERS, 1422-1509 6 vols. ed. by James Gairdner *Chatto* 1903-4; 2 vols. ed. by John Warrington *Dent* (*Everyman*) 1957 8s 6d each; ed. by Norman Davis *O.U.P.* (*Mediaeval and Tudor series*) 1958 15s (*Worlds Classics*) 1963 8s 6d
The first editor of these celebrated letters, a source for historians and of the greatest interest for the general reader, was Sir John Fenn, who published a selection in 1787. Gairdner's edition is still the standard one; but the new selection in *Everyman* (superseding the 1924 edition), is a very full selection collated with Gairdner's text, with the spelling, where necessary, modernised. The Pastons lived in the Norfolk village from which they took their name, from the fourteenth to sixteenth century. Their letters offer an incomparable account of social life in semi-feudal times. Professor Davis includes in his selection 95 letters by 26 writers, a glossary, notes, and introduction, and critical comments by noted

writers from Horace Walpole to Virginia Woolf. The new *Worlds
Classics* Selection of 142 Letters is in modern spelling.

Rhys, Ernest (Editor) *BRITISH ORATIONS (FROM ETHELBERT TO
CHURCHILL) *Dent (Everyman)* (1915) 1960 10s 6d
A selection of the most notable orations in English from the old
chronicles (A.D. 597) to 18 August, 1940, including in its progress through
the centuries speeches by Ethelbert, Queen Elizabeth I, James I, Charles I,
Cromwell, Burke, Chatham, Wilkes, Pitt, Fox, Canning, Brougham,
Macaulay, Peel, Cobden, Bright, Disraeli, Gladstone, Chamberlain,
Rosebery, Asquith, Lloyd George and Sir Winston Churchill.

THE GROWTH OF POLITICAL LIBERTY *Dent (Everyman)* 1921
'Designed to trace the slow political growth of the common folk, from
Alfred's time to our time.' It thus provides 'a source book of English
history', from about sixty sources, from histories, chronicles, charters,
letters, memoirs, and historical essays.

Turberville, A. S. (Editor) JOHNSON'S ENGLAND 2 vols. *O.U.P.*
1933 70s (the set) 846 pp 160 illus.
A collective work, offering 'an account of the life and manners of his age'.
This contribution to social history is similar to Sir Ernest Barker's general
work, for which see above, and to the companion set, published for the
tercentenary, called *Shakespeare's England*, 2 vols., O.U.P., 70s the set,
1192 pp, 197 illustrations, being a collective work by 43 contributors.

PHILOSOPHY AND RELIGION
(including political and social philosophy)

IN the seventeenth and eighteenth centuries speculation on scientific matters other than chemistry was called natural philosophy, a terminology inherited from the Middle Ages. Modern physics is applied and experimental natural philosophy. This provides a slight but convenient excuse for including here a few books strictly belonging to scientific speculation rather than to philosophy and ethics.

Apart from these, the selection falls into four main sections. In the leisurely centuries certain devotional classics and collections of sermons were household books. Together with the Holy Bible and Bunyan's *Pilgrim's Progress* (and probably Foxe's Book of Martyrs, 1563; 1776), this small collection appeared to be kept in many households for pious meditation and constant study. Baxter's *The Saints' Everlasting Rest* is still in print, but perhaps read now by relatively few. Readers of George Eliot's *The Mill on the Floss* may recall that this was the work Mrs. Glegg 'was accustomed to lay open before her on special occasions: on wet Sunday mornings, or when she heard of a death in the family'. Butler's *Sermons*, and similar collections doubtless had to take the place of an amusing novel for many a young man and woman. Law's *Serious Call* and Thomas à Kempis have been much-loved books and continue to attract thoughtful readers, even in the affluent society; perhaps because of it. In times when, though more is right, so much seems wrong and evil, the thoughts of those accustomed to seek wisdom and philosophy from 'the mighty dead', turn as did their ancestors to such works of wisdom offering guidance to the perplexed and solace to the troubled. Dr. Johnson, Edward Gibbon and John Wesley, all appreciated the wisdom of *A Serious Call*, and in our own time the late Dean Inge said it 'should be studied carefully by all who care for their Soul's health'. These books and others, such as John Woolman's minor writings beloved by Charles Lamb, and Hannah Smith's little book, must therefore rightly be accorded a place in the group that also contains the mightier Donne, whose prose style and imagery attract readers not greatly interested in theology and religion.

Then we have the larger group of seminal works whose influence has been prolonged and profound. In some instances as with the philosophy of Hobbes, Hume, and the reasonable John Locke; the sustained and elaborate treatises of Adam Smith and Thomas Malthus; the epoch-making work of Darwin, William Godwin and John Stuart Mill, these books have become part of Western civilisation. Controversies and counter-arguments aroused long ago on first publication have not yet died down. Hobbes, Hume and Locke in particular, continue to attract critical monographs. Other books, such as Owen's *A New View Of Society*, their work done, live on as historical landmarks and literary classics.

There remain the smaller group of personal statements, of which Cardinal Newman's *Apologia* is the greatest; the astonishing output of John Ruskin, one of the most salutary teachers of the nineteenth century; the notable translations of and monographs on the philosophers of ancient Greece; and modern books whose profound influence has been acknowledged by living writers in no uncertain terms.

F. H. Bradley's books are not for every reader, but we have recently been made aware of their influence, for example, on the thought and development of the poet T. S. Eliot, whose thesis *Knowledge and Experience in the Philosophy of F. H. Bradley*, written in 1916, and now in the archives of Harvard University, was published for the first time in 1963 by Faber and Faber. Sir James Frazer's *Golden Bough*, when finally assessed, may turn out to be the most influential work in the modern world; and the tributes paid by notable contemporaries to the *Principia Ethica* of the Cambridge philosopher G. E. Moore, make it clear that the philosophy of The Good Life has been more powerful than one might deduce from the history of the twentieth century so far.

Finally, since these subjects lend themselves to useful anthologies and selections, essential for many readers lacking the time or the application to study lengthy works, attention is called to the books edited by Sir Ernest Barker, Eric Colledge, H. Bettenson, T. E. Jessop (under Berkeley), A. J. Ayer, and to the paper back abridgement of Frazer's masterpiece in Macmillan's *St. Martins Library*.

For a concise summary A. D. Ritchie's *British Philosophers* published for the British Council by Longmans, 1951, 2s 6d, can scarcely be bettered; and Edward Gordon Selwyn's *A Short History of Christian Thought*, Geoffrey Bles, revised edition 1949, 5s, may be recommended with confidence as a notable example of an introduction to a great subject, likely to send the reader on to other and longer books.

Acton, John E. E. Dalberg (1st Baron) (1834-1902) ESSAYS ON CHURCH AND STATE ed. by Douglas Woodruff *Hollis and Carter* 1952 15s

The founder of the *Cambridge Modern History* made fugitive contributions, in the form of lectures and essays, to his lifelong study of history. In this collection, essays concerned with the relations between Church and State are brought together.

Alexander, Samuel (1859-1938) BEAUTY AND OTHER FORMS OF VALUE *Macmillan* 1933

PHILOSOPHICAL AND LITERARY PIECES ed. with a memoir by John Laud *Macmillan* 1939 15s

SPACE TIME AND DEITY 2 vols. *Macmillan* (1920) *Vision Press* 1950 80s (the set) 700 pp

Alexander's *Gifford Lectures*, 1916-18, being an advanced and sustained examination of the concepts of mental space-time.

*Ayer, A. J. and Raymond Winch (Editors) BRITISH EMPIRICAL
PHILOSOPHERS *Routledge* 1952 30s 560 pp
Two distinguished modern philosophers offer here a choice of characteristic writings by John Locke, Berkeley, David Hume, Thomas Reid
and John Stuart Mill, with an introduction and notes.

*Bacon, Sir Francis (Lord Verulam) (1561-1626) THE ADVANCE-
MENT OF LEARNING (1605) ed. by G. W. Kitchin *Dent* (*Everyman*)
(1915) 1962 8s 6d; ed. by W. Aldis Wright *O.U.P.* 1900 12s 6d;
(*Worlds Classics*) 1906 6s
A landmark in the literature of philosophy, in which Bacon approached
his subject historically and scientifically, examining the arguments for
unity in research and speculation, thus pointing to the future, when the
foundation of the Royal Society brought his ideas into practice. In the
Worlds Classics edition his unfinished *New Atlantis* (1627), is included.
It is an early example of a method of presenting a philosophical and
political argument in the form of an account of an imaginary country,
in this case, an island in the Pacific. The new edition in *Everyman* has a
glossary.

NEW ATLANTIS (1627) *O.U.P.* (*Worlds Classics*) 1906 6s; *Van
Nostrand* 1942 14s
See note under first book above. The Van Nostrand edition is included
in an edition of Bacon's essays, ed. by Gordon S. Haight, with annotations.

*Barker, Sir Ernest (1874-1960) GREEK POLITICAL THEORY *Methuen*
(1918) 1957 21s; 1960 12s 6d (*paperback*)
'Plato and his predecessors.'

NATIONAL CHARACTER AND FACTORS IN ITS FORMATION *Methuen*
(1927) 1948 21s

*Barker, Sir Ernest (Editor) SOCIAL CONTRACT: ESSAYS *O.U.P.*
(*Worlds Classics*) 1947 7s 6d
A collection, with an introduction, of essays by John Locke, and David
Hume, whose works are entered below, together with Rousseau's essay.
The common theme is the individual's relationship to the State; the
social contract; and Locke's 'Original Contract', by which a Society is
established, tempered by Hume's criticism. See below for the work of
Hobbes, whose *Leviathan* opposes this view.

Baxter, Richard (1615-91) THE SAINTS' EVERLASTING REST (1650)
ed. by John Wesley 1754; ed. by John T. Wilkinson *Epworth
Press* 1962 18s 6d
Once a household book, much studied by Nonconformists, this devotional work should be read in company with Baxter's autobiography,
which see in the first section. The new abridged edition has an interesting
introduction on Baxter.

*Bentham, Jeremy (1748-1832) PRINCIPLES OF MORALS AND LEGISLATION (1789; 1823) ed. by W. Harrison *Blackwell* 1948 30s
This edition includes Bentham's *A Fragment on Government* (1776; 1822). The *Introduction to the Principles of Morals* . . . presents the philosopher's ideas on the ethical basis of wise legislation, in which he states his utilitarian creed; the *Fragment* is 'an examination of what is delivered on the subject of government . . . in the introduction to Sir William Blackstone's *Commentaries*'. There is a standard, critical edition of Bentham's *Economic Writings* for advanced students, based on his printed and unprinted manuscripts, edited by Dr. W. Stark, 3 volumes, Allen and Unwin, 1952-4, 30s, 40s, and 45s each, 1470 pages.

*Berkeley, George (1685-1753) A NEW THEORY OF VISION (1709) ed. by A. D. Lindsay *Dent* (*Everyman*) (1910) 1954 8s 6d
Also contains *The Principles of Human Knowledge* (1710) and *The Three Dialogues* (between Hylas and Philonous) (1713) in opposition to sceptics and atheists. This volume contains therefore, 'the main exposition of his philosophy'.

THE PRINCIPLES OF HUMAN KNOWLEDGE (1710; 1734) ed. by T. E. Jessop *Nelson* 1937; ed. by G. J. Warnock *Collins* (*Fontana*) 1962 6s
The paperback reprint includes *The Three Dialogues* (1713).

SELECT PHILOSOPHICAL WRITINGS ed. by T. E. Jessop *Nelson* 1952 12s 6d
Excellent selection for general readers, and a good introduction for students, who will, however, if they wish to pursue the subject, consult the great definitive edition of Berkeley's *Complete Works*, edited by T. E. Jessop and A. A. Luce, 9 vols., Nelson, 1948-57, 30s each.

Bettenson, Henry (Editor) DOCUMENTS OF THE CHRISTIAN CHURCH *OUP* (*Worlds Classics*) 1943 8s 6d; 1963 18s 512 pp crown octavo
The selection ranges in time from the first years of the Church to the *Lambeth Appeal for Reunion* of recent years.

Bevan, Edwyn Robert (1870-1943) CHRISTIANITY *O.U.P.* (*Home University Library*) 1932 8s 6d
HOLY IMAGES *Allen and Unwin* 1940 7s 6d
The text of the Gifford Lectures, 1940.

SYMBOLISM AND BELIEF *Allen and Unwin* (1938); *Collins* (*Fontana*) 1962 10s 6d
The text of the Gifford Lectures, 1938. Bevan's controversial views are expressed in all three of the above books, dealing with image-worship and an inquiry into idolatry in the era of ancient paganism.

*THE BIBLE DESIGNED TO BE READ AS LITERATURE ed. by Ernest Sutherland Bates *Heinemann* (1937) 1962 30s 1243 pp

H

*THE READER'S BIBLE *O.U.P.* 1951 30s 1988 pp
The above are two popular editions of the Holy Bible in the A.V.,
designed for general reading.

THE NEW ENGLISH BIBLE: NEW TESTAMENT *O.U.P.* and *C.U.P.*
1961 21s (library edition)
The new translation into current English: 'neither a revision of the A.V.
nor intended to replace it'. For other editions see the Oxford Catalogue.

Bosanquet, Bernard (1848–1923) LOGIC *O.U.P.* (1888; 1911) 1931
A treatise on the morphology of knowledge, in which Bosanquet
discusses logic as a practical means to an end, and as a mental exercise.

Boyle, Robert (1627–91) THE SCEPTICAL CHYMIST (1661) *Dent*
(*Everyman*) 1911 6s 6d
Arguments for scientific method set forth by this famous natural philo-
sopher and physicist. The book is a landmark in the literature of science.

Bradley, Francis Herbert (1846–1924) APPEARANCE AND REALITY
O.U.P. (1893) 1930 25s
ESSAYS ON TRUTH AND REALITY *O.U.P.* 1914 25s
ETHICAL STUDIES *O.U.P.* (1896) 1927 21s; 1962 7s 6d (paperback)
PRINCIPLES OF LOGIC *O.U.P.* (1883) 2 vols. 1922 45s (the set)
The influence of this philosopher was profound and far-reaching.

Brooke, Zachary Nugent (1883–1946) THE ENGLISH CHURCH AND
THE PAPACY *C.U.P.* 1931 27s 6d
From the Norman Conquest to the reign of John: 1066 to 1210.

*Bunyan, John (1628–88) GRACE ABOUNDING (1666) *Dent* (*Everyman*) (1907) 1954 8s 6d; ed. by Roger Sharrock *O.U.P.* (*Oxford
English Texts*) 1962 35s; *S.C.M. Press* 1955 9s 6d
A personal narrative of spiritual revelation: 'Grace Abounding to the
Chief of Sinners, or the Brief Relation of the exceeding Mercy of God
in Christ to his Poor Servant'. The simple, Biblical power of Bunyan's
style, and the autobiographical element, make this a complementary
work to his masterpiece. Bound in *Everyman* with an early example of
didactic fiction in English: *The Life and Death of Mr. Badman*, an allegorical
dialogue between Mr. Attentive and Mr. Wiseman, the latter relating
the story of Mr. Badman. The *O.E.T.* edition is based on the 1666 text,
and is the nearest approach to a definitive edition. The volume contains
two posthumously published minor pieces.

THE PILGRIM'S PROGRESS (1678; 1679; 1684) ed. by James Blanton
Wharey; *O.U.P.* (*Oxford English Texts*) (1628) revised by Roger
Sharrock 1960 63s
A complete revision with rewritten introduction, to this standard
edition for scholars and literary students. The text is that of Bunyan's
first edition of 1678, with his afterthoughts and additions from the
earliest texts in which they appear. The commentary and bibliographical

information has been augmented. Other editions: *Collins (Classics)* 1954 5s; *Dent (Children's Illustrated Classics)* 1954 10s 6d; *(Everyman)* (1907) 1954 7s 6d; *Faber* 1947 15s illus. by Edward Ardizonne; *Nelson (Classics)* 1954 5s; *O.U.P. (Worlds Classics)* 1901 6s; *(Oxford Standard Authors)* (1904) 1959 12s 6d illus. by George Cruikshank.

The text of the last edition in *O.S.A.* is taken from the second edition of the First Part; and the first edition of the Second Part (1678 and 1684 respectively).

Burke, Edmund (1729-97) A PHILOSOPHICAL ENQUIRY INTO THE ORIGIN OF OUR IDEAS OF THE SUBLIME AND BEAUTIFUL (1756) ed. by J. T. Boulton *Routledge* 1958 32s
The first critical edition of a masterpiece once widely studied. The text used is from Burke's revision for a second edition. Notes and introduction complete this standard edition.

*Bury, John Bagnell (1861-1927) A HISTORY OF FREEDOM OF THOUGHT *O.U.P. (Home University Library)* (1913) ed. by H. J. Blackham 1952 8s 6d
A remarkable monograph by a great historian, in which man's struggles to assert the right to hold minority opinions and to teach and persuade others to hold beliefs against the prevailing ideas of their society, are recorded with balanced judgement. The editor of the last reprint adds an epilogue.

Butler, Joseph (1692-1752) THE ANALOGY OF RELIGION, NATURAL AND REVEALED (1736) *Dent (Everyman)* 1906
FIFTEEN SERMONS (1726) ed. by W. R. Matthews *Bell* (1914) 1949 10s 6d
Bishop Butler, eminent divine and preacher, left the Presbyterians for the Church of England, becoming preacher at the Rolls Chapel. Here he delivered the sermons reprinted from the 1729 edition, with 'a dissertation upon the nature of virtue'. The introduction, notes and analyses by the distinguished editor are of great value to students of ethics. Of the sermons and Butler's masterpiece, *The Analogy*, Professor Saintsbury observed that they 'occasionally contain aphorisms of beauty equal to their depth'.

Butler, Samuel (1835-1902) THE FAIR HAVEN (1873) *Cape* 1921 7s 6d
'In defence of the miraculous element in Our Lord's ministry'; 'by the late J.P.O. Memoir by W. B. Owen'. Thus disguised, the author of *Erewhon* published what is regarded as, next to that masterpiece, his most sustained ironic work.

Canton, William (1845-1926) A CHILD'S BOOK OF SAINTS (1898) *Dent (Everyman)* (1906) 1960 8s 6d
Short legends about St. Francis of Assisi, St. Dorothea, St. Basil the Hermit, and many other holy people. Suitable not only for general reading but also for reading aloud to children.

Carpenter, Edward (1844-1929) LOVE'S COMING-OF-AGE *Allen and Unwin* (1896) 1923 7s 6d (cloth); 6s (paperback)
A courageous, pioneer discussion of topics connected with the relations of the sexes, including the 'Intermediate Sex', and the place of woman in a modern free society.

*Chesterton, Gilbert Keith (1874-1936) ORTHODOXY *Bodley Head* (1908) 1950 12s 6d
ST. FRANCIS OF ASSISI *Hodder* (1923) 1949 7s 6d
The first book is a brilliant discussion of Chesterton's attitude to contemporary topics in religion and philosophy. The second, a sympathetic study of the founder of the Franciscans. This is regarded as one of Chesterton's best books.

Coleridge, Samuel Taylor (1772-1834) CONFESSIONS OF AN INQUIRING SPIRIT (1840) ed. by H. St. J. Hart *A. and C. Black* 1956 8s 6d
Modern reprint of the third edition of 1853 of this posthumously published work, with an introduction by J. H. Green, and a note contributed to the original edition by Sara Coleridge, the poet's daughter. The theme is the inspiration of the Bible, the arguments being presented in the form of letters.

Colledge, Eric (Editor) THE MEDIAEVAL MYSTICS OF ENGLAND *Murray* 1962 25s
A valuable anthology of characteristic writings of the English mystics, translated where necessary from the Latin, and given in standard versions. After a scholarly introduction of ninety pages, the editor provides an eleven-page bibliography. Among the mystics are Margery Kempe (see also in the *Autobiography* section), Julian of Norwich, Walter Hilton, and Richard Rolle, also entered below.

*Collingwood, Robin George (1889-1943) THE NEW LEVIATHAN *O.U.P.* 1942 35s
'Or, Man, Society, Civilisation and Barbarism'. A logical, sustained examination and discussion of modern ideas and trends by a distinguished historiographer and philosopher, whose *Idea of History*, O.U.P., 1946 28s, embodied many of his characteristic views on the theory of history.

Cornford, Francis Macdonald (1874-1943) BEFORE AND AFTER SOCRATES *C.U.P.* 1932 18s; 1960 7s 6d (paperback)
PLATO AND PARMENIDES *Routledge* 1939 24s
PLATO'S COSMOLOGY: THE TIMAEUS OF PLATO *Routledge* 1937 32s
PLATO'S THEORY OF KNOWLEDGE: THE THEAETETUS AND THE SOPHIST *Routledge* 1935 28s; 1960 10s 6d (paperback)
Before and After Socrates may be read with pleasure by the general reader interested in Greek thought and philosophy; the Platonic trilogy consists of monographs contributed to the *International Library of Psychology* for students.

*PLATO'S REPUBLIC translated by F. M. Cornford *O.U.P.* 1941 10s 6d
A notable translation for the general reader.

*Coulton, George Gordon (1858-1947) FIVE CENTURIES OF RELIGION 4 vols. *C.U.P.* 1923; 1927; 1936; 1950 72s 6d (volume IV only; others out of print)
The masterpiece of a great historian of the Middle Ages. Vol. 1: *St. Bernard, A.D. 1000-1200*; vol. 2: *The Friars and the Dead Weight of Tradition, A.D. 1200-1400*; vol. 3: *Getting and Spending*; vol. 4: *The Last Days of Mediaeval Monachism.*
The work as a whole provoked much criticism and controversy from Roman Catholic critics, notably from Coulton's contemporary, Hilaire Belloc.

Cranmer, Thomas (1489-1556) THE PRAYER BOOKS OF EDWARD VI (1549; 1552) ed. by E. C. S. Gibson *Dent (Everyman)* (1910) 1957 10s 6d
In his introduction, Bishop Gibson states that the Prayer Books were chiefly the work of Archbishop Cranmer, and of John Hooper, Bishop of Gloucester.

Crawley, Alfred Ernest (1869-1924) THE MYSTIC ROSE 2 vols. *Macmillan* (1902) ed. by Theodore Besterman *Methuen* (1927); *Mayflower Press (Meridian Books)* 1961 18s
The one-volume edition of this study of primitive marriage, 'and of primitive thought in its bearing on marriage', was revised and enlarged by its editor.

*Darwin, Charles Robert (1809-82) THE ORIGIN OF SPECIES BY MEANS OF NATURAL SELECTION (1859; 1872) *Dent (Everyman)* (1928) 1956 8s 6d; *O.U.P. (Worlds Classics)* (1902) 1951 7s 6d; *Watts* 1950 15s
This landmark in the literature of science presented the Darwinian theory of evolution based on the scientist's observations and researches. His final revised and corrected edition was the sixth of 1872. The Watts edition reprints Darwin's first text of 1859. The other two reprint the 1872 text. Sir Gavin de Beer has written an introduction on Darwin and his achievement for the *Worlds Classics* edition. Sub-title: 'The Preservation of Favoured Races in the Struggle for Life'.

THE DARWIN READER ed. by Marston Bates and Philip S. Humphrey *Macmillan* 1957 30s 481 pp
A choice from all of Darwin's principal writings: extracts from his *Autobiography* (1887); *The Voyage of the 'Beagle'* (1839); *The Origin of Species* (1859); *The Descent of Man* (1871); *The Expression of the Emotions in Man and Animals* (1873) and some of the lesser writings. There is a modern reprint of the last-named book in *The Thinker's Library*, Watts, 1934, 2s 6d.

*Dickinson, Goldsworthy Lowes (1862-1932) AFTER TWO
THOUSAND YEARS *Allen and Unwin* 1930 6s
'A dialogue between Plato and a modern young man.'

THE GREEK VIEW OF LIFE *Methuen* (1896) 1957 13s 6d; (*University
Paperbacks*) 1962 9s 6d
'I think I have got hold of the central thing, the thing that makes Greek
of permanent value to civilisation.' The reprint of a much-respected and
valuable book (the 23rd) has an introduction by the author's friend and
biographer, E. M. Forster.

JUSTICE AND LIBERTY *Allen and Unwin* 1908 6s
'A political dialogue.'

THE MEANING OF GOOD *Allen and Unwin* 1901 7s 6d
A discussion pursued in the author's favourite form—a dialogue.

A MODERN SYMPOSIUM *Allen and Unwin* (1905) 1930 7s 6d; 1962
4s 6d (paperback)
A notable discussion of topics in religion and politics, with an introduction by E. M. Forster.
PLATO AND HIS DIALOGUES *Allen and Unwin* 1931 9s 6d

Dixon, Richard Watson (1833-1900) A HISTORY OF THE CHURCH
OF ENGLAND 6 vols. *O.U.P.* (1878-91) 1902
'A treasure, if you can get it, or even a single volume of it.'—*Edmund
Blunden*. The period covered is from 'the Abolition of the Romish
Jurisdiction'.

*Dixon, William Macneile (1866-1946) THE HUMAN SITUATION
Edward Arnold 1937 15s; *Penguin Books* 1958 5s
The Gifford Lectures for 1935-7. 'A superbly written book.'—*A. D.
Ritchie* in *British Philosophers*, published by Longmans. The theme is
man's place in the universe.

Donne, John (1573?-1631) *DEVOTIONS UPON EMERGENT OCCASIONS
(1624) ed. by John Sparrow *C.U.P.* 1923
Bibliographical note by Geoffrey Keynes.

ESSAYS IN DIVINITY (1651) ed. by Evelyn M. Simpson *O.U.P.*
1952 18s
Written before Donne entered Holy Orders, and therefore of particular
interest to students of the poet's temperament.

*SERMONS ed. by Logan Pearsall Smith *O.U.P.* 1919 12s 6d
Selected passages, with an essay by the editor. These sermons are read as
examples of majestic prose, with many often quoted sentences of poetic
beauty and imagery. The definitive, monumental edition of Donne's
complete sermons is in progress, under the editorship of E. M. Simpson
and G. R. Potter, to be completed in ten volumes, C.U.P., 1953-.

Draper, John William (1811-82) HISTORY OF THE CONFLICT BETWEEN RELIGION AND SCIENCE (1874)
Once widely-read book by the British-born American historian; now used principally for reference.

*Eddington, Sir Arthur (1882-1944) THE NATURE OF THE PHYSICAL WORLD *C.U.P.* 1928 22s 6d; *Dent (Everyman)* (1935) 1955 10s 6d
A physicist's view of cosmology. It was one of the most widely-read and discussed books of its period. Here for the first time abstruse subjects such as the quantum theory and relativity were explained to the non-scientific general reader by a distinguished scientist writing in lucid English free from technical jargon.

Filmer, Sir Robert (c. 1590-1653) PATRIARCHA (1680) ed. by P. Laslett *Blackwell* 1949 17s 6d
A statement of the argument for absolute rule and for the theory of the divine right of kings. This edition contains other writings on political philosophy. See also Hobbes's *Leviathan*, below, and John Locke's refutation of Filmer's arguments in the first *Treatise on Government*. Students may be referred to the critical discussion of Filmer's and Locke's contentions in Chapter 1 of Namier's *England in the Age of the American Revolution* included in the *History* section.

*Frazer, Sir James George (1854-1941) THE GOLDEN BOUGH 13 vols. revised and enlarged *Macmillan* 1911-14 £18 18s (the set); Abridged one-volume edition 1922 25s; Paper edition *(St. Martins Library)* 1962 12s 6d 971 pp
'A study in magic and religion.' One of the seminal works of the century. It has influenced all students of comparative religion, and of related topics in ethnology, sociology, poetic myth and legend.

Galton, Sir Francis (1822-1911) HEREDITARY GENIUS *Macmillan* (1869); *Collins (Fontana)* 1962 8s 6d
INQUIRIES INTO HUMAN FACULTY AND ITS DEVELOPMENT (1883) *Dent (Everyman)* 1907
The author was one of the great pioneers in the development of the new science of eugenics and of a knowledge of finger-prints as a practical aid in identification of the individual.

George, Henry (1839-97) PROGRESS AND POVERTY (1879) *Dent (Everyman)* 1911
The argument put forward by this American social reformer made him known as 'Single-Tax George'. He advocated the gradual abolition of all taxes except a single one on land increments following the nationalisation of land, and examined with penetration causes of industrial depression and poverty in his own country.

Godwin, William (1756-1836) AN ENQUIRY CONCERNING POLITICAL JUSTICE (1793) 3 vols. ed. by F. E. L. Priestley (*Toronto*) *O.U.P.* 1946 100s 1438 pp

The definitive edition of a landmark in the literature of political philosophy. Godwin examined the effect of political justice on morals, general virtue and happiness. This edition is a photographic facsimile of the third, corrected edition, of 1798, with variant readings from the 1793 and 1796 texts.

Gore, Charles (1853-1932) THE PHILOSOPHY OF THE GOOD LIFE *Murray* (1934); *Dent* (*Everyman*) (1935) 1954 10s 6d
On the application of moral philosophy to everyday life.

Green, Thomas Hill (1836-82) PROLEGOMENA TO ETHICS *O.U.P.* (1883) 5th edn. ed. by A. C. Bradley 1906
Green was one of the great exponents of idealist philosophy.

Harrison, Jane Ellen (1850-1928) ANCIENT ART AND RITUAL *O.U.P.* (*Home University Library*) (1913) 1948 8s 6d
PROLEGOMENA TO THE STUDY OF GREEK RELIGION *Cambridge* (1903); *Merlin Press* 1961 36s Illus.
The greatest work of this remarkable scholar, providing an interpretation of the meaning of Greek religious beliefs, from the Olympian rites of the Homeric age to the mystic Dionysus. Professor Gilbert Murray said of this work: that it was 'a book that made an epoch'.

*Hobbes, Thomas (1588-1679) LEVIATHAN (1651) ed. by M. Oakeshott *Blackwell* 1946 21s; ed. by A. D. Lindsay *Dent* (*Everyman*) (1914) 1953 8s 6d; *Collins* (*Fontana*) 1962 7s 6d
A treatise on 'The Matter, Form and Power of a Commonwealth, Ecclesiastical and Civil'. The argument, pursued with power and cogency, has been the subject of much debate and controversy. The paperback edition is an abridgement made by John Plamenatz.

Hobson, John Atkinson (1858-1940) THE EVOLUTION OF MODERN CAPITALISM *Allen and Unwin* (1894) 1928 15s
'A study of machine production.'
IMPERIALISM (1902) *Allen and Unwin* 1938 15s
A study of the theory, with specific references to historical development.
THE SCIENCE OF WEALTH *O.U.P.* (*Home University Library*) (1911) rev. edn. by R. F. Harrod 1950

Hooker, Richard (1554?-1600) OF THE LAWS OF ECCLESIASTICAL POLITY (1594-1648) 2 vols. *Dent* (*Everyman*) (1907) 1954 10s 6d each
A classic statement of Anglican theology, and a famous example of Tudor prose. Hooker's *Complete Works*, 7th rev. edn. by R. W. Church and F. Paget, 3 vols., O.U.P. 1883-8, 70s the set, is available for students' reference, 1858 pages.

Hopkins, Gerard Manley (1844-89) SERMONS AND DEVOTIONAL WRITINGS ed. by Christopher Devlin *O.U.P.* 1959 42s

Contains all the sermons written by Hopkins, 1879-81, that is, mainly during the early years of his priesthood; his commentary on the *Spiritual Exercises* of Saint Ignatius; with concluding notes and discourses up to his death.

Hulme, Thomas Ernest (1883-1917) SPECULATIONS ed. by Sir Herbert Read *Routledge* (1924) 21s; 1960 8s 6d (paperback)
Essays on humanism and the philosophy of art by a young philosopher whose death in World War I deprived English thought of a luminous mind. Contains a frontispiece by Epstein; and the few poems left by Hulme. They founded the Imagist Movement of the 1920's.

Hume, David (1711-76) DIALOGUES CONCERNING NATURAL RELIGION (1779) ed. by Bruce M'Ewen *Blackwood* 1902 5s

*ENQUIRIES CONCERNING HUMAN UNDERSTANDING (1748) ed. by Sir L. A. Selby-Bigge *O.U.P.* (1894) 1902 15s

THE NATURAL HISTORY OF RELIGION (1757) ed. by H. E. Root *A. and C. Black* 1956 6s 6d
From *Four Dissertations* reprinted in 1760 with other essays.

THEORY OF KNOWLEDGE ed. by D. C. Yalden-Thomson *Nelson* 1951 12s 6d
Contains *Enquiries Concerning Human Understanding*; extracts from the *Treatise of Human Nature*, Book One (see also below); and Hume's *Abstract*.

THEORY OF POLITICS ed. by F. M. Watkins *Nelson* 1951 12s 6d
Contains Book Three, parts 1 and 2 of *The Treatise*, and thirteen of the *Essays: Moral, Political and Literary*.

*A TREATISE ON HUMAN NATURE (1739-40) ed. by Sir L. A. Selby-Bigge *O.U.P.* (1888) 1897 18s 734 pp; 2 vols. ed. by A. D. Lindsay *Dent (Everyman)* (1911) 1956 7s 6d each; *Collins (Fontana)* 1962 7s 6d
The paperback *Fontana* has Book One only. This supreme work was Hume's greatest contribution to philosophy. It is one of the great books of the modern world and has exerted considerable influence on European and American political theory. Refer also above under Sir Ernest Barker.

WRITINGS ON ECONOMICS ed. by Eugene Rotwein *Nelson* 1955
Collects into one volume all of Hume's economic essays, hitherto difficult to obtain, with both sides of the correspondence 'relevant to his economic thought'.

Inge, William Ralph (1860-1954) CHRISTIAN MYSTICISM *Methuen* (1899) 1948 12s 6d
These eight lectures delivered by 'the gloomy Dean', before the University of Oxford, seem likely to maintain their position as a standard exposition of the development of and changes in Christian mysticism from St. John and St. Paul to the nineteenth century. From 1911 the

H*

author was Dean of St. Paul's ('the wisest Dean since the last one' said his witty contemporary Bernard Shaw), and by his sermons and popular journalism earned his reputation as a pessimist.

James, William (1842-1910) *SELECTED PAPERS ON PHILOSOPHY *Dent (Everyman)* (1917) 1956 7s 6d
SELECTION OF WRITINGS ON PSYCHOLOGY *Penguin Books* 1950 2s 6d
*THE VARIETIES OF RELIGIOUS EXPERIENCE *Longmans* (1902) 1952
18s; *Collins (Fontana)* 1960 7s 6d; *W. H. Allen (Dolphin series)*
1962 10s
The Edinburgh *Gifford Lectures* on natural religion, 1901-2. Sub-title: 'A study in human nature'. James, the brother of the novelist Henry, was a notable American exponent of pragmatism.

Jeans, Sir James (1877-1946) *THE MYSTERIOUS UNIVERSE *C.U.P.*
1933 8s 6d
PHYSICS AND PHILOSOPHY *C.U.P.* 1942 15s
THE STARS IN THEIR COURSES *C.U.P.* 1931 15s
THE UNIVERSE AROUND US *C.U.P.* 1929 25s; 1960 13s 6d (paperback)
All of these popularisations of modern theories of astronomy and cosmology were bestsellers when first published.

Joad, C. E. M. (1891-1953) GUIDE TO MODERN THOUGHT *Faber*
1933 18s
INTRODUCTION TO MODERN PHILOSOPHY *O.U.P.* (*Worlds Manuals*) 1924 6s
*RETURN TO PHILOSOPHY *Faber* 1945 8s 6d
Representative popular books by a gifted teacher and broadcaster who did much to arouse public interest in philosophy and intellectual discussion. He also contributed an introduction on philosophy to the *Teach Yourself* series, E.U.P. (1944) 1946, 6s
*RECOVERY OF BELIEF *Faber* 1952 15s
A personal 'restatement of Christian philosophy', indicating that towards the end of his life the philosopher, inclined for so long to agnosticism, returned to a belief in Christianity as a way of life.

Joseph, Horace William Bundley (1867-1943) ESSAYS IN ANCIENT AND MODERN PHILOSOPHY *O.U.P.* 1935
INTRODUCTION TO LOGIC *O.U.P.* (1906) 1916 21s
SOME PROBLEMS IN ETHICS *O.U.P.* 1931

Jowett, Benjamin (1817-93) THE FOUR 'SOCRATIC' DIALOGUES translated by Benjamin Jowett *O.U.P.* 1903 10s
Euthyphro; the *Apology*, *Crito*, and *Phaedo.*, being the four great dialogues presenting the character, life and death of Socrates, selected from Jowett's standard translation of the *Dialogues* of Plato, published complete in four volumes, O.U.P. (1871) 1953, 126s (the set), 2992 pages.

SELECT PASSAGES FROM THE INTRODUCTIONS TO PLATO ed. by J. Lewis Campbell *Murray* (1902) 1950 4s
A selection for students, chosen from Jowett's introductions and analyses in the four-volumed work mentioned above.

*SELECTIONS FROM PLATO chosen from Jowett's translation by Sir Richard Livingstone O.U.P. (*Worlds Classics*) 1940 6s

THE 'POLITICS' OF ARISTOTLE translated by Benjamin Jowett O.U.P. (1885) ed. by H. W. C. Davis 1905 15s

*Kellett, Ernest Edward (1864-1950) A SHORT HISTORY OF RELIGIONS *Gollancz* 1933; *Penguin Books* 1962 7s 6d
A survey of all religions of the world, including minor, unusual beliefs, such as the Peculiar People, and the Shakers. It was highly praised when first published and is now an established standard work.

*Kenyon, Sir Frederic (1863-1952) OUR BIBLE AND THE ANCIENT MANUSCRIPTS (1895) *Eyre and Spottiswoode* (1939) rev. edn. by A. W. Adams 1957 42s Illus.
'How the text of the scriptures has come down to us, with an account of all the most recent discoveries in this field, including the Dead Sea Scrolls.' Introduction by G. R. Driver. Includes a study of the English printed Bible, from Coverdale to the American Revised Standard Version, and the translation by Monsignor Ronald Knox.

*Keynes, John Maynard (1st Baron) (1883-1946) ESSAYS IN PERSUASION *Macmillan* (1931); *Hart-Davis* 1951
'Here are collected croakings of twelve years—the croakings of a Cassandra who could never influence the course of events in time.' Thus wrote the author of these prophecies and discussions of current affairs, from the 1919 Peace Treaty of Versailles through the periods of inflation, deflation, the gold standard, and other political crises. An essay on one author, another prophet, is included—H. G. Wells.

THE GENERAL THEORY OF EMPLOYMENT, INTEREST AND MONEY *Macmillan* 1936 15s
This was Lord Keynes's most influential and controversial work. His most widely-read book was *The Economic Consequences of the Peace*, Macmillan, 1919.

Kidd, Benjamin (1858-1916) THE SCIENCE OF POWER *Methuen* 1918
A remarkable essay in social psychology, and a grim prophecy of the course of world affairs after World War I, under the influence of the current German philosophy of power politics.

Latimer, Hugh (1490?-1555) SERMONS 2 vols. (1758) *Dent* (*Everyman*) 1906
Sermons preached by the Protestant martyr from about 1529 to 1552. Introduction by Canon Beeching.

*Law, William (1686-1761) A SERIOUS CALL TO A DEVOUT AND HOLY LIFE (1728) *Dent (Everyman)* (1906) 1955 8s 6d; *Methuen* 1950 6s; *Epworth Press (Wyvern Books)* 1961 3s 6d
A much-loved classic of the Christian way of life 'adapted to the state and conditions of all Orders of Christians'.

Le Bon, Gustave (1841-1931) THE CROWD (1896; 1903) *Benn* 1952 8s 6d
A study of the popular or 'mass' mind, complementary in its way to Trotter's book, entered below. Coming prophetically at the turn of the century, it foreshadowed the influence of the type of newspaper then being developed by Northcliffe and others.

Lecky, William Edward Hartpole (1838-1903) HISTORY OF EURO-PEAN MORALS (1869) *W. H. Allen* 1955 35s; *Watts* 1930
Surveys the development of civilisation, and the changes in ethical concepts from Augustus to Charlemagne. The New York 1955 edition published in Great Britain by W. H. Allen, gives the complete text (2 vols. in 1), with a final chapter on the position of women, and an introduction by C. Wright Mills. This points out the classic nature of Lecky's inquiry, and emphasises his eminence as a philosophic historian.
THE HISTORY OF RATIONALISM IN EUROPE (1865) *Watts* 1946 7s 6d
A record of tolerance and the consequent development of civilisation in Europe.

Lindsay, Thomas Martin (1843-1914) A HISTORY OF THE REFORMA-TION IN EUROPE 2 vols. *T. and T. Clark (International Theological Library)* 1906-7 24s each
Vol. 1: *The Reformation in Germany*; vol. 2: *The Reformation in lands beyond Germany*. This is a standard work, not superseded, although specialists would require the great work on *Luther and the Reformation*, by James Mackinnon, 4 vols. Longmans, 1930; his two supplementary monographs, *Calvin, and the Reformation*, Longmans, 1936; and *The Origins of the Reformation*, Longmans, 1939.

Locke, John (1632-1704) *AN ESSAY CONCERNING HUMAN UNDER-STANDING (1690) 2 vols. ed. by John W. Yolton *Dent (Everyman)* (1947) 1961 12s 6d each
A supreme work, dealing with the limitations of the human mind, the scope of the mind in dealing with problems of state, the human comprehension of natural phenomena and allied topics. On these arguments and discussion has been erected the science of psychology as we now know it.
ON POLITICS AND EDUCATION ed by Howard Penniman *Van Nostrand* 1949 14s
Collects three major essays: *The Second Treatise on Civil Government*; *The First Letter on Toleration*; and *The Essay on Education*.
THE REASONABLENESS OF CHRISTIANITY (1695) AND OTHER WORKS ed. by I. T. Ramsey *A. and C. Black* 1958 12s 6d

The principal work is abridged, with introduction and notes; the other two are given in full: *A Discourse of Miracles* (1706); and *A Third Letter Concerning Toleration* (1692).

*TWO TREATISES OF CIVIL GOVERNMENT (1690) *Dent (Everyman)* (1924) 1953 7s 6d
The philosopher's arguments against the divine right of kings, and 'the false principles and foundation of Sir Robert Filmer', and allied topics. Refer also above to Sir Ernest Barker's selection from Locke and related works in a *Worlds Classics* volume; to Filmer's *Patriarcha*; and to Hobbes's *Leviathan*, entered above. Students will wish also to refer to an important edition of Locke's *Two Treatises of Government* (1690; 1694) with a critical introduction and notes by Peter Laslett, C.U.P., 1960, 55s. This provides an exact text, resulting from research in the Locke papers first made available to scholars in the Bodleian Library in 1946. Complicated bibliographical and textual problems are here resolved in a definitive text for students of philosophy and historiographers.

LOCKE AND LIBERTY ed. by Massimo Salvadori *Pall Mall Press* 1960 18s
A selection emphasising the 'reasonableness' of Locke's system. The choice is from *Human Understanding*; on *Education*; and from *The Letters On Toleration*.

McDougall, William (1871-1938) *CHARACTER AND CONDUCT OF LIFE *Methuen* (1927) 1949 12s 6d
'Practical psychology for everyman': how to make the best of oneself.

THE ENERGIES OF MEN *Methuen* (1932) 1950 12s 6d
'A study of the fundamentals of dynamic psychology': an introduction to the scientific study of men and society.

*AN INTRODUCTION TO SOCIAL PSYCHOLOGY *Methuen* (1908) 1950 21s; 1960 12s 6d (paperback) 424 pp
A standard work for students, now in its 30th edition, 'dealing with the motive forces which underlie all activities of individuals and societies'. Sir Cyril Burt said of it in a radio talk that 'it has attracted more readers than any other work on psychology published this century'.

AN OUTLINE OF PSYCHOLOGY *Methuen* (1923) 1949 25s
An introduction to the theory and terminology, intended for first-year students, but suitable also for lay readers.

*Malthus, Thomas (1766-1834) ESSAY ON THE PRINCIPLES OF POPULATION (1798; 1803) 2 vols. *Dent (Everyman)* (1914) 1958 10s 6d each
Epochal inquiry into the causes and the effects of the growth of populations in the modern industrial world, as Malthus foresaw them even before the industrial revolution had developed to expedite and increase his prophecies. Malthus also analysed checks on population in the history of mankind, such as want, disease, and wars.

Marett, Robert Ranulph (1866-1943) FAITH, HOPE AND CHARITY
IN PRIMITIVE RELIGION O.U.P. 1932
SACRAMENTS OF SIMPLE FOLK O.U.P. 1933
Two related monographs by a distinguished anthropologist and
euhemerist.

Maurice, Frederick Denison (1805-72) THEOLOGICAL ESSAYS (1853)
James Clarke 1957 15s
Once controversial and much-debated writings on the themes of atone-
ment and eternal life. Maurice was one of the founders of Christian
Socialism, and the founder of The Working-Man's College, London.
These essays were offered as 'deepest thoughts that are in me', and as
such, they do retain profound interest to modern theologians and to
those who study social problems from the Christian's viewpoint.

Mill, John Stuart (1806-73) ON BENTHAM AND COLERIDGE (1838;
1840) ed. by F. R. Leavis *Chatto* 1950
Critical essays of some length originally contributed to *The Westminster
Gazette*, with an editorial introduction of thirty-eight pages.

*ON LIBERTY (1859) ON REPRESENTATIVE GOVERNMENT (1861) ON
THE SUBJECTION OF WOMEN (1869) O.U.P. (*Worlds Classics*)
1912 6s
This volume of 568 pages, with an introduction by Millicent G. Fawcett,
collects the three great essays of Mill's maturity on the liberty of the
individual in the modern state, the political philosophy of democracy,
and the powerful argument for the emancipation of women. See also
under Mary Wollstonecraft below, for the edition of the last essay in
Everyman.

*UTILITARIANISM (1861) *Dent* (*Everyman*) (1910) 1954 7s 6d;
Collins (*Fontana Books*) 1962 7s 6d
The classic statement on the philosophy of 'the greatest good of the
greatest number' as a practical political doctrine. The *Everyman* edition
includes the essays on *Liberty*, and on *Representative Government*.

Milman, Henry Hart (1791-1868) THE HISTORY OF EARLY
CHRISTIANITY: from the birth of Christ to the abolition of
paganism in the Roman Empire. 3 vols. *Murray* (1840) 7s 6d
each

THE HISTORY OF LATIN CHRISTIANITY 9 vols. *Murray* (1854-6)
1883 67s 6d (the set)
'Including that of the Popes to the pontificate of Nicholas V.'

THE HISTORY OF THE JEWS (1829; 1866) 2 vols. *Dent* (*Everyman*)
1909
As a Dean of St. Paul's, Milman was also editor-compiler of a once
popular, and still interesting, volume called *Annals of St. Paul's
Cathedral*, 1868.

*Moore, George Edward (1873-1958) ETHICS *O.U.P.* (*Home University Library*) 1912 8s 6d

PHILOSOPHICAL STUDIES *Routledge* 1922 30s; 1960 (*paperback*) 10s 6d

PRINCIPIA ETHICA *C.U.P.* (1903) 1959 35s; 1960 (*paperback*) 13s 6d

This work, and Moore's thought, have influenced generations of intellectuals, and his advocacy of the Good Life made him revered by all who knew him at Cambridge, where he was a renowned Professor of Philosophy.

*More, Sir Thomas (1478-1535) UTOPIA (1516) translated from the Latin original by Ralph Robynson (1551) Text and translation ed. by J. H. Lupton *O.U.P.* 1895 25s; translation ed. by J. Churton Collins *O.U.P.* 1904 7s 6d; *Dent* (*Everyman*) (1910) 1955 7s 6d; ed. by J. R. Lumby *C.U.P.* 1879 9s 6d

The *Everyman* edition includes More's *A Dialogue of Comfort Against Tribulation* (1553), some *Letters*, and a glossary. A second translation was done by Gilbert Burnet in 1684. This was reprinted in 1906.

There is also a modern translation, with introduction and notes by G. C. Richards, Blackwell, 1923; and a separate edition of the *Dialogue of Comfort*, Sheed and Ward, 1951, 5s. The *Utopia*, with some of More's *Letters*, and with Roper's *Life of More* (1626), is available in a series of classics published in England by Van Nostrand, 1947, 14s.

Morley, John (1st Viscount) (1838-1923) ON COMPROMISE (1874) *Watts* 1944 2s 6d

A long essay in political philosophy, and a permanent contribution to any discussion of the subject. Morley's examination embraced such topics as the power of the press, State and Church, freedom of thought, and restraints in the interests of truth and posterity.

Mozley, John Kenneth (1883-1946) THE DOCTRINE OF GOD *S.P.C.K.* 1928 7s 6d

The text of three lectures.

THE HEART OF THE GOSPEL *S.P.C.K.* 1925 3s 6d

THE IMPASSIBILITY OF GOD *C.U.P.* 1926 15s

'A survey of Christian thought.'

SOME TENDENCIES IN BRITISH THEOLOGY *S.P.C.K.* 1951 10s 6d

'From the publication of *Lux Mundi* to the present day.' *Lux Mundi* was a restatement of aims in a series of Christian essays edited by Charles Gore in 1889 for the Broad-High Church movement.

Muirhead, John Henry (1855-1940) THE USE OF PHILOSOPHY *Allen and Unwin* 1928 10s 6d

Muirhead was a great teacher of philosophy. In addition to his original work he was editor of the standard series *Contemporary British Philosophy*, published by Allen and Unwin. These monographs are personal state-ments by distinguished philosophers of the twentieth century. Muirhead's original work for philosophers included a monograph on *Coleridge As Philosopher*, Allen and Unwin, 1930, 25s, and a contribution to Professor H. D. Lewis's series, named after him, the *Muirhead Library of Philosophy*.

*Murray, Gilbert (1866-1957) FIVE STAGES OF GREEK RELIGION *O.U.P.* (1925); *Watts* 1950 2s 6d
Based on a series of lectures given at Columbia University in April 1912.

GREEK STUDIES *O.U.P.* 1948 18s

STOIC, CHRISTIAN AND HUMANIST *Watts* (1940) 1950 6s
The related themes of all the above books emphasise the task the greatest humanist of his time had set himself: the interpretation of the wisdom of ancient Greece to the modern world. This aim he pursued in his notable series of translations of Greek drama, published by Allen and Unwin.

Myers, Frederick William Henry (1843-1901) HUMAN PER-SONALITY AND ITS SURVIVAL OF BODILY DEATH 2 vols. *Longmans* 1903
An abridged edition was published by Longmans in 1935. It is the most widely-studied work on the subject, discussing it with unusual comprehensiveness, detail and sympathy, and the citation of specific phenomena.

Nettleship, Richard Lewis (1846-92) LECTURES ON THE REPUBLIC OF PLATO ed. by R. G. Benson *Macmillan* (1898) 1901 (*Papermac*) 1962 10s 6d
Reissued from Nettleship's *Philosophical Lectures and Remains*, published posthumously in 1897, after the death of this classical scholar whilst making the ascent of Mont Blanc.

Newman, John Henry (1801-90) *APOLOGIA PRO VITA SUA (1864) *Dent* (*Everyman*) (1912) 1955 8s 6d; *Collins* (*Fontana*) 1959 3s 6d
An account of Cardinal Newman's religious opinions and of his spiritual development, presented in prose of singular grace and persuasion. Refer also to the omnibus selection of Newman's best work, entered in the *Essays and Belles Lettres* section.

ON THE SCOPE AND NATURE OF UNIVERSITY EDUCATION (1852) ed. by Wilfrid Ward *Dent* (*Everyman*) (1915) 1955 7s 6d
Bound with *Christianity and Scientific Investigations*. The first, and most widely-studied work consists of the lectures delivered at the Irish Catholic University, Dublin; the second, is the text of an undelivered lecture.

Oman, John Wood (1860-1939) GRACE AND PERSONALITY *C.U.P.* (1917) *Collins* (*Fontana*) 1960 6s

THE NATURAL AND THE SUPERNATURAL *C.U.P.* 1931
Discusses the metaphysical problems involved.

Owen, Robert (1771-1858) A NEW VIEW OF SOCIETY (1813; 1816) ed. by G. D. H. Cole *Dent* (*Everyman*) (1927) 1963 10s 6d

'This volume . . . contains all the best of Owen's writings with the exception of his unfinished Autobiography . . .' The essays 'on the principle of the formation of human character, and the application of the principle to practice' form the main section; the other essays are on poor relief, the employment of children in factories, and an address to the working classes on the rich and the poor, suggesting the bridging of the gap by rational, just, measures.

*Paine, Thomas (1737-1809) THE AGE OF REASON (1794-5) *Watts* 1947

Published originally in two parts but probably written during the Reign of Terror in Paris. It is a cogently expressed argument for deism and a rhetorical plea for rationalism in the conduct of human affairs.

THE RIGHTS OF MAN (1791-2) *Dent* (*Everyman*) (1915) 1954 8s 6d *Watts* 1949

'An answer to Mr. Burke's attack on the French Revolution.' Paine presented in this, his most widely-read and enduring polemic, the case for 'the principles of Freedom' from the point of view of a Rationalist.

Patmore, Coventry Kersey Dighton (1823-96) THE ROD, THE ROOT AND THE FLOWER (1895) ed. by Derek Patmore *Grey Walls Press* 1950

'In this last work he summed up his very personal philosophy about human and divine love', writes the poet's great-grandson. It consists of brief essays, aphorisms and reflections on many of the ideas about life, developed in *Sponsa Dei*, which Patmore burnt in manuscript in 1887.

Pearson, Karl (1857-1936) THE GRAMMAR OF SCIENCE (1892) *Dent* (*Everyman*) 1937 6s 6d

One of the great expositions of the principles of scientific thinking. It can scarcely be bettered as an introduction for the young student and the general reader.

Protheroe, Rowland Edmund (1st Baron Ernle) (1851-1937) THE PSALMS IN HUMAN LIFE *Murray* (1903) 1928 7s 6d

A type of anthology with commentaries, illustrating instances where recollections of the teachings of the Psalms have influenced the actions of men and women in the crises of their lives.

*Read, Carveth (1848-1931) MAN AND HIS SUPERSTITIONS *C.U.P.* (1920) 1925 35s

THE ORIGIN OF MAN *C.U.P.* (1920) 1925 17s 6d

*Ricardo, David (1772-1823) THE PRINCIPLES OF POLITICAL ECONOMY AND TAXATION (1817) *Dent* (*Everyman*) (1912) 1955 7s 6d

On the distribution of wealth, the theory of rent, wages, and allied topics, including the balance of trade, and in some ways, for students of economics, complementary to Adam Smith's *Wealth of Nations*, entered below.

Robinson, George Wade (1838-76) THE PHILOSOPHY OF THE ATONEMENT AND OTHER SERMONS (1875) *Dent* (*Everyman*) 1912 6s 6d

Characteristic sermons of a well-known Noncomformist.

Robinson, Henry Wheeler (1872-1945) THE HISTORY OF ISRAEL *Duckworth* 1938 9s 6d

A monograph in the *Studies in Theology* series.

INSPIRATION AND REVELATION IN THE OLD TESTAMENT *O.U.P.* 1946 21s; (*Paperbacks*) 1962 6s

THE RELIGIOUS IDEAS OF THE OLD TESTAMENT *Duckworth* (1913) revised edn. by L. H. Brockington 1956 9s 6d

Rolle, Richard (*c.* 1290-1349) ENGLISH WRITINGS ed. by Hope Emily Allen *O.U.P.* 1931 15s

A volume collecting the spiritual essays of the Saintly Hermit of Hampole, an English mystic, whose life, written by Frances M. M. Comper, Dent (1928), 1933, contained the first publication of his *English Lyrics*.

*Ruskin, John (1819-1900) UNTO THIS LAST (1862) *Allen and Unwin* 1906 7s 6d; *Dent* (*Everyman*) 1907

'Four essays on the first principles of political economy.' This remarkable book discusses with fluency and cogency the need for reforms that are now part of the Welfare State, but which in Ruskin's day must have appeared Utopian.

Rutherford, Samuel (*c.* 1600-61) SELECTED LETTERS (1664) ed. by Hugh Martin *S.C.M. Press* 1957

A choice of the letters of the Covenanter and theologian-controversialist. His life and work as a Calvinist belong to the history of the Church and to Protestantism.

Sackville-West, Victoria (1892-1962) THE EAGLE AND THE DOVE *Michael Joseph* (1943) 1953 (*Mermaid Books*) 4s 6d

'A study in contrasts': that is, in the lives and characters of two Carmelite saints.

Santayana, George (1863-1952) DOMINATIONS AND POWERS *Constable* 1951 42s

'Reflections on Liberty, Society and Government.' This, the philosopher's last book, was the fruit of many years of profound thought.

*THE LIFE OF REASON 5 vols. *Constable* (1923) new edn. in 1 vol. 1954 42s 504 pp

One of the great philosophical discussions of the twentieth century, presented systematically in five groups, with a general introduction. The sub-title, *The Phases of Human Progress*, indicates the approach to human problems of this aloof, uncompromising philosopher. The sections are: *Reason In Commonsense*; *In Art*; *In Religion*; *In Society*; *In Science*. These volumes were published between 1905 and 1906.

THE PHILOSOPHY OF SANTAYANA ed. by Irwin Edman *Constable* (1936) 1954 45s 966 pp
Presents a comprehensive selection of the work of this Spanish-American humanist, who lived in England, and towards the end of his life, in Italy, where he died.

SCEPTICISM AND ANIMAL FAITH (1923) *Constable* (*Dover Books*) 1955 12s

THE SENSE OF BEAUTY (1896) *Constable* (*Dover Books*) 1955 8s

Schiller, Ferdinand Canning Scott (1864-1937) HUMANISM *Macmillan* (1903) 1912

MUST PHILOSOPHERS DISAGREE? *Macmillan* 1934

STUDIES IN HUMANISM *Macmillan* (1907) 1912

Representative books of modern philosophical argument by a witty and graceful writer whose work may be read with enjoyment by the general reader as well as the student.

Seebohm, Frederic (1833-1912) THE OXFORD REFORMERS (1867) *Dent* (*Everyman*) 1914
A study of the religious movements at Oxford from 1496 to 1519, with specific reference to the teachings of John Colet, Erasmus, and Sir Thomas More.

Sidgwick, Alfred (1850-1943) THE PROCESS OF ARGUMENT *A. and C. Black* 1893

THE USE OF WORDS IN REASONING *A. and C. Black* 1901

Sidgwick, Henry (1838-1900) THE METHODS OF ETHICS *Macmillan* (1874) 1907 30s; (*Papermacs*) 1962 18s
A standard text, valued by students for its balanced, logical discussion of the subject.

OUTLINES OF THE HISTORY OF ETHICS FOR ENGLISH READERS *Macmillan* (1886) 1931 7s 6d
The last edition, the sixth, has an additional chapter by Professor A. G. Widgery.

*Smith, Adam (1723-90) AN INQUIRY INTO THE NATURE AND CAUSES OF THE WEALTH OF NATIONS 2 vols. (1776; 1791) *Dent* (*Everyman*) (1910) 1954 8s 6d each; ed. by Edwin Cannan *Methuen* (1904) 1950 25s each 968 pp; 1961 (*University Paperback*) 15s each
Cannan's standard edition of this classic statement of the principles of modern political economy and philosophy has a long introduction, notes and marginal summaries for students, and a full index. The notes on Smith's sources, with a record of the changes made in the five editions up to 1791, are the authorities for a definitive text.

Smith, Hannah (1832-1911) THE CHRISTIAN'S SECRET OF A HAPPY LIFE (1888) *Nisbet* 1945 3s 6d
A small book of personal devotion, much prized by those who know it, and referred to with affection by the author's distinguished son, the late Logan Pearsall Smith.

Smith, Herbert Maynard (1869-1949) HENRY VIII AND THE REFORMATION *Macmillan* (1948) 1962 30s
Praised when it was first published as a standard work, distinguished for 'the shrewd and sturdy independence of the author's judgements'— *Church Quarterly Review*.

PRE-REFORMATION ENGLAND *Macmillan* (1938)
Describes and discusses the background of social life and religious ideas that preceded the Reformation, and, in the author's view, made the development dealt with in the companion book inevitable.

Smith, Preserved (1880-1941) THE AGE OF THE REFORMATION *Cape* 1921 45s
A monograph originally published in the *American Historical Series*, New York.

Smith, William Robertson (1846-94) THE RELIGION OF THE SEMITES (1889) *New York, Meridian Books; Mayflower Press* 1957 16s
Standard, well-documented history of Hebrew religion as a social and cultural force in the ancient world, by the editor of the 9th edition of the *Encyclopaedia Britannica*. Developed from lectures delivered at Aberdeen in 1887, and still important to students of religion, sacrifice, taboo, rites and old Israel.

Sorley, William Ritchie (1855-1953) A HISTORY OF ENGLISH PHILOSOPHY *C.U.P.* 1920 30s
Probably the best one-volume survey there is of the British contribution to philosophical speculation up to the turn of the century.

THE MORAL LIFE AND MORAL WORTH *C.U.P.* (1911) 1930 7s 6d

*Spencer, Herbert (1820-1903) ESSAYS ON EDUCATION (1861) *Dent* (*Everyman*) (1911) 1962 10s 6d; *Watts* 1950 3s 6d
The *Everyman* edition includes essays on kindred subjects. In this once much-read statement of the nature of 'intellectual, moral and physical' education, the philosopher claims that a training in science is the best mental discipline for the modern world.

FIRST PRINCIPLES (1862) *Watts* 1946 3s 6d
A fundamental statement of the philosopher's system of evolutionary philosophy.

Stanley, Arthur Penrhyn (1815-81) HISTORICAL MEMORIALS OF CANTERBURY (1854) *Dent* (*Everyman*) 1906

Lectures and essays gathered to form a series of papers on the murder of Becket, Augustine and the bringing of Christianity to England, and allied topics.

LECTURES ON THE HISTORY OF THE EASTERN CHURCH (1861) *Dent* (*Everyman*) 1907
Twelve lectures. Little has been written in English on the subject, and the book retains its importance as an introduction.

*Stebbing, L. Susan (1885-1943) IDEALS AND ILLUSIONS *Watts* 1948 3s 6d

A MODERN ELEMENTARY LOGIC *Methuen* (1943) 1949 8s 6d; 1961 (*University Paperback*) 7s 6d

PHILOSOPHY AND THE PHYSICISTS *Methuen* (1937) *Constable* (*Dover Books*) 1959 13s 6d

THINKING TO SOME PURPOSE *Penguin Books* 1939 3s 6d
Hard thinking from a logical mind, clear expression, and an ability to discuss profound subjects in an interesting style, made all the books of this gifted woman as much valued by general readers as they were by students.

Stephen, Sir Leslie (1832-1904) AN AGNOSTIC'S APOLOGY *Murray* 1893
The title essay in this volume, originally contributed to a journal in 1876, is a notable statement of a rationalist on his agnosticism.

THE ENGLISH UTILITARIANS 3 vols. *Duckworth* 1900
A continuation of the following work. It discusses and explains the doctrines of Bentham and John Stuart Mill.

THE HISTORY OF ENGLISH THOUGHT IN THE 18TH CENTURY 2 vols. *Murray* (1876) 1902; *Hart-Davis* 1963 14s each 832 pp (paperbacks)
A standard work on rationalism and deism, with the beginnings of the utilitarian school of thought that flowered in the nineteenth century. See *The English Utilitarians*, above.

THE SCIENCE OF ETHICS *Murray* (1882) 1907 10s 6d

Stocks, John Leofric (1882-1937) THE LIMITS OF PURPOSE *Benn* 1932
Philosophical essays.

ON THE NATURE AND GROUNDS OF RELIGIOUS BELIEF O.U.P. 1934
TIME, CAUSE AND ETERNITY *Macmillan* 1938

Streeter, Burnett Hillman (1874-1937) THE BUDDHA AND THE CHRIST *Macmillan* 1932
Bampton Lectures on the meaning of the universe and the purpose of life.
*THE FOUR GOSPELS *Macmillan* 1924 30s
'A study of origins, treating of the manuscript tradition, sources, authorship and dates.'

REALITY *Macmillan* 1926
'A new correlation of science and religion.'

Taylor, Sir Henry (1800-86) THE STATESMAN (1836) *Cambridge, Heffer* 1957 18s
This belongs to the small class of books of which Machiavelli's *Il Principe* (1532) is the most famous example. As will be seen in Taylor's *Autobiography* (1885) he was able to observe at first hand the effect and power of the Civil Service in a democratic state.

★Taylor, Jeremy (1613-67) THE GOLDEN GROVE (1655) ed. by Logan Pearsall Smith *O.U.P.* 1930 15s
Selected passages from sermons and writings of a celebrated preacher famed for his splendid style.

HOLY LIVING AND HOLY DYING (1650-51) *Longmans*
This manual of personal devotions and religious reflections was once a household book.

Temple, William (1881-1944) CHRISTUS VERITAS *Macmillan* 1924 15s
MENS CREATRIX *Macmillan* 1917 21s
NATURE, MAN AND GOD *Macmillan* 1934 35s
READINGS IN ST. JOHN'S GOSPEL: 1st and 2nd series *Macmillan* 1945 18s; (*St. Martins Library*) 1961 6s
The writer of the above, wise, humanistic works was Archbishop of Canterbury. *Nature, Man and God* comprises the Gifford Lectures for 1932-3.

★Thomas à Kempis (1380-1471) THE IMITATION OF CHRIST (1471) translated from the Latin anonymously (1504)
A devotional work of personal reflections on Christ's teachings that is one of the most loved books of its kind. The sixteenth-century version has now been replaced in most modern editions. For example: newly translated by G. F. Maine *Collins* (*Classics*) 1957, 5s; newly, and anonymously translated *Dent* (*Everyman*) 1960, 12s 6d; translated by C. Bigg, *Methuen* (1905) 1954, 9s 6d; and a translation based on the work of F.B. (the Jesuit Anthony Hoskins) from c. 1613, *O.U.P.* (*Worlds Classics*) 1904, 7s 6d. This 'Ecclesiastical Music', as it was once termed, was thought to be the work of Jean Charlier de Gerson of France, but is now known to have been written by Thomas à Kempis, of Kempen, Cologne.

Traherne, Thomas (1634?-74) CENTURIES, POEMS, AND THANKS-GIVINGS 2 vols. ed. by H. M. Margoliouth *O.U.P.* 1958 84s (the set) 776 pp
Bertram Dobell, who published and first identified the manuscript of Traherne's writings, said in the first edition of 1908, revised 1928, that the work 'consists of a series of reflections on religious and moral subjects, divided into short numbered paragraphs . . . it contains his most mature thought'.

CHRISTIAN ETHICS; OR, DIVINE MORALITY (1675) *The Faith Press* 1962 18s

The only reprint after the first posthumous publication of this book of guidance on living a Christian life is given the title of *The Way of Blessedness*, with spelling and punctuation modernised by Margaret Bottrall.

Trotter, Wilfred (1872-1939) THE INSTINCTS OF THE HERD IN PEACE AND WAR *Benn* (1916) 1947

A study in social psychology with examples drawn from history up to the First World War.

Underhill, Evelyn (1875-1941) MYSTICISM *Methuen* (1911) 1942 30s; 1960 12s 6d (paperback)

'A study in the nature and development of man's spiritual consciousness' by one of the greatest English mystics of modern times.

PRACTICAL MYSTICISM *Dent* 1919 7s 6d

'A book for normal people.'

THE SCHOOL OF CHARITY, AND THE MYSTERY OF SACRIFICE *Longmans* 1954 10s 6d

Two separate works, published originally in 1934 and 1938 respectively. The first consists of 'meditations on the Chrisitian creed', and the second is 'a meditation on the liturgy'.

WORSHIP *Nisbet* (1936) 1937 12s 6d

Veblen, Thorstein (1857-1929) THE THEORY OF THE LEISURE CLASS (1899) *Allen and Unwin* 1925 18s

The best-known work of an American Left-wing economist and teacher. Its influence has been considerable in Left-wing circles in both the U.S.A., and Great Britain.

Wallas, Graham (1858-1932) *THE ART OF THOUGHT (1926) *Watts* 1948 3s 6d

*HUMAN NATURE IN POLITICS *Constable* (1908) 1938 10s

An introduction to the study of psychology in politics.

MEN AND IDEAS *Allen and Unwin* 1940 8s 6d

With a preface by Gilbert Murray.

Westermarck, Edward Alexander (1862-1939) THE ORIGIN AND DEVELOPMENT OF MORAL IDEAS 2 vols. *Macmillan* (1906-8) 1912-17

Influential work by a Finnish anthropologist who was Professor of Sociology at the University of London, and who wrote his scientific treatises in English. His major achievement was *The History of Human Marriage* Macmillan (1891), revised edition, in 3 vols. 1921.

White, Reginald James (Editor) POLITICAL TRACTS OF WORDSWORTH, COLERIDGE AND SHELLEY *C.U.P.* 1953 21s

After an introduction of forty-four pages, there follow the texts of
Coleridge's *A Lay Sermon* (1817), and *The Statesman's Manual* (1816);
Wordsworth's *The Convention of Cintra* (1809) and Shelley's *A Philo-
sophical View of Reform* (1819-1820), and *A Defence of Poetry* (1821).

★Whitehead, Alfred North (1861-1947) ADVENTURES OF IDEAS
C.U.P. (1934) 1938; 1960 10s 6d (paperback)
THE CONCEPT OF NATURE *C.U.P.* 1919 18s

AN INTRODUCTION TO MATHEMATICS *O.U.P.* (*Home University
Library*) (1911) 1946 8s 6d
A masterly exposition for the layman of the mathematician's way of
thinking, and of philosophical concepts in the science of mathematics.

SCIENCE AND THE MODERN WORLD *C.U.P.* 1925 12s 6d; *New
English Library Paperbacks* 1958 3s 6d
There is a selection of the most characteristic writings of this great
philosopher in *A Whitehead Anthology*, edited by F. S. C. Northrop and
M. W. Gross, C.U.P., 1954, 75s.

★Wollstonecraft, Mary (1759-97) A VINDICATION OF THE RIGHTS
OF WOMEN (1792) *Dent* (*Everyman*) (1929) 1955 10s 6d
In the reprint, John Stuart Mill's *The Subjection of Women* (which is
entered above) is bound with Mary Wollstonecraft Godwin's famous
manifesto. This expression of views on the equality of the sexes was
about a century in advance of its time.

★Woolman, John (1720-72) THE WISDOM OF JOHN WOOLMAN ed.
by Reginald Reynolds *Allen and Unwin* 1949
An introductory choice from writings of a celebrated Quaker, offered
by the editor 'as a guide to the seekers of today'. Refer also to John
Woolman's *Journal* entered in the *Autobiography* section.

★Yeats, William Butler (1865-1939) MYTHOLOGIES *Macmillan*
1959 25s
Collects into a single volume five works published separately. These
consisted of narratives of Irish country traditions and superstitions, with
stories of the uncanny and the supernatural based on folk-lore and oral
traditions. Yeats's commentary reveals his own esoteric philosophy. The
separate works were: *The Secret Rose* (1897); *The Celtic Twilight* (1893);
Stories of Red Hanrahan (1897); *Rosa Alchemica*, two minor pieces, and
Per Amica Silentia Lunae (1917).

Younghusband, Sir Francis Edward (1863-1942) VITAL RELIGION
Murray 1940 3s 6d
A little book, pleading for 'a brotherhood of faith'. Younghusband was
an explorer and a mountaineer as well as a soldier, and by temperament
was a man of deep religious feeling with more than a touch of the mystic.

POETRY AND POETIC DRAMA

No modern literature in the world surpasses English poetry and poetic drama, and perhaps none equals it. Rich with the products of poetic genius in every form: lyrical, epic, narrative, and dramatic, English poetry from Chaucer to W. B. Yeats displays a variety and versatility sustained throughout the centuries. If the eighteenth is the least of poetic centuries, it had the fortune to be brilliantly illuminated in four decades by the satire of Pope; and at the close, was distinguished by a literary landmark, never to be overlooked, in the publication of Coleridge and Wordsworth's *Lyrical Ballads*. The *Preface* and *Essay on Poetic Diction* by the latter in the second edition of 1800 and the third of 1802 were manifestos. Largely ignored by the general public for two decades, they nevertheless did something to inspire the early nineteenth century, and to rid poetry of eighteenth-century poetasters, ridiculed in *The Dunciad*, but never quite eliminated until public taste turned with greater judgement to the Romantic poets. Moreover, the century that included the poetry of the gentle Cowper, the lyrics of Burns, and Blake's best work, produced poetry of the first order, written against the prevailing current.

Narrative poetry by its very length and tendency is sometimes forced to relate in verse what prose can usually do so much better; nevertheless the works of Chaucer right at the outset of its history in English show what can be achieved in the hands of a supreme master. *The Canterbury Tales* and *Troilus and Criseyde* are almost poetic novels; the first being probably enjoyed by a greater circle of readers in every generation than anything else of its kind, while even the didactic Langland, in modern English versions, has never lacked an audience of common readers.

Pope's *The Rape of the Lock* has no equals as a mock-epic, and his satirical poems produced enough proverbial wit to fill a book of quotations that have passed into common currency. Lacking the highest gifts of the greatest poets able to express in golden lines truths and wisdom and to communicate with piercing insight the deepest thoughts of mankind, Pope yet became master of the language of his day, expressing his witty, graceful satire in lines that gleam in the mind and leap on the page like fish in the net.

In narrative poetry, Wordsworth was even able to give us the greatest autobiographical poem in literature; while Byron's *Don Juan* is certainly the most brilliantly amusing long poetic essay in sustained irony in any language. Byron had a European audience from the start: his life, character and poetic achievement were all inextricably intermingled. He was the least of our Romantics in poetic gifts; the greatest in his influence.

The epic needs scholarly appreciation and the leisure of the quiet library. Hence its virtual disappearance from the poetic scene. The severe criticism levelled by poets and critics at Milton's *Paradise Lost* can never depreciate the poet's achievement in his own age, nor his influence on those that followed. Nor can it relegate the poem and its companion piece to the library basement, alongside Foxe's *Book of Martyrs* and Dodsley's *Fugitive Pieces*. It was not intended to. What it has done in the last forty-five years is to persuade those who have been able to read Milton at length to do so with a critical mind and often, a healthy desire to form personal opinions instead of accepting textbook strictures.

Nothing could be better, and even if the epics emerge from re-scrutiny and new assessment somewhat lower in the lofty scale by which they can be measured, their readers will probably agree that Milton would still be a major poet had *Paradise Lost* and *Paradise Regained* never been published.

In the formal division that includes lyrical poetry English poetry has never faltered or failed to produce glittering masterpieces, from Wyatt's astonishing 'They flee from me, that sometime did me seek' to the modern work of the late Walter de la Mare, James Stephens, and Dylan Thomas. A lyric is more than a song. Its essence is comparative brevity; its characteristic the personal note. The first can be instanced by the carols and poems to be found in the anthologies of the thirteenth and fourteenth centuries; the second by Wyatt's poem quoted above, and by that poignant cry from the anonymous lover whose lyric graces the beginning of many an anthology of sixteenth-century poetry:

> 'Western wind, when wilt thou blow,
>   The small rain down can rain?
>   Christ, if my love were in my arms,
>   And I in my bed again!'

Is this exquisite quatrain minor or major poetry? In the strict sense there can surely be no such thing as minor poetry. A poem is either poetry or verse: the former a fusion of word magic and high, concentrated thought; the latter the expression of more mundane ideas in a style that appears to be accidental rather than inevitable. Changing fashions in poetic style and varying patterns of thought may push the work of a true poet into the background, but it must eventually emerge again by virtue of its power to light up the mind. Thus the poetry of a John Donne may be disregarded for a period. It was inevitable that it would in time reach again the hearts and minds of readers.

It is here that the labours and scholarship of editors play their part in the history of English literature. Editorial research establishes accurate texts; the skill and judgement of editors solves complicated biblio-graphical problems relating to authorship, dates, and textual authenticity. Critical editions, the discussion of a crux, the acceptance or rejection of a doubtful poem, the collation of manuscripts and previous editions, some-times involve a lifetime of research. Our debt to the great editors is con-siderable. Their work is almost creative in the preparation of standard, sometimes definitive editions, of poets for whom no holographs are extant. William A. Ringler's superb edition of Sir Philip Sidney's *Poems* is a recently published example of editorial research on this grand scale, and the emergence of a standard text of Donne, through the labours of editors culminating in Sir Herbert John Grierson's edition in the *Oxford English Texts* (1912), and John Hayward's *Nonesuch* Donne (1929) has vastly increased the range and number of the poet's admirers. Donne's self-confessed harshness no longer repels; in tune with the twentieth century, his poems have now taken their place with the greatest of the metaphysical poets. This convenient term, invented or developed from Dryden by Dr. Johnson in the essay on Cowley (see his *Lives of the Poets*) was once a depreciative label to attach to poets whose language and style favoured the use of conceits and involved, allusive symbols. It is now a term of classification only, as it was when Dryden first hinted at its future use as a critical term. A conceit is a fault if it intrudes itself between the poet and his readers, but when, like Richard Flecknoe's *Invocation of Silence*, in which we find the vivid metaphor, 'frost o' th' mouth; and thaw o' th' mind', it serves to impress itself imperishably on the mind, it is the hallmark of the true poet. Most of Flecknoe's work was minor; but here he wrote something worthy of preservation, and thanks to the discernment of a fine editor (H. J. Massingham), we have it in a *Treasury of Seventeenth Century Verse*.

The establishment of a definitive text of Shakespeare's plays is impossible, but research, scholarly conjecture, and inspired interpretation continue, starting on the grand scale, with Dr. Johnson's edition of Shakespeare in 1765. The monumental *Variorum Edition* by H. H. Furness and his successors, in progress from 1871, is itself proof of the inexhaustible theme. New editions of the *Arden* Shakespeare, now appearing, supersede those of a previous generation; the beautifully produced *New Shakespeare* published by Cambridge University Press, adds still further to our appreciation of the poet's supreme art; and the publication of scores of critical monographs on some aspect of the plays, every year, in many languages, itself creates a problem for the bibliographer, necessitating, after much too long a delay, the inauguration in 1948 of an annual *Shakespeare Survey of Study and Production* under the editorship of Professor Allardyce Nicoll, for Cambridge University Press, thus providing students with an English counterpart of the *Shakespeare Jahrbuch* founded in 1865.

This is a section particularly rich in anthologies and collections. Readers are reminded that many plays by writers of the seventeenth and eighteenth century will only be readily available in collections edited for *Everyman* and *Worlds Classics*. The selection of these volumes and of the standard anthologies of poetry is generous, but by no means exhaustive.

The historical surveys and critical monographs listed in *Essays and Belles Lettres* should not be overlooked by readers requiring stimulating and informative handbooks to widen the appreciation of this most difficult of all the literary arts. Group studies such as Robin Skelton's *The Cavalier Poets*, Longmans, 1960, 2s 6d, are especially helpful, and the critical essays in that choice anthology, Aldous Huxley's *Texts and Pretexts*, lift the anthologist's work to the creative level.

Lamborn's *Rudiments of Criticism* has not been bettered as a first book in appreciation of the poet's art and craft; Graham Hough's *The Romantic Poets*, Hutchinson, 1953 is now available as a *Grey Arrow* paperback, 1958, 3s 6d; and a notable critical survey of the development of poetry from the period of changing techniques to the difficulties of our own era bears the significant title of *Crisis in English Poetry, 1880-1940*, by Vivian de Sola Pinto, Hutchinson, 1951, 12s 6d.

Abercrombie, Lascelles (1881-1938) COLLECTED POEMS *O.U.P.* 1930
Abercrombie's verse dramas were influential in bringing back poetry to the British stage at festivals and non-professional productions, and his, lyric verse was representative of the Georgian contribution to poetry of the twenties.

Aldington, Richard (1892-1962) A DREAM IN THE LUXEMBOURG *Chatto* (1930); *Heinemann* 1947 5s
'Perhaps more evocative of the 1920s than much more pretentious poetry.' —*The Times* (obituary notice, 30 July, 1962).

Anonymous Poems and Dramatic Pieces *Everyman*
For this and other medieval dramatic pieces see under the editor, A. C. Cawley, in the next section of *Anthologies and Collections*.

THE FLOURE AND THE LEAFE (*c.* 1500) ed. by D. A. Pearsall *Nelson* (*Mediaeval and Renaissance Library*) 1962 16s
Wrongly ascribed to Chaucer and included in his collected works from 1598. This charming allegorical poem is now in the new series, with introduction, critical apparatus, notes and glossary. In the same little volume is a companion narrative poem called *The Assembly of Ladies*.

THE RETURN FROM PARNASSUS (1606) ed. by Oliphant Smeaton *Dent* (*Temple Dramatists*) 1905 7s 6d
'Or, The Scourge of Simony'; being part two of the *Parnassus Trilogy*, acted by students of St. John's College, Cambridge, with introduction, notes and glossary.

*SIR GAWAIN AND THE GREEN KNIGHT
Of all Arthurian romances apart from Malory's collection, this long alliterative poem from the fourteenth century is the most widely read. The delightful narrative of Sir Gawain's adventure and test has been translated into modern English several times, and the following versions are usually available: translated into English verse by Kenneth Hare, with introduction, notes and bibliography, Eyre and Spottiswoode (1918) 1948, 12s 6d; translated, with notes, into alliterative English verse by Brian Stone, Penguin Books, 1944, 2s 6d; translated into modern English

prose by M. R. Ridley, Edmund Ward (1944) 1962, 15s, with illustrations. For the *Everyman* edition of the text, see in the next section under Cawley, who has prepared an edition of this poem and of *Pearl*.

Arnold, Sir Edwin (1832-1904) THE LIGHT OF ASIA (1879) *Routledge* 1908 4s 6d

A narrative poem in blank verse, on 'the Great Renunciation and the Life and Teaching of Gautama'.

*Arnold, Matthew (1822-88) POETICAL WORKS (1877) ed. by C. B. Tinker and H. F. Lowry *O.U.P.* (*Standard Authors*) 1950 12s 6d 542 pp

The definitive edition, and the first to contain all the poems Arnold wrote. See also the standard commentary by Tinker and Lowry, *The Poetry of Matthew Arnold*, O.U.P., 1940.

POEMS ed. by R. A. Scott-James *Dent* (*Everyman*) 1955 10s 6d; *Nelson* (*Classics*) 1923 6s

Refer also to the selection of Arnold's prose and poetry in the *Reynard Library*, entered in the *Essays and Belles Lettres* section.

Barham, Richard Harris (1788-1845) THE INGOLDSBY LEGENDS; or, Mirth and Marvels (1840; 1847) *Dent* (*Everyman*) 1960 12s 6d; *Macmillan* 1951 6s

Amusing burlesques and comic, sometimes grotesque, verse, being medieval tales and legends cleverly mingled with nonsensical word-play. The world-famous *The Jackdaw of Rheims* is characteristic of the best of these legends by 'Thomas Ingoldsby, Esquire'.

Barnes William (1801-86) COLLECTED POEMS (1879) ed. and selected by Thomas Hardy *O.U.P.* (*Oxford Miscellany*) 1908 10s 6d; ed. and selected by Geoffrey Grigson *Routledge* (*Muses Library*) 1950 10s 6d

The selection in the *Muses Library* is arranged chronologically, some being *Poems in the Dorset Dialect*, chosen from the 1844 and 1862 *Poems of Rural Life*; the others in 'national English', including *Orra, a Lapland Tale* (1822) with glossary. For a fuller edition, in two volumes, edited by Bernard Jones, see Centaur Press, 1962, 168s the set, 1096 pp.

Beaumont, Francis (1584-1616) and John Fletcher (1579-1625) PLAYS (1679) 10 vols. ed. by A. R. Waller *C.U.P.* 1905-12 30s each (vols. 6-10 out of print)

BEST PLAYS 2 vols. ed. by J. St. Loe Strachey *Benn* (*Mermaid*) (1904) 1949-50 12s 6d each

*SELECTED PLAYS ed. by G. P. Baker *Dent* (*Everyman*) (1911) 1953 10s 6d

These two collaborators produced over fifty plays, of which their most popular are a comedy, *The Knight of the Burning Pestle*, and *The Maid's*

Tragedy, both in the *Everyman* edition, and also in *Mermaid*, vol. 1. Three plays are in separate editions: *The Faithful Shepherdess*; *Philaster*; and *The Knight of the Burning Pestle*, Dent (Temple Dramatists), 7s 6d each.

Beddoes, Thomas Lovell (1803-49) COLLECTED POEMS (1851) SELECTED PLAYS AND POEMS ed. by H. W. Donner *Routledge* (*Muses Library*) 1950 12s 6d
'The Last Elizabethan,' as Lytton Strachey termed him, wrote some well-known lyrics, often found in anthologies and *The Bride's Tragedy*, a play (1822).

*Belloc, Hilaire (1870-1953) SONNETS AND VERSE *Duckworth* (1949) 1954 15s; COLLECTED VERSE *Penguin Books* 1958 2s 6d; SONGS OF THE SOUTH COUNTRY *Duckworth* 1951 2s 6d 32 pp
The standard, revised edition, has a memoir by Reginald Jebb. See also *Essays and Belles Lettres* section, for collections of Belloc's prose and verse.

BEOWULF

The earliest poem of length in any modern language. The original text in Old English, discovered in the Cottonian Collection, British Museum, was transliterated by an Icelander, G. J. Thorkelin, in 1815. Standard editions of the text include those edited by A. J. Wyatt and R. W. Chambers, *C.U.P.* (1894) 1914, 35s; by C. L. Wrenn, *Harrap* (1953) 1958, 21s; and Fr. Klaeber, *Harrap* (for Heath, Boston, U.S.A.) (1922) 1936, 48s. These include *The Fight At Finnsburg* (*The Finnsburg Fragment*).

Translations

Translated into modern English prose, by John R. Clark Hall, *Allen and Unwin* (1911), revised by C. L. Wrenn (1940-50), 12s 6d, with *The Finnsburg Fragment*, and an introduction by J. R. R. Tolkien; into prose by Edwin Morgan, *Hand and Flower Press*, 1952, 12s 6d; into prose, by David Wright, *Penguin Books* (1957) 1959, 2s 6d; into prose, by R. K. Gordon, in the *Everyman* collection of *Anglo-Saxon Poetry*, Dent (1927) 1962, 7s 6d (this volume includes *The Finnsburg Fragment*).

Translated into modern English blank verse by Mary E. Waterhouse, *Bowes and Bowes*, 1950, 10s 6d. Among many out-of-print nineteenth-century versions, that by William Morris, in the metre of the original (1895) should be noted. Standard commentaries for students of Old English include *Beowulf*: an introduction, by R. W. Chambers, *C.U.P.* (1921) 1959, 55s; and *The Metre of Beowulf*, by A. J. Bliss, *Blackwell*, 1958, 25s.

Binyon, Robert Laurence (1869-1943) COLLECTED POEMS 2 vols. *Macmillan* 1931
Binyon translated Dante's *Inferno*, *Purgatorio*, and *Paradiso* into English triple rhyme, 3 vols. Macmillan, 1933-43, parallel Italian-English edition, 12s 6d each.

Blackmore, Richard Doddridge (1825-1900) THE GEORGICS OF
VIRGIL translated into English verse by R. D. Blackmore (1871)
1932
A delightful rendering by the author of *Lorna Doone*, who as a farmer,
was able to testify to the immortal and unchanging wisdom of the
instruction in this Latin classic. The 1932 edition was a beautiful quarto,
illustrated with woodcuts, 63s, with a collector's edition, bound in
vellum, £31 10s.

*Blake, William (1757-1827) POETICAL WORKS (1783-1804) ed. by
John Sampson O.U.P. (1905) 1913; (*Standard Authors*) 1921 16s
510 pp
COMPLETE WRITINGS ed. by Geoffrey Keynes *Nonesuch Press*
1957 63s 936 pp; POETRY AND PROSE ed. by Geoffrey Keynes
Nonesuch Press 1927 30s 1152 pp
Centenary editions 'of the whole of Blake's written work in a single
volume', including letters. The 1957 edition replaces a three-volume
collectors' edition, originally published in 1925, with illustrations from
engravings, and includes variant readings omitted in the 1927 edition.
Bound in quarter red buckram, with marbled boards.

POEMS AND PROPHECIES ed. by Max Plowman *Dent* (*Everyman*)
(1927) 1954 10s 6d including illustrated facsimile of *The Gates
of Paradise*, 1820

PROPHETIC WRITINGS 2 vols. ed. by D. J. Sloss and J. P. R.
Wallis O.U.P. 70s (the set) 1050 pp
The definitive text of the mystic writings, didactic and symbolic verse,
satires and apologues. The difficulties, obscurities and gnostic conun-
drums in these strange works have attracted many analytical and
elucidatory monographs. Some of the *Prophetic Books* are also included
in the *Oxford Standard Authors* Blake, entered above.

Selected by T. W. Bateson *Heinemann* (*Poetry Bookshelf*) 1957
9s 6d; by Ernest de Selincourt O.U.P. (*Worlds Classics*) 1927
7s 6d; and *Nelson* (*Classics*) 1937 6s

Bottomley, Gordon (1874-1948) POEMS AND PLAYS ed. and sel. by
Claud Colleer Abbott *Bodley Head* 1953 30s
Contains ninety pages of lyrics and other poems, with 464 pages of
dramatic writings—in all, ten poetic plays.

Bridges, Robert Seymour (1844-1930) *POEMS O.U.P. (*Standard
Authors*) (1912; 1936) 1953 12s 6d 722 pp
The latest edition includes *The Testament of Beauty*, but omits the eight
dramas.

THE SHORTER POEMS O.U.P. 1931 15s
*THE TESTAMENT OF BEAUTY O.U.P. 1929 18s
POETRY AND PROSE selected by John Sparrow O.U.P. 1955 8s 6d

Lyrics; excerpts from the longer poems; literary essays; and tributes
to Bridges by Gerard Manley Hopkins, Coventry Patmore, Lionel
Johnson, Laurence Binyon, and others.

Brontë, Anne (1820-49) COMPLETE POEMS ed. by Clement Shorter
and C. W. Hatfield *Hodder* 1923
Poems, 'by Currer, Ellis and Acton Bell' were published in 1846.

Brontë, Charlotte (1816-55) COMPLETE POEMS ed. by Clement
Shorter and C. W. Hatfield *Hodder* 1923
Some *Poems* and *Angrian Tales* are included in *Collins* (*Classics*) edition
of *The Professor*, entered in the *Fiction* section.

Brontë, Emily (1818-48) ★COMPLETE POEMS ed. by C. W. Hatfield
O.U.P. 1941 25s
The best edition, edited from the manuscripts. The poems are also
included in *Everyman* edition of *Wuthering Heights*.

GONDAL'S QUEEN ed. by Fannie E. Ratchford *Nelson* 1955 18s
'Presents a cycle of eighty-four poems by Emily Brontë, arranged for the
first time in logical sequence, to recreate the novel in verse which Emily
wrote for her beloved mystical kingdom of Gondal and its ruler, Augusta
Geraldine Almeda.'

★Brooke, Rupert (1887-1915) COMPLETE POEMS *Sidgwick and
Jackson* 1932 10s 6d with portrait and a facsimile of the MS. of
The Soldier

COLLECTED POEMS *Sidgwick and Jackson* 1918 16s
This edition, the first collection, contains a memoir by Sir Edward
Marsh, and two portraits from photographs.

POETICAL WORKS ed. by Geoffrey Keynes *Faber* 1946 12s 6d;
1960 (paperback) 5s
Selections: *Poems*, ed. by Geoffrey Keynes, *Nelson* (*Classics*) 1952, 5s;
1914 and Other Poems, *Faber* (Sesame Books), 1941, 3s 6d; *Twenty Poems*,
Sidgwick and Jackson, 1935, 2s.

Browne, William (1591-1643?) POEMS 2 vols. ed. by A. H. Bullen
Routledge (*Muses Library*) 1893
Browne of Tavistock wrote *Britannia's Pastorals* (1613 and 1616), and
The Shepherd's Pipe (1614). Part 3 of the *Pastorals* was not printed until
1852.

★Browning, Elizabeth Barrett (1806-61) POETICAL WORKS (1889)
O.U.P. (*Standard Authors*) 1904 12s 6d
The most read today, are the *Sonnets From the Portuguese* (1847). Separate,
pocket editions of this sequence are usually available, notably in the
American paperback series, W. H. Allen (*Dolphin Books*), 1962, 7s 6d.

★Browning, Robert (1812-89) COMPLETE POETICAL WORKS ed. by
Augustine Birrell and Sir Frederick Kenyon *Murray* (1919)
1945 30s 786 pp

The standard collection into one volume, by Browning's original publishers. It includes *The Ring and the Book*, which is also entered separately below.

POEMS, 1833-1868 *O.U.P.* (*Standard Authors*) (1905) 1940 15s 704 pp
Includes Browning's plays, and the shorter poems published after 1868.

POEMS AND PLAYS, 1833-1864 2 vols. *Dent* (*Everyman*) (1906) 1956 10s 6d each; POEMS, 1871-1890 (*Everyman*) 1940 6s 6d

SELECTED POEMS ed. by Edward Shanks *Macmillan* (*Golden Treasury series*) 1961 10s 6d; ed. by Sir Humphrey Milford *O.U.P.* (*Worlds Classics*) 1949 9s 6d 732 pp; ed. by James Reeves *Heinemann* (*Poetry Bookshelf*) 1956 8s 6d

THE RING AND THE BOOK (1868-9) *Dent* (*Everyman*) (1911) 1962 12s 6d; ed. by F. B. Pinion *Macmillan* (*Scholar's Library*) 1957 6s
A long dramatic poem, cast in the form of ten monologues, each of which presents a different view of the trial for murder of one Guido Franceschini, and his accomplices in the killing of his wife and foster-parents. Franceschini was put to death at Rome, 22 February, 1698. This extraordinary novel in verse was based on an account given in an old book picked up by Browning in Florence for a *lira*; the 'ring' in his title refers to the craftsmanship of the old Roman goldsmiths, in mingling 'gold with gold's alloy', akin to the poetic process inspired in Browning's mind by reading this old book.

Bryant, William Cullen (1794-1878) COLLECTED POEMS (1883) *O.U.P.* (*Standard Authors*) 1903
An American master of blank verse, in which medium he translated Homer, 1870-1. Bryant has been termed 'the Wordsworth of America', because of his insight into man in relation with nature.

*Burns, Robert (1759-96) POEMS, CHIEFLY IN SCOTTISH DIALECT (1786; 1787) POETICAL WORKS ed. by William Wallace *Chambers* (*Bicentenary Edition*) 1958 15s Illus.; POEMS AND SELECTED LETTERS ed. by Anthony Hepburn *Collins* (*Alloway Bicentenary Edition*) 1959 21s Illus.; ed. by J. Logie Robertson *O.U.P.* (*Standard Authors*) (1896) 1950 15s

POEMS AND SONGS ed. by James Barke *Collins* (*Classics*) 1955 7s 736 pp
'A completely new edition, including over sixty poems appearing in a collection for the first time.'

ed. by James Kinsley *Dent* (*Everyman*) (1906) 1958 10s 6d;
These are the principal editions of the complete poetical works, with introductions, notes, and glossaries.

ed. by G. S. Fraser *Heinemann* (*Poetry Bookshelf*) 1960 9s 6d; *Nelson* (*Classics*) 1954 7s; *Oliver and Boyd* 1951 10s 6d; *O.U.P.* (*Worlds Classics*) (1903) 1950 7s 6d

I

Butler, Samuel (1612–80) HUDIBRAS (1662; 1663; 1678) *C.U.P.*
1905

SATIRES AND MISCELLANEOUS POETRY AND PROSE ed. by R. Lamar
C.U.P. 1928 30s
The mock-epic *Hudibras* survives, and still gives pleasure to the general
reader for its proverbial wisdom and satire, expressed in vigorous
couplets.

Butler, Samuel (1835–1902) THE ILIAD OF HOMER rendered into
English prose by Samuel Butler (1898) ed. by Louise R. Loomis
Van Nostrand 1942 14s
This edition of an interesting prose translation by the author of *The Way
of All Flesh*, and *The Authoress of the Odyssey* (1897) reprints Butler's
original preface.

THE ODYSSEY OF HOMER rendered into English prose by Samuel
Butler (1900) ed. by Louise R. Loomis *Van Nostrand* 1944 14s
A companion volume to the above. That Butler held very unorthodox
views about the identity of the poet and the composition of the epic may
be gathered from the title of his book mentioned above.

*Byron, George Gordon Noel (*6th Baron*) (1788–1824) POEMS
(1806–1824) COMPLETE POETICAL AND DRAMATIC WORKS *Murray*
ed. with a memoir by E. Hartley Coleridge (1898–1904) 1947
35s; 3 vols. ed. by Guy Pocock *Dent* (*Everyman*) 1963 12s 6d
each; *O.U.P.* (*Standard Authors*) (1896; 1904) 1945 15s 924 pp;
SELECTED VERSE AND PROSE WORKS ed. by Peter Quennell
Collins (*Classics*) 1959 8s; SELECTED POEMS *O.U.P.* (*Worlds
Classics*) 1913 7s 6d
Refer also to the *Nonesuch* Byron, entered in the *Essays and Belles Lettres*
section.

Campbell, Roy (1901–57) COLLECTED POEMS 3 vols. *Bodley Head*
1949; 1957; 1960 21s; 21s; 18s
SONS OF THE MISTRAL *Faber* (*Sesame Books*) 1941 5s
Selected poems by a controversial, vigorous personality, writing in
traditional forms, with Swinburnian eloquence.

Campbell, Thomas (1777–1844) COMPLETE POETICAL WORKS (1805;
1890) ed. by J. Logie Robertson *O.U.P.* (*Standard Authors*) 1907
Campbell's longer narrative poems are little read now, but his songs and
lyrics, stirring military and naval poems, still give great enjoyment, and
are included in most anthologies.

*Campion, Thomas (1567–1619) WORKS ed. by Percival Vivian
O.U.P. (*Oxford English Texts*) 1909 21s
In addition to Campion's exquisite songs and ayres for music, published
in 1601, 1610, and 1617, this complete edition includes the Latin Poems,

and the prose works, of which his *Observations in the Arte of English Poesie* (1602) is notable for his plea for the writing of unrhymed verse, and *A New Waye in Counterpoint*, is a short treatise on his theories as a composer.

*Carew, Thomas (1595?-1639) POEMS ed. by Rhodes Dunlap *O.U.P.* (*Oxford English Texts*) 1949 35s
Refer also to Howarth's collection of *Minor Poets of the 17th Century*, entered in the next section of *Anthologies*.

Cary, Henry Francis (1772-1844) THE DIVINE COMEDY OF DANTE trans. by H. F. Cary (1814) *Dent* (*Everyman*) (1911) 1955 10s 6d; *O.U.P.* (*Standard Authors*) 1911 12s 6d
A version in blank verse that is regarded by Italian scholars as still a standard translation.

*Chapman, George (1559?-1634) BEST PLAYS ed. by W. L. Phelps *Benn* (*Mermaid Dramatists*) 1895
Chapman has not been well served by publishers and editors. T. M. Parrott's edition (Routledge, 1910-14) did not get beyond two volumes, and the old *Mermaid* selection has not been reprinted for many years. It contains his best comedy *All Fools*, the D'Ambois plays, and as examples of 'that full and heightened style' admired by his contemporary John Webster, *The Conspiracy*, and *The Tragedy of Charles, Duke of Byron*. R. H. Shepherd's edition in three volumes, 1874-5, 1889, is scarce.

POEMS ed. by P. B. Bartlett *O.U.P.* 1941
The best edition.

THE ILIAD AND THE ODYSSEY OF HOMER translated by George Chapman (1598; 1611; 1614; 1615) 2 vols. ed. by Allardyce Nicoll *Routledge* 1957 63s (the set)
This handsome edition is 'designed rather for the general reader and for the student engaged in exploring the literature of the Elizabethan period than for the scholar'. Volume Two contains *The Lesser Homerica*: that is, *The Homeric Hymns*, *The Batrachomyomachia*, and *Epigrams*, with notes, commentary and a glossary.

Chatterton, Thomas (1752-70) THE ROWLEY POEMS (1777; 1778) ed. by M. E. Hare *O.U.P.* 1911 15s
The text of T. Tyrwhitt's third edition of these poems, many of them of genuine beauty, that were originally said by Chatterton to be the work of a Tomas Rowley, a Bristol poet of the fifteenth century, but which were shown to be forgeries.

*Chaucer, Geoffrey (1340?-1400) WORKS 7 vols. ed. by W. W. Skeat *O.U.P.* 1894; 1897 252s (the set) 4314 pp
Volume 4 of this edition for students contains *The Canterbury Tales*; vol. 5, Skeat's notes; vol. 6 a glossarial index.

COMPLETE WORKS ed. by W. W. Skeat *O.U.P.* (*Standard Authors*) 1906 15s 906 pp; ed. by F. N. Robinson *O.U.P.* (1933) 1957

42s 1046 pp; ed. by A. W. Pollard *Macmillan (Globe Library)* (1898) 1953 15s 772 pp
Of the later editions, F. N. Robinson's critical edition, collated with many important manuscript sources, with glossary, a biography and detailed textual commentary and notes, is the best.

THE CANTERBURY TALES (1478) ed. by A. C. Cawley *Dent (Everyman)* (1908) 1958 12s 6d; ed. by W. W. Skeat *O.U.P. (Worlds Classics)* 1902 7s 6d
The new edition in *Everyman* is based on the Ellesmere MS. in the Huntingdon Library, California. This is an early fifteenth-century copy and is regarded by Dr. Cawley as of the greatest importance for the establishment of a standard text. Translations of *The Canterbury Tales* into modern English include Nevill Coghill's popular *Penguin*, 1951, 5s; and students may be referred to H. L. Hitchens's selection, edited for modern readers, presenting the best of the tales in Chaucer's own text, with obsolete words defined in the margin, and connecting notes, *Murray* (1946) 1956, 9s 6d; and to L. J. Lloyd's *A Chaucer Selection*, Harrap, 1952, 8s 6d, with introduction, glossary and notes.

TROILUS AND CRISEYDE (1482) ed. by John Warrington *Dent (Everyman)* 1953 8s 6d; ed. by W. W. Skeat *O.U.P. (Worlds Classics)* 1959 7s 6d
The *Everyman* edition has marginal glosses, with spelling slightly modernised; the *Worlds Classics* includes *The House of Fame* (1486). The story of Troilus and Cressida is one of the greatest achievements in English literature, and may indeed be regarded as the first novel in verse; derived from Boccaccio but enriched by Chaucer with his poetry and his extraordinary psychological insight. Of the hundreds of monographs on Chaucer and his work, one can refer only to *Chaucer's World*, by the American scholar, Edith Rickert, O.U.P. (1948) 1962, 21s; illustrated with thirty-five plates; *Chaucer*, by Raymond Preston, Sheed and Ward, 1952; and *Chaucer the Maker*, by John Speirs, Faber, 1960, 21s.

*Chesterton, Gilbert Keith (1874-1936) COLLECTED POEMS *Methuen* (1927) 1954 16s; ESSAYS AND POEMS ed. by Wilfrid Sheed *Penguin Books* 1958 2s 6d
THE BALLAD OF THE WHITE HORSE *Methuen* (1911) 1955 7s 6d

Churchill, Charles (1731-64) POETICAL WORKS ed. by Douglas Grant *O.U.P.* 1956 63s 610 pp
The first modern edition, with notes, of the work of a satirist who, observed Saintsbury in his *Short History*, is 'too much forgotten'.

Clare, John (1793-1864) POEMS 2 vols. ed. by J. W. Tibble *Dent* 1935 1126 pp.
The most comprehensive edition so far published of the work of this true poet of the English countryside. Forgotten in the twentieth century until Arthur Symons published a small selection in 1908, and Edmund

Blunden with Alan Porter, edited a selected volume in 1921, Clare is now a firmly re-established, frequently quoted, and fully appreciated poet. His *Poems, Descriptive of Rural Life* (1820) had some success when first published.

POEMS OF JOHN CLARE'S MADNESS ed. by Geoffrey Grigson *Routledge* 1949
'Here, for the first time, is a generous selection from all that Clare wrote between his first mental collapse and his death in 1864.'

*SELECTED POEMS ed. by Geoffrey Grigson *Routledge* (*Muses Library*) 1951 10s 6d; ed. by James Reeves *Heinemann* (*Poetry Bookshelf*) 1954 7s 6d

Clough, Arthur Hugh (1819-61) POEMS ed. by H. F. Lowry, A. L. P. Norrington and F. L. Mulhauser *O.U.P.* 1951 42s 610 pp
The definitive edition of all the poems by Matthew Arnold's friend, commemorated in Arnold's elegiac monody *Thyrsis*.

Coleridge, Hartley (1796-1849) COMPLETE POETICAL WORKS *Routledge* (*Muses Library*) 1908
In 1942 E. L. Griggs published *New Poems*, with a selection of others, by S. T. Coleridge's eldest son, O.U.P., now also out of print.

*Coleridge, Mary Elizabeth (1861-1907) COLLECTED POEMS ed. by Theresa Whistler *Hart-Davis* 1954 15s
The writer of these sensitive and graceful poems published two volumes in 1896 and 1897, under a pen-name, lest she should 'tarnish' the name 'which an ancestor had made illustrious in English poetry'. Sir Henry Newbolt's edition in 1907, in which he drew attention to this modesty on the part of Mary Coleridge, quickly proved how groundless were her fears, for the volume was much appreciated, and in two years went into five editions.

*Coleridge, Samuel Taylor (1772-1834) POETICAL WORKS AND DRAMAS 2 vols. ed. by E. H. Coleridge *O.U.P.* (*Oxford English Texts*) 1912 70s (the set) 1226 pp

POETICAL WORKS ed. by E. H. Coleridge and George Saintsbury *O.U.P.* (*Standard Authors*) (1912) 1954 15s 638 pp
Excluding the dramas. Summarises for students the various readings from published and unpublished sources.

COMPLETE POEMS ed. by Morchard Bishop *Macdonald* (*Illustrated Classics*) 1954 15s; selection ed. by John Beer *Dent* (*Everyman*) (1906) 1962 15s; POEMS *Nelson* (*Classics*) 1924 5s; ed. by Sir Arthur Quiller-Couch *O.U.P.* (*Worlds Classics*) (1912) 1959 7s 6d
Refer also to Stephen Potter's edition of Coleridge's *Complete Poems and Selected Prose*, in the *Nonesuch* series, entered in the *Essays and Belles Lettres* section.

THE LYRICAL BALLADS (1798; 1800; 1802; 1805)
For separate editions of these poems by Coleridge and Wordsworth see
under Wordsworth, below.

Collins, William (1721-59) POEMS (1765)
Bound with the poetical works of Thomas Gray in the *Oxford Standard
Authors* series, which see below; refer also to Fausset's *Minor Poets of the
18th Century* entered in the next section of *Anthologies*.

Constable, Henry (1562-1613) DIANA: TWENTY-THREE SONNETS
(1592) ed. by W. C. Hazlitt 1859; ed. by J. Gray 1897
Some sonnets by this minor poet will be found in the anthology known
as *England's Helicon* (1614) entered in the next section under Hugh
Macdonald, editor of the standard modern edition.

Corbet, Richard (1582-1635) POEMS ed. by J. A. W. Bennett and
H. R. Trevor-Roper O.U.P. 1955 30s
Bishop Corbet's minor and occasional verse sometimes produced charming lyrics, of which the delightful 'Farewell, rewards and fairies' is the
best known.

Cotton, Charles (1630-87) POEMS ed. by John Buxton *Routledge*
(*Muses Library*) 1958 18s
Provides for the first time a standard text of all of the poetry by Izaak
Walton's friend.

Cowley, Abraham (1618-1667) POEMS ed. by A. R. Waller
C.U.P. 1905; POETRY AND PROSE ed. by L. C. Martin O.U.P.
1949 8s 6d
It was in his essay on Cowley, in his *Lives of the Poets*, that Dr. Johnson
used the term 'metaphysical' to describe Cowley's style, thus adding a
literary epithet to the critic's vocabulary that has been used ever since,
although not in the pejorative sense that Johnson implied.

*Cowper, William (1731-1800) POETICAL WORKS ed. by Sir
Humphrey Milford O.U.P. (*Standard Authors*) (1905) 1950
12s 6d 710 pp; ed. by H. I'Anson Fausset *Dent* (*Everyman*) 1931
6s 6d
The *Everyman* is 'a comprehensive selection . . . designed to show his
many-sidedness in such varied examples of poetry as (amongst others)
The Task, John Gilpin, the *Olney Hymns* . . . and the satirical verses from
his *Table Talk*'.

Crabbe, George (1754-1832) POEMS (1834) ed. by Sir Adolphus
William Ward C.U.P. 1905-7; ed. by A. J. and R. M. Carlyle
O.U.P. (*Standard Authors*) (1908) 1914
*SELECTED POEMS ed. by Frank Whitehead *Chatto* (*Queen's
Classics*) 1956 6s 6d; THE BOROUGH (1810) *Dent* (*Temple Classics*)
1903 7s

From the original edition in seven volumes (1834) of Crabbe's complete poetical works, the editor of the selection has made a choice emphasising the poet's mastery of the short story in verse. Hence excerpts have been avoided except in the case of *The Parish Register*. The volume consists of complete 'Letters' from *The Borough* (1810) and some of the *Tales*. The narrative of *Peter Grimes* from which the libretto for Benjamin Britten's opera was taken, is given complete, from *The Borough*.

*Crashaw, Richard (1613?-49) THE POEMS: ENGLISH, LATIN AND GREEK ed. by L. C. Martin *O.U.P.* (1927) 1957 45s 572 pp
The definitive edition, with an introduction of ninety-four pages on the life of Crashaw; the text and the canon; and the order of the poems. Crashaw's poetry is ecstatic and devotional, sometimes that of a mystic, and is the best written in the characteristic 'metaphysical' style of the first half of the seventeenth century, in succession to Donne's.

Daniel, Samuel (1562-1619) THE CIVIL WARS (1595; 1599; 1609) ed. by Laurence Michel *O.U.P.* 1958
The completion of Daniel's *Civil Wars Between the Houses of Lancaster and York* in 1609 offered leisurely readers a long epic, that was later to be much admired by writers of the Romantic period, especially by Coleridge and Charles Lamb. This only modern edition since Grosart's of 1885 has a bibliographical and textual commentary, with sections on sources, Shakespeare's chronicle plays and allied topics of interest to students.

POEMS ed. by Arthur Colby Sprague *Routledge* (1930) 1950
An American edition containing the charming sonnet sequence *Delia* (1592). It includes a prose work *A Defence of Rhyme* (1603) which will also be founded in the *Everyman* volume called *The Prelude To Poetry*, for which see under Rhys, in the section of *Prose Anthologies*.

Darley, George (1795-1846) POETICAL WORKS *Routledge* (*Muses Library*) 1908
A minor Irish poet, still read for his lyrics and the longer poem *Nepenthe* (1839).

D'Avenant, Sir William (1606-68) LOVE AND HONOUR (1649) THE SIEGE OF RHODES (1656) ed. in one volume by J. W. Tupper *Harrap* 1909
The first actress to perform on an English stage appeared in D'Avenant's *The Siege of Rhodes*. In 1638 he was made Poet Laureate. *Gondibert* (1651) is forgotten, but *The Siege* is regarded as the foundation of English opera.

Davidson, John (1857-1909) POEMS AND BALLADS *Unicorn Press* 16s
A selection by R. D. Macleod, with an introduction, of a gifted poet of the *Yellow Book* Period, whose *Fleet Street Eclogues* (1893 and 1896), some ballads and songs, have outlived his attempt to bring poetic drama back to the English stage.

A SELECTION OF POEMS ed. by Maurice Lindsay *Hutchinson* 1961
25s

Davies, Sir John (1569-1626) ORCHESTRA (1596) ed. by E. M. W.
Tillyard *Chatto* 1945 5s
This poem is discussed and analysed at some length in Tillyard's
'elementary essay on the background of English Literature': *Five Poems,
1470-1870*, Chatto, 1948, 8s 6d. It is also to be found in Gerald Bullett's
Everyman anthology, *Silver Poets of the 16th Century*, entered in the next
section of *Anthologies*.

*Davies, William Henry (1871-1940) COMPLETE POEMS *Cape* (1942)
1963 25s
Poems of the 'Super-tramp', whose autobiography reveals the same
qualities of simplicity and fresh, uninhibited emotion, as his lyrics.

*de la Mare, Walter (1873-1956) COLLECTED POEMS *Faber* (1940)
1942 15s
Contains all the poems previously published in two volumes by Constable, and the 1935 volume, with the exception of the poems de la Mare
wrote for the enjoyment of young readers.

COLLECTED RHYMES AND VERSES *Faber* 1944 15s
A gathering of poems written for children from time to time.

SELECTED POEMS ed. by R. N. Green-Armytage *Faber* 1954
9s 6d
Refer also to the *Everyman* de la Mare entered in the *Essays and Belles
Lettres* section.

de Tabley, John Byrne Leicester Warren (3rd Baron) (1835-95)
COLLECTED POEMS (1903) SELECT POEMS ed. by John Drinkwater
O.U.P. 1924
The selection includes some pleasant lyrics, and Lord de Tabley's best
long poem, *Philoctetes* (1866), a metrical drama.

*Dekker, Thomas (1570?-1632) DRAMATIC WORKS 4 vols. ed. by
Fredson Bowers *C.U.P.* 1953-61 45s each 2130 pp
BEST PLAYS ed. by Ernest Rhys *Benn* (*Mermaid*) (1887) 1949
12s 6d
Contains the four most popular plays, one of which is the perennial
favourite, *The Shoemakers' Holiday* (1600). *Old Fortunatus* (1600) available separately, Dent (Temple Dramatists) 7s 6d

Denham, Sir John (1615-69) POETICAL WORKS ed. by T. H. Banks
O.U.P. 1928
A Yale University Press edition of a minor Caroline poet, whose
Cooper's Hill (1642), a pleasant pastoral, has a place in English poetry.

Diaper, William (1685-1717) COMPLETE WORKS ed. by D.
Broughton *Routledge* (*Muses Library*) 1952 15s

Forgotten since the first publication of these poems by a young Somerset poet in 1712-14, the work of Diaper is here introduced to readers in a scholarly, standard series.

*Dickinson, Emily (1830-86) SELECTED POEMS ed. by James Reeves *Heinemann* (*Poetry Bookshelf*) 1959 9s 6d; SELECTED POEMS AND LETTERS *W. H. Allen* (*Anchor Books*) 1959 10s
The definitive edition of the published poems of this major American poet has been issued by Harvard University Press, ed. by T. H. Johnson in three volumes, with variant readings, and twenty facsimiles, 1955, 200s. Poignant, lapidary, brief, these epigrammatic poems were treasured in secret by their writer, who passed most of her mature life in retirement. A critical study *Emily Dickinson's Poetry: Stairway of Surprise*, by Charles R. Anderson, Heinemann, 1963, 42s contains the authorised text of more than one hundred of her poems, thus providing an anthology as well as a guide.

Dixon, Richard Watson (1833-1900) LAST POEMS ed. by Robert Bridges *O.U.P.* 1905
A selection of lyrical verse by a saintly friend of Robert Bridges, who edited another selection in 1909, also out of print.

Dobson, Henry Austin (1840-1921) SELECTED POEMS *O.U.P.* (*Worlds Classics*) 1924 7s 6d
Pastiche, ballads, lyrics and occasional verse in the eighteenth-century manner.

Dolben, Digby Mackworth (1848-67) POEMS ed. by Robert Bridges *O.U.P.* 1911
With a memoir of this youthful poet, a monk, who was drowned before his poetic gifts could come to maturity.

*Donne, John (1573?-1631) POEMS (1633; 1635) 2 vols. ed. by Sir Herbert Grierson *O.U.P.* (*Oxford English Texts*) 1912 50s (the set) 928 pp
A notable example of bibliographical and textual research, establishing for the first time a full and authentic text. Donne's poems circulated in his lifetime only in manuscript, and authentic holographs are not extant to help editors with difficulties and obscurities.

POEMS ed. by Sir Herbert J. C. Grierson *O.U.P.* (*Standard Authors*) (1933) 1951 12s 6d
The 1912 text, without the notes, but with some corrections, and a number of poems assigned to Donne given in an appendix, with some textual variants indicated.

POEMS ed. by Hugh I'Anson Fausset *Dent* (*Everyman*) (1931) 1958 8s 6d
The editor's introduction is a notable biographical study of this greatest of all metaphysical poets of the seventeenth century.

I*

COMPLETE POETRY AND SELECTED PROSE ed. by John Hayward
Nonesuch Press 1929 21s 814 pp
A notable edition, and next to Grierson's in importance for the editor's
research towards the establishment of a definitive text.

THE DIVINE POEMS ed. by Helen Gardner *O.U.P.* 1952 28s
With a commentary of ninety-four pages of considerable value to
students.

THE SONGS AND SONETS (1633) ed. by Theodore Redpath
Methuen 1956 18s
'An *Editio Minor*, with introduction and explanatory notes . . . the first
separate edition . . . the notes on the poems are the fullest that have so
far appeared.'

SELECTED POEMS ed. by James Reeves *Heinemann* (*Poetry Bookshelf*) 1958 7s 6d
See also under *Essays and Belles Lettres* section.

Doughty, Charles Montagu (1843-1926) THE DAWN IN BRITAIN
7 vols. *Duckworth* 1906; one volume edition *Cape* 1943 692 pp
An epic poem, written in a sustained narrative style, demanding con-
centration, and in a vocabulary derived from that of Spenser and his
contemporaries.

Douglas, Lord Alfred Bruce (1870-1945) LYRIC POEMS *Unicorn
Press* 1935 7s 6d
SONNETS (1909) *Unicorn Press* 1935 4s 6d
The best verse of a sonneteer whose controversial life is part of the
literary history of the nineties and the Edwardian period.

Douglas, Gavin (1474?-1522) A SELECTION FROM HIS POETRY ed.
by Sydney Goodsir Smith *Oliver and Boyd* (*Saltire Classics*)
1959 7s 6d
'One of the first glories of Scottish literature,' writes the editor, who
devotes the greater part of his selection to Douglas's astonishingly
vigorous translation of Virgil's *Aeneid* (1553), with some of the original
prologues that Douglas himself wrote for each book, and the two
medieval allegories *King Hart* and *The Palice of Honour* (1553). Obsolete
words defined in footnotes.

Dowson, Ernest Christopher (1867-1900) COMPLETE POEMS
Unicorn Press 1947 7s 6d; ed. by Mark Longaker with annotations, *O.U.P.* 1963 48s
The first collection, published by the Bodley Head, in 1905, contained
a memoir by Arthur Symons, who knew the poet, four illustrations by
Aubrey Beardsley, and a portrait by William Rothenstein. 'He died
young, worn out by what was never really life to him, leaving a little
verse which has the pathos of things too young and too frail ever to
grown old.'—*Arthur Symons*.

*Drayton, Michael (1563-1631) POEMS 2 vols. ed. by John Buxton
  Routledge (Muses Library) 1953 30s (the set) 724 pp
  Text based on Drayton's collected editions of 1605 and succeeding
  volumes.

  MINOR POEMS, 1584-1630 ed. by C. Brett *O.U.P.* (*Tudor and
  Stuart Library*) 1907 15s
  Sonnets; odes; elegies; *Muses Elizium* (1630) and the exquisite *Nimphidia*
  (1627).

Drummond, William (1585-1649) POEMS 2 vols. ed. by William
  C. Ward *Routledge* (*Muses Library*) 1894; ed. by L. E. Kastner
  Manchester University Press 1913
  Sonnets, songs, the spiritual poems *Flowers of Sion*, and miscellanies of
  Drummond of Hawthornden. See his *Conversations with Jonson* (1618),
  entered in the *Essays and Belles Lettres* section.

*Dryden, John (1631-1700) COMPLETE WORKS ed. by Edward
  Niles Hooker and H. T. Swedenberg (*University of California
  Press*) *C.U.P.* 1956- *in progress*. Vol. 1: The Poems, 1649-80
  C.U.P. 1956 64s

  BEST PLAYS 2 vols. ed. by George Saintsbury *Benn* (*Mermaid*)
  (1904) 1949 18s; 12s 6d each
  Seven plays, including *All For Love*, on the theme of Antony and Cleopatra, but written from Cleopatra's point of view instead of Antony's;
  and the comedy *Marriage à la Mode*, which is also available separately,
  Dent (Temple Dramatists), 7s 6d.

  POEMS 4 vols. ed. by James Kinsley *O.U.P.* (*Oxford English
  Texts*) 1958 210s (the set) 2000 pp

  THE POEMS AND FABLES ed. by James Kinsley *O.U.P.* (*Standard
  Authors*) 1962 21s 864 pp
  For the one volume edition, the editor has selected from his definitive
  edition all of Dryden's original poems; poems of which he was part
  author; the prologues, epilogues, and songs from plays; a few pieces
  ascribed to him; and the complete text of *Fables, Ancient and Modern*
  (1700). Texts taken from the first editions, collated with all subsequent
  editions published in Dryden's lifetime.

  SELECTED POEMS ed. by Bonamy Dobrée *Dent* (*Everyman*)
  (1934) 1954 10s 6d; ed. by Douglas Grant *Penguin Books* 1955
  3s 6d; *Nelson* (*Classics*) 1956 6s; ed. by Roger Sharrock *Heinemann* (*Poetry Bookshelf*) 1963 9s 6d. Refer also to the Dryden
  volume in the *Reynard Library*, entered in the *Essays and Belles
  Lettres* section

  THE WORKS OF VIRGIL translated by John Dryden ed. by James
  Kinsley *O.U.P.* 1961 10s 6d
  The *Pastorals*; *Georgics*; and the *Aeneid* (1697), translated into English
  verse.

Dunbar, William (1460?-1530) POEMS ed. by James Kinsley
O.U.P. 1958 12s 6d
Introduction; text; notes; glossary; and five short appreciations.

POEMS ed. by W. Mackay Mackenzie *Faber* (1932) 1961 21s
A standard edition, with notes and a glossary.

*SELECTED POEMS ed. by Hugh Macdiarmid *Maclellan* 1955 6s
With a glossary and a bibliography.

Dyer, John (1699-1758) GRONGAR HILL AND OTHER POEMS (1726)
Included in *Minor Poets of the 18th Century*, edited by Hugh I'Anson
Fausset, listed in the next section of *Anthologies*.

*Emerson, Ralph Waldo (1803-82) POETICAL WORKS *Collins*
(*Classics*) 1954 7s
Included in a selection of Emerson's essays. Refer also to *Essays and Belles
Lettres* section for a collection of Emerson's characteristic prose, with the
poems, published by Van Nostrand.

Fergusson, Robert (1750-74) POEMS (1773) ed. by Alexander
Law *Oliver and Boyd* 1947
A selection of poems by a Scottish poet who was born and who died in
Edinburgh.

*FitzGerald, Edward (1809-83) THE RUBÁIYÁT OF OMAR KHAYYÁM
translated by Edward FitzGerald (1859-79) *A. and C. Black*
(1922) 1946 8s 6d Illustrated; *Collins* 30s (leather) 15s (cloth);
(*Classics*) 5s; *Dent* (*Everyman*) 1928; *Harrap* 1951 25s (leather)
10s 6d (cloth) illustrated by Willy Pogany; *Macmillan* (*Golden
Treasury series*) 1958 7s 6d; *Ward, Lock* 10s 6d (leather) 6s (cloth)
These are some of the many popular editions of the translation of which
G. K. Chesterton once wittily remarked that it was 'much too good to
be a good translation'. *Collins* (*Classics*) includes two minor works by
FitzGerald: *Euphranor: a Dialogue On Youth* (1851) and *Salámán and
Absál: an allegory* 'freely translated from the Persian of Jámi' (1856).
Everyman includes a translation of six plays by the Spanish dramatist
Calderón de la Barca (1853). The text of FitzGerald's first translation of
the *Rubáiyát* (1859) and the fourth (1879) is also included in Professor
A. J. Arberry's *Persian Poems*: an anthology of verse translations, Dent
(*Everyman*) 1954, 8s 6d, and in the *Reynard Library* omnibus entered in
the *Essays and Belles Lettres* section.

*Flecker, James Elroy (1884-1915) COLLECTED POEMS ed. by Sir
John Squire *Secker and Warburg* (1916) 1949 10s 6d; FORTY-TWO
POEMS, and THE GRECIANS *Dent* 1924 7s 6d
See also Flecker's play *Hassan* in the *Prose Drama* section. It contains
some well-known lyrics by this gifted young poet.

Fletcher, Giles (1588?-1623) and Phineas (1582-1650) POETICAL
WORKS 2 vols. ed. by F. S. Boas *C.U.P.* 1908-9

The chief work of these two poets (cousins of John Fletcher, the dramatist) is an ecstatic poem, *Christ's Victory and Triumph in Heaven and Earth*, by Giles Fletcher (1610) and *The Purple Island*, by Phineas Fletcher (1633)

*Ford, John (1586-1640) FIVE PLAYS ed. by Havelock Ellis *Benn (Mermaid)* (1888) 1961 16s
The Lover's Melancholy (1629); '*Tis Pity She's a Whore* (1633); *The Broken Heart* (1633); *Love's Sacrifice* (1633); and *Perkin Warbeck* (1634). The two that are sometimes revived, *The Broken Heart*, and '*Tis Pity*, are included in the *Everyman* edition of *Selected Plays of John Webster*, Dent, 1962, 8s 6d. '*Tis Pity* is one of *Five Stuart Tragedies*, selected by A. K. McIlwraith for the *Worlds Classics* volume entered in the next section.

Freeman, John (1880-1929) COLLECTED POEMS *Macmillan* 1928; LAST POEMS ed. by Sir John Squire *Macmillan* 1930
Of this Georgian poet Squire wrote in his memoir: 'He will be read by more people now (i.e. 1930), than when he was alive; alive, his chief readers were his brother-poets'.

Gascoigne, George (*C.* 1539-77) THE POSIES, AND OTHER WORKS (1575) *C.U.P.* 1904
A poet who interests scholars because he used forms in poetry before other English writers, and was one of the first to employ blank verse for tragedy, included in *The Posies*. He also wrote *The Glasse of Government*, satires, translations from Ariosto, and *The Supposes*, included in the *Worlds Classics* volume of *Five Pre-Shakespearean Comedies*, edited by F. S. Boas, and entered in the next section. Gascoigne's *Certain Notes or Instructions Concerning the Making of Verse or Rhyme in English* (1575), is the first thing of its kind in English and is an important example of critical prose.

Gay, John (1685-1732) POEMS (1720) 2 vols. *Routledge (Muses Library)* (1893) 1904
With the delightful *Trivia* (1716) and *Fables*, are ballads, and some of the well-known songs from Gay's two ballad operas, *The Beggar's Opera* (1728) and *Polly* (1729)

*Gilbert, Sir William Schwenck (1836-1911) THE BAB BALLADS (1869) 1904 *Macmillan* 6s Illus. by the author; THE BAB BALLADS and SONGS OF A SAVOYARD (1890) 1904 21s 564 pp Illus. by the author; THE SAVOY OPERAS, 1875-1896 *Macmillan* 1926 18s 698 pp; (*St. Martins Library*) 1962 8s 6d; 2 vols. *O.U.P.* (*Worlds Classics*) 1962-3 8s 6d each
The complete text of the Gilbert and Sullivan comic operas.

Golding, Arthur (1536?-1606) THE METAMORPHOSES OF OVID translated by Arthur Golding (1565) ed. by W. H. D. Rouse (1904) *Centaur Press* 1961 105s quarto; *Dent (Everyman)* (1939) 1955 8s 6d

Everyman is a volume of *Selected Works of Ovid* ed. by J. C. and M. J. Thornton, containing verse translations by Tudor and later poets: Golding, Turberville, Wolferston, Catlin, Marlowe, and Underdowne. The Centaur Press quarto is entitled *Shakespeare's Ovid*.

★Goldsmith, Oliver (1728-74) POEMS AND PLAYS ed. by Austin Dobson *Dent* (*Everyman*) (1910) 1954 8s 6d; *Nelson* (*Classics*) 1940 6s

Gordon, Adam Lindsay (1833-70) POEMS ed. by Frank M. Robb O.U.P. (1912) 1929 15s

Ballads and songs of the open air, by an Australian mounted policeman whose poetry has affinities with Kipling's.

Gorges, Sir Arthur (1557-1625) POEMS ed. by Helen Estabrook Sandison O.U.P. 1953 30s

Minor poems by a kinsman of Sir Walter Ralegh. He is the 'Alcyon' of Spenser's *Colin Clout*.

Gower, John (1330?-1408) COMPLETE WORKS 4 vols. ed. by G. C. Macaulay O.U.P. 1899-1902 Vols. 1 and 2 40s each (reprinted 1957)

The *Early English Texts* edition for students, the reprinted volumes being the English works, the chief of which is *Confessio Amantis*. A plain text edition is available, C.U.P., 4s 6d, of this long didactic poem. Chaucer's 'Moral Gower' was a court poet, and his best-known work is said to have been written at the request of Richard II.

Gray, David (1838-61) THE LUGGIE AND OTHER POEMS (1862) 1874

'A youth of genius,' wrote Matthew Arnold; he was befriended by Monckton-Milnes, Lord Houghton, who wrote the first biography of John Keats. Both poets died of consumption. Gray's principal poem celebrates the river Luggie in Dumbartonshire; his sonnet-sequence *In the Shadows* was written when he knew he was to suffer the same fate as Keats.

★Gray, Thomas (1716-71) POEMS O.U.P. (*Standard Authors*) (1919) revised edition by Leonard Whibley and Frederick Page 1937 12s 6d

Bound with the poems of William Collins.

POEMS, LETTERS AND ESSAYS *Dent* (*Everyman*) (1912) 1955 10s 6d

Green, Matthew (1696-1737) THE SPLEEN (1737)

This pleasant poem on the advantages of the contemplative life compared with the boredom of the envious and laboured, will be found in Hugh I'Anson Fausset's *Minor Poets of the 18th Century*, entered in the next section.

★GREENE, Robert (1558-92) COMPLETE PLAYS ed. by E. H. Dickinson *Benn* (*Mermaid*) 1909

PLAYS AND POEMS 2 vols. ed. by J. Churton Collins *O.U.P.* 1905
50s

THE TRAGICALL RAIGNE OF SELIMUS (1594) *Dent (Temple Dramatists)* 1898 7s 6d
Henry VI, the chronicle play which is in part credited to Greene, is included in editions of Shakespeare.

Greville, Sir Fulke (1st Baron Brooke) (1554-1628) POEMS AND DRAMAS 2 vols. ed. by Geoffrey Bullough *Oliver and Boyd* 1939
Sonnets, songs and tragedies, by an Elizabethan courtier, whose principal prose work was his *Life of Sidney* (1652).

Gurney, Ivor (1890-1937) POEMS ed. by Edmund Blunden *Hutchinson* 1954 7s 6d
Collects the songs and lyrics from two volumes by a poet whose work was written during World War I: *Severn and Somme* (1917), and *War's Embers* (1919).

*Hardy, Thomas (1840-1928) COLLECTED POEMS *Macmillan* (1919) 1932 21s 918 pp
SELECTED POEMS ed. by G. M. Young *Macmillan (Golden Treasury series)* (1940) 1951 8s 6d
THE DYNASTS 2 vols. *Macmillan* (1904; 1906; 1908) 1924 7s 6d each
An epic drama of the Napoleonic wars, in three parts, Volume 2 (part III) contains a verse play *The Queen of Cornwall* (1923).

Hawker, Robert Stephen (1803-75) CORNISH BALLADS AND OTHER POEMS (1879; 1899) ed. by C. E. Byles *Bodley Head* 1904 Illus.
The author of these narrative poems was a Cornish vicar. His *Song of the Western Men* will be found in some anthologies.

Hay, John (1838-1905) PIKE COUNTY BALLADS (1871)
Poems by an American ambassador to England. His travel book *Castilian Days* is a minor classic.

Hemans, Felicia Dorothea (1793-1835) POETICAL WORKS (1839) *Ward, Lock* 1920 12s 6d
Verses rather than poems, but the best of them, popular from their first appearance, continue to attract younger readers.

Henley, William Ernest (1849-1903) POEMS *Macmillan* 1921
Some of these lyrics have become popular as songs set to music.

Henryson, Robert (1430?-1505?) POEMS AND FABLES ed. by H. Harvey Wood *Oliver and Boyd* (1933) 1958 21s; SELECTED POEMS ed. by David Murison *Oliver and Boyd* 1952 5s
With notes, commentary and a glossary, in the full standard edition of this major Scottish poet.

THE TESTAMENT OF CRESSEID (1532; 1593) ed. by Bruce Dickins
Faber (1925) 1943 5s
In this poem Henryson continues the story related in Chaucer's great
poem, using rhyme-royal.

Herbert, Edward (Lord Herbert of Cherbury) (1583-1648) POEMS
ed. by G. C. Moore Smith O.U.P. 1923
A complete edition (seventy poems) will be found in Howarth's *Minor
Poets of the 17th Century*, listed in the next section. Lord Herbert, brother
to the greater poet, George, entered below, was a friend of John Donne,
whose metaphysical style may have influenced his own writing.

*Herbert, George (1593-1633) WORKS ed. by F. E. Hutchinson
O.U.P. (*Oxford English Texts*) 1941 42s 698 pp
A great piece of editing, probably as close to a definitive text as we are
likely to get.

POEMS O.U.P. (*Worlds Classics*) (1907) ed. by Helen Gardner
1961 7s 6d
The new edition is based on Hutchinson's text. The poems are arranged
in alphabetical order, with a notable introduction by the editor.

THE COUNTRY PARSON (1652) *S.C.M. Press* 1956 8s 6d
Herbert's prose work *A Priest To the Temple*, being advice to the country
parson, his character and rule of Holy Life, is here reprinted, together
with a selection of his poems.

*Herrick, Robert (1591-1674) POETICAL WORKS ed. by L. C.
Martin O.U.P. (*Oxford English Texts*) 1956 63s 631 pp
POEMS ed. by R. W. Moorman O.U.P. (*Oxford Standard
Authors*) 1921 12s 6d; (*Worlds Classics*) (1915) 1933 7s 6d
The *Worlds Classics* edition reproduces Moorman's text. Most of the
epigrams, included in Martin's edition, are omitted.

Hewlett, Maurice Henry (1861-1923) THE SONG OF THE PLOW
Macmillan 1916
'The English Chronicle,' devoted to the life of the agricultural peasant
from Norman times to the nineteenth century.

Heywood, Thomas (1575?-1641) BEST PLAYS *Benn* (*Mermaid*) 1888
*A WOMAN KILLED WITH KINDNESS (1607) ed. by R. W. Van
Fossen *Methuen* (*Revels Plays*) 1961 18s
Heywood's best and most frequently revived play. The new series uses
the quarto of 1607 as copy-text, with notes for students and a glossarial
index.

Hodgson, Ralph (1871-1962) COLLECTED POEMS *Macmillan* 1961
21s
The poet wrote comparatively little, with periods of complete silence
lasting decades. But when he published his last separate volume, *The*

Skylark and other poems, Macmillan, 1959, 15*s*, it was seen that his best work, including the much anthologised *The Bull*, and *Time, You Old Gypsy Man*, would certainly give him a permanent place in English poetry.

Hogg, James (1770-1835) THE POETIC MIRROR (1816) ed. by T. E. Welby *Scholartis Press* 1929
'Or *The Living Bards of Britain*,' being excellent parodies of the poetry of Coleridge, Byron, Scott, Wordsworth, and other contemporaries of 'the Ettrick Shepherd'.

Hood, Thomas (1799-1845) POEMS ed. by Walter Jerrold *O.U.P.* (*Worlds Classics*) (1906) 1917
Hood's best poems are widely known, and will be found in many anthologies: e.g. *I Remember*; *The Song of the Shirt*, and *The Bridge of Sighs*. Some were contributed to *Punch*.

*Hopkins, Gerard Manley (1844-89) POEMS ed. by Robert Bridges (1918); enlarged edition by W. H. Gardner *O.U.P.* 1948 16*s*
SELECTED POEMS ed. by James Reeves *Heinemann* (*Poetry Bookshelf*) 1953 6*s*; ed. by W. H. Gardner *Penguin Books* (1953) 1956 2*s* 6*d*
Notes in all of these editions elucidate difficulties in these influential poems, introduced to readers (apart from a few poems in older anthologies) by the writer's friend Robert Bridges.

*Housman, Albert Edward (1859-1936) COLLECTED POEMS *Cape* (1939) 1960 18*s*; *Penguin Books* 1956 3*s* 6*d*
This definitive edition includes all of Housman's work: *A Shropshire Lad* (1896); *Last Poems* (1922), and *More Poems* (1936) together with some additional poems printed in Laurence Housman's memoir of his brother, three chorus translations from the Greek, and a few not hitherto published in a book.

A SHROPSHIRE LAD *Richards Press* (1896) now *Unicorn Press* 7*s* 6*d* and 3*s* 6*d*; *Harrap* 1940 10*s* 6*d* Illus. with wood engravings by Agnes Miller Parker; LAST POEMS *Unicorn Press* 1922 7*s* 6*d* and 3*s* 6*d*

Hunt, James Henry Leigh (1784-1859) POETICAL WORKS ed. by H. S. Milford *O.U.P.* 1923
Minor verse; the best pieces are to be found in most anthologies.

Ingelow, Jean (1820-97) POEMS (1880; 1898) *O.U.P.* 1913
Once extremely popular, the minor poems by this writer of children's stories are now half-forgotten; her best pieces were *A Story of Doom* (1867) and *Divided*.

Johnson, Lionel Pigot (1867-1902) THE COMPLETE POEMS *Unicorn Press* 1953 26*s*

Introduction by Iain Fletcher. The *Poems* of 1895, revealed the grace and gift of melody of this minor poet, and assure him a place in the literary history of the nineties.

Johnson, Samuel (1709-84) POEMS ed. by David Nichol Smith and Edward L. McAdam *O.U.P.* (*Oxford English Texts*) 1941 38*s*
*PROSE AND POETRY ed. by R. W. Chapman *O.U.P.* 1922 8*s* 6*d*

Jones, Robert (*fl.* 1616) THE MUSES' GARDEN FOR DELIGHTS (1610) ed. by W. B. Squire *Blackwell* 1901
Songs and amatory lyrics written to be set to music.

Jonson, Ben (1572-1637) WORKS 11 vols. ed. by C. H. Herford and P. and E. Simpson *O.U.P.* 1925-51 55*s* each (75*s* each on hand-made paper) 7066 pp
A complete critical edition; vols. 1 and 2 are C. H. Herford's biography of *Ben Jonson: the Man and His Work* (1925). Vols. 3-6: *The Plays* (1927-38); 7-8: *The Sad Shepherd*; *Fall of Mortimer*; Masques and Entertainment; The Poems; and the Prose Works (1941-7); vol. 9: Historical Survey of the text; Stage History of the plays; Commentary on the Plays (1950); vol. 10: Commentary on the Masques (1950); vol. 11: Jonson's Literary Record; supplementary notes; index (1951).

*COMPLETE PLAYS 2 vols. ed. by Felix E. Schelling *Dent* (*Everyman*) (1910) 1962 10*s* 6*d* each; glossary to each volume
BEST PLAYS 2 vols. *Benn* (*Mermaid*) (1893-4) 1953 18*s* each
FIVE PLAYS *O.U.P.* (*Worlds Classics*) 1953 8*s* 6*d*
Contents: *Sejanus*; *The Alchemist*; *Volpone*; *Every Man In His Humour*; and *Bartholomew Fair*.

BARTHOLOMEW FAIR (1614) ed. by E. A. Horsman *Methuen* (*Revels Plays*) 1960 18*s*
Text based on the first edition, with notes for modern productions.

POEMS ed. by George Burke Johnstone *Routledge* (*Muses Library*) 1954 18*s*; 1962 9*s* (paperback)
Three collections from the folios, most of the uncollected poems, and a selection of lyrics from the masques and plays.

*Keats, John (1795-1821) POETICAL WORKS ed. by H. W. Garrod *O.U.P.* (*Oxford English Texts*) (1939) 1957 70*s* 676 pp
The definitive edition, with critical notes and introduction, embodying the knowledge gained from the latest research.

(*Oxford Standard Authors*) (1908) 1956 12*s* 6*d* 504 pp
Supersedes H. Buxton Forman's edition of 1908. The poems are placed in a new order, with critical notes.

ed. by J. Middleton Murry *Eyre and Spottiswoode* (1930) 1949 18*s*; *O.U.P.* (*Worlds Classics*) 1901 7*s* 6*d*; ed. by Ernest de

Selincourt *Methuen* (1905) 1954 35s; ed. by Edmund Blunden *Collins* (*Classics*) 1955 6s; *Nelson* (*Classics*) (1928) 1954 6s

Keble, John (1792-1866) THE CHRISTIAN YEAR (1827) *O.U.P.* (*Worlds Classics*) 1905
Devotional songs and lyrics: a poem for each Sunday of the year, and for Saints' Days. Once a household book, the familiar poems are still remembered as hymns. Keble initiated the Oxford Movement.

Keyes, Sidney (1922-43) COLLECTED POEMS ed. by Michael Meyer *Routledge* 1945 10s 6d
With notes, and a memoir of this gifted poet, who was killed in World War II.

Kingsley, Charles (1819-75) POEMS (1848; 1870) *Dent* (*Everyman*) 1927 6s 6d

Kipling, Rudyard (1865-1936) COLLECTED VERSE *Hodder* 1940 42s 845 pp
*A CHOICE OF KIPLING'S VERSE ed. by T. S. Eliot *Faber* 1941 15s Paperback 1963 6s
There are separate editions still available of the two most popular volumes: *Barrack-Room Ballads*, *Methuen* (1892) 1953, 12s 6d; and *Departmental Ditties*, Methuen (1886) 1950, 7s 6d.

Kyd, Thomas (1557?-1595?) WORKS ed. by Frederick S. Boas *O.U.P.* (1901) 1955 42s 586 pp
*THE SPANISH TRAGEDY (1594) *Dent* (*Temple Dramatists*) 1898 7s 6d; ed. by Philip Edwards *Methuen* (*Revels Plays*) 1959 18s
One of the first plays of its kind in English dramatic history, being written in blank verse, and produced in 1592. It was probably touched up by other dramatists, such as Ben Jonson, and it became one of the most popular tragedies of the Jacobean stage.

Lamb, Charles (1775-1834) POEMS *Collins* (*Classics*) 1953 6s
Included with a selection of Lamb's essays and letters.

Landor, Walter Savage (1775-1864) POEMS 3 vols. ed. by Stephen Wheeler *O.U.P.* 1937
The definitive edition, being the editor's part of an edition of Landor's complete works, edited with T. E. Welby, sixteen volumes 1927-36.

*POETRY AND PROSE ed. by Sir Edmund Chambers *O.U.P.* 1946 8s 6d
A selection of the poems will also be found in the *Everyman* edition of *Imaginary Conversations*, entered in the *Essays and Belles Lettres* section.

Langland, William (1330?-1400?) THE VISION OF WILLIAM CON-CERNING PIERCE THE PLOWMAN (1550) 2 vols. ed. by W. W. Skeat *O.U.P.* 1886 70s (the set) 1,216 pp

The principal edition of this narrative poem that has come down to us in no fewer than forty-seven manuscripts, probably dating from 1362 onwards. The language of the poem is Middle English.

*PIERS PLOWMAN translated into modern English by N. K. Coghill, *Phoenix House* 1949 12s 6d; by H. W. Wells *Sheed and Ward* 1935 18s; by Donald Attwater *Cassell* (1930) *Dent (Everyman)* 1957 12s 6d; by J. E. Goodrich *Penguin Books* 1959 3s 6d

The *Everyman* text is a new edition, revised by Rachel Attwater. Refer also to *Piers Plowman: an introduction*, by Elizabeth Salter, Blackwell, 1962, 15s, and note the new critical edition, in progress, edited by George Kane. When complete it will include all three versions of the poem and a comprehensive glossary. Volume 1: *The A Version: Will's Visions of Piers Plowman and Do-Well*, The Athlone Press, 1960, 70s. John Lawlor's *Piers Plowman: an Essay in Criticism*, Edward Arnold, 1962, 15s, is an outstandingly useful handbook written for the reader without academic knowledge of Middle English, elucidating difficulties, explaining allusions and obsolete words, and offering an invaluable reference book to students.

*Lawrence, David Herbert (1885-1930) COMPLETE POEMS 3 vols. 1957; 2 vols. ed. by Vivian de Sola Pinto and F. Warren Roberts 1963

SELECTED POEMS ed. by James Reeves *Heinemann (Poetry Bookshelf)* 1958 5s; ed. by W. E. Williams *Penguin Books* 1950 2s 6d

*Lawrence, Thomas Edward (1888-1935) THE ODYSSEY OF HOMER translated by T. E. Lawrence into English prose *O.U.P.* (1932) 1935 22s; with an introduction by Maurice Bowra *O.U.P. (Worlds Classics)* 1955 7s 6d

A modern version by Lawrence of Arabia, much admired for its manly, fluent narrative style.

Ledwidge, Francis (1891-1917) COMPLETE POEMS ed. by Lord Dunsany *Herbert Jenkins* (1919) 1955 12s 6d

A volume of lyrics collected from *Songs of the Field* (1915); *Songs of Peace* (1916) and *Last Songs* (1918) published after the poet's death in action in World War I.

Lewis, Alun (1915-44) HA! HA! AMONG THE TRUMPETS *Allen and Unwin* 1945 5s

With an appreciation by Robert Graves of the achievement of a young poet, killed in World War II.

Lindsay, Sir David (c. 1490-1555) POEMS ed. by Maurice Lindsay *Oliver and Boyd* 1948 5s

A selection of poems by the Scottish satirist whose masterpiece, entered below, was presented at the Edinburgh Festival in 1948.

THE SATYRE OF THE THRIE ESTAITS (1602) ed. by James Kinsley *Cassell* 1954 21*s*; ed. and adapted by Robert Kemp *Heinemann* (*Drama Library*) 5*s*
First performed before James V's court in 1540. The text of James Kinsley's edition is based on a rare copy of a quarto printed in 1602, with glossary and notes. Robert Kemp's abbreviation and adaptation for modern stage production where necessary translates the Scots dialect.

*Longfellow, Henry Wadsworth (1807-82) POETICAL WORKS *O.U.P.* (*Standard Authors*) 1925 12*s* 6*d* 886 pp; *Dent* (*Everyman*) (1909) 1961 10*s* 6*d*
Separate edition of the popular *Hiawatha* (1855) in Dent (*Children's Illustrated Classics*) 1960, 12*s* 6*d*.

*Lovelace, Richard (1618-57) POEMS ed. by C. H. Wilkinson *O.U.P.* (*Oxford English Texts*) 1930 30*s*
This definitive edition is also available in a collector's folio edition, 2 vols. O.U.P., 1925, 147*s*. The *Poems of Lovelace* will be found in the *Everyman* collection of *Minor Poets of the 17th Century*, edited by R. G. Howarth, entered in the next section.

*Macaulay, Thomas Babington (1st Baron) (1800-59) THE LAYS OF ANCIENT ROME (1842) *Dent* (*Everyman*) (1910) 1954 10*s* 6*d*
Also contains some other poems by Lord Macaulay, with miscellaneous essays. Refer also to the *Reynard Library* omnibus collection of Macaulay's *Prose and Poetry*, entered in the *Essays and Belles Lettres* section.

McGonagall, William (1830-?) POETIC GEMS (1890) *Duckworth* 1934 6*s*; MORE POETIC GEMS *Duckworth* 1962 12*s* 6*d*
A selection of the comic doggerel of a Scots handloom weaver, with a portrait and a brief autobiography. McGonagall was made much of by Edinburgh students, perhaps *pour rire*; nevertheless he took his verse seriously, and managed to publish it. Most of the poems are so very bad that they achieve a sort of distinction, and the fact that they have been many times reprinted (bound in tartan paper boards) indicates that they are still read and enjoyed. The last volume prints poems that have recently come to light in manuscript.

Mackail, John William (1859-1945) THE ODYSSEY OF HOMER trans. into English verse by J. W. Mackail *O.U.P.* (1912) 1932 25*s*

SELECT EPIGRAMS FROM THE GREEK ANTHOLOGY *Longmans* 1890

McNabb, Vincent Joseph (1868-1943) ANTHOLOGY ed. by Francis Edward Nugent *Blackfriars Press* 1955 13*s* 6*d*
Selections from the prose and verse of Father Vincent, a distinguished Dominican, friend of Belloc and G. K. Chesterton. Apart from devotional verse, the volume includes essays on Francis Thompson and on Chesterton.

Mangan, James Clarence (1803-49) POEMS ed. by L. I. Guiney
Dublin 1903
A selection of characteristic ballads by an Irish poet. His prose was
collected in a centenary edition, edited by D. J. O'Donoghue with an
essay by Lionel Johnson, Dublin, 1904.

Marlowe, Christopher (1564-93) WORKS ed. by R. H. Case
Methuen (1930-) rev. edition *in progress Tamburlaine the Great*
(1951); *The Tragicall History of Doctor Faustus* (1949); *Edward
the Second* (1955) 21s

WORKS ed. by C. F. Tucker *O.U.P.* 1910 17s 6d 682 pp
This volume includes the translations. Case's great edition for students
has a series of introductions by different scholars and authorities, with
detailed critical and other notes, to each volume.

*COMPLETE PLAYS *O.U.P.* (*Worlds Classics*) 1915 7s 6d and an
edition of FAUSTUS, with Goethe's *Faust* ed. by Sir Adolphus W.
Ward (*Worlds Classics*) 1908 7s 6d
The translation of Part I of Goethe's drama is by John Anster, first
published in 1853.

PLAYS ed. by Havelock Ellis *Benn* (*Mermaid*) (1887) 1951 12s 6d;
PLAYS AND POEMS ed. by M. R. Ridley *Dent* (*Everyman*) (1909)
1962 8s 6d; THREE PLAYS *Nelson* (*Classics*) 1954 7s

EDWARD THE SECOND (1594) *Dent* (*Temple Dramatists*) 1896 7s 6d;
DR. FAUSTUS (1604) *Dent* (*Temple Dramatists*) 1897 7s 6d; ed. by
John D. Jump *Methuen* (*The Revels Plays*) 1962 21s
This last edition of *The Tragical History of the Life and Death of Doctor
Faustus* is the first, complete edition for scholars to be prepared from the
early quartos, demonstrating acceptance of the opinion of Sir Walter
Greg that 'the 1616 version was closer to what Marlowe and another
wrote than was the 1604 version upon which editors had for a long time
been accustomed to rely'. The edition is in modern spelling, with a
glossarial appendix, and variant texts of five scenes.

Marston, John (1576-1634) PLAYS 3 vols. ed. by H. Harvey Wood
Oliver and Boyd 1938-43
Vol. 1: *The Dutch Courtesan*; *Antonis and Mellida*; *Antonio's Revenge*
(1602) 1938, 8s 6d. Vols. 2-3 out of print.

THE MALCONTENT (1604) *Dent* (*Temple Dramatists*) 1933 7s 6d
Marston's best play, *Eastward Ho!* is usually included in Ben Jonson's
plays.

Marvell, Andrew (1622-78) POEMS AND LETTERS 2 vols. ed. by
H. M. Margoliouth *O.U.P.* (*Oxford English Texts*) (1927) 1952
50s 746 pp Illus.
The definitive edition Vol. 1: the poems; vol. 2: the letters.

*POEMS ed. by Hugh Macdonald *Routledge (Muses Library)* 1952
12s 6d

From the British Museum's unique copy of *Miscellaneous Poems* (1681).
This contains three poems cancelled in ordinary copies of the folio. The
editor has also used a Bodleian Library manuscript copy of three poems
and some emendations.

Massinger, Philip (1583-1640) BEST PLAYS 2 vols. ed. by Arthur
Symons *Benn* (*Mermaid*) (1887)

*A NEW WAY TO PAY OLD DEBTS (1633) *Dent* (*Temple Dramatists*)
1904 7s 6d; ed. by Muriel St. Clare Byrne (1949) *Athlone Press*
1956 7s 6d

Massinger's most popular play. The last edition 'contains several original
features and is particularly suited to use in schools'.

Meredith, George (1828-1909) POETICAL WORKS ed. by G. M.
Trevelyan *Constable* 1912 640 pp

The definitive edition, with notes by the editor.

*SELECTED POETICAL WORKS ed. by G. M. Trevelyan *Longmans*
1955 16s 6d; SELECTED POEMS ed. by Graham Hough *O.U.P.*
1962 15s

This last selection includes *Modern Love* in two versions, the first one in
an appendix.

MODERN LOVE *Constable* (1862) *Hart-Davis* 1949 7s 6d

A tragic personal story told in fifty verses, each of sixteen lines, with the
sonnet-form rhyming scheme extended. This sequence contains
Meredith's finest and most enduring poetry.

Mew, Charlotte (1869-1928) COLLECTED POEMS *Duckworth* 1953
10s 6d

With a preface by Mrs. Harold Monro, whose husband published at his
Poetry Bookshop the separate volumes: *The Farmer's Bride* (1916); and
The Rambling Sailor (1929).

Meynell, Alice (1847-1922) COMPLETE POEMS *O.U.P.* (*Standard
Authors*) 1940; COLLECTED POEMS ed. by Sir Francis Meynell
Hollis and Carter 1947

Middleton, Thomas (1580-1627) BEST PLAYS 2 vols. ed. by A. C.
Swinburne *Benn* (*Mermaid*) (1887; 1890)

*THE CHANGELING (1653) ed. by N. W. Bawcutt *Methuen*
(*Revels Plays*) 1958 18s

This play was written in collaboration with William Rowley (1585?-
1642?) who was part-author, like Middleton himself, of many other
plays, including some of Dekker's.

*Milton, John (1608-74) POETICAL WORKS 2 vols. ed. by Helen
Darbishire *O.U.P.* (*Oxford English Texts*) 1952-5 35s each
760 pp

Vol. 1: *Paradise Lost*, based on the first edition of 1667, corrected by the second of 1674 and the manuscript. The value of retaining Milton's own punctuation and spelling for the full understanding and appreciation of the work is strongly emphasised. Vol. 2: *Paradise Regained*; *Samson Agonistes*; *Poems Upon Several Occasions, both English and Latin.*

POEMS ed. by Helen Darbishire *O.U.P.* 1961 25s 696 pp
'This edition . . . is a reprint, as careful as Editor and Printer can make it, from the printed copies published in the Poet's lifetime . . . *Paradise Lost* is given in the text of 1674 (the second edition), *Paradise Regained* and *Samson Agonistes* in that of 1671.'

THE POETICAL WORKS *O.U.P.* (*Standard Authors*) (1938) rev. edn. by Helen Darbishire 1958 16s 644 pp
This new edition for the series is based on the editor's *O.E.T.* edition in two volumes entered above. Also included are prose translations of all the foreign poems from the Columbia University Press edition of Milton.

THE ENGLISH POEMS ed. by H. C. Beeching *O.U.P.* (*Worlds Classics*) 1941 7s 6d
With an introduction by Charles Williams, and *A Reader's Guide to Milton*, by William Skeat. Spelling modernised.

COMPLETE ENGLISH POEMS ed. by John Gawsworth *Macdonald* (*Illustrated Classics*) 1953 15s; *Dent* (*Everyman*) (1909) ed. by B. A. Wright, with glossary and including the Latin poems 1956 10s 6d; *Nelson* (*Classics*) 1954 7s; *Macmillan* (*Globe Library*) (1877) 1955 16s 626 pp
See also the Nonesuch omnibus edition of Milton's *Complete Poetry and Selected Prose*, entered in the *Essays and Belles Lettres* section.

Moore, Thomas (1779-1852) POETICAL WORKS ed. by A. D. Godley *O.U.P.* (*Standard Authors*) 1910
Popular *Irish Melodies* (1807), *Lalla Rookh* (1818), and other minor verse by Byron's friend and biographer. The lyrics in the first-named were set to music by Sir John Stevenson.

Morris, William (1834-96) THE DEFENCE OF GUENEVERE; AND OTHER POEMS *O.U.P.* (*Worlds Classics*) 1914
This selection included *The Life and Death of Jason* (1867). Refer also to the Nonesuch omnibus of *Selected Writings in Prose and Poetry*, entered in the *Essays and Belles Lettres* section. The definitive edition of William Morris's *Complete Works* was published by Longmans, 1910-15, with introductions by May Morris, who wrote the indispensable biography of her father, *William Morris: Artist, Writer and Socialist*, 2 vols. Blackwell, 1936.

*Muir, Edwin (1887-1959) COLLECTED POEMS: 1921-58 *Faber* 1960 25s
Impressive, intellectual and sustained, these poems by a writer who was aloof from fashions and from the superficial approaches to the reading

public so damaging to some of his contemporaries, are likely to take their place with the best of the century's poetic output.

Newbolt, Sir Henry (1862-1938) POEMS NEW AND OLD *Murray* (1918) 1946 10s 6d
Ballads and lyrics, some of which have been set to music.

Newman, John Henry (1801-90) COLLECTED POEMS *O.U.P.* (*Standard Authors*) 1914
Refer also to the *Reynard Library* selection of Newman's prose and poetry, entered in the *Essays and Belles Lettres* section. The long, religious, dramatic monologue, *The Dream of Gerontius* (1866) is the principal poem, and many of the short ones are well-known hymns.

Noyes, Alfred (1880-1958) COLLECTED POEMS *Murray* (1950) 1963 30s
Lyrics, narrative poems, and an epic poem *Drake*, by a popular poet, who, wrote Walter Jerrold, was 'not ashamed of having sat at the feet of Tennyson.'

Oldham, John (1653-83) POEMS ed. by Bonamy Dobrée *Centaur Press* 1960 21s
Satirical verse admired by his contemporary John Dryden.

*Otway, Thomas (1652-85) PLAYS, POEMS AND LOVE-LETTERS 2 vols. ed. by J. Ghosh *O.U.P.* 70s 1084 pp
BEST PLAYS *Benn* (*Mermaid*) 1888
The best play, *Venice Preserv'd* (1682) is included in the *Worlds Classics* collection of *Five Restoration Tragedies*, edited by Bonamy Dobrée, entered in the next section.

*Owen, Wilfred (1893-1918) POEMS (1920) ed. by Edmund Blunden *Chatto* (1931) 1947 10s 6d
Owen was one of the best of all the young poets killed in World War I. Apart from their poignancy, his poems are greatly admired for the technical accomplishment they reveal, and for Owen's mastery of assonance.

Parnell, Thomas (1679-1718) POEMS (1722)
These are included in part (a total of thirty-nine poems) in *Minor Poets of the 18th Century*, edited by Hugh I'Anson Fausset, entered in the next section.

*Patmore, Coventry Kersey Dighton (1823-96) POEMS ed. by Frederick Page *O.U.P.* (*Standard Authors*) 1948 12s 6d 534 pp
The late Frederick Page wrote the standard critical biography of Patmore: *Patmore: A Study In Poetry*, O.U.P., 1933. The principal works read today are the narrative poem *The Angel In the House* (1858) an idealisation of the Victorian domestic woman; and the far profounder odes called collectively *The Unknown Eros* (1890) containing Patmore's best poetry.

Peacock, Thomas Love (1785-1866) POEMS ed. by Brimley
 Johnson *Routledge (Muses Library)* 1906
Scattered through the pages of Peacock's novels are some excellent
drinking songs and other poems. In this long out-of-print volume they
were collected for the first time, together with some longer pieces, such
as *Rhododaphne* (1818).

Peele, George (1554?-96) THE LIFE AND MINOR WORKS 3 vols. ed.
 by Charles T. Prouty *Yale University Press* 1953- *in progress*
This chief pre-Shakespearean playwright has been neglected by editors
since A. H. Bullen's two volumes published in 1888. But his best play
The Old Wives' Tale: a comedy (1595), is included in McIlwraith's *Five
Elizabethan Comedies*, entered in the next section,

*Poe, Edgar Allan (1809-49) POEMS AND ESSAYS ed. by Andrew
 Lang *Dent (Everyman)* (1927) 1955 8s 6d
All the poems are here, and among the prose pieces, the well-known
exposition of *The Poetic Principle*.

POEMS AND MISCELLANIES ed. by R. Brimley Johnson *O.U.P.
(Standard Authors)* (1927) 1947 12s 6d 578 pp
Includes the literary criticism, and *The Poetic Principle*.

TALES, POEMS AND ESSAYS *Collins (Classics)* 1953 7s

Pope, Alexander (1688-1744) THE TWICKENHAM EDITION OF THE
 POEMS OF ALEXANDER POPE 6 vols. (in seven parts) General
 Editor: John Butt *Methuen* 1939-54 (with revised editions of
 some volumes at later dates)
This great edition, one of the triumphs of post-war publishing, may be
bought separately or as a set: Vol. 1: *Pastoral Poetry* and the *Essay on
Criticism* (55s); vol. 2: *The Rape of the Lock, and Other Poems* (70s); vol. 3:
(Part 1): *An Essay on Man*; vol. 3: (Part 2): *Epistles To Several Persons*
(45s each part); vol. 4: *The Imitations of Horace* (42s); vol. 5: *The Dunciad*
(45s); and vol. 6: *Minor Poems* (45s).
Each volume is edited by a specialist, who provides a long introduction
and extensive notes.

*THE ONE VOLUME TWICKENHAM POPE ed. by John Butt *Methuen*
1963 40s 848 pp
'The first complete one volume edition of the poems (except the Homer
translation) for fifty years, with a selection of annotations from the
individual volumes of the Twickenham edition.'

COLLECTED POEMS ed. by Bonamy Dobrée *Dent (Everyman)*
(1924) 1962 7s 6d; ed. by M. A. W. Ward *Macmillan (Globe
Library)* (1869) 12s 6d 506 pp

POEMS *Nelson (Classics)* 1954 6s
Separate editions of *The Rape of the Lock* are available in students'
editions.

THE ILIAD OF HOMER translated by Alexander Pope (1715-20) *O.U.P. (Worlds Classics)* 1902 7s 6d; THE ODYSSEY OF HOMER translated by Alexander Pope (1725-6) *O.U.P. (Worlds Classics)* (1903)

Pope's translation of *The Iliad* into English heroic couplets, was probably the most popular translation ever made, and may still be read with pleasure.

Praed, Winthrop Mackworth (1802-39) SELECTED POEMS ed. by Kenneth Allott *Routledge (Muses Library)* 1953 18s

Some political poems, the full text of *Poems of Life and Manners*, and occasional poems: light, graceful verse, collected in 1864 by Derwent Coleridge.

Prior, Matthew (1664-1721) DIALOGUES OF THE DEAD ed. by A. R. Waller *C.U.P.* 1907 32s 6d

With other works in prose and verse.

POEMS ON SEVERAL OCCASIONS (1709; 1720) ed. by A. R. Waller *C.U.P.* 1905 35s

Charming *petit vers* and *vers de société*, with some social satires and longer pieces. The prose *Dialogues of the Dead* consist of four imaginary conversations between famous persons; for example: Oliver Cromwell talking to another; John Locke, conversing with Montaigne.

Quarles, Francis (1592-1644) EMBLEMS (1635) ed. by A. B. Grosart 1880-1

The only collected edition of Quarles's works was Grosart's in three volumes, which included *Emblems: Divine and Moral*. These consist of minor devotional verse, some epigrams, and some dull Biblical dialogues. On the whole, Quarles was the least interesting of the metaphysicals.

*Ralegh, Sir Walter (1552?-1618) POEMS ed. by Agnes M. C. Latham *Routledge (Muses Library)* 1951 10s 6d; 1962 7s 6d (paperback)

Collects all the poems now attributed to Ralegh; some have not appeared in any previous collection. Original spelling of the Hatfield House manuscripts is retained. Refer also to Gerald Bullett's anthology *Silver Poets of the 16th Century*, entered in the next section.

Ramsay, Allan (1686-1758) SELECTED POEMS ed. by H. Harvey Wood *Oliver and Boyd* (1940) 1946 5s

These pastorals and songs of a Scottish poet were first signs of the approaching era of the Romantic poets.

*Roberts, Michael (1902-48) COLLECTED POEMS *Faber* 1948 18s

One of the best poets of his generation, and a skilful, critical anthologist, Michael Roberts had barely reached his full stature as man of letters at his death.

*Rochester, John Wilmot (Earl of) (1647–80) POEMS ed. by Vivian de Sola Pinto *Routledge* (*Muses Library*) 1953 15s
A reliable text of everything that can be reasonably ascribed to Rochester, with an appendix of doubtful poems. Contains a long introduction, with notes, and for the first time autograph poems in the Duke of Portland's collection at the Library of the University of Nottingham, together with a selection of critical comments on Rochester's work from the seventeenth to the twentieth centuries, that is, from Marvell to F. R. Leavis. A classic edition of Rochester's *Collected Works*, edited by John Hayward, was published in a limited edition by the Nonesuch Press, 1926.

*Rosenberg, Isaac (1890–1918) COLLECTED POEMS *Chatto* 1950 15s
A foreword by Siegfried Sassoon pays a tribute to the splendid promise of the work left by this soldier-poet, who was killed in action in World War I. A volume of his prose and poetry was edited by Gordon Bottomley and Denys Harding in 1937.

*Rossetti, Christina Georgina (1830–94) GOBLIN MARKET AND OTHER POEMS (1862–9) *O.U.P.* (*Worlds Classics*) 1913 7s 6d
Includes *The Prince's Progress* (1866).

POEMS ed. by Kathleen Jarvis *Mowbray* 1955 6s

*Rossetti, Dante Gabriel (1828–82) POEMS (1870; 1881) ed. by Oswald Doughty *Dent* (*Everyman*) 1961 15s
Supersedes the *Everyman* edition of 1912 and takes its place as the best modern edition. It presents the text of the 1881 edition in full, plus some posthumously published poetry included in William Michael Rossetti's edition of his brother's works issued in 1886, and reprinted in 1911, together with a select bibliography and an introduction.

POEMS AND TRANSLATIONS *O.U.P.* (*Standard Authors*) (1913) 1960 18s
The 1850–70 texts, including a prose story *Hand and Soul*.

Rowe, Nicholas (1674–1718) THREE PLAYS ed. by J. R. Sutherland *Scholartis Press* 1929
Tamerlane (1701); *The Fair Penitent* (1703) and *Jane Shore* (1714) by one of Shakespeare's first editors (1709). Refer also to Bonamy Dobrée's collection of *Five Restoration Tragedies*, entered in the next section, for the text of *The Fair Penitent*.

Russell, George William (1867–1935) COLLECTED POEMS *Macmillan* 1926
Mystical and lyrical verse by an Irish poet, known by his pen-initials 'A.E.'.

*Sackville-West, Victoria (1892–1962) THE LAND *Heinemann* 1926 12s 6d Illus.
Georgics in praise of life on the land in the author's beloved Kent. This long, descriptive poem received the Hawthornden Prize.

Savage, Richard (1697–1743) POETICAL WORKS ed. by Clarence
Tracy *Cambridge University Press* 1962 35s
A definitive edition of the poetry of a minor poet, immortalised, not by
his own work, but by Dr. Samuel Johnson's sympathetic and appreciative *Account* (1744), later incorporated in Johnson's *Lives of the Poets*.

Scott, Alexander (1530–84) POEMS ed. by Alexander Scott *Oliver
and Boyd* 1952 7s 6d
Rare poems formerly collected by the Scottish Text Society, and in 1902
by the Early English Text Society.

*Scott, Sir Walter (1771–1832) POETICAL WORKS ed. by J. Logie
Robertson *O.U.P.* (*Standard Authors*) (1904) 1959 18s 978 pp
'This edition is believed to contain every known poem and fragment of
verse that Scott wrote. It is based on the standard text of Lockhart's
editions of 1833 and 1841, collated with more recent editions.'

SONGS AND LYRICS ed. by Sir Herbert Grierson *Oliver and Boyd*
1942 5s
A selection for general reading. The narrative poem *The Lady of the Lake*,
six cantos, 1810, is available separately in many editions for students.

Shadwell, Thomas (1642?–92) BEST PLAYS ed. by George Saintsbury *Benn* (*Mermaid*) 1903
A Whig poet and dramatist, who succeeded Dryden as poet laureate.
The four plays in the only selection are said to be worth the general
reader's attention, one, *The Sullen Lovers* (1668) being an adaptation of
Molière's *Les Fâcheux*. Montague Summers edited his *Complete Works*,
5 vols. Fortune Press, 1927.

*Shakespeare, William (1564–1616) WORKS (1623)

First Folio Facsimile

Kökeritz, Helge MR. WILLIAM SHAKESPEARE'S COMEDIES, HISTORIES
AND TRAGEDIES: a facsimile edition prepared by Helge Kökeritz
with an introduction by Charles Tyler Prouty *O.U.P.* 1955
90s 940 pp

Complete Works in One Volume
(*standard editions arranged under editors*)

Alexander, Peter THE TUDOR SHAKESPEARE edited with an introduction and glossary *Collins* 1951 17s 6d 1380 pp; and a
'Players' Edition', illustrated with twenty-four pictures of actors
from Burbage to Richard Burton 20s
Both editions have the preliminary matter to the First Folio.

Clark, W. G. and W. A. Wright THE GLOBE SHAKESPEARE *Macmillan* (1864) 1953 16s 1212 pp
The text, with glossary, follows the Cambridge Shakespeare.

Craig, W. J. THE OXFORD SHAKESPEARE *O.U.P.* (*Standard Authors*)
(1906) 1958 16s 1176 pp

The spelling has been modernised, and the punctuation revised; glossary;
index of characters and of first lines of songs.

THE OXFORD ILLUSTRATED SHAKESPEARE *O.U.P.* 1955 30s 1180 pp
Illus. with thirty-two plates from modern stage productions

Sisson, Charles Jasper ODHAMS' SHAKESPEARE *Odhams Press* 1954
30s 1376 pp Glossary; index of characters

Standard Edition in more than One Volume

Collins (*Classics*) 4 vols. ed. by Peter Alexander 1954 7s each;
Dent (*Everyman*) 3 vols. (1906) 1953 10s 6d each (the text follows
Clark and Wright's Cambridge Shakespeare; glossary); *Eyre
and Spottiswoode* (*The London Shakespeare*) 6 vols. ed. by John
Munro 1958 147s (the set) 5000 pp

(A new, annotated and critical edition, including 'an entirely fresh
recension of Shakespeare's text by John Munro', with introductions to
each play, a bibliography of the text, and the sources of the plot; printed
in single column throughout.)

OXFORD STANDARD AUTHORS 3 vols. *O.U.P.* 1911-12 21s each
(60s the set) Vol. 1: Comedies 1168 pp; vol. 2: Histories and
Poems 1220 pp; vol. 3: Tragedies 1312 pp

One Play—One Volume

THE ARDEN SHAKESPEARE general editors, Harold F. Brooks
and Harold Jenkins revised editions in progress *Methuen* 1951-
18s to 25s each volume

The new edition for students is nearly complete. Text, critical apparatus
and notes on same page, with long introductions. *The Poems*, edited
by F. T. Prince, was published in 1960, 21s.

THE NEW SHAKESPEARE ed. by Sir Arthur Quiller-Couch and
John Dover Wilson *C.U.P.* 1921 *in progress* 20s each

The *Cambridge Pocket Shakespeare*, *in progress*, reprints the text of the
parent series, in paperback editions, 5s each, without introductions and
notes, but with glossary.

THE NEW TEMPLE SHAKESPEARE ed. by M. R. Ridley *Dent*
1934-6 6s each (£24 the set of 40 volumes, in leather bindings)

Prefaces; glossary to each volume; with decorations by Eric Gill; pocket
size.

THE PENGUIN SHAKESPEARE ed. by G. B. Harrison *Penguin Books*
1937- *in progress* 2s 6d, 3s 6d and 5s each

Spelling and punctuation modernised. Includes *The Narrative Poems*
1959 2s 6d.

Facsimile editions of the quartos, edited by Sir Walter Greg, in collotype
reproduction, are in progress, ten plays available to date, O.U.P., 25s each.

The Sonnets

*SHAKESPEARE'S SONNETS ed. by Martin Seymour-Smith *Heinemann* (*Poetry Bookshelf*) 1963 10s 6d
This edition is notable for the editor's adherence to the old-spelling text, based on the 1609 quarto; for the long, critical introduction; and the detailed commentary, pages 119–90, in which linguistic and other difficulties are explained, and allusions interpreted.

THE SONNETS OF WILLIAM SHAKESPEARE *Blackwell* (*Shakespeare Head Press*) 1948 8s 6d; ed. by M. R. Ridley *Dent* (*New Temple Shakespeare* 1936 6s

The Poems

*THE POEMS OF SHAKESPEARE ed. by F. T. Prince *Methuen* (*Arden Shakespeare*) 1960 21s; THE NARRATIVE POEMS ed. by G. B. Harrison *Penguin Books* 1959 2s 6d
Students are referred to *A Complete Concordance or Verbal Index to Words, Phrases and Passages in the Dramatic Works of Shakespeare*, by John Bartlett, Macmillan (1894) 1910, 120s, quarto, with a supplement to the *Poems* in the current edition; and to *The Oxford Shakespeare Glossary*, by C. T. Onions, O.U.P., revised 1953, 15s. This useful reference work is 'an analysis of Shakespeare's vocabulary in the light of the results of the *Oxford Dictionary*'.

Shanks, Edward (1892–1953) POEMS, 1912–1932; POEMS, 1939–1952) *Macmillan* 1933; 1954 10s 6d each
POEMS *Sidgwick and Jackson* 1916 6s
Poems written in the traditional forms of English poetry, by a well-known journalist, novelist and man of letters.

*Shelley, Percy Bysshe (1792–1822) POEMS ed. by Thomas Hutchinson *O.U.P.* (*Standard Authors*) (1904) 1934 18s 936 pp
A new text, with variants at the foot of pages, with notes and a bibliography.

2 vols. *Dent* (*Everyman*) (1907) 1953 10s 6d each; *Macdonald* (*Illustrated Classics*) 1949 15s; selections ed. by Edmund Blunden *Collins* (*Classics*) 1954 7s; *Nelson* (*Classics*) (1929) 1954 7s; *O.U.P.* (*Worlds Classics*) 1913 7s 6d; *Penguin Books* 1956 3s 6d
Refer also to the *Nonesuch Press Shelley*, entered in the *Essays and Belles Lettres* section.

Shirley, James (1596–1666) BEST PLAYS ed. by Edmund Gosse *Benn* (*Mermaid*) 1888
Five representative plays, and a Masque: *The Triumph of Peace* (1633). Shirley was one of the most prolific dramatists of his period; his best poetry appears to be for the most part in his masques, that he wrote on the model set by Ben Jonson.

Sidney, Sir Philip (1554-86) POEMS (1591; 1598) ed. by William A. Ringler *O.U.P.* (*Oxford English Texts*) 1962 75s 578 pp
A superb critical edition with a long introduction of sixty-six pages and critical apparatus. No holographs exist, and this edition supersedes all others, since the editor analysed more than a hundred manuscripts and prints, most of which were unknown to previous editors. Refer also to Gerald Bullett's *Silver Poets of the 16th Century*, entered in the next section. It includes 108 sonnets, poems from *Arcadia*, and some other songs and sonnets.

*Skelton, John (1460-1529) COMPLETE POEMS ed. by Philip Henderson *Dent* (1931) 1949 20s 510 pp
The spelling has been modernised in this edition of the works of the greatest poet between Chaucer and Wyatt.

POEMS ed. by Vivian de Sola Pinto *Sidgwick and Jackson* 1950 6s
A selection that includes the best of the shorter poems, extracts from the longer poems, *Philip Sparrow*, and *Colin Clout*, with an index of obsolete words.

*Smart, Christopher (1722-71) COLLECTED POEMS 2 vols. ed. by Norman Callan *Routledge* (*Muses Library*) 1949 25s (the set)
Smart's *Song to David* (1763), his most famous poem, will be found in many anthologies.

JUBILATE AGNO ed. by William H. Bond *Hart-Davis* 1954 15s
The editorial notes and introduction of this important edition of Smart's *Rejoice In the Lamb*, first edited by William F. Stead, as 'A Song From Bedlam', Cape, 1939, limited edition, suggest that the poem was meant to be read antiphonally, in the manner of Hebrew poetry. Christopher Smart wrote it between 1756 and 1764, while he was in an asylum, and the manuscript is in the Library of Harvard University.

Smith, Horatio (1779-1849) and James (1775-1839) REJECTED ADDRESSES (1812) *Routledge* 1907; *Methuen* 1903
'Or, The New Theatrum Poetarum.' These amusing parodies of poetry and prose styles of the brothers' distinguished contemporaries are amongst the most brilliant in the language. The brothers pretended that Mr. William Wordsworth, Lord Byron, William Cobbett, etc., had submitted addresses to be read at the re-opening of Drury Lane Theatre, 10 October, 1812. Thus *The Baby's Debut*, in the simple style of the common man, takes off admirably the Wordsworthian style advocated in *The Lyrical Ballads* of 1800, and the prose piece *A Hampshire Farmer's Address*, is a delightful parody of Cobbett's forthright self-opinionated pronouncements.

*Sorley, Charles Hamilton (1895-1915) MARLBOROUGH, AND OTHER POEMS *C.U.P.* 1916 8s 6d
Apart from the most memorable title-poem, this small volume contains some short pieces of great promise, never fulfilled, owing to the young soldier-poet's death in action in World War I.

Southey, Robert (1774-1843) POEMS ed. by M. H. Fitzgerald
O.U.P. (*Standard Authors*) 1909
Minor poems, and the once-popular narrative poems *Thalaba the
Destroyer* (1801); *The Curse of Kehama* (1810); *Roderick, the Last of the
Goths* (1814); *Madoc* (1805), and *A Tale of Paraguay* (1825), together with
The Vision of Judgement (1821) that provoked Byron's famous parody
in 1823.

*Spenser, Edmund (1552?-99) POETICAL WORKS ed. by J. C. Smith
and Ernest de Selincourt O.U.P. (*Standard Authors*) 1912 15*s*
814 pp
With critical notes, a biographical and critical essay by de Selincourt, a
glossary by H. Alexander, together with a reprint from the 1580 edition
of *The Correspondence of Spenser and Harvey* (*Three Letters Between two
Universitie Men*).

MINOR POEMS ed. by Ernest de Selincourt O.U.P. (*Oxford
English Texts*) 1910 30*s* 590 pp
These are *The Shepheard's Calender* (1579); *Complaints* (1591); *Daphnaida*
(1591); *Colin Clout* (1595); *Fowre Hymns* (1596), *Prothalamion* (1596) and
miscellaneous sonnets.

THE FAERIE QUEENE 2 vols. ed. by J. C. Smith O.U.P. (*Oxford
English Texts*) 1909 50*s* 1066 pp
Contains other poems, and is complementary to the above volume of
Minor Poems.

THE FAERIE QUEENE 2 vols. ed. by J. W. Hales Dent (*Everyman*)
1955 10*s* 6*d* each
With a glossary.

THE SHEPHEARDE'S CALENDER AND OTHER POEMS ed. by Philip
Henderson Dent (*Everyman*) (1932) 1956 10*s* 6*d*
Completes the *Everyman* Spenser.

*Squire, Sir John Collings (1884-1958) COLLECTED POEMS *Mac-
millan* 1959 25*s*
With an appreciation by John Betjeman.

Stanley, Thomas (1625-78) POEMS AND TRANSLATIONS (1647;
1651) ed. by Galbraith Miller Crump O.U.P. (*Oxford English
(Texts*) 1962 70*s*
The first edition of this minor poet's work to include as far as is known,
everything he wrote. Editorial annotations and collation with extant
manuscripts and early editions for variant readings, a life of Stanley,
sources and a commentary, make this as near to a definitive edition as
modern scholarship can achieve.

*Stephens, James (1882-1950) COLLECTED POEMS *Macmillan* (1926)
1954 15*s*
An Irish poet with the gift of phrase and more than a touch of fantasy.

K

*Stevenson, Robert Louis (1850-94) COLLECTED POEMS ed. by Janet Adam Smith *Hart-Davis* 1950 18s 572 pp
All of the poems published during Stevenson's lifetime, a selection of those left unpublished in book form; a thirty-page introduction and editorial notes.

POEMS ed. by Ernest Rhys *Dent (Everyman)* 1925 6s 6d
Contains *Underwoods* (1887) *A Child's Garden of Verses, Songs of Travel,* and *Ballads* (1890).

A CHILD'S GARDEN OF VERSES (1885) *Bodley Head* 1895 9s 6d
Illus. quarto; *Collins (Classics)* (1928) 1958 5s Illus.; *Harrap* 6s 6d Illus.; *Nelson Classics)* 1926 5s; *Dent (Children's Illustrated Classics)* 1960 10s 6d
The last edition contains other poems for children, with an introduction by D. C. Browning, and with colour drawings by Mary Shillabeer.

Suckling, Sir John (1609-42) POEMS
The most complete text known, of seventy-eight poems, will be found in R. G. Howarth's *Minor Poets of the 17th Century*, entered in the next section.

Surrey, Henry Howard (Earl of) (1517?-1547) POEMS
These will be found in Gerald Bullett's *Silver Poets of the 16th Century* entered in the next section.

*Swift, Jonathan (1667-1745) POEMS 3 vols. ed. by Sir Harold Williams *O.U.P.* (1938) 1957 105s (the set) 1316 pp Illus.
One of the greatest editorial achievements of the twentieth century.

2 vols. ed. by Joseph Horrell *Routledge (Muses Library)* 1958 42s (the set)
A collated text of everything 'now accepted in Swift's canon', in which the arrangement of the poems is by subject and 'kind', thus displaying and emphasising, suggests the editor, Swift's 'range and diversity'. Refer also to John Hayward's edition of Swift's *Gulliver's Travels* for the *Nonesuch Library*, which includes a selection of poems, and is entered in the *Essays and Belles Lettres* section.

*Swinburne, Algernon Charles (1837-1909) SELECTED POEMS ed. by Edward Shanks *Macmillan* 1950 8s 6d; ed. by Laurence Binyon *O.U.P. (Worlds Classics)* 1939 7s 6d; ed. by Bonamy Dobrée *Penguin Books* 1961 3s 6d
The *Golden Pine* edition of Swinburne's collected poetical works was last published by Heinemann, in six vols. 1917. Another selection in addition to the above will be found in Richard Church's *Everyman* volume of Swinburne's *Poems and Prose*, entered in the *Essays and Belles Lettres* section.

Symons, Arthur (1865-1945) POEMS 2 vols. *Heinemann* 1902
Remembered chiefly by his essays on art, and Italy, Paris and its people,

Symons here collected his lyrics and verse, written for the most part in the tradition of Victorian verse.

*Synge, John Millington (1871-1909) POEMS ed. by Robin Skelton O.U.P. 1962 21s
Volume 1 of a definitive edition of Synge's *Collected Works*, in progress. This edition more than doubles the text of his verse hitherto published, and includes translations, with variant readings.

Tabb, John Bannister (1845-1909) THE POETRY OF FATHER TABB ed. by Francis A. Litz *Bodley Head* 1928
Collects the poetry in a number of small volumes published from 1882 to 1902. Father Tabb was an American of Richmond, Virginia, of Scottish descent. He held the view that 'the ultimate, perhaps if we except the dramatic, the only authentic art form is the lyric'.

*Tennyson, Alfred (*1st Baron*) (1809-92) THE POEMS AND PLAYS O.U.P. (*Standard Authors*) (1914) 1953 12s 6d 884 pp
The revised edition supersedes the first by the addition of the later poems up to the poet's death, and the plays *Queen Mary* (1875); *Harold* (1876); *Becket* (1884) and other dramatic pieces.

POETICAL WORKS *Macmillan* (*Globe*) (1894) 1899 12s 6d 648 pp; ed. and sel. by Sir Charles Tennyson *Collins* (*Classics*) 1956 7s; and, 'The Idylls of the King'; and 'The Princess' *Collins* (*Classics*) 1954 7s; Poems 2 vols. ed. by Mildred Bozman *Dent* (*Everyman*) 1950 6s 6d each; sel. by Edmund Blunden *Heinemann* (*Poetry Bookshelf*) 1950 8s 6d; sel. by John Gawsworth *Macdonald* (*Illustrated Classics*) 1951 15s; sel. by Sir John Squire *Macmillan* (*Golden Treasury series*) (1947) 1959 7s 6d; *Nelson* (*Classics*) 1954 7s; sel. by Stephen Gwynn O.U.P. (*Worlds Classics*) 1950 6s

*Thomas, Dylan (1914-1953) COLLECTED POEMS, 1934-52 *Dent* 1952 18s
It is not often that a twentieth-century poet has produced work with the stamp of genius recognised by critics and the great public during his lifetime, but in this small class Dylan Thomas made his mark. His collected volume became a bestseller; his personality legendary.

UNDER MILK WOOD *Dent* 1954 10s 6d; (*Aldine Paperbacks*) 1962 5s
'A play for voices.' It had remarkable success both on the radio for which it was written and on the stage.

*Thomas, Edward (1878-1917) COLLECTED POEMS *Faber* 1917 15s
THE TRUMPET AND OTHER POEMS *Faber* (*Sesame Books*) 1940 3s 6d
Edward Thomas, poet and essayist, was a true poet of the countryside, and the selection contains many poems with the stamp of immortality upon them. He was killed in action in World War I.

*Thompson, Francis (1859-1907) COLLECTED POEMS ed. by
Wilfrid Meynell *O.U.P. (Standard Authors)* (1937) 1951 12s 6d

SELECTED POEMS ed. by Wilfrid Meynell *Cape* 1929 6s; *Nelson
(Classics)* 1954 6s
Wilfrid Meynell, editor and discerning friend of poets, without whose
help it is doubtful if Francis Thompson would have survived, has provided a biographical note to the standard selection.

*Thomson, James (1700-48) POETICAL WORKS ed. by J. Logie
Robertson *O.U.P. (Standard Authors)* 1908 12s 6d 540 pp
The Castle of Indolence (1748) Thomson's most enduring long poem,
written in Spenserian stanzas, is available separately, ed. by Alec M.
Hardie, with an introduction by Edmund Blunden, O.U.P., 1956,
12s 6d. Extracts from *The Seasons*, a poem in blank verse, in four books
(1726-30), are to be found in some anthologies of longer poems.

*Thomson, James ('B.V.') (1834-82) THE CITY OF DREADFUL NIGHT
and other poems (1880) ed. by Edmund Blunden *Methuen* 1932
'B.V.' (for Bysshe Vanolis) was Thomson's pen-name. His masterpiece,
a gloomy, but powerful poem, was first contributed to a periodical (1874)
and earned him the soubriquet 'The Pessimist'.

*Tourneur, Cyril (1575?-1626) BEST PLAYS *Benn (Mermaid)* (1888)
1954 16s
Included in the *Mermaid Dramatists* with the plays of John Webster,
entered below. The two chosen are *The Revenger's Tragedy* (1607) and
The Atheist's Tragedy (1611). Allardyce Nicoll edited Tourneur's *Complete Works* in a limited edition for collectors, published 1930.

*Traherne, Thomas (1637-74) CENTURIES, POEMS AND THANKS-
GIVINGS 2 vols. ed. by H. M. Margoliouth *O.U.P. (Oxford
English Texts)* 1958 84s (the set) 700 pp
Supersedes all other editions of the poems and spiritual meditations, and
includes twelve early poems now assigned to Traherne. The original
spelling and punctuation is retained, with variants indicated, and altera-
tions made by the poet's brother Philip printed parallel with the originals.

POEMS OF FELICITY ed. by Sir H. I. Bell *O.U.P. (Tudor and
Stuart Library)* 1910 15s
'Containing Divine Reflections on the Native Objects of and Infant-Ey.'
This selection was edited from a manuscript prepared by Traherne, but
never published.

CENTURIES ed. by H. M. Margoliouth and Hilda Vaughan
Faith Press 1960 15s
Bertram Dobell first established the authorship of these *Centuries of
Meditation*, and published them in 1908.

*Trevelyan, Robert Calverley (1872-1951) SELECTED POEMS
MacGibbon and Kee 1953 8s 6d

In the preface to Trevelyan's *Collected Works*, 2 vols. Longmans, 1939, Sir Desmond MacCarthy wrote: 'I do not think his good work will be forgotten.'

*Turner, Charles Tennyson (1808-79) A HUNDRED SONNETS ed. by Sir Charles Tennyson and John Betjeman *Hart-Davis* 1960 15s
Lord Tennyson's eldest brother, who added the surname Turner in 1837, contributed to *Poems of Two Brothers* (1827) in which appeared the first work of his great brother. The *Hundred Sonnets* have been selected from Tennyson Turner's *Collected Sonnets* (1880). Sir Harold Nicolson wrote that he was 'a true poet, whose talents, though restricted, were original, delicate, sincere, and above all refreshingly spontaneous'.

Urquhart, Sir Thomas (1611-60) SELECTED POEMS ed. by John Purves *Oliver and Boyd* 1942 5s
Sir Thomas Urquhart of Cromarty was the first English translator of the first books of the works of Rabelais, entered in the *Essays and Belles Lettres* section.

*Vaughan, Henry (1622-95) WORKS ed. by L. C. Martin *O.U.P.* (*Oxford English Texts*) (1914) 1958 65s 771 pp; (*Standard Authors*) 1963 30s
The revised and expanded edition includes letters and all the poems known to have been written by Vaughan 'The Silurist', the greatest religious poet in the language next to Herbert. He got his soubriquet from that part of South Wales, his native country, now called Brecknockshire, which in ancient times was inhabited by a tribe known as the Silures. The new *OSA* edition contains all the poetry and selected prose.

*Waller, Edmund (1606-87) POEMS 2 vols. ed. by G. Thorn Drury *Routledge* (*Muses Library*) 1901
The best lyrics by this Cavalier poet will be found in all anthologies.

*Webster, John (1580?-1625) PLAYS 4 vols. ed. by F. L. Lucas *Chatto* 1927
The best edition of the complete dramatic works.

BEST PLAYS ed. by J. A. Symonds *Benn* (*Mermaid*) (1888) 1954 16s
Bound with two plays of Cyril Tourneur, entered above.

PLAYS ed. by G. B. Harrison *Dent* (*Everyman*) (1933) 1962 8s 6d
Bound with the plays of John Ford, entered above.

THE DUCHESS OF MALFI (1623) and THE WHITE DEVIL (1612) ed. by F. L. Lucas *Chatto* 1957 18s each
The two plays, reissued, with the original introductions, and revised notes, from the standard edition in four volumes, entered above.

THE WHITE DEVIL ed. by G. B. Harrison *Dent* (*Temple Dramatists*) 1933 7s 6d; ed. by John Russell Brown *Methuen* (*Revels Plays*) 1960 21s

*Whitman, Walt (1819-92) LEAVES OF GRASS (1855) ed. by Emory
Holloway *Dent (Everyman)* (1944) 1957 10s 6d; ed. by Malcolm
Cowley *Secker and Warburg* 1960 21s
Everyman includes all that Whitman included in his last edition of *Leaves
of Grass*, the twelfth of 1892. Malcolm Cowley's text is that of the
important first edition of 1855, and was originally reprinted in New
York, 1959. A facsimile edition of the 1860 text, with an introduction
by R. H. Pearce, is available as a paperback, O.U.P., 1962, 18s. Refer
also to the *Nonesuch* Whitman, *Complete Poetry and Selected Prose*,
entered in the *Essays and Belles Lettres* section.

Whittier, John Greenleaf (1807-92) POEMS (1888-9) ed. by
W. Garrett Horder *O.U.P. (Standard Authors)* 1904
A once widely-read American poet, whose narrative poems have now
almost been forgotten. His well-known short poems such as *Barbara
Frietchie*, and *Snowbound*, are in nearly all anthologies.

*Wilde, Oscar (1854-1900) POEMS *Methuen* (1909) 1951 5s
There is a separate edition of *The Ballad of Reading Gaol* (1898), Wilde's
best long poem, published by the Unicorn Press, 1944, 4s 6d. The poems
are also reprinted in the omnibus editions entered in the *Essays and Belles
Lettres* section.

Williams, Charles (1886-1945) COLLECTED PLAYS *O.U.P.* 1963 30s
Nine distinguished plays, chiefly in verse, and on religious themes,
introduced by John Heath-Stubbs, who says Williams here made 'a
very distinctive and original contribution both to the tradition of
religious drama, and to the development of the verse-play as a living
form in our time.'

Winchilsea, Anne Kingsmill Finch, Countess of (1666?-1720)
POEMS ed. by J. Middleton Murry *Cape* 1928
Many of these exquisite poems deserve constant reading; there are eighty-
five in H. I'Anson Fausset's collection of *Minor Poets of the 18th Century*
entered in the next section.

Wither, George (1588-1667) POEMS 2 vols. ed. by Frank Sidgwick
Bullen 1903
Pastorals, lyrics, and *Hymns and Songs of the Church* (1623), together with
Mistress of Phil'arete and the well-known and anthologised 'Shall I,
wasting in despaire Dye, because a woman's fair?'

*Wordsworth, William (1770-1850) THE POETICAL WORKS 5 vols.
ed. by Ernest de Selincourt and Helen Darbishire *O.U.P.*
(Oxford English Texts) 1940-9 201s (the set) 2078 pp
The definitive edition, and one of the great editorial achievements of the
twentieth century. The volumes, separately priced according to length,
from 30s to 42s each, follows the poet's systematic classification of the
poems in groups. Vol. 2 was re-issued in 1952 and vol. 3 in 1954.

POETICAL WORKS ed. by Thomas Hutchinson O.U.P. (*Standard Authors*) (1895; 1904) 1953 16s 1018 pp; 3 vols. ed. by Philip Wayne *Dent* (*Everyman*) (1907-8) 1954 10s 6d each 1373 pp
In the *Everyman* edition the poems are arranged in the order of publication.

THE LYRICAL BALLADS (1798; 1800; 1802; 1805) ed. by H. Littledale O.U.P. 1911 8s 6d; ed. by George Sampson *Methuen* (*English Classics*) (1903; 10th edn. 1940) 1956 8s 6d; *W. H. Allen* (*Dolphin Books*) 1962 7s 6d; *Methuen* 1963 32s 6d
The Lyrical Ballads is reprinted separately for students because the volume is a landmark in the history of English poetry, and is usually regarded as the dawn of the Romantic Movement, long heralded, but here fully and historically affirmed in the famous preface and *Essay On Poetic Diction* Wordsworth wrote for the 2 volumed edition of 1800 and its successors. *The Lyrical Ballads* contained Coleridge's *The Rime of the Ancient Mariner*, and other, shorter pieces, as well as Wordsworth's *Lines Composed Above Tintern Abbey*. The effect of these poems and theories was scarcely felt until 1820.

*THE PRELUDE; OR, GROWTH OF A POET'S MIND ed. by Ernest de Selincourt O.U.P. (*Oxford English Texts*) (1926) revised edition by Helen Darbishire 1959 75s 676 pp
An autobiographical poem, here edited from the manuscripts, and providing for the first time the text of the first version of 1805-6, with revisions in 1817-19, parallel with that of the 1850 edition published posthumously, with critical apparatus, introduction and notes.

ed. by Ernest de Selincourt O.U.P. (*Standard Authors*) 1934 16s
This edition gives the text of the 1805 version, with introduction and notes, based on the parallel text edition noted above.

THE PRELUDE (1850) ed. by E. E. Reynolds *Macmillan* (*Golden Treasury*) 1932 6s 6d
See also volume 3 of the *Everyman* Wordsworth, containing *The Prelude* (1850), together with the companion pieces of an autobiographical nature, *The Excursion* (1814), which was the second part of a projected, but unfinished poetic autobiography called *The Recluse; or Views of Nature, Man and Society* (1888).

SELECTED POETICAL WORKS ed. by H. M. Margoliouth *Collins* (*Classics*) 1959 8s; ed. by W. M. Merchant *Hart-Davis* (*Reynard Library*) 1955 27s 6d 880 pp; ed. by Roger Sharrock *Heinemann* (*Poetry Bookshelf*) 1958 8s 6d; ed. by Matthew Arnold *Macmillan* (*Golden Treasury*) (1879) 1934 8s 6d; *Nelson* (*Classics*) 1928 7s; O.U.P. (*Worlds Classics*) 1913 7s 6d
The selection in the *Reynard Library* contains some of Wordsworth's prose.

*Wyatt, Sir Thomas (1503?-42) COLLECTED POEMS ed. by Kenneth Muir *Routledge* (*Muses Library*) 1949 12s 6d

The poems and songs of the greatest lyric poet of the Tudor period, who shared with Surrey the distinction of introducing the Petrarchan sonnet form into English poetry, are included in Gerald Bullett's collection of *Silver Poets of the 16th Century*, entered in the next section.

*Yeats, William Butler (1865-1939) COLLECTED PLAYS *Macmillan* (1934) 1952 25s 705 pp
COLLECTED POEMS *Macmillan* (1933) 1950 21s 566 pp
The definitive editions of all the dramatic, lyrical and narrative work. The appendix of notes on Gaelic mythology, and events in Irish history of his own time, indicate the occasional sources of Yeats's inspiration. A great edition, with variant readings, somewhat loosely, if not in-accurately, called 'The Variorum Edition' of the *Poems*, edited by Peter Allt and Russell K. Alspach, was published by Macmillan, 1957, 126s, 884 pp, quarto.

SELECTED POEMS ed. by Norman Jeffares *Macmillan* (*Scholars Library*) (1929) 1962 7s 6d
An enlarged edition of a *Golden Treasury* series selection, with notes on difficulties, allusions, legends and the identities of persons.

Young, Edward (1683-1765) POETICAL WORKS (1741; 1752) *Bell* (1896)
Some of Young's lines in his masterpiece, *The Complaint, or Night Thoughts* (1742-5) have a proverbial simplicity, and have passed into the language of common speech.

ANTHOLOGIES OF POETRY AND POETIC DRAMA
(arranged under editors)

Aldington, Richard POETRY OF THE ENGLISH-SPEAKING WORLD *Heinemann* (1947) 1956 30s 963 pp
From Chaucer to T. S. Eliot and W. H. Auden.

Allen, John THREE MEDIEVAL PLAYS *Heinemann* (*Drama Library*) 1953 6s
Everyman; *Master Pierre Pathelin* (a farce); and *The Coventry Nativity Play*. This edition is based on a text edited by Hardin Craig. The farce is translated into English prose from medieval French rhyming couplets. All three plays were written to be acted; hence the editor has had the producer in mind when preparing this edition.

*Auden, Wystan Hugh THE OXFORD BOOK OF LIGHT VERSE *O.U.P.* (1938) 1962 21s 578 pp
'Light verse is used for the purpose of this anthology in a far wider sense than that commonly accorded to the phrase today. It has been taken by the editor to include all verse which is popular in its forms and easily understood, verse which is neither deeply emotional nor obscure, nor

personal, but is casual in its content and unpretentious in its form.' In these words the publisher describes this best of all anthologies of its type. The range in time is from Chaucer to the twentieth century.

THE POET'S TONGUE ed. with John Garrett *Bell* (1935) 1948 13s 6d
'A first approach to poetry.' Balladry is foremost, and the lighter forms of verse from Chaucer and Skelton to T. S. Eliot.

*Auden, Wystan Hugh and Norman Holmes Pearson POETS OF THE ENGLISH LANGUAGE 5 vols. *Eyre and Spottiswoode* 1952 15s each
The most comprehensive collection of its kind in modern anthologies, with notes and biographical summaries. Vol. 1: Langland to Spenser; vol. 2: Marlowe to Marvell; vol. 3: Milton to Goldsmith; vol. 4: Blake to Poe; vol. 5: Tennyson to Yeats.

Ault, Norman ELIZABETHAN LYRICS *Longmans* (1925) 1949 SEVEN-TEENTH CENTURY LYRICS *Longmans* (1928) 1950
Standard anthologies, compiled from an unusually wide variety of sources, including manuscript collections of ballads, old plays and drolleries, with scholarly notes, both biographical and textual, bibliography, and a subject index.

Beattie, William BORDER BALLADS *Penguin Books* 1952 2s 6d
Based on Scott's *Minstrelsy of the Scottish Border*, which see below.

*Boas, Frederick Samuel FIVE PRE-SHAKESPEAREAN COMEDIES *O.U.P.* (*Worlds Classics*) 1934 7s 6d
From the early Tudor period, the editor has chosen: *Fulgens and Lucrece*, by Henry Medwell (1497); *The Four PP*, by John Heywood (1545?); *Ralph Roister Doister*, by Nicolas Udall (1566); *The Supposes*, by George Gascoigne (1566); and *Gammer Gurton's Needle*, by William Stevenson? (1575). The last play is published separately in the *Percy Reprint* series, edited by H. F. B. Brett-Smith, Blackwell 1920, 7s 6d.

SONGS AND LYRICS FROM THE ENGLISH PLAYBOOKS *Cresset Press* 1945 15s

*Bottrall, Ronald and Margaret COLLECTED ENGLISH VERSE *Sidgwick and Jackson* (1947) 1962 21s
'The principles of choice incorporate the standards of the best contemporary literary criticism.'

*Bridges, Robert THE SPIRIT OF MAN *Longmans* 1916 8s 6d
An anthology of prose and poetry, with some French, originally compiled for the troubled years of World War I. Notes and authors are given in an appendix, so that the reader's critical faculties are kept on the alert when reading the extracts, which are arranged in four books under headings such as 'Ideal Love'; 'The Idea of God'; 'Melancholy'.

K*

Brook, G. L. THE HARLEY LYRICS *Manchester University Press* (1948) 1956 12s 6d
The Middle English lyrics of the MS. Harley 2253, of which that great scholar W. P. Ker, said, it contains 'everything best worth remembering in the old lyrical poetry'.

Brown, Carleton ENGLISH LYRICS OF THE THIRTEENTH CENTURY O.U.P. 1932 18s

ENGLISH LYRICS OF THE FOURTEENTH CENTURY O.U.P. (1924) revised by G. V. Smithers 1952 21s

ENGLISH LYRICS OF THE FIFTEENTH CENTURY O.U.P. 1939 21s
Brown's work in this field was completed by R. H. Robbins, entered below.

*Buchan, John (1st Baron Tweedsmuir) THE NORTHERN MUSE *Nelson* 1931 8s 6d
An anthology of Scots vernacular poetry.

*Bullett, Gerald THE ENGLISH GALAXY OF SHORTER POEMS *Dent* (*Everyman*) 1933 6s 6d

SILVER POETS OF THE SIXTEENTH CENTURY *Dent* (*Everyman*) (1947) 1955 8s 6d
A volume of exceptional interest, since it gives the works of Sir Thomas Wyatt; Henry Howard, Earl of Surrey; Sir Philip Sidney; Sir Walter Ralegh; and Sir John Davies. The editor provides a glossary, and introduction, and notes.

Butler, Guy A BOOK OF SOUTH AFRICAN VERSE O.U.P. 1959 18s
Thirty-four poets are represented from Thomas Pringle (born 1789) to Peter Jackson (born 1928).

*Cawley, A. C. EVERYMAN AND MEDIEVAL MIRACLE PLAYS *Dent* (*Everyman*) 1956 7s 6d
Contains the most famous morality play that gave the title to the series, and a new selection of Biblical plays enacted as pageants at Corpus Christi or guild pageants for which sometimes the whole cycle would be played. A little-known piece called *Death of Pilate* comes from Cornwall. Spellings slightly modernised, but the original text retained with glosses and footnotes. An introduction and bibliography add to the value of this collection for students of the beginnings of English drama.

*Cawley, A. C. PEARL; and SIR GAWAIN AND THE GREEN KNIGHT *Dent* (*Everyman*) 1962 10s 6d
Pearl, a religious poem, survives in the British Museum in a unique fourteenth-century manuscript written in the north-west Midland dialect. Professor Cawley, in this notable new *Everyman*, presents the text of the alliterative poem, with some modernisation of spelling, but very restricted; marginal glosses and footnote paraphrases assist readers with other difficulties. In the same manuscript is preserved the narrative poem, *Sir Gawain*, a superb example of medieval romance. For details of

translation into modern English see in the preceding section under the group of anonymous works: *Sir Gawain and the Green Knight*, pages 252-3.

★Cecil, Lord David THE OXFORD BOOK OF CHRISTIAN VERSE *O.U.P.* 1940 18s
The choice is from poems expressing Christian faith and experience: the time range is from fourteenth century and early anonyma to twentieth-century poets.

★Cecil, Lord David and Allen Tate MODERN VERSE IN ENGLISH, 1900-1950 *Eyre and Spottiswoode* 1958 25s 704 pp
'With critical introductions on British and American poetry and biographical notes on the poets included.'

★Chambers, Sir Edmund Kerchever THE OXFORD BOOK OF SIXTEENTH CENTURY VERSE *O.U.P.* 1932 21s 920 pp

Chapman, Robert and Jonathan Bennett AN ANTHOLOGY OF NEW ZEALAND VERSE *O.U.P.* 1956 21s

★Child, Francis James (1825-96) THE ENGLISH AND SCOTTISH POPULAR BALLADS 10 parts in 5 vols. Boston 1882-98; ed. by G. L. Kittredge 5 vols. in 3 *O.U.P.* 19.6 320s (the set) 2712 pp
The greatest anthology of balladry, providing texts of extant versions of 305 traditional ballads, with notes, sources, historical material, textual analysis and 'a description of comparable foreign analogues'. Francis Child, like his eighteenth-century predecessor Bishop Percy, entered below, drew some of his material from the seventeenth-century manuscript known as *The Percy Folio*, in the British Museum.

★Church, Richard and two others POEMS OF OUR TIME *Dent (Everyman)* (1945) 1962 8s 6d
Presents in a choice made by the principal editor and Mildred Bozman, and Dame Edith Sitwell, characteristic work by 150 poets writing from 1900 to 1946, with a supplement to 1960 by the last-named.

Cohen, John Michael THE PENGUIN BOOK OF COMIC AND CURIOUS VERSE *Penguin Books* 1952 3s 6d
MORE COMIC AND CURIOUS VERSE *Penguin Books* 1956 3s 6d
Includes contemporary poets as well as the classics of humorous writing in verse.

Collins, Vere Henry A BOOK OF NARRATIVE VERSE *O.U.P.* (*Worlds Classics*) 1930 6s
Contains forty-three poems from Chaucer to Kipling, some being given complete: for example, *Peter Grimes* (Crabbe) and *The Rape of the Lock* (Pope). Introduced by an essay on the nature of narrative poetry by Edmund Blunden.

Cunliffe, John William EARLY ENGLISH CLASSICAL TRAGEDIES *O.U.P.* 1912 25s

Texts, with introduction, glossary and notes of: *Gorboduc* (1565); *Jocasta* (1575); *Gismond of Salerne* (*Tancred and Gismund*) (1591); and *The Misfortunes of Arthur*, performed in 1587.

Daglish, Jack EIGHT METAPHYSICAL POETS *Heinemann* 1962 9s 6d
A representative selection of poems by Donne, Herbert, Carew, Crashaw, Vaughan, King, Marvell, and Cowley. Includes notes, a critical estimate, and a biography of each poet.

*de la Mare, Walter (1873-1956) COME HITHER *Constable* (1923) 1949 30s 824 pp Illus.
'A collection of rhymes and poems for the young of all ages.'

*de Sola Pinto, Vivian and Allan Edwin Rodway THE COMMON MUSE *Chatto* 1957 25s Illus.
A scholarly anthology of popular British ballads, broadside poetry, doggerel from street rhymes. A long introduction and copious notes, with reproductions of old prints, title-pages and printers' devices, add to the attraction of the book. Poems are classed in groups: historical; crime and punishment; rural; marital; vocational, etc., and the time range is from traditional verse of the fifteenth century, to popular songs of the twentieth century

Dearmer, Percy and others THE OXFORD BOOK OF CAROLS *O.U.P.* 1928 12s 6d; words only 4s 6d

*Dobrée, Bonamy FIVE HEROIC PLAYS *O.U.P.* (*Worlds Classics*) 1960 8s 6d
Complementary anthology to *Five Restoration Tragedies*. The new volume contains: *The Tragedy of Mustapha*, by Robert Boyle; *The Empress of Morocco*, by Elkaneh Settle; *The Destruction of Jerusalem*, by John Crowne; *Sophonisba*, by Nathaniel Lee; and *Aureng-Zebe*, by John Dryden. These dramas were all performed between 1665 and 1667.

*Dobrée, Bonamy FIVE RESTORATION TRAGEDIES *O.U.P.* (*Worlds Classics*) 1928 6s
Contents: *All For Love*, by John Dryden (1678); *Venice Preserv'd*, by Otway (1682); *Oroonoko*, by Southerne (1696); *The Fair Penitent*, by Rowe (1703); and *Cato*, by Addison (1713).

*Dobrée, Bonamy and Sir Herbert Read THE LONDON BOOK OF ENGLISH VERSE *Eyre and Spottiswoode* (1930) 1956 21s 928 pp
About one-third of the poems are not in other anthologies. The collection is classified under appropriate headings: narrative verse; descriptive; metaphysical; and so on.

*Fausset, Hugh I'Anson MINOR POETS OF THE EIGHTEENTH CENTURY *Dent* (*Everyman*) 1930
Thomas Parnell; Matthew Green; John Dyer; William Collins; Anne, Countess of Winchilsea.

*Fellowes, Edmund Horace ENGLISH MADRIGAL VERSE, 1588-1632 *O.U.P.* (1920) 1931 21*s*
Edited from the original song books.

Fergusson, Sir James THE GREEN GARDEN *Oliver and Boyd* 1946 5*s*
A collection of Scottish poetry ranging from thirteenth to eighteenth century, emphasising lesser-known verse.

*Flower, Desmond and Margaret CASSELL'S ANTHOLOGY OF ENGLISH POETRY *Cassell* (1938) 1946 12*s* 6*d* 512 pp

Franklin, Alexander SEVEN MIRACLE PLAYS *O.U.P.* 1963 10*s* 6*d*
Adaptations for modern readers, of *Noah's Flood*, and two others from the *Chester Cycle*, together with a *Towneley* play, two from the *York Cycle*, the *Norwich* play of *Adam and Eve*, and a version of *Abraham and Isaac* from the Brome and Dublin manuscripts.

*Gardner, Helen THE METAPHYSICAL POETS *O.U.P.* 1961 18*s*
Published originally in 1957 as a Penguin anthology. This library edition provides readers with a masterly anthology in a format worthy of its scholarship. The selection consists of 200 poems from about forty authors from Shakespeare to Herrick and Richard Leigh, who wrote either occasionally or entirely, in the style termed 'metaphysical'. The editor adds biographical notes.

*Gordon, Robert Kay ANGLO-SAXON POETRY *Dent (Everyman)* (1927) 1962 7*s* 6*d*
Professor Gordon has selected and translated poetry written between A.D. 650 and 1000, from *Beowulf* and *Widsith*, to *The Battle of Maldon*. English versions in prose include *The Dream of the Rood*, *The Finnesburg Fragment*, *Genesis*, *Judith*, *The Ruin*, and *The Seafarer*. This volume includes 'almost the entire contents of the famous Exeter and Vercelli manuscripts'.

*Graves, Robert ENGLISH AND SCOTTISH BALLADS *Heinemann* 1957 9*s* 6*d*
A selection of forty of the best ballads made by a modern poet from what he terms 'the golden age of balladry', that is, the early fourteenth to mid-sixteenth centuries, with a long introduction and critical notes. Obsolete words are explained in footnotes.

*Green, Roger Lancelyn A CENTURY OF HUMOROUS VERSE, 1850-1950 *Dent (Everyman)* 1959 10*s* 6*d*
Includes some limericks. The anthology provides specimens of the best work of 120 authors, some well-known, some practically unknown, with a sprinkling of 'anon'.

*Greene, Richard L. A SELECTION OF ENGLISH CAROLS *O.U.P.* (*Mediaeval and Tudor series*) 1962 25*s*

*Grierson, Sir Herbert John Clifford (1866-1960) METAPHYSICAL LYRICS AND POEMS O.U.P. 1921 10s 6d
Gathered from the seventeenth century: John Donne to Butler.

THE OXFORD BOOK OF SEVENTEENTH CENTURY VERSE O.U.P. 1934 21s 988 pp
Edited with Geoffrey Bullough.

*Hayward, John THE PENGUIN BOOK OF ENGLISH VERSE *Penguin Books* 1956 4s 6d
A choice from the work of 150 poets from the Elizabethans to the present day.
SEVENTEENTH CENTURY POETRY *Chatto* 1948 8s 6d
NINETEENTH CENTURY POETRY *Chatto* 1932 8s 6d

Honey, W. B. THE BROADWAY BOOK OF ENGLISH VERSE *Routledge* 1939 12s 6d 488 pp
'English poems from the fourteenth century to the present day.'

Housman, John E. BRITISH POPULAR BALLADS *Harrap* 1952 7s 6d
A long introduction, with notes, and a selection of ballads from the fifteenth to the eighteenth centuries, arranged in groups: religious; tragic; love; historical; and supernatural.

*Howarth, Robert Guy MINOR POETS OF THE SEVENTEENTH CENTURY *Dent (Everyman)* (1931) 1952 12s 6d
Thomas Carew; Sir John Suckling; Lord Herbert; and Richard Lovelace. Edward, Lord Herbert's poems are given complete (70 poems); so too are Carew's 125 poems; and Suckling's 78 poems, with the complete modern text of Lovelace, 103 poems and 42 translations.

Hussey, Maurice THE CHESTER MYSTERY PLAYS *Heinemann (Drama Library)* 1957 8s 6d
The texts of sixteen pageant plays from the Chester Craft cycle, from *The Fall of Lucifer* to *The Last Judgement*. The texts are based on the best extant editions issued in the *Early English Text Society* series, slightly modernised where necessary for pleasurable reading, with introduction and notes to help producers of pageants.

*Huxley, Aldous TEXTS AND PRETEXTS *Chatto* 1932 10s 6d
This is an anthology chosen with exquisite discrimination, but throughout, displaying the critical individuality of the compiler both in the choice and in the commentary. It is the impact of the poems (including some French verse) on the compiler's mind, that is revealed.

Johnson, Reginald Brimley A BOOK OF BRITISH BALLADS *Dent (Everyman)* 1912 6s 6d
About 130 ballads from the earliest to Kipling and Yeats, grouped as Old Ballads; Modern Ballads; Peasant Ballads; Irish Ballads; and Miscellaneous.

Jones, Gwyn WACE AND LAYAMON: ARTHURIAN CHRONICLES *Dent* (*Everyman*) (1912) 1962 10s 6d
See also under *History* section, for Geoffrey of Monmouth's *Histories of the Kings of Britain*, which was adapted by Wace *c.* 1154, in *Geste des Bretons*. Later, a priest known as Layamon produced an alliterative poem in Old English based, it is thought, on Wace, with additions. The interest and importance of these *Arthurian Chronicles*, Wace's *Roman de Brut*, and Layamon's *Brut*, introduced by Professor Gwyn Jones, lies in the stories of the legendary kings later used by Shakespeare and others. Layamon's work is the source from which sprang *King Lear*, *Cymbeline*, and the Arthurian histories.

Kennedy, Charles EARLY ENGLISH CHRISTIAN POETRY *O.U.P.* (*Galaxy Books*) 1963 10s 6d
Translations of selected poetry from Caedmon, Cynewulf, and other Old English poets of the 7th and 8th centuries.

Kermode, Frank ENGLISH PASTORAL POETRY *Harrap* 1952 7s 6d
From early English translations (the Pastorals of Theocritus); anonymous lyrics; translations of Tasso; to songs from Spenser, Marlowe, Ben Jonson and Milton, and five poems of Marvell, with an introduction of thirty-four pages.

Knowland, A. S. SIX CAROLINE PLAYS *O.U.P.* (*Worlds Classics*) 1962 9s 6d 553 pp
Professor Knowland's selections, which he introduces, are: *The Lady of Pleasure*; and *The Wedding*, by James Shirley (1596-1666); *A Mad Couple Well Matched*; and *The Antipodes*, by Richard Brome (1590-1652); Sir William Davenant's *The Wits* (1605-68); and, Thomas Killigrew's *The Parson's Wedding* (1611-82). Authors' dates doubtful within a year or two. All of these plays were acted or written during the reign of Charles I; and all are comedies, with the exception of *The Wedding*.

Lamb, Charles SPECIMENS OF ENGLISH DRAMATIC POETS (1808) *Routledge* 1907
This creative anthology is a landmark in literature, since the choice from the old dramatists 'who lived about the time of Shakespeare', with Lamb's notes, directed the attention of readers, critics and others to plays that in Lamb's time were forgotten and neglected.

*Lawrence, R. G. EARLY SEVENTEENTH CENTURY DRAMA *Dent* (*Everyman*) 1962 12s 6d
Collects, with an introduction, plays by Dekker, Heywood, Marston, Middleton and Rowley, and Massinger.

*Lewis, D. B. Wyndham and Charles Lee THE STUFFED OWL *Dent* (1930) 1948 15s Illus. by Max Beerbohm
The eight cartoons by 'the incomparable Max' add relish to an appreciative anthology of bad verse, much of it so bad that it is memorable and remembered.

MacDiarmid, Hugh THE GOLDEN TREASURY OF SCOTTISH POETRY *Macmillan* 1940 6s

MacDonagh, Donagh and Lennox Robinson THE OXFORD BOOK OF IRISH VERSE *O.U.P.* 1958 21s
From Nahum (1652-1715) to Cecil Day Lewis and some other twentieth-century poets.

*Macdonald, Hugh ENGLAND'S HELICON (1600; 1614) *Routledge* (*Muses Library*) 1950 10s 6d; 1962 7s 6d (paperback)
This famous anthology of Elizabethan times ranks next to Tottel's *Miscellany* (1577) in literary importance and general interest. It includes the best lyrical and pastoral poetry from Drayton, Lodge, Greene, Ralegh, Spenser and other poets of the period up to Shakespeare. Hugh Macdonald's modern edition is from the 1600 edition, with some additional poems taken from the second edition of 1614.

*McIlwraith, Archibald Kennedy FIVE ELIZABETHAN COMEDIES *O.U.P.* (*Worlds Classics*) 1934 7s 6d
Campaspe, by John Lyly (1584); *The Old Wives' Tale*, by George Peele (1595); *Friar Bacon and Friar Bungay*, by Robert Greene (1594); *The Shoemakers' Holiday*, by Thomas Dekker (1600); and *The Merry Devil of Edmonton* (anonymous, 1608). Introduction and notes included.

FIVE ELIZABETHAN TRAGEDIES *O.U.P.* (*Worlds Classics*) 1938 7s 6d
The *Thyestes* of Seneca, translated and adapted by Jasper Heywood (1560); *Gorboduc*, by Sackville and Norton (1565); *The Spanish Tragedy*, by Thomas Kyd (1592); *Arden of Feversham* (anonymous, 1592); and *A Woman Killed With Kindness*, by Thomas Heywood (1607). Introduction and notes for students.

FIVE STUART TRAGEDIES *O.U.P.* (*Worlds Classics*) 1953 9s 6d
Bussy D'Ambois, by George Chapman (1607); *The Maid's Tragedy*, by Beaumont and Fletcher (1619); *The Duchess of Malfi*, by John Webster (1623); *The Roman Actor*, by Philip Massinger (1629); and *'Tis Pity She's a Whore*, by John Ford (1633). Introduction; footnotes; and with spelling modernised from standard texts.

Mackail, John William (1859-1945) SELECT EPIGRAMS FROM THE GREEK ANTHOLOGY *Longmans* 1890
These rendering are much admired for their neatness and pointed wit.

Mackie, Robert Laird A BOOK OF SCOTTISH VERSE *O.U.P.* (*Worlds Classics*) 1934 7s 6d
Collects some of the old Scottish ballads, and characteristic work of forty-nine authors from the thirteenth to the beginning of the twentieth century.

Manning-Sanders, Ruth A BUNDLE OF BALLADS *O.U.P.* 1959 15s Illus.
A prettily decorated volume of border ballads, in slightly modernised language, other well-known ballads, and some unfamiliar examples.

*Marshall, Leslie Birkett RARE POEMS OF THE SEVENTEENTH CENTURY *C.U.P.* 1936 17s 6d
Selected from manuscripts in the British Museum Collection, from old miscellanies, and similar sources. In all there are about 200 poems, most of which have not appeared in any other anthology. Glossary of obsolete words and phrases.

*Massingham, Harold John A TREASURY OF SEVENTEENTH CENTURY VERSE *Macmillan* 1920 6s
The selection is made with rare judgement, from the period stretching from the death of Shakespeare to the Restoration, 1616-60, with valuable notes.

*Matthiessen, Francis Otto THE OXFORD BOOK OF AMERICAN VERSE *O.U.P.* 1950 50s 1118 pp

*May, G. Lacey ENGLISH RELIGIOUS VERSE *Dent* (*Everyman*) 1937 6s 6d
Poems from the Middle Ages to the present day: about 300 selected from 140 authors.

*Methuen, Sir Algernon AN ANTHOLOGY OF MODERN VERSE, 1900-1920 *Methuen* (1921) 1960 9s 6d
Robert Lynd introduced this most popular anthology. In its latest edition (the thirty-ninth) frequent reprinting testifies to its well-established authority.

SHAKESPEARE TO HARDY *Methuen* (1922) 1951
A school anthology of English lyrics.

*Milford, Sir Humphrey Sumner THE OXFORD BOOK OF ENGLISH VERSE OF THE ROMANTIC PERIOD, 1798-1837 *O.U.P.* 1928 21s 896 pp
Of especial value to students of literary history who are interested in the period as a whole, and who require an anthology to use with such critical monographs as *The Visionary Company: a Reading of English Romantic Poetry*, by Harold Bloom, Faber, 1962, 36s.

Monro, Harold TWENTIETH CENTURY POETRY *Chatto* 1929 8s 6d
From Hardy to Robert Bridges and Walter de la Mare, and through the Georgian period.

*Muir, Kenneth ELIZABETHAN LYRICS *Harrap* 1952 8s 6d
A critical anthology, with an introduction of forty-two pages and notes. The poems are arranged in groups; with a selection from the Elizabethan miscellanies, masques and plays.

Murdoch, Walter and Alan Mulgan A BOOK OF AUSTRALIAN AND NEW ZEALAND VERSE *O.U.P.* 1951 15s
Based on a superseded anthology, *The Oxford Book of Australian Verse* (1918). Contemporary poets are included.

Nichols, John Bowyer WORDS AND DAYS O.U.P. (1895) 1941
'A table book of prose and verse', with an introduction and appreciation
by George Saintsbury, and in the last edition, an additional appreciation
by Logan Pearsall Smith.

*Nicholson, Daniel H. S. and A. H. E. Lee THE OXFORD BOOK OF
ENGLISH MYSTICAL VERSE O.U.P. 1916 18s 660 pp
From the thirteenth to the twentieth century.

Oliver, John W. and J. C. Smith A SCOTS ANTHOLOGY *Oliver and
Boyd* 1949 20s 556 pp
'All that is best in Scottish poetry is represented here.' Arranged chrono-
logically from the thirteenth to the twentieth century.

*Palgrave, Francis Turner (1824-97) THE GOLDEN TREASURY OF
ENGLISH SONGS AND LYRICS (1861; 1896) ed. and extended by
C. Day Lewis *Collins (Classics)* 1959 7s; *Dent (Everyman)* (1906)
enlarged edition 1955 7s 6d; *Macmillan (Golden Treasury series)*
enlarged and ed. by Laurence Binyon 1926 7s 6d; O.U.P.
(Standard Authors) (1907) enlarged edition (1940) 1956 15s;
(Worlds Classics) (1907) enlarged edition 1956 6s
The above are the series editions of this most famous of all modern
anthologies, brought up to date, in some cases considerably extended:
for example, the *Worlds Classics* contains 220 pages of additional poems
from Landor to Dylan Thomas; the *Everyman* has an eighty-eight-page
supplement of poems 'chosen to conform to the Palgrave tradition'.

*Peacock, William ENGLISH VERSE 5 vols. O.U.P. *(Worlds Classics)*
1928-31 7s 6d each
Vol. 1: Early lyrics to Shakespeare; vol. 2: Campion to the ballads;
vol. 3: Dryden to Wordsworth; vol. 4: Scott to E. B. Browning;
vol. 5: Longfellow to Rupert Brooke. The series includes some longer
poems in full; for example, Chaucer's *Prologue* and two of the *Canterbury Tales* in the first volume; and Coleridge's *Ancient Mariner* in the
fourth volume.

Percy, Thomas (1729-1811) RELIQUES OF ANCIENT POETRY (1765)
3 vols. ed. by H. B. Wheatley *Allen and Unwin* 1876-7; 2 vols.
Dent (Everyman) 1906
A literary landmark was created when Bishop Percy first published this
collection of ballads, metrical romances and shorter poems. It stimulated
interest of writers and readers of his time in early poetry, traditional
ballads, and did much to influence those who responded to the romance
of the Middle Ages, and who prepared the way for the flowering of the
romantic poets of the early nineteenth century. The compiler drew upon
the seventeenth-century manuscript collection known as the Percy
Folio, adding further items in his successive editions of 1775, 1794 and
1812.

*Pollard, Alfred William ENGLISH MIRACLE PLAYS, MORALITIES AND INTERLUDES O.U.P. (1890; 1923) 1927 15s
'Specimens of the pre-Elizabethan drama, with introduction, notes and glossary.'

Purvis, J. S. THE YORK CYCLE OF MYSTERY PLAYS S.P.C.K. 1957 27s 6d
A modernised text that was prepared for the York Festival presentations of 1951: but, said *The Times Literary Supplement* reviewer in 1957, 'Dr. Purvis has had to alter astonishingly little'. There are forty-eight plays, with notes on the productions.

*Quiller-Couch, Sir Arthur (1863-1944) THE OXFORD BOOK OF BALLADS O.U.P. 1910 18s 896 pp

THE OXFORD BOOK OF ENGLISH VERSE, 1250-1918 O.U.P. (1900; 1939) 1953 21s 1200 pp

THE OXFORD BOOK OF VICTORIAN VERSE O.U.P. 1912 21s 1040 pp
These are all well-established favourites, especially the general anthology as revised by the original editor.

*Reeves, James THE EVERLASTING CIRCLE *Heinemann* 1960 25s
An anthology of 'English traditional verse'. There are 142 songs and fragments in this notable collection.

A GOLDEN LAND *Constable* 1958 25s 512 pp Illus.
Intended chiefly for younger readers, but like de la Mare's *Come Hither*, a pleasant anthology for all readers.

THE IDIOM OF THE PEOPLE *Heinemann* 1958 21s (*Mercury Books*) 1961 8s 6d
Masterly presentation of English folk-songs based on the unbowderlised versions in the Cecil Sharp collection.

THE MODERN POET'S WORLD *Heinemann* (*Poetry Bookshelf*) 1957 8s 6d
A creative anthology with helpful commentary elucidating difficulties and explaining allusions. Includes some modern American work.

*Rhys, Ernest THE NEW GOLDEN TREASURY OF SONGS AND LYRICS *Dent* (*Everyman*) 1914 6s 6d
A companion to Palgrave's *Golden Treasury*, beginning earlier and ending later: from Chaucer to Swinburne.

THE GOLDEN TREASURY OF LONGER POEMS *Dent* (*Everyman*) (1921) 1953 8s 6d
From Chaucer to de la Mare. The selection includes a number of narrative poems: stories in verse.

Robbins, Rosswell Hope SECULAR LYRICS OF THE FOURTEENTH AND FIFTEENTH CENTURIES O.U.P. 1955 30s
A Middle English anthology, completing the work of Carleton Brown, entered above, with notes and glossary.

*Roberts, Denys Kilham THE CENTURIES POETRY 5 vols. *Penguin Books* 1938-53 2s 6d each
Vol. 1: Chaucer to Shakespeare; vol. 2: Donne to Dryden; vol. 3: Pope to Keats; vol. 4: Hood to Hardy; vol. 5: Bridges to the Present Day.

Rollins, Hyder Edward A PEPYSIAN GARLAND *C.U.P.* 1922
Ballads of the period 1595-1639, transcribed chiefly from the Pepys Library now in the Library of Magdalene College, Cambridge. Chiefly blackletter broadside ballads, this selection was later followed by the editor's larger series of *Pepys Ballads*, 8 vols., O.U.P., 1929-32, 28s each, covering the period from 1535 to 1702. Volume 3 is out of print.

Rose, Martial THE WAKEFIELD MYSTERY PLAYS *Evans* 1961 35s
The text of the complete cycle of thirty-two plays, with long introduction of particular interest to producers.

*Rylands, George THE AGES OF MAN *Heinemann* 1939 13s 6d; (*Mercury Books*) 1962 9s 6d
A Shakespeare anthology of passages from the plays and poems, chosen to display Shakespeare's 'image of man and nature'.

*Saintsbury, George (1845-1933) MINOR POETS OF THE CAROLINE PERIOD 3 vols. *O.U.P.* 1905; 1906; 1921
An anthology of classic permanence. Vol. 1: Chamberlayne; Benlowes; Katherine Philips; Hannay; Philomela. Vol. 2: Marmion; Kynaston; Hall; Godolphin; Ayres; Chalkhill; Carey; Hammond; Bosworth. Vol. 3: Cleveland; Stanley; King; Flatman; Whiting.

Scott, Sir Walter (1771-1832) MINSTRELSY OF THE SCOTTISH BORDER (1802-3) 4 vols. revised and edited by T. F. Henderson *Oliver and Boyd* 1932
Interest in the old ballads, stimulated by Bishop Percy's *Reliques*, entered above, was sustained and increased by Scott's great collection. He was assisted by James Hogg, 'the Ettrick Shepherd', in the research and collecting of these traditional ballads, with some contemporary imitations. See also under Beattie above, for the Penguin anthology, based on Scott's work.

Smith, A. J. M. THE OXFORD BOOK OF CANADIAN VERSE *O.U.P.* 1960 40s 502 pp
A chronologically arranged selection of everything of value in Canadian poetry from Standish O'Grady (1793-1841) to twentieth-century poets, including some French poems by French Canadians.

*Smith, David Nichol THE OXFORD BOOK OF EIGHTEENTH CENTURY VERSE *O.U.P.* 1926 21s 740 pp

Stewart, Douglas and Nancy Keesing AUSTRALIAN BUSH BALLADS *Angus and Robertson* 1956 30s
The first volume of a standard collection to be completed by a further volume. Thus the whole of Australian balladry will be anthologised

from the settlements of the nineteenth century to the present time, including many anonymous ballads.

Taylor, Geoffrey IRISH POETS OF THE NINETEENTH CENTURY *Routledge (Muses Library)* 1954 12s 6d
An anthology of poets of Irish birth, whose work has some Irish reference, topographical or historical. Both major and minor work is included, and each poet is introduced with a biographical essay and a bibliography.

*Thorndike, Ashley Horace MINOR ELIZABETHAN DRAMA 2 vols. *Dent (Everyman)* (1910) 1959 8s 6d each
Vol. 1: (Pre-Shakespearean Tragedies)-*Gorboduc*, by Norton and Sackville (1565); *Arden of Feversham* (anonymous, 1592); *David and Bethsabe*, by George Peele (1599); *The Spanish Tragedy*, by Thomas Kyd (1592); *Cambyses, King of Persia*, by Thomas Preston (1569).

Vol. 2: (Pre-Shakespearean Comedies)-*Friar Bacon and Friar Bungay*, by Robert Greene (1594); *Ralph Roister Doister* (1566?); *Endimion*, by John Lyly (1591); *The Old Wives' Tale*, by George Peele (1595); *James the Fourth*, by Robert Greene (1598).

The revised edition of this standard collection is by Howarth, and each volume has a glossary.

*Wavell, Archibald Perceval, *1st Earl* (1883-1950) OTHER MEN'S FLOWERS *Cape* (1944) 1959 18s
The last edition of this popular personal anthology is a memorial edition, with an introduction by Wavell's son. The choice is restricted to those poems that this great soldier admired and loved all his life.

*Wheeler, Charles Bickersteth SIX PLAYS BY CONTEMPORARIES OF SHAKESPEARE *O.U.P. (Worlds Classics)* 1915 8s 6d
Three comedies: *The Shoemaker's Holiday*, by Thomas Dekker (1600); *The Knight of the Burning Pestle*, by Beaumont and Fletcher (1613); and *A New Way to Pay Old Debts*, by Philip Massinger (1633). Two tragedies: John Webster's *The White Devil* (1612), and *The Duchess of Malfi* (1623); and a romantic drama, *Philaster*, by Beaumont and Fletcher (1620), with an historical introduction to each play and a general preface to the whole collection.

Wright, Judith A BOOK OF AUSTRALIAN VERSE *O.U.P.* 1956 15s
A chronologically arranged selection, emphasising the work of the last thirty years.

*Young, Douglas SCOTTISH VERSE, 1851-1951 *Nelson* 1952 18s
A complementary anthology to Buchan's *Northern Muse* entered above.

PROSE DRAMA

No form of art is more fleeting and fugitive than prose drama. Plays that charm and thrill thousands of playgoers of one generation, filling theatres with delighted, applauding audiences for months, even years, are withdrawn and forgotten, save perhaps for a few occasional revivals from time to time. Of these, a very small number continue to be read.

Hence the brief contents of this section. In considering what to put in and what to leave out of twentieth-century drama by playwrights no longer living, the availability of a printed text for general reading was taken as a fair indication of chances of survival as literature. The specialist firm of Samuel French maintain an extensive back list of acting editions of thousands of plays. Professional players as well as amateur productions rely very much on these editions, but they do not come within the scope of this select bibliography. Specialists are therefore referred to French's current catalogues, and to the great catalogue of the Library of the British Drama League, published by Faber, 1950, 30s, 1115 pp; with three supplements, 1951, 1954, 1956, 8s 6d, 21s and 21s each. It includes books on the theatre and drama, with a section of *Plays in French* in the third supplement. *The Player's Library*, as it is called, is an invaluable reference work without a rival.

Thus, if playgoers who may remember, for example, the pleasure of seeing that sensitive study in the Tchehovian style, *Musical Chairs*, by the late Ronald Mackenzie, do not find it listed here, they are asked to agree that as it is no longer available for reading, and has not been revived for some years, it was proper to omit mention of its publication by Victor Gollancz in the year of its author's untimely death. This is but one of many similar examples.

Attention is called, however, to the collections entered in the sub-section. These include some volumes reprinting plays by A. A. Milne, Arnold Bennett; a selection of Barnstormer Plays; and an anthology of representative drama of the nineteenth century.

For the substantial remainder, the wit and elegance of the Restoration dramatists, and of Sheridan and Wilde, entirely dominate the scene until the advent of Bernard Shaw, the world's greatest prose playwright. Eugene O'Neill, his only rival, had to be omitted as a twentieth-century American. Indeed, the drama as a form of literature enjoyed as much in the armchair as in the theatre, appears to be chiefly due to the genius of Irish-born playwrights. The glittering nine were, with only two exceptions, all either Irishmen or, like Congreve, were educated in Ireland. Vanbrugh and Wycherley alone represent English playwrights, and the former was of Dutch descent.

Professor Allardyce Nicoll, the learned Director of the Shakespeare Institute, Stratford on Avon, is the greatest bibliographer and historian of the drama and theatre. His books are essential to students, and his

British Drama, Harrap, 4th revised edition 1949, 21s, 540 pp has not been surpassed as a standard short survey. There is also an interesting new historical study of the development of British drama from the miracle plays of the Middle Ages, up to Bernard Shaw and Emlyn Williams with the allusive, but concealing, title of *The Golden Labyrinth*. Its author, Professor G. Wilson Knight, has here provided what should become a standard book for all who are interested in the play as a form of English literature rather than a part of the history of the theatre. An admirable companion to Walter Allen's book on the English novel (noted in the introduction to the *Fiction* section) and published by Phoenix House, 1962, 30s, 402 pp, it is written in a lucid, fluent style likely to attract the general reader, yet the treatment is comprehensive enough to satisfy the student.

But it is almost invidious to name only two books on such a vast subject. The history and criticism of the drama have together attracted enough books to form a library within a library at the British Drama League.

Archer, William (1856-1924) THE GREEN GODDESS *Heinemann* 1923
A successful melodrama by the pioneer translator of Ibsen's plays, and the dramatic critic of the new theatre inaugurated by Bernard Shaw in the nineties.

Baring, Maurice (1874-1945) TEN DIMINUTIVE DRAMAS *Heinemann* (1911) 1952 5s
The reprint has an introduction by Sir Desmond MacCarthy. These plays are suitable for puppets as well as ordinary stage production.

Barrie, Sir James (1860-1937) COLLECTED PLAYS *Hodder* (1928) 1942 35s 1284 pp
The definitive edition in one volume. Separate editions of some of the most popular plays are also available: *The Admirable Crichton* (1902) (7s 6d); *Dear Brutus* (1917) (7s 6d); *Mary Rose* (1920) (6s); *Peter Pan* (1904) (7s 6d); and *Quality Street* (1913) (7s 6d).

*PLAYS AND STORIES *Dent* (*Everyman*) 1962 12s 6d
This latest addition to the series includes *The Admirable Crichton*; *Dear Brutus*; and the one-acter *Shall We Join the Ladies* (1921).

Bennett, Arnold (1867-1931) THE GREAT ADVENTURE *Methuen* (1913) and MILESTONES (1912) 1953 4s
Of these two popular plays, the first was based on Bennett's novel, *Buried Alive*, and the second was written in collaboration with Edward Knoblock. This one is included in the *Everyman* volume of *Modern Plays*, edited by John Hadfield, entered in next section, and also in the collected edition of Knoblock's plays, for which see below.

Berkeley, Reginald (1890-1935) THE LADY WITH A LAMP (Gollancz, 1929); *Longmans* 1949 5s
A play on the life and work of Florence Nightingale.

*Besier, Rudolf (1878-1942) THE BARRETTS OF WIMPOLE STREET
(1930) *Longmans* 1948 3s 6d
Presents in dramatic form the love story and elopement of Elizabeth
Barrett with Robert Browning.

*Bridie, James (Osborne Henry Mavor) (1888-1951) COLONEL
WOTHERSPOON AND OTHER PLAYS *Constable* (1934) 1950 10s

MORAL PLAYS *Constable* (1936) 1950 10s
Bridie's eighteen plays are available in separate editions, in a paperback
series, Constable, 5s each. *Tobias and the Angel*, and *The Anatomist*, were
two of the best and most popular.

Chapin, Harold (1886-1915) COMEDIES *Chatto* 1921
Sir James Barrie introduced this memorial edition of the charming
Edwardian plays of a victim of World War I. '*The New Morality*,' wrote
Barrie, 'would merit a high place in any gathering together of the best
English comedies of recent years.' The companion pieces are *Art and
Opportunity*; *Elaine*; and *The Marriage of Columbine*.

*Chesterton, Gilbert Keith (1874-1936) THE JUDGMENT OF DOCTOR
JOHNSON *Sheed and Ward* 1927

MAGIC (1913) *Dent* 1925
A fantasy of a moving and haunting kind. The last act is included in the
G.K.C. *Worlds Classics* volume, for which see in the *Essays and Belles
Lettres* sections.

*Congreve, William (1670-1729) COMPLETE PLAYS ed. by A. C.
Ewald *Benn* (*Mermaid series*) (1887) 1962 18s; *MacGibbon and
Kee* (Dramabooks) 1958 12s 6d
The four famous comedies, and Congreve's tragedy in verse: *The
Mourning Bride* (1710).

COMEDIES ed. by Bonamy Dobrée *O.U.P.* (*Worlds Classics*)
1929 7s 6d
The Way of the World (1700); *The Old Bachelor* (1693); *The Double
Dealer* (1694); and *Love For Love* (1695). The first of these available
separately *Dent* (*Temple Dramatists*), 7s 6d

Drinkwater, John (1882-1937) ABRAHAM LINCOLN *Sidgwick and
Jackson* (1918) 1928 3s 6d
A popular biographical play.

Etherege, Sir George (1635-91) DRAMATIC WORKS 2 vols.
ed. by H. F. B. Brett-Smith *Blackwell* 1927
Edited from original quartos, with an introduction of 108 pages, and
notes. Principal contents: *Love In a Tub* (1664); *She Wou'd If She Cou'd*
(1668); and *The Man of Mode; or, Sir Fopling Flutter* (1676). The last-
named is included in Gosse's *Everyman* collection of *Restoration Plays*,
entered in the next section.

*Farquhar, George (1678-1707) FOUR PLAYS *Benn (Mermaid series)* (1906) 1949 12s 6d; *MacGibbon and Kee (Dramabooks)* 1958 16s 6d
These lively comedies, two of which are revived from time to time, are: *The Beaux Stratagem* (1707); *The Recruiting Officer* (1706) and the lesser, *The Constant Couple* (1700); and *The Twin Rivals* (1702). The first-named also available separately, Dent *(Temple Dramatists)*, 7s 6d.

Field, Nathan (1587?-1633) PLAYS ed. by William Peery *Nelson* 1951 12s 6d
The work of a minor dramatist and an actor, who may have collaborated with Beaumont and Fletcher, and who is known to have been in Ben Jonson's circle. His best plays are said to be *A Woman is a Weathercocke* (1609); and *Amends For Ladies* (1611). The above edition (from the University of Texas) is the only reprint since 1888.

Flecker, James Elroy (1884-1915) DON JUAN *Heinemann* 1925 HASSAN *Heinemann* (1922) 1951 6s
A play with an Arabian Nights atmosphere and plot, with some memorable lyrics, written by the young poet, who was killed in World War I.

*Galsworthy, John (1867-1933) TEN FAMOUS PLAYS *Duckworth* (1941) 1952 21s
Strife; Justice; Loyalties; The Silver box; The Skin Game; Old English; Joy; Escape; The Roof; and *Windows.* Most of these are available separately, 3s 6d each.

SIX SHORT PLAYS *Duckworth* 1921 3s 6d
The First and the Last; The Little Man; Hall-Marked; Defeat; The Sun; and *Punch and Go.*

*Gay, John (1685-1732) THE BEGGAR'S OPERA (1728) POLLY (1729)
'A Newgate Pastoral' and its lively sequel, both very popular when revived as ballad operas, with music to the lyrics, usually to traditional airs. *The Beggar's Opera* is included in John Hampden's *Everyman* selection, entered in the next section, and also in W. D. Taylor's *Worlds Classics* volume.

*Goldsmith, Oliver (1728-74) PLAYS *Dent (Everyman)* (1910) 1948 8s 6d; *MacGibbon and Kee (Dramabooks)* 1958 10s 6d; *Nelson (Classics)* 1954 6s
She Stoops To Conquer (1773) and *The Good-Natured Man* (1768). The former is one of the most popular and much-loved plays in the language. In the *Everyman* and the Nelson edition the poems of Goldsmith are also included; and there is a text of *She Stoops To Conquer* in the *Collins Classics* edition of Goldsmith's novel *The Vicar of Wakefield*, entered in the *Fiction* section. This play also available separately, Dent *(Temple Dramatists)*, 7s 6d.

*Granville-Barker, Harley (1877-1946) MADRAS HOUSE *Sidgwick and Jackson* (1910) 1925

THE VOYSEY INHERITANCE *Sidgwick and Jackson* (1909; 1913) 1934 3s 6d

WASTE *Sidgwick and Jackson* (1909) 1926 3s 6d

Three social dramas of distinction and power, written by a famous producer and Shakespearean commentator. The last editions were his revised, definitive texts for production.

*Gregory, Augusta (Lady) (1852-1932) SELECTED PLAYS ed. by Elizabeth Coxhead *Putnam* 1962 25s

Sean O'Casey adds an appreciation of one of the founders of the Abbey Theatre to this selection of Lady Gregory's comedies and short plays. These contributions to the Irish dramatic renaissance were all written for Dublin production and were published in various separate volumes from time to time.

Hamilton, Patrick (1904-62) ROPE *Constable* 1929 5s

A classic thriller on the theme of the motiveless murder. It was a great success when first produced and has been frequently revived on both stage and radio.

Holcroft, Thomas (1745-1809) THE ROAD TO RUIN (1792)

Popular melodrama, sometimes revised *pour rire*. Holcroft was a journalist in the Godwin-Tom Paine circle.

Houghton, William Stanley (1881-1913) HINDLE WAKES *Sidgwick and Jackson* 1912 5s

A popular play of the 'Manchester School' of realism, in which Houghton drew upon his own knowledge of the Lancashire cotton mill workers.

*Housman, Laurence (1865-1959) VICTORIA REGINA: a dramatic biography *Cape* (1934) 1950 15s Illus. by E. H. Shepard

These plays on Queen Victoria were banned from the stage until 1937 when some of them were allowed to be produced as a sort of centenary tribute.

THE LITTLE PLAYS OF SAINT FRANCIS 3 vols. *Sidgwick and Jackson* 1922 7s 6d each

James, Henry (1843-1916) COMPLETE PLAYS *Hart-Davis* 1949 35s 846 pp

Edited by James's biographer and bibliographer, Leon Edel, who also has published a separate edition of the principal play, *Guy Domville*, Hart-Davis, 1961, 16s, with a long introduction of 121 pages, which is almost a book in itself. Here is told the full story of the production, and the disastrous reception in London 1895, together with critical appraisals by some of James's famous contemporaries, Bernard Shaw, Arnold Bennett, and H. G. Wells. The complete volume contains two dramas based on two of James's best long-short stories: *Daisy Miller*; and *The Other House*.

*Joyce, James (1882-1941) EXILES *Cape* (1924) 1952 12s 6d; *Four Square Books* 1962 2s 6d
The definitive edition of 1952, published by Cape, contains the author's notes, with an introduction by Padraic Colum.

Knoblock, Edward (1874-1945) KISMET AND OTHER PLAYS *Chapman and Hall* 1957 18s
The principal play is given in the original version instead of the much-altered text used for the musical comedy of the same title; of the other plays, the best-known is *Milestones*, written in collaboration with Arnold Bennett, entered above. The volume includes an essay on the art of play writing, based on Knoblock's own experience, and recommended to beginners and aspirants.

Lawrence, David Herbert (1885-1930) THE WIDOWING OF MRS. HOLROYD *Duckworth* 1914
A drama in three acts. The action takes place in the kitchen of a miner's small cottage. The play was written soon after the death of Lawrence's mother, about the same time as his masterpiece, *Sons and Lovers*.

Lillo, George (1693-1739) THE LONDON MERCHANT; OR GEORGE BARNWELL (1731) *Harvill Press* 1949 5s
A domestic drama which has a place in the history of English dramatic literature, and so is also included in Hampden's *Everyman* collection entered in the next section.

Lonsdale, Frederick (Frederick Leonard) (1881-1954) CANARIES SOMETIMES SING *Methuen* 1929

THE LAST OF MRS. CHEYNEY *Collins* 1925

ON APPROVAL *Collins* 1927
Three light, amusing social comedies of the twenties, once very popular on the stage. They are available, with others by the same author, in French's acting editions.

Pinero, Sir Arthur Wing (1855-1934) DANDY DICK *Heinemann* (1893) 1959 6s 6d
A farce, first produced in 1887.

THE MAGISTRATE *Heinemann* 1895
Another farce, successfully revived from time to time.

THE SECOND MRS. TANQUERAY *Heinemann* 1895
Pinero's principal drama, and the only play of his that is likely to be accorded a place of importance in the history of the nineteenth-century English stage.

THE THUNDERBOLT *Heinemann* 1908
Most of Pinero's plays are usually available in French's acting editions. They helped to bridge the gap between the period when British dramatic literature was in the doldrums, and the advent of Shaw and Wilde.

Robertson, Thomas William (1829-71) CASTE (1867) *Bodley Head*
1951 *4s 6d*; *Nelson* 1932

SOCIETY (1865)

These two 'Barnstormer Plays' heralded a change in English drama.
When Robertson wrote them, the British theatre had sunk into
mediocrity and insignificance, notable only for melodramatic exaggera-
tions that sometimes gave enjoyment in the hands of capable producers
and outstanding actors. Robertson's *David Garrick*, and *Ours*, together
with his best play, *Caste*, have been successfully revived, and are included
in the collection of his best work, published in two volumes in 1889.
Caste is also given in George Rowell's *Worlds Classics* volume, and in
Montagu Slater's collection, both entered in the next section.

Shairp, Mordaunt (1887-1939) THE CRIME AT BLOSSOMS *Allen and
Unwin* 1932 *4s 6d*

THE GREEN BAY TREE *Allen and Unwin* 1933

Two successful plays, sometimes revived, the first being a thriller, and
the second a remarkable study in the possessive nature of an unhealthy
affection between a mature man and a younger.

*Shaw, George Bernard (1856-1950) COLLECTED PLAYS *Constable*
(*Standard Edition*) 17 vols. 1931-2 *15s* each (reprints of *Man and
Superman* (*18s*), *Plays Pleasant* (*21s*), *St. Joan* and *The Apple Cart*
(*18s*), and *Three Plays For Puritans* (*21s*))

SIX PLAYS *Constable* 1962 *40s* 668 pp

An omnibus selection, without the prefaces, of *Arms and the Man* (1898);
Man and Superman (1903); *Major Barbara* (1905); *Pygmalion* (1912);
Heartbreak House (1919); and *St. Joan* (1924). Paperback editions of some
of Shaw's plays are available from time to time in Penguin Books, *2s 6d*
each, and there are four available in Constable's edition, *5s* each.

*Sheridan, Richard Brinsley (1751-1816) PLAYS 3 vols. ed. by
R. C. Rhodes *Blackwell* 1928

The best collected edition.

COMPLETE PLAYS *Collins* (*Classics*) 1955 *6s*; *Dent* (*Everyman*)
(1906) 1956 *8s 6d*; *O.U.P.* (*Worlds Classics*) (1906) 1956 *6s*;
MacGibbon and Kee (*Dramabooks*) 1958 *12s 6d*

These editions give all of Sheridan's plays written by him and accepted
without question as his work. Separate editions of the most frequently
revived are available: *The Rivals* (1775); *The School for Scandal* (1777);
The Critic (1779); in Dent's (*Temple Dramatists*), *7s 6d* each. The definitive
edition in three volumes includes *St. Patrick's Day* (1775); *The Duenna*
(1775); and *Pizarro* (1799), the last being a drama adapted from Kotzebue.
The *Worlds Classics* edition is a revised text 'after a detailed comparison
of early issues of Sheridan, who remains after nearly two hundred years
the unequalled master of the Comedy of Manners in English'. This
volume contains Sheridan's *Verses to the Memory of Garrick*, and a chronology of his life.

Steele, Sir Richard (1672-1729) PLAYS *Benn* (*Mermaid series*) 1926
The volume contains all the comedies by Steele, who was Addison's gay
collaborator in the *Spectator* essays. These are *The Lying Lover*; *The Tender
Husband*; *The Conscious Lovers*; *The Funeral*; and two unfinished plays.
The best play, *The Conscious Lovers*, is included in W. D. Taylor's
Worlds Classics collection, entered in the next section.

THE FUNERAL; OR, GRIEF A LA MODE (1702) *Blackie* 1957 7s Illus.

*Synge, John Millington (1871-1909) COLLECTED PLAYS *Allen and
Unwin* (1932) 1959 15s
This is volume 1 of the complete works of this Irish writer. The six
plays are usually also available separately in pocket editions.

THE PLAYBOY OF THE WESTERN WORLD *Allen and Unwin* (1907)
1957 7s 6d; 1962 4s 6d (paperback); *Methuen* (1907) 1961 4s;
Four Square Paperbacks 1962 3s 6d
The Methuen edition of Synge's masterpiece has a thirty-page introduction by T. R. Henn, on the Abbey Theatre, the personality of the
playwright, and the significance of the play.

FOUR PLAYS and THE ARAN ISLANDS ed. by Robin Skelton O.U.P.
(*Worlds Classics*) 1962 8s 6d
Contents: *Riders to the Sea*; *The Shadow of the Glen*; *The Tinker's Wed-
ding*; and *The Playboy of the Western World*; and the study of *The Aran
Islands*. Contains a bibliography and a list of books on Synge and his
work.

PLAYS, POEMS AND PROSE *Dent* (*Everyman*) (1954) 1962 8s 6d
See also the preceding section *Poetry*, for details of the first volume
(*Poems*) of a definitive edition of Synge's *Collected Works in progress*,
5 volumes, 1962-.

*Vanbrugh, Sir John (1664-1726) PLAYS (1730) *Benn* (*Mermaid*)
(1896) 1949 12s 6d
Contents: *The Relapse; or, Virtue In Danger* (1697); *The Provok'd Wife*
(1697); *The Confederacy* (1705); and *A Journey To London; or, The
Provok'd Husband* (1728). The last was finished by Colley Cibber. *The
Provok'd Wife* is included in a volume of *Restoration Plays*, edited by
Edmund Gosse, entered in the next section.

*Wilde, Oscar (1854-1900) FIVE FAMOUS PLAYS *Duckworth* 1952 18s
An Ideal Husband (1899); *The Importance of Being Earnest* (1899); *Lady
Windermere's Fan* (1893); *A Woman of No Importance* (1893); and *Salome*
(1894).
The last play is given in the original French, with a parallel English
translation.

FOUR PLAYS *Unicorn Press* 1944 12s 6d

THE IMPORTANCE OF BEING EARNEST *Methuen* 1957 15s
The first publication of the full original text in four acts, with a preface
by Vyvyan Holland, explaining how Sir George Alexander asked Wilde

to cut his first draft to three acts, for the initial production of this delightful comedy.

SALOME *Unicorn Press* 1947 4s 6d

COMPLETE PLAYS *Collins (Classics)* 1954 6s

Refer also to the collected works of Wilde, etc., entered in the *Essays and Belles Lettres* section.

*Wycherley, William (1640-1716) PLAYS *Benn (Mermaid series)* (1888) 1948 12s 6d

Love In a Wood (1672); *The Gentleman Dancing-Master* (1673); *The Country Wife* (1675); and *The Plain Dealer* (1677).

The Plain Dealer is an adaptation of Molière's masterpiece *Le Misanthrope*. In spite of its coarseness *The Country Wife* is frequently revived, and is one of the amusing Restoration comedies that is rather more enjoyable to see than to read. It is included in Gosse's collection of *Restoration Plays*, entered in the next section.

PROSE DRAMA
(Collections)

Arranged under editors; and including miscellaneous collections of plays in both prose and verse

*Gosse, Sir Edmund (1849-1928) RESTORATION PLAYS: FROM DRYDEN TO FARQUHAR *Dent (Everyman)* (1912) 1953 8s 6d

All For Love, by John Dryden; *The Country Wife*, by William Wycherley; *The Way of the World*, by William Congreve; *Venice Preserv'd*, by Thomas Otway; *The Beaux Stratagem*, by George Farquhar; *The Provok'd Wife*, by Sir John Vanbrugh; and *The Man of Mode*, by Sir George Etherege.

*Hadfield, John MODERN PLAYS *Dent (Everyman)* (1937) 1962 8s 6d

Journey's End, by R. C. Sherriff; *For Services Rendered*, by W. Somerset Maugham; *Hay Fever*, by Noël Coward; *The Dover Road*, by A. A. Milne; and *Milestones*, by Arnold Bennett and Edward Knoblock.

*Hampden, John EIGHTEENTH CENTURY PLAYS *Dent (Everyman)* (1928) 1954 12s 6d

The Beggar's Opera, by John Gay; *The Clandestine Marriage*, by George Colman and David Garrick; *Cato*, by Joseph Addison; *Jane Shore*, by Nicholas Rowe; *Tom Thumb the Great*, by Henry Fielding; *The London Merchant*, by George Lillo; and *The West Indian*, by Richard Cumberland.

Knowland, A. S. SIX CAROLINE PLAYS *O.U.P. (Worlds Classics)* 1962 9s 6d

This new volume presents plays that were written wholly or in part during the reign of Charles I. It contains *The Parson's Wedding*, by Sir

William Killigrew; *The Lady of Pleasure*, and *The Wedding*, both by James Shirley; Richard Brome's *A Mad Couple Well Matcht*, and *The Antipodes*; and *The Wits*, by Sir William D'Avenant.

Morrell, Janet Margaret FOUR ENGLISH COMEDIES OF THE 17TH AND 18TH CENTURIES *Penguin Books* 1950 3s 6d
Volpone, by Ben Jonson; *The Way of the World*, by William Congreve; *She Stoops to Conquer*, by Oliver Goldsmith; and *The School For Scandal*, by R. B. Sheridan.

*Rowell, George NINETEENTH CENTURY PLAYS *O.U.P.* (*Worlds Classics*) 1953 9s 6d 580 pp
Collects ten melodramas, popular in their period, that was one in which the British stage sank to its lowest level. All of these plays had some qualities that enabled them to hold their place in public estimation: *Black-Ey'd Susan*, by Douglas Jerrold; *Money*, by Edward Bulwer-Lytton; *Masks and Faces*, by Tom Taylor and Charles Reade; *The Colleen Bawn*, by Dion Boucicault; *Lady Audley's Secret*, by C. H. Hazlewood; *The Ticket-of-Leave Man*, by Tom Taylor; *Caste*, by T. W. Robertson; *Two Roses*, by James Albery; *The Bells*, by Leopold Lewis; and *A Pair of Spectacles*, by Sidney Grundy.

Slater, Montagu BARNSTORMER PLAYS *Bodley Head* 1928–51 4s 6d each
Modern editions of popular melodramas of the nineteenth-century travelling companies, known as barnstormers. In the series are such one-time favourites as *Caste*, by T. W. Robertson; *Sweeney Todd, the Demon Barber of Fleet Street*, by George Dobdin Pitt, and *Maria Marten; or, The Murder in the Red Barn*, an anonymous masterpiece which is sometimes revived *pour rire*.

*Taylor, William Duncan EIGHTEENTH CENTURY COMEDY *O.U.P.* (*Worlds Classics*) 1929 7s 6d
The Beaux Stratagem, by George Farquhar (1707); *The Conscious Lovers*, by Sir Richard Steele (1722); *The Beggar's Opera*, by John Gay (1728); *Tom Thumb the Great*, by John Fielding (1731); and *She Stoops to Conquer*, by Oliver Goldsmith (1773).

TRAVEL, DESCRIPTION AND TOPOGRAPHY
(including personal narratives of adventure and exploration)

CLASSIFIERS evolve logical schedules, but books refuse to conform. There is nothing precise in those we group together under the heading of Travel. It will be seen that they comprise personal narratives, usually written in recollection 'when the journey's over'; systematically recorded accounts and formal logs, often taking the shape of a diary or journal; and substantial works about expeditions and explorations in which are unfolded chapters in the story of man's gradual discovery of the earth and its peoples; the development of maps and charts; and scientific description of countries and regions. Even guide books occasionally achieve the status of literature: Wordsworth's *Guide To the Lakes* has some literary interest as well as practical value.

Travellers' tales, then, are apt to be a fusion of autobiography, history, formal handbooks, topographical and scientific description. They offer a diverting miscellany of adventure, sport, social history and purely factual information. That is why the literature of travel rivals the novel in popularity with the reading public.

'Ay, now am I in Arden; the more fool I; when I was at home, I was in a better place: but travellers must be content.' Thus *As You Like It* offers a chapter heading for many a narrative of peril and adventure listed below, for Touchstone's nostalgic sigh is echoed in books we enjoy in the comfort of an armchair.

In English we are fortunate in having the firm foundation built by the industry and scholarship of Richard Hakluyt: his monumental *Principal Navigations*, truly, as Froude said, a prose epic, is without a peer in world literature, combining as it does a literary classic of picturesque charm from an age when English prose, if somewhat prolix, was alive with youthful vigour, freshly minted and colourful; and an historical narrative of priceless value. Wisest of editors, Hakluyt's masterly redaction of the personal documents he had acquired retained the individuality of the several writers. He established a tradition, and his literary heir, Samuel Purchas, although scarcely in the same class, helped to preserve the subsequent records. Some excellent modern anthologies and collections grouped together in the sub-section continue the tradition with distinction.

Detailed descriptions, or topography proper, also got off with a good start with Camden's *Britannia*, notably rendered by Philemon Holland into sturdy English prose, followed by the immensely interesting Stow; with later contributions of abounding, permanent social interest by Defoe and Cobbett. Here too, as in autobiography, the amateur has occasionally scored a bull's eye, beating the professionals at their own game: we would certainly be the poorer if the account of her journeys kept by Celia Fiennes had not survived to attract eventually a distinguished editor and publisher; and John Byng's diaries of his tours in England and Wales, a companion for Cobbett's *Rural Rides* from an aristocratic amateur with a social conscience, is certainly a treasure as a bedside book. It has an added entry here; cannot it be granted a permanent place in *Everyman* or *Nelson Classics* to keep it in print? And in our own time, few who possess H. J. Massingham's pleasant regional descriptions of 'the coloured counties' he knew and loved, would wish to part with them.

The works of A. R. Wallace, Charles Darwin, A. W. Bates and Charles Waterton belong to science and natural history; A. F. Mummery, A. W. Moore, Sir Leslie Stephen and Edward Whymper contributed to the literature of an adventurous sport; Mungo Park, J. H. Speke, Livingstone, Captain Scott, Shackleton and Cherry-Garrard to the history of exploration; and so on: their books have also a secure place in English literature.

In a class apart are travel essays and informal personal narratives, belonging as much to Belles Lettres as to Travel. That most light-hearted and gay of all travel essayists, Robert Louis Stevenson, exclaimed in his evergreen *Travels with a Donkey*: 'I travel for travel's sake. The great affair is to move', and that is the impulse behind all travellers of his restless, literary kind. With Kinglake's *Eothen* we realise that we are reading a delightful narrative not as a traveller's tale, but for the pleasure received from being allowed to keep company with the author. The personal touch is the important element; and the narrative style the quality that endears it to our hearts. The Italy of Gissing's *By the Ionian Sea* is not our Italy, which is largely the creation of the travel agency and the jet: but once read, Gissing's best book is a delight to return to. Strangely, Italy drew another masterpiece from a later angry man, that most peevish and hot-tempered of all modern travellers, D. H. Lawrence. If the island that inspired it becomes a wilderness of skyscrapers, industrial concerns, and over-populated bathing beaches, Lawrence's greatest nonfiction book, *Sea and Sardinia*, will always be read with delight and relish, for its self-revelation and the intense, glowing prose spontaneously flowing from his pen in moments of supreme communication with sea, sailors, passengers, peasants and landscapes.

How near to autobiography such writing steers is seldom more plainly displayed than in *Sea and Sardinia*. Even Joseph Conrad, a man of precision, could scarcely separate the two, for his *Mirror of the Sea* and *A Personal Record* are complementary.

The extraordinary attraction for the English of the Near and Middle East is well known; by lucky chance, travellers to Arabia, Syria, and the surrounding countries, have been writers of high distinction, adding books of enduring quality to travel literature. Their contributions, in fact, are so considerable that they have attracted a monograph in the British Council series of *Writers and Their Work*: Robin Fedden's *English Travellers In the Near East*, Longmans, 1958, 2s 6d. In the same series, Oliver Warner, that urbane authority on matters maritime and Nelson, has contributed a

L

handbook on *British Maritime Writing: Hakluyt to Cook*, Longmans, 1958, 2s 6d, that should not be missed. Within the limits of this series, it could scarcely be bettered.

Little wonder, then, that travel literature finds so many readers. 'We set out for places which we do not reach, or reach too late; and, on the way, there befall us all manner of things which we could never have awaited,' wrote Hilaire Belloc in his *The Cruise of the 'Nona'*. A sort of serendipity, in fact, luring and rewarding the traveller, whether he ventures 'On the shores of Asia, or in the Edgware Road'.

*Anson, George (1697-1762) A VOYAGE ROUND THE WORLD, 1740-4 (1748) *Dent (Everyman)* 1912
The narrative of the voyage undertaken between 1740 and 1744 by the first Lord of the Admiralty, with a squadron of seven ships. It was drafted by the Chaplain, the Rev. R. Walters. Lord Anson, 'the father of the Royal Navy', revised and approved the final text for publication. Introduction by John Masefield.

Baker, Sir Samuel White (1821-93) THE ALBERT N'YANZA (1866) 2 vols. *Sidgwick and Jackson* 1962 84s (the set) 567 pp
The handsome modern edition of this account of exploration and adventure, complete with maps, illustrations and portraits, has a preface taken by permission from Alan Moorehead's book *The White Nile* (Hamish Hamilton, 1960) in which he states that 'it is the most readable of explorers' books'. In his exploration of the Great Basin of the Nile and its sources, from 1861 to 1865, Baker and his intrepid companion, Lady Baker, saw strange and dreadful things, and had much to do with the eventual suppression of the cruel slave trade.

THE NILE TRIBUTARIES OF ABYSSINIA *Macmillan* 1867
Adventures in search of sport and discoveries amongst 'the Sword Hunters of the Hamran Arabs'.

Barrow, Sir John (1764-1848) TRAVELS INTO THE INTERIOR OF SOUTHERN AFRICA (1801-4)
A VOYAGE TO COCHIN-CHINA, 1792-3 (1806)
Narratives of adventurous journeys, by the Founder of the Geographical Society.

*Bates, Henry Walter (1825-92) THE NATURALIST ON THE RIVER AMAZONS (1863) *Dent (Everyman)* 1910; *Murray* 1910; *C.U.P. (University of California Paperbacks)* 1962 21s
'A record of adventures, habits of animals, and sketches of Brazilian and Indian life during eleven years of travel.' This delightful narrative describes the scientific expedition the naturalist made from 1851 onwards. It resulted in thousands of new species being discovered and named.

*Beckford, William (1759-1844) JOURNAL IN PORTUGAL AND SPAIN, 1787-1788 ed. by Boyd Alexander *Hart-Davis* 1954 30s

A transcript made for the first time of the journal kept by Beckford, the eccentric author of *Vathek*, during a journey which he was compelled by his family to make, because they wished to get him out of their way by sending him to Jamaica. But he slipped ship at Lisbon.

TRAVEL DIARIES 2 vols. ed. by Guy Chapman *Constable* 1928
The best edition, with a memoir and notes, and including the *Recollections of an Excursion to the Monasteries of Alcobaca and Batalha*. These volumes, wrote John Beresford in his introduction to the first edition of the *Torrington Diaries*, 'contain enthralling descriptions and brilliant writing'.

Bell, Aubrey Fitzgerald (1881-1950) A PILGRIM IN SPAIN *Methuen* 1924
SPANISH GALICIA *Bodley Head* 1922
Two books that were compared in an obituary notice in *The Times* with the classic narratives of travel in Spain by Borrow and Ford, entered below.

Bell, Sir Charles Alfred (1870-1945) THE PEOPLE OF TIBET *O.U.P.* 1928
TIBET: PAST AND PRESENT *O.U.P.* 1924

*Bell, Gertrude Lowthian (1868-1926) FROM AMURATH TO AMURATH *Heinemann* 1911
THE DESERT AND THE SOWN *Heinemann* 1907
'Tales of Syrian travel.'

PERSIAN PICTURES *Benn* (1928) 1947
Three books of travel in the Near East where the author lived and worked for many years. See also her celebrated *Letters* entered in the *Autobiography* section.

*Belloc, Hilaire (1870-1953) THE CRUISE OF THE 'NONA' *Constable* (1925) 1955 20s; *Penguin Books* 1958 2s 6d
Introduction by Lord Stanley. This lively log of Belloc's experiences with his old-fashioned 10-ton cutter (not for him the elegance of an expensive yacht) is one of his best books.

THE FOUR MEN *Nelson* 1912
An old favourite. In characteristic style Belloc recalls walking with friends through his beloved Sussex, a county that he celebrated in song and prose throughout his life.

THE OLD ROAD *Constable* (1904) 1921 8s 6d
That is, the road from Canterbury to Winchester. An entertaining mixture of archaeology, history and topography.

ON SAILING THE SEA *Hart-Davis* (*Mariners Library*) 1951 12s 6d
A choice of passages from Belloc's travel books, many of which are now out of print. Notable selections are from *The Cruise of the 'Nona'* (entered above) and *The Hills and the Sea* (1906).

THE PATH TO ROME *Allen and Unwin* 1902 18s Illustrated by Belloc; *Penguin Books* 1958 3s 6d

Perhaps the most enduring of all Belloc's out-of-doors books. He describes a walk from Lorraine in the valley of the Moselle in the old days at the turn of the century when a man could walk on traffic-free lanes and eat and drink liberally for a few francs a day. 'My enchanted pilgrimage' he termed it.

Belt, Thomas (1832–78) THE NATURALIST IN NICARAGUA (1874) *Dent (Everyman)* 1911

Belt was a geologist working and prospecting in the country from 1868.

Borrow, George (1803–81) *THE BIBLE IN SPAIN (1843) *Dent (Everyman)* (1906) 1961 12s 6d; *Macdonald (Illustrated Classics)* 1959 15s

The long title of this best of all travel narratives concerned with Spain, is 'The Journey, Adventures and Imprisonments of an Englishman in an Attempt to Circulate the Scriptures in the Peninsula'. Borrow was a colporteur for the British and Foreign Bible Society. The *Everyman* edition is introduced by Dr. Walter Starkie; and the other standard edition, by Peter Quennell, with Richard Ford's pictures, reproducing paintings of landscapes and towns of old Spain.

THE GYPSIES OF SPAIN *Murray* (1841) 1901 6s

'The Zincali; or, An Account of the Gypsies of Spain, with an original collection of their songs and poetry, and a copious dictionary of their language.'

ROMANO LAVO-LIL *Murray* (1874) 1908 6s

The Word Book of the Romany; or, English Gypsy Language; 'With many pieces in Gypsy, illustrative of the way of speaking and thinking of the English Gypsies; with specimens of their poetry, and an account of certain Gypsyries or places inhabited by them, and of various things relating to Gypsy life in England.'

*WILD WALES *Murray* (1862) *Collins* 1957 9s 6d Illus.; (*Classics*) 1955 6s; *Dent (Everyman)* (1906) 1958 12s 6d; *O.U.P. (Worlds Classics)* 1920 7s 6d

A vivid, descriptive account of a visit and journey made from July 1854: '. . . a simple, uncoloured record of a walking tour,' wrote Theodore Watts-Dunton, who knew Borrow. The Collins illustrated edition has over 100 photographs of places in North Wales, visited by Borrow.

Boswell, James (1740–95) JOURNAL OF A TOUR TO CORSICA (1768) ed. by Sir Sydney Roberts *C.U.P.* 1923 12s 6d

Boswell's *An Account of Corsica: the Journal of a Tour to that Island*; and *Memoirs of Pascal Paoli*, was Boswell's first noteworthy publication, and his support of Paoli's bid for the independence of Corsica followed a meeting with the general during his tour.

*JOURNAL OF A TOUR TO THE HEBRIDES WITH SAMUEL JOHNSON
(1786) *Collins (Classics)* 1955 6s; ed. by L. F. Powell *Dent
(Everyman)* (1909) 1958 10s 6d; *Macdonald (Illustrated Classics)*
1956 15s; ed. by R. W. Chapman *O.U.P. (Oxford Standard
Authors)* 1924 12s 6d; ed. by F. A. Pottle and C. H. Bennett
Heinemann 1963 50s
Macdonald's series edition is illustrated with twenty caricatures by
Thomas Rowlandson; the *O.S.A.* edition is bound with Dr. Johnson's
Journey To the Western Islands of Scotland (1775) entered below.

Brewster, Ralph H. (1904-51) THE 6,000 BEARDS OF ATHOS *Duckworth* 1935 15s
Brewster was a mystic, and his sympathetic description of the ancient,
remote monastery in Greece, and of the life of the bearded monks, is
enlivened by many amusing stories. See also Robert Byron's book
entered below.

*Browne, Edward Granville (1862-1926) A YEAR AMONGST THE
PERSIANS *C.U.P.* (1893) new edition, with a memoir by Sir
E. Denison Ross *A. and C. Black* (1926) 1950 35s 650 pp
Browne was one of the greatest Orientalists of his time. His other master-
piece was the standard *Literary History of Persia*, 4 vols. C.U.P. (1902-24)
1928, 45s each.

Bruce, James (1730-94) TRAVELS TO DISCOVER THE SOURCES OF THE
NILE 5 vols. (1790)
A famous narrative of the author's explorations in Egypt, from Cairo,
through to Abyssinia, during which in 1770 he discovered the source of
the main stream of the Blue Nile. He was known as 'The Abyssinian'.
See Perham's anthology, entered below, for selected passages.

*Bullen, Frank Thomas (1857-1915) THE CRUISE OF THE 'CACHA-
LOT' ROUND THE WORLD *Murray* (1898) 1948 7s 6d; *Collins
(Classics)* 1953 6s
Plain tale of the sea, which in the Collins *Classics* edition is bound with
Bullen's *The Log of a Sea Waif* (1899). The 'Cachalot' was hunting sperm
whales in the old days and by the old ways; the *Log* is an autobiographical
account of 'the first four years of my sea life'.

Burckhardt, John Lewis (1784-1817) TRAVELS IN ARABIA 2 vols.
1829
The most celebrated of the early narratives of travel in Arabia (Aleppo
and Mecca), by an explorer who lived the life of a Moslem. This Swiss
author wrote his travel memoirs in English.

Burton, Sir Richard Francis (1821-90) FIRST FOOTSTEPS IN EAST
AFRICA (1856) *Dent (Everyman)* 1910
An account of Burton's pioneer journey into the Somali country, 1854-5.

THE LAKE REGION OF CENTRAL AFRICA 2 vols. (1860) ed. by Alan Moorehead *Sidgwick and Jackson* 1961 84s (the set) 880 pp Illus. A diary kept by the explorer, on a journey which was the first penetration into the interior of Africa on such a scale. The editor of the modern reprint says: '. . . not only his best book but, also, in a field of writing that was remarkably good, one of the best explorer journals ever written'.

PILGRIMAGE TO EL MEDINAH AND MECCA (1855) *Bell* 1913
Perhaps the most widely read of Burton's travel books.

*Butler, Samuel (1835-1902) ALPS AND SANCTUARIES (1881) *Cape* 1925
R. A. Streatfeild, who edited a new and revised edition in 1913, with some additions to the 1881 text, considered this to be 'one of the wisest, wittiest and tenderest of Butler's books'. An enchanting book it is even in these post-war days, when the St. Gothard tunnel and railways, and motorways, and travel agencies, have changed the quietude of Piedmont and the Canton Ticino for ever.

Byron, Robert (1905-41) THE ROAD TO OXIANA *Macmillan* (1937) *Lehmann* 1950
THE STATION: ATHOS-TREASURES AND MEN *Duckworth* (1928) *Lehmann* 1949
Books by a writer of rare talent, lost to literature during World War II. His two passions were architecture and travel. An appreciation will be found in *Four Studies in Loyalty*, by Christopher Sykes, Collins, 1946.

Calderón de la Barca, Frances Inglis (1804-82) LIFE IN MEXICO (1843) *Dent* (*Everyman*) (1913) 1954 12s 6d
A contemporary survey and description written by the Scottish wife of the Spanish Ambassador to Mexico.

Camden, William (1551-1623) BRITANNIA (1586; 1607) translated from the Latin by Philemon Holland (1610)
A survey of the British Isles made by the first of the great scholar-antiquarians. Another standard English translation was made in 1789 by Richard Gough, revised in 1806.

Candler, Edmund (1874-1926) THE UNVEILING OF LHASA *Edward Arnold* 1905
Of historical interest because it gives an account of the British Expedition to the Forbidden City, at that time hitherto visited by only one Englishman.

*Cherry-Garrard, Apsley (1886-1959) THE WORST JOURNEY IN THE WORLD *Chatto* (1922) 1951 Illus.; maps
The personal narrative of the author's experiences with the British Antarctic Expedition, 1910-13. Refer also to Captain Scott's Journals, entered below. The maps and illustrations were by the author and his colleague, Dr. E. A. Wilson, who did not survive.

*Cobbett, William (1763-1835) RURAL RIDES (1830) 2 vols. ed. by
Asa Briggs *Dent (Everyman)* (1912) 1953 8s 6d each; ed. by
E. W. Martin *Macdonald (Illustrated Classics)* 1959 15s
Narrative of tours made from 1821; Cobbett wanted 'to see for himself'
the state of England in the agricultural districts and towns, the villages
and farms, from the south country to the north. His political comments,
and frequently racy descriptions, give us a picture of rural England at
the period of change and hardship. The illustrated series edition reproduces Gilray's contemporary cartoons from the *Life of Cobbett*, by
himself, and other contemporary prints.

Collingwood, Robin George (1889-1943) THE FIRST MATE'S LOG
O.U.P. 1940
This entertaining log was kept by the distinguished historiographer and
philosopher on a voyage to Greece in the schooner-yacht *Fleur de Lys*
in 1939, in the company of some undergraduate friends.

*Conrad, Joseph (1857-1924) THE MIRROR OF THE SEA (1906) *Dent*
(1912) 1946 11s 6d
Bound with *A Personal Record*. The two books are complementary, being
personal reminiscences of the novelist's early manhood in the Merchant
Service.

Conway, William Martin (Lord Conway of Allington) (1856-
1937) THE ALPS FROM END TO END *Constable* (1895) *Nelson* 1917
A survey of permanent interest, made by a well-known mountaineer,
and still of value to the twentieth-century Alpine climber.

Cook, Captain James (1728-79) THE JOURNALS OF CAPT. JAMES
COOK ON HIS VOYAGES OF DISCOVERY ed. by J. C. Beaglehole
and three others *C.U.P.* 1955- *in progress*
A definitive edition published for the Hakluyt Society. Vol. 1: (1955)—
The Voyage of the 'Endeavour', 1768-71 (80s); vol. 2: (1961)—The
Voyage of the 'Resolution' and the 'Adventure' (120s). To accompany
the above C.U.P. have published a *Portfolio of Charts and Views*, drawn
by Captain Cook and his officers, and reproduced from the original
manuscripts, 50s.

*VOYAGES OF DISCOVERY (1773; 1777; 1784) *Cresset Press* 1950
12s 6d; *Dent (Everyman)* (1906) 1954 10s 6d
First voyage, 1771; second (towards the South Pole) and round the world,
1772-5; third to the Pacific Ocean, 1776-80. The record of these voyages,
selected in the two series editions, were written in part by Captain Cook
himself, and in part by Captain King. The Cresset Press selection has an
introduction by Christopher Lloyd, an authority on naval history.

Coryate, Thomas (1577?-1617) CRUDITIES (1611) 2 vols. *Macle-
hose* 1905
Record of a journey made on foot from 1608, across Europe, to Venice.
'Coryat's Crudities Hastily Gobled Up in Five Moneths' Travels', are

read sometimes for the pleasure to be savoured from the high-flown,
picturesque style of the narrative.

Crèvecoeur, Michel-Guillaume Jean de (1735-1813) LETTERS FROM
AN AMERICAN FARMER (1782) *Chatto* (1909); *Dent* (*Everyman*)
(1912) 1962 10s 6d
A naturalised British subject who settled in Orange County, New York,
and who became a farmer, wrote these letters in English. They were
translated into his native French, and are said to have encouraged many
French families to emigrate to America in search of farms and work on
the land.

Curzon, Robert (Lord Zouche) (1810-73) VISITS TO MONASTERIES
IN THE LEVANT (1849) *O.U.P.* 1916; *Arthur Barker* 1955 25s
Illus.
The author was a diplomat, in office in Constantinople. This pleasant
travel book is a record of his visits to Mount Athos (refer also above to
Brewster and Byron), and to the Near East.

*Dampier, William (1652-1715) A NEW VOYAGE ROUND THE
WORLD (1697) ed. by Sir Albert Gray *A. and C. Black* 1937
18s Illus.; maps

VOYAGES AND DESCRIPTIONS (1699) 2 vols. ed. by John Masefield
Richards Press 1906
This picturesque narrative and record of adventures voyaging to the
South Seas, the East Indies, New Holland, and Australia, is bound with
Dampier's *New Voyage*.

*Dana, Richard Henry (1815-1882) TWO YEARS BEFORE THE MAST
(1840) *Dent* (*Everyman*) 1912; *Nelson* (*Classics*) 1956 5s
A narrative of personal experiences by an American who worked on
board a merchant vessel in the old, hard, days of the sailing craft. In the
Everyman edition a later, shorter work is given, *Twenty-Four Years After*
(1869), in which is described another voyage.

*Darwin, Charles Robert (1809-82) JOURNAL OF RESEARCHES (THE
VOYAGE OF THE 'BEAGLE') (1839) *Dent* (*Everyman*) (1906) 1955
10s 6d Illus.; *Hamish Hamilton* 1962 26s
Full title: 'Journal of Researches into the Geology and Natural History
of the Various Countries Visited during the Voyage of "H.M.S. Beagle"
Round the World, 1832-6'. The 'Beagle' went to South America,
Patagonia, Chili, Peru, and the Pacific Islands, and it was there that
Darwin made his most interesting and important observations on
certain aspects of natural evolution of the species, adaptation to environment, and related topics. The Hamish Hamilton edition is from Harper,
New York, and is a skilful abridgement, with editorial comment,
drawings and maps, suitable not only for general readers, but also for
older children interested in science.

*Defoe, Daniel (1661?-1731) A TOUR THROUGH THE WHOLE ISLAND
OF GREAT BRITAIN (1724-7) 2 vols. ed. by G. D. H. Cole *Peter
Davies* (1927); *Dent (Everyman)* (1928) 1962 15s each
The best edition had a set of maps by Hermann Moll. The new *Everyman*
now includes the complete, unabridged text (including the Scottish tour
formerly omitted). Defoe's record of social and economic conditions is,
says the editor, 'by far the most graphic contemporary account' of its
period. See also the later tours of John Byng and Cobbett.

Dickens, Charles (1812-70) AMERICAN NOTES (1842) and PICTURES
FROM ITALY (1846) introduction by Sacheverell Sitwell *O.U.P.*
1957 15s Illus.
'The two lesser works, here presented, show the sparks of his talent,
and if they do not enhance, still less do they tarnish his great name.'—
Sacheverell Sitwell. The illustrations are by Marcus Stone, Samuel Palmer
and Clarkson Stanfield.

*Doughty, Charles Montagu (1843-1926) TRAVELS IN ARABIA
DESERTA (1888) 2 vols. introduction by T. E. Lawrence *Cape*
1936 105s (the set) 1313 pp Illus.
PASSAGES FROM 'ARABIA DESERTA' selected by Edward Garnett
Cape 1931 16s
The quartos of the complete, standard edition, contain all the illustrations, maps and drawings from the original edition, together with a
glossary of Arabic words and an index. Doughty travelled in Arabia,
and lived with Arabs, as one of themselves, from 1876 to 1878. T. E.
Lawrence of Arabia, said that Doughty's was 'a book not like other
books; but something particular, a bible of its kind'. Doughty, he added,
'by being always Arab in manner and European in mind maintained a
perfect judgement'.

WANDERINGS IN ARABIA *Duckworth* (1908) 1948 15s 608 pp
An authorised abridgement by Edward Garnett.

*Douglas, Norman (1868-1952) OLD CALABRIA (1915) *Secker and
Warburg* 1955 30s; *Penguin Books* 1962 12s 6d
SIREN LAND (1911) and FOUNTAINS IN THE SAND (1912) *Secker
and Warburg* 1957 30s
The last edition brings together into one volume two modern classics of
travel in which the writer first evokes the landscape, and the life of the
region surrounding Naples, and then follows this with a description of
the more exotic scene in Tunisia. Douglas is said to have been delighted
when a British officer told him that during the war *Fountains in the Sand*
had been 'more useful to us than anything prepared by our experts'.

Du Chaillu, Paul Belloni (c. 1835-1903) EXPLORATION AND
ADVENTURES IN EQUATORIAL AFRICA (1861) revised edition 1871
ed. by L. Stanley Jast *Werner Laurie* 1945
Apart from its interest for the general reader as a record of an adventurous, pioneer journey, the narrative was valued for the scientific

L*

information Du Chaillu accumulated on the geography, fauna and
tribes, of the West African region he explored.

Dufferin and Ava (Marquess of) (1826-1902) LETTERS FROM HIGH
LATITUDES (1859) *Murray* 1903; *O.U.P.* 1915
'Being some account of a voyage in 1856 in the schooner-yacht *Foam* to
Iceland, Jan Meyen and Spitzbergen.'

Eden, Emily (1797-1869) UP THE COUNTRY 2 vols. (1866-7) ed. by
Edward Thompson *O.U.P.* 1930
'Letters written to her sister from the Upper Province of India,' where
Emily Eden lived from 1835 to 1842, having accompanied her brother
on his appointment as Governor-General of India.

*Fielding, Henry (1707-54) JOURNAL OF A VOYAGE TO LISBON
(1755) *Dent* (*Everyman*) (1932) 1958 8s 6d
In 1754 Fielding went to Lisbon to regain broken health, and although
he did not succeed, he left this delightful, posthumous journal as his last
prose writing, for he died soon after his arrival in Portugal, and was
buried at Lisbon. The work is bound with the novel *Jonathan Wild*.

*Fiennes, Celia (1662-1741) JOURNEYS (1888) ed. by Christopher
Morris *Cresset Press* (1947) 1949 12s 6d
The first edition of 1888, states the editor of the only modern edition,
was 'incomplete, inaccurate, and unannotated'; it has long been a scarce
book. The new edition established a definitive text from the original
manuscript. The record Celia Fiennes kept on her extensive journeys
throughout England, into Wales, and to the Scottish Border counties,
reveals her sharp observation concerning details of social, economic,
architectural and topographical interest, and it thus provides a valuable
survey to set beside Defoe and Cobbett. Preface by G. M. Trevelyan.

Ford, Ford Madox (F. M. Hueffer) (1873-1939) PROVENCE *Allen
and Unwin* 1935 16s
A study of this southern region of France, 'from minstrels to the machine'.

Ford, Richard (1796-1858) GATHERINGS FROM SPAIN (1846) *Dent*
(*Everyman*) 1906
Ford's *Handbook for Travellers in Spain*, prepared in 1845 for John
Murray's standard series, attracted admiration for its literary style as well
as for its practical value, and this selection and revision, introduced in
Everyman by Thomas Okey, for general reading, has since maintained a
position as a minor classic of travel literature.

Franklin, Sir John (1786-1847) A JOURNEY TO THE SHORES OF THE
POLAR SEA, 1819-1822 (1823) *Dent* (*Everyman*) 1910
First of two narratives of Arctic exploration, introduced in *Everyman* by
Captain Robert Falcon Scott. On a later expedition in 1845, from which
Franklin did not return, it is thought that he discovered the North-West
Passage.

Gage, Thomas (1603?-56) THE ENGLISH-AMERICAN: HIS TRAVAIL
BY SEA AND LAND (1648) ed. by A. P. Newton *Routledge (Broad-
way Travellers series)* (1928) 1946; ed. by J. Eric S. Thompson
University of Oklahoma 1958 $5.00
'A New Survey of the West Indies'; a travel narrative of the New World,
by a naval chaplain.

*Gibbings, Robert (1889-1958) COMING DOWN THE WYE *Dent*
1942 18s

OVER THE REEFS *Dent* 1948 18s

SWEET THAMES RUN SOFTLY *Dent* 1940 18s
All of these pleasant travel and descriptive narratives were made
beautiful books by the wood engravings with which the author-
traveller-artist illustrated them. He was the greatest wood engraver of
his time, and a delightful personality. *Over the Reefs* describes his sojourn
and experiences in the South Seas. For the complete list of his many
books and his bibliography refer to his publisher's current catalogue.

Gibbs, J. Arthur (1878-1909) A COTSWOLD VILLAGE *Murray* (1898)
1942 7s 6d Illus.; *Cape* 1929
'Country life and pursuits in Gloucestershire.'

Gill, William John (1843-82) THE RIVER OF GOLDEN SAND 2 vols.
Murray 1882
'A journey through China and Eastern Tibet to Burma.'

Giraldus de Barri ('Cambrensis') (1146?-1220?) THE ITINERARY OF
ARCHBISHOP BALDWIN THROUGH WALES (1585) translated by
Sir R. C. Hoare (1806) *Dent (Everyman)* 1908
The series edition includes the *Descriptio Cambriae (Description of Wales)*.
Both works are source books for the legends and topography of Wales
in the twelfth century.

*Gissing, George (1857-1903) BY THE IONIAN SEA (1901) *Unicorn
Press* 1956 12s 6d
Gissing's happiest work describes the holiday of his lifetime, and
although he seems to have met with indifferent hospitality at Italian inns,
he responded with so much appreciation to the beauty of scene and stone
that his book is treasured by all modern travellers in search of the
emotional link between landscape and literature. The introduction is by
Frank Swinnerton.

Graham, R. B. Cunninghame (1852-1936) MOGREB-EL-ACKSA
Heinemann (1898); *Duckworth* 1921
A description of a journey in Morocco.

*Grenfell, Sir Wilfred Thomason (1865-1940) A LABRADOR
DOCTOR *Hodder* (1920) 1948 21s
An autobiographical record of travel, and of heroic work as a missionary
doctor in the Far North.

*Hakluyt, Richard (1552?-1616) PRINCIPAL NAVIGATIONS (1589; 1599) 10 vols. *Dent* 1927 Illus.; 8 vols. (*Everyman*) (1907-9) 1962 15s each; sel. by A. S. Mott *Blackwell* 1929 12s 6d Illus.; sel. by Janet Hampden *O.U.P.* (*Worlds Classics*) 1958 8s 6d

Dent's standard set of this prose epic contained reproductions of contemporary maps, drawings and illustrations, in crown octavo volumes. The new *Everyman* edition in library format reprints the same text, with minor omissions of certain Latin items and some few in foreign originals. The introduction is by John Masefield. *Worlds Classics* is an excellent selection that includes the famous narratives of the Tudor seamen, and of other travellers and explorers, including the account of the defeat of the Spanish Armada, Drake's voyage round the world, the famous fight of the *Revenge*, together with a glossary, chronology, and a select bibliography. Hakluyt himself collected and edited these first-hand narratives, and the whole work is an example of Tudor prose at its most vigorous and picturesque. The full title is *The Principal Navigations Voyages Traffiques and Discoveries of the English Nation.*

Hall, Basil (1788-1844) TRAVELS IN INDIA, CEYLON AND BORNEO (1831-3) ed. by H. G. Rawlinson *Routledge* (*Broadway Travellers series*) 1931

Selected passages from nine volumes, issued in three series, under the title of *Fragments of Voyages and Travels, 1831-3*. The choice is from Chapters I, VI, and VII of volume 2 (second series); and volume 2 (third series). The editor writes: 'These nine little volumes, once well-known, are now comparatively rare and almost forgotten . . . They are, indeed a lasting joy to the reader . . . Few books ever penned give a more graphic and entertaining picture of the Royal Navy a century ago.'

Herbert, Aubrey Nigel H. Molyneux (1880-1923) BEN KENDIM ed. by Sir Desmond MacCarthy *Putnam* 1924

Desmond MacCarthy edited this posthumous record of Eastern travel as yet another literary testimony of the fascination of the Near and Middle East experienced by many English travellers from the eighteenth century to the twentieth.

Herbert, Sir Thomas (1606-82) TRAVELS IN PERSIA, 1627-9 (1634) ed. by Sir William Foster *Routledge* (*Broadway Travellers series*) 1928

An abridgement of a work entitled *A Relation of Some Yeares Travaile Into Afrique and the Greater Asia Especially the Territories of the Persian Monarchie* selecting for modern readers the most interesting passages.

*Hudson, William Henry (1841-1922) AFOOT IN ENGLAND (1909) *Dent* (*Open-Air Library*) 1933 Illus. by Eric Fitch Daglish

Essays on guide-books, walking and cycling in the English countryside, following a river, and towns and villages in the south.

HAMPSHIRE DAYS (1903) *Dent* 1923

On the New Forest, and Selborne, and many other villages and landscapes in Hampshire, south England, with essays on bird life.

A HIND IN RICHMOND PARK (1922) *Dent* 1951 11*s* 6*d*
Included in this collection of essays is the piece *An Old Thorn*.

IDLE DAYS IN PATAGONIA (1893) *Dent* 1954 11*s* 6*d*
A narrative of travel and sojourn from youthful years and early man-hood, spent by Hudson in South America, before he came to live and work as a naturalist-writer in England.

NATURE IN DOWNLAND (1900) *Dent* 1951 11*s* 6*d*
A naturalist's description of birds and landscapes observed during walks on the Sussex Downs.

James, Henry (1843-1916) ENGLISH HOURS (1905) ed. by A. L. Lowe *Heinemann* 1960 25*s* Illus. by Anthony Gross; (*Mercury Books*) 1963 12*s* 6*d*

A LITTLE TOUR IN FRANCE *Heinemann* (1884) *Benn* 1948
'. . . impressions, immediate, lazy and consciously limited.' Places visited include Tours, Blois, Bourges, Poitiers, Toulouse, Carcassonne, Nimes, Tarascon, Arles, Les Baux, Avignon, Orange, Macon, and Dijon.

PARISIAN SKETCHES ed. by Leon Edel and Ilse Dusoir Lind *Hart-Davis* 1958 25*s*
A collection of letters to the *New York Tribune*, from 1875 to 1876, in which James described the literary and artistic life of Paris.

*Johnson, Samuel (1709-84) A JOURNEY TO THE WESTERN ISLANDS OF SCOTLAND (1775) ed. by R. W. Chapman *O.U.P.* (*Standard Authors*) 1924 12*s* 6*d*
In this series edition Johnson's account is bound with Boswell's *Tour to the Hebrides* (1785), a companion piece describing the journey they took together in 1773, from August to November. Other editions of Boswell's *Journal* are entered above.

Jones, Henry Festing (1851-1928) CASTELLINARIA, AND OTHER SICILIAN DIVERSIONS (1911; 1920)

DIVERSIONS IN SICILY (1909; 1920) *Cape* 1929

MOUNT ERYX, AND OTHER DIVERSIONS OF TRAVEL *Cape* 1921
Individual in his absorption of Mediterranean landscape and of the past, displayed in classical antiquities, Festing Jones's travel books reveal affinities with those of his friend, whose biography he wrote, Samuel Butler, author of *Erewhon* and *The Way of All Flesh*.

King, Clarence (1842-1901) MOUNTAINEERING IN THE SIERRA NEVADA (1872) *A. and C. Black* 1947
An American classic of mountaineering literature. King was a professional geologist.

*Kingdon-Ward, Frank (1885-1958) BURMA'S ICY MOUNTAINS *Cape* 1949 15*s* Illus.
The story of two expeditions, 1937-9, into mountains 20,000 feet high. Kingdon-Ward was one of the greatest plant-hunters of his time.

MODERN EXPLORATION *Cape* 1945 6s

*Kinglake, Alexander William (1809-91) EOTHEN (1844) *Dent* (1908) 1954 8s 6d; ed. by Robin Fedden *Methuen* 1948 6s
'Traces of Travel Brought Home from the East'—from the dawn. *Eothen* is one of the first nineteenth-century travel books to be enjoyed as a masterpiece of literature, apart from its value as a work of description. It is a delightful and at times, amusing record, of Kinglake's leisurely travels in countries of the Near East.

Kingsley, Mary Henrietta (1862-1900) TRAVELS IN WEST AFRICA *Macmillan* (1896)
This courageous traveller (niece of the novelist Charles Kingsley) ventured into remote regions, including the Congo and the Cameroons, observing native customs not witnessed by white travellers before, especially those connected with fetish worship. She recounted her experiences with humour and her book is excellent reading, deserving at least a modern edition in an abridged form.

Kipling, Rudyard (1865-1936) FROM SEA TO SEA 2 vols. *Macmillan* (1899) 1938
'Letters of Travel' written for *The Pioneer* from 1889; *Letters of Marque*; *The City of Dreadful Night*, and other essays.

*Knight, Edward Frederick (1852-1925) THE CRUISE OF THE 'ALERTE' (1890) *Hart-Davis* (*Mariners Library*) 1952 10s 6d
'Search for treasure on Trinidad.'

THE 'FALCON' ON THE BALTIC (1888) *Hart-Davis* (*Mariners Library*) 1951 10s 6d
This is an old favourite with yachtsmen and cruising enthusiasts, here introduced to a new generation in this standard series.

Lane, Edward William (1801-76) MANNERS AND CUSTOMS OF THE MODERN EGYPTIANS (1836) ed. by E. Stanley Poole *Dent* (*Everyman*) (1908) 1954 10s 6d Illus.
Introduced and recommended by Moursi Saad el-Din, of the Egyptian Ministry of Education. It is said that time has not outdated this entertaining travel book as a reliable and authentic picture of Egypt and its people.

*Lawrence, David Herbert (1885-1930) MORNINGS IN MEXICO (1927) and ETRUSCAN PLACES (1932) *Heinemann* 1950 12s 6d
The impressions of Mexico includes a famous essay on 'The Hopi Snake Dance'.

SEA AND SARDINIA (1923) *Heinemann* 1952 12s 6d and 8s 6d
One of Lawrence's greatest books. To say that it describes a journey from Palermo in Sicily to Cagliari, the capital of Sardinia, thence inland to Nuoro, and back via Terranova, is merely geographical information; it's the style of the narrative that matters. The prose is as alive as the

movement of a lizard; as glowing as the Sardinian sun. Richard Aldington, who writes the introduction to the reprint in the collected edition, says: 'A quite unconscious portrait of the author, that irresistibly charming Lawrence who had the gift of making even the most commonplace things seem wonderful'.

TWILIGHT IN ITALY *Duckworth* (1916); *Heinemann* 1950 12s 6d and 8s 6d

Leake, William Martin (1777-1860) JOURNAL OF A TOUR IN ASIA MINOR (1824)
TRAVELS IN NORTHERN GREECE 4 vols. (1835)
There have been no modern editions of these works by a distinguished geographer, but they are held in great esteem by authorities on nineteenth-century travel books.

Lewis, Matthew Gregory (1775-1818) THE JOURNAL OF A WEST-INDIAN PROPRIETOR, 1815-1817 (1834) ed. by M. Wilson *Routledge* 1929
The best book by 'Monk' Lewis, as he became known after the publication of his licentious novel, *The Monk*, entered in the *Fiction* section. Having inherited Jamaican plantations, Lewis went to see for himself the conditions of slave labour obtaining, and what he saw made him improve things. Hence the historical interest of his posthumously published journal.

*Livingstone, David (1813-73) MISSIONARY TRAVELS AND RE-SEARCHES IN SOUTH AFRICA (1857) ed. and compiled from Livingstone's own published diaries and journals by James I. Macnair *Dent* 1954 21s Illus.; maps

Lowell, James Russell (1819-91) FIRESIDE TRAVELS (1864) ed. by E. V. Lucas *O.U.P.* 1909
Of these once popular six discursive essays on Italy, the Mediterranean, voyages by sea, and kindred subjects, the editor said: 'The neglect of *Fireside Travels*, on both sides of the Atlantic has been a mistake, for it has meant the loss of much wisdom and wit, fancy and learning, wise humanity and not a little beauty'.

*Lubbock, Alfred Basil (1876-1944) ROUND THE HORN BEFORE THE MAST *Murray* (1902) 1946 8s 6d Illus.
An account of a voyage from San Francisco round Cape Horn to Liverpool in a four-masted windjammer. Lubbock, from his own experiences, and his researches, was an authority on the old clippers. For a complete list of his standard monographs on The China Clippers, The Colonial Clippers, the 'Cutty Sark', The Opium Clippers, etc., see the annotated current catalogue of the firm of marine book publishers, Brown, Son and Ferguson, of Glasgow.

*Macaulay, Dame Rose (1881-1958) FABLED SHORE *Hamish Hamilton* (1949) 1956 21s; *Arrow Books* 1960 5s
A witty and diverting account of a car journey from the Pyrenees to Cape St. Vincent in Portugal. With great skill the writer links the history of this vast stretch of the Mediterranean with landscape, people and things seen.

*Macdonald, John (1741-?) MEMOIRS OF AN EIGHTEENTH-CENTURY FOOTMAN (1790) ed. by John Beresford *Routledge* (*Broadway Travellers series*) 1927 16s
The original title was *Travels In Various Parts of Europe, Asia and Africa, 1745-1779*. It is a racy, amusing personal narrative of a poverty-stricken childhood; service under twenty-seven masters; and contains a notable account of the occasion when the footman was sent by his master to call on 'Mr. Sterne, the celebrated author', when Yorick lay dying. Lecky the historian thought Macdonald was the first known man to have had the courage to walk about London under the shelter of an umbrella, although others say this credit is due to Jonas Hanway. The modern edition appears to have been the only reprint.

*MacGregor, John (1825-92) THE VOYAGE ALONE IN THE YAWL 'ROB ROY' (1867) *Hart-Davis* (*Mariners Library*) 1954 10s 6d
A narrative of adventures in a canoe: 'London to Paris and back'. The barrister-author wrote other books of a similar kind under the pseudonym of his canoe-name: 'Rob Roy'.

*McMullen, Richard Turrill (1830-91) DOWN CHANNEL (1869; 1893) *Hart-Davis* (*Mariners Library*) 1949 10s 6d
One of the most treasured books of sea adventure. None of the voyages was outside the home waters, but yachtsmen regard the narrative as a classic of the sport. The introductions to the series edition are by Canon Dixon Kemp and Arthur Ransome.

Malcolm, Sir John (1769-1833) SKETCHES OF PERSIA 2 vols. (1827-8) *Cassell* 1888
'From the journals of a traveller in the East.' The author was a soldier, but later was three times ambassador to Persia, and did much to arouse and sustain British interest in Persia at the beginning of the nineteenth century.

Mallock, William Hurrell (1849-1923) IN AN ENCHANTED ISLAND (1889)
A record of 'a winter Retreat in Cyprus', by the brilliant satirist who wrote on labour problems, and is famed still for his ironic masterpiece, *The New Republic*, for which see in the *Fiction* section.

*Mandeville, Sir John (1300?-1372?) TRAVELS (1496) *Dent* (*Everyman*) 1928; translated from Jean d'Outremeuse; 2 vols. ed. by P. Hamelius *O.U.P.* (1919; 1923) 1960-1 25s each
'The Voiage and Travayle of Syr John Mandeville, Knight.' Scholars think this extraordinary work must be a redaction of a number of travel

books, taking the reader to the Holy Land, Turkey, Persia, Egypt, India, and Tartary. The French original was attributed to Jean de Bourgogne, perhaps an assumed name of Sir John Mandeville. *Everyman* offers a modernised translation, together with a fragment known as *The Journal of Frier Odoricus*. Odoric may have been one of the authors edited by Mandeville for his *Travels*. The Middle English text published for the *Early English Text Society* by O.U.P. is for scholars and students rather than the general reader.

*Massingham, Harold John (1888-1952) CHILTERN COUNTRY *Batsford* (1940) 1949 12s 6d (and 6s 6d paperback); ENGLISH DOWNLAND *Batsford* (1936) 1949 12s 6d (and 6s 6d paperback)
Profusely illustrated topographical descriptions of characteristic regions of southern England, by a gifted journalist.

THE SOUTHERN MARCHES *Robert Hale* 1952 21s Illus.
A standard work in *The Regional Books*, and the best modern topographical description of the beautiful landscape and villages of the English-Welsh border 'twixt Wye and Usk'.

Montague, Charles Edward (1867-1928) THE RIGHT PLACE *Chatto* 1924
Informal essays on the art of travel, with some personal experiences of journeys in Europe, 'when the map was in tune'.

Moore, Adolphus W. (1841-87) THE ALPS IN 1864 2 vols. ed. by E. H. Stevens *Blackwell* 1939
A private journal of a mountaineer.

*Muhlauser, George Henry Pasche (1870?-1923) THE CRUISE OF THE 'AMARYLLIS' (1924) *Hart-Davis* (*Mariners Library*) 1950 10s 6d
With a memoir of the author, by E. Keble Chatterton.

*Mummery, Albert Frederick (1855-95) MY CLIMBS IN THE ALPS AND CAUCASUS (1895) *Blackwell* 1947 9s 6d
A classic of mountaineering literature, by one of the greatest of the Victorian climbers.

*Newton, Arthur Percival (1873-1942) TRAVEL AND TRAVELLERS OF THE MIDDLE AGES *Routledge* 1926 25s Illus.; maps
A volume in the standard series *The History of Civilisation*.

*Noyce, Wilfrid (1917-62) SOUTH COL *Heinemann* 1954 10s 6d Illus.
The 1953 Everest Expedition described in vivid detail by a great mountaineer whose gifts as a writer enabled him to make the reader feel what it was like to open up the route, as he did with Sherpa Annulla.

TO THE UNKNOWN MOUNTAIN *Heinemann* 1962 21s Illus.
The last mountaineering book of this quiet, resourceful, modest climber who here gave readers a personal narrative about the ascent of 'the

unknown peak' called *Trivor* (23,370 feet) in the Karakoram region of the Himalayas. The earlier conquest of Machapuchare in the Himalayas was described in his *Climbing the Fish's Tail*, Heinemann, 1958 18s

Palgrave, William Gifford (1826-88) A NARRATIVE OF A YEAR'S JOURNEY THROUGH CENTRAL AND EASTERN ARABIA 2 vols. 1865
The journey was undertaken when Palgrave was a Jesuit missionary working in Syria and Arabia. He was the son of F. T. Palgrave, compiler of the anthology, *The Golden Treasury*.

*Park, Mungo (1771-1806) TRAVELS IN INTERIOR DISTRICTS OF AFRICA, 1795-7 (1799) *Dent* (*Everyman*) (1907) ed. by Ronald Miller 1954 10s 6d
Includes the explorer's *Journal of a Mission to the Interior of Africa in 1805*. In this expedition the discoverer of the River Niger lost his life, and the editor has added material to give a complete account of the 1805-6 journey.

*Parkman, Francis (1823-93) THE OREGON TRAIL (1849) ed. by H. S. Commager *O.U.P.* 1944; (*Mentor Books*) 1956 4s
'Sketches of prairie and Rocky Mountain life', being a narrative of Parkman's life with the Indians during a sojourn with them in 1846. This is Parkman's most widely read book. For related works conceived when he was writing *The Oregon Trail*, as a sort of 'history of the American forest', refer to the *History* section.

Purchas, Samuel (1575-1626) PURCHAS HIS PILGRIMES (1612; 1619; 1625) ed. and selected by H. G. Rawlinson *C.U.P.* 1931
Purchas continued the work of Hakluyt, entered above, and is thought to have acquired his papers and documents for these diffuse travel narratives, now of antiquarian interest only. Yet the three compilations are source books for picturesque accounts of the 'History of the World in Sea Voyages and Land Travell by Englishmen and others'. See, for example, *The First Englishman in Japan*, by P. G. Rogers, with a foreword by Edmund Blunden, Harvill Press, 1956, 12s 6d. The original record of William Adams (1564-1620), who served two Japanese emperors for twenty years, was preserved by Purchas. The standard edition of the complete Purchas narratives was published by Maclehose, in twenty volumes, 1905-7.

Reade, William Winwood (1838-75) SAVAGE AFRICA (1863)
Reade (nephew of Charles, the author of *The Cloister and the Hearth*) travelled to West Africa in 1862, and with few resources, went up the Congo for about 150 miles. He then spent a year journeying into the interior, studying the slave trade. 'The feat was one worthy to rank with those of much more renowned travellers and has never received half the credit it deserves,' wrote F. Legge, in his biographical introduction to Winwood Reade's much more famous work, *The Martyrdom of Man*, entered in the *History* section.

Ross, Sir John (1777-1856) A VOYAGE OF DISCOVERY (1819; 1835) *Murray* 1847
Record of an early attempt to discover the North-West Passage, and to explore Baffin Bay, 1829-33.

Scott, Robert Falcon (1868-1912) THE VOYAGE OF THE 'DISCOVERY' 2 vols. *Murray* (1905) 1929 15s
The reprint of this record of Antarctic exploration on the expedition of 1900-4, was an abridged, popular edition.

SCOTT'S LAST EXPEDITION: JOURNALS AND REPORTS 2 vols. ed. by Leonard Huxley *Murray* 1913 25s (the set) Illus.; maps
Sir James Barrie contributed a biographical appreciation of the great explorer, and there is a preface by Sir Clements Markham. Vol. 1 prints Scott's Journals; vol. 2 the reports of the journeys and the scientific work undertaken by Dr. E. A. Wilson and others on the ill-fated expedition.

*SCOTT'S LAST EXPEDITION: THE PERSONAL JOURNALS *Murray* 1923 15s Illus.; map
This is the popular edition of the main work, and prints the personal journals kept by Captain Scott on his journey to the South Pole.

Shackleton, Sir Ernest (1874-1922) SOUTH *Heinemann* (1919) 1951 Illus.
A record of Antarctic exploration, 1914-17, the author's last expedition to the South Pole.

Shelvocke, George (*fl.* 1690-1728) A VOYAGE ROUND THE WORLD (1726) ed. by W. G. Perrin *Cassell* 1928 Illus.; *Cape* 1930
The Cape edition was issued under the title of *A Privateer's Voyage Round the World.*

Sherley, Sir Anthony (1565-1635?) RELATION OF HIS TRAVELS INTO PERSIA (1613) ed. by Sir E. Denison Ross *Routledge* (*Broadway Travellers series*) 1933 Illus.
The series reprint was issued under the title of *Sir Anthony Sherley and his Persian Adventure*, and included four contemporary narratives relating to Sherley's journey to and sojourn in Persia, extracts from his *Relation*, together with a long introduction, a bibliography, and a life of the author.

*Slocum, Captain Joshua (1844-19?) SAILING ALONE AROUND THE WORLD (1900) *Hart-Davis* (*Mariners Library*) 1948 12s 6d
This was one of the most famous voyages of which we have a record, for Captain Slocum sailed 46,000 miles in his sloop *Spray*. He ventured a second time, but never returned. Refer also to *The Life and Voyages of Captain Joshua Slocum*, by Victor Slocum, Hart-Davis, 1952, 21s.

Smith, Captain John (1580-1631) TRUE TRAVELS AND ADVENTURES INTO EUROPE, ASIA, AFRICA AND AMERICA, 1593-1629 (1630) *Routledge* 1907

THE GENERALL HISTORIE OF VIRGINIA, NEW ENGLAND AND THE
SUMMER ISLES (1624) 2 vols. *Maclehose* 1907
'Together with *True Travels* . . . and a sea grammar.' This edition thus
brought together the works of the pioneer who colonised Virginia, of
which state he became president in 1608.

Smollett, Tobias (1721-1771) TRAVELS THROUGH FRANCE AND
ITALY (1766) *O.U.P.* (*Worlds Classics*) 1907
John Lehmann also published in 1949 an edition of this narrative of a
tour of two years. The novelist's work is distinguished for its shrewd,
individual and sometimes caustic comments on manners and customs,
art and architecture.

Smythe, Frank Sydney (1900-49) THE ADVENTURES OF A MOUN-
TAINEER *Dent* (1940) 1950 Illus.

KAMET CONQUERED *Hodder* (1932) 1948 Illus.
These two notable mountaineering books by a great climber and
mountain explorer display some of his own photographs, for which he
was famous.

MY ALPINE ALBUM *A. and C. Black* 1947 12s 6d Illustrated; map
SNOW ON THE HILLS *A. and C. Black* 1948 12s 6d Illus.
SWISS WINTER *A. and C. Black* 1948 12s 6d Illus.
All of the above quartos are profusely illustrated with reproductions of
the author's photographs, some in colour.

Speke, John Hanning (1827-64) JOURNAL OF THE DISCOVERY OF
THE SOURCE OF THE NILE (1863) *Dent* (*Everyman*) 1906
The record of the famous journey sponsored by the Royal Geographical
Society, during which Speke discovered the Victoria Nyanza, and the
source of the River Nile.

Stanley, Sir Henry Morton (1841-1904) HOW I FOUND LIVINGSTONE
(1872)

IN DARKEST AFRICA; OR, THE RESCUE OF EMIN 2 vols. (1890)

THROUGH THE DARK CONTINENT 2 vols. (1878)
Once frequently reprinted, these popular narratives of exploration and
adventure, are now reference books for details of Stanley's adventures
when carrying out his editor's instructions 'Find Livingstone'; his subsequent explorations along the course of the river Congo; and his last
expedition to rescue Emin Pasha, which he accomplished in 1888.

Stein, Sir Aurel (1862-1943) RUINS OF DESERT CATHAY 2 vols.
Macmillan 1912
This distinguished archaeologist and traveller undertook many journeys
for the Government of India. All of his books are of permanent import-
ance, but are now somewhat scarce. The others include: *On Alexander's
Track to the Indus* (1929); *On Ancient Central Asian Tracks* (1933); *On Old
Routes of Western Iran* (1940) and *Sand-Buried Ruins of Khotan* (1903), all
published by Macmillan, and long out of print.

*Stephen, Sir Leslie (1823-1904) THE PLAYGROUND OF EUROPE (1871) *Blackwell* 1947 9s 6d
The author was a President of the Alpine Club for some years; and this book on climbing in Switzerland and the Alps did much to popularise the sport in Victorian times.

Stevenson, Robert Louis (1850-94) ACROSS THE PLAINS *Chatto* 1892
With other memories and essays.' See *Essays of Travel*, below.

EDINBURGH (1879; 1888) *Hart-Davis* (1954) 1961 12s 6d
'Picturesque notes, with etchings.' The reprint has twenty-three photographs by Alvin Langdon Coburn.

ESSAYS OF TRAVEL *Chatto* 1905
A miscellaneous collection, eight essays being under the title of *The Amateur Emigrant*, being impressions of the voyage from Glasgow to America. This is an introduction to *Across the Plains*, entered above, in which Stevenson recounted his experiences as an emigrant travelling from New York to San Francisco. See *Travels With a Donkey (Collins Classics)* below.

AN INLAND VOYAGE (1878)
See *Travels With a Donkey*, entered below.

IN THE SOUTH SEAS *Chatto* 1896
'An account of experiences and observations in the Marquesas, Paumotus and Gilbert Islands in the course of two cruises on the yacht *Casco* (1888) and the schooner *Equator* (1889).'

THE SILVERADO SQUATTERS (1883)
'Sketches from a Californian mountain' . . . a sojourn at Calistoga in a deserted mining camp. See *Travels With a Donkey*, below.

*TRAVELS WITH A DONKEY IN THE CEVENNES (1879) *Collins (Classics)* 1956 6s; *Dent (Everyman)* (1925) 1954 8s 6d; *Nelson (Classics)* 1954 6s
This delightful and much-loved narrative of a journey from Monastier is bound in all the series with other works, listed above: Collins—*An Inland Voyage*; *The Silverado Squatters* and *The Amateur Emigrant*, from *Essays of Travel*; Everyman—*An Inland Voyage*; and *The Silverado Squatters*; Nelson—*An Inland Voyage*.

*Stow, John (1525?-1605) A SURVEY OF LONDON (1598; 1603) ed. by H. B. Wheatley *Dent (Everyman)* (1912) 1956 12s 6d; 2 vols. ed. by C. L. Kingsford *O.U.P.* 1908 50s 932 pp
The text of the standard edition in two volumes is from the 1603 edition, also used in *Everyman*, with John Norden's map. This is the principal authority for our knowledge of life and topography in Elizabethan London: its thoroughfares, people and social conditions. C. L. Kingsford adds a biography of John Stow; and *Everyman* provides many notes and corrections, with a useful topographical index.

Sturt, Charles (1795-1869) TWO EXPEDITIONS INTO THE INTERIOR OF SOUTHERN AUSTRALIA 2 vols. 1833; 1848
Sturt led three expeditions into hitherto unexplored regions.

Sykes, Sir Percy Molesworth (1867-1945) *A HISTORY OF EXPLORATION *Routledge* 1934 Illus.
Records and summarises in masterly style the whole of geographical discovery from the earliest times to the twentieth century, with twenty-four plates and thirty-five maps.

TEN THOUSAND MILES IN PERSIA *Murray* 1902

Symons, Arthur (1865-1945) CITIES *Dent* 1903 CITIES OF ITALY *Dent* 1907
COLOUR STUDIES IN PARIS *Chapman and Hall* 1918
Of particular interest for its vivid impressions of Parisian artists and poets of the nineties, including a sketch of Yvette Guilbert, the music-hall entertainer, and material on the two poets, Paul Verlaine and Stéphane Mallarmé.

*Synge, John Millington (1871-1909) THE ARAN ISLANDS *Allen and Unwin* (1907) 1961 18s; *O.U.P.* (*Worlds Classics*) 1962 8s 6d
'In the pages that follow I have given a direct account of my life on the islands, and of what I met with among them, inventing nothing, and changing nothing that is essential.' *Worlds Classics* edition is included with the *Four Plays* entered in the *Prose Drama* section.

*Thomas, Edward (1878-1917) THE HEART OF ENGLAND *Dent* (1906) (*Open-Air Library*) 1932 Illus. by Erich Fitch Daglish
THE SOUTH COUNTRY *Dent* (1909) 1932 Illus. with wood engravings by Eric Fitch Daglish
'This, then, is my South Country. It covers the North Downs and the South Downs, the Icknield Way and the Pilgrims' Way, and the cross-roads between them and the Thames and the sea.' Helen Thomas, the poet's wife, said that this was 'one of the happiest of the prose works of Edward Thomas'.

*Tomlinson, H. M. (1873-1958) THE SEA AND THE JUNGLE *Duckworth* 1912 6s; *Penguin Books* 1953 2s 6d
'The story of a journey in a tramp steamer 2,000 miles up the Amazon.

*Torrington, John Byng, *5th Viscount* (1740-1813) TRAVEL DIARIES *Eyre and Spottiswoode* 1954
See under *Autobiographies* for details of the original edition and the abridgement.

Trollope, Frances (1780-1863) DOMESTIC MANNERS OF THE AMERICANS (1832) ed. by Michael Sadleir *Routledge* 1927
An entertaining account of Mrs. Trollope's three years in America, garnished with some frank and caustic comments said to have been

resented by Americans at the time of the first publication. Mrs. Trollope, mother of Anthony, herself wrote many novels.

*Tschiffely, Aimé Felix (1895-1953) TSCHIFFELY'S RIDE *Heinemann* (1933) *Hodder* (1947) 1952 20s Illus.
Personal narrative of one of the greatest horse rides in history: 'being the account of 10,000 miles in the saddle through the Americas from Argentina to Washington'.

Twain, Mark (Samuel Langhorne Clemens) (1835-1910) THE INNOCENTS ABROAD (1869) *Collins* (*Classics*) 1930 6s
'A record of a pleasure-trip.' This travel journal, written in Mark Twain's humorous style, continues to amuse readers of generation after generation. Europe, Egypt and the Holy Land, are visited by Americans temperamentally unable to appreciate guide-book scenes, buildings, and native art. The book established Clemens as an American humorist with a completely individual style, owing nothing to English writers in this form of literature.

*LIFE ON THE MISSISSIPPI *Chatto* (1883) 1928; *O.U.P.* (*Worlds Classics*) 1962 9s 6d
An autobiographical narrative of Twain's early life as a journeyman pilot on the Mississippi; in these days he found the pen-name that he was to use for the rest of his working life and which soon became familiar all over the world. 'Mark Twain' was the call of the boatmen, sounding the river depth as they drew in to the shore.

A TRAMP ABROAD *Chatto* (1880) MORE TRAMPS ABROAD *Chatto* (1897)
Facetious, semi-fictional accounts of travel in Europe, similar in style to the much more amusing *Innocents Abroad*.

*Voss, John Claus (1854-1922) VENTURESOME VOYAGES (1913) *Hart-Davis* (*Mariners Library*) 1949 12s 6d
The preface by Richard Hughes emphasises the great achievement of Captain Voss in circumnavigating the globe in his small boat.

*Wallace, Alfred Russel (1823-1913) THE MALAY ARCHIPELAGO *Macmillan* (1869; 1892) 1922; *New York, Dover* 1962 $2.00 Maps
After travelling on the Amazon with H. W. Bates, whose book is entered above, Wallace spent many years making scientific observations on the fauna of the Malay islands, 'the land of the orangutan and the Bird of Paradise', writing later 'this narrative of travel, with studies of man and nature'. The only modern reprint of this fascinating book is the American.

TRAVELS ON THE AMAZON AND RIO NEGRO *Macmillan* (1853) *Ward, Lock* 1911
Wallace's journey with Bates was made from 1848 to 1850. The naturalist specialised in entomology, and their expedition was mainly

for the purpose of collecting specimens. Wallace's observations did much to support Darwin's theory of natural selection, and were coincident with Darwin's own work.

Waterton, Charles (1782-1865) WANDERINGS IN SOUTH AMERICA (1825; 1866) *Dent (Everyman)* 1925 6s 6d
A naturalist's travels and scientific observations in 'South America, the North-West of the United States, and the Antilles, in 1812, 1816, 1820, and 1824'.

Whitman, Walt (1819-92) SPECIMEN DAYS IN AMERICA (1882) *Routledge* 1906
Personal impressions of Boston, Washington, and elsewhere, recollected from the years spent as a volunteer nurse in soldiers' hospitals. There are some interesting reports of conversations with Emerson and other eminent contemporaries.

Whymper, Edward (1840-1911) SCRAMBLES AMONGST THE ALPS *Murray* (1871) revised and enlarged by H. E. G. Tyndale 1936 25s
This is the most famous of all the Victorian mountaineering narratives. Whymper recounts many climbs, some of them pioneer ascents of peaks, including the Matterhorn, from 1860 onwards. The revised edition includes additional material taken from Whymper's unpublished diaries.

Wood, Thomas (1892-1950) COBBERS *O.U.P.* (1934) 1953 18s; 1961 *(paperback)* 7s 6d
'A personal record of a journey from Essex, England, to Australia, Tasmania, and some of the reefs and islands in the Coral Sea, made in the years 1930, 1931 and 1932.'

Wordsworth, William (1770-1850) A GUIDE THROUGH THE DISTRICT OF THE LAKES (1810; 1835) *Hart-Davis* 1951 9s 6d; 4s *(paperback)* Illus. by John Piper
Apart from its literary interest as the prose of a poet, the guide is still of practical use to fell-walkers. The earlier editions of 1810, 1820, and 1822, were published under slightly different titles, and sometimes with other works, such as Joseph Wilkinson's *Select Views in Cumberland*, and later, with Wordsworth's volume *The River Duddon and other poems*.

Young, Arthur (1741-1820) TRAVELS IN FRANCE, 1787,8,9 ed. by C. Maxwell *C.U.P.* 1929 25s
Young was a pioneer worker in scientific agronomy and agriculture. This, his most enduring work, has considerable interest because it offers an account of social and agricultural conditions in France just before the Revolution, although it lacks qualities required to make it readable as a travel book.

Younghusband, Sir Frances Edward (1863-1942) THE EPIC OF MOUNT EVEREST *Edward Arnold* 1926 8s 6d

THE WONDERS OF THE HIMALAYAS *Murray* 1924
Colonel Younghusband was a rare combination of a man of action, an explorer, and a mystic philosopher. In addition he was a writer of distinction.

THE LITERATURE OF TRAVEL
(*Anthologies and collections*)

*Axelson, Eric (Editor) SOUTH AFRICAN EXPLORERS O.U.P. (*Worlds Classics*) 1954 7s 6d
An anthology of notable extracts from famous travel books, and the personal narratives of pioneer explorers.

Blakeney, Edward Henry (1869-1955) (Editor) PEAKS, PASSES AND GLACIERS *Dent* (*Everyman*) 1926
A selection from three volumes of records of the mountaineering achievements and adventures of members of the Alpine Club, 1859-62, together with additional essays by Edward Whymper, Sir Alfred Wills and Sir Leslie Stephen, whose own books are listed in this section.

*Crone, G. R. (Editor) THE EXPLORERS *Cassell* 1962 25s
An anthology of first-hand accounts of adventures taken from the writings of the famous explorers. The editor, Librarian of the Royal Geographical Society, has arranged the extracts chronologically in groups, with maps showing routes taken.

*Howard, Cecil (Editor) WEST AFRICAN EXPLORERS O.U.P. (*Worlds Classics*) 1951 9s 6d 610 pp
Selections from classic and other well-known travel narratives with an introduction by J. H. Plumb.

*Ley, Charles David (Editor and Translator) PORTUGUESE VOYAGES, 1498-1663 *Dent* (*Everyman*) (1947) 1953 10s 6d
An anthology of narratives of explorations made during the golden age of Porguguese discovery, which included the colonisation of Brazil. The extracts are translated by the editor and other scholars, and include selections from Dr. Johnson's translation of Father Jerome Lobo's *A Voyage To Abyssinia* (*The Jesuits In Abyssinia*) *1625-1634*, published in 1735. This notable collection therefore deserves a place in *An English Library*, although the original texts were Portuguese.

Marsh, Zoë (Editor) EAST AFRICA THROUGH CONTEMPORARY RECORDS *C.U.P.* 1961 25s Illus.; maps; school edition: 13s 6d
An anthology with notes, offering a unique selection of extracts illustrating the history of Kenya, Uganda, Tanganyika, and Zanzibar, from the earliest times onwards. Official reports, travel narratives, letters, and similar sources have been the sources of this valuable survey. Refer also to the *Worlds Classics* anthology entered under Richards below.

*Massingham, Hugh and Pauline THE ENGLISHMAN ABROAD
Phoenix House 1962 30s Illus.
'These pages can be seen as a painless armchair journey. No bother about
tickets,' write the compilers of this amusing anthology of personal descriptions through the centuries penned by famous and unknown Britons
who have crossed the Channel to grumble at the French for being so
different, to be rude to the Italians, for not understanding English, and
so on. For many of these travellers the negroes really did begin at Calais:
that is why their letters and diaries provide such a diverting miscellany,
with illustrations from the period.

*Perham, Margery and Jack Simmons (Editors) AFRICAN DIS-
COVERY *Faber* (1942) 1957 30s Illus.; maps
'An anthology of exploration'; being the best passages from the writings
of the great British explorers, from James Bruce's journey to Ethiopia in
1769, to Livingstone's death in 1873. Between these two dates the
explorers of note were Mungo Park, Hugh Clapperton, W. B. Baikie,
Sir Richard Burton, J. H. Speke, Sir Samuel Baker, and Sir H. M.
Stanley. Biographies are added by the editors, and the illustrations and
maps are reproduced from the original editions.

*Richards, Charles and James Place (Editors) EAST AFRICAN
EXPLORERS *O.U.P.* (*Worlds Classics*) 1960 8s 6d
The extracts in this anthology are chosen from travellers' narratives,
journals, and other records of early travel from 1843 to 1903. Refer also
to Zoë Marsh's anthology entered above.

A BOOKMAN'S REFERENCE LIBRARY

THE compiler of *An English Library* is indebted to every one of the books recommended in this section: they have been referred to throughout the labour of checking entries, accumulating facts, and verifying bibliographical details. There are perhaps few general readers who would wish to add the complete collection to their personal libraries, but all the volumes mentioned would or should be in every public reference library as a matter of course.

Specific acknowledgement and thanks should be made to the compilers of the key books. These are A. J. Hoppé's perfect *Reader's Guide to Everyman's Library*, a bibliographical tool fully worthy of the great series it records in such detail, than which there can be no greater praise; *The Cambridge Bibliography of English Literature*, together with George Watson's handy concise edition in one volume, extended to the literature of the present century; Professor Baugh's masterly encyclopaedic *Literary History of England*, packed with useful bibliographical data; D. C. Browning's *Dictionary of Literary Biography*; the Cresset Press series of *Introductions to English Literature*, edited by Professor Bonamy Dobrée to provide a unique literary history with bibliographies of great value to students; the excellent *Annals of English Literature*, now once more back in print in a fully revised edition; Bessie Graham's standard *Reader's Adviser and Bookman's Manual*; the invaluable series of *Oxford Companions*; the H. W. Wilson series, without a rival in Great Britain; Cassell's *Encyclopaedia of Literature*; Benet's *The Reader's Encyclopaedia*; and the revised edition of Chambers's *Biographical Dictionary*, distinguished above all other reference books of its kind by the care taken to include references to notable books by and about the persons whose lives are so concisely, and sometimes so brilliantly, summarised by the editor and his contributors.

To these one should add that admirable bibliographical tool known as *British National Bibliography*, which from 1950 onwards, under the meticulous direction of A. J. Wells, has provided librarians, booksellers, and research workers in every subject upon which books are published, with a systematically and closely classified record of British book publishing, and with index cumulations. There is no parallel in the world of national bibliography. The latest editions of the book trade bibliographies, known as *Whitaker's Cumulative Book List*, and its companion, *The Reference Catalogue of Current Literature*, have also been very useful for the checking of editions in print up to 1960; and the various volumes of *The English Catalogue of Books* have been frequently referred to for dates of first editions.

Baker, Ernest A. A GUIDE TO HISTORICAL FICTION *Routledge* 1914
Standard work, now outdated, but useful for the classics and early twentieth-century novels. Arranged by country and period.

A GUIDE TO THE BEST FICTION *Routledge* 1932 634 pp quarto
Still of great value on account of the thoroughness of the editorial work, which was done in collaboration with James Packman. Every novel entered is annotated and sometimes shrewdly evaluated. The choice is wide, and includes American novels, and translations of foreign fiction.

Bartholomew, John George AN ATLAS OF ANCIENT AND CLASSICAL GEOGRAPHY *Dent* (*Reference Library*) (1907) 1952 18s
The fully revised edition was the work of John Warrington. There are sixty-four maps in colour and others, with a gazetteer and index.

*Bartlett, John (1820-1905) FAMILIAR QUOTATIONS *Macmillan* (1855) Centennial (the 13th) edition 1956 50s 1648 pp
'A collection of passages, phrases and proverbs, traced to their sources in ancient and modern literature.' Arrangement: chronologically under authors, with an index of 113,500 entries. Another edition, published by Routledge, 12s 6d, is the compiler's original collection.

*Bateson, Frederick W. THE CAMBRIDGE BIBLIOGRAPHY OF ENGLISH LITERATURE 5 vols. *C.U.P.* 1940; 1957 200s (Vols. 1-4); and 70s (Vol. 5) 4000 pp (double-columns)
Vol. 1: A.D. 600-1660; vol. 2: 1660-1800; vol. 3: 1800-1900; vol. 5: Supplement edited by George Watson, recording works published between 1935 and 1955 relating to the subjects and authors in the main bibliographies; vol. 4: Subject index of names in vols. 1-3, and of anonymous titles. 'Sets out to record, as far as possible in chronological order, the authors, titles and editions, with relevant critical matter, of all writings in book-form (whether in English or Latin) that can still be said to possess some literary interest, by natives of what is now the British Empire, up to the year 1900.'—*Editor's preface* (*1940*). See also under Watson below, for details of the abridgement.

*Baugh, Albert C. and four others A LITERARY HISTORY OF ENGLAND *Routledge* 1950 63s 1673 pp
An outstanding, encyclopaedic survey, notable for shrewd judgements, bibliographical information and lucid style.

Beckson, Karl and Arthur Ganz A READER'S GUIDE TO LITERARY TERMS *Thames and Hudson* 1961 21s
Definitions arranged alphabetically to provide a dictionary of all the terms used in literary histories, criticism, and analytical discussion of literary forms.

Benét, William Rose THE READER'S ENCYCLOPAEDIA *Harrap* (1948) 1955 50s 1242 pp
'An encyclopaedia of world literature and the arts.'

Benham, Sir W. Gurney (1859-1944) BOOK OF QUOTATIONS
Harrap (1907) rev. edn. 1947 30s 1392 pp
Originally published by Ward, Lock. It is, with Bartlett's collection, see
above, the most popular of the older reference works of this type.
Arrangement: alphabetical, with author index, thus differing from Bart-
lett, which is chronological. Includes Latin quotations.

*Brewer, Ebenezer Cobham (1810-97) A DICTIONARY OF PHRASE
AND FABLE (1895) rev. by Desmond Flower and Arthur L. Hayward *Cassell* 1957 30s 984 pp
In the revision, American and Australian phrases in common use are
included; literary allusions and historic phrases are traced to sources,
and anecdotes associated with them recorded.

*British Council WRITERS AND THEIR WORK *Longmans* 1950- *in
progress* 2s 6d each
Standard series of paperback supplements to *British Book News*, a monthly
magazine of classified book reviews published monthly by The British
Council, 2s 6d, with an annual author and title index. The supplements
by 1962 had reached a total of 140 monographs, providing masterly
summaries of the lives and works of British authors from Malory and
Chaucer to living writers, together with bibliographies of principal
books and of critical monographs. There are also a few devoted to
classified specific topics, such as *English Maritime Writing: Hakluyt to
Cook*; *English Translators and Translations*; *English Travellers in the Near
East*; and *Cavalier Poets*. The authors contributing to this notable series
are all well-known authorities and scholars.

Browning, D. C. *A DICTIONARY OF LITERARY BIOGRAPHY: ENGLISH
AND AMERICAN *Dent* (*Reference Library*) (1958) 1960 20s 752 pp
A new work, superseding *Everyman's Biographical Dictionary* (1910).
It provides in alphabetical order 2,300 literary biographies in brief, with
details of works and publication years. Of the authors, 650 are twentieth-
century additions.

A DICTIONARY OF QUOTATIONS AND PROVERBS *Dent* (*Reference
Library*) 1951 18s 766 pp
About 6,000 quotations are arranged under authors. Then follow about
4,000 proverbs.

A DICTIONARY OF SHAKESPEARE QUOTATIONS *Dent* (*Reference
Library*) 1953 18s 572 pp
About 4,000 quotations and extracts, are arranged in the usual order
observed when presenting the plays and poems; with extracts from contemporary writings on Shakespeare, and an index to key words to help
the reader in tracking down quotations to their sources.

*Cam, Helen HISTORICAL NOVELS *Routledge* (for *Historical Asso-
ciation*) 1961 2s 6d (1s 6d to members) 26 pp
The author of this most useful summary, appraisal and evaluation, is
Professor Emerita, Harvard University. She ranges over European

fiction to give examples of historical novels she recommends. She provides an appendix of a select bibliography, arranged chronologically from Ancient Greece to Boston (U.S.A.) in the seventies, with grading marks to indicate novels of outstanding value. Refer also to the National Book League Readers Guide to *Historical Fiction*, entered under Duggan below.

*Carter, John ABC FOR BOOK-COLLECTORS *Hart-Davis* (1952) 1961 16*s*; and *Mercury Books* (1961) 7*s* 6*d*
Third revision of the standard handbook of guidance and essential information. The author is an expert and an acknowledged authority on bibliographical subjects connected with first editions and book-collecting. The definitions and data are arranged alphabetically under subjects.

*Cary, Max and others THE OXFORD CLASSICAL DICTIONARY *O.U.P.* 1949 55*s* 992 pp quarto
Collective scholarship of 164 contributors has here produced the standard reference work on this subject, under the editorship of six eminent classicists.

*Cohen, J. M. and M. J. THE PENGUIN DICTIONARY OF QUOTATIONS (1960) New edition *Cape* 1962 42*s* 672 pp
A hard cover, royal octavo edition, with some additional material, of a popular compendium, in which more emphasis is laid on modern and contemporary quotations than on the familiar passages from the classics. About 12,000 quotations are arranged under the names of the authors, with a detailed index, and with translations of quotations in foreign languages.

*Collins, F. Howard AUTHORS' AND PRINTERS' DICTIONARY *O.U.P.* (1905) 1956 10*s* 6*d*
Authoritative guidance for writers, editors, printers and proof correctors, and for typists dealing with literary copy. The rules and decisions regarding treatment of proper names, spellings, plurals, foreign words, abbreviations and similar difficulties that crop up from time to time are those followed by the Clarendon Press for their house style.

*Collison, Robert NEWNES DICTIONARY OF DATES AND ANNIVERSARIES *Newnes* 1962 35*s*
A chronology of about 10,000 world events and important people: historical, political, economic, scientific and cultural. Arranged in two parts: alphabetical order under names; and chronologically through the calendar from 1 January to 31 December.

*Dobrée, Bonamy (Editor) INTRODUCTIONS TO ENGLISH LITERATURE 5 vols. *Cresset Press* (1938-40) revised editions 1950-8 21*s* each
The best series for students and general readers, requiring not only authoritative, scholarly critical and historical summaries, but also bibliographical information. The general editor writes: 'The purpose of these volumes . . . is to introduce people to the pleasures of literature by

putting those who enjoy reading in touch with books and authors unfamiliar to them, and by helping them to satisfy and extend those appetencies of mind and sensibility which literature, in its manifold variety, serves.'

*Duggan, Alfred HISTORICAL FICTION *National Book League* (*Readers Guides*) 1957 3s 48 pp
Bibliographical summary of historical novels of note, published between 1923 and 1956, with an introductory essay by our leading historical novelist. Refer also to Helen Cam's companion pamphlet entered above.

*Fowler, Henry Watson A DICTIONARY OF MODERN ENGLISH USAGE *O.U.P.* 1926 18s 750 pp
The standard guide to the correct use of words and phrases, constructions and spellings; arranged alphabetically to supplement the ordinary dictionary.

Fowler, Henry Watson and F. G. THE KING'S ENGLISH *O.U.P.* 3rd edn. 1930 12s 6d
Standard guide to grammar and diction.

*Ghosh, Jyotish Chandra and others ANNALS OF ENGLISH LITERATURE, 1475-1950 *O.U.P.* (1936) 1961 25s
'The principal publications of each year together with an alphabetical index of authors and their works.' This invaluable reference work 'has its origin in an aspiration of Sir Walter Raleigh . . .' stated the preface to the first edition. The revision, bringing the data up to the end of 1950, was done by R. W. Chapman and others. It is next to the *Cambridge Bibliography of English Literature* in usefulness as an everyday reference book.

*Graham, Bessie READER'S ADVISER AND BOOKMAN'S MANUAL *New York, Bowker; Great Britain, Whitaker* (1921) rev. by Esther R. Hoffman 9th edition 1960 110s 900 pp
Systematically arranged, this standard reference book for students, booksellers, librarians and general readers, is a comprehensive guide to classical and standard works of creative literature and to reference books, excluding technical subjects. American imprints and prices given.

*Haines, Helen E. LIVING WITH BOOKS *Columbia University Press* (1935) 1950 48s 636 pp
An American handbook. It is intended primarily for librarians, but the illuminating discussion and appreciation of the great books of the literature of the world, including evaluation and guidance regarding best editions, are of great value for booksellers and students.

*Halliday, Frank Ernest A SHAKESPEARE COMPANION, 1550-1950 *Duckworth* 1952 50s 743 pp Illus.
A useful reference book on the life, the plays, the productions, the characters and the literature on Shakespeare.

*Hart, James D. THE OXFORD COMPANION TO AMERICAN LITERA-
TURE *O.U.P.* (1941) 1956 65s 898 pp
Information and facts arranged alphabetically under the names of
authors, the titles of books, the names of characters, and under general
literary topics and allusions.

*Harvey, Sir Paul THE OXFORD COMPANION TO ENGLISH LITERA-
TURE *O.U.P.* (1932) 1947 38s 940 pp
THE CONCISE OXFORD DICTIONARY OF ENGLISH LITERATURE
O.U.P. 1939 18s 576 pp
Based on the parent work.

THE OXFORD COMPANION TO CLASSICAL LITERATURE *O.U.P.* 1937
18s 480 pp
Indispensable reference dictionaries for all users of books and general
readers. Similar in arrangement to J. D. Hart's *Companion*, which see
above.

Harvey, Sir Paul and J. E. Heseltine THE OXFORD COMPANION
TO FRENCH LITERATURE *O.U.P.* 1959 45s 771 pp
Information and facts on French authors and their books from the
beginnings to the post-war (1945-55) writers and existentialists, with
brief discussions of allied matters and literary topics generally, and some
attention to Belgian authors, such as Maeterlinck and Georges Simenon.

*Hoppé, A. J. THE READER'S GUIDE TO EVERYMAN'S LIBRARY *Dent*
(1932) 1960 12s 6d
The preface by E. F. Bozman is an interesting chapter in the history of
publishing, summarising as it does the splendid achievement of the firm
of J. M. Dent and Sons, Ltd., from 1906 onwards, in providing a whole
library of the classics and standard books in creative literature in English
or in translation at modest prices. Volumes 1 and 2 in EML (May 1906)
were the two volumes of Boswell's *Johnson*, price sixpence each. The
thousandth *Everyman*, was a new translation of Aristotle's *Metaphysics*,
published in 1956. This handbook, with dates, descriptive annotations,
and other information, is one of the most useful quick-reference books
in current literature.

Horwill, Herbert William A DICTIONARY OF MODERN AMERICAN
USAGE *O.U.P.* (1935) 1944 18s
A companion work to Fowler's *Modern English Usage*.

Hyamson, Albert Montefiore A DICTIONARY OF UNIVERSAL BIOG-
RAPHY *Routledge* (1916) 1950 84s 680 pp quarto
'All ages; all people.' Not a biographical dictionary, but rather a guide to
sources of information, such as standard biographies. The briefest details
of dates and achievements are given in a line or two for each entry.

Johnson, Samuel (1709-1784) A DICTIONARY OF THE ENGLISH
LANGUAGE 2 vols. (1755; 1773) A Modern Selection, ed. by
E. L. McAdam and George Milne *Gollancz* 1963 25s 480 pp

From the 2,300 pages of the original edition of this monumental work, the editors have retained 'most of the entries which can no longer be found in most modern dictionaries.' Johnson's wit, prejudices, and vigorous style are here, and the selection provides a fascinating book to browse in, especially for the changes in meanings of certain words, the rich variety of words now lost from our vocabulary, and the illuminating clarity of the original definitions.

Keller, Helen Rex THE READER'S DIGEST OF BOOKS (1896) rev. and enl. edn. *Allen and Unwin* 1947 42s 1447 pp
Summarises the contents, themes, and plots of over four hundred standard books, fiction and non-fiction. Arranged alphabetically by titles, with an author index.

*Kunitz, Stanley J. and Howard Haycraft AMERICAN AUTHORS, 1600-1900 *New York, The H. W. Wilson Co.* 1938 846 pp
BRITISH AUTHORS BEFORE 1800 *New York, The H. W. Wilson Co.* 1952 584 pp
BRITISH AUTHORS OF THE NINETEENTH CENTURY *New York, The H. W. Wilson Co.* 1936 677 pp
TWENTIETH CENTURY AUTHORS *New York, The H. W. Wilson Co.* 1942 1577 pp
FIRST SUPPLEMENT TO TWENTIETH CENTURY AUTHORS *New York, The H. W. Wilson Co.* 1955 60s 1577 pp
An invaluable series of standard biographical dictionaries, illustrated with portraits, and providing bibliographical details of principal works, with references to other sources of information. Some of the material in the twentieth-century volumes is quoted from personal statements made by the authors in response to editorial requests. The series is usually available in all large reference libraries, and is obtainable in Great Britain from the British agents of the H. W. Wilson Co., from whom current British prices can be obtained on application.

Lee, Sir Sidney (1859-1926) and Sir Edmund Chambers (1866-1954) SHAKESPEARE REFERENCE LIBRARY *O.U.P.* 1925 5s
A useful bibliography for students and librarians, in an English Association pamphlet series.

Lemprière, John (*c.* 1765-1824) A CLASSICAL DICTIONARY (1788) rev. by F. A. Wright *Routledge* 1950 18s 704 pp
A dictionary 'of proper names mentioned by ancient authors, with a chronological table'.

Marriott, Sir John Arthur Ransome (1859-1945) ENGLISH HISTORY IN ENGLISH FICTION *Blackie* 1940
Useful appraisal and evaluation of novels recommended by this distinguished professional historian as accurate (or reasonably so) presentations of history from the Roman era in Britain up to the end of the Victorian era. To be recommended to librarians and teachers as a guide to

M

background reading for older children. Refer also to Helen Cam's
pamphlet entered above.

*Onions, Charles Talbut THE OXFORD SHAKESPEARE GLOSSARY
O.U.P. (1911; 1919) 1953 15s
A double-columned reference glossary, presenting in this form an
analysis of Shakespeare's vocabulary 'in the light of the results of the
Oxford Dictionary', which see below.

*Onions, C. T. and others THE SHORTER OXFORD ENGLISH DIC-
TIONARY *O.U.P.* 3rd revised edn. (1944) 1955 from £6 15s
(cloth) 2538 pp quarto
The great, indispensable dictionary 'on historical principles', prepared
from the parent work (1884-1928) in thirteen volumes, by William
Little, H. W. Fowler and Jessie Coulson, revised and edited, with
appendix, and addenda up to 1955, by Dr. C. T. Onions, and with
corrections up to 1959 in the latest editions.

*THE OXFORD DICTIONARY OF QUOTATIONS *O.U.P.* (1941) 1953
45s 1003 pp quarto
Following the preface by Bernard Darwin, are some thousands of extracts
or briefer quotations from English writings, with a group devoted to the
Bible, and a small selection of famous sayings from French writers or
statesmen, and a few from the classics. The arrangement is in one
alphabetical sequence under authors' names, with a full index to the key
or the purposive words. This is a standard work that may be used as an
anthology as well as a ready-reference book.

Patrick, David and William Geddie CHAMBERS'S CYCLOPAEDIA OF
ENGLISH LITERATURE 3 vols. *Chambers* rev. edn. 1922 2570 pp
Illus. folios
Although in need of further revision, and of new material relating to the
twentieth century, this invaluable reference work is still the best thing of
its kind ever published. Biographical, bibliographical and critical articles,
arranged chronologically in systematic groups, together with portraits,
etc., and lengthy extracts from characteristic works, make it a most useful
aid to students.

Purvis, J. S. DICTIONARY OF ECCLESIASTICAL TERMS *Nelson* 1962 30s
A reference work for students of theology, librarians, the clergy, and
general readers of theological books, defining and explaining more than
a thousand terms used in books and in worship.

*Roget, Peter Mark (1779-1869) A THESAURUS OF ENGLISH WORDS
AND PHRASES (1852) rev. and enl. by S. R. Roget *Longmans*
(1925) 1962 30s 1364 pp
An English vocabulary arranged 'so as to facilitate the expression of ideas
and assist in literary composition'. Thus, associated words, synonyms,
antonyms, and phrases are grouped systematically in a classification
eme, bringing like near to like, and presenting the opposing groups in

parallel columns: opposition: co-operation; fasting: gluttony; and so on, with a complete index of words. The 1962 volume is a completely revised and enlarged edition. Other editions of this famous desk book for writers are in Dent's Reference Library series, revised by D. C. Browning, 1952, 18s; and in Penguin Books (a smaller edition) 1953, 6s.

*Sampson, George CONCISE CAMBRIDGE HISTORY OF ENGLISH LITERATURE *C.U.P.* (1941) 1961 25s 1072 pp
Based on the parent work in fifteen volumes, for which see below under Ward. The new edition has an additional chapter on 'The Age of T. S. Eliot', by R. C. Churchill.

*Scholes, Percy A. THE OXFORD COMPANION TO MUSIC *O.U.P.* (1938) 9th rev. ed. 1955 75s 1256 pp quarto
A standard reference work, the material being arranged alphabetically, with 1100 illustrations and plates. A smaller coverage of the subject is given in *The Oxford Junior Companion To Music*, O.U.P. 1954, 42s, 464 pp Illus. quarto; and still smaller in *The Concise Oxford Dictionary of Music*, O.U.P. 1952, 25s, 686 pp Illus.

Smith, Frank Seymour THE CLASSICS IN TRANSLATION *Scribners* 1930
An annotated bibliography of the best translations to 1930 of Greek and Latin classics into English, with an introductory essay on theories of translation.

AN ENGLISH LIBRARY (*C.U.P.* for N.B.L., 1943; 1950) *André Deutsch* 1963 30s

KNOW-HOW BOOKS *Thames and Hudson* 1956 21s
An annotated bibliography of Do-It-Yourself books for handymen, and of introductions to science, art, history and literature for beginners.

WHAT SHALL I READ NEXT? *C.U.P.* for *N.B.L.* 1953 12s 6d
A personal selection of twentieth-century books, annotated for general readers, and arranged in similar groups to *An English Library* to which it is complementary.

*Smith, Horatio A DICTIONARY OF MODERN EUROPEAN LITERATURE *O.U.P.* 1947 80s 914 pp
Authors; their books; literary themes and movements from about 1870. Excludes English literature.

*Smith, William George THE OXFORD DICTIONARY OF ENGLISH PROVERBS *O.U.P.* (1935) rev. edn. by Sir Paul Harvey 1948 45s 772 pp
Detailed index compiled by Janet E. Heseltine.

*Steinberg, S. H. CASSELL'S ENCYCLOPAEDIA OF LITERATURE 2 vols. *Cassell* 1953 42s each (one volume edition bound in leather, 105s) 2120 pp

Vol. 1: Historical surveys of the literatures of all countries of the world from oral traditions to the latest trends; discussions of literary forms, schools and genres of literature. Subject matter arranged in alphabetical dictionary order. Followed by part of a group of brief biographies, with bibliographical details, including translations of foreign works into English and dates, of writers who died before 1 August, 1914. Vol. 2: Continues, to page 1669, the biographies of part 1; and the remainder of the volume then contains biographies of a second group, authors from 1914 to date.

*Stephen, Sir Leslie (1832-1904) and Sir Sidney Lee (1859-1926) THE CONCISE DICTIONARY OF NATIONAL BIOGRAPHY 2 vols. O.U.P. 1930; 1961 60s and 42s 1648 pp; 528 pp
Part 1 epitomises the main work, which is in twenty-two volumes, £60 the set, 30500 pages, to the year 1900.
Part 2 is an epitome of the supplementary years from 1901 to 1950, dealt with in the set of five volumes, under other editors, published from 1912 to 1959, one for each decade, 55s each (Vols. 1-4), 105s (Vol. 5).

*Stevenson, Burton Egbert BOOK OF QUOTATIONS *Cassell* (1934) 1947 84s 2856 pp quarto
The most comprehensive work of its kind. The selection includes quotations from the English classics and other notable books; from Greek, Latin, Italian, Spanish, German and French works, in the original languages, with translations into English; all quotations being arranged under subjects, with a very detailed index.

'The Sunday Times' 101 GREAT BOOKS OF OUR TIME *Sunday Times* 1961 2s 6d
Annotated list selected by the literary staff of *The Sunday Times*, with an introduction by John Braine, and an index-bibliography of current editions. The first book is Kipling's *Kim* (1901); the last *A Land*, by Jacquetta Hawkes (1951); with two additions made by readers who responded to an invitation to vote by nominating one fiction and one non-fiction to bring the total to 101. The readers' choices were: *Precious Bane*, by Mary Webb (1924); and *The Human Situation*, by W. Macneile Dixon (1937).

Sykes, Egerton A DICTIONARY OF NON-CLASSICAL MYTHOLOGY *Dent* (*Reference Library*) 1952 18s

*Thorne, J. O. CHAMBERS'S BIOGRAPHICAL DICTIONARY *Chambers* (1897) 1961 70s 1432 pp
Biographies in brief, varying from a paragraph to a couple of pages, of notable people of all times, and all countries. Apart from its use as a desk book, this standard work is useful to the reader and literary student for its bibliographical information relating to books by classical and other authors, and to the books written about them. An appendix lists pen-names and pseudonyms.

Treble, Henry Arthur and G. H. Vallins AN ABC OF ENGLISH
USAGE *O.U.P.* 1936 6s 6d
Derived from the parent work, for which see above under Fowler.

*Ward, Sir Adolphus William (1837-1924) and A. R. Waller
THE CAMBRIDGE HISTORY OF ENGLISH LITERATURE 15 vols. *C.U.P.*
1907-16 25s each
Collective work with a general index, 1927. Also issued in a cheaper
edition omitting the bibliographies, 1932, 21s each. In need of revision,
but still of great importance as a reference work for students. See also
Sampson, above, for a *Concise History*.

Warrington, John EVERYMAN'S CLASSICAL DICTIONARY *Dent*
(*Reference Library*) 1961 20s
An entirely new work, superseding the former standard reference work
Smith's *Smaller Classical Dictionary*. The compiler has arranged the
articles alphabetically, and covers his subject from Homer (eighth
century B.C.) to the death of Constantine, A.D. 337.

Watson, George THE CONCISE CAMBRIDGE BIBLIOGRAPHY OF
ENGLISH LITERATURE, 600-1950 *C.U.P.* 1958 20s 272 pp
After a general introduction relating to reference books, collections and
bibliographies, this useful abridgement of the parent work (see Bateson
above) gives brief bibliographical details of important and secondary
works from Caedmon to Dylan Thomas. Thus the scope of the main
work is extended to twentieth-century literature in English up to 1950.
The arrangement differs from the parent work, in that within each period
the entries are arranged alphabetically under the authors. Students having
access to the five-volumed work will therefore still find the *Concise
Bibliography* of great use as a quick-reference work.

*West, Michael and P. F. Kimber DESKBOOK OF CORRECT ENGLISH
Longmans 1957 10 6d
'A dictionary of spelling, punctuation, grammar and usage.'

AUTHOR INDEX

This index includes names of editors of reference books, and of anthologies and collections; it does not include editors of specific texts and standard editions. Consult the Title Index for anonymous works, such as 'Everyman'; and for critical and biographical monographs, entered therein under the surnames of the authors and people written about, e.g., 'Austen, Jane'; 'Nelson, Lord'; 'Shakespeare'.

Hyphened surnames will be found under the first part; that is, look for 'Sackville-West' under 'Sackville-'. Authors using well-established, familiar pen-names, such as 'George Orwell', 'Katherine Mansfield' and others, are entered only under pen-names, and not under real names.

Page references following names of foreign authors refer to the translators; for example: Rabelais directs the reader to Urquhart's classic translation. Authors mentioned in notes are indicated by 'n' after the page numbers.

TITLE INDEX

Formal titles such as 'Poems'; Collected Works'; 'Poetical Works'; 'Essays'; 'Plays'; 'Letters'; 'Selections'; 'Diary'; 'Journal', and 'Anthologies' have been omitted; so too, have Autobiographies, unless the books have distinctive titles, such as, 'Far Away and Long Ago'. For details of such books refer direct to the appropriate section or to the author index. Look for the subjects of biographical and critical monographs under surnames; that is, look under 'Austen, Jane'. These names are in italics, indicating that they are title-subjects.

Titles beginning with 'The History of' . ., will be found under the first word indicating the subject; e.g., 'English Literature' (Saintsbury); 'Europe' (Fisher; Grant); 'European Morals' (Lecky), and so on. The conventional short title of many novels is used: e.g. 'The History of Mr. Polly', will be found under 'Mr. Polly'; 'Henry Esmond' is under that shortened version of the full title. Only those collections and anthologies in the sub-sections, bearing distinctive titles, have been indexed: e.g. 'Golden Treasury, The' (Palgrave). As in the author index, books mentioned in notes are indicated by 'n' after page numbers.

378   TITLE INDEX

LIST OF PAPERBACK SERIES